Sue Pemberton

Cambridge IGCSE® and O Level Additional Mathematics

Coursebook

Second edition

CAMBRIDGE
UNIVERSITY PRESS

Shaftesbury Road, Cambridge CB2 8EA, United Kingdom

One Liberty Plaza, 20th Floor, New York, NY 10006, USA

477 Williamstown Road, Port Melbourne, VIC 3207, Australia

314–321, 3rd Floor, Plot 3, Splendor Forum, Jasola District Centre, New Delhi – 110025, India

103 Penang Road, #05-06/07, Visioncrest Commercial, Singapore 238467

Cambridge University Press is part of the University of Cambridge.

It furthers the University's mission by disseminating knowledge in the pursuit of education, learning and research at the highest international levels of excellence.

www.cambridge.org

Information on this title: cambridge.org/9781108411660

First published 2016

20 19 18 17 16 15 14 13 12

Printed in India by Multivista Global Pvt Ltd

A catalogue record for this publication is available from the British Library

ISBN 978-1-108-41166-0 Paperback

Contents

Acknowledgements

Past examination paper questions throughout are reproduced by permission of Cambridge Assessment International Education.

Thanks to the following for permission to reproduce images:

Cover artwork: Shestakovych/Shutterstock
Chapter 1 Fan jianhua/Shutterstock; Chapter 2 zhu difeng/Shutterstock; Chapter 3 LAGUNA DESIGN/Getty Images; Chapter 4 Michael Dechev/Shutterstock; Fig. 4.1 Steve Bower/Shutterstock; Fig. 4.2 Laboko/Shutterstock; Fig. 4.3 irin-k/Shutterstock; Chapter 5 zentilia/Shutterstock; Chapter 6 Peshkova/Shutterstock; Chapter 7 ittipon/Shutterstock; Chapter 8 Zhu Qiu/EyeEm/Getty Images; Chapter 9 paul downing/Getty Images; Fig. 9.1 aarrows/Shutterstock; Chapter 10 Gino Santa Maria/Shutterstock; Fig. 10.1snake3d/Shutterstock; Fig. 10.2 Keith Publicover/Shutterstock; Fig. 10.3 Aleksandr Kurganov/Shutterstock; Fig. 10.4 Africa Studio/Shutterstock; Chapter 11 elfinadesign/Shutterstock; Chapter 12 AlenKadr/Shutterstock; Chapter 13 muratart/Shutterstock; Chapter 14 Neamov/Shutterstock; Chapter 15 Ahuli Labutin/Shutterstock; Chapter 16 AlexLMX/Getty

Introduction

This highly illustrated coursebook covers the *Cambridge IGCSE®* and *O Level Additional Mathematics* syllabuses (0606 and 4037). The course is aimed at students who are currently studying or have previously studied *Cambridge IGCSE® Mathematics* (0580) or *Cambridge O Level Mathematics* (4024).

Where the content in one chapter includes topics that should have already been covered in previous studies, a recap section has been provided so that students can build on their prior knowledge.

'Class discussion' sections have been included to provide students with the opportunity to discuss and learn new mathematical concepts with their classmates, with their class teacher acting as the facilitator. The aim of these class discussion sections is to improve the student's reasoning and oral communication skills.

'Challenge' questions have been included at the end of most exercises to challenge and stretch high-ability students.

Towards the end of each chapter, there is a summary of the key concepts to help students consolidate what they have just learnt. This is followed by a 'Past paper' questions section, which contains *real* questions taken from past examination papers.

A Practice Book is also available in the *Cambridge IGCSE® Additional Mathematics* series, which offers students further targeted practice. This book closely follows the chapters and topics of the coursebook offering additional exercises to help students to consolidate concepts learnt and to assess their learning after each chapter. A Teacher's Resource, to offer support and advice, is also available.

How to use this book

Chapter – each chapter begins with a set of learning objectives to explain what you will learn in this chapter.

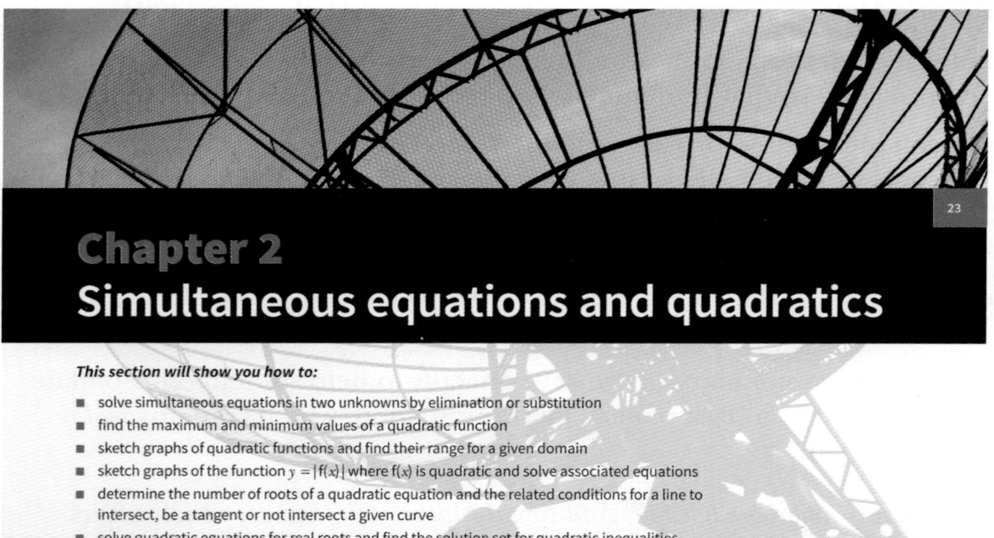

23

Chapter 2
Simultaneous equations and quadratics

This section will show you how to:

- solve simultaneous equations in two unknowns by elimination or substitution
- find the maximum and minimum values of a quadratic function
- sketch graphs of quadratic functions and find their range for a given domain
- sketch graphs of the function $y = |f(x)|$ where $f(x)$ is quadratic and solve associated equations
- determine the number of roots of a quadratic equation and the related conditions for a line to intersect, be a tangent or not intersect a given curve
- solve quadratic equations for real roots and find the solution set for quadratic inequalities.

Recap – check that you are familiar with the introductory skills required for the chapter.

RECAP

You should already know how to solve linear inequalities.

Two examples are shown below.

Solve $2(x-5) < 9$	expand brackets
$2x - 10 < 9$	add 10 to both sides
$2x < 19$	divide both sides by 2
$x < 9.5$	

Solve $5 - 3x \geqslant 17$	subtract 5 from both sides
$-3x \geqslant 12$	divide both sides by -3
$x \leqslant -4$	

Class Discussion – additional activities to be done in the classroom for enrichment.

CLASS DISCUSSION

Solve each of these three pairs of simultaneous equations.

$8x + 3y = 7$
$3x + 5y = -9$

$3x + y = 10$
$2y = 15 - 6x$

$2x + 5 = 3y$
$10 - 6y = -4x$

Discuss your answers with your classmates.

Discuss what the graphs would be like for each pair of equations.

Worked Example – detailed step-by-step approaches to help students solve problems.

WORKED EXAMPLE 1

Find the value of:

a $\frac{8!}{5!}$ b $\frac{11!}{8!3!}$

Answers

a $\frac{8!}{5!} = \frac{8\times 7\times 6\times 5\times 4\times 3\times 2\times 1}{5\times 4\times 3\times 2\times 1}$

$= 8\times 7\times 6$

$= 336$

b $\frac{11!}{8!3!} = \frac{11\times 10\times 9\times 8\times 7\times 6\times 5\times 4\times 3\times 2\times 1}{8\times 7\times 6\times 5\times 4\times 3\times 2\times 1\times 3\times 2\times 1}$

$= \frac{990}{6}$

$= 165$

Note – quick suggestions to remind you about key facts and highlight important points.

Note:
$\log_{10} 30$ can also be written as $\lg 30$ or $\log 30$.

Challenge – challenge yourself with tougher questions that stretch your skills.

CHALLENGE Q

6 This design is made from 1 blue circle, 4 orange circles and 16 green circles. The circles touch each other. Given that the radius of each green circle is 1 unit, find the exact radius of

a the orange circles,

b the blue circle.

Summary – at the end of each chapter to review what you have learnt.

Summary

One radian (1^c) is the size of the angle subtended at the centre of a circle, radius r, by an arc of length r.

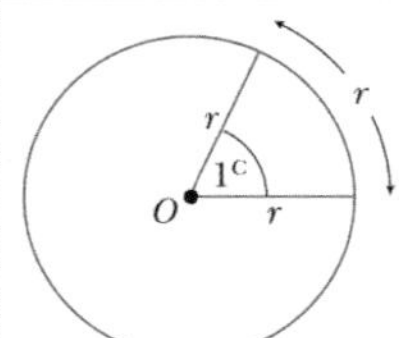

When θ is measured in radians:

- the length of arc $AB = r\theta$
- the area of sector $AOB = \frac{1}{2}r^2\theta$.

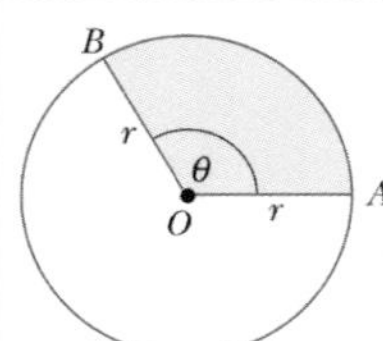

Examination questions – exam-style questions for you to test your knowledge and understanding at the end of each chapter.

Examination questions

Worked example

The function f is such that $f(x) = 4x^3 - 8x^2 + ax + b$, where a and b are constants. It is given that $2x - 1$ is a factor of $f(x)$ and that when $f(x)$ is divided by $x + 2$ the remainder is 20. Find the remainder when $f(x)$ is divided by $x - 1$. [6]

Cambridge IGCSE Additional Mathematics 0606 Paper 11 Q2 Nov 2011

Answer

$f(x) = 4x^3 - 8x^2 + ax + b$

If $2x - 1$ is a factor, then $f\left(\frac{1}{2}\right) = 0$.

$$4\left(\frac{1}{2}\right)^3 - 8\left(\frac{1}{2}\right)^2 + a\left(\frac{1}{2}\right) + b = 0$$

$$\frac{1}{2} - 2 + a\left(\frac{1}{2}\right) + b = 0$$

$$a\left(\frac{1}{2}\right) + b = 1\frac{1}{2}$$

$$a + 2b = 3 \quad \text{----------------------(1)}$$

Remainder $= 20$ when divided by $x + 2$, means that $f(-2) = 20$.

$$4(-2)^3 - 8(-2)^2 + a(-2) + b = 20$$

$$-32 - 32 - 2a + b = 20$$

$$-2a + b = 84 \quad \text{--------------------(2)}$$

From (1) $a = 3 - 2b$.

Substituting in (2), gives: $-2(3 - 2b) + b = 84$

$$-6 + 4b + b = 84$$

$$5b = 90$$

$$b = 18$$

So $a = -33$, $b = 18$.

Remainder when $f(x) = 4x^3 - 8x^2 - 33x + 18$ is divided by $(x - 1)$ is $f(1)$.

Remainder $= 4(1)^3 - 8(1)^2 - 33(1) + 18$

$= 4 - 8 - 33 + 18$

$= -19$

Activity – for you to apply your theoretical knowledge to a practical task.

ACTIVITY

Use graphing software to confirm that:

- $y = \cos x + 1$ is a translation of $y = \cos x$ by the vector $\begin{pmatrix} 0 \\ 1 \end{pmatrix}$
- $y = \cos x + 2$ is a translation of $y = \cos x$ by the vector $\begin{pmatrix} 0 \\ 2 \end{pmatrix}$
- $y = \cos x - 3$ is a translation of $y = \cos x$ by the vector $\begin{pmatrix} 0 \\ -3 \end{pmatrix}$

and

- $y = \tan x + 1$ is a translation of $y = \tan x$ by the vector $\begin{pmatrix} 0 \\ 1 \end{pmatrix}$
- $y = \tan x - 2$ is a translation of $y = \tan x$ by the vector $\begin{pmatrix} 0 \\ -2 \end{pmatrix}$

Chapter 1
Functions

This section will show you how to:

- understand and use the terms: function, domain, range (image set), one-one function, inverse function and composition of functions
- use the notation $f(x) = 2x^3 + 5$, $f : x \mapsto 5x - 3$, $f^{-1}(x)$ and $f^2(x)$
- understand the relationship between $y = f(x)$ and $y = |f(x)|$
- solve graphically or algebraically equations of the type $|ax + b| = c$ and $|ax + b| = cx + d$
- explain in words why a given function is a function or why it does not have an inverse
- find the inverse of a one-one function and form composite functions
- use sketch graphs to show the relationship between a function and its inverse.

1.1 Mappings

Input		Output
1	→	2
2	→	3
3	→	4
4	→	5

is called a **mapping diagram**.

The rule connecting the input and output values can be written algebraically as: $x \mapsto x + 1$.

This is read as 'x is mapped to $x + 1$'.

The mapping can be represented graphically by plotting values of $x + 1$ against values of x.

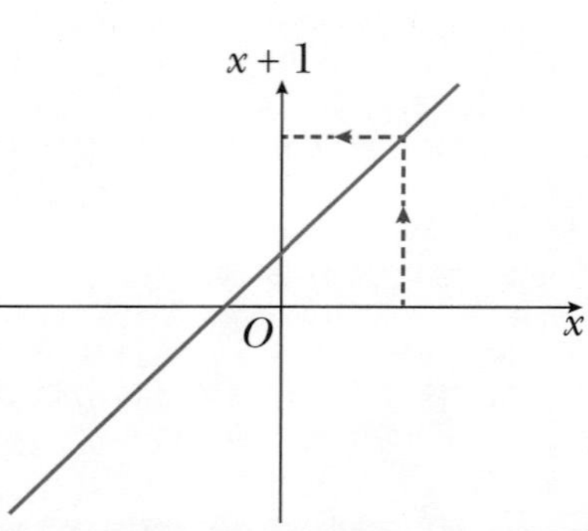

The diagram shows that for one input value there is just one output value.

It is called a **one-one** mapping.

The table below shows one-one, many-one and one-many mappings.

one-one	many-one	one-many
$x + 1$, O, x	x^2, O, x	$\pm\sqrt{x}$, O, x
For one input value there is just one output value.	For two input values there is one output value.	For one input value there are two output values.

Exercise 1.1

Determine whether each of these mappings is one-one, many-one or one-many.

1 $x \mapsto x + 1 \quad x \in \mathbb{R}$

2 $x \mapsto x^2 + 5 \quad x \in \mathbb{R}$

3 $x \mapsto x^3 \quad x \in \mathbb{R}$

4 $x \mapsto 2^x \quad x \in \mathbb{R}$

5 $x \mapsto \dfrac{1}{x} \quad x \in \mathbb{R},\ x > 0$

6 $x \mapsto x^2 + 1 \quad x \in \mathbb{R},\ x \geqslant 0$

7 $x \mapsto \dfrac{12}{x} \quad x \in \mathbb{R},\ x > 0$

8 $x \mapsto \pm x \quad x \in \mathbb{R},\ x \geqslant 0$

1.2 Definition of a function

A **function** is a rule that maps each x value to just one y value for a defined set of input values.

This means that mappings that are either $\left\{\begin{array}{l}\text{one-one}\\\text{many-one}\end{array}\right.$ are called functions.

The mapping $x \mapsto x+1$ where $x \in \mathbb{R}$, is a one-one function.

It can be written as $\left\{\begin{array}{ll}\text{f}: x \mapsto x+1 & x \in \mathbb{R}\\ \text{f}(x) = x+1 & x \in \mathbb{R}\end{array}\right.$

($\text{f} : x \mapsto x+1$ is read as 'the function f is such that x is mapped to $x+1$')

$\text{f}(x)$ represents the output values for the function f.

So when $\text{f}(x) = x+1$, $\text{f}(2) = 2+1 = 3$.

The set of input values for a function is called the **domain** of the function.

The set of output values for a function is called the **range** (or image set) of the function.

WORKED EXAMPLE 1

$\text{f}(x) = 2x - 1 \quad x \in \mathbb{R}, -1 \leqslant x \leqslant 3$

a Write down the domain of the function f.

b Sketch the graph of the function f.

c Write down the range of the function f.

Answers

a The domain is $-1 \leqslant x \leqslant 3$.

b The graph of $y = 2x - 1$ has gradient 2 and a y-intercept of -1.

When $x = -1$, $y = 2(-1) - 1 = -3$

When $x = 3$, $y = 2(3) - 1 = 5$

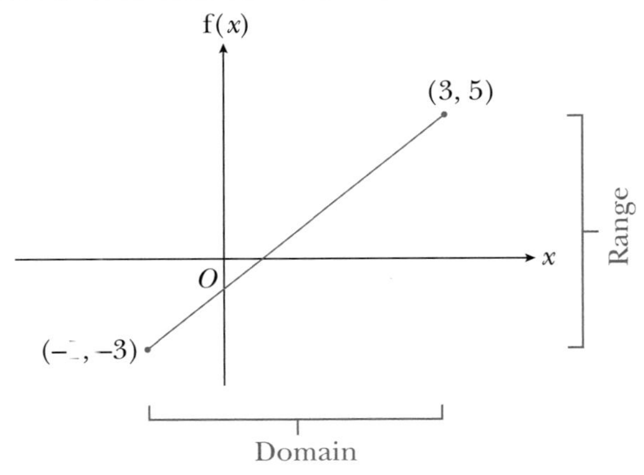

c The range is $-3 \leqslant \text{f}(x) \leqslant 5$.

WORKED EXAMPLE 2

The function f is defined by $f(x) = (x-2)^2 + 3$ for $0 \leqslant x \leqslant 6$.
Sketch the graph of the function.
Find the range of f.

Answers

$f(x) = (x-2)^2 + 3$ is a positive quadratic function so the graph will be of the form $\bigvee$

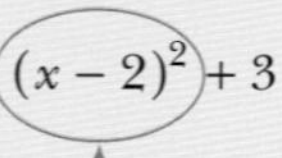

This part of the expression is a square so it will always be $\geqslant 0$. The smallest value it can be is 0. This occurs when $x = 2$.

The minimum value of the expression is $0 + 3 = 3$ and this minimum occurs when $x = 2$.

So the function $f(x) = (x-2)^2 + 3$ will have a minimum point at the point (2, 3).

When $x = 0$, $y = (0-2)^2 + 3 = 7$.

When $x = 6$, $y = (6-2)^2 + 3 = 19$.

The range is $3 \leqslant f(x) \leqslant 19$.

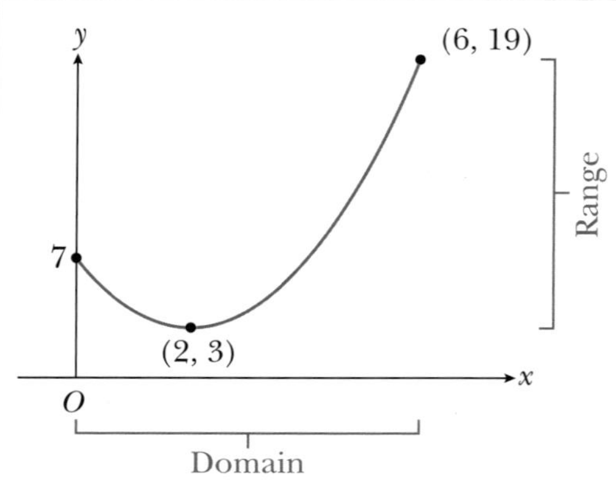

Exercise 1.2

1 Which of the mappings in **Exercise 1.1** are functions?

2 Find the range for each of these functions.

a $f(x) = x - 5$, $\quad -2 \leqslant x \leqslant 7$

b $f(x) = 3x + 2$, $\quad 0 \leqslant x \leqslant 5$

c $f(x) = 7 - 2x$, $\quad -1 \leqslant x \leqslant 4$

d $f(x) = x^2$, $\quad -3 \leqslant x \leqslant 3$

e $f(x) = 2^x$, $\quad -3 \leqslant x \leqslant 3$

f $f(x) = \frac{1}{x}$, $\quad 1 \leqslant x \leqslant 5$

3 The function g is defined as $g(x) = x^2 + 2$ for $x \geqslant 0$.
Write down the range of g.

4 The function f is defined by $f(x) = x^2 - 4$ for $x \in \mathbb{R}$.
Find the range of f.

5 The function f is defined by $f(x) = (x-1)^2 + 5$ for $x \geqslant 1$.
Find the range of f.

6 The function f is defined by $f(x) = (2x+1)^2 - 5$ for $x \geqslant -\frac{1}{2}$.
Find the range of f.

7 The function f is defined by $f : x \mapsto 10 - (x-3)^2$ for $2 \leqslant x \leqslant 7$.
Find the range of f.

8 The function f is defined by $f(x) = 3 + \sqrt{x - 2}$ for $x \geqslant 2$.
Find the range of f.

1.3 Composite functions

Most functions that you meet are combinations of two or more functions.

For example, the function $x \mapsto 2x + 5$ is the function 'multiply by 2 and then add 5'. It is a combination of the two functions g and f where:

$g : x \mapsto 2x$ (the function 'multiply by 2')

$f : x \mapsto x + 5$ (the function 'add 5')

So, $x \mapsto 2x + 5$ is the function 'first do g then do f'.

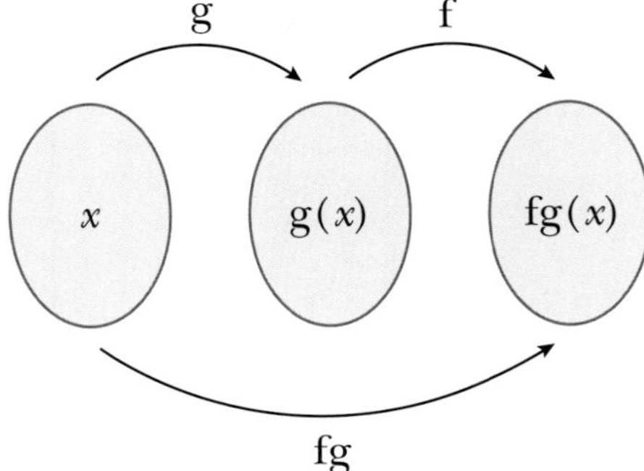

When one function is followed by another function, the resulting function is called a **composite function**.

fg(x) means the function g acts on x first, then f acts on the result.

Note:
$f^2(x)$ means ff(x), so you apply the function f twice.

WORKED EXAMPLE 3

The function f is defined by $f(x) = (x - 2)^2 - 3$ for $x > -2$.

The function g is defined by $g(x) = \dfrac{2x + 6}{x - 2}$ for $x > 2$.

Find fg(7).

Answers

fg(7)	g acts on 7 first and $g(7) = \dfrac{2(7) + 6}{7 - 2} = 4$
$= f(4)$	f is the function 'take 2, square and then take 3'
$= (4 - 2)^2 - 3$	
$= 1$	

WORKED EXAMPLE 4

$f(x) = 2x - 1$ for $x \in \mathbb{R}$ $\quad$ $g(x) = x^2 + 5$ for $x \in \mathbb{R}$

Find **a** $fg(x)$ **b** $gf(x)$ **c** $f^2(x)$.

Answers

a $fg(x)$ — g acts on x first and $g(x) = x^2 + 5$

$= f(x^2 + 5)$ — f is the function 'double and take 1'

$= 2(x^2 + 5) - 1$

$= 2x^2 + 9$

b $gf(x)$ — f acts on x first and $f(x) = 2x - 1$

$= g(2x - 1)$ — g is the function 'square and add 5'

$= (2x - 1)^2 + 5$ — expand brackets

$= 4x^2 - 4x + 1 + 5$

$= 4x^2 - 4x + 6$

c $f^2(x)$ — $f^2(x)$ means $ff(x)$

$= ff(x)$ — f acts on x first and $f(x) = 2x - 1$

$= f(2x - 1)$ — f is the function 'double and take 1'

$= 2(2x - 1) - 1$

$= 4x - 3$

Exercise 1.3

1 $f : x \mapsto 2x + 3$ for $x \in \mathbb{R}$

$g : x \mapsto x^2 - 1$ for $x \in \mathbb{R}$

Find $fg(2)$.

2 $f(x) = x^2 - 1$ for $x \in \mathbb{R}$

$g(x) = 2x + 3$ for $x \in \mathbb{R}$

Find the value of $gf(5)$.

3 $f(x) = (x + 2)^2 - 1$ for $x \in \mathbb{R}$

Find $f^2(3)$.

4 The function f is defined by $f(x) = 1 + \sqrt{x - 2}$ for $x \geqslant 2$.

The function g is defined by $g(x) = \dfrac{10}{x} - 1$ for $x > 0$.

Find $gf(18)$.

5 The function f is defined by $f(x) = (x - 1)^2 + 3$ for $x > -1$.

The function g is defined by $g(x) = \dfrac{2x + 4}{x - 5}$ for $x > 5$.

Find $fg(7)$.

6 $\text{h} : x \mapsto x + 2$ for $x > 0$

$\text{k} : x \mapsto \sqrt{x}$ for $x > 0$

Express each of the following in terms of h and k.

a $x \mapsto \sqrt{x} + 2$ **b** $x \mapsto \sqrt{x + 2}$

7 The function f is defined by $\text{f} : x \mapsto 3x + 1$ for $x \in \mathbb{R}$.

The function g is defined by $\text{g} : x \mapsto \dfrac{10}{2 - x}$ for $x \neq 2$.

Solve the equation $\text{gf}(x) = 5$.

8 $\text{g}(x) = x^2 + 2$ for $x \in \mathbb{R}$

$\text{h}(x) = 3x - 5$ for $x \in \mathbb{R}$

Solve the equation $\text{gh}(x) = 51$.

9 $\text{f}(x) = x^2 - 3$ for $x > 0$

$\text{g}(x) = \dfrac{3}{x}$ for $x > 0$

Solve the equation $\text{fg}(x) = 13$.

10 The function f is defined, for $x \in \mathbb{R}$, by $\text{f} : x \mapsto \dfrac{3x + 5}{x - 2}$, $x \neq 2$.

The function g is defined, for $x \in \mathbb{R}$, by $\text{g} : x \mapsto \dfrac{x - 1}{2}$.

Solve the equation $\text{gf}(x) = 12$.

11 $\text{f}(x) = (x + 4)^2 + 3$ for $x > 0$

$\text{g}(x) = \dfrac{10}{x}$ for $x > 0$

Solve the equation $\text{fg}(x) = 39$.

12 The function g is defined by $\text{g}(x) = x^2 - 1$ for $x \geqslant 0$.

The function h is defined by $\text{h}(x) = 2x - 7$ for $x \geqslant 0$.

Solve the equation $\text{gh}(x) = 0$.

13 The function f is defined by $\text{f} : x \mapsto x^3$ for $x \in \mathbb{R}$.

The function g is defined by $\text{g} : x \mapsto x - 1$ for $x \in \mathbb{R}$.

Express each of the following as a composite function, using only f and/or g:

a $x \mapsto (x - 1)^3$ **b** $x \mapsto x^3 - 1$ **c** $x \mapsto x - 2$ **d** $x \mapsto x^9$

1.4 Modulus functions

The **modulus** of a number is the magnitude of the number without a sign attached.

The modulus of 4 is written $|4|$.

$|4| = 4$ and $|-4| = 4$

It is important to note that the modulus of any number (positive or negative) is always a positive number.

The modulus of a number is also called the **absolute value**.

The modulus of x, written as $|x|$, is defined as:

$$|x| = \begin{cases} x & \text{if } x > 0 \\ 0 & \text{if } x = 0 \\ -x & \text{if } x < 0 \end{cases}$$

CLASS DISCUSSION

Ali says that these are all rules for absolute values:

$$|x+y| = |x| + |y| \qquad |x-y| = |x| - |y|$$

$$|xy| = |x| \times |y| \qquad \left|\frac{x}{y}\right| = \frac{|x|}{|y|} \qquad (|x|)^2 = x^2$$

Discuss each of these statements with your classmates and decide if they are:

Always true	Sometimes true	Never true

You must justify your decisions.

The statement $|x| = k$, where $k \geqslant 0$, means that $x = k$ or $x = -k$.

This property is used to solve equations that involve modulus functions.

So, if you are solving equations of the form $|ax + b| = k$, you solve the equations

$ax + b = k$ and $ax + b = -k$

If you are solving harder equations of the form $|ax + b| = cx + d$, you solve the equations

$ax + b = cx + d$ and $ax + b = -(cx + d)$.

When solving these more complicated equations you must always check your answers to make sure that they satisfy the original equation.

WORKED EXAMPLE 5

Solve.

a $|2x+1| = 5$ **b** $|4x-3| = x$ **c** $|x^2-10| = 6$ **d** $|x-3| = 2x$

Answers

a $|2x+1| = 5$

$2x+1 = 5$ or $2x+1 = -5$

$2x = 4$ $\quad 2x = -6$

$x = 2$ $\quad x = -3$

CHECK: $|2\times 2+1| = 5$ ✓ and $|2\times -3+1| = 5$ ✓

Solution is: $x = -3$ or 2.

b $|4x-3| = x$

$4x-3 = x$ or $4x-3 = -x$

$3x = 3$ $\quad 5x = 3$

$x = 1$ $\quad x = 0.6$

CHECK: $|4\times 0.6-3| = 0.6$ ✓ and $|4\times 1-3| = 1$ ✓

Solution is: $x = 0.6$ or 1.

c $|x^2-10| = 6$

$x^2-10 = 6$ or $x^2-10 = -6$

$x^2 = 16$ $\quad x^2 = 4$

$x = \pm 4$ $\quad x = \pm 2$

CHECK: $|(-4)^2-10| = 6$ ✓, $|(-2)^2-10| = 6$ ✓, $|(2)^2-10| = 6$ ✓ and $|(4)^2-10| = 6$ ✓

Solution is: $x = -4, -2, 2$ or 4.

d $|x-3| = 2x$

$x-3 = 2x$ or $x-3 = -2x$

$x = -3$ $\quad 3x = 3$

$x = 1$

CHECK: $|-3-3| = 2\times -3$ ✗ and $|1-3| = 2\times 1$ ✓

Solution is: $x = 1$.

Exercise 1.4

1 Solve

a $|3x-2| = 10$ **b** $|2x+9| = 5$ **c** $|6-5x| = 2$

d $\left|\frac{x-1}{4}\right| = 6$ **e** $\left|\frac{2x+7}{3}\right| = 1$ **f** $\left|\frac{7-2x}{2}\right| = 4$

g $\left|\frac{x}{4}-5\right| = 1$ **h** $\left|\frac{x+1}{2}+\frac{2x}{5}\right| = 4$ **i** $|2x-5| = x$

2 Solve

a $\left|\frac{2x-5}{x+3}\right| = 8$ **b** $\left|\frac{3x+2}{x+1}\right| = 2$ **c** $\left|1+\frac{x+12}{x+4}\right| = 3$

d $|3x-5| = x+2$ **e** $x+|x-5| = 8$ **f** $9-|1-x| = 2x$

3 Solve

a $|x^2-1| = 3$ **b** $|x^2+1| = 10$ **c** $|4-x^2| = 2-x$

d $|x^2-5x| = x$ **e** $|x^2-4| = x+2$ **f** $|x^2-3| = x+3$

g $|2x^2+1| = 3x$ **h** $|2x^2-3x| = 4-x$ **i** $|x^2-7x+6| = 6-x$

4 Solve each of the following pairs of simultaneous equations

a $y = x+4$, $y = |x^2-16|$ **b** $y = x$, $y = |3x-2x^2|$ **c** $y = 3x$, $y = |2x^2-5|$

1.5 Graphs of $y = |f(x)|$ where f(x) is linear

Consider drawing the graph of $y = |x|$.

First draw the graph of $y = x$.

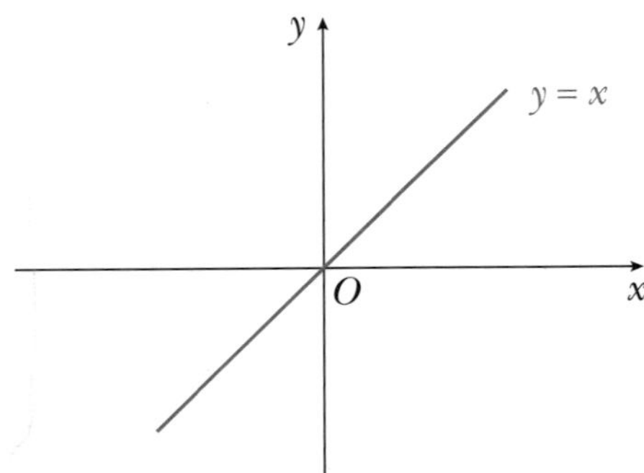

You then reflect in the x-axis the part of the line that is below the x-axis.

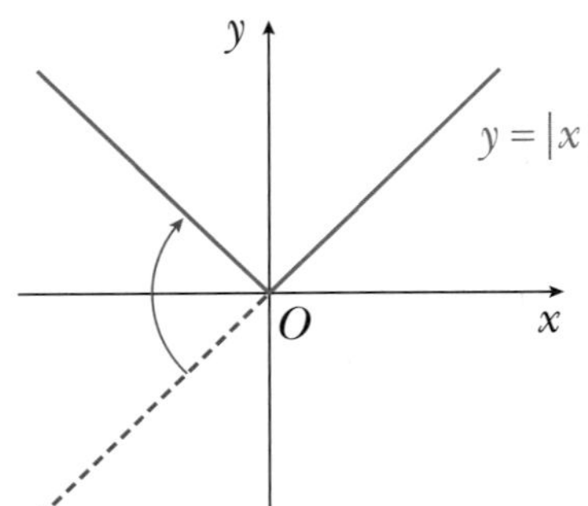

WORKED EXAMPLE 6

Sketch the graph of $y = \left|\frac{1}{2}x - 1\right|$, showing the coordinates of the points where the graph meets the axes.

Answers

First sketch the graph of $y = \frac{1}{2}x - 1$.

The line has gradient $\frac{1}{2}$ and a y-intercept of -1.

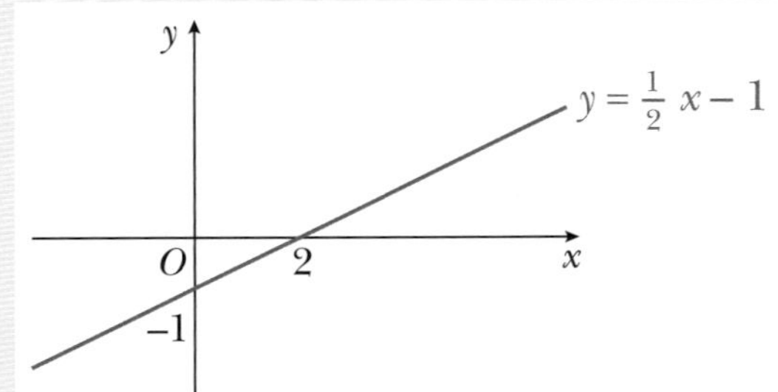

You then reflect in the x-axis the part of the line that is below the x-axis.

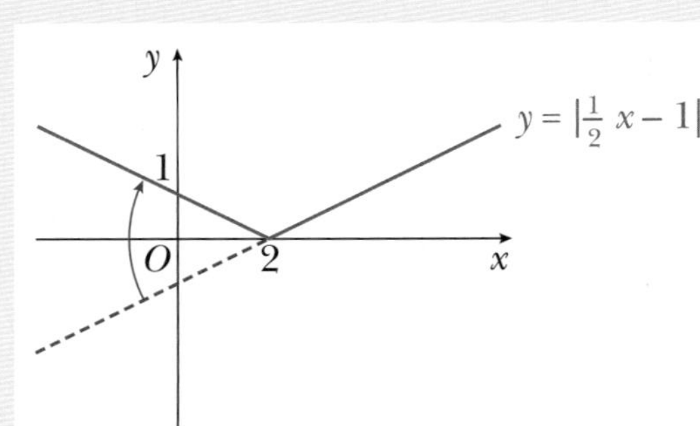

In **Worked example 5** you saw that there were two answers, $x = -3$ or $x = 2$, to the equation $|2x + 1| = 5$.

These can also be found graphically by finding the x-coordinates of the points of intersection of the graphs of $y = |2x + 1|$ and $y = 5$ as shown.

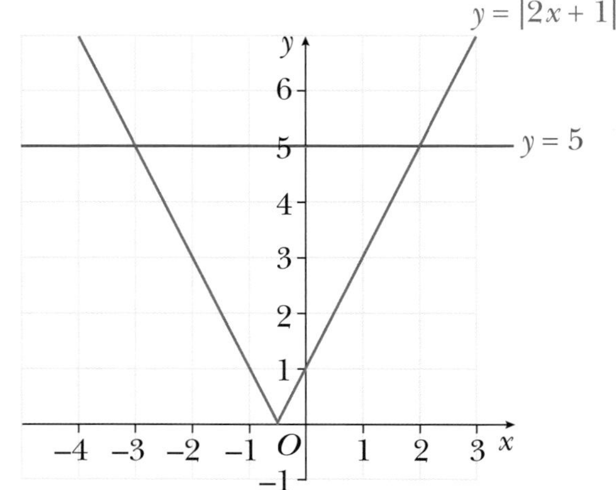

In the same worked example you also saw that there was only one answer, $x = 1$, to the equation $|x - 3| = 2x$.

This can also be found graphically by finding the x-coordinates of the points of intersection of the graphs of $y = |x - 3|$ and $y = 2x$ as shown.

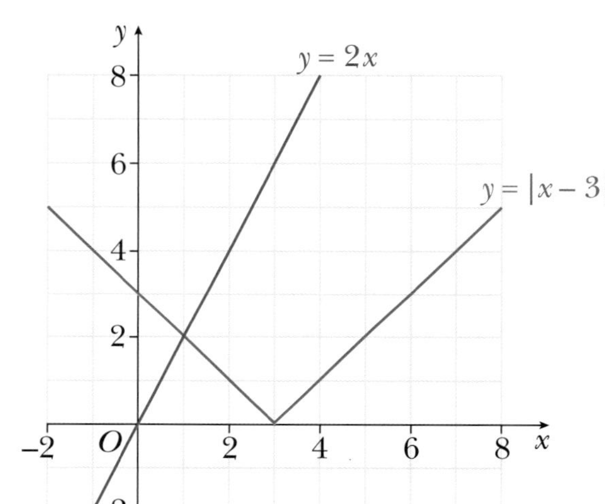

Exercise 1.5

1 Sketch the graphs of each of the following functions showing the coordinates of the points where the graph meets the axes.

a $y = |x + 1|$ **b** $y = |2x - 3|$ **c** $y = |5 - x|$

d $y = \left|\frac{1}{2}x + 3\right|$ **e** $y = |10 - 2x|$ **f** $y = \left|6 - \frac{1}{3}x\right|$

2 **a** Complete the table of values for $y = |x - 2| + 3$.

x	−2	−1	0	1	2	3	4
y		6		4			

b Draw the graph of $y = |x - 2| + 3$ for $-2 \leqslant x \leqslant 4$.

3 Draw the graphs of each of the following functions.

a $y = |x| + 1$ **b** $y = |x| - 3$ **c** $y = 2 - |x|$

d $y = |x - 3| + 1$ **e** $y = |2x + 6| - 3$

4 Given that each of these functions is defined for the domain $-3 \leqslant x \leqslant 4$, find the range of

a $\mathrm{f} : x \mapsto 5 - 2x$ **b** $\mathrm{g} : x \mapsto |5 - 2x|$ **c** $\mathrm{h} : x \mapsto 5 - |2x|$.

5 $f : x \mapsto 3 - 2x$ for $-1 \leqslant x \leqslant 4$
$g : x \mapsto |3 - 2x|$ for $-1 \leqslant x \leqslant 4$
$h : x \mapsto 3 - |2x|$ for $-1 \leqslant x \leqslant 4$
Find the range of each function.

6 **a** Sketch the graph of $y = |2x + 4|$ for $-6 < x < 2$, showing the coordinates of the points where the graph meets the axes.
b On the same diagram, sketch the graph of $y = x + 5$.
c Solve the equation $|2x + 4| = x + 5$.

7 A function f is defined by $f(x) = |2x - 6| - 3$, for $-1 \leqslant x \leqslant 8$.
a Sketch the graph of $y = f(x)$.
b State the range of f.
c Solve the equation $f(x) = 2$.

8 **a** Sketch the graph of $y = |3x - 4|$ for $-2 < x < 5$, showing the coordinates of the points where the graph meets the axes.
b On the same diagram, sketch the graph of $y = 2x$.
c Solve the equation $2x = |3x - 4|$.

CHALLENGE Q

9 **a** Sketch the graph of $f(x) = |x + 2| + |x - 2|$.
b Use your graph to solve the equation $|x + 2| + |x - 2| = 6$.

1.6 Inverse functions

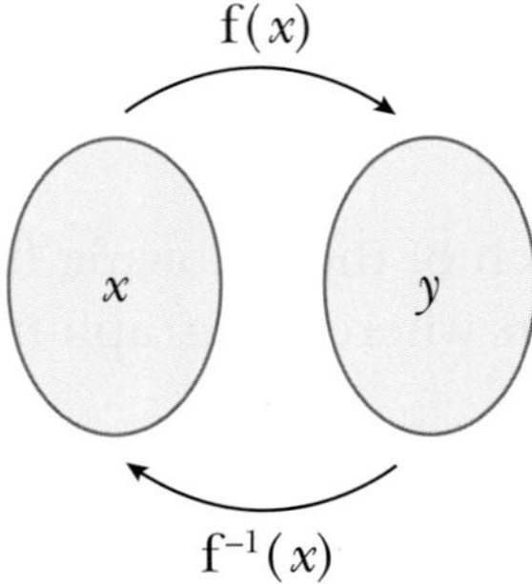

The inverse of a function $f(x)$ is the function that undoes what $f(x)$ has done.

The inverse of the function $f(x)$ is written as $f^{-1}(x)$.

The domain of $f^{-1}(x)$ is the range of $f(x)$.

The range of $f^{-1}(x)$ is the domain of $f(x)$.

It is important to remember that not every function has an inverse.

An inverse function $f^{-1}(x)$ can exist if, and only if, the function $f(x)$ is a one-one mapping.

You should already know how to find the inverse function of some simple one-one mappings.

The steps to find the inverse of the function $f(x) = 5x - 2$ are:

Step 1: Write the function as $y =$ ⟶ $y = 5x - 2$

Step 2: Interchange the x and y variables. ⟶ $x = 5y - 2$

Step 3: Rearrange to make y the subject. ⟶ $y = \dfrac{x + 2}{5}$

$$f^{-1}(x) = \frac{x + 2}{5}$$

CLASS DISCUSSION

Discuss the function $f(x) = x^2$ for $x \in \mathbb{R}$.

Does the function f have an inverse?

Explain your answer.

How could you change the domain of f so that $f(x) = x^2$ does have an inverse?

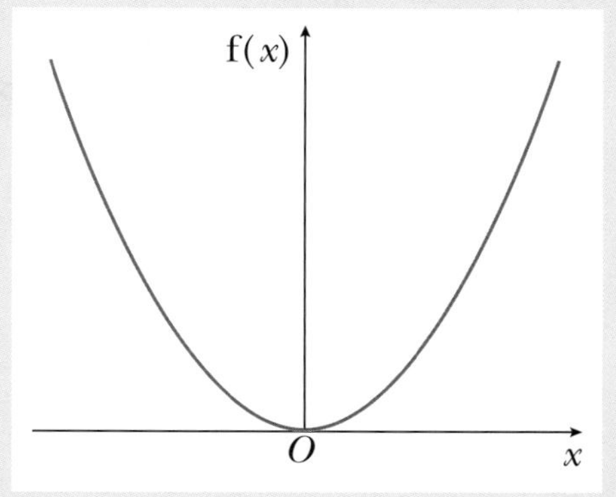

WORKED EXAMPLE 7

$f(x) = \sqrt{x+1} - 5$ for $x \geqslant -1$

a Find an expression for $f^{-1}(x)$.

b Solve the equation $f^{-1}(x) = f(35)$.

Answers

a $f(x) = \sqrt{x+1} - 5$ for $x \geqslant -1$

Step 1: Write the function as $y =$ → $y = \sqrt{x+1} - 5$

Step 2: Interchange the x and y variables. → $x = \sqrt{y+1} - 5$

Step 3: Rearrange to make y the subject. → $x + 5 = \sqrt{y+1}$

$$(x+5)^2 = y + 1$$

$$y = (x+5)^2 - 1$$

$f^{-1}(x) = (x+5)^2 - 1$

b $f(35) = \sqrt{35+1} - 5 = 1$

$(x+5)^2 - 1 = 1$

$(x+5)^2 = 2$

$x + 5 = \pm\sqrt{2}$

$x = -5 \pm \sqrt{2}$

$x = -5 + \sqrt{2}$ or $x = -5 - \sqrt{2}$

The range of f is $f(x) \geqslant -5$ so the domain of f^{-1} is $x \geqslant -5$.

Hence the only solution of $f^{-1}(x) = f(35)$ is $x = -5 + \sqrt{2}$.

Exercise 1.6

1 $f(x) = (x+5)^2 - 7$ for $x \geqslant -5$. Find an expression for $f^{-1}(x)$.

2 $f(x) = \dfrac{6}{x+2}$ for $x \geqslant 0$. Find an expression for $f^{-1}(x)$.

3 $f(x) = (2x-3)^2 + 1$ for $x \geqslant 1\frac{1}{2}$. Find an expression for $f^{-1}(x)$.

4 $f(x) = 8 - \sqrt{x-3}$ for $x \geqslant 3$. Find an expression for $f^{-1}(x)$.

5 $f : x \mapsto 5x - 3$ for $x > 0$ $\qquad g : x \mapsto \dfrac{7}{2-x}$ for $x \neq 2$

Express $f^{-1}(x)$ and $g^{-1}(x)$ in terms of x.

6 $f : x \to (x+2)^2 - 5$ for $x > -2$

a Find an expression for $f^{-1}(x)$. **b** Solve the equation $f^{-1}(x) = 3$.

7 $f(x) = (x-4)^2 + 5$ for $x > 4$

a Find an expression for $f^{-1}(x)$. **b** Solve the equation $f^{-1}(x) = f(0)$.

8 $g(x) = \dfrac{2x+3}{x-1}$ for $x > 1$

a Find an expression for $g^{-1}(x)$. **b** Solve the equation $g^{-1}(x) = 5$.

9 $f(x) = \dfrac{x}{2} + 2$ for $x \in \mathbb{R}$ $\qquad g(x) = x^2 - 2x$ for $x \in \mathbb{R}$

a Find $f^{-1}(x)$. **b** Solve $fg(x) = f^{-1}(x)$.

10 $f(x) = x^2 + 2$ for $x \in \mathbb{R}$ $\qquad g(x) = 2x + 3$ for $x \in \mathbb{R}$

Solve the equation $gf(x) = g^{-1}(17)$.

11 $f : x \mapsto \dfrac{2x+8}{x-2}$ for $x \neq 2$ $\qquad g : x \mapsto \dfrac{x-3}{2}$ for $x > -5$

Solve the equation $f(x) = g^{-1}(x)$.

12 $f(x) = 3x - 24$ for $x \geqslant 0$. Write down the range of f^{-1}.

13 $f : x \mapsto x + 6$ for $x > 0$ $\qquad g : x \mapsto \sqrt{x}$ for $x > 0$

Express $x \mapsto x^2 - 6$ in terms of f and g.

14 $f : x \mapsto 3 - 2x$ for $0 \leqslant x \leqslant 5$

$g : x \mapsto |3 - 2x|$ for $0 \leqslant x \leqslant 5$

$h : x \mapsto 3 - |2x|$ for $0 \leqslant x \leqslant 5$

State which of the functions f, g and h has an inverse.

15 $f(x) = x^2 + 2$ for $x \geqslant 0$ $\qquad g(x) = 5x - 4$ for $x \geqslant 0$

a Write down the domain of f^{-1}. **b** Write down the range of g^{-1}.

16 The functions f and g are defined, for $x \in \mathbb{R}$, by

$f : x \mapsto 3x - k$, where k is a positive constant

$g : x \mapsto \dfrac{5x-14}{x+1}$, where $x \neq -1$.

a Find expressions for f^{-1} and g^{-1}.

b Find the value of k for which $f^{-1}(5) = 6$.

c Simplify $g^{-1}g(x)$.

17 $f : x \mapsto x^3$ for $x \in \mathbb{R}$ $\quad$ $g : x \mapsto x - 8$ for $x \in \mathbb{R}$

Express each of the following as a composite function, using only f, g, f^{-1} and/or g^{-1}:

a $x \mapsto (x-8)^{\frac{1}{3}}$ **b** $x \mapsto x^3 + 8$ **c** $x \mapsto x^{\frac{1}{3}} - 8$

d $x \mapsto (x+8)^{\frac{1}{3}}$

1.7 The graph of a function and its inverse

In **Worked example 1** you considered the function $f(x) = 2x - 1$ $x \in \mathbb{R}$, $-1 \leqslant x \leqslant 3$.
The domain of f was $-1 \leqslant x \leqslant 3$ and the range of f was $-3 \leqslant f(x) \leqslant 5$.

The inverse function is $f^{-1}(x) = \dfrac{x+1}{2}$.
The domain of f^{-1} is $-3 \leqslant x \leqslant 5$ and the range of f^{-1} is $-1 \leqslant f^{-1}(x) \leqslant 3$.

Drawing f and f^{-1} on the same graph gives:

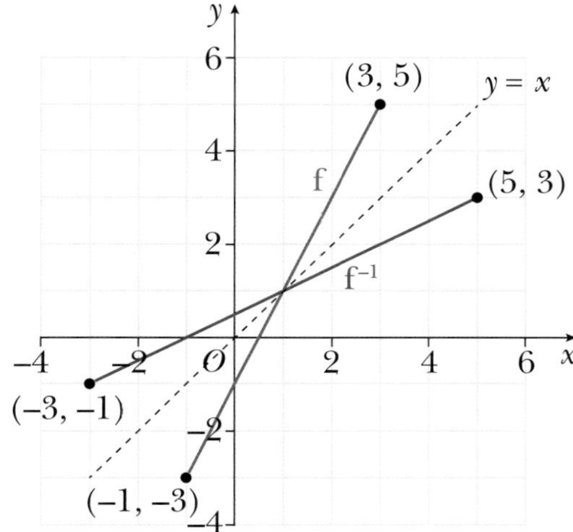

Note:
The graphs of f and f^{-1} are reflections of each other in the line $y = x$.
This is true for all one-one functions and their inverse functions.
This is because: $ff^{-1}(x) = x = f^{-1}f(x)$.

Some functions are called **self-inverse functions** because f and its inverse f^{-1} are the same.
If $f(x) = \dfrac{1}{x}$ for $x \neq 0$, then $f^{-1}(x) = \dfrac{1}{x}$ for $x \neq 0$.

So $f(x) = \dfrac{1}{x}$ for $x \neq 0$ is an example of a self-inverse function.
When a function f is self-inverse, the graph of f will be symmetrical about the line $y = x$.

WORKED EXAMPLE 8

$f(x) = (x - 2)^2, \ 2 \leqslant x \leqslant 5.$

On the same axes, sketch the graphs of $y = f(x)$ and $y = f^{-1}(x)$, showing clearly the points where the curves meet the coordinate axes.

Answers

$y = (x - 2)^2$

This part of the expression is a square so it will always be $\geqslant 0$. The smallest value it can be is 0. This occurs when $x = 2$.

When $x = 5$, $y = 9$.

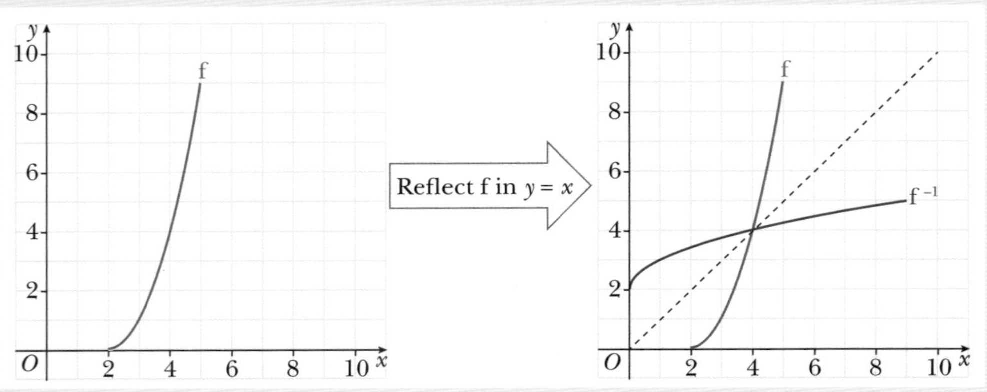

CLASS DISCUSSION

Sundeep says that the diagram shows the graph of the function $f(x) = x^x$ for $x > 0$, together with its inverse function $y = f^{-1}(x)$.

Is Sundeep correct?

Explain your answer.

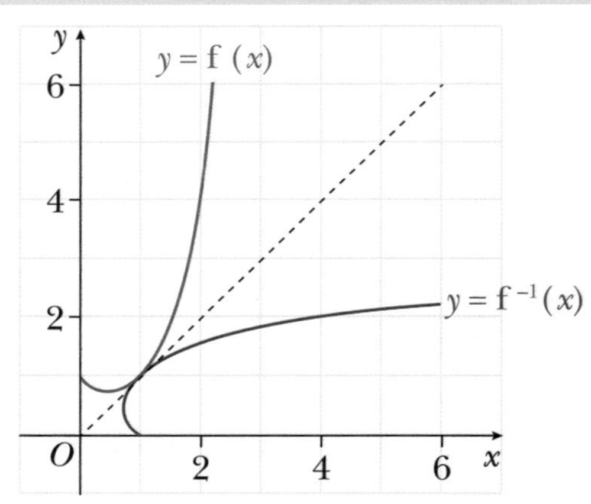

Exercise 1.7

1 On a copy of the grid, draw the graph of the inverse of the function f.

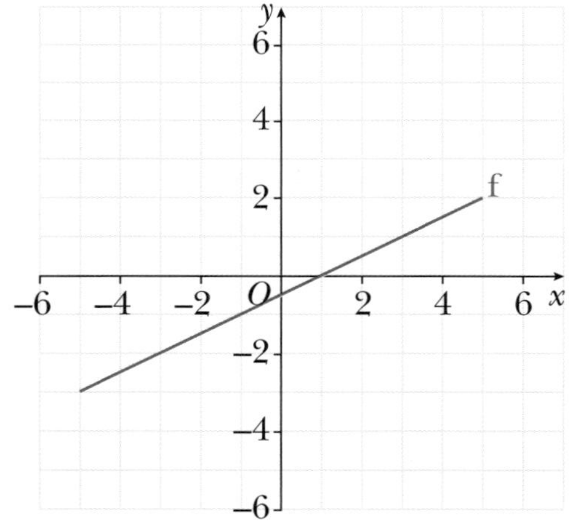

2 On a copy of the grid, draw the graph of the inverse of the function g.

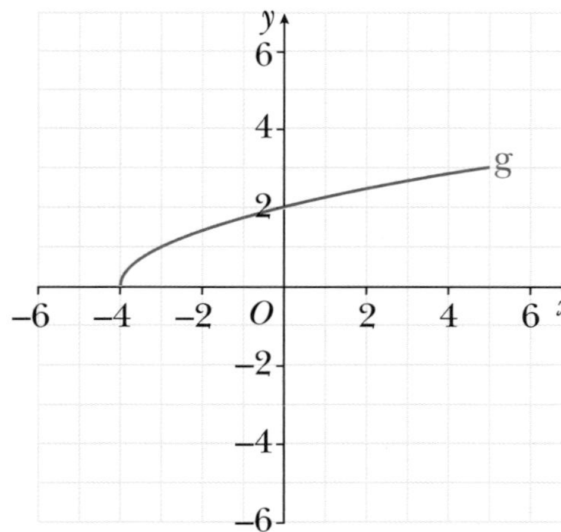

3 $f(x) = x^2 + 3, x \geqslant 0.$

On the same axes, sketch the graphs of $y = f(x)$ and $y = f^{-1}(x)$, showing the coordinates of any points where the curves meet the coordinate axes.

4 $g(x) = 2^x$ for $x \in \mathbb{R}$

On the same axes, sketch the graphs of $y = g(x)$ and $y = g^{-1}(x)$, showing the coordinates of any points where the curves meet the coordinate axes.

5 $g(x) = x^2 - 1$ for $x \geqslant 0.$

Sketch, on a single diagram, the graphs of $y = g(x)$ and $y = g^{-1}(x)$, showing the coordinates of any points where the curves meet the coordinate axes.

6 $f(x) = 4x - 2$ for $-1 \leqslant x \leqslant 3.$

Sketch, on a single diagram, the graphs of $y = f(x)$ and $y = f^{-1}(x)$, showing the coordinates of any points where the lines meet the coordinate axes.

7 The function f is defined by $f : x \mapsto 3 - (x + 1)^2$ for $x \geqslant -1.$

a Explain why f has an inverse.

b Find an expression for f^{-1} in terms of x.

c On the same axes, sketch the graphs of $y = f(x)$ and $y = f^{-1}(x)$, showing the coordinates of any points where the curves meet the coordinate axes.

CHALLENGE Q

8 $f : x \mapsto \dfrac{2x + 7}{x - 2}$ for $x \neq 2$

a Find f^{-1} in terms of x.

b Explain what this implies about the symmetry of the graph of $y = f(x)$.

Summary

Functions

A function is a rule that maps each x-value to just one y-value for a defined set of input values.

Mappings that are either $\begin{cases} \text{one-one} \\ \text{many-one} \end{cases}$ are called functions.

The set of input values for a function is called the **domain** of the function.

The set of output values for a function is called the **range** (or image set) of the function.

Modulus function

The modulus of x, written as $|x|$, is defined as:

$$|x| = \begin{cases} x & \text{if } x > 0 \\ 0 & \text{if } x = 0 \\ -x & \text{if } x < 0 \end{cases}$$

Composite functions

$fg(x)$ means the function g acts on x first, then f acts on the result.

$f^2(x)$ means $ff(x)$.

Inverse functions

The inverse of a function $f(x)$ is the function that undoes what $f(x)$ has done.

The inverse of the function $f(x)$ is written as $f^{-1}(x)$.

The domain of $f^{-1}(x)$ is the range of $f(x)$.

The range of $f^{-1}(x)$ is the domain of $f(x)$.

An inverse function $f^{-1}(x)$ can exist if, and only if, the function $f(x)$ is a one-one mapping.

The graphs of f and f^{-1} are reflections of each other in the line $y = x$.

Examination questions

Worked example

The functions f and g are defined by

$$f(x) = \frac{2x}{x+1} \quad \text{for} \quad x > 0,$$

$$g(x) = \sqrt{x+1} \quad \text{for} \quad x > -1.$$

a Find fg(8). [2]

b Find an expression for $f^2(x)$, giving your answer in the form $\frac{ax}{bx+c}$ where a, b and c are integers to be found. [3]

c Find an expression for $g^{-1}(x)$, stating its domain and range. [4]

Cambridge IGCSE Additional Mathematics 0606 Paper 21 Q12i,ii,iii Jun 2014

Answers

a $g(8) = \sqrt{8+1} = 3$

$fg(8) = f(3)$ — substitute 3 for x in $\frac{2x}{x+1}$

$= \frac{2(3)}{3+1}$

$= 1.5$

b $f^2(x) = ff(x)$

$= f\left(\frac{2x}{x+1}\right)$ — substitute $\frac{2x}{x+1}$ for x in $\frac{2x}{x+1}$

$= \frac{2\left(\frac{2x}{x+1}\right)}{\left(\frac{2x}{x+1}\right)+1}$ — simplify

$= \frac{\frac{4x}{x+1}}{\frac{3x+1}{x+1}}$ — multiply numerator and denominator by $x + 1$

$= \frac{4x}{3x+1}$

$a = 4$, $b = 3$ and $c = 1$

c $g(x) = \sqrt{x+1}$ for $x > -1$

Step 1: Write the function as $y =$ ⟶ $y = \sqrt{x+1}$

Step 2: Interchange the x and y variables. ⟶ $x = \sqrt{y+1}$

Step 3: Rearrange to make y the subject. ⟶ $x^2 = y + 1$

$y = x^2 - 1$

$g^{-1}(x) = x^2 - 1$

The range of g is $g(x) > 0$ so the domain of g^{-1} is $x > 0$.

The domain of g is $x > -1$ so the range of g^{-1} is $x > -1$.

Exercise 1.8

Exam Exercise

1 Solve the equation $|4x - 5| = 21$. [3]

Cambridge IGCSE Additional Mathematics 0606 Paper 21 Q1 Nov 2011

2 **a** Sketch the graph of $y = |3 + 5x|$, showing the coordinates of the points where your graph meets the coordinate axes. [2]

b Solve the equation $|3 + 5x| = 2$. [2]

Cambridge IGCSE Additional Mathematics 0606 Paper 11 Q1i,ii Nov 2012

3 **a** Sketch the graph of $y = |2x - 5|$, showing the coordinates of the points where the graph meets the coordinate axes. [2]

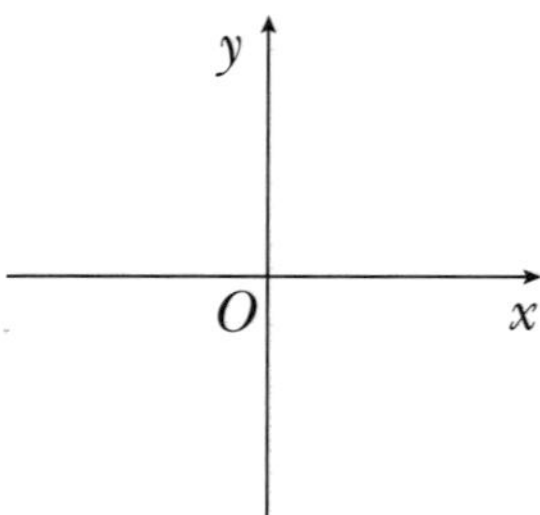

b Solve $|2x - 5| = 3$. [2]

Cambridge IGCSE Additional Mathematics 0606 Paper 11 Q1i,ii Jun 2012

4 A function f is such that $f(x) = 3x^2 - 1$ for $-10 \leqslant x \leqslant 8$.

a Find the range of f. [3]

b Write down a suitable domain for f for which f^{-1} exists. [1]

Cambridge IGCSE Additional Mathematics 0606 Paper 11 Q12ai,ii Nov 2013

5 The functions f and g are defined for real values of x by

$$f(x) = \sqrt{x-1} - 3 \quad \text{for } x > 1,$$

$$g(x) = \frac{x-2}{2x-3} \quad \text{for } x > 2.$$

a Find gf(37). [2]

b Find an expression for $f^{-1}(x)$. [2]

c Find an expression for $g^{-1}(x)$. [2]

Cambridge IGCSE Additional Mathematics 0606 Paper 21 Q4 Nov 2014

6 A function g is such that $g(x) = \frac{1}{2x-1}$ for $1 \leqslant x \leqslant 3$.

a Find the range of g. [1]

b Find $g^{-1}(x)$. [2]

c Write down the domain of $g^{-1}(x)$. [1]

d Solve $g^2(x) = 3$. [3]

Cambridge IGCSE Additional Mathematics 0606 Paper 11 Q9i-iv Nov 2012

7 **a** The functions f and g are defined, for $x \in \mathbb{R}$, by

$$f : x \mapsto 2x + 3$$

$$g : x \mapsto x^2 - 1.$$

Find fg(4). [2]

b The functions h and k are defined, for $x > 0$, by

$$h : x \mapsto x + 4$$

$$k : x \mapsto \sqrt{x}.$$

Express each of the following in terms of h and k.

i $x \mapsto \sqrt{x+4}$ [1]

ii $x \mapsto x + 8$ [1]

iii $x \mapsto x^2 - 4$ [2]

Cambridge IGCSE Additional Mathematics 0606 Paper 21 Q5a,bi,ii,iii Nov 2011

8 The function f is defined by $f(x) = 2 - \sqrt{x+5}$ for $-5 \leqslant x < 0$.

i Write down the range of f. [2]

ii Find $f^{-1}(x)$ and state its domain and range. [4]

The function g is defined by $g(x) = \frac{4}{x}$ for $-5 \leqslant x < -1$.

iii Solve $fg(x) = 0$. [3]

Cambridge IGCSE Additional Mathematics 0606 Paper 11 Q6 Jun 2016

9 **a** The function f is such that $f(x) = 2x^2 - 8x + 5$.

i Show that $f(x) = 2(x + a)^2 + b$, where a and b are to be found. [2]

ii Hence, or otherwise, write down a suitable domain for f so that f^{-1} exists. [1]

b The functions g and h are defined respectively by

$$g(x) = x^2 + 4,\ x \geqslant 0, \quad h(x) = 4x - 25,\ x \geqslant 0,$$

i Write down the range of g and of h^{-1}. [2]

ii On a copy of the axes below sketch the graphs of $y = g(x)$ and of $y = g^{-1}(x)$, showing the coordinates of any points where the curves meet the coordinate axes. [3]

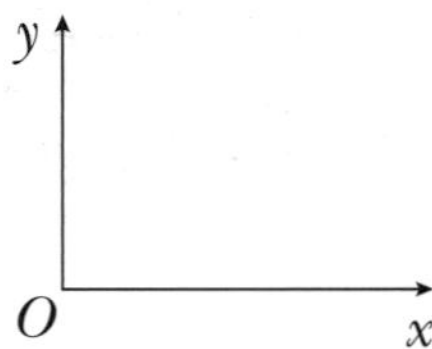

iii Find the value of x for which $gh(x) = 85$. [4]

Cambridge IGCSE Additional Mathematics 0606 Paper 11 Q11ai,ii,bi,ii,iii Jun 2011

10 i On the axes below, sketch the graphs of $y = 2 - x$ and $y = |3 + 2x|$. [4]

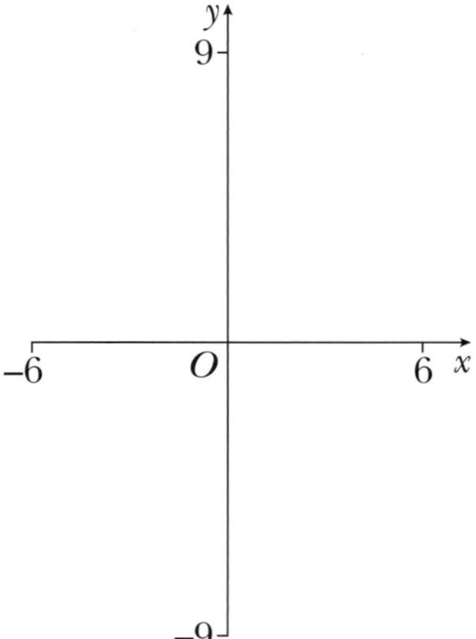

ii Solve $|3 + 2x| = 2 - x$. [3]

Cambridge IGCSE Additional Mathematics 0606 Paper 12 Q4 Mar 2016

Chapter 2
Simultaneous equations and quadratics

This section will show you how to:

- solve simultaneous equations in two unknowns by elimination or substitution
- find the maximum and minimum values of a quadratic function
- sketch graphs of quadratic functions and find their range for a given domain
- sketch graphs of the function $y = |f(x)|$ where $f(x)$ is quadratic and solve associated equations
- determine the number of roots of a quadratic equation and the related conditions for a line to intersect, be a tangent or not intersect a given curve
- solve quadratic equations for real roots and find the solution set for quadratic inequalities.

RECAP (simultaneous equations)

You should already know how to use a graphical method or an algebraic method to solve simultaneous equations where both equations are linear.

To solve simultaneous linear equations algebraically you should know both the elimination method and the substitution method.

Elimination method

Solve $5x + 2y = 25$ ----------------(1)

$2x - y = 1$ ----------------(2)

Multiply (2) by 2.

$5x + 2y = 25$

$4x - 2y = 2$

Add the equations to eliminate y.

$9x = 27$

$x = 3$

Substitute for x in equation (2).

$6 - y = 1$

$y = 5$

Solution is $x = 3$, $y = 5$.

Substitution method

Solve $5x + 2y = 25$ --------------(1)

$2x - y = 1$ --------------(2)

Make y the subject of equation (2).

$y = 2x - 1$

Substitute for y in equation (1).

$5x + 2(2x - 1) = 25$

$9x - 2 = 25$

$9x = 27$

$x = 3$

Substitute for x in equation (2).

$6 - y = 1$

$y = 5$

Solution is $x = 3$, $y = 5$.

CLASS DISCUSSION

Solve each of these three pairs of simultaneous equations.

$8x + 3y = 7$
$3x + 5y = -9$

$3x + y = 10$
$2y = 15 - 6x$

$2x + 5 = 3y$
$10 - 6y = -4x$

Discuss your answers with your classmates.

Discuss what the graphs would be like for each pair of equations.

RECAP (quadratic equations)

You should already know how to use a graphical method or an algebraic method to solve quadratic equations.

To solve quadratic equations algebraically you should know the factorisation method, the quadratic formula method and the completing the square method.

Factorisation method

Solve $x^2 - 4x - 12 = 0.$

Factorise:

$$(x - 6)(x + 2) = 0$$

$$x - 6 = 0 \quad \text{or} \quad x + 2 = 0$$

Solution is $x = 6$ or $x = -2.$

Completing the square method

Solve $x^2 - 4x - 12 = 0.$

Complete the square.

$$(x - 2)^2 - 4 - 12 = 0$$

$$(x - 2)^2 = 16$$

Square root both sides.

$$x - 2 = \pm 4$$

$$x - 2 = 4 \quad \text{or} \quad x - 2 = -4$$

Solution is $x = 6$ or $x = -2.$

Quadratic formula method

Solve $x^2 - 4x - 12 = 0.$

Identify a, b and c

$a = 1$, $b = -4$ and $c = -12.$

Use the formula:

$$x = \frac{-b \pm \sqrt{b^2 - 4ac}}{2a}$$

Substitute for a, b and c.

$$x = \frac{4 \pm \sqrt{(-4)^2 - 4 \times 1 \times (-12)}}{2 \times 1}$$

$$x = \frac{4 \pm \sqrt{64}}{2}$$

$$x = \frac{4 \pm 8}{2}$$

$$x = \frac{4 + 8}{2} \quad \text{or} \quad x = \frac{4 - 8}{2}$$

Solution is $x = 6$ or $x = -2.$

CLASS DISCUSSION

Solve each of these quadratic equations.

$x^2 - 8x + 15 = 0$ $\quad$ $x^2 + 4x + 4 = 0$ $\quad$ $x^2 + 2x + 4 = 0$

Discuss your answers with your classmates. Discuss what the graphs would be like for each of the functions $y = x^2 - 8x + 15$, $y = x^2 + 4x + 4$ and $y = x^2 + 2x + 4$.

2.1 Simultaneous equations (one linear and one non-linear)

In this section you will learn how to solve simultaneous equations where one equation is linear and the second equation is not linear.

The diagram shows the graphs of $y = x + 1$ and $y = x^2 - 5$.

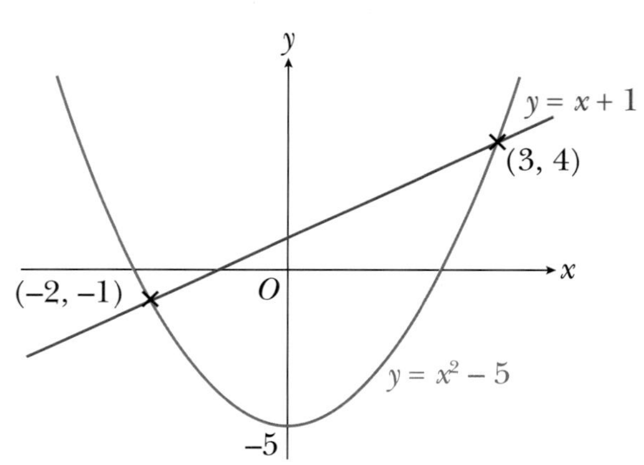

The coordinates of the points of intersection of the two graphs are (–2, –1) and (3, 4).

We say that $x = -2$, $y = -1$ and $x = 3$, $y = 4$ are the solutions of the simultaneous equations $y = x + 1$ and $y = x^2 - 5$.

The solutions can also be found algebraically:

$y = x + 1$ -------(1)
$y = x^2 - 5$ ------(2)

Substitute for y from (1) into (2):

$$x + 1 = x^2 - 5 \quad \text{rearrange}$$
$$x^2 - x - 6 = 0 \quad \text{factorise}$$
$$(x + 2)(x - 3) = 0$$
$$x = -2 \text{ or } x = 3$$

Substituting $x = -2$ into (1) gives $y = -2 + 1 = -1$.
Substituting $x = 3$ into (1) gives $y = 3 + 1 = 4$.
The solutions are: $x = -2$, $y = -1$ and $x = 3$, $y = 4$.

WORKED EXAMPLE 1

Solve the simultaneous equations.

$2x + 2y = 7$

$x^2 - 4y^2 = 8$

Answers

$2x + 2y = 7$ -------(1)
$x^2 - 4y^2 = 8$ ------(2)

From (1), $x = \dfrac{7 - 2y}{2}$.
Substitute for x in (2):

$$\left(\frac{7 - 2y}{2}\right)^2 - 4y^2 = 8 \quad \text{expand brackets}$$

$$\frac{49 - 28y + 4y^2}{4} - 4y^2 = 8 \quad \text{multiply both sides by 4}$$

$$49 - 28y + 4y^2 - 16y^2 = 32 \quad \text{rearrange}$$

$$12y^2 + 28y - 17 = 0 \quad \text{factorise}$$

$$(6y + 17)(2y - 1) = 0$$

$$y = -2\frac{5}{6} \text{ or } y = \frac{1}{2}$$

Substituting $y = -2\dfrac{5}{6}$ into (1) gives $x = 6\dfrac{1}{3}$.

Substituting $y = \dfrac{1}{2}$ into (1) gives $x = 3$.

The solutions are: $x = 6\dfrac{1}{3}$, $y = -2\dfrac{5}{6}$ and $x = 3$, $y = \dfrac{1}{2}$.

Exercise 2.1

Solve the following simultaneous equations.

1 $y = x^2$
$y = x + 6$

2 $y = x - 6$
$x^2 + xy = 8$

3 $y = x - 1$
$x^2 + y^2 = 25$

4 $xy = 4$
$y = 2x + 2$

5 $x^2 - xy = 0$
$x + y = 1$

6 $3y = 4x - 5$
$x^2 + 3xy = 10$

7 $2x + y = 7$
$xy = 6$

8 $x - y = 2$
$2x^2 - 3y^2 = 15$

9 $x + 2y = 7$
$x^2 + y^2 = 10$

10 $y = 2x$
$x^2 + xy = 3$

11 $xy = 2$
$x + y = 3$

12 $y^2 = 4x$
$2x + y = 4$

13 $x + 3y = 0$
$2x^2 + 3y = 1$

14 $x + y = 4$
$x^2 + y^2 = 10$

15 $y = 3x$
$2y^2 - xy = 15$

16 $x - 2y = 1$
$4y^2 - 3x^2 = 1$

17 $3 + x + xy = 0$
$2x + 5y = 8$

18 $xy = 12$
$(x - 1)(y + 2) = 15$

19 Calculate the coordinates of the points where the line $y = 1 - 2x$ cuts the curve $x^2 + y^2 = 2$.

20 The sum of two numbers x and y is 11.

The product of the two numbers is 21.25.

a Write down two equations in x and y.

b Solve your equations to find the possible values of x and y.

21 The sum of the areas of two squares is $818\,\text{cm}^2$.

The sum of the perimeters is 160 cm.

Find the lengths of the sides of the squares.

22 The line $y = 2 - 2x$ cuts the curve $3x^2 - y^2 = 3$ at the points A and B.

Find the length of the line AB.

23 The line $2x + 5y = 1$ meets the curve $x^2 + 5xy - 4y^2 + 10 = 0$ at the points A and B.

Find the coordinates of the midpoint of AB.

24 The line $y = x - 10$ intersects the curve $x^2 + y^2 + 4x + 6y - 40 = 0$ at the points A and B.

Find the length of the line AB.

25 The straight line $y = 2x - 2$ intersects the curve $x^2 - y = 5$ at the points A and B.

Given that A lies below the x-axis and the point P lies on AB such that $AP : PB = 3 : 1$, find the coordinates of P.

26 The line $x - 2y = 2$ intersects the curve $x + y^2 = 10$ at two points A and B.

Find the equation of the perpendicular bisector of the line AB.

2.2 Maximum and minimum values of a quadratic function

RECAP

The general equation of a quadratic function is $f(x) = ax^2 + bx + c$, where a, b and c are constants and $a \neq 0$.

The graph of the function $y = ax^2 + bx + c$ is called a **parabola**. The orientation of the parabola depends on the value of a, the coefficient of x^2.

If $a > 0$, the curve has a **minimum point** which occurs at the lowest point of the curve.

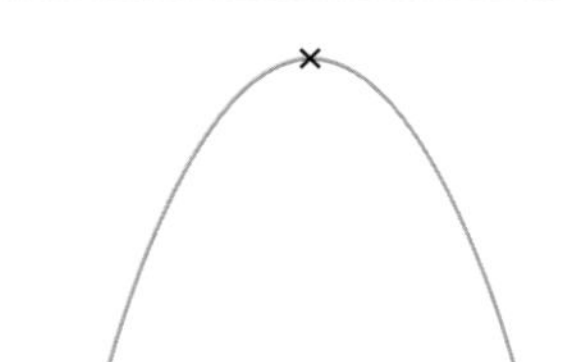

If $a < 0$, the curve has a **maximum point** which occurs at the highest point of the curve.

The maximum and minimum points can also be called **turning points or stationary points.**
Every parabola has a line of symmetry that passes through the maximum or minimum point.

WORKED EXAMPLE 2

$f(x) = x^2 - 3x - 4 \qquad x \in \mathbb{R}$

a Find the axis crossing points for the graph of $y = f(x)$.

b Sketch the graph of $y = f(x)$ and use the symmetry of the curve to find the coordinates of the minimum point.

c State the range of the function $f(x)$.

Answers

a $y = x^2 - 3x - 4$

When $x = 0$, $y = -4$.

When $y = 0$,

$x^2 - 3x - 4 = 0$

$(x + 1)(x - 4) = 0$

$x = -1$ or $x = 4$

Axes crossing points are: $(0, -4)$, $(-1, 0)$ and $(4, 0)$.

b The line of symmetry cuts the x-axis midway between -1 and 4.

So the line of symmetry is $x = 1.5$

When $x = 1.5$, $y = (1.5)^2 - 3(1.5) - 4$.

$y = -6.25$.

Minimum point $= (1.5, -6.25)$.

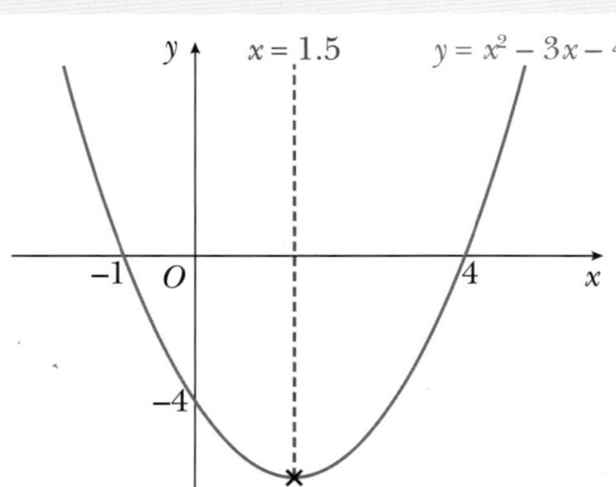

c The range is $f(x) \geqslant -6.25$.

Completing the square

If you expand the expressions $(x+d)^2$ and $(x-d)^2$ you obtain the results:

$$(x+d)^2 = x^2 + 2dx + d^2 \quad \text{and} \quad (x-d)^2 = x^2 - 2dx + d^2$$

Rearranging these give the following important results:

$$x^2 + 2dx = (x+d)^2 - d^2$$

$$x^2 - 2dx = (x-d)^2 - d^2$$

This is known as **completing the square**.

To complete the square for $x^2 + 8x$:

$$8 \div 2 = 4$$

$$x^2 + 8x = (x+4)^2 - 4^2$$

$$x^2 + 8x = (x+4)^2 - 16$$

To complete the square for $x^2 + 10x - 3$:

$$10 \div 2 = 5$$

$$x^2 + 10x - 3 = (x+5)^2 - 5^2 - 3$$

$$x^2 + 10x - 3 = (x+5)^2 - 28$$

To complete the square for $2x^2 - 8x + 14$ you must first take a factor of 2 out of the expression:

$$2x^2 - 8x + 14 = 2[x^2 - 4x + 7]$$

$$4 \div 2 = 2$$

$$x^2 - 4x + 7 = (x-2)^2 - 2^2 + 7$$

$$x^2 - 4x + 3 = (x-2)^2 + 3$$

So, $2x^2 - 8x + 6 = 2[(x-2)^2 + 3] = 2(x-2)^2 + 6$

You can also use an algebraic method for completing the square, as shown in the following example.

WORKED EXAMPLE 3

Express $2x^2 - 4x + 5$ in the form $p(x-q)^2 + r$, where p, q and r are constants to be found.

Answers

$2x^2 - 4x + 5 = p(x-q)^2 + r$

Expanding the brackets and simplifying gives:

$2x^2 - 4x + 5 = px^2 - 2pqx + pq^2 + r$

Comparing coefficients of x^2, coefficients of x and the constant gives:

$2 = p$ --------(1) $\quad -4 = -2pq$ -------(2) $\quad 5 = pq^2 + r$ -------(3)

Substituting $p = 2$ in equation (2) gives $q = 1$.

Substituting $p = 2$ and $q = 1$ in equation (3) gives $r = 3$.

So $2x^2 - 4x + 5 = 2(x-1)^2 + 3$.

Completing the square for a quadratic expression or function enables you to:

- write down the maximum or minimum value of the expression
- write down the coordinates of the maximum or minimum point of the function
- sketch the graph of the function
- write down the line of symmetry of the function
- state the range of the function.

In **Worked example 3** you found that:

$$2x^2 - 4x + 5 = 2(x-1)^2 + 3$$

This part of the expression is a square so it will always be $\geqslant 0$. The smallest value it can be is 0. This occurs when $x = 1$.

The minimum value of the expression is $2 \times 0 + 3 = 3$ and this minimum occurs when $x = 1$.

So the function $y = 2x^2 - 4x + 5$ will have a minimum point at the point (1, 3).

When $x = 0$, $y = 5$.

The graph of $y = 2x^2 - 4x + 5$

can now be sketched:

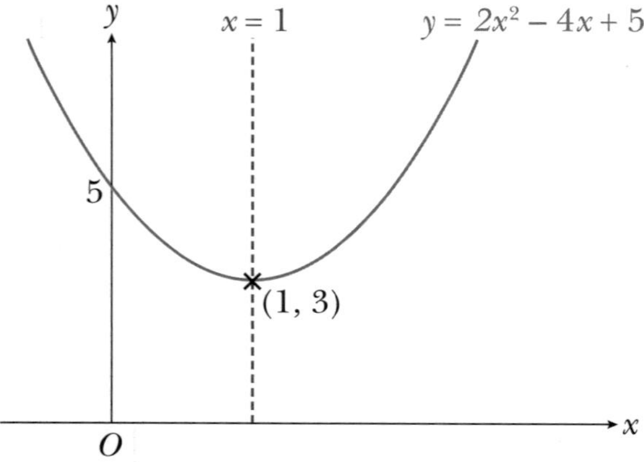

The line of symmetry is $x = 1$.

The range is $y \geqslant 3$.

The general rule is:

For a quadratic function $f(x) = ax^2 + bx + c$ that is written in the form $f(x) = a(x-h)^2 + k$,

i if $a > 0$, the minimum point is (h, k)

ii if $a < 0$, the maximum point is (h, k).

WORKED EXAMPLE 4

$f(x) = 2 + 8x - 2x^2 \qquad x \in \mathbb{R}$

a Find the value of a, the value of b and the value of c for which $f(x) = a - b(x + c)^2$.

b Write down the coordinates of the maximum point on the curve $y = f(x)$.

c Sketch the graph of $y = f(x)$, showing the coordinates of the points where the graph intersects the x and y-axes.

d State the range of the function $f(x)$.

Answers

a $2 + 8x - 2x^2 = a - b(x + c)^2$

$2 + 8x - 2x^2 = a - b(x^2 + 2cx + c^2)$

$2 + 8x - 2x^2 = a - bx^2 - 2bcx - bc^2$

Comparing coefficients of x^2, coefficients of x and the constant gives:

$-2 = -b$ --------(1) $\qquad 8 = -2bc$ --------(2) $\qquad 2 = a - bc^2$ --------(3)

Substituting $b = 2$ in equation (2) gives $c = -2$.

Substituting $b = 2$ and $c = -2$ in equation (3) gives $a = 10$.

So $a = 10$, $b = 2$ and $c = -2$.

b $y = 10 - 2(x - 2)^2$

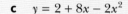

This part of the expression is a square so it will always be $\geqslant 0$. The smallest value it can be is 0. This occurs when $x = 2$.

The maximum value of the expression is $10 - 2 \times 0 = 10$ and this maximum occurs when $x = 2$.

So the function $y = 2 + 8x - 2x^2$ will have maximum point at the point $(2, 10)$.

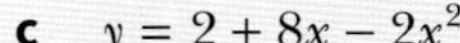

c $y = 2 + 8x - 2x^2$

When $x = 0$, $y = 2$.

When $y = 0$,

$10 - 2(x - 2)^2 = 0$

$2(x - 2)^2 = 10$

$(x - 2)^2 = 5$

$x - 2 = \pm\sqrt{5}$

$x = 2 \pm \sqrt{5}$

$x = 2 - \sqrt{5}$ or $x = 2 + \sqrt{5}$

($x = -0.236$ or $x = 4.24$ to 3 sf).

Axes crossing points are: $(0, 2)$, $(2 - \sqrt{5}, 0)$ and $(2 + \sqrt{5}, 0)$.

d The range is $f(x) \leqslant 10$.

Exercise 2.2

1 Use the symmetry of each quadratic function to find the maximum or minimum points.

Sketch each graph, showing all axis crossing points.

a $y = x^2 - 5x - 6$ **b** $y = x^2 - x - 20$ **c** $y = x^2 + 4x - 21$

d $y = x^2 + 3x - 28$ **e** $y = x^2 + 4x + 1$ **f** $y = 15 + 2x - x^2$

2 Express each of the following in the form $(x - m)^2 + n$.

a $x^2 - 8x$ **b** $x^2 - 10x$ **c** $x^2 - 5x$ **d** $x^2 - 3x$

e $x^2 + 4x$ **f** $x^2 + 7x$ **g** $x^2 + 9x$ **h** $x^2 + 3x$

3 Express each of the following in the form $(x - m)^2 + n$.

a $x^2 - 8x + 15$ **b** $x^2 - 10x - 5$ **c** $x^2 - 6x + 2$ **d** $x^2 - 3x + 4$

e $x^2 + 6x + 5$ **f** $x^2 + 6x + 9$ **g** $x^2 + 4x - 17$ **h** $x^2 + 5x + 6$

4 Express each of the following in the form $a(x - p)^2 + q$.

a $2x^2 - 8x + 3$ **b** $2x^2 - 12x + 1$ **c** $3x^2 - 12x + 5$ **d** $2x^2 - 3x + 2$

e $2x^2 + 4x + 1$ **f** $2x^2 + 7x - 3$ **g** $2x^2 - 3x + 5$ **h** $3x^2 - x + 6$

5 Express each of the following in the form $m - (x - n)^2$.

a $6x - x^2$ **b** $10x - x^2$ **c** $3x - x^2$ **d** $8x - x^2$

6 Express each of the following in the form $a - (x + b)^2$.

a $5 - 2x - x^2$ **b** $8 - 4x - x^2$ **c** $10 - 5x - x^2$ **d** $7 + 3x - x^2$

7 Express each of the following in the form $a - p(x + q)^2$.

a $9 - 6x - 2x^2$ **b** $1 - 4x - 2x^2$ **c** $7 + 8x - 2x^2$ **d** $2 + 5x - 3x^2$

8 **a** Express $4x^2 + 2x + 5$ in the form $a(x + b)^2 + c$, where a, b and c are constants.

b Does the function $y = 4x^2 + 2x + 5$ meet the x-axis? Explain your answer.

9 $f(x) = 2x^2 - 8x + 1$

a Express $2x^2 - 8x + 1$ in the form $a(x + b)^2 + c$, where a and b are integers.

b Find the coordinates of the stationary point on the graph of $y = f(x)$.

10 $f(x) = x^2 - x - 5$ for $x \in \mathbb{R}$

a Find the smallest value of $f(x)$ and the corresponding value of x.

b Hence write down a suitable domain for $f(x)$ in order that $f^{-1}(x)$ exists.

11 $f(x) = 5 - 7x - 2x^2$ for $x \in \mathbb{R}$

a Write $f(x)$ in the form $p - 2(x - q)^2$, where p and q are constants to be found.

b Write down the range of the function $f(x)$.

12 $f(x) = 14 + 6x - 2x^2$ for $x \in \mathbb{R}$

a Express $14 + 6x - 2x^2$ in the form $a + b(x + c)^2$, where a, b and c are constants.

b Write down the coordinates of the stationary point on the graph of $y = f(x)$.

c Sketch the graph of $y = f(x)$.

13 $f(x) = 7 + 5x - x^2$ for $0 \leqslant x \leqslant 7$

a Express $7 + 5x - x^2$ in the form $a - (x + b)^2$, where a, and b are constants.

b Find the coordinates of the turning point of the function $f(x)$, stating whether it is a maximum or minimum point.

c Find the range of f.

d State, giving a reason, whether or not f has an inverse.

14 The function f is such that $f(x) = 2x^2 - 8x + 3$.

a Write $f(x)$ in the form $2(x + a)^2 + b$, where a, and b are constants to be found.

b Write down a suitable domain for f so that f^{-1} exists.

15 $f(x) = 4x^2 + 6x - 8$ where $x \geqslant m$

Find the smallest value of m for which f has an inverse.

16 $f(x) = 1 + 4x - x^2$ for $x \geqslant 2$

a Express $1 + 4x - x^2$ in the form $a - (x + b)^2$, where a and b are constants to be found.

b Find the coordinates of the turning point of the function $f(x)$, stating whether it is a maximum or minimum point.

c Explain why $f(x)$ has an inverse and find an expression for $f^{-1}(x)$ in terms of x.

2.3 Graphs of $y = |f(x)|$ where $f(x)$ is quadratic

To sketch the graph of the modulus function $y = |ax^2 + bx + c|$, you must:

- first sketch the graph of $y = ax^2 + bx + c$
- reflect in the x-axis the part of the curve $y = ax^2 + bx + c$ that is below the x-axis.

WORKED EXAMPLE 5

Sketch the graph of $y = |x^2 - 2x - 3|$.

Answers

First sketch the graph of $y = x^2 - 2x - 3$.

When $x = 0$, $y = -3$.

So the y-intercept is -3.

When $y = 0$,

$$x^2 - 2x - 3 = 0$$

$$(x + 1)(x - 3) = 0$$

$$x = -1 \text{ or } x = 3.$$

So the x-intercepts are -1 and 3.

The x-coordinate of the minimum point $= \dfrac{-1 + 3}{2} = 1$.

The y-coordinate of the minimum point $= (1)^2 - 2(1) - 3 = -4$.

The minimum point is $(1, -4)$.

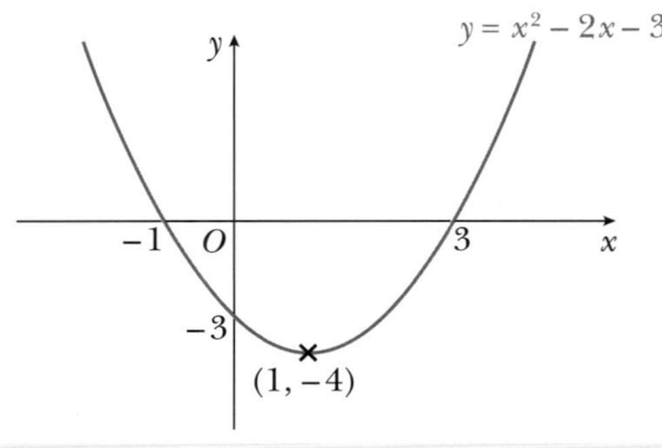

Now reflect in the x-axis the part of the curve $y = x^2 - 2x - 3$ that is below the x-axis.

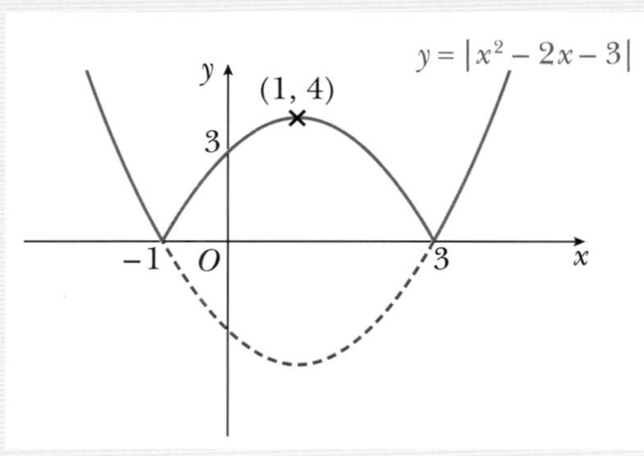

A sketch of the function $y = |x^2 + 4x - 12|$ is shown below.

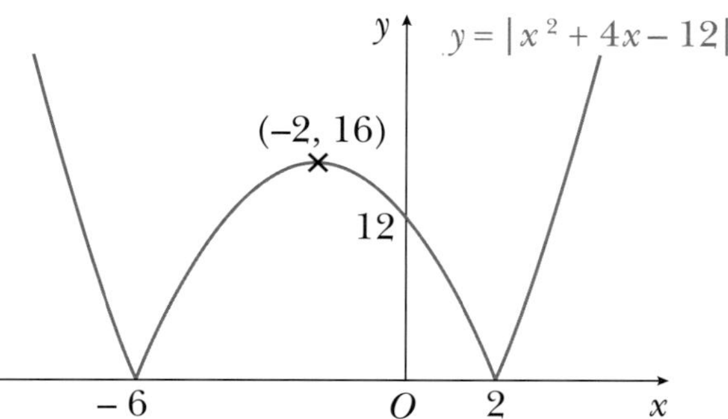

Now consider using this graph to find the number of solutions of the equation $|x^2 + 4x - 12| = k$ where $k \geqslant 0$.

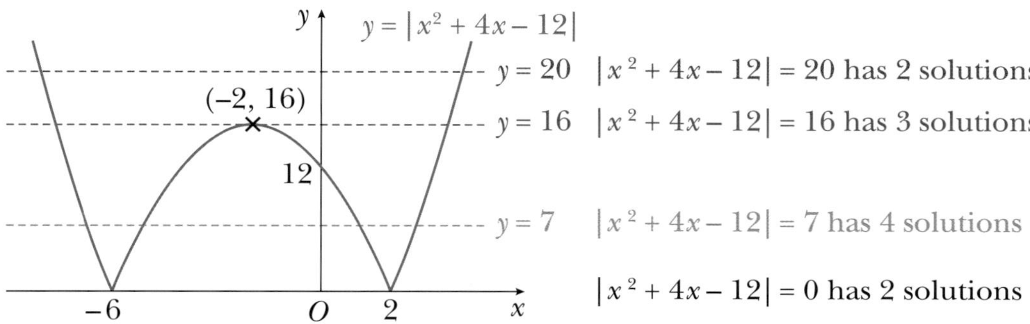

The conditions for the number of solutions of the equation $|x^2 + 4x - 12| = k$ are:

Value of k	$k = 0$	$0 < k < 16$	$k = 16$	$k > 16$
Number of solutions	2	4	3	2

Equations involving $|f(x)|$, where $f(x)$ is quadratic, can be solved algebraically:

To solve $|x^2 + 4x - 12| = 16$:

$x^2 + 4x - 12 = 16$ or $x^2 + 4x - 12 = -16$

$x^2 + 4x - 28 = 0$ or $x^2 + 4x + 4 = 0$

$x = \dfrac{-4 \pm \sqrt{4^2 - 4 \times 1 \times (-28)}}{2 \times 1}$ or $(x + 2)(x + 2) = 0$

$x = \dfrac{-4 \pm \sqrt{128}}{2}$ or $x = -2$

$x = -2 \pm 4\sqrt{2}$

($x = 3.66$ or $x = -7.66$ to 3 sf)

The exact solutions are $x = -2 - 4\sqrt{2}$ or $x = -2$ or $x = -2 + 4\sqrt{2}$.

Note:
The graph of $y = |x^2 + 4x - 12|$ is sketched below showing these three solutions.

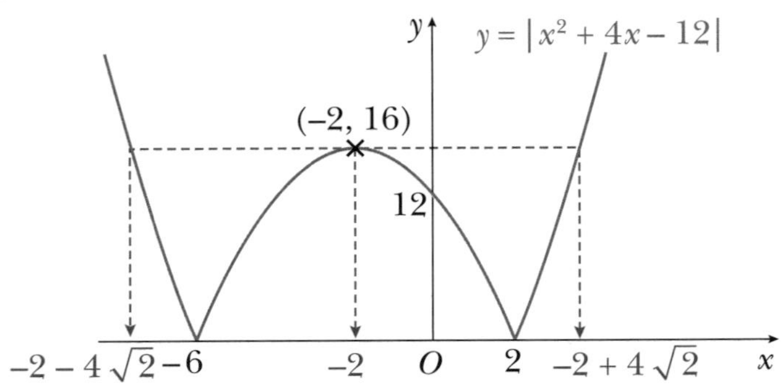

Exercise 2.3

1 Sketch the graphs of each of the following functions.

a $y = |x^2 - 4x + 3|$ **b** $y = |x^2 - 2x - 3|$ **c** $y = |x^2 - 5x + 4|$

d $y = |x^2 - 2x - 8|$ **e** $y = |2x^2 - 11x - 6|$ **f** $y = |3x^2 + 5x - 2|$

2 $f(x) = 1 - 4x - x^2$

a Write f(x) in the form $a - (x + b)^2$, where a and b are constants.

b Sketch the graph of $y = f(x)$.

c Sketch the graph of $y = |f(x)|$.

3 $f(x) = 2x^2 + x - 3$

a Write f(x) in the form $a(x + b)^2 + c$, where a, b and c are constants.

b Sketch the graph of $y = |f(x)|$.

4 **a** Find the coordinates of the stationary point on the curve $y = |(x - 7)(x + 1)|$.

b Sketch the graph of $y = |(x - 7)(x + 1)|$.

c Find the set of values of k for which $|(x - 7)(x + 1)| = k$ has four solutions.

5 **a** Find the coordinates of the stationary point on the curve $y = |(x + 5)(x + 1)|$.

b Find the set of values of k for which $|(x + 5)(x + 1)| = k$ has two solutions.

6 **a** Find the coordinates of the stationary point on the curve $y = |(x - 8)(x - 3)|$.

b Find the value of k for which $|(x - 8)(x - 3)| = k$ has three solutions.

7 Solve these equations.

a $|x^2 - 6| = 10$ **b** $|x^2 - 2| = 2$ **c** $|x^2 - 5x| = 6$

d $|x^2 + 2x| = 24$ **e** $|x^2 - 5x + 1| = 3$ **f** $|x^2 + 3x - 1| = 3$

g $|x^2 + 2x - 4| = 5$ **h** $|2x^2 - 3| = 2x$ **i** $|x^2 - 4x + 7| = 4$

CHALLENGE Q

8 Solve these simultaneous equations.

a $y = x + 1$
$y = |x^2 - 2x - 3|$

b $2y = x + 4$
$y = \left|\frac{1}{2}x^2 - x - 3\right|$

c $y = 2x$
$y = |2x^2 - 4|$

2.4 Quadratic inequalities

RECAP

You should already know how to solve linear inequalities.

Two examples are shown below.

Solve $2(x - 5) < 9$	expand brackets
$2x - 10 < 9$	add 10 to both sides
$2x < 19$	divide both sides by 2
$x < 9.5$	

Solve $5 - 3x \geqslant 17$	subtract 5 from both sides
$-3x \geqslant 12$	divide both sides by -3
$x \leqslant -4$	

Note:
It is very important that you remember the rule that when you multiply or divide both sides of an inequality by a negative number then the inequality sign must be reversed. This is illustrated in the second example above, when both sides of the inequality were divided by –3.

CLASS DISCUSSION

Robert is asked to solve the inequality $\frac{7x + 12}{x} \geqslant 3$.

He writes: $7x + 12 \geqslant 3x$
$4x \geqslant -12$
so $x \geqslant -3$

Anna checks his answer using the number –4.

She writes: When $x = -4$,
$(7 \times (-4) + 12) \div (-4) = (-16) \div (-4) = 4$
Hence $x = -4$ is a value of x that satisfies the original inequality
So Robert's answer must be incorrect!

Discuss Robert's working out with your classmates and explain Robert's error.

Now solve the inequality $\frac{7x + 12}{x} \geqslant 3$ correctly.

Quadratic inequalities can be solved by sketching a graph and considering when the graph is above or below the x-axis.

WORKED EXAMPLE 6

Solve $x^2 - 3x - 4 > 0$.

Answers

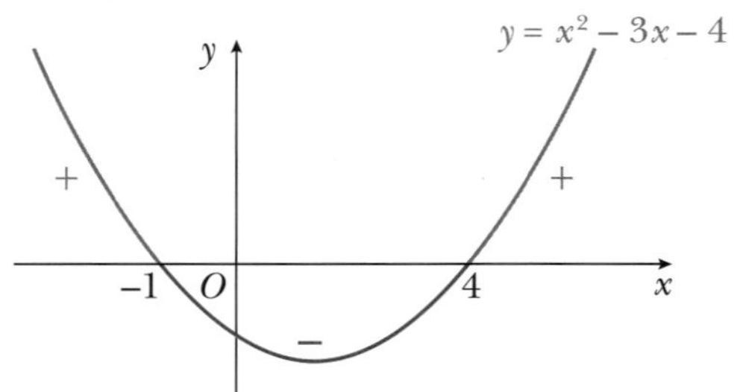

Sketch the graph of $y = x^2 - 3x - 4$.

When $y = 0$, $x^2 - 3x - 4 = 0$

$(x + 1)(x - 4) = 0$

$x = -1$ or $x = 4$.

So the x-axis crossing points are -1 and 4.

For $x^2 - 3x - 4 > 0$ you need to find the range of values of x for which the curve is positive (above the x-axis).

The solution is $x < -1$ and $x > 4$.

WORKED EXAMPLE 7

Solve $2x^2 \leqslant 15 - x$.

Answers

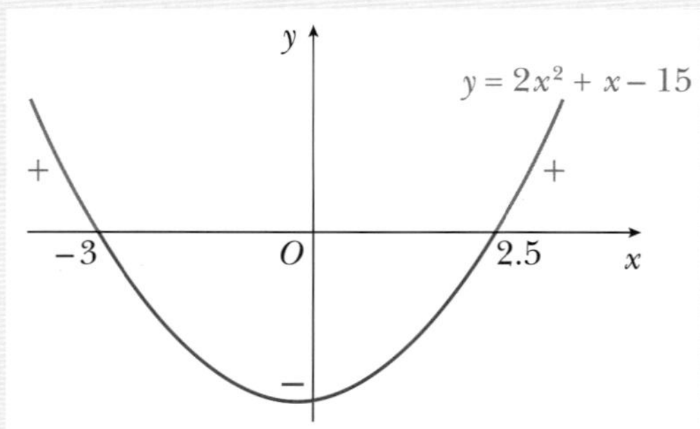

Rearranging: $2x^2 + x - 15 \leqslant 0$.

Sketch the graph of $y = 2x^2 + x - 15$.

When $y = 0$, $2x^2 + x - 15 = 0$

$(2x - 5)(x + 3) = 0$

$x = 2.5$ or $x = -3$.

So the x-axis crossing points are -3 and 2.5.

For $2x^2 + x - 15 \leqslant 0$ you need to find the range of values of x for which the curve is either zero or negative (below the x-axis).

The solution is $-3 \leqslant x \leqslant 2.5$.

Exercise 2.4

1 Solve.

a $(x + 3)(x - 4) > 0$ **b** $(x - 5)(x - 1) \leqslant 0$ **c** $(x - 3)(x + 7) \geqslant 0$

d $x(x - 5) < 0$ **e** $(2x + 1)(x - 4) < 0$ **f** $(3 - x)(x + 1) \geqslant 0$

g $(2x + 3)(x - 5) < 0$ **h** $(x - 5)^2 \geqslant 0$ **i** $(x - 3)^2 \leqslant 0$

2 Solve.

a $x^2 + 5x - 14 < 0$ **b** $x^2 + x - 6 \geqslant 0$ **c** $x^2 - 9x + 20 \leqslant 0$

d $x^2 + 2x - 48 > 0$ **e** $2x^2 - x - 15 \leqslant 0$ **f** $5x^2 + 9x + 4 > 0$

3 Solve.

a $x^2 < 18 - 3x$ **b** $12x < x^2 + 35$

c $x(3 - 2x) \leqslant 1$ **d** $x^2 + 4x < 3(x + 2)$

e $(x + 3)(1 - x) < x - 1$ **f** $(4x + 3)(3x - 1) < 2x(x + 3)$

4 Find the set of values of x for which

a $x^2 - 11x + 24 < 0$ and $2x + 3 < 13$

b $x^2 - 4x \leqslant 12$ and $4x - 3 > 1$

c $x(2x - 1) < 1$ and $7 - 2x < 6$

d $x^2 - 3x - 10 < 0$ and $x^2 - 10x + 21 < 0$

e $x^2 + x - 2 > 0$ and $x^2 - 2x - 3 \geqslant 0.$

5 Solve.

a $|x^2 + 2x - 2| < 13$ **b** $|x^2 - 8x + 6| < 6$ **c** $|x^2 - 6x + 4| < 4$

CHALLENGE Q

6 Find the range of values of x for which $\dfrac{4}{3x^2 - 2x - 8} < 0.$

2.5 Roots of quadratic equations

The answers to an equation are called the **roots** of the equation.

Consider solving the following three quadratic equations using the formula $x = \dfrac{-b \pm \sqrt{b^2 - 4ac}}{2a}$.

$x^2 + 2x - 8 = 0$ $x = \dfrac{-2 \pm \sqrt{2^2 - 4 \times 1 \times (-8)}}{2 \times 1}$ $x = \dfrac{-2 \pm \sqrt{36}}{2}$ $x = 2$ or $x = -4$	$x^2 + 6x + 9 = 0$ $x = \dfrac{-6 \pm \sqrt{6^2 - 4 \times 1 \times 9}}{2 \times 1}$ $x = \dfrac{-2 \pm \sqrt{0}}{2}$ $x = -1$ or $x = -1$	$x^2 + 2x + 6 = 0$ $x = \dfrac{-2 \pm \sqrt{2^2 - 4 \times 1 \times 6}}{2 \times 1}$ $x = \dfrac{-2 \pm \sqrt{-20}}{2}$ no solution
2 distinct roots	**2 equal roots**	**0 roots**

The part of the quadratic formula underneath the square root sign is called the **discriminant**.

$$\text{discriminant} = b^2 - 4ac$$

The sign (positive, zero or negative) of the discriminant tells you how many roots there are for a particular quadratic equation.

$b^2 - 4ac$	Nature of roots
> 0	2 real distinct roots
$= 0$	2 real equal roots
< 0	0 real roots

There is a connection between the roots of the quadratic equation $ax^2 + bx + c = 0$ and the corresponding curve $y = ax^2 + bx + c$.

$b^2 - 4ac$	Nature of roots of $ax^2 + bx + c = 0$	Shape of curve $y = ax^2 + bx + c$
> 0	2 real distinct roots	$a > 0$ x or $a < 0$ x The curve cuts the x-axis at 2 distinct points.
$= 0$	2 real equal roots	$a > 0$ x or $a < 0$ x The curve touches the x-axis at 1 point.
< 0	0 real roots	$a > 0$ x or $a < 0$ x The curve is entirely above or entirely below the x-axis.

WORKED EXAMPLE 8

Find the values of k for which $x^2 - 3x + 6 = k(x - 2)$ has two equal roots.

Answers

$$x^2 - 3x + 6 = k(x - 2)$$

$$x^2 - 3x + 6 - kx + 2k = 0$$

$$x^2 - (3 + k)x + 6 + 2k = 0$$

For two equal roots $b^2 - 4ac = 0$.

$$(3 + k)^2 - 4 \times 1 \times (6 + 2k) = 0$$

$$k^2 + 6k + 9 - 24 - 8k = 0$$

$$k^2 - 2k - 15 = 0$$

$$(k + 3)(k - 5) = 0$$

So $k = -3$ or $k = 5$.

WORKED EXAMPLE 9

Find the values of k for which $x^2 + (k-2)x + 4 = 0$ has two distinct roots.

Answers

$x^2 + (k-2)x + 4 = 0$

For two distinct roots $b^2 - 4ac > 0$

$$(k-2)^2 - 4 \times 1 \times 4 > 0$$

$$k^2 - 4k + 4 - 16 > 0$$

$$k^2 - 4k - 12 > 0$$

$$(k+2)(k-6) > 0$$

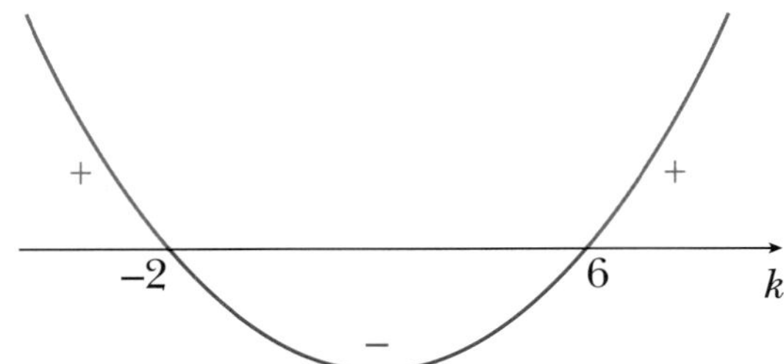

Critical values are −2 and 6.

So $k < -2$ or $k > 6$.

Exercise 2.5

1 State whether these equations have two distinct roots, two equal roots or no roots.

a $x^2 + 4x + 4$ **b** $x^2 + 4x - 21$ **c** $x^2 + 9x + 1$ **d** $x^2 - 3x + 15$

e $x^2 - 6x + 2$ **f** $4x^2 + 20x + 25$ **g** $3x^2 + 2x + 7$ **h** $5x^2 - 2x - 9$

2 Find the values of k for which $x^2 + kx + 9 = 0$ has two equal roots.

3 Find the values of k for which $kx^2 - 4x + 8 = 0$ has two distinct roots.

4 Find the values of k for which $3x^2 + 2x + k = 0$ has no real roots.

5 Find the values of k for which $(k+1)x^2 + kx - 2k = 0$ has two equal roots.

6 Find the values of k for which $kx^2 + 2(k+3)x + k = 0$ has two distinct roots.

7 Find the values of k for which $3x^2 - 4x + 5 - k = 0$ has two distinct roots.

8 Find the values of k for which $4x^2 - (k-2)x + 9 = 0$ has two equal roots.

9 Find the values of k for which $4x^2 + 4(k-2)x + k = 0$ has two equal roots.

10 Show that the roots of the equation $x^2 + (k-2)x - 2k = 0$ are real and distinct for all real values of k.

11 Show that the roots of the equation $kx^2 + 5x - 2k = 0$ are real and distinct for all real values of k.

2.6 Intersection of a line and a curve

When considering the intersection of a straight line and a parabola, there are three possible situations.

Situation 1	Situation 2	Situation 3
2 points of intersection	1 point of intersection	0 points of intersection
The line cuts the curve at two distinct points.	The line touches the curve at one point. This means that the line is a **tangent** to the curve.	The line does not intersect the curve.

You have already learnt that to find the points of intersection of the line $y = x - 6$ with the parabola $y = x^2 - 3x - 4$ you solve the two equations simultaneously.

This would give $x^2 - 3x - 4 = x - 6$

$$x^2 - 4x + 2 = 0.$$

The resulting quadratic equation can then be solved using the quadratic formula:

$$x = \frac{-b \pm \sqrt{b^2 - 4ac}}{2a}$$

The number of points of intersection will depend on the value of $b^2 - 4ac$.

The different situations are given in the table below.

$b^2 - 4ac$	Nature of roots	Line and curve
> 0	2 real distinct roots	2 distinct points of intersection
$= 0$	2 real equal roots	1 point of intersection (line is a tangent)
< 0	0 real roots	no points of intersection

The condition for a quadratic equation to have real roots is $b^2 - 4ac \geqslant 0$.

WORKED EXAMPLE 10

Find the value of k for which $y = 2x + k$ is a tangent to the curve $y = x^2 - 4x + 4$.

Answers

$x^2 - 4x + 4 = 2x + k$

$x^2 - 6x + (4 - k) = 0$

Since the line is a tangent to the curve,

$b^2 - 4ac = 0.$

$(-6)^2 - 4 \times 1 \times (4 - k) = 0$

$36 - 16 + 4k = 0$

$k = -5$

WORKED EXAMPLE 11

Find the range of values of k for which $y = x - 5$ intersects the curve $y = kx^2 - 6$ at two distinct points.

Answers

$kx^2 - 6 = x - 5$

$kx^2 - x - 1 = 0$

Since the line intersects the curve at two distinct points,

$b^2 - 4ac > 0.$

$(-1)^2 - 4 \times k \times (-1) > 0$

$1 + 4k > 0$

$k > -\frac{1}{4}$

WORKED EXAMPLE 12

Find the values of k for which $y = kx - 3$ does not intersect the curve $y = x^2 - 2x + 1$.

Answers

$x^2 - 2x + 1 = kx - 3$

$x^2 - x(2 + k) + 4 = 0$

Since the line and curve do not intersect,

$b^2 - 4ac < 0.$

$(2 + k)^2 - 4 \times 1 \times 4 < 0$

$k^2 + 4k + 4 - 16 < 0$

$k^2 + 4k - 12 < 0$

$(k + 6)(k - 2) < 0$

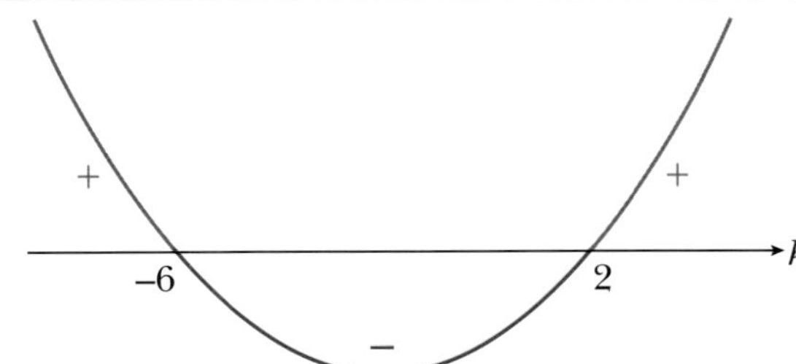

Critical values are –6 and 2.

So $-6 < k < 2$.

Exercise 2.6

1 Find the values of k for which $y = kx + 1$ is a tangent to the curve $y = 2x^2 + x + 3$.

2 Find the value of k for which the x-axis is a tangent to the curve $y = x^2 + (3 - k)x - (4k + 3)$.

3 Find the values of the constant c for which the line $y = x + c$ is a tangent to the curve $y = 3x + \frac{2}{x}$.

4 Find the set of values of k for which the line $y = 3x + 1$ cuts the curve $y = x^2 + kx + 2$ in two distinct points.

5 The line $y = 2x + k$ is a tangent to the curve $x^2 + 2xy + 20 = 0$.

- **a** Find the possible values of k.
- **b** For each of these values of k, find the coordinates of the point of contact of the tangent with the curve.

6 Find the set of values of k for which the line $y = k - x$ cuts the curve $y = x^2 - 7x + 4$ in two distinct points.

7 Find the values of k for which the line $y = kx - 10$ meets the curve $x^2 + y^2 = 10x$.

8 Find the set of values of m for which the line $y = mx - 5$ does not meet the curve $y = x^2 - 5x + 4$.

9 The line $y = mx + 6$ is a tangent to the curve $y = x^2 - 4x + 7$.
Find the possible values of m..

Summary

Completing the square

For a quadratic function $f(x) = ax^2 + bx + c$ that is written in the form $f(x) = a(x - h)^2 + k$,

i if $a > 0$, the minimum point is (h, k) **ii** if $a < 0$, the maximum point is (h, k).

Quadratic equation ($ax^2 + bx + c = 0$) and corresponding curve ($y = ax^2 + bx + c$)

$b^2 - 4ac$	Nature of roots of $ax^2 + bx + c = 0$	Shape of curve $y = ax^2 + bx + c$
> 0	2 real distinct roots	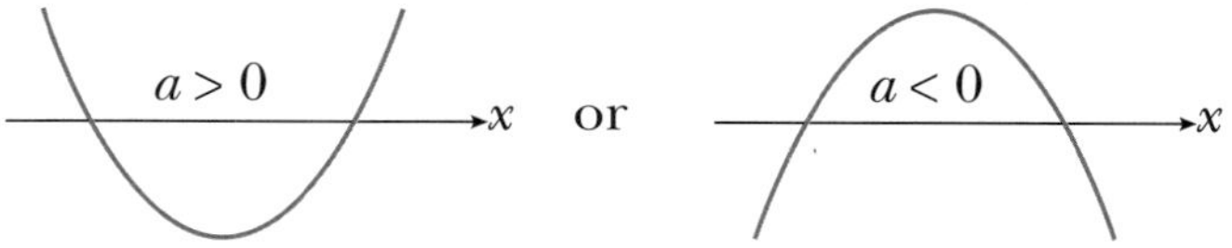 $a > 0$ x or $a < 0$ x The curve cuts the x-axis at 2 distinct points.
$= 0$	2 real equal roots	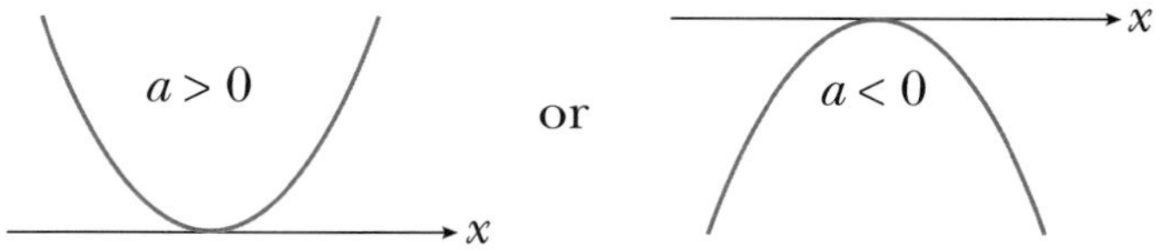 $a > 0$ x or $a < 0$ x The curve touches the x-axis at 1 point.
< 0	0 real roots	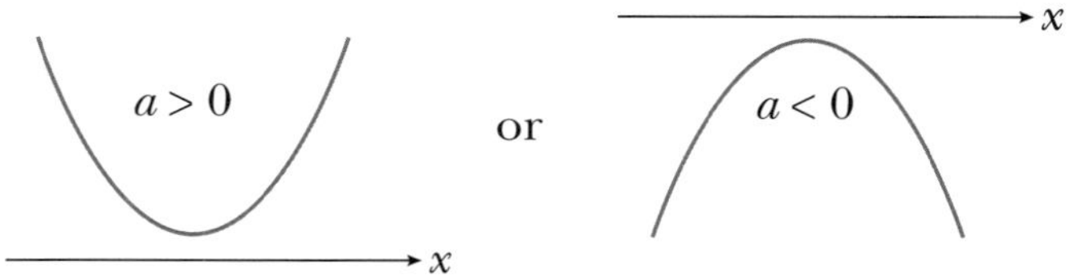 $a > 0$ x or $a < 0$ x The curve is entirely above or entirely below the x-axis.

Quadratic curve and straight line

Situation 1	Situation 2	Situation 3
2 points of intersection	1 point of intersection	0 points of intersection
The line cuts the curve at two distinct points.	The line touches the curve at one point. This means that the line is a **tangent** to the curve.	The line does not intersect the curve.

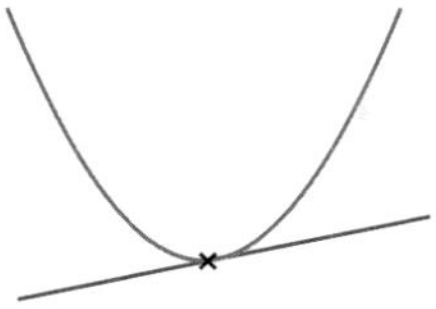

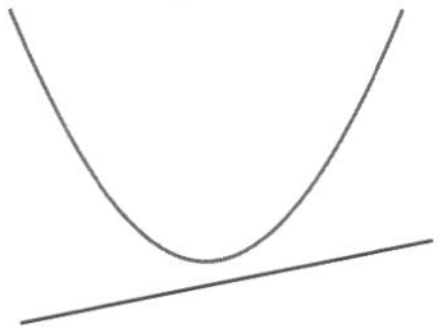

Solving simultaneously the equation of the curve with the equation of the line will give a quadratic equation of the form $ax^2 + bx + c = 0$. The discriminant $b^2 - 4ac$, gives information about the roots of the equation and also about the intersection of the curve with the line.

$b^2 - 4ac$	Nature of roots	Line and curve
> 0	2 real distinct roots	2 distinct points of intersection
$= 0$	2 real equal roots	1 point of intersection (line is a tangent)
< 0	no real roots	no points of intersection

The condition for a quadratic equation to have real roots is $b^2 - 4ac \geqslant 0$.

Examination questions

Worked example

The line $y = 2x - 8$ cuts the curve $2x^2 + y^2 - 5xy + 32 = 0$ at the points A and B.

Find the length of the line AB. [7]

Cambridge IGCSE Additional Mathematics 0606 Paper 21 Q8 Jun 2013

Answers

$y = 2x - 8$ ----------------------------(1)

$2x^2 + y^2 - 5xy + 32 = 0$ ----------(2)

Substitute for y from (1) in (2):

$$2x^2 + (2x - 8)^2 - 5x(2x - 8) + 32 = 0 \quad \text{expand brackets}$$

$$2x^2 + 4x^2 - 32x + 64 - 10x^2 + 40x + 32 = 0 \quad \text{collect like terms}$$

$$-4x^2 + 8x + 96 = 0 \quad \text{divide by } -4$$

$$x^2 - 2x - 24 = 0 \quad \text{factorise}$$

$$(x - 6)(x + 4) = 0$$

$$x = 6 \text{ or } x = -4$$

When $x = 6$, $y = 2(6) - 8 = 4$.

When $x = -4$, $y = 2(-4) - 8 = -16$.

The points of intersection are A (6, 4) and B (–4, –16).

Using Pythagoras: $AB^2 = 20^2 + 10^2$

$AB^2 = 500$

$AB = \sqrt{500}$

$AB = 22.4$ to 3 sf

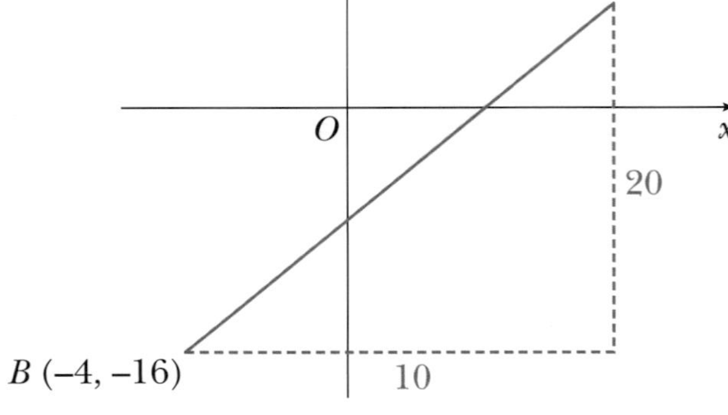

Exercise 2.7

Exam Exercise

1 Find the set of values of k for which the line $y = k(4x - 3)$ does not intersect the curve $y = 4x^2 + 8x - 8$. [5]

Cambridge IGCSE Additional Mathematics 0606 Paper 11 Q4 Jun 2014

2 Find the set of values of x for which $x(x + 2) < x$. [3]

Cambridge IGCSE Additional Mathematics 0606 Paper 21 Q1 Jun 2014

3 **a** Express $2x^2 - x + 6$ in the form $p(x - q)^2 + r$, where p, q and r are constants to be found. [3]

b Hence state the least value of $2x^2 - x + 6$ and the value of x at which this occurs. [2]

Cambridge IGCSE Additional Mathematics 0606 Paper 21 Q5i,ii Jun 2014

4 Find the set of values of k for which the curve $y = (k+1)x^2 - 3x + (k+1)$ lies below the x-axis. [4]

Cambridge IGCSE Additional Mathematics 0606 Paper 11 Q2 Nov 2013

5 Find the set of values of x for which $x^2 < 6 - 5x$. [3]

Cambridge IGCSE Additional Mathematics 0606 Paper 21 Q1 Nov 2013

6 Find the values of k for which the line $y = k - 6x$ is a tangent to the curve $y = x(2x + k)$. [4]

Cambridge IGCSE Additional Mathematics 0606 Paper 11 Q2 Nov 2012

7 It is given that $f(x) = 4 + 8x - x^2$.

a Find the value of a and of b for which $f(x) = a - (x+b)^2$ and hence write down the coordinates of the stationary point of the curve $y = f(x)$. [3]

b On the axes below, sketch the graph of $y = f(x)$, showing the coordinates of the point where your graph intersects the y-axis.

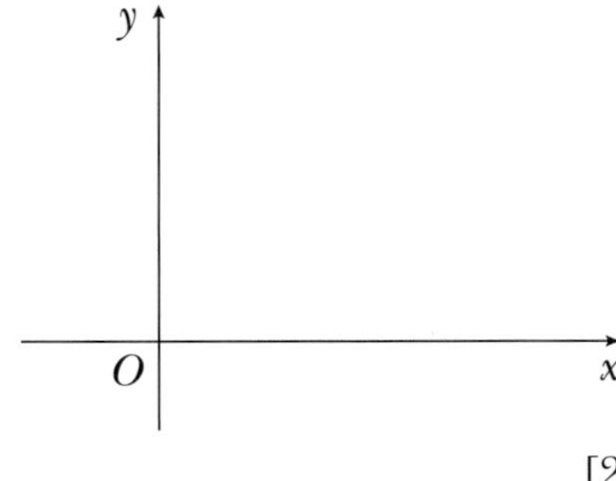

[2]

Cambridge IGCSE Additional Mathematics 0606 Paper 21 Q4i,ii Nov 2012

8 Given that the straight line $y = 3x + c$ is a tangent to the curve $y = x^2 + 9x + k$, express k in terms of c. [4]

Cambridge IGCSE Additional Mathematics 0606 Paper 21 Q2 Nov 2011

9 Find the set of values of k for which the line $y = 2x - 5$ cuts the curve $y = x^2 + kx + 11$ in two distinct points. [6]

Cambridge IGCSE Additional Mathematics 0606 Paper 21 Q4 Jun 2011

10 The equation of a curve is given by $y = 2x^2 + ax - 14$, where a is a constant.

Given that this equation can also be written as $y = 2(x-3)^2 + b$, where b is a constant, find

a the value of a and of b, [2]

b the minimum value of y. [1]

Cambridge IGCSE Additional Mathematics 0606 Paper 11 Q1i,ii Nov 2010

11 Find the set of values of m for which the line $y = mx - 2$ cuts the curve $y = x^2 + 8x + 7$ in two distinct points. [6]

Cambridge IGCSE Additional Mathematics 0606 Paper 21 Q5 Nov 2010

12 a On a copy of the grid to the right, sketch the graph of $y = |(x-2)(x+3)|$ for $-5 \leqslant x \leqslant 4$, and state the coordinates of the points where the curve meets the coordinate axes. [4]

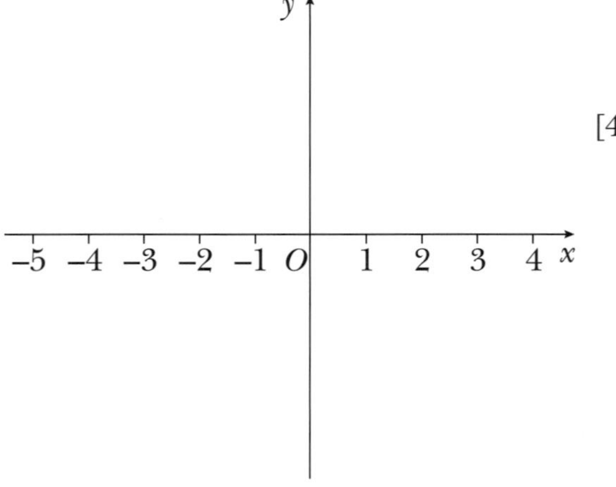

b Find the coordinates of the stationary point on the curve $y = |(x-2)(x+3)|$. [3]

c Given that k is a positive constant, state the set of values of k for which $|(x-2)(x+3)| = k$ has 2 solutions only. [3]

Cambridge IGCSE Additional Mathematics 0606 Paper 11 Q8i,ii,iii Nov 2013

13 Find the value of k for which the curve $y = 2x^2 - 3x + k$

i passes through the point $(4, -7)$, [1]

ii meets the x-axis at one point only. [2]

Cambridge IGCSE Additional Mathematics 0606 Paper 11 Q1 Jun 2016

14 Find the range of values of k for which the equation $kx^2 + k = 8x - 2xk$ has 2 real distinct roots. [4]

Cambridge IGCSE Additional Mathematics 0606 Paper 11 Q1 Nov 2015

15 a Find the set of values of x for which $4x^2 + 19x - 5 \leqslant 0$. [3]

b i Express $x^2 + 8x - 9$ in the form $(x + a)^2 + b$. where a and b are integers. [2]

ii Use your answer to **part i** to find the greatest value of $9 - 8x - x^2$ and the value of x at which this occurs. [2]

iii Sketch the graph of $y = 9 - 8x - x^2$, indicating the coordinates of any points of intersection with the coordinate axes. [2]

Cambridge IGCSE Additional Mathematics 0606 Paper 21 Q9 Jun 2015

Chapter 3
Indices and Surds

This section will show you how to:

- perform simple operations with indices and surds, including rationalising the denominator.

RECAP

You should already know the meaning of the words index, power, exponent and base:

$$2 \times 2 \times 2 \times 2 = 2^4$$

(the 4 is the index, exponent or power; the 2 is the base)

The plural of the word index is indices.

You should also know and be able to apply the following rules of indices:

(These rules are always true if the bases a and b are positive real numbers and the indices m and n are real numbers.)

RULE 1:	$a^m \times a^n = a^{m+n}$	RULE 6:	$a^0 = 1$
RULE 2:	$a^m \div a^n = a^{m-n}$ or $\frac{a^m}{a^n} = a^{m-n}$	RULE 7:	$a^{-n} = \frac{1}{a^n}$
RULE 3:	$(a^m)^n = a^{mn}$	RULE 8:	$a^{\frac{1}{n}} = \sqrt[n]{a}$
RULE 4:	$a^n \times b^n = (ab)^n$	RULE 9:	$a^{\frac{m}{n}} = (\sqrt[n]{a})^m = \sqrt[n]{a^m}$
RULE 5:	$\frac{a^n}{b^n} = \left(\frac{a}{b}\right)^n$		

Note:

- If the bases a and b are negative then the indices m and n must be integers for Rules 1–5 to be always true.
- Rules 6 and 7 are also true if base a is negative.

3.1 Simplifying expressions involving indices

When simplifying expressions involving indices you often need to use more than one of the rules for indices.

In Worked Example 1 and Exercise 3.1 you may assume that all bases are positive real numbers.

WORKED EXAMPLE 1

Simplify $\dfrac{(4x^2y)^2 \times \sqrt{9x^6y^2}}{(x^3y^2)^{-2}}$.

Answers

$$\frac{(4x^2y)^2 \times \sqrt{9x^6y^2}}{(x^3y^2)^{-2}} = \frac{(4)^2(x^2)^2(y)^2 \times (9)^{\frac{1}{2}}(x^6)^{\frac{1}{2}}(y^2)^{\frac{1}{2}}}{(x^3)^{-2}(y^2)^{-2}}$$

$$= \frac{16x^4y^2 \times 3x^3y}{x^{-6}y^{-4}}$$

$$= \frac{48x^7y^3}{x^{-6}y^{-4}}$$

$$= 48x^{13}y^7$$

Exercise 3.1

1 Simplify each of the following.

a $(x^5)^3$ **b** $x^7 \times x^9$ **c** $x^5 \div x^8$

d $\sqrt{x^{10}}$ **e** $\sqrt{x^{-4}}$ **f** $(x^{-3})^5$

g $\sqrt[3]{x^6}$ **h** $(x^{-1})^2 \times \left(x^{\frac{1}{2}}\right)^8$ **i** $3x^2 y \times 5x^4 y^3$

j $\sqrt{25x^6 y^{-4}}$ **k** $\left(2x^3 y^{\frac{3}{2}}\right)^4$ **l** $\sqrt{9x^8 y^{-4}} \times \sqrt[3]{8x^6 y^{-3}}$

2 Simplify each of the following.

a $\dfrac{\sqrt[3]{x} \times \sqrt[3]{x^5}}{x^{-2}}$ **b** $\dfrac{x^2 \times \sqrt{x^5}}{x^{-\frac{1}{2}}}$

c $\dfrac{(\sqrt[3]{x})^2 \times \sqrt{x^6}}{x^{-\frac{1}{3}}}$ **d** $\dfrac{(3xy)^2 \times \sqrt{x^4 y^6}}{(2x^4 y^3)^2}$

3 Given that $\dfrac{(36x^4)^2}{8x^2 \times 3x} = 2^a\, 3^b\, x^c$, evaluate a, b and c.

4 Given that $\dfrac{\sqrt{x^{-1}} \times \sqrt[3]{y^2}}{\sqrt{x^6 y^{-\frac{2}{3}}}} = x^a\, y^b$, find the value of a and the value of b.

5 Given that $\dfrac{\sqrt{a^{\frac{4}{5}}\, b^{-\frac{2}{3}}}}{a^{-\frac{1}{5}}\, b^{\frac{2}{3}}} = a^x\, b^y$, find the value of x and the value of y.

6 Given that $\dfrac{(a^x)^2}{b^{5-x}} \times \dfrac{b^{y-4}}{a^y} = a^2\, b^4$, find the value of x and the value of y.

7 Simplify $(1 + x)^{\frac{3}{2}} - (1 + x)^{\frac{1}{2}}$.

3.2 Solving equations involving indices

Consider the equation $2^x = 64$.

The equation has an unknown exponent (or index) and is called an **exponential equation**. You have already learnt how to solve simple exponential equations such as $2^x = 64$. In this section, you will learn how to solve more complicated exponential equations.

CLASS DISCUSSION

The diagram shows the graph of $y = 2^x$ for $-3 \leqslant x \leqslant 3$.

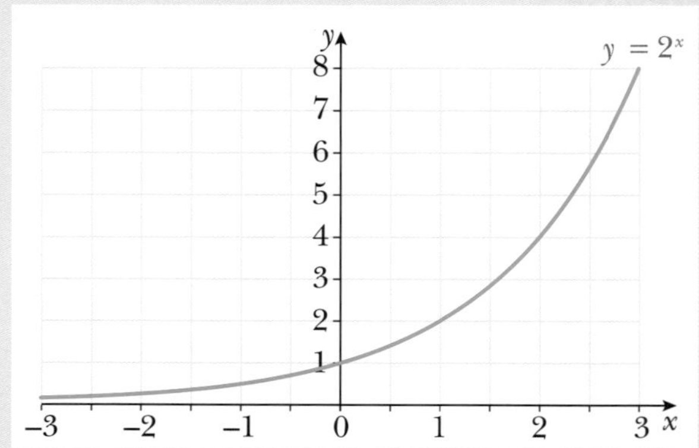

Discuss the following questions with your classmates:

- How does the graph behave when $x > 3$?
- How does the graph behave when $x < -3$?
- How does the graph of $y = 3^x$ compare with the graph of $y = 2^x$?
- How does the graph of $y = 4^x$ compare with the graphs of $y = 2^x$ and $y = 3^x$?

Now answer the following question:

- If $a > 0$, is it possible to find a value of x for which a^x is either 0 or negative?

WORKED EXAMPLE 2

Solve the equation $2^{3x+1} = 8$.

Answers

$2^{3x+1} = 8$ change 8 to 2^3

$2^{3x+1} = 2^3$ equate the indices

$3x + 1 = 3$ solve for x

$3x = 2$

$x = \frac{2}{3}$

WORKED EXAMPLE 3

Solve the equation $3^{2x-1} \times 9^{x-1} = 243$.

Answers

$3^{2x-1} \times 9^{x-1} = 243$ change to base 3

$3^{2x-1} \times (3^2)^{x-1} = 3^5$

$3^{2x-1} \times 3^{2x-2} = 3^5$ add the indices on the left hand side

$3^{4x-3} = 3^5$ equate the indices

$4x - 3 = 5$ solve for x

$4x = 8$

$x = 2$

WORKED EXAMPLE 4

Solve the simultaneous equations.

$9^x(27^y) = 1$

$4^x \div (\sqrt{2})^y = 128$

Answers

$9^x(27^y) = 1$ change to base 3

$4^x \div (\sqrt{2})^y = 128$ change to base 2

$3^{2x} \times 3^{3y} = 3^0$ add indices on the left hand side

$2^{2x} \div 2^{\frac{1}{2}y} = 2^7$ subtract indices on the left hand side

$3^{2x+3y} = 3^0$ equating the indices gives $2x + 3y = 0$

$2^{2x-\frac{1}{2}y} = 2^7$ equating the indices gives $2x - \frac{1}{2}y = 7$

$2x + 3y = 0$ subtract the two equations

$2x - \frac{1}{2}y = 7$

$3\frac{1}{2}y = -7$, so $y = -2$.

Substituting $y = -2$ into $2x + 3y = 0$ gives $x = 3$.

The solution is $x = 3$, $y = -2$.

WORKED EXAMPLE 5

a Solve the equation $4y^2 + 3y - 1 = 0$.

b Use your answer to **part a** to solve the equation $4(2^x)^2 + 3(2^x) - 1 = 0$.

Answers

a $4y^2 + 3y - 1 = 0$ factorise

$(4y - 1)(y + 1) = 0$

$4y - 1 = 0$ or $y + 1 = 0$

$y = \frac{1}{4}$ or $y = -1$

b $4(2^x)^2 + 3(2^x) - 1 = 0$ comparing with $4y^2 + 3y - 1 = 0$ gives $y = 2^x$

$2^x = \frac{1}{4}$ or $2^x = -1$ replace $\frac{1}{4}$ with 2^{-2}

$2^x = 2^{-2}$ or $2^x = -1$

Solving $2^x = 2^{-2}$, gives $x = -2$.

There is no solution to $2^x = -1$, since $2^x > 0$ for all real values of x.

The solution is $x = -2$.

Exercise 3.2

1 Solve each of the following equations.

a $5^{2x} = 5^{7x-1}$ **b** $4^{2x+1} = 4^{3x-2}$

c $7^{x^2} = 7^{6-x}$ **d** $3^{2x^2} = 3^{9x+5}$

2 Solve each of the following equations.

a $2^{n+1} = 32$ **b** $4^{2n} = 256$ **c** $2^{n+2} = 128$

d $3^{2n+1} = 27$ **e** $2^{n-1} = \frac{1}{4}$ **f** $2^{3n+2} = \frac{1}{128}$

g $5^{n+1} = \frac{1}{125}$ **h** $5^{x^2-16} = 1$

3 Solve each of the following equations.

a $2^x = 4^3$ **b** $3^{2x-1} = 27^x$ **c** $5^{3x-7} = 25^{2x}$

d $3^x = 9^{x+5}$ **e** $4^{3x+4} = 8^{4x+12}$ **f** $25^{2x+1} = 125^{3x+2}$

g $\left(\frac{1}{4}\right)^x = 64$ **h** $4^{5-3x} = \frac{1}{8^{x+1}}$ **i** $8^{4x-3} = \left(\frac{1}{16}\right)^{x+1}$

j $5^{x^2+3} = 25^{2x}$ **k** $3^{x^2-4} = 27^x$ **l** $2^{2x^2-2} - 8^x = 0$

4 Solve each of the following equations.

a $2^{3x} \times 4^{x+1} = 64$ **b** $2^{3x+1} \times 8^{x-1} = 128$

c $(2^{2-x})(4^{2x+3}) = 8$ **d** $3^{x+1} \times 9^{2-x} = \frac{1}{27}$

5 Solve each of the following equations.

a $\frac{27^{2x}}{3^{5-x}} = \frac{3^{2x+1}}{9^{x+3}}$ **b** $\frac{4^x}{2^{3-x}} = \frac{2^{3x}}{8^{x-2}}$

c $\frac{2^{x+4}}{8^{-x}} = \frac{64}{4^{\frac{1}{2}x}}$ **d** $\frac{27^{2x}}{3^{6-x}} = \frac{3^{2x+1}}{9^{x+3}}$

6 Solve each of the following equations.

a $3^{2x} \times 2^x = \frac{1}{18}$ **b** $2^{2x} \times 5^x = 8000$ **c** $5^{2x} \times 4^x = \frac{1}{1000}$

7 Solve each of the following pairs of simultaneous equations.

a $4^x \div 2^y = 16$ **b** $27^x = 9(3^y)$ **c** $125^x \div 5^y = 25$

$3^{2x} \times 9^y = 27$ $2^x \div 8^y = 1$ $2^{3x} \times \left(\frac{1}{8}\right)^{1-y} = 32$

8 a Solve the equation $2y^2 - 7y - 4 = 0$.

b Use your answer to **part a** to solve the equation $2(2^x)^2 - 7(2^x) - 4 = 0$.

9 a Solve the equation $4y^2 = 15 + 7y$.

b Use your answer to **part a** to solve the equation $4(9^x) = 15 + 7(3^x)$.

10 a Solve the equation $3y = 8 + \frac{3}{y}$.

b Use your answer to **part a** to solve the equation $3x^{\frac{1}{2}} = 8 + 3x^{-\frac{1}{2}}$.

3.3 Surds

A surd is an irrational number of the form $\sqrt{n}$, where n is a positive integer that is not a perfect square.

$\sqrt{2}$, $\sqrt{5}$ and $\sqrt{12}$ are all surds.

$\sqrt{9}$ is not a surd because $\sqrt{9} = \sqrt{3^2} = 3$.

Other examples of surds are $2 + \sqrt{5}$, $\sqrt{7} - \sqrt{2}$ and $\frac{3 - \sqrt{2}}{5}$.

When an answer is given using a surd, it is an exact answer.

CLASS DISCUSSION

The frog can only hop onto lily pads that contain surds.

It is allowed to move along a row (west or east) or a column (north or south) but is not allowed to move diagonally.

Find the route that the frog must take to catch the fly.

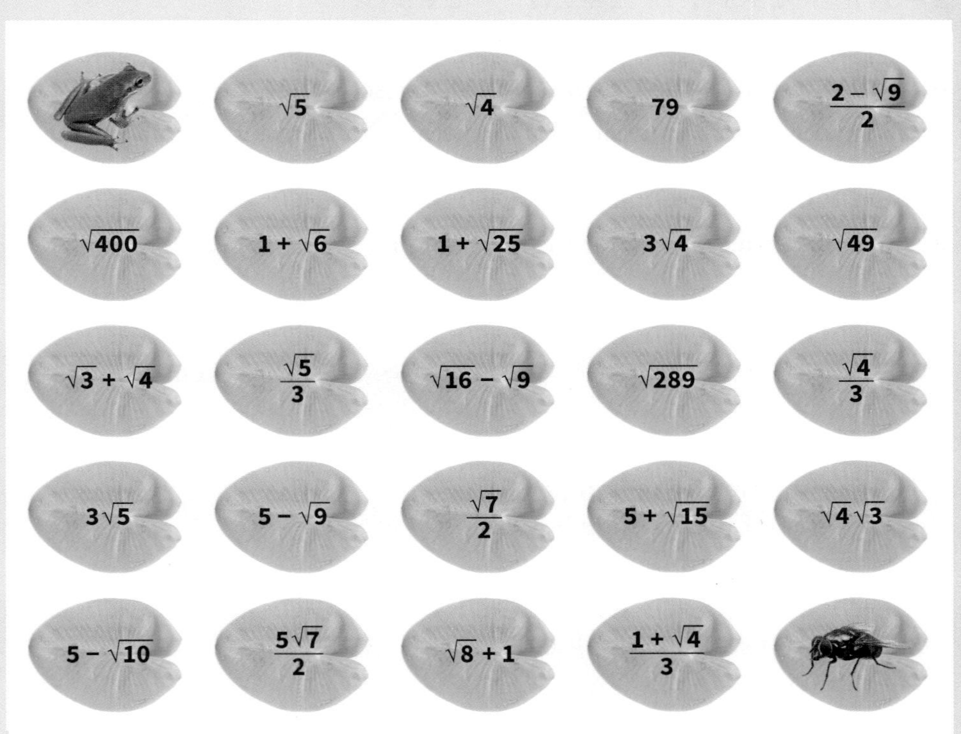

You can collect like terms together.

$6\sqrt{11} + 3\sqrt{11} = 9\sqrt{11}$ and $5\sqrt{7} - 2\sqrt{7} = 3\sqrt{7}$

WORKED EXAMPLE 6

Simplify $4(5 - \sqrt{3}) - 2(5\sqrt{3} - 1)$.

Answers

$4(5 - \sqrt{3}) - 2(5\sqrt{3} - 1)$	expand the brackets
$= 20 - 4\sqrt{3} - 10\sqrt{3} + 2$	collect like terms
$= 22 - 14\sqrt{3}$	

Exercise 3.3

1 Simplify.

a $3\sqrt{5} + 7\sqrt{5}$ **b** $3\sqrt{10} + 2\sqrt{10}$ **c** $8\sqrt{11} + \sqrt{11}$ **d** $6\sqrt{3} - \sqrt{3}$

2 A $3\sqrt{5} + 7\sqrt{3}$ B $2\sqrt{5} - 3\sqrt{3}$ C $2\sqrt{3} - \sqrt{5}$

Simplify.

a A + B **b** A − C **c** 2A + 3B **d** 5A + 2B − C

3 The first 4 terms of a sequence are

$2 + 3\sqrt{7}$ $2 + 5\sqrt{7}$ $2 + 7\sqrt{7}$ $2 + 9\sqrt{7}$.

a Write down the 6th term of this sequence.

b Find the sum of the first 5 terms of this sequence.

c Write down an expression for the nth term of this sequence.

4 **a** Find the exact length of AB.

b Find the exact perimeter of the triangle.

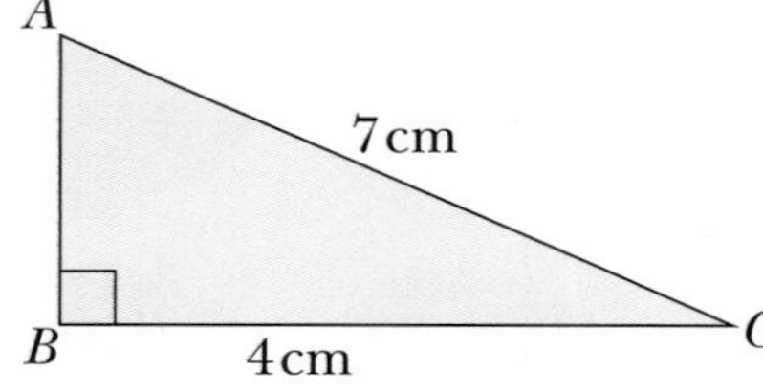

CHALLENGE Q

5 The number in the rectangle on the side of the triangle is the **sum** of the numbers at the adjacent vertices.

Find the value of x, the value of y and the value of z.

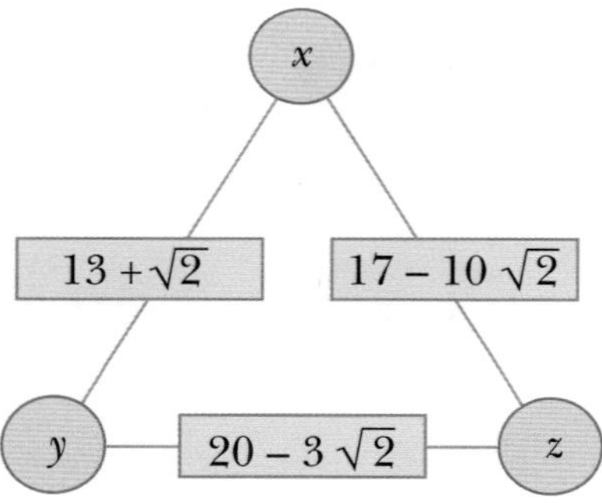

CHALLENGE Q

6 This design is made from 1 blue circle, 4 orange circles and 16 green circles.
The circles touch each other.
Given that the radius of each green circle is 1 unit, find the exact radius of

a the orange circles,

b the blue circle.

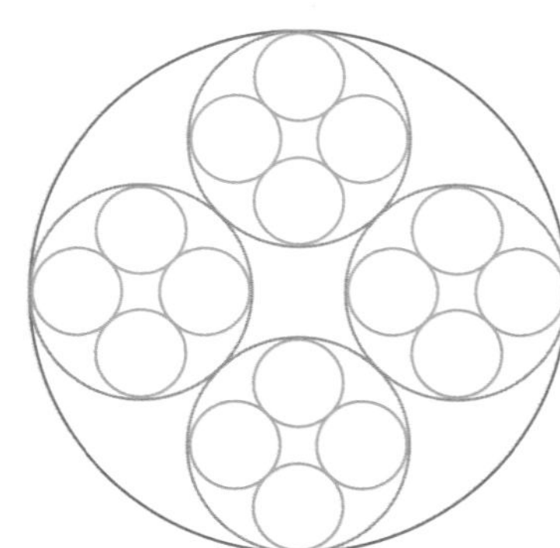

3.4 Multiplication, division and simplification of surds

You can multiply surds using the rule: $\sqrt{a} \times \sqrt{b} = \sqrt{ab}$

WORKED EXAMPLE 7

Simplify.

a $\sqrt{3} \times \sqrt{5}$ **b** $(\sqrt{8})^2$ **c** $2\sqrt{5} \times 3\sqrt{3}$

Answers

a $\sqrt{3} \times \sqrt{5} = \sqrt{3 \times 5} = \sqrt{15}$

b $(\sqrt{8})^2 = \sqrt{8} \times \sqrt{8} = \sqrt{64} = 8$ **Note:** $\sqrt{n} \times \sqrt{n} = n$

c $2\sqrt{5} \times 3\sqrt{3} = 6\sqrt{15}$

WORKED EXAMPLE 8

Expand and simplify.

a $(4 - \sqrt{3})^2$ **b** $(\sqrt{3} + 5\sqrt{2})(\sqrt{2} + \sqrt{3})$

Answers

a $(4 - \sqrt{3})^2$ square means multiply by itself

$= (4 - \sqrt{3})(4 - \sqrt{3})$ expand the brackets

$= 16 - 4\sqrt{3} - 4\sqrt{3} + 3$ collect like terms

$= 19 - 8\sqrt{3}$

b $(\sqrt{3} + 5\sqrt{2})(\sqrt{2} + \sqrt{3})$ expand the brackets

$= \sqrt{6} + 3 + 10 + 5\sqrt{6}$ collect like terms

$= 13 + 6\sqrt{6}$

$\sqrt{98}$ can be simplified using the multiplication rule.

$\sqrt{98} = \sqrt{49 \times 2} = \sqrt{49} \times \sqrt{2} = 7\sqrt{2}$

WORKED EXAMPLE 9

Simplify $\sqrt{75} - \sqrt{12}$.

Answers

$\sqrt{75} - \sqrt{12}$	$75 = 25 \times 3$ and $12 = 4 \times 3$
$= \sqrt{25} \times \sqrt{3} - \sqrt{4} \times \sqrt{3}$	$\sqrt{25} = 5$ and $\sqrt{4} = 2$
$= 5 \times \sqrt{3} - 2 \times \sqrt{3}$	collect like terms
$= 3\sqrt{3}$	

You can divide surds using the rule: $\dfrac{\sqrt{a}}{\sqrt{b}} = \sqrt{\dfrac{a}{b}}$

WORKED EXAMPLE 10

Simplify $\dfrac{\sqrt{77}}{\sqrt{11}}$.

Answers

$\dfrac{\sqrt{77}}{\sqrt{11}} = \sqrt{\dfrac{77}{11}} = \sqrt{7}$

Exercise 3.4

1 Simplify.

a $\sqrt{18} \times \sqrt{2}$ **b** $\sqrt{2} \times \sqrt{72}$ **c** $\sqrt{5} \times \sqrt{6}$ **d** $(\sqrt{2})^2$

e $(\sqrt{13})^2$ **f** $(\sqrt{5})^3$ **g** $3\sqrt{2} \times 5\sqrt{3}$ **h** $7\sqrt{5} \times 2\sqrt{7}$

2 Simplify.

a $\dfrac{\sqrt{112}}{\sqrt{28}}$ **b** $\dfrac{\sqrt{52}}{\sqrt{26}}$ **c** $\dfrac{\sqrt{12}}{\sqrt{3}}$ **d** $\dfrac{\sqrt{17}}{\sqrt{68}}$

e $\dfrac{\sqrt{12}}{\sqrt{108}}$ **f** $\dfrac{\sqrt{15}}{\sqrt{3}}$ **g** $\dfrac{\sqrt{54}}{\sqrt{6}}$ **h** $\dfrac{\sqrt{4}}{\sqrt{25}}$

i $\dfrac{\sqrt{5}}{\sqrt{81}}$ **j** $\dfrac{\sqrt{88}}{2\sqrt{11}}$ **k** $\dfrac{9\sqrt{20}}{3\sqrt{5}}$ **l** $\dfrac{\sqrt{120}}{\sqrt{24}}$

3 Simplify.

a $\sqrt{8}$ **b** $\sqrt{12}$ **c** $\sqrt{20}$ **d** $\sqrt{28}$

e $\sqrt{50}$ **f** $\sqrt{72}$ **g** $\sqrt{18}$ **h** $\sqrt{32}$

i $\sqrt{80}$ **j** $\sqrt{90}$ **k** $\sqrt{63}$ **l** $\sqrt{99}$

m $\sqrt{45}$ **n** $\sqrt{125}$ **o** $\sqrt{117}$ **p** $\sqrt{200}$

q $\sqrt{75}$ **r** $\sqrt{3000}$ **s** $\frac{\sqrt{20}}{2}$ **t** $\frac{\sqrt{27}}{3}$

u $\frac{\sqrt{500}}{5}$ **v** $\sqrt{20} \times \sqrt{10}$ **w** $\sqrt{8} \times \sqrt{5}$ **x** $\sqrt{8} \times \sqrt{6}$

y $\sqrt{245} \times \sqrt{5}$

4 Simplify.

a $5\sqrt{3} + \sqrt{48}$ **b** $\sqrt{12} + \sqrt{3}$ **c** $\sqrt{20} + 3\sqrt{5}$

d $\sqrt{75} + 2\sqrt{3}$ **e** $\sqrt{32} - 2\sqrt{8}$ **f** $\sqrt{125} + \sqrt{80}$

g $\sqrt{45} - \sqrt{5}$ **h** $\sqrt{20} - 5\sqrt{5}$ **i** $\sqrt{175} - \sqrt{28} + \sqrt{63}$

j $\sqrt{50} + \sqrt{72} - \sqrt{18}$ **k** $\sqrt{200} - 2\sqrt{18} + \sqrt{72}$ **l** $5\sqrt{28} - 3\sqrt{63} - \sqrt{7}$

m $\sqrt{80} + 2\sqrt{20} + 4\sqrt{45}$ **n** $5\sqrt{12} - 3\sqrt{48} + 2\sqrt{75}$ **o** $\sqrt{72} + \sqrt{8} - \sqrt{98} + \sqrt{50}$

5 Expand and simplify.

a $\sqrt{2}(3 + \sqrt{2})$ **b** $\sqrt{3}(2\sqrt{3} + \sqrt{12})$ **c** $\sqrt{2}(5 - 2\sqrt{2})$

d $\sqrt{3}(\sqrt{27} + 5)$ **e** $\sqrt{3}(\sqrt{3} - 1)$ **f** $\sqrt{5}(2\sqrt{5} + \sqrt{20})$

g $(\sqrt{2} + 1)(\sqrt{2} - 1)$ **h** $(\sqrt{3} + 5)(\sqrt{3} - 1)$ **i** $(2 + \sqrt{5})(2\sqrt{5} + 1)$

j $(3 - \sqrt{2})(3 + \sqrt{2})$ **k** $(4 + \sqrt{3})(4 - \sqrt{3})$ **l** $(1 + \sqrt{5})(1 - \sqrt{5})$

m $(4 + 2\sqrt{3})(4 - 2\sqrt{3})$ **n** $(\sqrt{7} + \sqrt{5})(\sqrt{7} + 2\sqrt{5})$ **o** $(3 + 2\sqrt{2})(5 + 2\sqrt{2})$

6 Expand and simplify.

a $(2 + \sqrt{5})^2$ **b** $(5 - \sqrt{3})^2$ **c** $(4 + 5\sqrt{3})^2$ **d** $(\sqrt{2} + \sqrt{3})^2$

7 A rectangle has sides of length $(2 + \sqrt{8})$ cm and $(7 - \sqrt{2})$ cm.
Find the area of the rectangle.
Express your answer in the form $a + b\sqrt{2}$, where a and b are integers.

8 **a** Find the value of AC^2.

b Find the value of tan x.
Write your answer in the form $\frac{a\sqrt{6}}{b}$,
where a and b are integers.

c Find the area of the triangle.
Write your answer in the form $\frac{p\sqrt{6}}{q}$,
where p and q are integers.

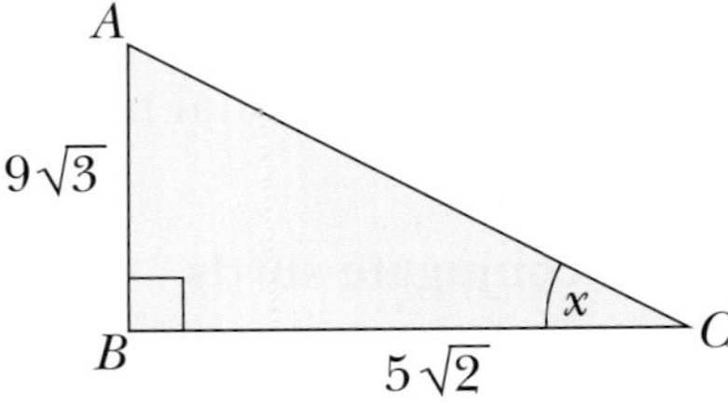

9 A cuboid has a square base.
The sides of the square are of length $(1 + \sqrt{2})$ cm.
The height of the cuboid is $(5 - \sqrt{2})$ cm.
Find the volume of the cuboid.
Express your answer in the form $a + b\sqrt{2}$, where a and b are integers.

CHALLENGE Q

10 Find the exact value of $\sqrt{2+\sqrt{3}} - \sqrt{2-\sqrt{3}}$.

(Hint: let $x = \sqrt{2+\sqrt{3}} - \sqrt{2-\sqrt{3}}$ and then square both sides of the equation.)

CHALLENGE Q

11 a Given that $\sqrt{6-4\sqrt{2}} = \sqrt{a} - \sqrt{b}$, find the value of a and the value of b.

b Given that $\sqrt{23-6\sqrt{6-4\sqrt{2}}} = \sqrt{c} + \sqrt{d}$, find the value of c and the value of d.

3.5 Rationalising the denominator of a fraction

CLASS DISCUSSION

Khadeeja says that:

'The product of two irrational numbers is irrational.'

Discuss this statement with your classmates and decide if this statement is:

Always true	Sometimes true	Never true

You must justify your decision.

You rationalise the denominator of a fraction when it is a surd.

To rationalise the denominator of a fraction means to turn an irrational denominator into a rational number.

In **Exercise 3.4, question 5m** you found that

$$(4+2\sqrt{3})(4-2\sqrt{3}) = (4)^2 - 8\sqrt{3} + 8\sqrt{3} - (2\sqrt{3})^2 = 16 - 12 = 4$$

This is an example of the product of two irrational numbers $(4+2\sqrt{3})$ and $(4-2\sqrt{3})$ giving a rational number (4).

$4+2\sqrt{3}$ and $4-2\sqrt{3}$ are called **conjugate surds**.

The product of two conjugate surds always gives a rational number.

The product of conjugate surds $a+b\sqrt{c}$ and $a-b\sqrt{c}$ is a rational number.

So you can rationalise the denominator of a fraction using these rules:

- For fractions of the form $\frac{1}{\sqrt{a}}$, multiply numerator and denominator by $\sqrt{a}$.
- For fractions of the form $\frac{1}{a+b\sqrt{c}}$, multiply numerator and denominator by $a-b\sqrt{c}$.
- For fractions of the form $\frac{1}{a-b\sqrt{c}}$, multiply numerator and denominator by $a+b\sqrt{c}$.

Note:
To find products such as $(4 + 2\sqrt{3})(4 - 2\sqrt{3})$, it is quicker to use the algebraic identity:

$$(x + y)(x - y) = x^2 - y^2$$

So $(4 + 2\sqrt{3})(4 - 2\sqrt{3}) = 4^2 - (2\sqrt{3})^2 = 16 - 12 = 4$

WORKED EXAMPLE 11

Rationalise the denominators of

a $\frac{2}{\sqrt{5}}$ **b** $\frac{5}{2 + \sqrt{3}}$ **c** $\frac{\sqrt{7} + 3\sqrt{2}}{\sqrt{7} - \sqrt{2}}$.

Answers

a $\frac{2}{\sqrt{5}}$ multiply numerator and denominator by $\sqrt{5}$

$= \frac{2\sqrt{5}}{\sqrt{5}\sqrt{5}}$

$= \frac{2\sqrt{5}}{5}$

b $\frac{5}{2 + \sqrt{3}}$ multiply numerator and denominator by $(2 - \sqrt{3})$

$= \frac{5(2 - \sqrt{3})}{(2 + \sqrt{3})(2 - \sqrt{3})}$ use $(x + y)(x - y) = x^2 - y^2$ to expand the denominator

$= \frac{10 - 5\sqrt{3}}{(2)^2 - (\sqrt{3})^2}$

$= 10 - 5\sqrt{3}$

c $\frac{\sqrt{7} + 3\sqrt{2}}{\sqrt{7} - \sqrt{2}}$ multiply numerator and denominator by $(\sqrt{7} + \sqrt{2})$

$= \frac{(\sqrt{7} + 3\sqrt{2})(\sqrt{7} + \sqrt{2})}{(\sqrt{7} - \sqrt{2})(\sqrt{7} + \sqrt{2})}$ use $(x + y)(x - y) = x^2 - y^2$ to expand the denominator

$= \frac{7 + \sqrt{14} + 3\sqrt{14} + 6}{(\sqrt{7})^2 - (\sqrt{2})^2}$

$= \frac{13 + 4\sqrt{14}}{5}$

Exercise 3.5

1 Rationalise the denominators.

a $\frac{1}{\sqrt{5}}$ **b** $\frac{3}{\sqrt{2}}$ **c** $\frac{9}{\sqrt{3}}$ **d** $\frac{\sqrt{2}}{\sqrt{6}}$

e $\frac{4}{\sqrt{5}}$ **f** $\frac{12}{\sqrt{3}}$ **g** $\frac{4}{\sqrt{12}}$ **h** $\frac{10}{\sqrt{8}}$

i $\frac{3}{\sqrt{8}}$ **j** $\frac{\sqrt{2}}{\sqrt{32}}$ **k** $\frac{\sqrt{3}}{\sqrt{15}}$ **l** $\frac{\sqrt{12}}{\sqrt{156}}$

m $\frac{5}{2\sqrt{2}}$ **n** $\frac{7}{2\sqrt{3}}$ **o** $\frac{1 + \sqrt{5}}{\sqrt{5}}$ **p** $\frac{\sqrt{3} - 1}{\sqrt{3}}$

q $\frac{3 - \sqrt{2}}{\sqrt{2}}$ **r** $\frac{14 - \sqrt{7}}{\sqrt{7}}$

2 Rationalise the denominators and simplify.

a $\dfrac{1}{1+\sqrt{2}}$ **b** $\dfrac{1}{3+\sqrt{5}}$ **c** $\dfrac{1}{3+\sqrt{7}}$ **d** $\dfrac{4}{3-\sqrt{5}}$

e $\dfrac{5}{2+\sqrt{5}}$ **f** $\dfrac{\sqrt{7}}{2-\sqrt{7}}$ **g** $\dfrac{2}{2-\sqrt{3}}$ **h** $\dfrac{5}{2\sqrt{3}-3}$

i $\dfrac{1}{2\sqrt{3}-\sqrt{2}}$ **j** $\dfrac{8}{\sqrt{7}-\sqrt{5}}$

3 Rationalise the denominators and simplify.

a $\dfrac{2-\sqrt{3}}{2+\sqrt{3}}$ **b** $\dfrac{1+\sqrt{2}}{3-\sqrt{2}}$ **c** $\dfrac{\sqrt{2}+1}{2\sqrt{2}-1}$ **d** $\dfrac{\sqrt{7}-\sqrt{2}}{\sqrt{7}+\sqrt{2}}$

e $\dfrac{\sqrt{5}+1}{3-\sqrt{5}}$ **f** $\dfrac{\sqrt{17}-\sqrt{11}}{\sqrt{17}+\sqrt{11}}$ **g** $\dfrac{\sqrt{3}-\sqrt{7}}{\sqrt{3}+\sqrt{7}}$ **h** $\dfrac{\sqrt{23}+\sqrt{37}}{\sqrt{37}-\sqrt{23}}$

4 Write as a single fraction.

a $\dfrac{1}{\sqrt{3}+1}+\dfrac{1}{\sqrt{3}-1}$ **b** $\dfrac{2}{\sqrt{7}+\sqrt{2}}+\dfrac{1}{\sqrt{7}-\sqrt{2}}$ **c** $\dfrac{2}{4-\sqrt{3}}+\dfrac{1}{4+\sqrt{3}}$

5 The area of a rectangle is $(8+\sqrt{10})\text{ cm}^2$.

The length of one side is $(\sqrt{5}+\sqrt{2})$ cm.

Find the length of the other side in the form $a\sqrt{5}+b\sqrt{2}$, where a and b are integers.

6 A cuboid has a square base of length $(2+\sqrt{5})$ cm.

The volume of the cuboid is $(16+7\sqrt{5})\text{ cm}^3$.

Find the height of the cuboid.

Express your answer in the form $a+b\sqrt{5}$, where a and b are integers.

7 A right circular cylinder has a volume of $(25+14\sqrt{3})\pi\text{ cm}^3$ and a base radius of $(2+\sqrt{3})$ cm.

Find its height in the form $(a+b\sqrt{3})$ cm, where a and b are integers.

8 **a** Find the value of $\tan x$.

Write your answer in the form $\dfrac{a+b\sqrt{2}}{c}$, where a, b and c are integers.

b Find the area of the triangle.

Write your answer in the form $\dfrac{p+q\sqrt{2}}{r}$, where p, q and r are integers.

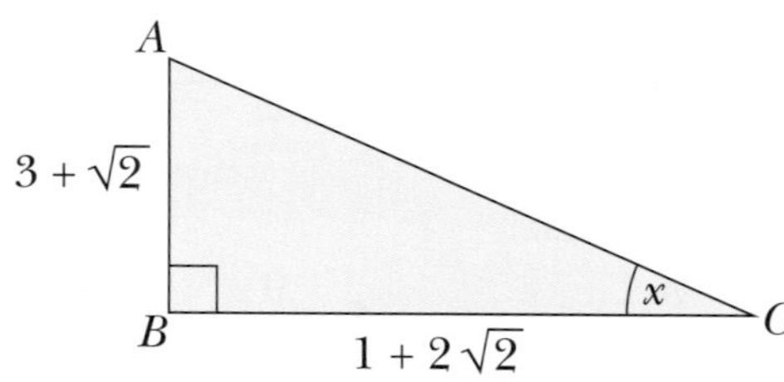

9 Find the value of $\cos\theta$.

Write your answer in the form $\dfrac{a+b\sqrt{7}}{c}$, where a, b and c are integers.

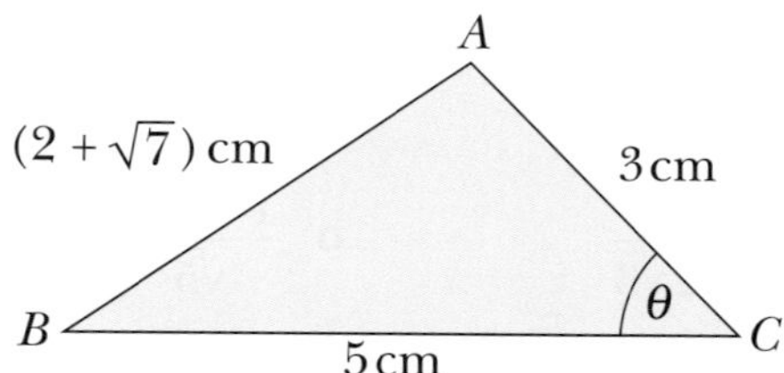

CHALLENGE Q

10 The blue circle has radius 2 and the green circle has radius 1. AB is a common tangent and all three circles touch each other.

Find the radius of the smaller circle.

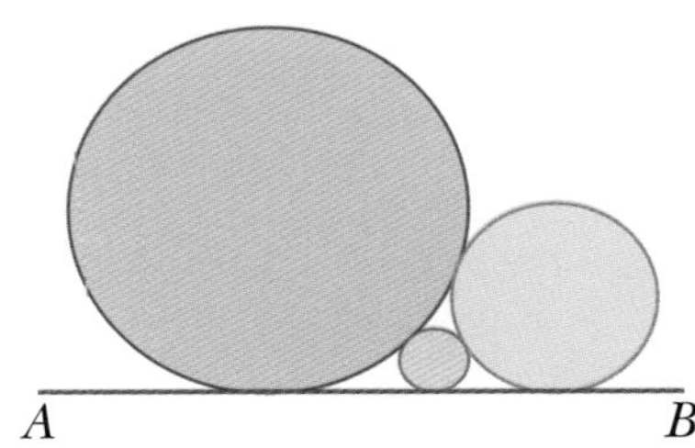

3.6 Solving equations involving surds

WORKED EXAMPLE 12

Solve $\sqrt{5}\,x = \sqrt{2}\,x + \sqrt{7}$.

Answers

$\sqrt{5}\,x = \sqrt{2}\,x + \sqrt{7}$	collect x's on one side
$\sqrt{5}\,x - \sqrt{2}\,x = \sqrt{7}$	factorise
$x(\sqrt{5} - \sqrt{2}) = \sqrt{7}$	divide both sides by $(\sqrt{5} - \sqrt{2})$
$x = \dfrac{\sqrt{7}}{\sqrt{5} - \sqrt{2}}$	multiply numerator and denominator by $(\sqrt{5} + \sqrt{2})$
$x = \dfrac{\sqrt{7}(\sqrt{5} + \sqrt{2})}{(\sqrt{5} - \sqrt{2})(\sqrt{5} + \sqrt{2})}$	use $(x + y)(x - y) = x^2 - y^2$ to expand the denominator
$x = \dfrac{\sqrt{35} + \sqrt{14}}{(\sqrt{5})^2 - (\sqrt{2})^2}$	
$x = \dfrac{\sqrt{35} + \sqrt{14}}{5 - 2}$	
$x = \dfrac{\sqrt{35} + \sqrt{14}}{3}$	

WORKED EXAMPLE 13

Solve the simultaneous equations.

$$3x + 5y = 20$$
$$\sqrt{2}\,x - 5\sqrt{2}\,y = 8$$

Answers

$$3x + 5y = 20 \qquad \text{multiply the first equation by } \sqrt{2}$$
$$\sqrt{2}\,x - 5\sqrt{2}\,y = 8$$

$$3\sqrt{2}\,x + 5\sqrt{2}\,y = 20\sqrt{2} \qquad \text{add the two equations to eliminate } y$$
$$\sqrt{2}\,x - 5\sqrt{2}\,y = 8$$

$$4\sqrt{2}\,x = 20\sqrt{2} + 8 \qquad \text{divide both sides by } 4\sqrt{2}$$

$$x = \frac{20\sqrt{2} + 8}{4\sqrt{2}} \qquad \text{multiply numerator and denominator by } \sqrt{2}$$

$$x = \frac{(20\sqrt{2} + 8) \times \sqrt{2}}{4\sqrt{2} \times \sqrt{2}}$$

$$x = \frac{40 + 8\sqrt{2}}{8}$$

$$x = 5 + \sqrt{2}$$

Substituting $x = 5 + \sqrt{2}$ in the first equation gives

$$3(5 + \sqrt{2}) + 5y = 20$$
$$15 + 3\sqrt{2} + 5y = 20$$
$$5y = 5 - 3\sqrt{2}$$
$$y = \frac{5 - 3\sqrt{2}}{5}$$

So the solution is $x = 5 + \sqrt{2}$, $y = \dfrac{5 - 3\sqrt{2}}{5}$.

CLASS DISCUSSION

Haroon writes:

$$x = 2$$
$$x + 2 = 4$$
$$x^2 + 4x + 4 = 16$$
$$x^2 + 4x - 12 = 0$$
$$(x + 6)(x - 2) = 0$$
$$\text{So } x = -6 \text{ or } x = 2$$

Discuss this with your classmates.

Explain why he now has two values for x.

In the class discussion you found that if you square both sides of an equation and then solve the resulting equation, you sometimes find that you have an answer that is not a valid solution of the original equation. Hence, it is always important to check your answers by substituting the answers back into the original equation.

WORKED EXAMPLE 14

Solve $\sqrt{x} = 2x - 6$.

Answers

$$\begin{aligned} \sqrt{x} &= 2x - 6 && \text{square both sides} \\ x &= (2x-6)(2x-6) && \text{expand the brackets} \\ x &= 4x^2 - 24x + 36 && \text{collect like terms} \\ 4x^2 - 25x + 36 &= 0 && \text{factorise} \\ (4x-9)(x-4) &= 0 \\ x &= \frac{9}{4} \text{ or } x = 4 \end{aligned}$$

Check $x = \frac{9}{4}$ in the original equation:

$\sqrt{\frac{9}{4}} = \frac{3}{2}$ and $2 \times \frac{9}{4} - 6 = -\frac{3}{2}$, so $x = \frac{9}{4}$ is not a valid solution of the original equation.

Check $x = 4$ in the original equation:

$\sqrt{4} = 2$ and $2 \times 4 - 6 = 2$, so $x = 4$ is a solution of the original equation.

So the final answer is $x = 4$.

WORKED EXAMPLE 15

Solve $\sqrt{3x+4} - \sqrt{2x+1} = 1$

Answers

$$\begin{aligned} \sqrt{3x+4} - \sqrt{2x+1} &= 1 && \text{isolate one of the square roots} \\ \sqrt{3x+4} &= 1 + \sqrt{2x+1} && \text{square both sides} \\ 3x+4 &= \left(1 + \sqrt{2x+1}\right)\left(1 + \sqrt{2x+1}\right) && \text{expand the brackets} \\ 3x+4 &= 1 + 2\sqrt{2x+1} + 2x + 1 && \text{isolate the square root and collect like terms} \\ x+2 &= 2\sqrt{2x+1} && \text{square both sides} \\ (x+2)^2 &= 4(2x+1) && \text{expand the brackets} \\ x^2 + 4x + 4 &= 8x + 4 && \text{collect like terms} \\ x^2 - 4x &= 0 && \text{factorise} \\ x(x-4) &= 0 \\ x = 0 \text{ or } x &= 4 \end{aligned}$$

Check $x = 0$ in the original equation:

$\sqrt{3 \times 0 + 4} - \sqrt{2 \times 0 + 1} = \sqrt{4} - \sqrt{1} = 1$, so $x = 0$ is a solution of the original equation.

Check $x = 4$ in the original equation:

$\sqrt{3 \times 4 + 4} - \sqrt{2 \times 4 + 1} = \sqrt{16} - \sqrt{9} = 1$, so $x = 0$ is also a solution of the original equation.

So the final answer is $x = 0$ or $x = 4$.

Exercise 3.6

1 Solve these equations.

a $\sqrt{12}\,x - \sqrt{5}\,x = \sqrt{3}$ **b** $\sqrt{10}\,x = \sqrt{5}\,x + \sqrt{2}$ **c** $\sqrt{17}\,x = 2\sqrt{3}\,x + \sqrt{5}$

2 Solve these simultaneous equations.

a $3x - y = 5\sqrt{2}$
$2x + y = 5$

b $x + y = 5$
$\sqrt{6}x + 2y = 12$

c $3x + y = 6$
$4x + 3y = 8 - 5\sqrt{5}$

d $2x + y = 11$
$5x - 3y = 11\sqrt{7}$

e $x + \sqrt{2}\,y = 5 + 4\sqrt{2}$
$x + y = 8$

3 Solve these equations.

a $10\sqrt{x} - 4 = 7\sqrt{x} + 6$ **b** $6\sqrt{x} + 4 = 9\sqrt{x} + 3$ **c** $7\sqrt{x} + 9 = 10\sqrt{x} + 10$

d $\sqrt{2x - 1} - 3 = 0$ **e** $\sqrt{2x - 3} = 6$ **f** $\sqrt{5x - 1} = \sqrt{x + 7}$

g $3 + \sqrt{5x + 6} = 12$ **h** $\sqrt{5x^2 - 8} = 2x$ **i** $12 - \sqrt{x + 5} = 7$

4 Solve these equations.

a $\sqrt{2x - 1} = x$ **b** $\sqrt{x + 6} = x$ **c** $\sqrt{2x + 3} - x = 0$

d $\sqrt{10 - 2x} + x = 1$ **e** $\sqrt{x + 15} = x + 3$ **f** $\sqrt{x + 4} + 2 = x$

g $\sqrt{x + 5} + 1 = x$ **h** $\sqrt{4x - 3} + 2x - 1 = 0$ **i** $\sqrt{x} = 2x - 6$

j $\sqrt{3x + 1} - x - 1 = 0$ **k** $2x + 3 - \sqrt{20x + 9} = 0$

5 Solve these equations.

a $\sqrt{2x + 7} = \sqrt{x + 3} + 1$ **b** $\sqrt{x} = \sqrt{x - 5} + 1$

c $\sqrt{3x + 4} - \sqrt{2x + 1} = 1$ **d** $\sqrt{x + 1} - \sqrt{x} = 1$

e $\sqrt{x + 1} + \sqrt{2x + 3} = 5$ **f** $\sqrt{16 - 2x} = 2 + \sqrt{36 + 6x}$

6 The roots of the equation $x^2 - 2\sqrt{6}\,x + 5 = 0$ are p and q, where $p > q$.

Write $\frac{p}{q}$ in the form $\frac{a + b\sqrt{6}}{c}$, where a, b and c are integers.

7 Find the positive root of the equation $(4 - \sqrt{2})\,x^2 - (1 + 2\sqrt{2})\,x - 1 = 0$.

Write your answer in the form $\frac{a + b\sqrt{2}}{c}$, where a, b and c are integers.

Summary

Rules of indices

RULE 1: $a^m \times a^n = a^{m+n}$

RULE 2: $a^m \div a^n = a^{(m-n)}$ or $\frac{a^m}{a^n} = a^{m-n}$

RULE 3: $(a^m)^n = a^{mn}$

RULE 4: $a^n \times b^n = (ab)^n$

RULE 5: $\frac{a^n}{b^n} = \left(\frac{a}{b}\right)^n$

RULE 6: $a^0 = 1$

RULE 7: $a^{-n} = \frac{1}{a^n}$

RULE 8: $a^{\frac{1}{n}} = \sqrt[n]{a}$

RULE 9: $a^{\frac{m}{n}} = (\sqrt[n]{a})^m = \sqrt[n]{a^m}$

Rules of surds

RULE 1: $\sqrt{ab} = \sqrt{a} \times \sqrt{b}$

RULE 2: $\sqrt{\frac{a}{b}} = \frac{\sqrt{a}}{\sqrt{b}}$

RULE 3: $\sqrt{a} \times \sqrt{a} = a$

The product of conjugate surds $a + b\sqrt{c}$ and $a - b\sqrt{c}$ is a rational number.

Examination questions

Worked example

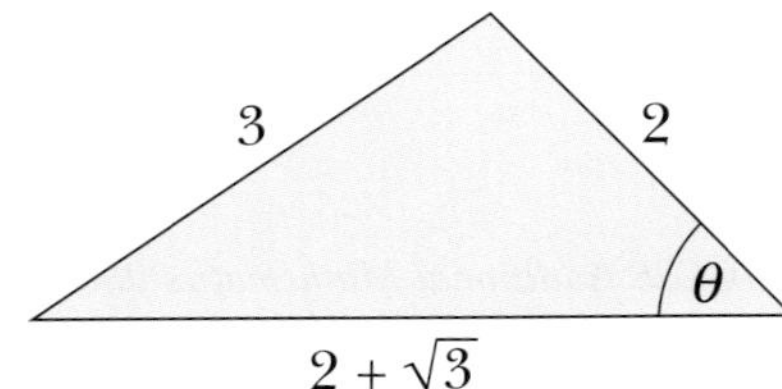

Without using a calculator, find the value of $\cos \theta$, giving your answer in the form $\frac{a + b\sqrt{3}}{c}$, where a, b and c are integers.

Cambridge IGCSE Additional Mathematics 0606 Paper 21 Q3 Nov 2011

Answers

Using the cosine rule:

$$3^2 = (2 + \sqrt{3})^2 + 2^2 - 2 \times (2 + \sqrt{3}) \times 2 \times \cos\theta$$

Rearrange to make $\cos\theta$ the subject:

$$\cos\theta = \frac{(2 + \sqrt{3})^2 + 2^2 - 3^2}{2 \times (2 + \sqrt{3}) \times 2}$$

square brackets in the numerator

$$(2 + \sqrt{3})^2 = 4 + 2\sqrt{3} + 2\sqrt{3} + 3 = 7 + 4\sqrt{3}$$

$$\cos\theta = \frac{7 + 4\sqrt{3} + 4 - 9}{4(2 + \sqrt{3})}$$

collect like terms in the numerator

$$\cos\theta = \frac{2 + 4\sqrt{3}}{4(2 + \sqrt{3})}$$

multiply numerator and denominator by $(2 - \sqrt{3})$

$$\cos\theta = \frac{(2 + 4\sqrt{3})(2 - \sqrt{3})}{4(2 + \sqrt{3})(2 - \sqrt{3})}$$

$$(2 + 4\sqrt{3})(2 - \sqrt{3}) = 4 - 2\sqrt{3} + 8\sqrt{3} - 12 = -8 + 6\sqrt{3}$$

$$(2 + \sqrt{3})(2 - \sqrt{3}) = 2^2 - (\sqrt{3})^2 = 1$$

$$\cos\theta = \frac{-8 + 6\sqrt{3}}{4}$$

divide numerator and denominator by 2

$$\cos\theta = \frac{-4 + 3\sqrt{3}}{2}$$

Exercise 3.7

Exam exercise

1 Solve $2^{x^2 - 5x} = \frac{1}{64}$. [4]

Cambridge IGCSE Additional Mathematics 0606 Paper 21 Q11a Jun 2014

2 Solve the simultaneous equations,

$$\frac{4^x}{256^y} = 1024$$

$$3^{2x} \times 9^y = 243$$ [5]

Cambridge IGCSE Additional Mathematics 0606 Paper 21 Q5 Nov 2013

3 Solve the equation $\frac{36^{2y-5}}{6^{3y}} = \frac{6^{2y-1}}{216^{y+6}}$. [4]

Cambridge IGCSE Additional Mathematics 0606 Paper 21 Q5b Jun 2012

4 Integers a and b are such that $(a + 3\sqrt{5})^2 + a - b\sqrt{5} = 51$. Find the possible values of a and the corresponding values of b. [6]

Cambridge IGCSE Additional Mathematics 0606 Paper 21 Q9 Nov 2014

5 **Without using a calculator**, express $6(1 + \sqrt{3})^{-2}$ in the form $a + b\sqrt{3}$, where a and b are integers to be found. [4]

Cambridge IGCSE Additional Mathematics 0606 Paper 21 Q2 Jun 2014

6 **Do not use a calculator in this question.**

Express $\dfrac{(4\sqrt{5}-2)^2}{\sqrt{5}-1}$ in the form $p\sqrt{5}+q$, where p and q are integers. [4]

Cambridge IGCSE Additional Mathematics 0606 Paper 21 Q2 Nov 2013

7 **Do not use a calculator in any part of this question.**

a **i** Show that $3\sqrt{5}-2\sqrt{2}$ is a square root of $53-12\sqrt{10}$. [1]

ii State the other square root of $53-12\sqrt{10}$. [1]

b Express $\dfrac{6\sqrt{3}+7\sqrt{2}}{4\sqrt{3}+5\sqrt{2}}$ in the form $a+b\sqrt{6}$, where a and b are integers to be found. [4]

Cambridge IGCSE Additional Mathematics 0606 Paper 11 Q7a,bi,ii Nov 2012

8 **Calculators must not be used in this question.**

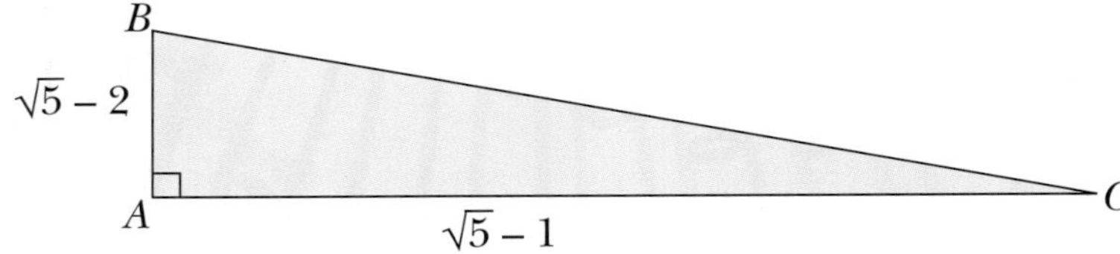

The diagram shows a triangle ABC in which angle $A = 90°$.

Sides AB and AC are $\sqrt{5}-2$ and $\sqrt{5}+1$ respectively.

Find $\tan B$ in the form $a+b\sqrt{5}$, where a and b are integers. [3]

Cambridge IGCSE Additional Mathematics 0606 Paper 11 Q7i Jun 2013

9 Given that $\dfrac{p^{-2}qr^{-\frac{1}{2}}}{\sqrt{p^{\frac{1}{3}}q^{2}r^{-3}}} = p^a q^b r^c$, find the values of a, b, and c. [3]

Cambridge IGCSE Additional Mathematics 0606 Paper 12 Q2 Mar 2016

10 **Do not use a calculator in this question.**

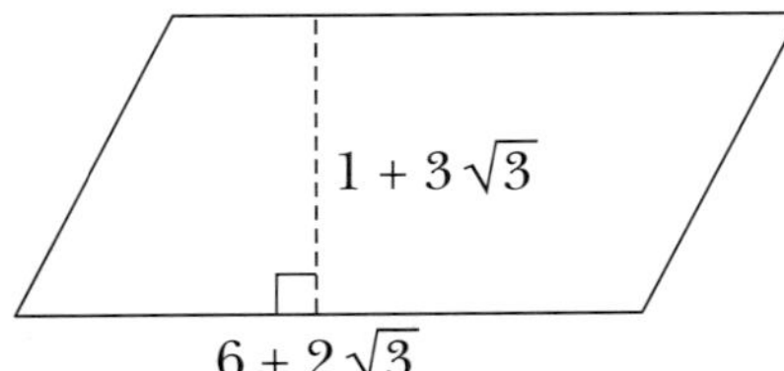

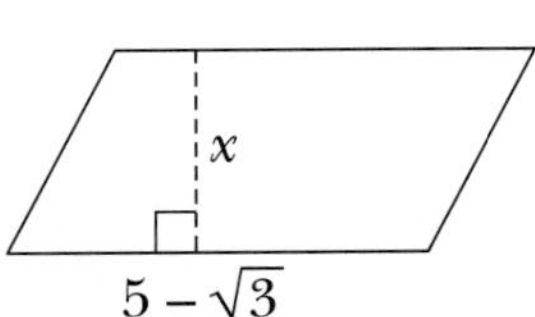

The diagram shows two parallelograms that are similar. The base and height, in centimetres, of each parallelogram is shown. Given that x, the height of the smaller parallelogram,

is $\dfrac{p+q\sqrt{3}}{6}$, find the value of each of the integers p and q. [5]

Cambridge IGCSE Additional Mathematics 0606 Paper 22 Q6 Mar 2016

Chapter 4
Factors and polynomials

This section will show you how to:

- use the remainder and factor theorems
- find factors of polynomials
- solve cubic equations.

4.1 Adding, subtracting and multiplying polynomials

A **polynomial** is a an expression of the form

$$a_n x^n + a_{n-1}x^{n-1} + a_{n-2}x^{n-2} + \ldots + a_2x^2 + a_1x^1 + a_0$$

where:

- x is a variable
- n is a non-negative integer
- the coefficients $a_n, a_{n-1}, a_{n-2}, \ldots, a_2, a_1, a_0$ are constants
- a_n is called the leading coefficient and $a_n \neq 0$
- a_0 is called the constant term.

The highest power of x in the polynomial is called the **degree** of the polynomial.

You already know the special names for polynomials of degree 1, 2 and 3. These are shown in the table below together with the special name for a polynomial of degree 4.

Polynomial expression	Degree	Name
$ax + b, \quad a \neq 0$	1	linear
$ax^2 + bx + c, \quad a \neq 0$	2	quadratic
$ax^3 + bx^2 + cx + d, \quad a \neq 0$	3	cubic
$ax^4 + bx^3 + cx^2 + dx + e, \quad a \neq 0$	4	quartic

The next example is a recap on how to add, subtract and multiply polynomials.

WORKED EXAMPLE 1

If $\text{P}(x) = 2x^3 - 6x^2 - 5$ and $\text{Q}(x) = x^3 + 2x - 1$, find an expression for

a $\text{P}(x) + \text{Q}(x)$, **b** $\text{P}(x) - \text{Q}(x)$, **c** $2\text{Q}(x)$, **d** $\text{P}(x)\text{Q}(x)$.

Answers

a $\text{P}(x) + \text{Q}(x) = 2x^3 - 6x^2 - 5 + x^3 + 2x - 1$ collect like terms

$= 3x^3 - 6x^2 + 2x - 6$

b $\text{P}(x) - \text{Q}(x) = (2x^3 - 6x^2 - 5) - (x^3 + 2x - 1)$ remove brackets

$= 2x^3 - 6x^2 - 5 - x^3 - 2x + 1$ collect like terms

$= x^3 - 6x^2 - 2x - 4$

c $2\text{Q}(x) = 2(x^3 + 2x - 1)$

$= 2x^3 + 4x - 2$

d $\text{P}(x)\text{Q}(x) = (2x^3 - 6x^2 - 5)(x^3 + 2x - 1)$

$= 2x^3(x^3 + 2x - 1) - 6x^2(x^3 + 2x - 1) - 5(x^3 + 2x - 1)$

$= 2x^6 + 4x^4 - 2x^3 - 6x^5 - 12x^3 + 6x^2 - 5x^3 - 10x + 5$

$= 2x^6 - 6x^5 + 4x^4 - 19x^3 + 6x^2 - 10x + 5$

CLASS DISCUSSION

P(x) is a polynomial of degree p and Q(x) is a polynomial of degree q, where $p > q$.
Discuss with your classmates what the degree of each of the following polynomials is:

$P(x) + Q(x)$	$2P(x)$	$Q(x) + 5$
$-3Q(x)$	$P^2(x)$	$[Q(x)]^2$
$P(x)Q(x)$	$QP(x)$	$Q(x) - P(x)$

Exercise 4.1

1 If $P(x) = 3x^4 + 2x^2 - 1$ and $Q(x) = 2x^3 + x^2 + 1$, find an expression for

a $P(x) + Q(x)$

b $3P(x) + Q(x)$

c $P(x) - 2Q(x)$

d $P(x)Q(x)$.

2 Find the following products.

a $(2x-1)(4x^3 + x + 2)$

b $(x^3 + 2x^2 - 1)(3x + 2)$

c $(3x^2 + 2x - 5)(x^3 + x^2 + 4)$

d $(x+2)^2(3x^3 + x - 1)$

e $(x^2 - 5x + 2)^2$

f $(3x-1)^3$

3 Simplify each of the following.

a $(2x-3)(x+2) + (x+1)(x-1)$

b $(3x+1)(x^2 + 5x + 2) - (x^2 - 4x + 2)(x+3)$

c $(2x^3 + x - 1)(x^2 + 3x - 4) - (x+2)(x^3 - x^2 + 5x + 2)$

4 If $f(x) = 2x^2 - x - 4$ and $g(x) = x^2 + 5x + 2$, find an expression for

a $f(x) + xg(x)$

b $[f(x)]^2$

c $f^2(x)$

d $gf(x)$.

4.2 Division of polynomials

To be able to divide a polynomial by another polynomial you first need to remember how to do long division with numbers.

The steps for calculating $5508 \div 17$ are:

324	
$17\overline{)5508}$	Divide 55 by 17
51	$3 \times 17 = 51$
40	$55 - 51 = 4$, bring down the 0 from the next column
34	Divide 40 by 17, $2 \times 17 = 34$
68	$40 - 34 = 6$, bring down the 8 from the next column
68	Divide 68 by 17, $4 \times 17 = 68$
0	$68 - 68 = 0$

So $\qquad 5508 \div 17 = 324$

dividend $\qquad$ divisor $\qquad$ quotient

The same process can be applied to the division of polynomials.

WORKED EXAMPLE 2

Divide $x^3 - 5x^2 + 8x - 4$ by $x - 2$.

Answers

Step 1:

x^2	
$x - 2\overline{)x^3 - 5x^2 + 8x - 4}$	divide the first term of the polynomial by x, $x^3 \div x = x^2$
$x^3 - 2x^2$	multiply $(x - 2)$ by x^2, $x^2(x - 2) = x^3 - 2x^2$
$-3x^2 + 8x$	subtract, $(x^3 - 5x^2) - (x^3 - 2x^2) = -3x^2$
	bring down the $8x$ from the next column

Step 2: Repeat the process

$x^2 - 3x$	
$x - 2\overline{)x^3 - 5x^2 + 8x - 4}$	
$x^3 - 2x^2$	
$-3x^2 + 8x$	divide $-3x^2$ by x, $-3x^2 \div x = -3x$
$-3x^2 + 6x$	multiply $(x - 2)$ by $-3x$, $-3x(x - 2) = -3x^2 + 6x$
$2x - 4$	subtract, $(-3x^2 + 8x) - (-3x^2 + 6x) = 2x$
	bring down the -4 from the next column

Step 3: Repeat the process

$x^2 - 3x + 2$	
$x - 2\overline{)x^3 - 5x^2 + 8x - 4}$	
$x^3 - 2x^2$	
$-3x^2 + 8x$	
$-3x^2 + 6x$	
$2x - 4$	divide $2x$ by x, $2x \div x = 2$
$2x - 4$	multiply $(x - 2)$ by 2, $2(x - 2) = 2x - 4$
0	subtract, $(2x - 4) - (2x - 4) = 0$

So $(x^3 - 5x^2 + 8x - 4) \div (x - 2) = x^2 - 3x + 2$.

WORKED EXAMPLE 3

Divide $2x^3 - x + 51$ by $x + 3$.

There are no x^2 terms in $2x^3 - x + 51$ so we write it as $2x^3 + 0x^2 - x + 51$.

Answers

Step 1:

$$\begin{array}{r|l} & 2x^2 \\ x+3 & 2x^3 + 0x^2 - x + 51 \\ & 2x^3 + 6x^2 \\ & \quad\;\; -6x^2 - x \end{array}$$

divide the first term of the polynomial by x, $2x^3 \div x = 2x^2$

multiply $(x + 3)$ by $2x^2$, $2x^2(x + 3) = 2x^3 + 6x^2$

subtract, $(2x^3 + 0x^2) - (2x^3 + 6x^2) = -6x^2$

bring down the $-x$ from the next column

Step 2: Repeat the process

$$\begin{array}{r|l} & 2x^2 - 6x \\ x+3 & 2x^3 + 0x^2 - x + 51 \\ & 2x^3 + 6x^2 \\ & \quad\;\; -6x^2 - x \\ & \quad\;\; -6x^2 - 18x \\ & \qquad\qquad 17x + 51 \end{array}$$

divide $-6x^2$ by x, $-6x^2 \div x = -6x$

multiply $(x + 3)$ by $-6x$, $-6x(x + 3) = -6x^2 - 18x$

subtract, $(-6x^2 - x) - (-6x^2 - 18x) = 17x$

bring down the 51 from the next column

Step 3: Repeat the process

$$\begin{array}{r|l} & x^2 - 6x + 17 \\ x+3 & 2x^3 + 0x^2 - x + 51 \\ & 2x^3 + 6x^2 \\ & \quad\;\; -6x^2 - x \\ & \quad\;\; -6x^2 - 18x \\ & \qquad\qquad 17x + 51 \\ & \qquad\qquad 17x + 51 \\ & \qquad\qquad\qquad 0 \end{array}$$

divide $17x$ by x, $17x \div x = 17$

multiply $(x + 3)$ by 17, $17(x + 3) = 17x + 51$

subtract, $(17x + 51) - (17x + 51) = 0$

So $(2x^3 - x + 51) \div (x + 3) = 2x^2 - 6x + 17$.

Exercise 4.2

1 Simplify each of the following.

- **a** $(x^3 + 3x^2 - 46x - 48) \div (x + 1)$
- **b** $(x^3 - x^2 - 3x + 2) \div (x - 2)$
- **c** $(x^3 - 20x^2 + 100x - 125) \div (x - 5)$
- **d** $(x^3 - 3x - 2) \div (x - 2)$
- **e** $(x^3 - 3x^2 - 33x + 35) \div (x - 7)$
- **f** $(x^3 + 2x^2 - 9x - 18) \div (x + 2)$

2 Simplify each of the following.

- **a** $(3x^3 + 8x^2 + 3x - 2) \div (x + 2)$
- **b** $(6x^3 + 11x^2 - 3x - 2) \div (3x + 1)$
- **c** $(3x^3 - 11x^2 + 20) \div (x - 2)$
- **d** $(3x^3 - 21x^2 + 4x - 28) \div (x - 7)$

3 Simplify.

a $\dfrac{3x^3 - 3x^2 - 4x + 4}{x - 1}$ **b** $\dfrac{2x^3 + 9x^2 + 25}{x + 5}$

c $\dfrac{3x^3 - 50x + 8}{3x^2 + 12x - 2}$ **d** $\dfrac{x^3 - 14x - 15}{x^2 - 3x - 5}$

4 **a** Divide $x^4 - 1$ by $(x + 1)$. **b** Divide $x^3 - 8$ by $(x - 2)$.

4.3 The factor theorem

In **Worked example 2** you found that $x - 2$ divided exactly into $(x^3 - 5x^2 + 8x - 4)$.

$$(x^3 - 5x^2 + 8x - 4) \div (x - 2) = x^2 - 3x + 2$$

This can also be written as:

$$(x^3 - 5x^2 + 8x - 4) = (x - 2)(x^2 - 3x + 2)$$

If a polynomial $P(x)$ is divided exactly by a linear factor $x - c$ to give the polynomial $Q(x)$, then

$$P(x) = (x - c)Q(x).$$

Substituting $x = c$ into this formula gives $P(c) = 0$.

Hence:

> If for a polynomial $P(x)$, $P(c) = 0$ then $x - c$ is a factor of $P(x)$.

This is known as the **factor theorem**.

For example, when $x = 2$,

$$4x^3 - 8x^2 - x + 2 = 4(2)^3 - 8(2)^2 - 2 + 2 = 32 - 32 - 2 + 2 = 0.$$

Therefore $x - 2$ is a factor of $4x^3 - 8x^2 - x + 2$.

The factor theorem can be extended to:

> If for a polynomial $P(x)$, $P\left(\dfrac{b}{a}\right) = 0$ then $ax - b$ is a factor of $P(x)$.

For example, when $x = \dfrac{1}{2}$,

$$4x^3 - 2x^2 + 8x - 4 = 4\left(\frac{1}{2}\right)^3 - 2\left(\frac{1}{2}\right)^2 + 8\left(\frac{1}{2}\right) - 4 = \frac{1}{2} - \frac{1}{2} + 4 - 4 = 0.$$

Therefore $2x - 1$ is a factor of $4x^3 - 2x^2 + 8x - 4$.

CLASS DISCUSSION

Discuss with your classmates which of the following expressions are exactly divisible by $x - 2$.

$x^3 - x^2 - x - 2$	$2x^3 + 5x^2 - 4x - 3$	$x^3 - 4x^2 + 8x - 8$
$2x^4 - x^3 + 3x^2 - 2x - 5$	$x^3 - 8$	$3x^3 - 8x - 8$
$6x^3 - 10x^2 - 18$	$x^3 + x^2 - 4x - 4$	$x^3 + x + 10$

WORKED EXAMPLE 4

Show that $x - 3$ is a factor of $x^3 - 6x^2 + 11x - 6$ by

a algebraic division

b the factor theorem.

Answers

a Divide $x^3 - 6x^2 + 11x - 6$ by $x - 3$.

$$
\begin{array}{r|l}
 & x^2 - 3x + 2 \\
x - 3 & x^3 - 6x^2 + 11x - 6 \\
 & \underline{x^3 - 3x^2} \\
 & -3x^2 + 11x \\
 & \underline{-3x^2 + 9x} \\
 & 2x - 6 \\
 & \underline{2x - 6} \\
 & 0
\end{array}
$$

The remainder $= 0$, so $x - 3$ is a factor of $x^3 - 6x^2 + 11x - 6$.

b Let $f(x) = x^3 - 6x^2 + 11x - 6$ if $f(3) = 0$, then $x - 3$ is a factor.

$$
\begin{aligned}
f(3) &= (3)^3 - 6(3)^2 + 11(3) - 6 \\
&= 27 - 54 + 33 - 6 \\
&= 0
\end{aligned}
$$

So $x - 3$ is a factor of $x^3 - 6x^2 + 11x - 6$.

WORKED EXAMPLE 5

$2x^2 + x - 1$ is a factor of $2x^3 - x^2 + ax + b$.

Find the value of a and the value of b.

Answers

Let $f(x) = 2x^3 - x^2 + ax + b$.

If $2x^2 + x - 1 = (2x - 1)(x + 1)$ is a factor of $f(x)$, then $2x - 1$ and $x + 1$ are also factors of $f(x)$.

Using the factor theorem $f\left(\frac{1}{2}\right) = 0$ and $f(-1) = 0$.

$f\left(\frac{1}{2}\right) = 0$ gives $2\left(\frac{1}{2}\right)^3 - \left(\frac{1}{2}\right)^2 + a\left(\frac{1}{2}\right) + b = 0$

$$\frac{1}{4} - \frac{1}{4} + \frac{a}{2} + b = 0$$

$$a = -2b \quad \text{--------------------(1)}$$

$f(-1) = 0$ gives $2(-1)^3 - (-1)^2 + a(-1) + b = 0$

$$-2 - 1 - a + b = 0$$

$$a = b - 3 \quad \text{--------------------(2)}$$

(2) = (1) gives $b - 3 = -2b$

$$3b = 3$$

$$b = 1$$

Substituting in (2) gives $a = -2$.

So $a = -2$, $b = 1$.

Exercise 4.3

1 Use the factor theorem to show:

a $x - 4$ is a factor of $x^3 - 3x^2 - 6x + 8$

b $x + 1$ is a factor of $x^3 - 3x - 2$

c $x - 2$ is a factor of $5x^3 - 17x^2 + 28$

d $3x + 1$ is a factor of $6x^3 + 11x^2 - 3x - 2$.

2 Find the value of a in each of the following.

a $x + 1$ is a factor of $6x^3 + 27x^2 + ax + 8$.

b $x + 7$ is a factor of $x^3 - 5x^2 - 6x + a$.

c $2x + 3$ is a factor of $4x^3 + ax^2 + 29x + 30$.

3 $x - 2$ is a factor of $x^3 + ax^2 + bx - 4$.

Express b in terms of a.

4 Find the value of a and the value of b in each of the following.

a $x^2 + 3x - 10$ is a factor of $x^3 + ax^2 + bx + 30$.

b $2x^2 - 11x + 5$ is a factor of $ax^3 - 17x^2 + bx - 15$.

c $4x^2 - 4x - 15$ is a factor of $4x^3 + ax^2 + bx + 30$.

5 It is given that $x^2 - 5x + 6$ and $x^3 - 6x^2 + 11x + a$ have a common factor.
Find the possible value of a.

6 $x - 2$ is a common factor of $3x^3 - (a - b)x - 8$ and $x^3 - (a + b)x + 30$.
Find the value of a and the value of b.

7 $x - 3$ and $2x - 1$ are factors of $2x^3 - px^2 - 2qx + q$.

a Find the value of p and the value of q.

b Explain why $x + 3$ is also a factor of the expression.

8 $x + a$ is a factor of $x^3 + 8x^2 + 4ax - 3a$.

a Show that $a^3 - 4a^2 + 3a = 0$.

b Find the possible values of a.

4.4 Cubic expressions and equations

Consider factorising $x^3 - 5x^2 + 8x - 4$ completely.

In **Worked example 2** you found that $(x^3 - 5x^2 + 8x - 4) \div (x - 2) = x^2 - 3x + 2$.

This can be rewritten as: $x^3 - 5x^2 + 8x - 4 = (x - 2)(x^2 - 3x + 2)$.

Factorising completely gives: $x^3 - 5x^2 + 8x - 4 = (x - 2)(x - 2)(x - 1)$.

Hence if you know one factor of a cubic expression it is possible to then factorise the expression completely. The next example illustrates three different methods for doing this.

WORKED EXAMPLE 6

Factorise $x^3 - 3x^2 - 13x + 15$ completely.

Answers

Let $f(x) = x^3 - 3x^2 - 13x + 15$.
The positive and negative factors of 15 are ±1, ±3, ±5 and ±15.
$f(1) = (1)^3 - 3 \times (1)^2 - 13 \times (1) + 15 = 0$
So $x - 1$ is a factor of $f(x)$.
The other factors can be found by any of the following methods.

Method 1 (by trial and error)
$f(x) = x^3 - 3x^2 - 13x + 15$

$f(1) = (1)^3 - 3 \times (1)^2 - 13 \times (1) + 15 = 0$
So $x - 1$ is a factor of $f(x)$.

$f(-3) = (-3)^3 - 3 \times (-3)^2 - 13 \times (-3) + 15 = 0$
So $x + 3$ is a factor of $f(x)$.

$f(5) = (5)^3 - 3 \times (5)^2 - 13 \times (5) + 15 = 0$

So $x - 5$ is a factor of $f(x)$.
Hence $f(x) = (x - 1)(x - 5)(x + 3)$

Method 2 (by long division)

$$\begin{array}{r} x^2 - 2x - 15 \\ x-1\overline{)\,x^3 - 3x^2 - 13x + 15} \\ \underline{x^3 - x^2} \qquad\qquad \\ -2x^2 - 13x \qquad \\ \underline{-2x^2 + 2x} \qquad \\ -15x + 15 \\ \underline{-15x + 15} \\ 0 \end{array}$$

$$\begin{aligned} f(x) &= (x-1)(x^2 - 2x - 15) \\ &= (x-1)(x-5)(x+3) \end{aligned}$$

Method 3 (by equating coefficients)

Since $x - 1$ is a factor, $x^3 - 3x^2 - 13x + 15$ can be written as:

$$x^3 - 3x^2 - 13x + 15 = (x-1)(ax^2 + bx + c)$$

coefficient of x^3 is 1, so $a = 1$ since $1 \times 1 = 1$

constant term is -15, so $c = -15$ since $-1 \times -15 = 15$

$$x^3 - 3x^2 - 13x + 15 = (x-1)(x^2 + bx - 15)$$ expand and collect like terms

$$x^3 - 3x^2 - 13x + 15 = x^3 + (b-1)x^2 + (-b-15)x + 15$$

Equating coefficients of x^2: $b - 1 = -3$

$$b = -2$$

$$\begin{aligned} f(x) &= (x-1)(x^2 - 2x - 15) \\ &= (x-1)(x-5)(x+3) \end{aligned}$$

WORKED EXAMPLE 7

Solve $2x^3 - 3x^2 - 18x - 8 = 0$.

Answers

Let $f(x) = 2x^3 - 3x^2 - 18x - 8$.

The positive and negative factors of 8 are ±1, ±2, ±4 and ±8.

$f(-2) = 2(-2)^3 - 3 \times (-2)^2 - 18 \times (-2) - 8 = 0$

So $x + 2$ is a factor of $f(x)$.

$$2x^3 - 3x^2 - 18x - 8 = (x+2)(ax^2 + bx + c)$$

coefficient of x^3 is 2, so $a = 2$ since $1 \times 2 = 2$

constant term is -8, so $c = -4$ since $2 \times -4 = -8$

$$2x^3 - 3x^2 - 18x - 8 = (x+2)(2x^2 + bx - 4)$$ expand and collect like terms

$$2x^3 - 3x^2 - 18x - 8 = 2x^3 + (b+4)x^2 + (2b-4)x - 8$$

Equating coefficients of x^2: $b + 4 = -3$

$$b = -7$$

$$f(x) = (x+2)(2x^2 - 7x - 4)$$
$$= (x+2)(2x+1)(x-4)$$

Hence $(x+2)(2x+1)(x-4) = 0$.

So $x = -2$ or $x = -\frac{1}{2}$ or $x = 4$.

WORKED EXAMPLE 8

Solve $2x^3 + 7x^2 - 2x - 1 = 0$.

Answers

Let $f(x) = 2x^3 + 7x^2 - 2x - 1$.

The positive and negative factors of -1 are ±1.

$$f(-1) = 2(-1)^3 + 7\times(-1)^2 - 2\times(-1) - 1 \neq 0$$
$$f(1) = 2(1)^3 + 7\times(1)^2 - 2\times(1) - 1 \neq 0$$

So $x - 1$ and $x + 1$ are not factors of $f(x)$.

By inspection, $f\left(\frac{1}{2}\right) = 2\left(\frac{1}{2}\right)^3 + 7\times\left(\frac{1}{2}\right)^2 - 2\times\left(\frac{1}{2}\right) - 1 = 0$.

So $2x - 1$ is a factor of:

$$2x^3 + 7x^2 - 2x - 1 = (2x-1)(ax^2 + bx + c)$$

coefficient of x^3 is 2, so $a = 1$ since $2 \times 1 = 2$

constant term is -1, so $c = 1$ since $-1 \times 1 = -1$

$$2x^3 + 7x^2 - 2x - 1 = (2x-1)(x^2 + bx + 1)$$
$$2x^3 + 7x^2 - 2x - 1 = 2x^3 + (2b-1)x^2 + (2-b)x - 1$$

Equating coefficients of x^2: $2b - 1 = 7$

$$b = 4$$

So $2x^3 + 7x^2 - 2x - 1 = (2x-1)(x^2 + 4x + 1)$.

$$x = \frac{1}{2} \text{ or } x = \frac{-4 \pm \sqrt{4^2 - 4\times1\times1}}{2\times1}$$

$$x = \frac{1}{2} \text{ or } x = \frac{-4 \pm 2\sqrt{3}}{2}$$

$$x = \frac{1}{2} \text{ or } x = -2 + \sqrt{3} \text{ or } x = -2 - \sqrt{3}$$

Not all cubic expressions can be factorised into 3 linear factors.

Consider the cubic expression $x^3 + x^2 - 36$.

Let $f(x) = x^3 + x^2 - 36$.

$$f(3) = (3)^3 + (3)^2 - 36 = 0$$

So $x - 3$ is a factor of $f(x)$.

$$x^3 + x^2 - 36 = (x-3)(ax^2 + bx + c)$$

coefficient of x^3 is 1, so $a = 1$ since $1 \times 1 = 1$	constant term is -36, so $c = 12$ since $-3 \times 12 = -36$

$$x^3 + x^2 - 36 = (x-3)(x^2 + bx + 12)$$

$$x^3 + x^2 - 36 = x^3 + (b-3)x^2 + (12 - 3b)x - 36$$

Equating coefficients of x^2: $b - 3 = 1$

$$b = 4$$

So $x^3 + x^2 - 36 = (x-3)(x^2 + 4x + 12)$

(Note: $x^2 + 4x + 12$ cannot be factorised into two further linear factors, since the discriminant < 0.)

Exercise 4.4

1 a Show that $x - 1$ is a factor of $2x^3 - x^2 - 2x + 1$.

 b Hence factorise $2x^3 - x^2 - 2x + 1$ completely.

2 Factorise these cubic expressions completely.

 a $x^3 + 2x^2 - 3x - 10$ b $x^3 + 4x^2 - 4x - 16$

 c $2x^3 - 9x^2 - 18x$ d $x^3 - 8x^2 + 5x + 14$

 e $2x^3 - 13x^2 + 17x + 12$ f $3x^3 + 2x^2 - 19x + 6$

 g $4x^3 - 8x^2 - x + 2$ h $2x^3 + 3x^2 - 32x + 15$

3 Solve the following equations.

 a $x^3 - 3x^2 - 33x + 35 = 0$ b $x^3 - 6x^2 + 11x - 6 = 0$

 c $3x^3 + 17x^2 + 18x - 8 = 0$ d $2x^3 + 3x^2 - 17x + 12 = 0$

 e $2x^3 - 3x^2 - 11x + 6 = 0$ f $2x^3 + 7x^2 - 5x - 4 = 0$

 g $4x^3 + 12x^2 + 5x - 6 = 0$ h $2x^3 - 3x^2 - 29x + 60 = 0$

4 Solve the following equations.

 Express roots in the form $a \pm b\sqrt{c}$, where necessary.

 a $x^3 + 5x^2 - 4x - 2 = 0$ b $x^3 + 8x^2 + 12x - 9 = 0$

 c $x^3 + 2x^2 - 7x - 2 = 0$ d $2x^3 + 3x^2 - 17x + 12 = 0$

5 Solve the equation $2x^3 + 9x^2 - 14x - 9 = 0$.

 Express roots in the form $a \pm b\sqrt{c}$, where necessary.

6 Solve the equation $x^3 + 8x^2 + 12x = 9$.

Write your answers correct to 2 decimal places where necessary.

7 **a** Show that $x - 2$ is a factor of $x^3 - x^2 - x - 2$.

b Hence show that $x^3 - x^2 - x - 2 = 0$ has only one real root and state the value of this root.

8 $f(x)$ is a cubic polynomial where the coefficient of x^3 is 1.

Find $f(x)$ when the roots of $f(x) = 0$ are

a -2, 1 and 5 **b** -5, -2 and 4 **c** -3, 0 and 2.

9 $f(x)$ is a cubic polynomial where the coefficient of x^3 is 2.

Find $f(x)$ when the roots of $f(x) = 0$ are

a -0.5, 2 and 4 **b** 0.5, 1 and 2 **c** -1.5, 1 and 5.

10 $f(x)$ is a cubic polynomial where the coefficient of x^3 is 1.

The roots of $f(x) = 0$ are -3, $1 + \sqrt{2}$ and $1 - \sqrt{2}$.

Express $f(x)$ as a cubic polynomial in x with integer coefficients.

11 $f(x)$ is a cubic polynomial where the coefficient of x^3 is 2.

The roots of $f(x) = 0$ are $\frac{1}{2}$, $2 + \sqrt{3}$ and $2 - \sqrt{3}$.

Express $f(x)$ as a cubic polynomial in x with integer coefficients.

12 $2x + 3$ is a factor of $2x^4 + (a^2 + 1)x^3 - 3x^2 + (1 - a^3)x + 3$.

a Show that $4a^3 - 9a^2 + 4 = 0$.

b Find the possible values of a.

4.5 The remainder theorem

Consider $f(x) = 2x^3 - 4x^2 + 7x - 37$.

Substituting $x = 3$ in the polynomial gives $f(3) = 2(3)^3 - 4(3)^2 + 7(3) - 37 = 2$.

When $2x^3 - 4x^2 + 7x - 37$ is divided by $x - 3$, there is a remainder.

$$
\begin{array}{r}
2x^2 + 2x + 13 \\
x - 3 \,\big)\, \overline{2x^3 - 4x^2 + 7x - 37} \\
\underline{2x^3 - 6x^2 } \\
2x^2 + 7x \\
\underline{2x^2 - 6x } \\
13x - 37 \\
\underline{13x - 39} \\
2
\end{array}
$$

The remainder is 2. This is the same value as $f(3)$.

$f(x) = 2x^3 - 4x^2 + 7x - 36$, can be written as

$f(x) = (x - 3)(2x^2 + 2x + 13) + 2$.

In general:

If a polynomial $\mathrm{P}(x)$ is divided by $x - c$ to give the polynomial $\mathrm{Q}(x)$ and a remainder R, then

$$\mathrm{P}(x) = (x - c)\mathrm{Q}(x) + R.$$

Substituting $x = c$ into this formula gives $\mathrm{P}(c) = R$.

This leads to the **remainder theorem**:

> If a polynomial $\mathrm{P}(x)$ is divided by $x - c$, the remainder is $\mathrm{P}(c)$.

The Remainder Theorem can be extended to:

> If a polynomial $\mathrm{P}(x)$ is divided by $ax - b$, the remainder is $\mathrm{P}\left(\dfrac{b}{a}\right)$.

WORKED EXAMPLE 9

Find the remainder when $7x^3 + 6x^2 - 40x + 17$ is divided by $(x + 3)$ by using

a algebraic division **b** the factor theorem.

Answers

a Divide $7x^3 + 6x^2 - 40x + 17$ by $(x + 3)$.

$$
\begin{array}{r|l}
 & 7x^2 + 15x + 5 \\
\hline
x + 3 & 7x^3 + 6x^2 - 40x + 17 \\
 & 7x^3 + 21x^2 \\
\hline
 & -15x^2 - 40x \\
 & -15x^2 - 45x \\
\hline
 & 5x + 17 \\
 & 5x + 15 \\
\hline
 & 2
\end{array}
$$

The remainder is 2.

b Let $\mathrm{f}(x) = 7x^3 + 6x^2 - 40x + 17$.

$$
\begin{aligned}
\text{Remainder} &= \mathrm{f}(-3) \\
&= 7(-3)^3 + 6(-3)^2 - 40(-3) + 17 \\
&= -189 + 54 + 120 + 17 \\
&= 2
\end{aligned}
$$

WORKED EXAMPLE 10

$f(x) = 2x^3 + ax^2 - 9x + b$

When $f(x)$ is divided by $x - 1$, the remainder is 1.

When $f(x)$ is divided by $x + 2$, the remainder is 19.

Find the value of a and of b.

Answers

$f(x) = 2x^3 + ax^2 - 9x + b$

When $f(x)$ is divided by $x - 1$, the remainder is 1 means that: $f(1) = 1$.

$$2(1)^3 + a(1)^2 - 9(1) + b = 1$$
$$2 + a - 9 + b = 1$$
$$a + b = 8 \text{ ------------------(1)}$$

When $f(x)$ is divided by $x + 2$, the remainder is 19 means that: $f(-2) = 19$.

$$2(-2)^3 + a(-2)^2 - 9(-2) + b = 19$$
$$-16 + 4a + 18 + b = 19$$
$$4a + b = 17 \text{ --------(2)}$$

(2) − (1) gives $3a = 9$

$$a = 3$$

Substituting $a = 3$ in equation (2) gives $b = 5$.

$a = 3$ and $b = 5$

Exercise 4.5

1 Find the remainder when

- **a** $x^3 + 2x^2 - x + 3$ is divided by $x - 1$
- **b** $x^3 - 6x^2 + 11x - 7$ is divided by $x - 2$
- **c** $x^3 - 3x^2 - 33x + 30$ is divided by $x + 2$
- **d** $2x^3 - x^2 - 18x + 11$ is divided by $2x - 1$.

2 **a** When $x^3 + x^2 + ax - 2$ is divided by $x - 1$, the remainder is 5.
Find the value of a.

b When $2x^3 - 6x^2 + 7x + b$ is divided by $x + 2$, the remainder is 3.
Find the value of b.

c When $2x^3 + x^2 + cx - 10$ is divided by $2x - 1$, the remainder is −4.
Find the value of c.

3 $f(x) = x^3 + ax^2 + bx - 5$

$f(x)$ has a factor of $x - 1$ and leaves a remainder of 3 when divided by $x + 2$.

Find the value of a and of b.

4 $f(x) = x^3 + ax^2 + 11x + b$

$f(x)$ has a factor of $x - 2$ and leaves a remainder of 24 when divided by $x - 5$.

Find the value of a and of b.

5 $f(x) = x^3 - 2x^2 + ax + b$

$f(x)$ has a factor of $x - 3$ and leaves a remainder of 15 when divided by $x + 2$.

a Find the value of a and of b.

b Solve the equation $f(x) = 0$.

6 $f(x) = 4x^3 + 8x^2 + ax + b$

$f(x)$ has a factor of $2x - 1$ and leaves a remainder of 48 when divided by $x - 2$.

a Find the value of a and of b.

b Find the remainder when $f(x)$ is divided by $x - 1$.

7 $f(x) = 2x^3 + (a + 1)x^2 - ax + b$

When $f(x)$ is divided by $x - 1$, the remainder is 5.

When $f(x)$ is divided by $x - 2$, the remainder is 14.

Show that $a = -4$ and find the value of b.

8 $f(x) = ax^3 + bx^2 + 5x - 2$

When $f(x)$ is divided by $x - 1$, the remainder is 6.

When $f(x)$ is divided by $2x + 1$, the remainder is -6.

Find the value of a and of b.

9 $f(x) = x^3 - 5x^2 + ax + b$

$f(x)$ has a factor of $x - 2$.

a Express b in terms of a.

b When $f(x)$ is divided by $x + 1$, the remainder is -9.

Find the value of a and of b.

10 $f(x) = x^3 + ax^2 + bx + c$

The roots of $f(x) = 0$ are 2, 3, and k.

When $f(x)$ is divided by $x - 1$, the remainder is -8.

a Find the value of k.

b Find the remainder when $f(x)$ is divided by $x + 1$.

11 $f(x) = 4x^3 + ax^2 + 13x + b$

$f(x)$ has a factor of $2x - 1$ and leaves a remainder of 21 when divided by $x - 2$.

a Find the value of a and of b.

b Find the remainder when the expression is divided by $x + 1$.

12 $f(x) = x^3 - 8x^2 + kx - 20$

When $f(x)$ is divided by $x - 1$, the remainder is R.

When $f(x)$ is divided by $x - 2$, the remainder is $4R$.

Find the value of k.

13 $f(x) = x^3 + 2x^2 - 6x + 9$

When $f(x)$ is divided by $x + a$, the remainder is R.

When $f(x)$ is divided by $x - a$, the remainder is $2R$.

a Show that $3a^3 - 2a^2 - 18a - 9 = 0$.

b Solve the equation in **part a** completely.

14 $f(x) = x^3 + 6x^2 + kx - 15$

When $f(x)$ is divided by $x - 1$, the remainder is R.

When $f(x)$ is divided by $x + 4$, the remainder is $-R$.

a Find the value of k.

b Hence find the remainder when the expression is divided by $x + 2$.

15 $P(x) = 5(x-1)(x-2)(x-3) + a(x-1)(x-2) + b(x-1) + c$

It is given that when $P(x)$ is divided by each of $x - 1$, $x - 2$ and $x - 3$ the remainders are 7, 2 and 1 respectively. Find the values of a, b, and c.

CHALLENGE Q

16 $f(x) = x^3 + ax^2 + bx + c$

The roots of $f(x) = 0$ are 1, k, and $k + 1$.

When $f(x)$ is divided by $x - 2$, the remainder is 20.

a Show that $k^2 - 3k - 18 = 0$.

b Hence find the possible values of k.

Summary

The **factor theorem**:

If, for a polynomial $P(x)$, $P(c) = 0$ then $x - c$ is a factor of $P(x)$.

If, for a polynomial $P(x)$, $P\left(\frac{b}{a}\right) = 0$ then $ax - b$ is a factor of $P(x)$.

The **remainder theorem**:

If a polynomial $P(x)$ is divided by $x - c$, the remainder is $P(c)$.

If a polynomial $P(x)$ is divided by $ax - b$, the remainder is $P\left(\frac{b}{a}\right)$.

Examination questions

Worked example

The function f is such that $f(x) = 4x^3 - 8x^2 + ax + b$, where a and b are constants. It is given that $2x - 1$ is a factor of $f(x)$ and that when $f(x)$ is divided by $x + 2$ the remainder is 20. Find the remainder when $f(x)$ is divided by $x - 1$. [6]

Cambridge IGCSE Additional Mathematics 0606 Paper 11 Q2 Nov 2011

Answer

$f(x) = 4x^3 - 8x^2 + ax + b$

If $2x - 1$ is a factor, then $f\left(\frac{1}{2}\right) = 0$.

$$4\left(\frac{1}{2}\right)^3 - 8\left(\frac{1}{2}\right)^2 + a\left(\frac{1}{2}\right) + b = 0$$

$$\frac{1}{2} - 2 + a\left(\frac{1}{2}\right) + b = 0$$

$$a\left(\frac{1}{2}\right) + b = 1\frac{1}{2}$$

$$a + 2b = 3 \quad \text{-----------------------(1)}$$

Remainder = 20 when divided by $x + 2$, means that $f(-2) = 20$.

$$4(-2)^3 - 8(-2)^2 + a(-2) + b = 20$$

$$-32 - 32 - 2a + b = 20$$

$$-2a + b = 84 \quad \text{---------------------(2)}$$

From (1) $a = 3 - 2b$.

Substituting in (2), gives: $-2(3 - 2b) + b = 84$

$$-6 + 4b + b = 84$$

$$5b = 90$$

$$b = 18$$

So $a = -33$, $b = 18$.

Remainder when $f(x) = 4x^3 - 8x^2 - 33x + 18$ is divided by $(x - 1)$ is $f(1)$.

Remainder $= 4(1)^3 - 8(1)^2 - 33(1) + 18$

$= 4 - 8 - 33 + 18$

$= -19$

Exercise 4.6

Exam Exercise

1 **a** Show that $x - 2$ is a factor of $3x^3 - 14x^2 + 32$. [1]

b Hence factorise $3x^3 - 14x^2 + 32$ completely. [4]

Cambridge IGCSE Additional Mathematics 0606 Paper 21 Q12i,ii Nov 2012

2 The function $f(x) = ax^3 + 4x^2 + bx - 2$, where a and b are constants, is such that $2x - 1$ is a factor. Given that the remainder when $f(x)$ is divided by $x - 2$ is twice the remainder when $f(x)$ is divided by $x + 1$, find the value of a and of b. [6]

Cambridge IGCSE Additional Mathematics 0606 Paper 11 Q6 Nov 2013

3 **a** The remainder when the expression $x^3 + 9x^2 + bx + c$ is divided by $x - 2$ is twice the remainder when the expression is divided by $x - 1$. Show that $c = 24$. [5]

b Given that $x + 8$ is a factor of $x^3 + 9x^2 + bx + 24$, show that the equation $x^3 + 9x^2 + bx + 24 = 0$ has only one real root. [4]

Cambridge IGCSE Additional Mathematics 0606 Paper 21 Q10i,ii Nov 2012

4 The expression $x^3 + 8x^2 + px - 25$ leaves a remainder of R when divided by $x - 1$ and a remainder of $-R$ when divided by $x + 2$.

a Find the value of p. [4]

b Hence find the remainder when the expression is divided by $x + 3$. [2]

Cambridge IGCSE Additional Mathematics 0606 Paper 21 Q5i,ii Jun 2011

5 Factorise completely the expression $2x^3 - 11x^2 - 20x - 7$. [5]

Cambridge IGCSE Additional Mathematics 0606 Paper 11 Q4 Nov 2010

6 The expression $x^3 + ax^2 - 15x + b$ has a factor of $x - 2$ and leaves a remainder 75 when divided by $x + 3$. Find the value of a and of b. [5]

Cambridge IGCSE Additional Mathematics 0606 Paper 21 Q2 Nov 2010

7 The polynomial $f(x) = ax^3 + 7x^2 - 9x + b$ is divisible by $2x - 1$. The remainder when $f(x)$ is divided by $x - 2$ is 5 times the remainder when $f(x)$ is divided by $x + 1$.

i Show that $a = 6$ and find the value of b. [4]

ii Using the values from **part a**, show that $f(x) = (2x - 1)(cx^2 + dx + e)$, where c, d and e are integers to be found. [2]

iii Hence factorise $f(x)$ completely. [2]

Cambridge IGCSE Additional Mathematics 0606 Paper 12 Q7 Mar 2016

Chapter 5
Equations, inequalities and graphs

This section will show you how to:

- solve graphically or algebraically equations of the type $|ax+b|=|cx+d|$
- solve graphically or algebraically inequalities of the type $|ax+b|>c \ (c \geqslant 0)$, $|ax+b| \leqslant c \ (c>0)$ and $|ax+b| \leqslant |cx+d|$
- solve cubic inequalities in the form $k(x-a)(x-b)(x-c) \leqslant d$ graphically
- sketch the graphs of cubic polynomials and their moduli, when given in factorised form
- use substitution to form and solve quadratic equations.

5.1 Solving equations of the type $|ax + b| = |cx + d|$

CLASS DISCUSSION

Using the fact that $|p|^2 = p^2$ and $|q|^2 = q^2$ you can say that:

$$p^2 - q^2 = |p|^2 - |q|^2$$

Using the difference of two squares then gives:

$$p^2 - q^2 = (|p| - |q|)(|p| + |q|)$$

Using the statement above, explain how these three important results can be obtained:

(The symbol $\Leftrightarrow$ means 'is equivalent to'.)

- $|p| = |q| \Leftrightarrow p^2 = q^2$
- $|p| > |q| \Leftrightarrow p^2 > q^2$
- $|p| < |q| \Leftrightarrow p^2 < q^2$, if $q \neq 0$

The next worked example shows you how to solve equations of the form $|ax + b| = |cx + d|$ using algebra. To solve this type of equation you can use the techniques that you learnt in Chapter 1 or you can use the rule:

$$|p| = |q| \Leftrightarrow p^2 = q^2$$

WORKED EXAMPLE 1

Solve the equation $|x - 5| = |x + 1|$ using an algebraic method.

Answers

Method 1

$|x - 5| = |x + 1|$

$x - 5 = x + 1$ or $x - 5 = -(x + 1)$

$0 = 6$ or $2x = 4$ — $0 = 6$ is false

$x = 2$

CHECK: $|2 - 5| = |2 + 1|$ ✓

The solution is $x = 2$

Method 2

$|x - 5| = |x + 1|$ — use $|p| = |q| \Leftrightarrow p^2 = q^2$

$(x - 5)^2 = (x + 1)^2$ — expand

$x^2 - 10x + 25 = x^2 + 2x + 1$ — simplify

$12x = 24$

$x = 2$

The equation $|x-5|=|x+1|$ could also have been solved graphically.

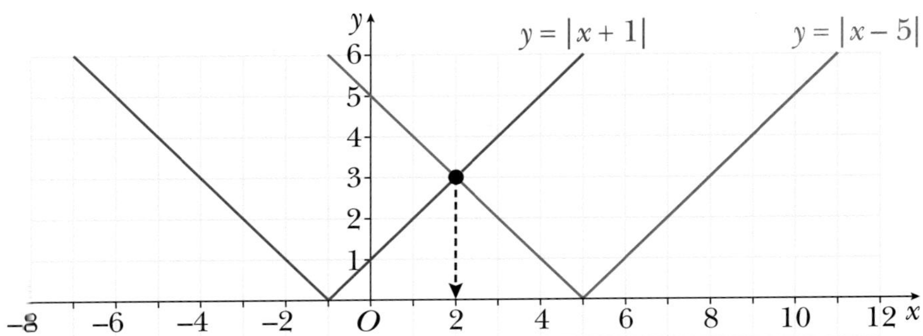

The solution is the x-coordinate where the two graphs intersect.

WORKED EXAMPLE 2

Solve the equation $|2x+1| = |x-3|$ using an algebraic method.

Answers

Method 1

$|2x+1| = |x-3|$

$2x+1 = x-3$ or $2x+1 = -(x-3)$

$x = -4$ or $3x = 2$

$x = \frac{2}{3}$

CHECK: $|2(-4)+1| = |-4-3|$ ✓, $\left|2 \times \frac{2}{3} + 1\right| = \left|\frac{2}{3} - 3\right|$ ✓

Solution is $x = \frac{2}{3}$ or $x = -4$

Method 2

$|2x+1| = |x-3|$ — use $|p| = |q| \Leftrightarrow p^2 = q^2$

$(2x+1)^2 = (x-3)^2$ — expand

$4x^2 + 4x + 1 = x^2 - 6x + 9$ — simplify

$3x^2 + 10x - 8 = 0$ — factorise

$(3x-2)(x+4) = 0$

$x = \frac{2}{3}$ or $x = -4$

The equation $|2x+1|=|x-3|$ could also be solved graphically.

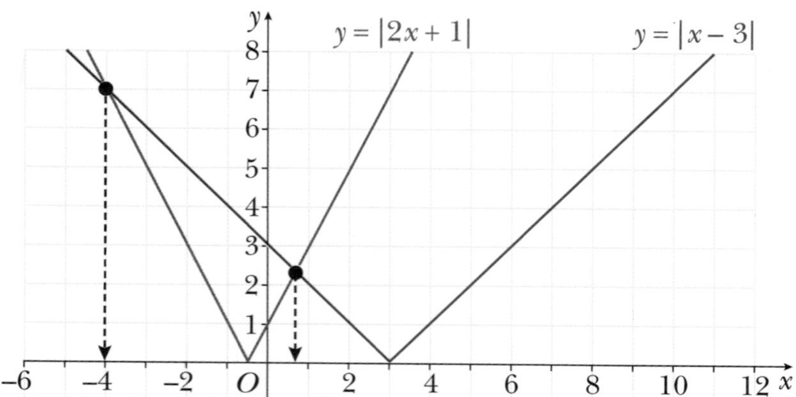

From the graph, one of the answers is clearly $x=-4$. The exact value of the other answer is not so obvious and algebra is needed to find this exact value.

The graph of $y=|x-3|$ can be written as:

$y=x-3$ if $x \geqslant 3$

$y=-(x-3)$ if $x<3$

The graph of $y=|2x+1|$ can be written as:

$y=2x+1$ if $x \geqslant -\frac{1}{2}$

$y=-(2x+1)$ if $x<-\frac{1}{2}$

The second answer is found by finding the x value at the point where $y=-(x-3)$ and $y=2x+1$ intersect.

$$2x+1=-x-3$$

$$2x+1=-x+3$$

$$3x=2$$

$$x=\frac{2}{3}$$

Hence the solution is $x=-4$ or $x=\frac{2}{3}$.

WORKED EXAMPLE 3

Solve $|x + 4| + |x - 5| = 11$.

Answers

$|x + 4| + |x - 5| = 11$ — subtract $|x - 5|$ from both sides

$|x + 4| = 11 - |x - 5|$ — split the equation into two parts

$x + 4 = 11 - |x - 5|$ ------(1)

$x + 4 = |x - 5| - 11$ ------(2)

Using equation (1)

$|x - 5| = 7 - x$ — split this equation into two parts

$x - 5 = 7 - x$ or $x - 5 = -(7 - x)$

$2x = 12$ or $0 = -2$ — $0 = -2$ is false

$x = 6$

Using equation (2)

$|x - 5| = x + 15$ — split this equation into two parts

$x - 5 = x + 15$ or $x - 5 = -(x + 15)$

$0 = 20$ or $2x = -10$ — $0 = 20$ is false

$x = -5$

CHECK: $|6 + 4| + |6 - 5| = 11$ ✓, $|-5 + 4| + |-5 - 5| = 11$ ✓

The solution is $x = 6$ or $x = -5$.

Exercise 5.1

1 Solve.

a $|2x-1|=|x|$ **b** $|x+5|=|x-4|$ **c** $|2x-3|=|4-x|$

d $|5x+1|=|1-3x|$ **e** $|1-4x|=|2-x|$ **f** $\left|1-\frac{x}{2}\right|=|3x+2|$

g $|3x-2|=|2x+5|$ **h** $|2x-1|=2|3-x|$ **i** $|2-x|=5\left|\frac{1}{2}x+1\right|$

2 Solve the simultaneous equations $y=|x-5|$ and $y=|8-x|$.

3 Solve the equation $6|x+2|^2+7|x+2|-3=0$.

4 **a** Solve the equation $x^2-6|x|+8=0$.

b Use graphing software to draw the graph of $f(x)=x^2-6|x|+8$.

c Use your graph in **part b** to find the range of the function f.

CHALLENGE Q

5 Solve the equation $|x+1|+|2x-3|=8$.

CHALLENGE Q

6 Solve the simultaneous equations $y = |x - 5|$ and $y = |3 - 2x| + 2$.

CHALLENGE Q

7 Solve the equation $2|3x + 4y - 2| + 3\sqrt{25 - 5x + 2y} = 0$.

5.2 Solving modulus inequalities

Two useful properties that can be used when solving modulus inequalities are:

$|p| \leqslant q \Leftrightarrow -q \leqslant p \leqslant q$ and $|p| \geqslant q \Leftrightarrow p \leqslant -q$ or $p \geqslant q$

The following examples illustrate the different methods that can be used when solving modulus inequalities.

WORKED EXAMPLE 4

Solve $|2x - 1| < 3$.

Answers

Method 1 (using algebra)

$|2x - 1| < 3$ use $|p| < q \Leftrightarrow -q < p < q$

$-3 < 2x - 1 < 3$

$-2 < 2x < 4$

$-1 < x < 2$

Method 2 (using a graph)

The graphs of $y = |2x - 1|$ and $y = 3$ intersect at the points A and B.

$$|2x-1| = \begin{cases} 2x-1 & \text{if } x \geqslant \frac{1}{2} \\ -(2x-1) & \text{if } x < \frac{1}{2} \end{cases}$$

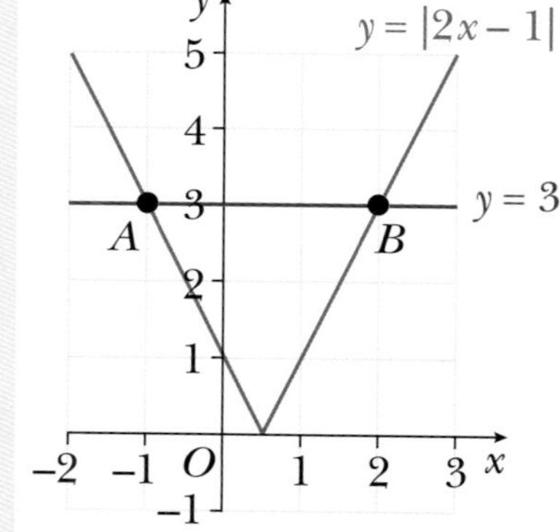

At A, the line $y = -(2x - 1)$ intersects the line $y = 3$.

$-(2x - 1) = 3$

$-2x + 1 = 3$

$2x = -2$

$x = -1$

At B, the line $y = 2x - 1$ intersects the line $y = 3$.

$2x - 1 = 3$

$2x = 4$

$x = 2$

To solve the inequality $|2x - 1| < 3$ you must find where the graph of the function $y = |2x - 1|$ is below the graph of $y = 3$.

Hence, the solution is $-1 < x < 2$.

WORKED EXAMPLE 5

Solve $|2x + 3| > 4$.

Answers

Method 1 (using algebra)

$|2x + 3| > 4$ use $|p| > q \Leftrightarrow p < -q$ or $p > q$

$2x + 3 < -4$ or $2x + 3 > 4$

$2x < -7$ or $2x > 1$

$x < -\frac{7}{2}$ or $x > \frac{1}{2}$

Method 2 (using a graph)

The graphs of $y = |2x + 3|$ and $y = 4$ intersect at the points A and B.

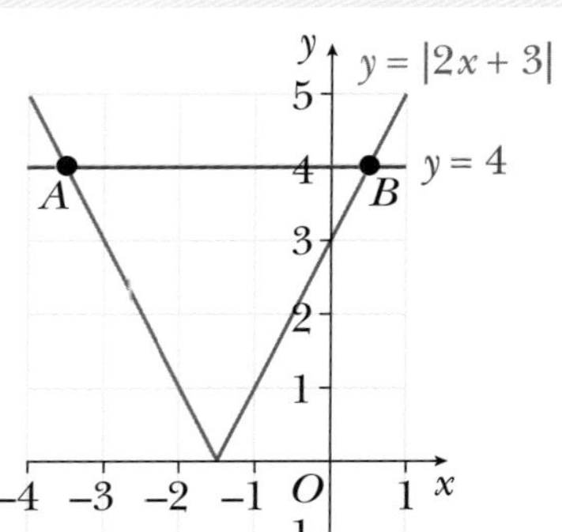

$$|2x + 3| = \begin{cases} 2x + 3 & \text{if } x \geqslant -1\frac{1}{2} \\ -(2x + 3) & \text{if } x < -1\frac{1}{2} \end{cases}$$

At A, the line $y = -(2x + 3)$ intersects the line $y = 4$.

$-(2x + 3) = 4$

$-2x - 3 = 4$

$2x = -7$

$x = -\frac{7}{2}$

At B, the line $y = 2x + 3$ intersects the line $y = 4$.

$2x + 3 = 4$

$2x = 1$

$x = \frac{1}{2}$

To solve the inequality $|2x + 3| > 4$ you must find where the graph of the function $y = |2x + 3|$ is above the graph of $y = 4$.

Hence, the solution is $x < -\frac{7}{2}$ or $x > \frac{1}{2}$.

WORKED EXAMPLE 6

Solve the inequality $|2x+1| \geqslant |3-x|$.

Answers

Method 1 (using algebra)

$$|2x+1| \geqslant |3-x| \qquad \text{use } |p| \geqslant |q| \Leftrightarrow p^2 \geqslant q^2$$

$$(2x+1)^2 \geqslant (3-x)^2$$

$$4x^2+4x+1 \geqslant 9-6x+x^2$$

$$3x^2+10x-8 \geqslant 0 \qquad \text{factorise}$$

$$(3x-2)(x+4) \geqslant 0$$

Critical values are $\frac{2}{3}$ and -4.

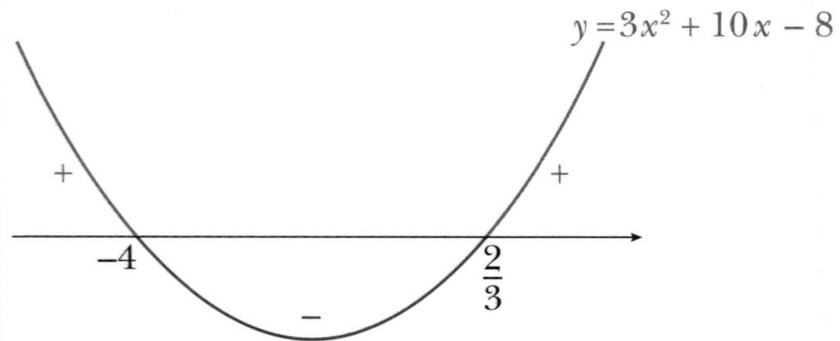

Hence, $x \leqslant -4$ or $x \geqslant \frac{2}{3}$.

Method 2 (using a graph)

The graphs of $y=|2x+1|$ and $y=|3-x|$ intersect at the points A and B.

$$|2x+1| = \begin{cases} 2x+1 & \text{if } x \geqslant -\frac{1}{2} \\ -(2x+1) & \text{if } x < -\frac{1}{2} \end{cases}$$

$$|3-x| = |x-3| = \begin{cases} x-3 & \text{if } x \geqslant 3 \\ -(x-3) & \text{if } x < 3 \end{cases}$$

At A, the line $y=-(2x+1)$ intersects the line $y=-(x-3)$.

$$2x+1 = x-3$$

$$x = -4$$

At B, the line $y=2x+1$ intersects the line $y=-(x-3)$.

$$2x+1 = -(x-3)$$

$$3x = 2$$

$$x = \frac{2}{3}$$

To solve the inequality $|2x+1| \geqslant |3-x|$ you must find where the graph of the function $y=|2x+1|$ is above the graph of $y=|3-x|$.

Hence, $x \leqslant -4$ or $x \geqslant \frac{2}{3}$.

Exercise 5.2

1

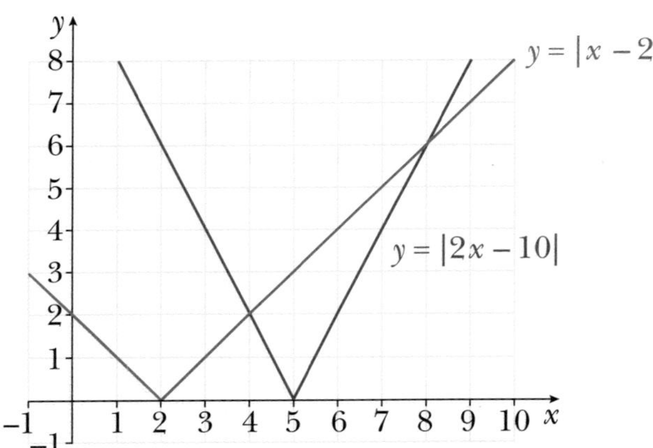

The graphs of $y=|x-2|$ and $y=|2x-10|$ are shown on the grid.

Write down the set of values of x that satisfy the inequality $|x-2|>|2x-10|$.

2 **a** On the same axes sketch the graphs of $y=|3x-6|$ and $y=|4-x|$.

b Solve the inequality $|3x-6| \geqslant |4-x|$.

3 Solve.

a $|2x-3|>5$	**b** $|4-5x| \leqslant 9$	**c** $|8-3x|<2$
d $|2x-7|>3$	**e** $|3x+1|>8$	**f** $|5-2x| \leqslant 7$

4 Solve.

a $|2x-3| \leqslant x-1$	**b** $|5+x|>7-2x$	**c** $|x-2|-3x \leqslant 1$

5 Solve.

a $|2x-1| \leqslant |3x|$	**b** $|x+1|>|x|$	**c** $|x|>|3x-2|$
d $|4x+3|>|x|$	**e** $|x+3| \geqslant |2x|$	**f** $|2x|<|x-3|$

6 Solve.

a $|x+1|>|x-4|$ **b** $|x-2|\geqslant|x+5|$ **c** $|x+1|\leqslant|3x+5|$

d $|2x+3|\leqslant|x-3|$ **e** $|x+2|<\left|\frac{1}{2}x-5\right|$ **f** $|3x-2|\geqslant|x+4|$

7 Solve.

a $2|x-3|>|3x+1|$ **b** $3|x-1|<|2x+1|$ **c** $|2x-5|\leqslant 3|2x+1|$

8 Solve the inequality $|x+2k|\geqslant|x-3k|$ where k is a positive constant.

9 Solve the inequality $|x+3k|<4|x-k|$ where k is a positive constant.

CHALLENGE Q

10 Solve $|3x+2|+|3x-2|\leqslant 8$.

5.3 Sketching graphs of cubic polynomials and their moduli

In this section you will learn how to sketch graphs of functions of the form $y=k(x-a)(x-b)(x-c)$ and their moduli.

When sketching graphs of this form you should show the general shape of the curve and all of the axis intercepts.

To help find the general shape of the curve you need to consider what happens to

- y as x tends to positive infinity (i.e. as $x \to +\infty$)
- y as x tends to negative infinity (i.e. as $x \to -\infty$)

WORKED EXAMPLE 7

a Sketch the graph of the function $y=(2x-1)(2-x)(x+1)$.

b Hence sketch the graph of $y=|(2x-1)(2-x)(x+1)|$

Answers

a When $x=0$, $y=-1\times 2\times 1=-2$.

$\therefore$ The curve intercepts the y-axis at $(0, -2)$.

When $y=0$, $(2x-1)(2-x)(x+1)=0$

$$2x-1=0 \qquad 2-x=0 \qquad x+1=0$$

$$x=\frac{1}{2} \qquad x=2 \qquad x=-1$$

$\therefore$ The curve intercepts the x-axis at $\left(\frac{1}{2}, 0\right)$, $(2, 0)$ and $(-1, 0)$.

As $x \to +\infty$, $y \to -\infty$

As $x \to -\infty$, $y \to +\infty$

The graph of the function $y = (2x-1)(2-x)(x+1)$ is:

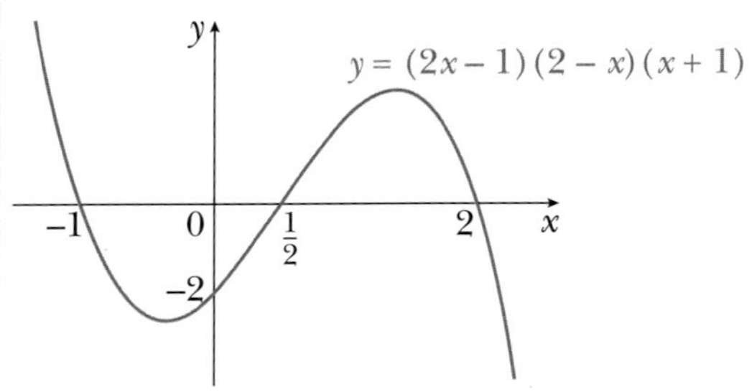

b To sketch the curve $y = |(2x-1)(2-x)(x+1)|$ you reflect in the x-axis the parts of the curve $y = (2x-1)(2-x)(x+1)$ that are below the x-axis.

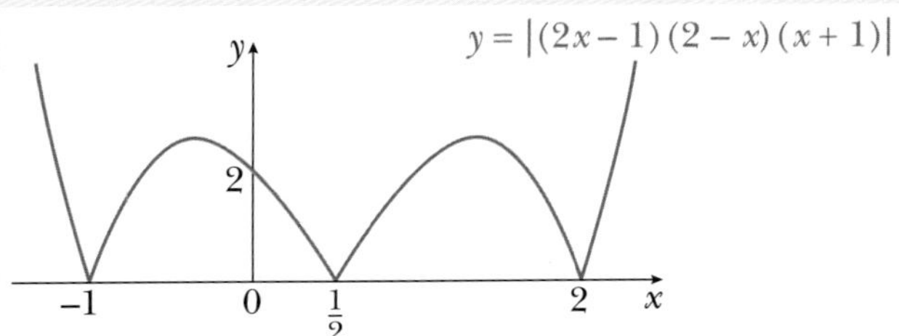

WORKED EXAMPLE 8

a Sketch the graph of the function $y = (x-1)^2(x+1)$.

b Hence sketch the graph of $y = |(x-1)^2(x+1)|$.

Answers

a When $x = 0$, $y = (-1)^2 \times 1 = 1$.

$\therefore$ The curve intercepts the y-axis at $(0, 1)$.

When $y = 0$, $(x-1)(x-1)(x+1) = 0$

$x - 1 = 0 \qquad x - 1 = 0 \qquad x + 1 = 0$

$x = 1$ (repeated root) $\qquad x = -1$

$\therefore$ The curve intercepts the x-axis at $(1, 0)$ and $(-1, 0)$.

As $x \to +\infty$, $y \to +\infty$

As $x \to -\infty$, $y \to -\infty$

The graph of the function $y = (x - 1)^2 (x + 1)$ is:

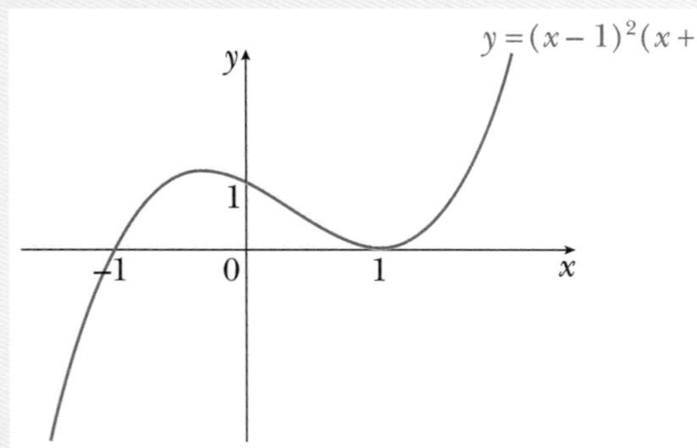

b To sketch the curve $y = |(x - 1)^2 (x + 1)|$ you reflect in the x-axis the part of the curve $y = (x - 1)^2 (x + 1)$ that is below the x-axis.

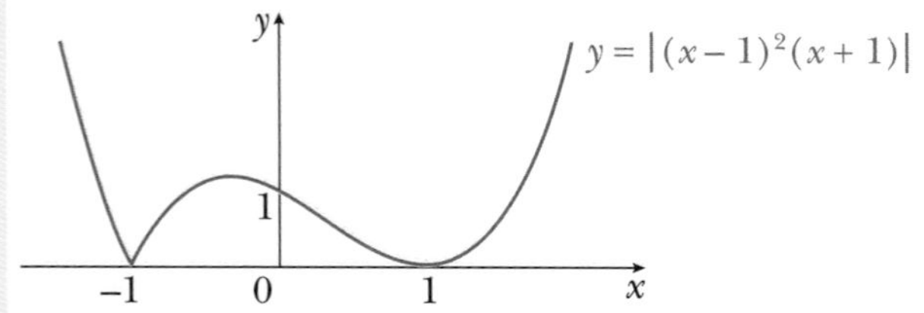

In worked examples 7 and 8, you considered the value of y as $x \to \pm\infty$ to determine the shape of the cubic curve. It is often easier to remember that for a curve with equation $y = k(x - a)(x - b)(x - c)$ the shape of the graph is:

if k is positive   if k is negative

Exercise 5.3

1 Find the coordinates of the points A, B and C where the curve intercepts the x-axis and the point D where the curve intercepts the positive y-axis.

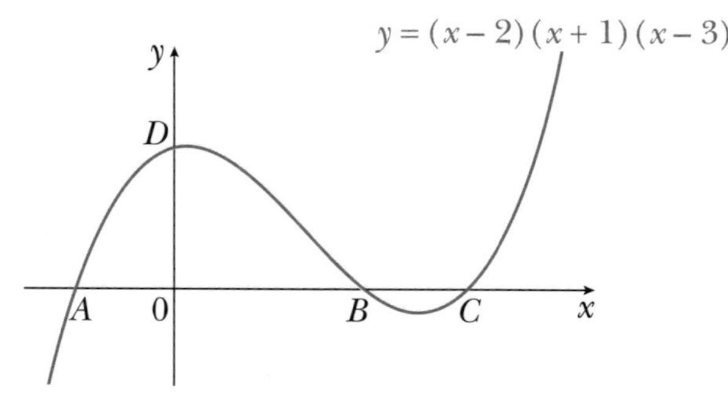

2 Sketch each of these curves and indicate clearly the axis intercepts.

a $y = (x - 2)(x - 4)(x + 3)$

b $y = (x + 2)(x + 1)(3 - x)$

c $y = (2x + 1)(x + 2)(x - 2)$

d $y = (3 - 2x)(x - 1)(x + 2)$

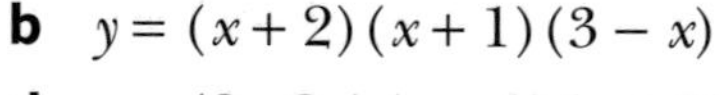

3 Find the coordinates of the point A and the point B, where A is the point where the curve intercepts the positive x-axis and B is the point where the curve intercepts the positive y-axis.

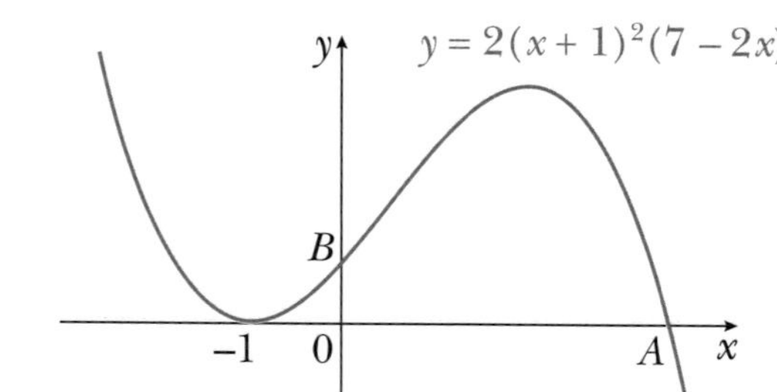

4 Sketch each of these curves and indicate clearly the axis intercepts.

a $y=x^2(x+2)$ **b** $y=x^2(5-2x)$

c $y=(x+1)^2(x-2)$ **d** $y=(x-2)^2(10-3x)$

5 Sketch each of these curves and indicate clearly the axis intercepts.

a $y=|(x+1)(x-2)(x-3)|$ **b** $y=|2(5-2x)(x+1)(x+2)|$

c $y=|x(9-x^2)|$ **d** $y=|3(x-1)^2(x+1)|$

6 Factorise each of these functions and then sketch the graph of each function indicating clearly the axis intercepts.

a $y = 9x - x^3$ **b** $y = x^3 + 4x^2 + x - 6$

c $y = 2x^3 + x^2 - 25x + 12$ **d** $y = 2x^3 + 3x^2 - 29x - 60$

7 **a** On the same axes sketch the graphs of $y=x(x-5)(x-7)$ and $y=x(7-x)$, showing clearly the points at which the curves meet the coordinate axes.

b Use algebra to find the coordinates of all the points where the graphs intersect.

8 **a** On the same axes sketch the graphs of $y=(2x-1)(x+2)(x+1)$ and $y=(x+1)(4-x)$, showing clearly the points at which the curves meet the coordinate axes.

b Use algebra to find the coordinates of all the points where the graphs intersect.

CHALLENGE Q

9 The diagram shows the graph of $y=k(x-a)^2(x-b)$.

Find the values of a, b and k.

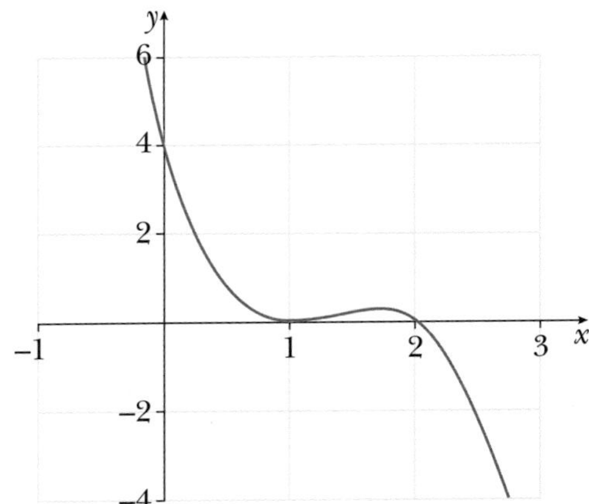

CHALLENGE Q

10 The diagram shows the graph of $y=|k(x-a)(x-b)(x-c)|$ where $a<b<c$.

Find the values of a, b, c and k.

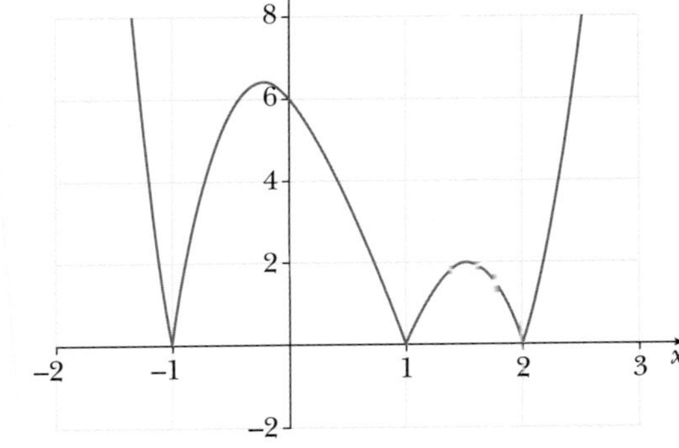

5.4 Solving cubic inequalities graphically

In this section you will learn how to use a graphical method to solve inequalities of the form $k(x-a)(x-b)(x-c) \leqslant d$.

WORKED EXAMPLE 9

The diagram shows part of the graph of $y = \frac{1}{6}(x-3)(x-2)(x+2)$.

Use the graph to solve the inequality $(x-3)(x-2)(x+2) \leqslant 6$.

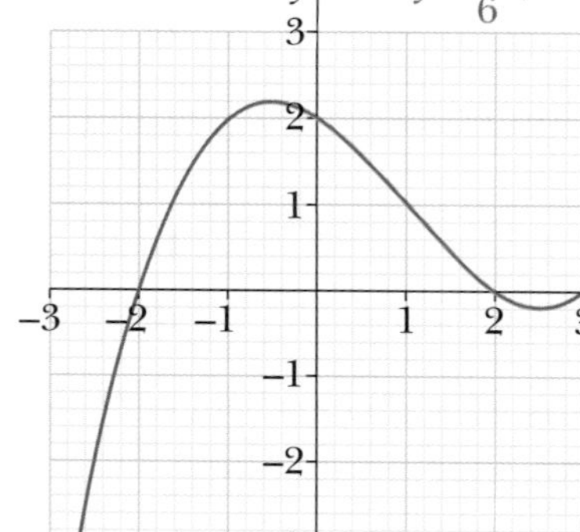

Answers

$(x-3)(x-2)(x+2) \leqslant 6$ — divide both sides by 6

$\frac{1}{6}(x-3)(x-2)(x+2) \leqslant 1$

You need to find where the curve $y = \frac{1}{6}(x-3)(x-2)(x+2)$ is below the line $y = 1$.

The red sections of the graph represent where the curve $y = \frac{1}{6}(x-3)(x-2)(x+2)$ is the line $y = 1$.

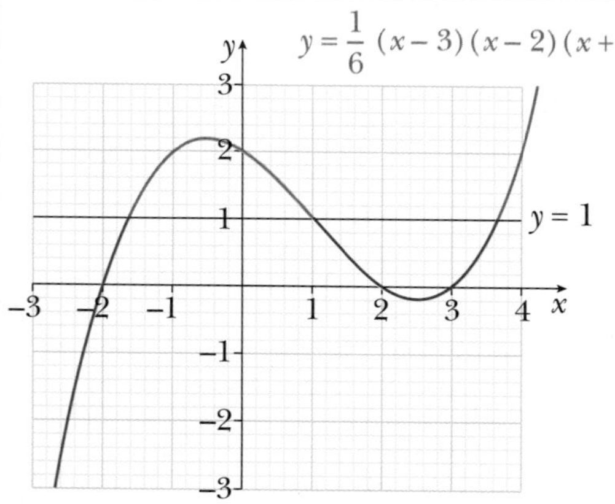

The solution is $x \leqslant -1.6$ or $1 \leqslant x \leqslant 3.6$.

Exercise 5.4

1 The diagram shows part of the graph of $y = x(x-2)(x+1)$.

Use the graph to solve each of the following inequalities

a $x(x-2)(x+1) \leqslant 0$,

b $x(x-2)(x+1) \geqslant 1$,

c $x(x-2)(x+1) \leqslant -2$.

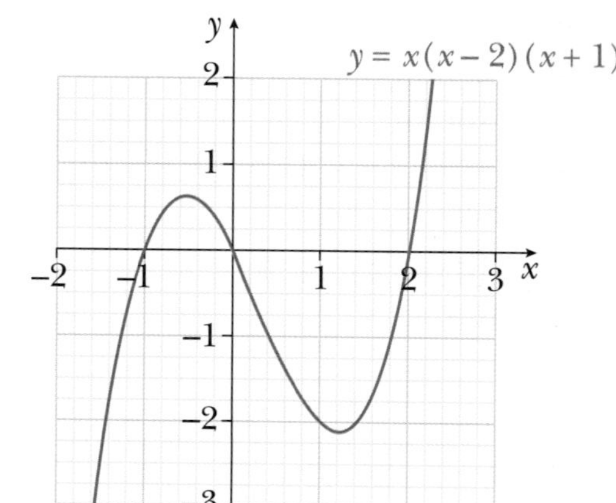

2 The diagram shows part of the graph of $y=(x+1)^2(2-x)$.
Use the graph to solve each of the following inequalities

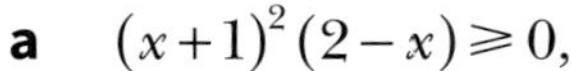

a $(x+1)^2(2-x)\geqslant 0$,

b $(x+1)^2(2-x)\leqslant 4$,

c $(x+1)^2(2-x)\leqslant 3$.

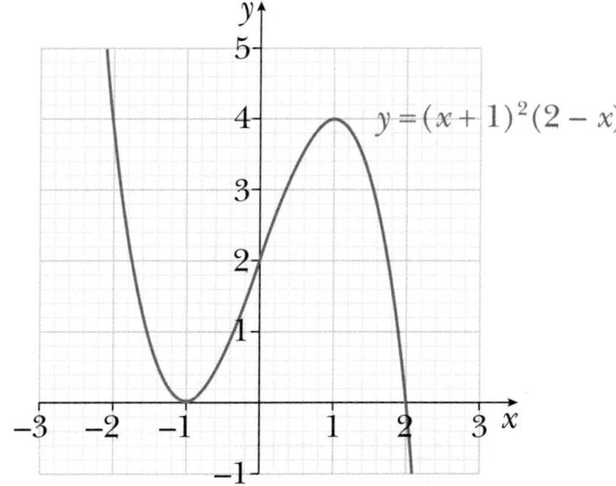

3 The diagram shows part of the graph of $y=(1-x)(x-2)(x+1)$.
Use the graph to solve each of the following inequalities

a $(1-x)(x-2)(x+1)\leqslant -3$,

b $(1-x)(x-2)(x+1)\leqslant 0$,

c $(1-x)(x-2)(x+1)\geqslant -1$.

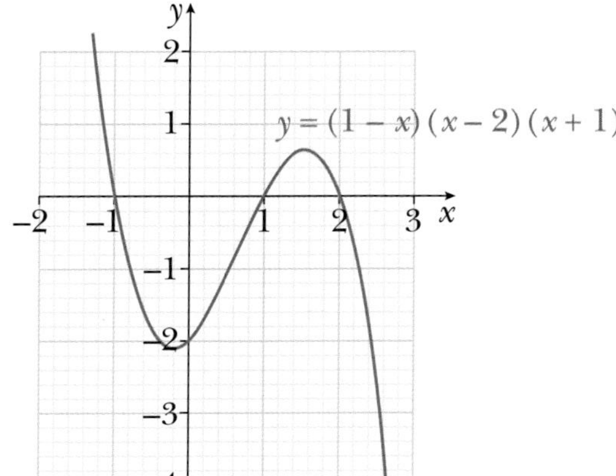

5.5 Solving more complex quadratic equations

You may be asked to solve an equation that is quadratic in some function of x.

WORKED EXAMPLE 10

Solve the equation $4x^4-17x^2+4=0$.

Answers

Method 1 (substitution method)

$4x^4-17x^2+4=0$ — use the substitution $y=x^2$

$4y^2-17y+4=0$ — factorise

$(4y-1)(y-4)=0$ — solve

$4y-1=0$ or $y-4=0$

$y=\frac{1}{4}$ or $y=4$ — substitute x^2 for y

$x^2=\frac{1}{4}$ or $x^2=4$

$x=\pm\frac{1}{2}$ or $x=\pm 2$

Method 2 (factorise directly)

$$4x^4 - 17x^2 + 4 = 0$$
$$(4x^2 - 1)(x^2 - 4) = 0$$
$$4x^2 - 1 = 0 \quad \text{or} \quad x^2 - 4 = 0$$
$$x^2 = \frac{1}{4} \quad \text{or} \quad x^2 = 4$$
$$x = \pm\frac{1}{2} \quad \text{or} \quad x = \pm 2$$

WORKED EXAMPLE 11

Use the substitution $y = x^{\frac{1}{3}}$ to solve the equation $3x^{\frac{2}{3}} - 5x^{\frac{1}{3}} + 2 = 0$.

Answers

$$3x^{\frac{2}{3}} - 5x^{\frac{1}{3}} + 2 = 0 \qquad \text{let } y = x^{\frac{1}{3}}$$
$$3y^2 - 5y + 2 = 0 \qquad \text{factorise}$$
$$(3y - 2)(y - 1) = 0 \qquad \text{solve}$$
$$3y - 2 = 0 \quad \text{or} \quad y - 1 = 0$$
$$y = \frac{2}{3} \quad \text{or} \quad y = 1 \qquad \text{substitute } x^{\frac{1}{3}} \text{ for } y$$
$$x^{\frac{1}{3}} = \frac{2}{3} \quad \text{or} \quad x^{\frac{1}{3}} = 1 \qquad \text{cube both sides}$$
$$x = \left(\frac{2}{3}\right)^3 \quad \text{or} \quad x = (1)^3$$
$$x = \frac{8}{27} \quad \text{or} \quad x = 1$$

WORKED EXAMPLE 12

Solve the equation $x - 4\sqrt{x} - 21 = 0$.

Answers

$$x - 4\sqrt{x} - 21 = 0 \qquad \text{use the substitution } y = \sqrt{x}$$
$$y^2 - 4y - 21 = 0$$
$$(y - 7)(y + 3) = 0$$
$$y - 7 = 0 \quad \text{or} \quad y + 3 = 0$$
$$y = 7 \quad \text{or} \quad y = -3 \qquad \text{substitute } \sqrt{x} \text{ for } y$$
$$\sqrt{x} = 7 \quad \text{or} \quad \sqrt{x} = -3 \qquad \sqrt{x} = -3 \text{ has no real solutions}$$
$$\therefore x = 49$$

WORKED EXAMPLE 13

Solve the equation $8(4^x)-33(2^x)+4=0$.

Answers

$8(4^x)-33(2^x)+4=0$ — 4^x can be written as $(2^2)^x=(2^x)^2$

$8(2^x)^2-33(2^x)+4=0$ — let $y=2^x$

$8y^2-33y+4=0$

$(8y-1)(y-4)=0$

$y=\frac{1}{8}$ or $y=4$ — substitute 2^x for y

$2^x=\frac{1}{8}$ or $2^x=4$ — $\frac{1}{8}=2^{-3}$ and $4=2^2$

$x=-3$ or $x=2$

Exercise 5.5

1 Find the real values of x satisfying the following equations.

a $x^4-5x^2+4=0$ **b** $x^4+x^2-6=0$ **c** $x^4-20x^2+64=0$

d $x^4+2x^2-8=0$ **e** $x^4-4x^2-21=0$ **f** $2x^4-17x^2-9=0$

g $4x^4+6=11x^2$ **h** $\frac{2}{x^4}+\frac{1}{x^2}=6$ **i** $\frac{8}{x^6}+\frac{7}{x^3}=1$

2 Use the quadratic formula to solve these equations.
Write your answers correct to 3 significant figures.

a $x^4-8x^2+1=0$ **b** $x^4-5x^2-2=0$ **c** $2x^4-x^2-5=0$

d $2x^6-3x^3-8=0$ **e** $3x^6-5x^3-2=0$ **f** $2x^8-7x^4-3=0$

3 Solve.

a $x-7\sqrt{x}+10=0$ **b** $x-\sqrt{x}-12=0$ **c** $x+5\sqrt{x}-24=0$

d $\sqrt{x}(2+\sqrt{x})=35$ **e** $8x-18\sqrt{x}+9=0$ **f** $6x+11\sqrt{x}-35=0$

g $2x+4=9\sqrt{x}$ **h** $3\sqrt{x}+\frac{5}{\sqrt{x}}=16$ **i** $2\sqrt{x}+\frac{4}{\sqrt{x}}=9$

4 Solve the equation $2x^{\frac{2}{3}}-7x^{\frac{1}{3}}+6=0$.

5 The curve $y=\sqrt{x}$ and the line $5y=x+4$ intersect at the points P and Q.

a Write down an equation satisfied by the x-coordinates of P and Q.

b Solve your equation in **part a** and hence find the coordinates of P and Q.

6 Solve

a $2^{2x}-6(2^x)+8=0$ **b** $3^{2x}-10(3^x)+9=0$ **c** $2(2^{2x})-9(2^x)+4=0$

c $3^{2x+1}-28(3^x)+9=0$ **d** $2^{2x+2}-33(2^x)+8=0$ **e** $3^{2x+2}+3(3^x)-2=0$

7 $f(x) = 2^x$ and $g(x) = 4x^2 + 7x$. Solve $gf(x) = 2$.

8 $f(x) = x^3 - 2$ and $g(x) = x^2 - 5x$. Solve $gf(x) = 6$.

9 $f(x) = x^2 + 3x$ and $g(x) = x^2 - 4x$. Solve $gf(x) = 0$.

Summary

Solving modulus equations

To solve modulus equations you can use the property:

$$|a| = |b| \Leftrightarrow a^2 = b^2$$

Solving modulus inequalities

To solve modulus inequalities you can use the properties:

$$|a| \leqslant b \Leftrightarrow -b \leqslant a \leqslant b$$

$$|a| \geqslant b \Leftrightarrow a \leqslant -b \text{ or } a \geqslant b$$

$$|a| > |b| \Leftrightarrow a^2 > b^2$$

$$|a| < |b| \Leftrightarrow a^2 < b^2,\ b \neq 0$$

The graph of $y = k(x-a)(x-b)(x-c)$

The x-axis intercepts are $(a, 0)$, $(b, 0)$ and $(c, 0)$.

The shape of the graph is

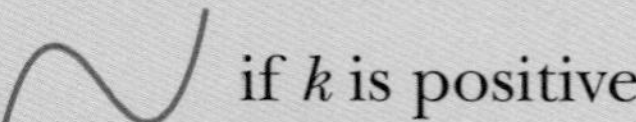 if k is positive   if k is negative

The graph of $y = |k(x-a)(x-b)(x-c)|$

To sketch the curve $y = |k(x-a)(x-b)(x-c)|$ you reflect in the x-axis the parts of the curve $y = k(x-a)(x-b)(x-c)$ that are below the x-axis.

Examination questions

Worked example

a On the same axes sketch the graphs of $y = x^2(x - 2)$ and $y = x(6 - x)$, showing clearly the points at which the curves meet the coordinate axes. [5]

b Use algebra to find the coordinates of the points where the graphs intersect. [6]

Examination style question

Answers

a The graph of $y = x^2(x - 2)$:

When $x = 0$, $y = 0^2 \times (-2) = 0$.

$\therefore$ The curve intercepts the y-axis at $(0, 0)$.

When $y = 0$, $x^2(x - 2) = 0$

$x = 0 \qquad x = 0 \qquad x - 2 = 0$

$x = 0 \quad \text{(repeated root)} \qquad x = 2$

$\therefore$ The curve intercepts the x-axis at $(0, 0)$ and $(2, 0)$.

As $x \to +\infty$, $y \to +\infty$
As $x \to -\infty$, $y \to -\infty$

The graph of $y = x(6 - x)$:

When $x = 0$, $y = 0 \times 6 = 0$.

$\therefore$ The curve intercepts the y-axis at $(0, 0)$.

When $y = 0$, $x(6 - x) = 0$

$x = 0 \qquad 6 - x = 0$

$x = 0 \qquad x = 6$

$\therefore$ The curve intercepts the x-axis at $(0, 0)$ and $(6, 0)$.

As $x \to +\infty$, $y \to -\infty$
As $x \to -\infty$, $y \to -\infty$

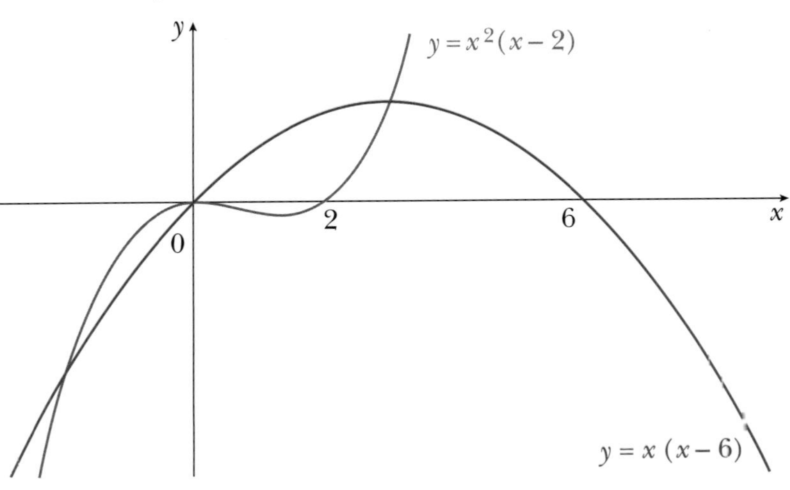

b At the points of intersection:

$$x^2(x-2) = x(6-x)$$
$$x^2(x-2) - x(6-x) = 0$$
$$x[x(x-2) - (6-x)] = 0$$
$$x(x^2 - x - 6) = 0$$
$$x(x-3)(x+2) = 0$$

$x = 0$ or $x = 3$ or $x = -2$

$x = 0 \Rightarrow y = 0$

$x = 3 \Rightarrow y = 9$

$x = -2 \Rightarrow y = -16$

The points of intersection are $(-2, -16)$, $(0, 0)$ and $(3, 9)$.

Exercise 5.6

Exam Style Exercise

1 Solve the equation $|2x - 3| = |3x - 5|$. [3]

Examination style question

2 Solve the inequality $|2x - 1| > 7$. [3]

Examination style question

3 Solve the inequality $|7 - 5x| < 3$. [3]

Examination style question

4 Solve the inequality $|x| > |3x - 2|$. [4]

Examination style question

5 Solve the inequality $|x - 1| \leqslant |x + 2|$. [4]

Examination style question

6 Solve the inequality $|x + 2| < \left|\frac{1}{2}x - 1\right|$. [4]

Examination style question

7 Solve the inequality $|x + 2k| > |x - k|$ where k is a positive constant. [4]

Examination style question

8 **a** Solve the equation $|x - 13| = 14$. [3]

b Hence solve the equation $|y^3 - 13| = 14$. [1]

Examination style question

9 Sketch the graph of $y = x(3-2x)(x-4)$, showing clearly the points at which the curve meets the coordinate axes. [3]

Examination style question

10 Sketch the graph of $y = 2(2x-1)(x-3)(x+1)$ showing clearly the points at which the curve meets the coordinate axes. [4]

Examination style question

11

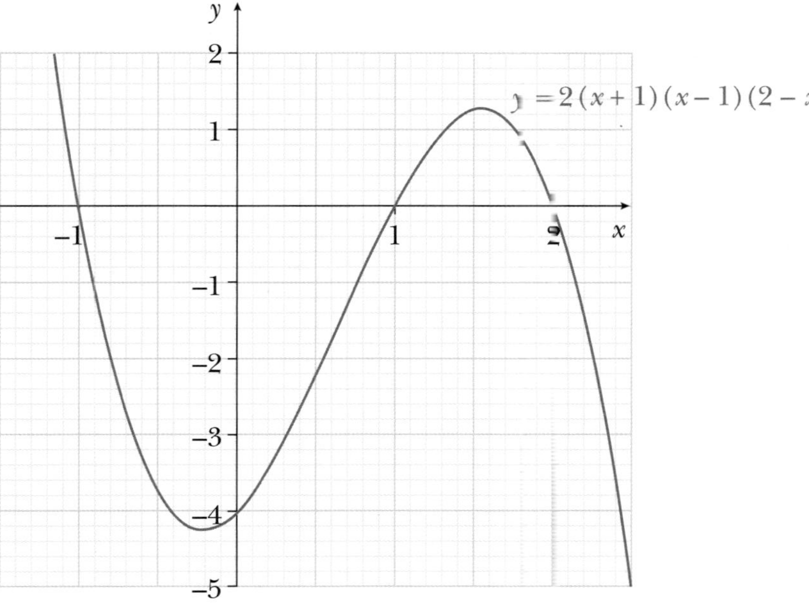

The diagram shows part of the graph of $y = 2(x+1)(x-1)(2-x)$.

Use the graph to solve the inequality $(x+1)(x-1)(2-x) > -1$. [3]

Examination style question

12 a Sketch the graph of $y = (x-4)(x-1)(x+2)$, showing clearly the points at which the curve meets the coordinate axes. [4]

b Hence sketch the curve $y = |(x-4)(x-1)(x+2)|$. [1]

Examination style question

13 a Factorise completely $x^3 + x^2 - 6x$. [3]

b Hence sketch the curve with equation $y = x^3 + x^2 - 6x$, showing clearly the points at which the curve meets the coordinate axes. [3]

Examination style question

14 a On the same axes sketch the graphs of $y = (x-3)(x+1)^2$ and $y = \frac{6}{x}$, showing clearly the points at which the curves meet the coordinate axes. [5]

b Hence state the number of real roots of the equation $(x-3)(x+1)^2 = \frac{6}{x}$. [1]

Examination style question

15 a Factorise completely $2x^3 + x^2 - 25x + 12$. [5]

b Hence sketch the curve with equation $y = 2x^3 + x^2 - 25x + 12$, showing clearly the points at which the curve meets the coordinate axes. [4]

Examination style question

16 a On the same axes sketch the graphs of $y = x^2(6 - x)$ and $y = 4x(4 - x)$, showing the points at which the curves meet the coordinate axes. [5]

b Use algebra to find the coordinates of the points where the graphs intersect. [6]

Examination style question

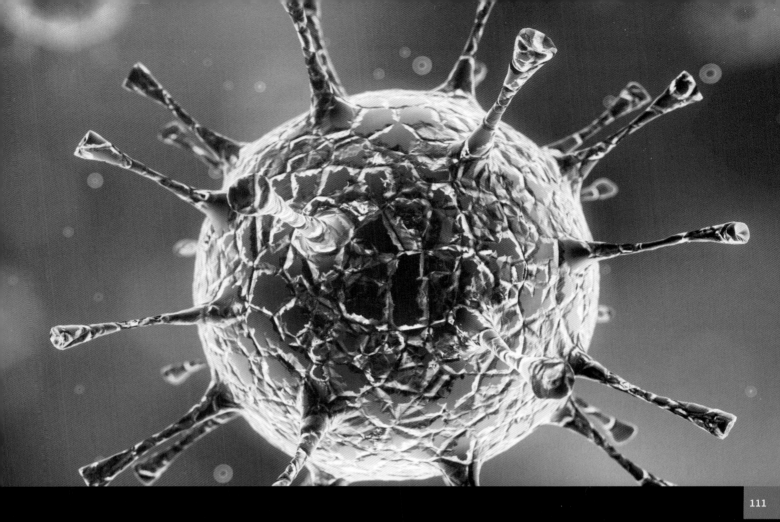

Chapter 6
Logarithmic and exponential functions

This section will show you how to:

- use simple properties of the logarithmic and exponential functions including $\ln x$ and e^x
- use graphs of the logarithmic and exponential functions including $\ln x$ and e^x and graphs of $ke^{nx} + a$ and $k\ln(ax + b)$ where n, k, a and b are integers
- use the laws of logarithms, including change of base of logarithms
- solve equations of the form $a^x = b$.

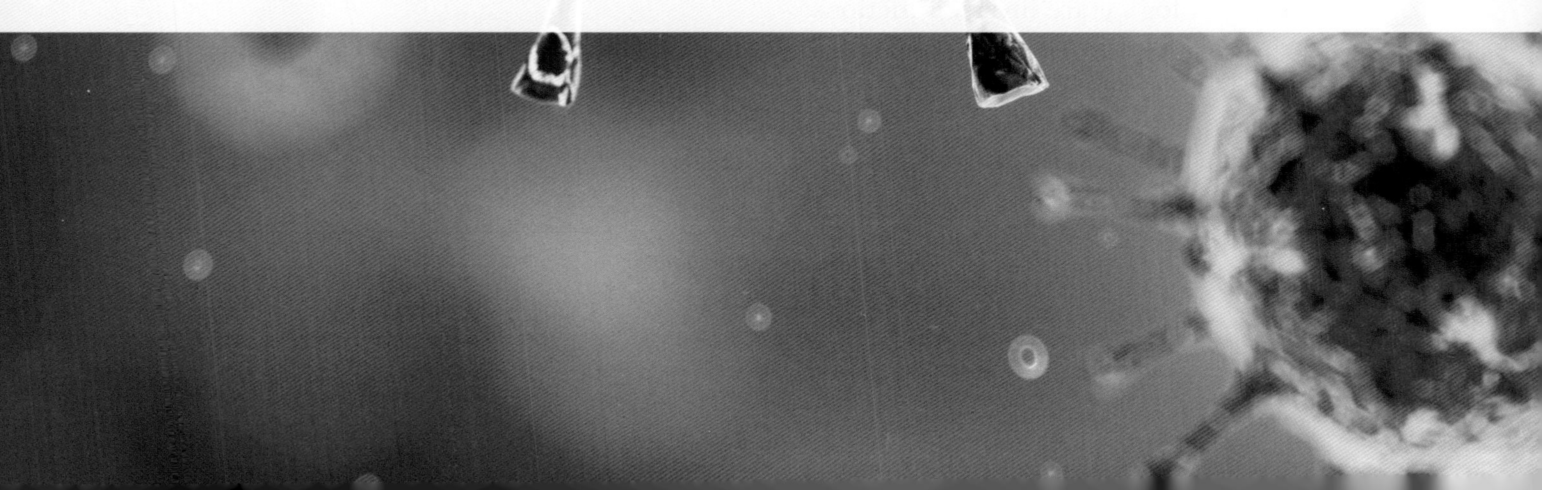

6.1 Logarithms to base 10

Consider the exponential function $f(x) = 10^x$.

To solve $10^x = 30$.
You can say $10^1 = 10$ and $10^2 = 100$.
So $1 < x < 2$.

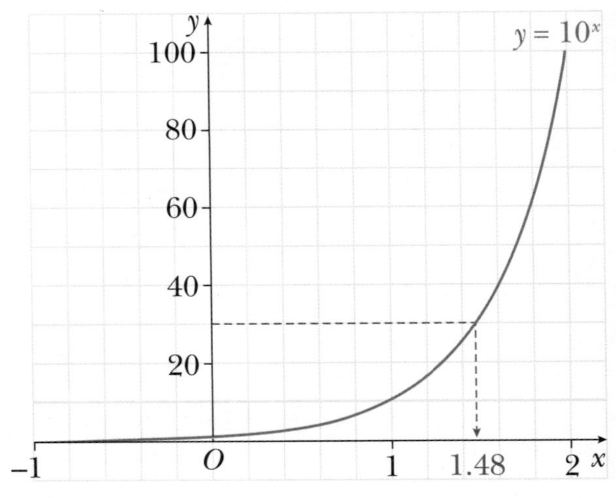

The graph of $y = 10^x$ could be used to give a more accurate value for x when $10^x = 30$.
From the graph, $x \approx 1.48$.

There is a function that gives the value of x directly.

If $10^x = 30$ then $x = \log_{10}30$.
$\log_{10}30$ is read as 'log 30 to base 10'.
log is short for **logarithm**.

Note:
$\log_{10}30$ can also be written as lg 30 or log 30.

On your calculator, for logs to the base 10, you use the **log** or **lg** key.

So if $10^x = 30$

then $x = \log_{10}30$

$x = 1.477$ to 4 sf.

Hence the rule for base 10 is:

If $y = 10^x$ then $x = \log_{10}y$.

This rule can be described in words as:

$\log_{10}y$ is the power that 10 must be raised to in order to obtain y.

For example, $\log_{10}100 = 2$ since $100 = 10^2$.

$y = 10^x$ and $y = \log_{10}x$ are inverse functions.

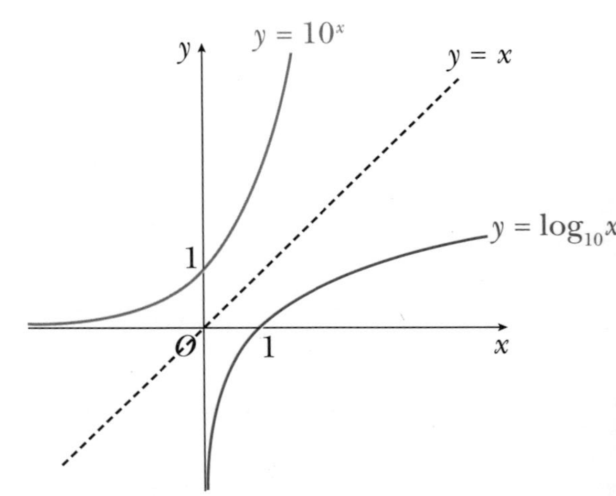

CLASS DISCUSSION

Discuss with your classmates why each of these four statements is true.

$\log_{10} 10 = 1$	$\log_{10} 1 = 0$	$\log_{10} 10^x = x$ for $x \in \mathbb{R}$	$x = 10^{\log_{10} x}$ for $x > 0$

WORKED EXAMPLE 1

a Convert $10^x = 45$ to logarithmic form.

b Solve $10^x = 45$ giving your answer correct to 3 sf.

Answers

a **Method 1**

$10^x = 45$

Step 1: Identify the base and index: The base is 10. The index is x.

Step 2: Start to write in log form: In log form the index always goes on its own and the base goes at the base of the logarithm. So $x = \log_{10}?$

Step 3: Complete the log form: Fill in the last number. $x = \log_{10}45$

So $x = \log_{10}45$.

Method 2

$10^x = 45$

$\log_{10}10^x = \log_{10}45$ Take logs to base 10 of both sides. $\log_{10}10^x = x$

$x = \log_{10}45$

b $10^x = 45$

$x = \log_{10}45$

$x \approx 1.65$

WORKED EXAMPLE 2

a Convert $\log_{10}x = 2.9$ to exponential form.

b Solve $\log_{10}x = 2.9$ giving your answer correct to 3 sf.

Answers

a **Method 1**

$\log_{10}x = 2.9$

Step 1: Identify the base and index: The base is 10. The index is 2.9. (In log form the index is always on its own.)

Step 2: Start to write in exponential form: Write the base and the index first. So $10^{2.9} = ?$

Step 3: Complete the exponential form: $x = 10^{2.9}$

So $x = 10^{2.9}$

Method 2

$\log_{10}x = 2.9$

$10^{\log_{10}x} = 10^{2.9}$ $\quad 10^{\log_{10}x} = x$

$x = 10^{2.9}$

b $\log_{10}x = 2.9$

$x = 10^{2.9}$

$x \approx 794$

WORKED EXAMPLE 3

Find the value of

a $\log_{10}100\ 000$ **b** $\log_{10}0.001$ **c** $\log_{10}100\sqrt{10}$.

Answers

a $\log_{10}100\ 000 = \log_{10}10^5$ write 100 000 as a power of 10, $100\,000 = 10^5$

$= 5$

b $\log_{10}0.001 = \log_{10}10^{-3}$ write 0.001 as a power of 10, $0.001 = 10^{-3}$

$= -3$

c $\log_{10}100\sqrt{10} = \log_{10}10^{2.5}$ write $100\sqrt{10}$ as a power of 10

$= 2.5$ $\quad 100\sqrt{10} = 10^2 \times 10^{0.5} = 10^{2.5}$

Exercise 6.1

1 Convert from exponential form to logarithmic form.

a $10^3 = 1000$ b $10^2 = 100$ c $10^6 = 1000000$

d $10^x = 2$ e $10^x = 15$ f $10^x = 0.06$

2 Solve each of these equations, giving your answers correct to 3 sf.

a $10^x = 75$ b $10^x = 300$ c $10^x = 720$

d $10^x = 15.6$ e $10^x = 0.02$ f $10^x = 0.005$

3 Convert from logarithmic form to exponential form.

a $\lg 100000 = 5$ b $\lg 10 = 1$ c $\lg \frac{1}{1000} = -3$

d $\lg x = 7.5$ e $\lg x = 1.7$ f $\lg x = -0.8$

4 Solve each of these equations, giving your answers correct to 3 sf.

a $\lg x = 5.1$ b $\lg x = 3.16$ c $\lg x = 2.16$

d $\lg x = -0.3$ e $\lg x = -1.5$ f $\lg x = -2.84$

5 Without using a calculator, find the value of

a $\lg 10000$ b $\lg 0.01$ c $\lg \sqrt{10}$

d $\lg\left(\sqrt[3]{10}\right)$ e $\lg\left(10\sqrt{10}\right)$ f $\lg\left(\frac{1000}{\sqrt{10}}\right)$.

6.2 Logarithms to base *a*

In the last section you learnt about logarithms to the base of 10.

The same principles can be applied to define logarithms in other bases.

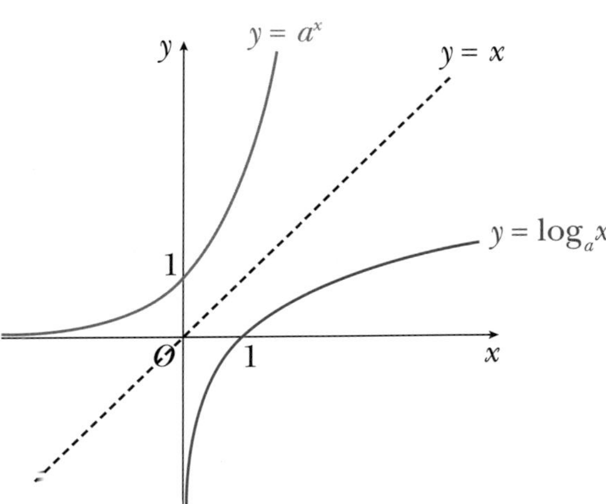

> If $y = a^x$ then $x = \log_a y$.
>
> $\log_a a = 1$ $\log_a 1 = 0$
>
> $\log_a a^x = x$ $x = a^{\log_a x}$

The conditions for $\log_a x$ to be defined are:

- $a > 0$ and $a \neq 1$
- $x > 0$

WORKED EXAMPLE 4

Convert $2^4 = 16$ to logarithmic form.

Answers

Method 1

$2^4 = 16$

Step 1: Identify the base and index: The base is 2. The index is 4.

Step 2: Start to write in log form: In log form the index always goes on its own and the base goes at the base of the logarithm. So $4 = \log_2 ?$

Step 3: Complete the log form: Fill in the last number. $4 = \log_2 16$

So $4 = \log_2 16$.

Method 2

$2^4 = 16$

$\log_2 2^4 = \log_2 16$ — Take logs to base 2 of both sides, $\log_2 2^4 = 4$.

$4 = \log_2 16$

WORKED EXAMPLE 5

Convert $\log_7 49 = 2$ to exponential form.

Answers

Method 1

$\log_7 49 = 2$

Step 1: Identify the base and index: The base is 7. The index is 2. (In log form the index is always on its own.)

Step 2: Start to write in exponential form: Write the base and the index first. So $7^2 = ?$

Step 3: Complete the exponential form: $7^2 = 49$

So $7^2 = 49$

Method 2

$\log_7 49 = 2$

$7^{\log_7 49} = 7^2$ — $7^{\log_7 49} = 49$

$49 = 7^2$

WORKED EXAMPLE 6

Find the value of

a $\log_3 81$ **b** $\log_2 128$ **c** $\log_4 \frac{1}{16}$

Answers

a $\log_3 81 = \log_3 3^4$ write 81 as a power of 3, $81 = 3^4$
$= 4$

b $\log_2 128 = \log_2 2^7$ write 128 as a power of 2, $128 = 2^7$
$= 7$

c $\log_4 \frac{1}{16} = \log_4 4^{-2}$ write $\frac{1}{16}$ as a power of 4, $\frac{1}{16} = 4^{-2}$
$= -2$

Exercise 6.2

1 Convert from exponential form to logarithmic form.

a $4^3 = 64$ **b** $2^5 = 32$ **c** $5^3 = 125$

d $6^2 = 36$ **e** $2^{-5} = \frac{1}{32}$ **f** $3^{-4} = \frac{1}{81}$

g $a^2 = b$ **h** $x^y = 4$ **i** $a^b = c$

2 Convert from logarithmic form to exponential form.

a $\log_2 4 = 2$ **b** $\log_2 64 = 6$ **c** $\log_5 1 = 0$

d $\log_3 9 = 2$ **e** $\log_{36} 6 = \frac{1}{2}$ **f** $\log_8 2 = \frac{1}{3}$

g $\log_x 1 = 0$ **h** $\log_x 8 = y$ **i** $\log_a b = c$

3 Solve.

a $\log_2 x = 4$ **b** $\log_3 x = 2$ **c** $\log_5 x = 4$

d $\log_3 x = \frac{1}{2}$ **e** $\log_x 144 = 2$ **f** $\log_x 27 = 3$

g $\log_2 (x - 1) = 4$ **h** $\log_3 (2x + 1) = 2$ **i** $\log_5 (2 - 3x) = 3$

4 Find the value of

a $\log_4 16$ **b** $\log_3 81$ **c** $\log_4 64$ **d** $\log_2 0.25$

e $\log_3 243$ **f** $\log_2 \left(8\sqrt{2}\right)$ **g** $\log_5 \left(25\sqrt{5}\right)$ **h** $\log_2 \left(\frac{1}{\sqrt{8}}\right)$

i $\log_{64} 8$ **j** $\log_7 \left(\frac{\sqrt{7}}{7}\right)$ **k** $\log_5 \sqrt[3]{5}$ **l** $\log_3 \frac{1}{\sqrt{3}}$

5 Simplify.

a $\log_x x^2$ **b** $\log_x \sqrt[3]{x}$ **c** $\log_x \left(x\sqrt{x}\right)$ **d** $\log_x \frac{1}{x^2}$

e $\log_x \left(\frac{1}{x^2}\right)^3$ **f** $\log_x \left(\sqrt{x^7}\right)$ **g** $\log_x \left(\frac{x}{\sqrt[3]{x}}\right)$ **h** $\log_x \left(\frac{x\sqrt{x}}{\sqrt[3]{x}}\right)$

6 Solve.

a $\log_3 (\log_2 x) = 1$ **b** $\log_2 (\log_5 x) = 2$

6.3 The laws of logarithms

If x and y are both positive and $a > 0$ and $a \neq 1$, then the following **laws of logarithms** can be used:

Multiplication law

$$\log_a(xy) = \log_a x + \log_a y$$

Division law

$$\log_a\left(\frac{x}{y}\right) = \log_a x - \log_a y$$

Power law

$$\log_a(x)^m = m\log_a x$$

Proofs:

$$\begin{aligned}&\log_a(xy)\\ &= \log_a\left(a^{\log_a x} \times a^{\log_a y}\right)\\ &= \log_a\left(a^{\log_a x + \log_a y}\right)\\ &= \log_a x + \log_a y\end{aligned}$$

$$\begin{aligned}&\log_a\left(\frac{x}{y}\right)\\ &= \log_a\left(\frac{a^{\log_a x}}{a^{\log_a y}}\right)\\ &= \log_a\left(a^{\log_a x - \log_a y}\right)\\ &= \log_a x - \log_a y\end{aligned}$$

$$\begin{aligned}&\log_a(x)^m\\ &= \log_a\left(\left(a^{\log_a x}\right)^m\right)\\ &= \log_a\left(a^{m\log_a x}\right)\\ &= m\log_a x\end{aligned}$$

Using the power law, $\log_a\left(\frac{1}{x}\right) = \log_a x^{-1}$

$= -\log_a x$

This gives another useful rule to remember:

$$\log_a\left(\frac{1}{x}\right) = -\log_a x$$

WORKED EXAMPLE 7

Use the laws of logarithms to simplify these expressions.

a $\lg 8 + \lg 2$ **b** $\log_4 15 \div \log_4 5$ **c** $2\log_3 4 + 5\log_3 2$

Answers

a $\lg 8 + \lg 2$

$= \lg(8 \times 2)$

$= \lg 16$

b $\log_4 15 \div \log_4 5$

$= \log_4\left(\frac{15}{5}\right)$

$= \log_4 3$

c $2\log_3 4 + 5\log_3 2$

$= \log_3 4^2 + \log_3 2^5$

$= \log_3(16 \times 32)$

$= \log_3 512$

WORKED EXAMPLE 8

Given that $\log_5 p = x$ and $\log_5 q = y$, express in terms of x and/or y

a $\log_5 p + \log_5 q^3$ **b** $\log_5 p^2 - \log_5 \sqrt{q}$ **c** $\log_5\left(\frac{q}{5}\right)$

Answers

a $\log_5 p + \log_5 q^3$
$= \log_5 p + 3\log_5 q$
$= x + 3y$

b $\log_5 p^2 - \log_5 \sqrt{q}$
$= 2\log_5 p - \frac{1}{2}\log_5 q$
$= 2x - \frac{1}{2}y$

c $\log_5\left(\frac{q}{5}\right)$
$= \log_5 q - \log_5 5$
$= y - 1$

Exercise 6.3

1 Write as a single logarithm.

a $\log_2 5 + \log_2 3$ **b** $\log_3 12 - \log_3 2$ **c** $3\log_5 2 + \log_5 8$

d $2\log_7 4 - 3\log_7 2$ **e** $\frac{1}{2}\log_3 25 + \log_3 4$ **f** $2\log_7\left(\frac{1}{4}\right) + \log_7 8$

g $1 + \log_4 3$ **h** $\lg 5 - 2$ **i** $3 - \log_4 10$

2 Write as a single logarithm, then simplify your answer.

a $\log_2 56 - \log_2 7$ **b** $\log_6 12 + \log_6 3$ **c** $\frac{1}{2}\log_2 36 - \log_2 3$

d $\log_3 15 - \frac{1}{2}\log_3 25$ **e** $\log_4 40 - \frac{1}{3}\log_4 125$ **f** $\frac{1}{2}\log_3 16 - 2\log_3 6$

3 Simplify.

a $2\log_5 3 - \frac{1}{2}\log_5 4 + \log_5 8$ **b** $2 + \frac{1}{2}\log_2 49 - \log_2 21$

4 **a** Express 16 and 0.25 as powers of 2.

b Hence, simplify $\frac{\log_3 16}{\log_3 0.25}$.

5 Simplify.

a $\frac{\log_7 4}{\log_7 2}$ **b** $\frac{\log_7 27}{\log_7 3}$ **c** $\frac{\log_3 64}{\log_3 0.25}$ **d** $\frac{\log_5 100}{\log_5 0.01}$

6 Given that $u = \log_5 x$, find, in simplest form in terms of u

a x **b** $\log_5\left(\frac{x}{25}\right)$ **c** $\log_5\left(5\sqrt{x}\right)$ **d** $\log_5\left(\frac{x\sqrt{x}}{125}\right)$.

7 Given that $\log_4 p = x$ and $\log_4 q = y$, express in terms of x and/or y

a $\log_4(4p)$ **b** $\log_4\left(\frac{16}{p}\right)$ **c** $\log_4 p + \log_4 q^2$ **d** pq.

8 Given that $\log_a x = 5$ and $\log_a y = 8$, find

a $\log_a\left(\frac{1}{y}\right)$ **b** $\log_a\left(\frac{\sqrt{x}}{y}\right)$ **c** $\log_a(xy)$ **d** $\log_a(x^2y^3)$.

9 Given that $\log_a x = 12$ and $\log_a y = 4$, find the value of

a $\log_a\left(\frac{x}{y}\right)$ **b** $\log_a\left(\frac{x^2}{y}\right)$ **c** $\log_a\left(x\sqrt{y}\right)$ **d** $\log_a\left(\frac{y}{\sqrt[3]{x}}\right)$.

6.4 Solving logarithmic equations

You have already learnt how to solve simple logarithmic equations.

In this section you will learn how to solve more complicated equations.

It is essential, when solving equations involving logs, that all roots are checked in the original equation.

WORKED EXAMPLE 9

Solve.

a $2\log_8(x+2) = \log_8(2x+19)$ **b** $4\log_x 2 - \log_x 4 = 8$

Answers

a
$2\log_8(x+2) = \log_8(2x+19)$ use the power law

$\log_8(x+2)^2 = \log_8(2x+19)$ use equality of logarithms

$(x+2)^2 = 2x+19$ expand brackets

$x^2+4x+4 = 2x+19$

$x^2+2x-15 = 0$

$(x-3)(x+5) = 0$

$x = 3$ or $x = -5$

Check when $x = 3$: $2\log_8(x+2) = 2\log_8 5 = \log_8 25$ is defined

$\log_8(2x+19) = \log_8 25$ is defined

So $x = 3$ is a solution, since both sides of the equation are defined and equivalent in value.

Check when $x = -5$: $2\log_8(x+2) = 2\log_8(-3)$ is not defined

So $x = -5$ is not a solution of the original equation.

Hence, the solution is $x = 3$.

b
$4\log_x 2 - \log_x 4 = 2$ use the power law

$\log_x 2^4 - \log_x 2^2 = 2$ use the division law

$\log_x 2^{4-2} = 2$

$\log_x 2^2 = 2$

$\log_x 4 = 2$ convert to exponential form

$x^2 = 4$

$x = \pm 2$

Since logarithms only exist for positive bases, $x = -2$ is not a solution.

Check when $x = 2$: $4\log_2 2 - \log_2 4 = 4 - 2\log_2 2$

$= 4 - 2$

$= 2$

So $x = 2$ satisfies the original equation.

Hence, the solution is $x = 2$.

Exercise 6.4

1 Solve.

a $\log_2 x + \log_2 4 = \log_2 20$

b $\log_4 2x - \log_4 5 = \log_4 3$

c $\log_4 (x-5) + \log_4 5 = 2\log_4 10$

d $\log_3 (x+3) = 2\log_3 4 + \log_3 5$

2 Solve.

a $\log_6 x + \log_6 3 = 2$

b $\lg(5x) - \lg(x-4) = 1$

c $\log_2 (x+4) = 1 + \log_2 (x-3)$

d $\log_3 (2x+3) = 2 + \log_3 (2x-5)$

e $\log_5 (10x+3) - \log_5 (2x-1) = 2$

f $\lg($[illegible]$ - 5) + 2\lg 2 = 1 + \lg(2x-1)$

3 Solve.

a $\log_5 (x+8) + \log_5 (x+2) = \log_5 20x$

b $\log_3 x + \log_3 (x-2) = \log_3 15$

c $2\log_4 x - \log_4 (x+3) = 1$

d $\lg x - \lg(x+1) = \lg 20$

e $\log_3 x + \log_3 (2x-5) = 1$

f $3 + 2\log_2 x = \log_2 (14x-3)$

g $\lg(x+5) + \lg 2x = 2$

h $\lg x + \lg(x-15) = 2$

4 Solve.

a $\log_x 64 - \log_x 4 = 1$

b $\log_x 16 - \log_x 4 = 3$

c $\log_x 4 - 2\log_x 3 = 2$

d $\log_x 15 = 2 + \log_x 5$

5 Solve.

a $(\log_5 x)^2 - 3\log_5 (x) + 2 = 0$

b $(\log_5 x)^2 - \log_5 (x^2) = 15$

c $(\log_5 x)^2 - \log_5 (x^3) = 18$

d $2(\log_2 x)^2 + 5\log_2 (x^2) = 72$

CHALLENGE Q

6 Solve the simultaneous equations.

a $xy = 64$
$\log_x y = 2$

b $2^x = 4^y$
$2\lg y = \lg x + \lg 5$

c $\log_4 (x+y) = 2\log_4 x$
$\log_4 y = \log_4 3 + \log_4 x$

d $xy = 640$
$2\log_{10} x - \log_{10} y = 2$

e $\log_{10} a = 2\log_{10} b$
$\log_{10} (2a - b) = 1$

f $4^{xy} = 2^{x+5}$
$\log_2 y - \log_2 x = 1$

CHALLENGE Q

7 **a** Show that $\lg(x^2 y) = 18$ can be written as $2\lg x + \lg y = 18$.

b $\lg(x^2 y) = 18$ and $\lg\left(\frac{x}{y^3}\right) = 2$.

Find the value of $\lg x$ and $\lg y$.

6.5 Solving exponential equations

In Chapter 3 you learnt how to solve exponential equations whose terms could be converted to the same base. In this section you will learn how to solve exponential equations whose terms cannot be converted to the same base.

WORKED EXAMPLE 10

Solve, giving your answers correct to 3 sf.

a $3^x = 40$ **b** $5^{2x+1} = 200$

Answers

a

$3^x = 40$ take logs of both sides

$\lg 3^x = \lg 40$ use the power rule

$x \lg 3 = \lg 40$ divide both sides by lg 3

$x = \dfrac{\lg 40}{\lg 3}$

$x \approx 3.36$

b

$5^{2x+1} = 200$ take logs of both sides

$\lg 5^{2x+1} = \lg 200$ use the power rule

$(2x+1)\lg 5 = \lg 200$ divide both sides by lg 5

$2x + 1 = \dfrac{\lg 200}{\lg 5}$

$2x + 1 = 3.292\ldots$

$2x = 2.292\ldots$

$x \approx 1.15$

WORKED EXAMPLE 11

Solve $3(2^{2x}) - 2^{x+1} - 8 = 0$.

Answers

$3(2^{2x}) - 2^{x+1} - 8 = 0$ replace 2^{x+1} with $2(2^x)$

$3(2^{2x}) - 2(2^x) - 8 = 0$ use the substitution $y = 2^x$

$3y^2 - 2y - 8 = 0$ factorise

$(y-2)(3y+4) = 0$

When $y = 2$

$2 = 2^x$

$x = 1$

When $y = -\dfrac{4}{3}$

$-\dfrac{4}{3} = 2^x$ there are no solutions to this equation since 2^x is always positive

Hence, the solution is $x = 1$.

Exercise 6.5

1 Solve, giving your answers correct to 3 sf.

a $2^x = 70$ **b** $3^x = 20$ **c** $5^x = 4$ **d** $2^{3x} = 150$

e $3^{x+1} = 55$ **f** $2^{2x+1} = 20$ **g** $7^{x-5} = 50$ **h** $7^x = 3^{x+4}$

i $5^{x+1} = 3^{x+2}$ **j** $4^{x-1} = 5^{x+1}$ **k** $3^{2x+3} = 5^{3x+1}$ **l** $3^{4-5x} = 2^{x+4}$

2 **a** Show that $2^{x+1} - 2^{x-1} = 15$ can be written as $2(2^x) - \frac{1}{2}(2^x) = 15$.

b Hence find the value of 2^x.

c Find the value of x.

3 Solve, giving your answers correct to 3 sf.

a $2^{x+2} - 2^x = 4$ **b** $2^{x+1} - 2^{x-1} - 8 = 0$

c $3^{x+1} - 8(3^{x-1}) - 5 = 0$ **d** $2^{x+2} - 2^{x-3} = 12$

e $5^x - 5^{x+2} + 125 = 0$

4 Use the substitution $y = 3^x$ to solve the equation $3^{2x} + 2 = 5(3^x)$.

5 Solve, giving your answers correct to 3 sf.

a $3^{2x} - 6 \times 3^x + 5 = 0$ **b** $4^{2x} - 6 \times 4^x - 7 = 0$

c $2^{2x} - 2^x - 20 = 0$ **d** $5^{2x} - 2(5^x) - 3 = 0$

6 Use the substitution $u = 5^x$ to solve the equation $5^{2x} - 2(5^{x+1}) + 21 = 0$.

7 Solve, giving your answers correct to 3 sf.

a $2^{2x} + 2^{x+1} - 15 = 0$ **b** $6^{2x} - 6^{x+1} + 7 = 0$

c $3^{2x} - 2(3^{x+1}) + 8 = 0$ **d** $4^{2x+1} = 17(4^x) - 15$

8 Solve, giving your answers correct to 3 sf.

a $4^x - 3(2^x) - 10 = 0$ **b** $16^x + 2(4^x) - 35 = 0$

c $9^x - 2(3^{x+1}) + 8 = 0$ **d** $25^x + 20 = 12(5^x)$

CHALLENGE Q

9 $3^{2x+1} \times 5^{x-1} = 27^x \times 5^{2x}$

Find the value of **a** 15^x **b** x.

CHALLENGE Q

10 Solve the equations, giving your answers correct to 3 significant figures.

a $|3^x + 2| = |3^x - 10|$ **b** $|2^{x+1} + 3| = |2^x + 10|$

c $3^{2|x|} = 5(3^{|x|}) + 24$ **d** $4^{|x|} = 5(2^{|x|}) + 14$

CHALLENGE Q

11 Solve the inequality $|2^{x+1}-1|<|2^x-8|$ giving your answer in exact form.

6.6 Change of base of logarithms

You sometimes need to change the base of a logarithm.

A logarithm in base b can be written with a different base c using the **change of base rule**.

If $a, b, c > 0$ and $b, c \neq 1$, then:

$$\log_b a = \frac{\log_c a}{\log_c b}$$

Proof:

If $x = \log_b a$, then $b^x = a$ — take logs of both sides

$\log_c b^x = \log_c a$ — use the power rule

$x \log_c b = \log_c a$ — divide both sides by $\log_c b$

$$x = \frac{\log_c a}{\log_c b}$$

$$\log_b a = \frac{\log_c a}{\log_c b}$$

If $c = a$ in the change of base rule, then the rule gives:

$$\log_b a = \frac{1}{\log_a b}$$

WORKED EXAMPLE 12

Change $\log_2 7$ to base 10. Hence evaluate $\log_2 7$ correct to 3 sf.

Answers

$\log_2 7 = \dfrac{\lg 7}{\lg 2} \approx 2.81$

Note:

Some calculators have a $\log_{\blacksquare}\square$ key.

This can be used to evaluate $\log_2 7$ directly.

The change of base rule can be used to solve equations involving logarithms with different bases.

WORKED EXAMPLE 13

Solve $\log_3 x = \log_9(x+6)$.

Answers

$\log_3 x = \log_9(x+6)$	change $\log_9(x+6)$ to base 3
$\log_3 x = \dfrac{\log_3(x+6)}{\log_3 9}$	$\log_3 9 = \log_3 3^2 = 2$
$\log_3 x = \dfrac{\log_3(x+6)}{2}$	multiply both sides by 2
$2\log_3 x = \log_3(x+6)$	use the power rule
$\log_3 x^2 = \log_3(x+6)$	use equality of logs
$x^2 = x+6$	
$x^2 - x - 6 = 0$	
$(x-3)(x+2) = 0$	
$x = 3$ or $x = -2$	

Check when $x = 3$: $\log_3 3$ is defined and is equal to 1
$\log_9(3+6) = \log_9 9$ is defined and is equal to 1

So $x = 3$ is a solution, since both sides of the equation are defined and equivalent in value.

Check when $x = -2$: $\log_3(-2)$ is not defined

So $x = -2$ is not a solution of the original equation.

Hence, the solution is $x = 3$.

Exercise 6.6

1 Use the rule $\log_b a = \dfrac{\log_{10} a}{\log_{10} b}$ to evaluate these correct to 3 sf.

a $\log_2 10$ b $\log_3 33$ c $\log_5 8$ d $\log_7 0.0025$

2 Given that $u = \log_4 x$, find, in simplest form in terms of u.

a $\log_x 4$, b $\log_x 16$, c $\log_x 2$, d $\log_x 8$.

3 Given that $\log_9 y = x$, express in terms of x.

a $\log_y 9$, b $\log_9(9y)$, c $\log_3 y$, d $\log_3(81y)$.

4 a Given that $\log_p x = 20$ and $\log_p y = 5$, find $\log_y x$.

b Given that $\log_p X = 15$ and $\log_p Y = 6$, find the value of $\log_X Y$.

5 Evaluate $\log_p 2 \times \log_8 p$.

6 Solve.

a $\log_9 3 + \log_9(x+4) = \log_5 25$ b $2\log_4 2 + \log_7(2x+3) = \log_3 27$

7 a Express $\log_4 x$ in terms of $\log_2 x$.

b Using your answer of **part a**, and the substitution $u = \log_2 x$, solve the equation $\log_4 x + \log_2 x = 12$.

8 Solve.

a $\log_2 x + 5\log_4 x = 14$ **b** $\log_3 x + 2\log_9 x = 4$

c $5\log_2 x - \log_4 x = 3$ **d** $4\log_3 x = \log_9 x + 2$

9 **a** Express $\log_x 3$ in terms of a logarithm to base 3.

b Using your answer of **part a**, and the substitution $u = \log_3 x$, solve the equation $\log_3 x = 3 - 2\log_x 3$.

10 Solve.

a $\log_3 x = 9\log_x 3$ **b** $\log_5 x + \log_x 5 = 2$

c $\log_4 x - 4\log_x 4 + 3 = 0$ **d** $\log_4 x + 6\log_x 4 - 5 = 0$

e $\log_2 x - 9\log_x 2 = 8$ **f** $\log_5 y = 4 - 4\log_y 5$

11 **a** Express $\log_4 x$ in terms of $\log_2 x$.

b Express $\log_8 y$ in terms of $\log_2 y$.

c Hence solve, the simultaneous equations

$6\log_4 x + 3\log_8 y = 16$

$\log_2 x - 2\log_4 y = 4$.

CHALLENGE Q

12 Solve the simultaneous equations

$2\log_3 y = \log_5 125 + \log_3 x$

$2^y = 4^x$.

6.7 Natural logarithms

There is another type of logarithm to a special base called e.

The number e is an irrational number and $e \approx 2.718$.

The number e is a very important number in mathematics as it has very special properties. You will learn about these special properties in Chapters 15 and 16.

Logarithms to the base of e are called **natural logarithms**.

$\ln x$ is used to represent $\log_e x$.

If $y = e^x$ then $x = \ln y$.

$y = \ln x$ is the reflection of $y = e^x$ in the line $y = x$.
$y = \ln x$ and $y = e^x$ are inverse functions.

All the rules of logarithms that you have learnt so far also apply for natural logarithms.

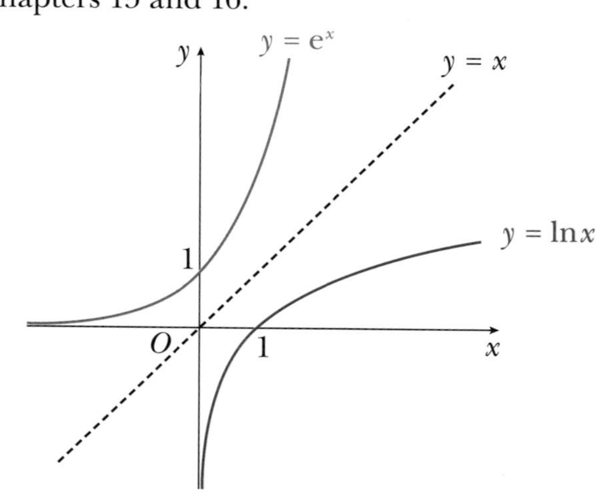

Exercise 6.7

1 Use a calculator to evaluate correct to 3 sf.

a e^2 **b** $e^{1.5}$ **c** $e^{0.2}$ **d** e^{-3}

2 Use a calculator to evaluate correct to 3 sf.

a $\ln 4$ **b** $\ln 2.1$ **c** $\ln 0.7$ **d** $\ln 0.39$

3 Without using a calculator find the value of

a $e^{\ln 5}$ **b** $e^{\frac{1}{2}\ln 64}$ **c** $3e^{\ln 2}$ **d** $-e^{-\ln\frac{1}{2}}$

4 Solve.

a $e^{\ln x} = 7$ **b** $\ln e^x = 2.5$ **c** $e^{2\ln x} = 36$ **d** $e^{-\ln x} = 20$

5 Solve, giving your answers correct to 3 sf.

a $e^x = 70$ **b** $e^{2x} = 28$ **c** $e^{x+1} = 16$ **d** $e^{2x-1} = 5$

6 Solve, giving your answers in terms of natural logarithms.

a $e^x = 7$ **b** $2e^x + 1 = 7$ **c** $e^{2x-5} = 3$ **d** $\frac{1}{2}e^{3x-1} = 4$

7 Solve, giving your answers correct to 3 sf.

a $\ln x = 3$ **b** $\ln x = -2$ **c** $\ln(x+1) =$ [illegible] **d** $\ln(2x-5) = 3$

8 Solve, giving your answers correct to 3 sf.

a $\ln x^3 + \ln x = 5$ **b** $e^{3x+4} = 2e^{x-1}$ **c** $\ln(x+5) - \ln x = 3$

9 Solve, giving your answers in exact form.

a $\ln(x-3) = 2$ **b** $e^{2x-1} = 7$ **c** $e^{2x} - 4e^x = 0$

d $e^x = 2e^{-x}$ **e** $e^{2x} - 9e^x + 20 = 0$ **f** $e^x + 6e^{-x} = 5$

10 Solve, giving your answers correct to 3 sf.

a $e^{2x} - 2e^x - 24 = 0$ **b** $e^{2x} - 5e^x + 4 = 0$ **c** $e^x +$ [illegible]$e^{-x} = 80$

11 Solve the simultaneous equations, giving your answers in exact form.

a $\ln x = 2\ln y$

$\ln y - \ln x = 1$

b $e^{5x-y} = 3e^{3x}$

$e^{2x} = 5e^{x+y}$

12 Solve $5\ln(7-e^{2x}) = 3$, giving your answer correct to 3 significant figures.

13 Solve $ex - xe^{5x-1} = 0$.

CHALLENGE Q

14 Solve $5x^2 - x^2e^{2x} + 2e^{2x} = 10$ giving your answers in exact form.

6.8 Practical applications of exponential equations

In this section you will see how exponential equations can be applied to real-life situations.

WORKED EXAMPLE 14

The temperature, T °C, of a hot drink, t minutes after it is made, is given by

$$T = 75e^{-0.02t} + 20.$$

a Find the temperature of the drink when it was made.

b Find the temperature of the drink when $t = 6$.

c Find the value of t when $T = 65$.

Answers

a When $t = 0$,

$T = 75e^{-0.02 \times 0} + 20$
$= 75e^0 + 20$ — use $e^0 = 1$
$= 95$

Temperature of the drink when first made is 95 °C.

b When $t = 6$,

$T = 75e^{-0.02 \times 6} + 20$
$= 86.5$

Temperature of the drink when $t = 6$ is 86.5 °C.

c When $T = 65$,

$65 = 75e^{-0.02t} + 20$ — subtract 20 from both sides
$45 = 75e^{-0.02t}$ — divide both sides by 75
$0.6 = e^{-0.02t}$ — take ln of both sides
$\ln 0.6 = -0.02t$ — divide both sides by −0.02
$t = \dfrac{\ln 0.6}{-0.02}$
$t = 25.5$ to 3 sf

Exercise 6.8

1 At the start of an experiment the number of bacteria was 100.

This number increases so that after t minutes the number of bacteria, N, is given by the formula

$$N = 100 \times 2^t.$$

a Estimate the number of bacteria after 12 minutes.

b Estimate the time, in minutes, it takes for the number of bacteria to exceed 10 000 000.

2 At the beginning of 2015, the population of a species of animals was estimated at 50 000.

This number decreased so that, after a period of n years, the population was

$$50000e^{-0.03n}.$$

a Estimate the population at the beginning of 2020.

b Estimate the year in which the population would be expected to have first decreased to 5000.

3 The volume of water in a container, $V\,\text{cm}^3$, at time t minutes, is given by the formula

$$V = 2000\,\text{e}^{-kt}.$$

When $V = 1000$, $t = 15$.

a Find the value of k.

b Find the value of V when $t = 22$.

4 A species of fish is introduced to a lake.

The population, N, of this species of fish after t weeks is given by the formula

$$N = 500\,\text{e}^{-0.3t}.$$

a Find the initial population of these fish.

b Estimate the number of these fish after 6 weeks.

c Estimate the number of weeks it takes for the number of these fish to have fallen to $\frac{1}{2}$ of the number introduced.

5 The value, $\$V$, of a house n years after it was built is given by the formula

$$V = 250\,000\,\text{e}^{an}.$$

When $n = 3$, $V = 350\,000$.

a Find the initial value of this house.

b Find the value of a.

c Estimate the number of years for this house to double in value.

6 The area, $A\,\text{cm}^2$, of a patch of mould is measured daily.

The area, n days after the measurements started, is given by the formula

$$A = A_0 b^n.$$

When $n = 2$, $A = 1.8$ and when $n = 3$, $A = 2.4$.

a Find the value of b.

b Find the value of A_0 and explain what A_0 represents.

c Estimate the number of days for the area of this patch of mould to exceed $7\,\text{cm}^2$.

6.9 The graphs of simple logarithmic and exponential functions

You should already know the properties of the graphs $y = \text{e}^x$ and $y = \ln x$.

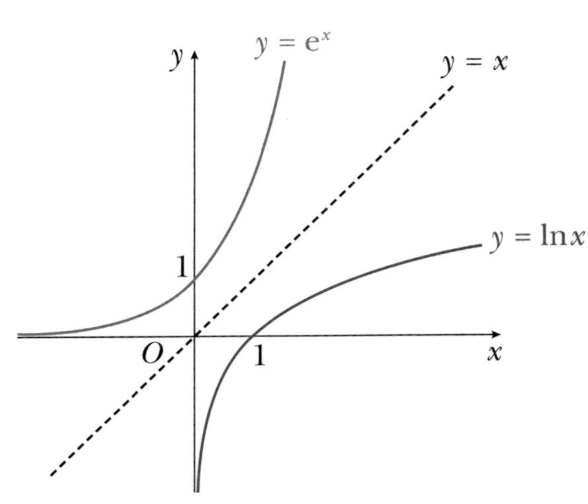

The graph of $y = \text{e}^x$

- $y = \text{e}^x$ intercepts the y-axis at $(0, 1)$.
- $\text{e}^x > 0$ for all values of x.
- When x gets closer to $-\infty$, then y gets closer to 0.
- This can be written as: As $x \to -\infty$, then $y \to 0$.
- The graph is said to be asymptotic to the negative x-axis.
- Also, as $x \to +\infty$, then $y \to +\infty$.

The graph of $y = \ln x$

- $y = \ln x$ intercepts the x-axis at (1, 0).
- $\ln x$ only exists for positive values of x.
- As $x \to 0$, then $y \to -\infty$.
- The graph is asymptotic to the negative y-axis.
- As $x \to +\infty$, then $y \to +\infty$.

$y = e^x$ and $y = \ln x$ are inverse functions, so they are mirror images of each other in the line $y = x$.

Exercise 6.9

1 Use a graphing software package to plot each of the following family of curves for $k = 3, 2, 1, -1, -2$ and -3.

a $y = e^{kx}$ **b** $y = ke^x$ **c** $y = e^x + k$

Describe the properties of each family of curves.

2 Use a graphing software package to plot each of the following family of curves for $k = 3, 2, 1, -1, -2$ and -3.

a $y = \ln kx$ **b** $y = k \ln x$ **c** $y = \ln(x + k)$

Describe the properties of each family of curves.

6.10 The graphs of $y = ke^{nx} + a$ and $y = k\ln(ax + b)$ where n, k, a and b are integers

CLASS DISCUSSION

Consider the function $y = 2e^{3x} + 1$.

Discuss the following and decide on the missing answers:

1 When $x = 0$, $y = \ldots$

2 The y-intercept is $(\ldots, \ldots)$

3 When $y = 0$, x is …

4 As $x \to +\infty$, $y \to \ldots$

5 As $x \to -\infty$, $y \to \ldots$

6 The line $y = \ldots$ is an …

Now sketch the graph of $y = 2e^{3x} + 1$ and compare your answer with your classmates.

(Remember to show any axis crossing points and asymptotes on your sketch graph.)

WORKED EXAMPLE 15

Sketch the graph of $y = 3e^{-2x} - 5$.

Answers

When $x = 0$, $\quad y = 3e^0 - 5$

$= 3 - 5$

$= -2$ $\qquad$ hence the y-intercept is $(0, -2)$

When $y = 0$, $0 = 3e^{-2x} - 5$

$$\frac{5}{3} = e^{-2x}$$

$$\ln\left(\frac{5}{3}\right) = -2x$$

$$x = -\frac{1}{2}\ln\left(\frac{5}{3}\right)$$

$x \approx -0.255$ $\qquad$ hence the x-intercept is $(-0.255, 0)$

As $x \to +\infty$, $e^{-2x} \to 0$ so $y \to -5$ $\qquad$ hence the asymptote is $y = -5$

As $x \to -\infty$, $e^{-2x} \to \infty$ so $y \to \infty$

The sketch graph of $y = 3e^{-2x} - 5$ is:

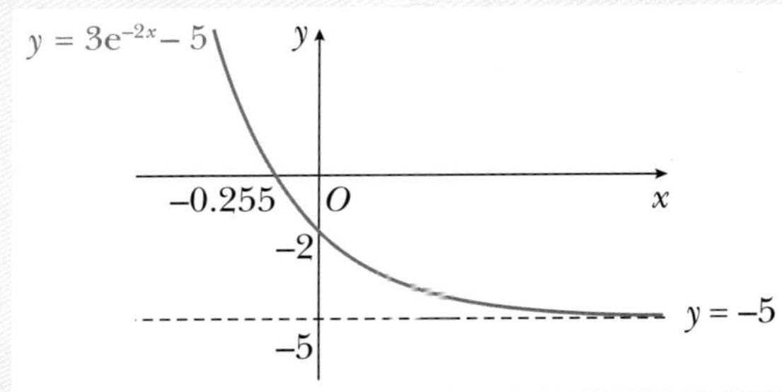

WORKED EXAMPLE 16

Sketch the graph of $y = 4\ln(2x + 5)$.

Answers

When $x = 0$, $y = 4\ln 5$,
≈ 6.44 hence the y-intercept is $(0, 4\ln 5)$

When $y = 0$, $0 = 4\ln(2x + 5)$

$0 = \ln(2x + 5)$

$e^0 = 2x + 5$

$1 = 2x + 5$

$x = -2$ hence the x-intercept is $(-2, 0)$

$\ln x$ only exists for positive values of x.

So $4\ln(2x + 5)$ only exists for $2x + 5 > 0$
$x > -2.5$.

As $x \to +\infty$, $y \to \infty$

As $x \to -2.5$, $y \to -\infty$ hence the asymptote is $x = -2.5$

The sketch graph of $y = 4\ln(2x + 5)$ is:

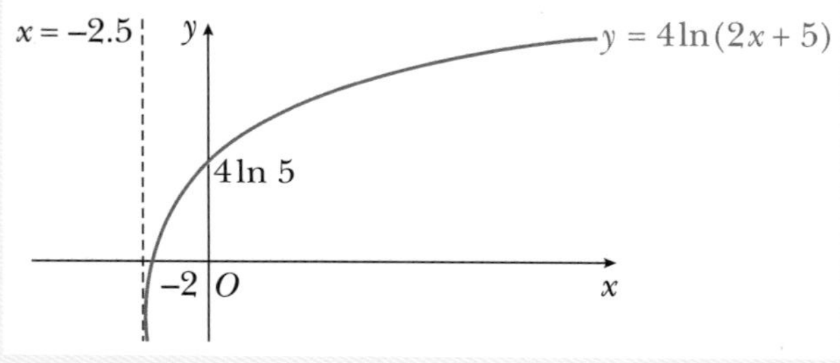

Exercise 6.10

1 Sketch the graphs of each of the following exponential functions.
[Remember to show the axis crossing points and the asymptotes.]

a $y = 2e^x - 4$ **b** $y = 3e^x + 6$ **c** $y = 5e^x + 2$

d $y = 2e^{-x} + 6$ **e** $y = 3e^{-x} - 1$ **f** $y = -2e^{-x} + 4$

g $y = 4e^{2x} + 1$ **h** $y = 2e^{-5x} + 8$ **i** $y = -e^{4x} + 2$

2 Sketch the graphs of each of the following logarithmic functions.
[Remember to show the axis crossing points and the asymptotes.]

a $y = \ln(2x + 4)$ **b** $y = \ln(3x - 6)$ **c** $y = \ln(8 - 2x)$

d $y = 2\ln(2x + 2)$ **e** $y = 4\ln(2x - 4)$ **f** $y = -3\ln(6x - 9)$

6.11 The inverse of logarithmic and exponential functions

In Chapter 1 you learnt how to find the inverse of a one-one function.

This section shows you how to find the inverse of exponential and logarithmic functions.

WORKED EXAMPLE 17

Find the inverse of each function and state its domain.

a $f(x) = 2e^{-4x} + 3$ for $x \in \mathbb{R}$ **b** $f(x) = 3\ln(2x - 4)$ for $x > 2$

Answers

a $f(x) = 2e^{-4x} + 3$ for $x \in \mathbb{R}$

Step 1: Write the function as $y =$ ⟶ $y = 2e^{-4x} + 3$

Step 2: Interchange the x and y variables. ⟶ $x = 2e^{-4y} + 3$

Step 3: Rearrange to make y the subject. ⟶ $x - 3 = 2e^{-4y}$

$$\frac{x-3}{2} = e^{-4y}$$

$$\ln\left(\frac{x-3}{2}\right) = -4y$$

$$y = -\frac{1}{4}\ln\left(\frac{x-3}{2}\right)$$

$f^{-1}(x) = -\frac{1}{4}\ln\left(\frac{x-3}{2}\right)$ for $x > 3$

b $f(x) = 3\ln(2x - 4)$, $x > 2$

Step 1: Write the function as $y =$ ⟶ $y = 3\ln(2x - 4)$

Step 2: Interchange the x and y variables. ⟶ $x = 3\ln(2y - 4)$

Step 3: Rearrange to make y the subject. ⟶ $\frac{x}{3} = \ln(2y - 4)$

$$e^{\frac{x}{3}} = 2y - 4$$

$$2y = e^{\frac{x}{3}} + 4$$

$$y = \frac{1}{2}e^{\frac{x}{3}} + 2$$

$f^{-1}(x) = \frac{1}{2}e^{\frac{x}{3}} + 2$ for $x \in \mathbb{R}$

Exercise 6.11

1 The following functions are each defined for $x \in \mathbb{R}$.

Find $f^{-1}(x)$ for each function and state its domain.

a $f(x) = e^x + 4$ **b** $f(x) = e^x - 2$ **c** $f(x) = 5e^x - 1$

d $f(x) = 3e^{2x} + 1$ **e** $f(x) = 5e^{2x} + 3$ **f** $f(x) = 4e^{-3x} + 5$

g $f(x) = 2 - e^x$ **h** $f(x) = 5 - 2e^{-2x}$

2 Find $f^{-1}(x)$ for each function.

a $f(x) = \ln(x+1),\ x > -1$

b $f(x) = \ln(x-3),\ x > 3$

c $f(x) = 2\ln(x+2),\ x > -2$

d $f(x) = 2\ln(2x+1),\ x > -\frac{1}{2}$

e $f(x) = 3\ln(2x-5),\ x > \frac{5}{2}$

f $f(x) = -5\ln(3x-1),\ x > \frac{1}{3}$

3 $f(x) = e^{2x} + 1$ for $x \in \mathbb{R}$

a State the range of $f(x)$.

b Find $f^{-1}(x)$.

c State the domain of $f^{-1}(x)$.

d Find $f^{-1}f(x)$.

4 $f(x) = e^{x}$ for $x \in \mathbb{R}$ $\qquad$ $g(x) = \ln 5x$ for $x > 0$

a Find **i** $fg(x)$ **ii** $gf(x)$.

b Solve $g(x) = 3f^{-1}(x)$.

5 $f(x) = e^{3x}$ for $x \in \mathbb{R}$ $\qquad$ $g(x) = \ln x$ for $x > 0$

a Find **i** $fg(x)$ **ii** $gf(x)$.

b Solve $f(x) = 2g^{-1}(x)$.

6 $f(x) = e^{2x}$ for $x \in \mathbb{R}$ $\qquad$ $g(x) = \ln(2x+1)$ for $x > -\frac{1}{2}$

a Find $fg(x)$.

b Solve $f(x) = 8g^{-1}(x)$.

Summary

The rules of logarithms

If $y = a^x$ then $x = \log_a y$.

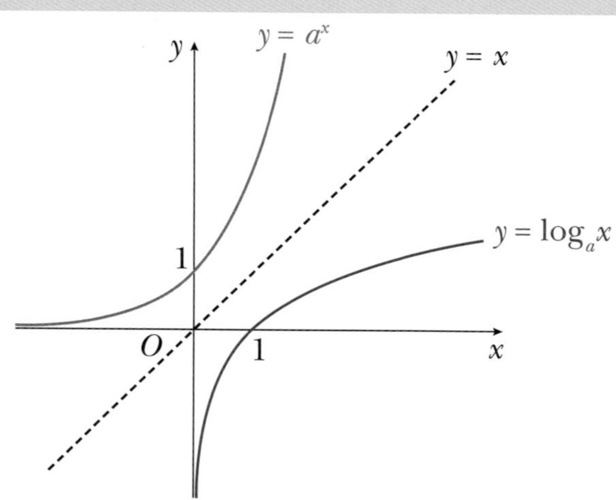

$\log_a a = 1 \qquad \log_a 1 = 0$

$\log_a a^x = x \qquad x = a^{\log_a x}$

Product rule: $\log_a(xy) = \log_a x + \log_a y$

Division rule: $\log_a\left(\frac{x}{y}\right) = \log_a x - \log_a y$

Power rule: $\log_a(x)^m = m\log_a x$ $\qquad$ [special case: $\log_a\left(\frac{1}{x}\right) = -\log_a x$]

Change of base: $\log_b a = \frac{\log_c a}{\log_c b}$ $\qquad$ [special case: $\log_b a = \frac{1}{\log_a b}$]

Natural logarithms

Logarithms to the base of e are called natural logarithms.
$\ln x$ is used to represent $\log_e x$.

If $y = e^x$ then $x = \ln y$.

All the rules of logarithms apply for natural logarithms.

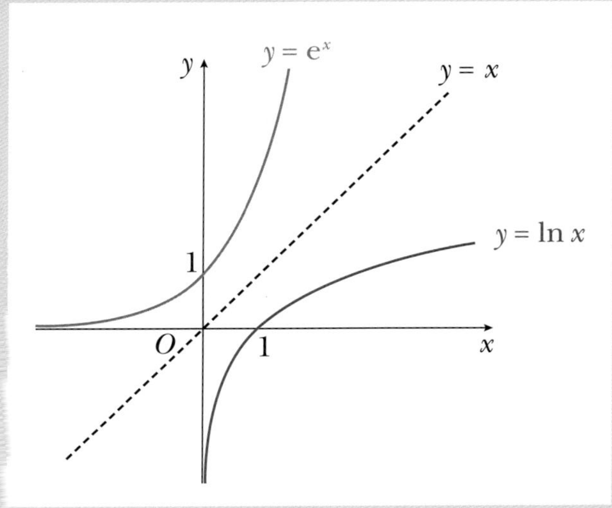

Examination questions

Worked example

By changing the base of $\log_{2a} 4$, express $(\log_{2a} 4)(1 + \log_a 2)$ as a single logarithm to base a. [4]

Cambridge IGCSE Additional Mathematics 0606 Paper 21 Q11b Jun 2014

Answer

$$\log_{2a} 4 = \frac{\log_a 4}{\log_a 2a}$$ use the product rule on the denominator

$$= \frac{\log_a 4}{\log_a 2 + \log_a a}$$ remember that $\log_a a = 1$

$$= \frac{\log_a 4}{1 + \log_a 2}$$

$$(\log_{2a} 4)(1 + \log_a 2) = \left(\frac{\log_a 4}{1 + \log_a 2}\right)(1 + \log_a 2)$$

$$= \frac{(\log_a 4)(1 + \log_a 2)}{1 + \log_a 2}$$ divide numerator and denominator by $(1 + \log_a 2)$

$$= \log_a 4$$

Exercise 6.12

Exam Exercise

1 **a** Using the substitution $y = 5^x$, show that the equation $5^{2x+1} - 5^{x+1} + 2 = 2(5^x)$ can be written in the form $ay^2 + by + 2 = 0$, where a and b are constants to be found. [2]

b Hence solve the equation $5^{2x+1} - 5^{x+1} + 2 = 2(5^x)$. [4]

Cambridge IGCSE Additional Mathematics 0606 Paper 11 Q4i,ii Nov 2014

2 Solve the following simultaneous equations.

$$\log_2(x+3) = 2 + \log_2 y$$

$$\log_2(x+y) = 3$$ [5]

Cambridge IGCSE Additional Mathematics 0606 Paper 21 Q3 Nov 2014

3 Functions g and h are defined by

$$g(x) = 4e^x - 2 \quad \text{for } x \in \mathbb{R},$$

$$h(x) = \ln 5x \quad \text{for } x > 0.$$

a Find $g^{-1}(x)$. [2]

b Solve $gh(x) = 18$. [3]

Cambridge IGCSE Additional Mathematics 0606 Paper 11 Q12bi,ii Nov 2013

4 Given that $\log_p X = 5$ and $\log_p Y = 2$, find

a $\log_p X^2$, [1]

b $\log_p \frac{1}{X}$, [1]

c $\log_{XY} p$. [2]

Cambridge IGCSE Additional Mathematics 0606 Paper 21 Q4i,ii,iii Nov 2013

5 **a** Given that $\log_4 x = \frac{1}{2}$, find the value of x. [1]

b Solve $2\log_4 y - \log_4(5y - 12) = \frac{1}{2}$. [4]

Cambridge IGCSE Additional Mathematics 0606 Paper 11 Q4i,ii Jun 2013

6 Solve the equation $3^{2x} = 1000$, giving your answer to 2 decimal places. [2]

Cambridge IGCSE Additional Mathematics 0606 Paper 21 Q5a Jun 2012

7 Express $\lg a + 3\lg b - 3$ as a single logarithm. [3]

Cambridge IGCSE Additional Mathematics 0606 Paper 11 Q2 Jun 2011

8 Using the substitution $u = 5^x$, or otherwise, solve

$$5^{2x+1} = 7(5^x) - 2.$$ [5]

Cambridge IGCSE Additional Mathematics 0606 Paper 11 Q4 Nov 2012

9 The temperature, T° Celsius, of an object, t minutes after it is removed from a heat source, is given by

$$T = 55\,e^{-0.1t} + 15.$$

a Find the temperature of the object at the instant it is removed from the heat source. [1]

b Find the temperature of the object when $t = 3$. [1]

c Find the value of t when $T = 25$. [3]

Cambridge IGCSE Additional Mathematics 0606 Paper 21 Q8i,ii,iii Jun 2011

10 a Write $\log_{27} x$ as a logarithm to base 3. [2]

b Given that $\log_a y = 3(\log_a 15 - \log_a 3) + 1$, express y in terms of a. [3]

Cambridge IGCSE Additional Mathematics 0606 Paper 21 Q1 Jun 2015

11 Do not use a calculator in this question.

i Find the value of $-\log_p p^2$. [1]

ii Find $\lg\left(\frac{1}{10^n}\right)$. [1]

iii Show that $\frac{\lg 20 - \lg 4}{\log_5 10} = (\lg y)^2$, where y is a constant to be found. [2]

iv Solve $\log_r 2x + \log_r 3x = \log_r 600$. [2]

Cambridge IGCSE Additional Mathematics 0606 Paper 21 Q3 Jun 2016

12 a i Sketch the graph of $y = e^x - 5$, showing the exact coordinates of any points where the graph meets the coordinate axes. [3]

ii Find the range of values of k for which the equation $e^x - 5 = k$ has no solutions. [1]

b Simplify $\log_a \sqrt{2} + \log_a 8 + \log_a\left(\frac{1}{2}\right)$, giving your answer in the form $p\log_a 2$, where p is a constant. [2]

c Solve the equation $\log_3 x - \log_9 4x = 1$. [4]

Cambridge IGCSE Additional Mathematics 0606 Paper 22 Q10 Mar 2015

13 a Solve the following equations to find p and q.

$$8^{q-1} \times 2^{2p+1} = 4^7$$

$$9^{p-4} \times 3^q = 81$$ [4]

b Solve the equation $\lg(3x-2) + \lg(x+1) = 2 - \lg 2$. [5]

Cambridge IGCSE Additional Mathematics 0606 Paper 21 Q5 Nov 2015

Chapter 7
Straight-line graphs

This section will show you how to:

- solve questions involving midpoint and length of a line
- use the condition for two lines to be parallel or perpendicular
- interpret the equation of a straight-line graph in the form $y = mx + c$
- transform given relationships, including $y = ax^n$ and $y = ab^x$, to straight-line form and hence determine unknown constants by calculating the gradient or intercept of the transformed graph.

RECAP

You should already be familiar with the following coordinate geometry work:

Length of a line, gradient and midpoint

P is the point (x_1, y_1) and Q is the point (x_2, y_2).
M is the midpoint of the line PQ.

The length of the line $PQ = \sqrt{(x_2 - x_1)^2 + (y_2 - y_1)^2}$.

The gradient of the line $PQ = \dfrac{y_2 - y_1}{x_2 - x_1}$.

The coordinates of M are $\left(\dfrac{x_1 + x_2}{2}, \dfrac{y_1 + y_2}{2}\right)$.

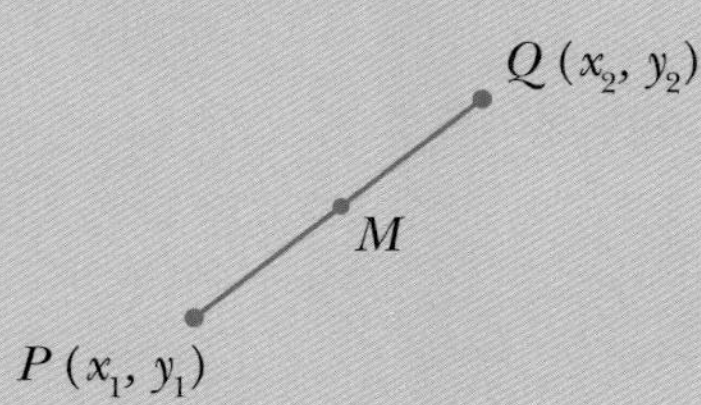

Gradients of parallel lines

If two lines are parallel then their gradients are equal.

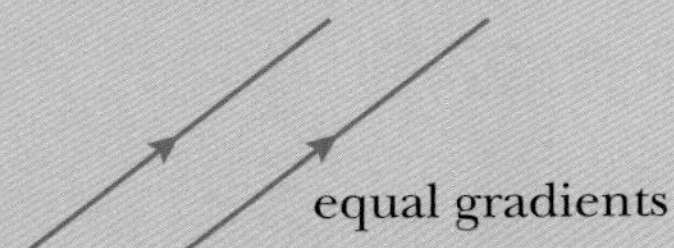

Gradients of perpendicular lines

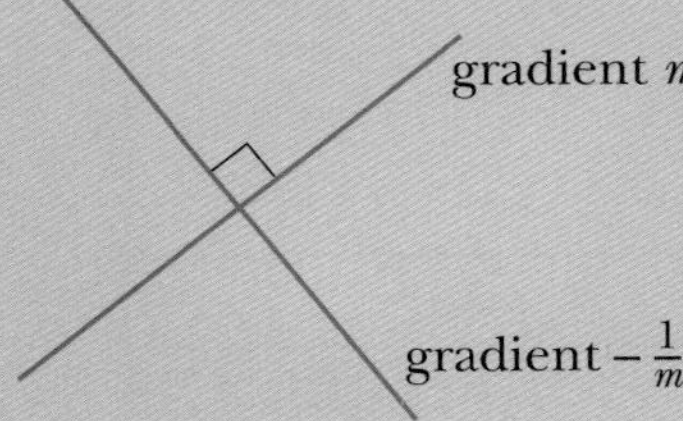

If a line has a gradient of m, a line perpendicular to it has a gradient of $-\dfrac{1}{m}$.

This rule can also be written as:

If the gradients of the two perpendicular lines are m_1 and m_2, then $m_1 \times m_2 = -1$.

The equation of a straight line

The equation of a straight line is $y = mx + c$ where m = the gradient and c = the y-intercept.

7.1 Problems involving length of a line and midpoint

You need to know how to apply the formulae for the midpoint and the length of a line segment to solve problems.

WORKED EXAMPLE 1

A is the point $(-3, 7)$ and B is the point $(6, -2)$.

a Find the length of AB.

b Find the midpoint of AB.

Answers

a $(-3, 7)$ ↑↑ (x_1, y_1) $\quad$ $(6, -2)$ ↑↑ (x_2, y_2) $\quad$ decide which values to use for x_1, y_1, x_2, y_2

$$AB = \sqrt{(x_2 - x_1)^2 + (y_2 - y_1)^2}$$
$$= \sqrt{(6 - -3)^2 + (-2 - 7)^2}$$
$$= 9\sqrt{2}$$

b $$\text{Midpoint} = \left(\frac{x_1 + x_2}{2}, \frac{y_1 + y_2}{2}\right)$$
$$= \left(\frac{-3 + 6}{2}, \frac{7 + -2}{2}\right)$$
$$= (1.5, 2.5)$$

WORKED EXAMPLE 2

The distance between two points $P(7, a)$ and $Q(a + 1, 9)$ is 15.

Find the two possible values of a.

Answers

$(7, a)$ ↑↑ (x_1, y_1) $\quad$ $(a + 1, 9)$ ↑↑ (x_2, y_2) $\quad$ decide which values to use for x_1, y_1, x_2, y_2

Using $PQ = \sqrt{(x_2 - x_1)^2 + (y_2 - y_1)^2}$ and $PQ = 15$.

$$\sqrt{(a + 1 - 7)^2 + (9 - a)^2} = 15$$

$$\sqrt{(a - 6)^2 + (9 - a)^2} = 15 \quad \text{square both sides}$$

$$(a - 6)^2 + (9 - a)^2 = 225$$

$$a^2 - 12a + 36 + 81 - 18a + a^2 = 225 \quad \text{collect terms on one side}$$

$$2a^2 - 30a - 108 = 0 \quad \text{divide both sides by 2}$$

$$a^2 - 15a - 54 = 0 \quad \text{factorise}$$

$$(a - 18)(a + 3) = 0 \quad \text{solve}$$

$$a - 18 = 0 \text{ or } a + 3 = 0$$

Hence $a = 18$ or $a = -3$.

WORKED EXAMPLE 3

The coordinates of the midpoint of the line segment joining $A(-5, 11)$ and $B(p, q)$, are $(2.5, -6)$.

Find the value of p and the value of q.

Answers

$(-5, 11)$ (p, q) decide which values to use for x_1, y_1, x_2, y_2

(x_1, y_1) (x_2, y_2)

Using $\left(\frac{x_1 + x_2}{2}, \frac{y_1 + y_2}{2}\right)$ and midpoint $= (2.5, -6)$.

$$\left(\frac{x_1 + x_2}{2}, \frac{y_1 + y_2}{2}\right) = (2.5, -6)$$

$$\left(\frac{-5 + p}{2}, \frac{11 + q}{2}\right) = (2.5, -6)$$

Equating the x-coordinates gives: $\frac{-5 + p}{2} = 2.5$

$-5 + p = 5$

$p = 10$

Equating the y-coordinates gives: $\frac{11 + q}{2} = -6$

$11 + q = -12$

$q = -23$

Hence $p = 10$ and $q = -23$.

WORKED EXAMPLE 4

Three of the vertices of a parallelogram $ABCD$ are $A(-10, 1)$, $B(6, -2)$ and $C(14, 4)$.

a Find the midpoint of AC.

b Find the coordinates of D.

Answers

a Midpoint of $AC = \left(\frac{-10 + 14}{2}, \frac{1 + 4}{2}\right) = (2, 2.5)$.

b Let the coordinates of D be (m, n).

Since $ABCD$ is a parallelogram, the midpoint of BD is the same as the midpoint of AC.

Midpoint of $BD = \left(\frac{6 + m}{2}, \frac{-2 + n}{2}\right) = (2, 2.5)$

Equating the x-coordinates gives: $\frac{6 + m}{2} = 2$

$6 + m = 4$

$m = -2$

Equating the y-coordinates gives: $\frac{-2 + n}{2} = 2.5$

$-2 + n = 5$

$n = 7$

The coordinates of D are $(-2, 7)$.

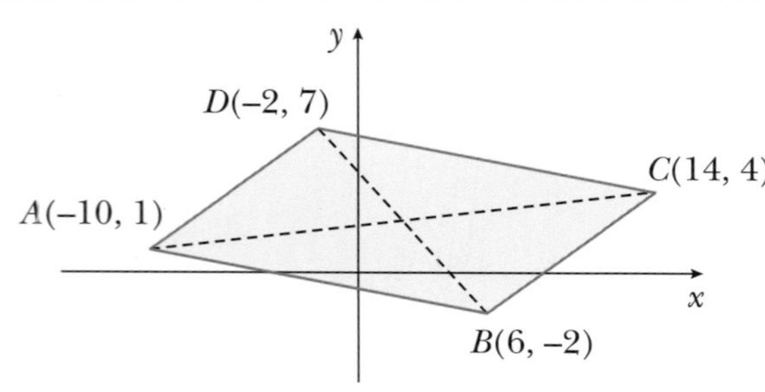

CLASS DISCUSSION

This triangle has sides of length $5\sqrt{3}$ cm, $2\sqrt{6}$ cm and $7\sqrt{2}$ cm.
Priya says that the triangle is right-angled.
Discuss whether she is correct.
Explain your reasoning.

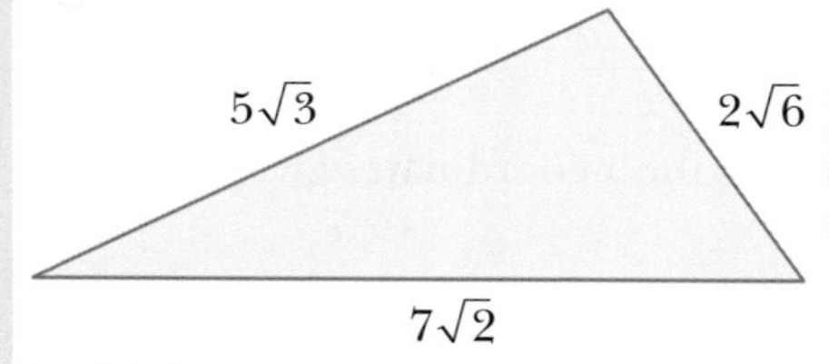

Exercise 7.1

1 Find the length of the line segment joining

a $(2, 0)$ and $(5, 0)$ **b** $(-7, 4)$ and $(-7, 8)$ **c** $(2, 1)$ and $(8, 9)$

d $(-3, 1)$ and $(2, 13)$ **e** $(5, -2)$ and $(2, -6)$ **f** $(4, 4)$ and $(-20, -3)$

g $(6, -5)$ and $(1, 2)$ **h** $(-3, -2)$ and $(-1, -5)$ **i** $(-7, 7)$ and $(5, -5)$.

2 Calculate the lengths of the sides of the triangle PQR.
Use your answers to determine whether or not the triangle is right-angled.

a $P(3, 11)$, $Q(5, 7)$, $R(11, 10)$

b $P(-7, 8)$, $Q(-1, 4)$, $R(5, 12)$

c $P(-8, -3)$, $Q(-4, 5)$, $R(-2, -6)$

3 $A(-1, 0)$, $B(1, 6)$ and $C(7, 4)$.
Show that triangle ABC is a right-angled isosceles triangle.

4 The distance between two points $P(10, 2b)$ and $Q(b, -5)$ is $5\sqrt{10}$.
Find the two possible values of b.

5 The distance between two points $P(6, -2)$ and $Q(2a, a)$ is 5.
Find the two possible values of a.

6 Find the coordinates of the midpoint of the line segment joining

a $(5, 2)$ and $(7, 6)$ **b** $(4, 3)$ and $(9, 11)$ **c** $(8, 6)$ and $(-2, 10)$

d $(-1, 7)$ and $(2, -4)$ **e** $(-7, -8)$ and $(-2, 3)$ **f** $(2a, -3b)$ and $(4a, 5b)$.

7 The coordinates of the midpoint of the line segment joining $P(-8, 2)$ and $Q(a, b)$, are $(5, -3)$.

Find the value of a and the value of b.

8 Three of the vertices of a parallelogram $ABCD$ are $A(-7, 6)$, $B(-1, 8)$ and $C(7, 3)$.

a Find the midpoint of AC.

b Find the coordinates of D.

9 The point $P(2k, k)$ is equidistant from $A(-2, 4)$ and $B(7, -5)$.

Find the value of k.

10 In triangle ABC, the midpoints of the sides AB, BC and AC are $P(2, 3)$, $Q(3, 5)$ and $R(-4, 4)$ respectively. Find the coordinates of A, B and C.

7.2 Parallel and perpendicular lines

You need to know how to apply the rules for gradients to solve problems involving parallel and perpendicular lines.

WORKED EXAMPLE 5

The coordinates of 3 points are $A(8 - k, 2)$, $B(-2, k)$ and $C(-8, 2k)$.
Find the possible values of k if A, B and C are collinear.

Answers

If A, B and C are collinear then they lie on the same line.

gradient of AB = gradient of BC

$$\frac{k-2}{-2-(8-k)} = \frac{2k-k}{-8-(-2)}$$

$$\frac{k-2}{k-10} = \frac{k}{-6}$$ cross multiply

$$-6(k-2) = k(k-10)$$ expand brackets

$$-6k + 12 = k^2 - 10k$$ collect terms on one side

$$k^2 - 4k - 12 = 0$$ factorise

$$(k-6)(k+2) = 0$$ solve

$k - 6 = 0$ or $k + 2 = 0$

Hence $k = 6$ or $k = -2$.

WORKED EXAMPLE 6

The vertices of triangle ABC are $A(-4, 2)$, $B(5, -5)$ and $C(k, k+2)$.
Find the possible values of k if angle ACB is 90°.

Answers

Since angle ACB is 90°,
gradient of AC × gradient of $BC = -1$.

$$\frac{(k+2)-2}{k-(-4)} \times \frac{(k+2)-(-5)}{k-5} = -1$$

$$\frac{k}{k+4} \times \frac{k+7}{k-5} = -1$$

$$k(k+7) = -(k+4)(k-5)$$

$$k^2 + 7k = -(k^2 - k - 20)$$

$$k^2 + 7k = -k^2 + k + 20$$

$$2k^2 + 6k - 20 = 0$$

$$k^2 + 3k - 10 = 0$$

$$(k+5)(k-2) = 0$$

$$k + 5 = 0 \text{ or } k - 2 = 0$$

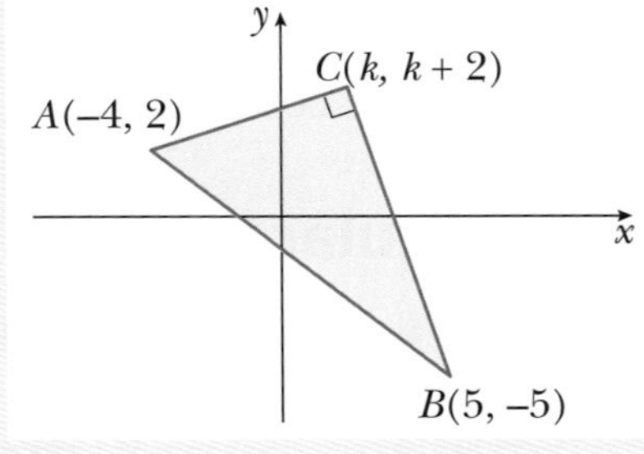

Hence $k = -5$ or $k = 2$.

The two possible situations are:

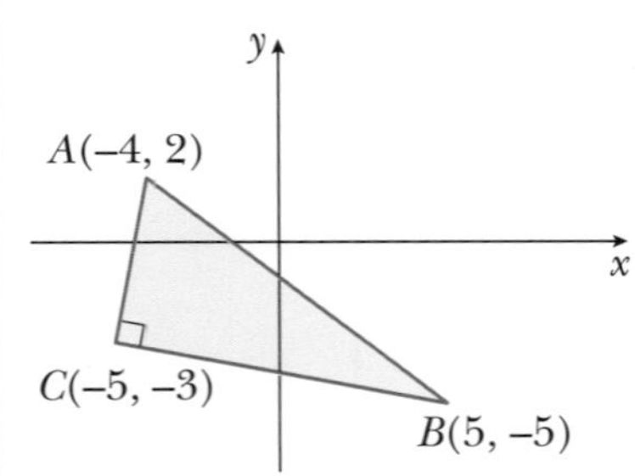

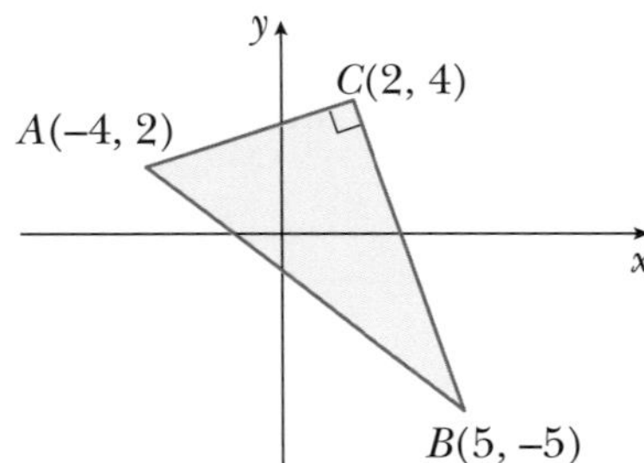

Exercise 7.2

1 Find the gradient of the line AB for each of the following pairs of points.

a $A(1, 2)$ $B(3, -2)$ **b** $A(4, 3)$ $B(5, 0)$

c $A(-4, 4)$ $B(7, 4)$ **d** $A(1, -9)$ $B(4, 1)$

e $A(-4, -3)$ $B(5, 0)$ **f** $A(6, -7)$ $B(2, -4)$

2 Write down the gradient of lines perpendicular to a line with gradient

a 3 **b** $-\frac{1}{2}$ **c** $\frac{2}{5}$ **d** $1\frac{1}{4}$ **e** $-2\frac{1}{2}$

3 Two vertices of a rectangle $ABCD$ are $A(3, -5)$ and $B(6, -3)$.

a Find the gradient of CD.

b Find the gradient of BC.

4 $A(-1, -5)$, $B(5, -2)$ and $C(1, 1)$.
$ABCD$ is a trapezium.
AB is parallel to DC and angle BAD is 90°.
Find the coordinates of D.

5 The midpoint of the line segment joining $P(-2, 3)$ and $Q(4, -1)$ is M.
The point C has coordinates $(-1, -2)$.
Show that CM is perpendicular to PQ.

6 $A(-2, 2)$, $B(3, -1)$ and $C(9, -4)$.
  a Find the gradient of AB and the gradient of BC.
  b Use your answer to **part a** to decide whether or not the points A, B and C are collinear.

7 The coordinates of 3 points are $A(-4, 4)$, $B(k, -2)$ and $C(2k + 1, -6)$.
Find the value of k if A, B and C are collinear.

8 The vertices of triangle ABC are $A(-k, -2)$, $B(k, -4)$ and $C(4, k - 2)$.
Find the possible values of k if angle ABC is 90°.

CHALLENGE Q

9 A is the point $(-2, 0)$ and B is the point $(2, 6)$.
Find the point C on the x-axis such that angle ABC is 90°.

7.3 Equations of straight lines

You should already know that the equation of a straight line is

$$y = mx + c$$

where m = the gradient and c = the y-intercept.

There is an alternative formula that can be used when you know the gradient of the straight line and a point on the line.

Consider a line, with gradient m, which passes through the known point $A(x_1, y_1)$ and whose general point is $P(x, y)$.

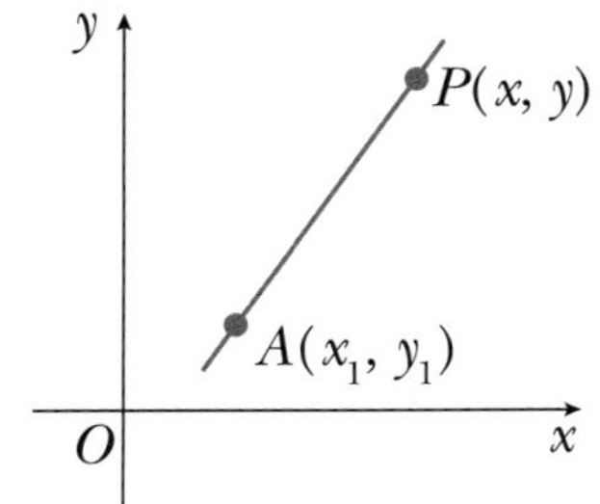

Gradient of $AP = m$, hence $\dfrac{y - y_1}{x - x_1} = m$ multiply both sides by $(x - x_1)$

$$y - y_1 = m(x - x_1).$$

The equation of a straight line, with gradient m, which passes through the point (x_1, y_1) is:

$$y - y_1 = m(x - x_1)$$

WORKED EXAMPLE 7

Find the equation of the straight line

a with gradient 2 and passing through the point (4, 7)

b passing through the points (–5, 8) and (1, –4).

Answers

a Using $y - y_1 = m(x - x_1)$ with $m = 2$, $x_1 = 4$ and $y_1 = 7$

$$y - 7 = 2(x - 4)$$
$$y - 7 = 2x - 8$$
$$y = 2x - 1$$

b (–5, 8) (1, –4) decide which values to use for x_1, y_1, x_2, y_2

(x_1, y_1) (x_2, y_2)

$$\text{Gradient} = m = \frac{y_2 - y_1}{x_2 - x_1} = \frac{(-4) - 8}{1 - (-5)} = -2$$

Using $y - y_1 = m(x - x_1)$ with $m = -2$, $x_1 = -5$ and $y_1 = 8$.

$$y - 8 = -2(x + 5)$$
$$y - 8 = -2x - 10$$
$$y = -2x - 2$$

WORKED EXAMPLE 8

Find the equation of the perpendicular bisector of the line joining $A(3, 2)$ and $B(7, 10)$.

Answers

Gradient of $AB = \frac{10-2}{7-3} = \frac{8}{4} = 2$. using $\frac{y_2 - y_1}{x_2 - x_1}$

Gradient of the perpendicular is $-\frac{1}{2}$. using $m_1 \times m_2 = -1$

Midpoint of $AB = \left(\frac{3+7}{2}, \frac{2+10}{2}\right) = (5, 6)$. using $\left(\frac{x_1 + x_2}{2}, \frac{y_1 + y_2}{2}\right)$

So the perpendicular bisector is the line passing through the point (5, 6) with gradient $-\frac{1}{2}$.

Using $y - y_1 = m(x - x_1)$ with $x_1 = 5$, $y_1 = 6$ and $m = -\frac{1}{2}$.

$$y - 6 = -\frac{1}{2}(x - 5)$$

$$y - 6 = -\frac{1}{2}x + \frac{5}{2}$$

$$y = -\frac{1}{2}x + 8.5$$

multiply both sides by 2 and rearrange

$$x + 2y = 17$$

Exercise 7.3

1 Find the equation of the line with

a gradient 3 and passing through the point (6, 5)

b gradient –4 and passing through the point (2, –1)

c gradient $-\frac{1}{2}$ and passing through the point (8, –3).

2 Find the equation of the line passing through

a (3, 2) and (5, 7) **b** (–1, 6) and (5, –3) **c** (5, –2) and (–7, 4).

3 Find the equation of the line

a parallel to the line $y = 2x + 4$, passing through the point (6, 2)

b parallel to the line $x + 2y = 5$, passing through the point (2, –5)

c perpendicular to the line $2x + 3y = 12$, passing through the point (7, 3)

d perpendicular to the line $4x - y = 6$, passing through the point (4, –1).

4 P is the point (2, 5) and Q is the point (6, 0).
A line l is drawn through P perpendicular to PQ to meet the y-axis at the point R.

a Find the equation of the line l.

b Find the coordinates of the point R.

c Find the area of triangle OPR where O is the origin.

5 Find the equation of the perpendicular bisector of the line segment joining the points

a (1, 3) and (–3, 1) **b** (–1, –5) and (5, 3) **c** (0, –9) and (5, –2).

6 The perpendicular bisector of the line joining $A(-1, 4)$ and $B(2, 2)$ intersects the x-axis at P and the y-axis at Q.
 a Find the coordinates of P and of Q.
 b Find the length of PQ.
 c Find the area of triangle OPQ where O is the origin.

7 The line l_1 has equation $3x + 2y = 12$.
The line l_2 has equation $y = 2x - 1$.
The lines l_1 and l_2 intersect at the point A.
 a Find the coordinates of A.
 b Find the equation of the line through A which is perpendicular to the line l_1.

8 The coordinates of three points are $A(1, 5)$, $B(9, 7)$ and $C(k, -6)$.
M is the midpoint of AB and MC is perpendicular to AB.
 a Find the coordinates of M.
 b Find the value of k.

9 The coordinates of triangle ABC are $A(2, -1)$, $B(3, 7)$ and $C(14, 5)$.
P is the foot of the perpendicular from B to AC.
 a Find the equation of BP.
 b Find the coordinates of P.
 c Find the lengths of AC and BP.
 d Use your answers to **part c** to find the area of triangle ABC.

CHALLENGE Q

10 The coordinates of triangle PQR are $P(-3, -2)$, $Q(5, 10)$ and $R(11, -2)$.
 a Find the equation of the perpendicular bisectors of **i** PQ **ii** QR.
 b Find the coordinates of the point which is equidistant from P, Q and R.

Note:
The point is where the perpendicular bisectors of the sides intersect.

7.4 Areas of rectilinear figures

CLASS DISCUSSION

Discuss with your classmates, how you can find the area of triangle ABC.

Try to find as many different methods as possible.

Compare the ease of use of each of these methods.

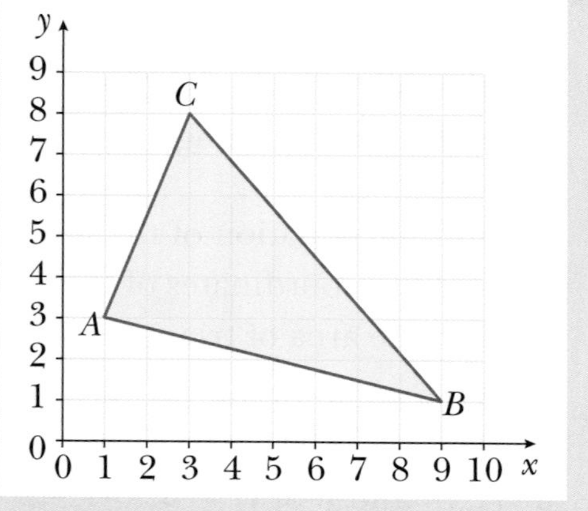

There is a method that you might not have seen before. It is often referred to as the 'shoestring' or 'shoelace' method. You do not have to know this method for the examination, but you may find it useful to know.

If the vertices of triangle ABC are $A(x_1, y_1)$, $B(x_2, y_2)$ and $C(x_3, y_3)$, then:

$$\text{Area of triangle } ABC = \frac{1}{2}\left| x_1y_2 + x_2y_3 + x_3y_1 - x_2y_1 - x_3y_2 - x_1y_3 \right|$$

This complicated formula can be written as: $\frac{1}{2}\begin{vmatrix} x_1 & x_2 & x_3 & x_1 \\ y_1 & y_2 & y_3 & y_1 \end{vmatrix}$

The products in the direction ↘ are given positive signs and the products in the direction ↗ are given negative signs.

For the triangle in the class discussion $A(1, 3)$, $B(9, 1)$ and $C(3, 8)$: $\frac{1}{2}\begin{vmatrix} 1 & 9 & 3 & 1 \\ 3 & 1 & 8 & 3 \end{vmatrix}$

$$\begin{aligned}\text{area of triangle } ABC &= \frac{1}{2}|1\times1 + 9\times8 + 3\times3 - 3\times9 - 1\times3 - 8\times1| \\ &= \frac{1}{2}|1 + 72 + 9 - 27 - 3 - 8| \\ &= \frac{1}{2}|44| \\ &= 22 \text{ units}^2\end{aligned}$$

This method can be extended for use with polygons with more than 3 sides.

Note:
If you take the vertices in an anticlockwise direction around a shape, then the inside of the modulus sign will be positive. If you take the vertices in a clockwise direction, then the inside of the modulus sign will be negative.

149

WORKED EXAMPLE 9

The vertices of a pentagon $ABCDE$ are $A(0, -1)$, $B(5, 1)$, $C(3, 4)$, $B(-1, 6)$ and $C(-3, 2)$.

a Find the area of the pentagon using the 'shoestring' method.

b Find the area of the pentagon using the 'boxing in' method.

Answers

a $\frac{1}{2}\begin{vmatrix} 0 & 5 & 3 & -1 & -3 & 0 \\ -1 & 1 & 4 & 6 & 2 & -1 \end{vmatrix}$

$$\begin{aligned}\text{Area of pentagon} &= \frac{1}{2}|0 + 20 + 18 + (-2) + 3 - (-5) - 3 - (-4) - (-18) - 0| \\ &= \frac{1}{2}|63| \\ &= 31.5 \text{ units}^2\end{aligned}$$

b For the 'boxing in' method, you draw a rectangle around the outside of the pentagon.

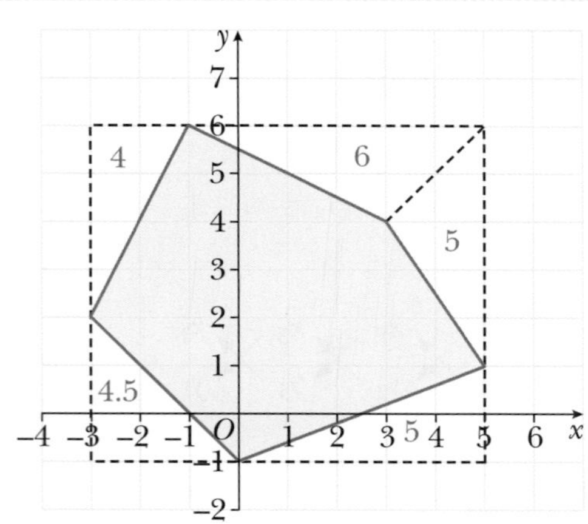

Area of pentagon = area of rectangle – sum of the outside areas

$= (8 \times 7) - (4 + 6 + 5 + 5 + 4.5)$

$= 56 - 24.5$

$= 31.5 \text{ units}^2$

Exercise 7.4

1 Find the area of these triangles.

a $A(-2, 3)$, $B(0, -4)$, $C(5, 6)$ **b** $P(-3, 1)$, $Q(5, -3)$, $R(2, 4)$

2 Find the area of these quadrilaterals.

a $A(1, 8)$, $B(-4, 5)$, $C(-2, -3)$, $D(4, -2)$

b $P(2, 7)$, $Q(-5, 6)$, $R(-3, -4)$, $S(7, 2)$

3 Triangle PQR where $P(1, 4)$, $Q(-3, -4)$ and $R(7, k)$ is right-angled at Q.

a Find the value of k. **b** Find the area of triangle PQR.

4 A is the point $(-4, 0)$ and B is the point $(2, 3)$.

M is the midpoint of the line AB.

Point C is such that $\overrightarrow{MC} = \begin{pmatrix} 3 \\ -6 \end{pmatrix}$.

a Find the coordinates of M and C.

b Show that CM is perpendicular to AB.

c Find the area of triangle ABC.

5 Angle ABC is 90° and M is the midpoint of the line AB.

The point C lies on the y-axis.

a Find the coordinates of B and C.

b Find the area of triangle ABC.

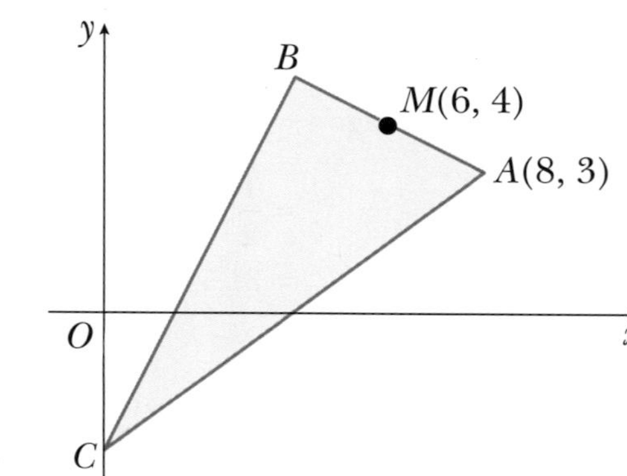

6 A is the point $(-4, 5)$ and B is the point $(5, 8)$.

The perpendicular to the line AB at the point [illegible] crosses the y-axis at the point C.

a Find the coordinates of C.

b Find the area of triangle ABC.

7 AB is parallel to DC and BC is perpendicular to AB.

a Find the coordinates of C.

b Find the area of trapezium $ABCD$.

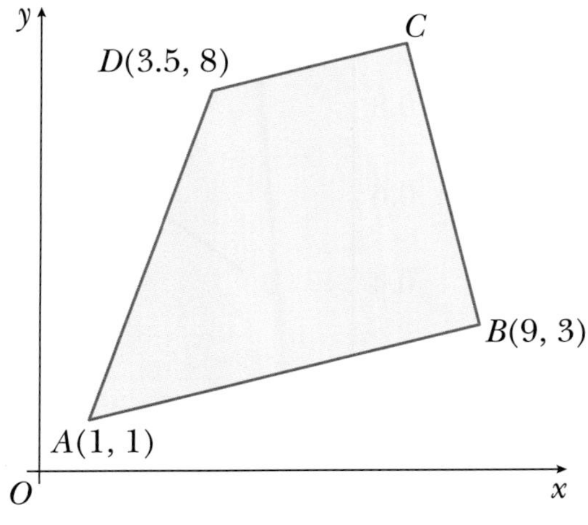

8 $ABCD$ is a square.

A is the point $(-2, 0)$ and C is the point $(6, 4)$.

AC and BD are diagonals of the square, which intersect at M.

a Find the coordinates of M, B and D.

b Find the area of $ABCD$.

9 The coordinates of 3 of the vertices of a parallelogram $ABCD$ are $A(-4, 3)$, $B(5, -5)$ and $C(15, -1)$.

a Find the coordinates of the points of intersection of the diagonals.

b Find the coordinates of the point D.

c Find the area of parallelogram $ABCD$.

7.5 Converting from a non-linear equation to linear form

Some situations in the real world can be modelled using an equation.

Consider an experiment where a simple pendulum, of length L cm, travels from A to B and back to A in a time of T seconds. The table shows the time taken, T, for different lengths L.

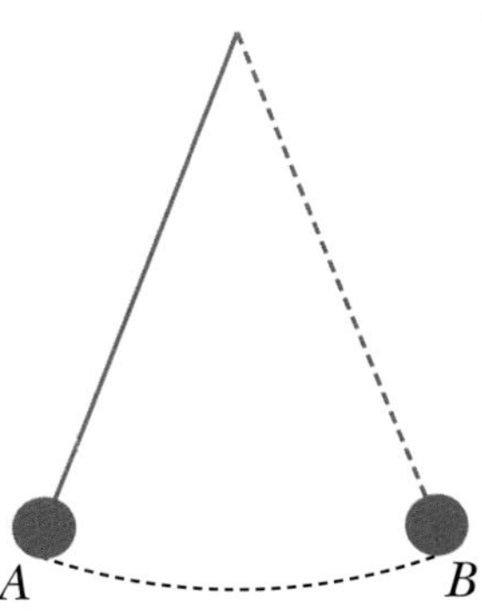

L	5	10	15	20	25	30
T	0.45	0.63	0.78	0.90	1.00	1.10

When the graph of T against L is drawn, the points lie on a curve. They do not lie on a straight line.

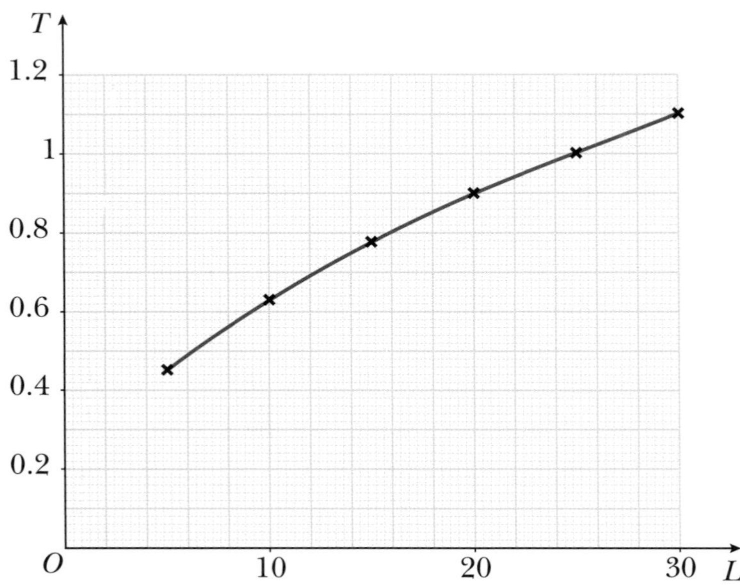

So how can you find the equation of the curve?

If you are told that the rule connecting the variables T and L is believed to be $T = a\sqrt{L}$, you should draw the graph of T against $\sqrt{L}$. To do this, you must first make a table of values for T and $\sqrt{L}$.

$\sqrt{L}$	2.24	3.16	3.87	4.47	5.00	5.48
T	0.45	0.63	0.78	0.90	1.00	1.10

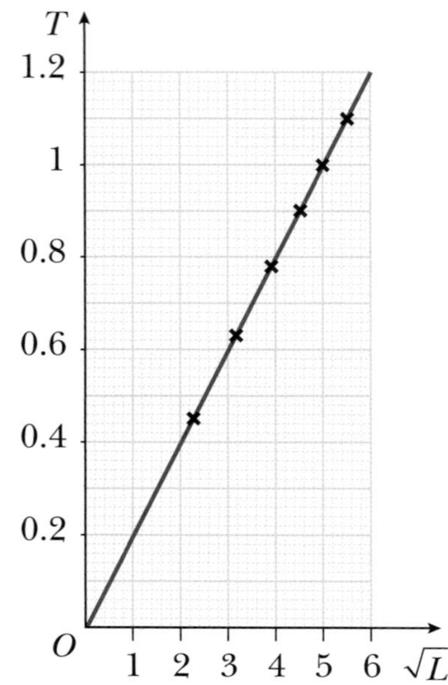

The fact that the points now lie on a straight line confirms the belief that the rule connecting the variables T and L is $T = a\sqrt{L}$.

The gradient of the straight line tells you the value of a.

Using the two end points, gradient $= \dfrac{1.1 - 0.45}{5.48 - 2.24} \approx 0.2$.

Hence the approximate rule connecting T and L is

$$T = 0.2\sqrt{L}$$

In the example above you have converted from a non-linear graph to a linear graph.

Before you can model more complicated relationships, you must first learn how to choose suitable variables for Y and X to convert from a non-linear equation into the linear form $Y = mX + c$ where m is the gradient of the straight line and c is the Y-intercept.

WORKED EXAMPLE 10

Convert $y = ax + \dfrac{b}{x}$, where a and b are constants, into the form $Y = mX + c$.

Answers

Method 1 $\quad y = ax + \dfrac{b}{x}$

Multiplying both sides of the equation by x gives:

$$xy = ax^2 + b$$

Now compare $xy = ax^2 + b$ with $Y = mX + c$:

$$\begin{array}{ccccccc} \boxed{xy} & = & a & \boxed{x^2} & + & b \\ \uparrow & & \uparrow & \uparrow & & \uparrow \\ Y & = & m & X & + & c \end{array}$$

The non-linear equation $y = ax + \dfrac{b}{x}$ becomes the linear equation:

$Y = mX + c$, where $Y = xy$, $X = x^2$, $m = a$ and $c = b$

Method 2 $\quad y = ax + \dfrac{b}{x}$

Dividing both sides of the equation by x gives:

$$\frac{y}{x} = a + \frac{b}{x^2}$$

Now compare $\dfrac{y}{x} = a + \dfrac{b}{x^2}$ with $Y = mX + c$:

$$\begin{array}{ccccccc} \boxed{\frac{y}{x}} & = & b & \boxed{\frac{1}{x^2}} & + & a \\ \uparrow & & \uparrow & \uparrow & & \uparrow \\ Y & = & m & X & + & c \end{array}$$

The non-linear equation $y = ax + \dfrac{b}{x}$ becomes the linear equation:

$Y = mX + c$, where $Y = \dfrac{y}{x}$, $X = \dfrac{1}{x^2}$, $m = b$ and $c = a$

It is important to note that the variables X and Y in $Y = mX + c$ must contain only the original variables x and y. They must not contain the unknown constants a and b.

Similarly the constants m and c must contain only the original unknown constants a and b. They must not contain the variables x and y.

WORKED EXAMPLE 11

Convert $y = ae^{-bx}$, where a and b are constants, into the form $Y = mX + c$.

Answers

$$y = ae^{-bx}$$

Taking natural logarithms of both sides gives

$$\ln y = \ln (ae^{-bx})$$
$$\ln y = \ln a + \ln e^{-bx}$$
$$\ln y = \ln a - bx$$
$$\ln y = -bx + \ln a$$

Now compare $\ln y = -bx + \ln a$ with $Y = mX + c$:

$$\ln y = -b\,x + \ln a$$
$$Y = m\,X + c$$

The non-linear equation $y = ae^{-bx}$ becomes the linear equation:

$Y = mX + c$, where $Y = \ln y$, $X = x$, $m = -b$ and $c = \ln a$

Exercise 7.5

1 Convert each of these non-linear equations into the form $Y = mX + c$, where a and b are constants. State clearly what the variables X and Y and the constants m and c represent.

(Note: there may be more than one way to do this.)

a $y = ax^2 + b$ **b** $y = ax + \frac{b}{x}$ **c** $y = ax^2 - bx$

d $y(a - x) = bx$ **e** $y = a\sqrt{x} + \frac{b}{\sqrt{x}}$ **f** $y = \frac{a}{x^2} + b$

g $x = axy + by$ **h** $\frac{1}{y} = a\sqrt{x} - \frac{b}{\sqrt{x}}$

2 Convert each of these non-linear equations into the form $Y = mX + c$, where a and b are constants. State clearly what the variables X and Y and the constants m and c represent.

(Note: there may be more than one way to do this.)

a $y = 10^{ax+b}$ **b** $y = e^{ax-b}$ **c** $y = ax^b$

d $y = ab^x$ **e** $x^a y^b = e^2$ **f** $xa^y = b$

g $a = e^{x^2+by}$ **h** $y = ae^{bx}$

7.6 Converting from linear form to a non-linear equation

WORKED EXAMPLE 12

Find y in terms of x.

a

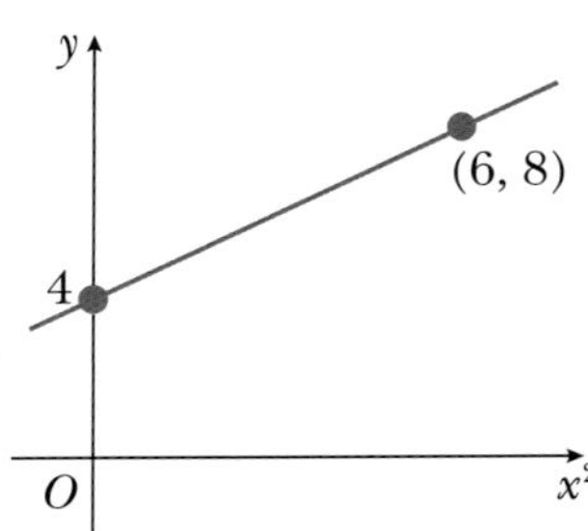

b

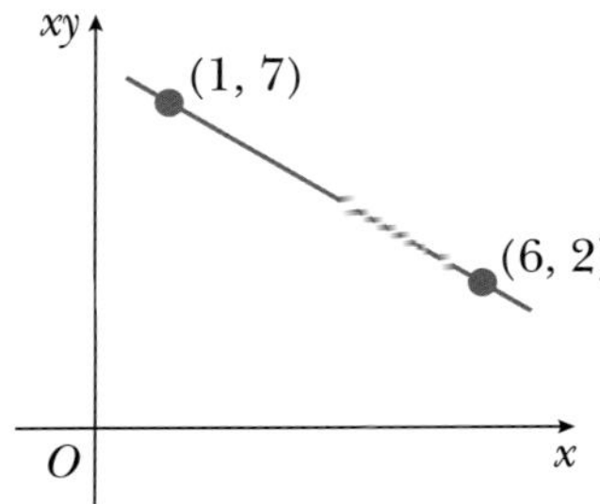

Answers

a The linear equation is $Y = mX + c$, where $Y = y$ and $X = x^2$.

Gradient $= m = \dfrac{8-4}{6-0} = \dfrac{2}{3}$

Y-intercept $= c = 4$

Hence $Y = \dfrac{2}{3}X + 4$.

The non-linear equation is $y = \dfrac{2}{3}x^2 + 4$.

b The linear equation is $Y = mX + c$, where $Y = xy$ and $X = x$.

Gradient $= m = \dfrac{2-7}{6-1} = -1$

Using $Y = mX + c$, $m = -1$, $X = 6$ and $Y = 2$

$2 = -1 \times 6 + c$

$c = 8$

Hence $Y = -X + 8$.

The non-linear equation is $xy = -x + 8$

$y = -1 + \dfrac{8}{x}$.

WORKED EXAMPLE 13

Variables x and y are such that $y = a \times b^x$, where a and b are constants.

The diagram shows the graph of $\lg y$ against x, passing through the points $(2, 5)$ and $(6, 13)$.

Find the value of a and the value of b.

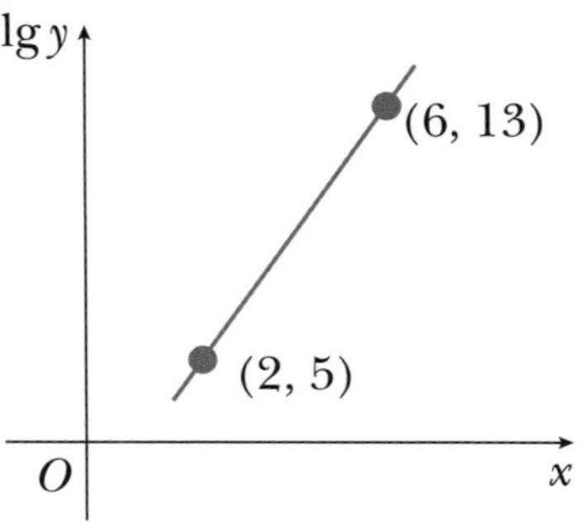

Answers

$$y = a \times b^x$$

Taking logarithms of both sides gives:

$$\lg y = \lg\ (a \times b^x)$$

$$\lg y = \lg a + \lg b^x$$

$$\lg y = x \lg b + \lg a$$

Now compare $\lg y = x \lg b + \lg a$ with $Y = mX + c$:

$$\lg y = \lg b \ x + \lg a$$

$$Y = m \ X + c$$

Gradient $= m = \dfrac{13 - 5}{6 - 2} = 2$

$$\lg b = 2$$

$$b = 10^2$$

Using $Y = mX + c$, $m = 2$, $X = 2$ and $Y = 5$

$$5 = 2 \times 2 + c$$

$$c = 1$$

$$\lg a = 1$$

$$a = 10^1$$

Hence $a = 10$ and $b = 100$.

Exercise 7.6

1 The graphs show part of a straight line obtained by plotting y against some function of x.

For each graph, express y in terms of x.

a

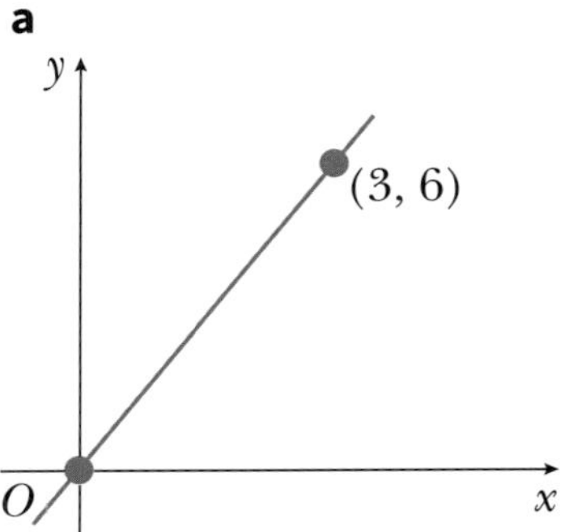

b

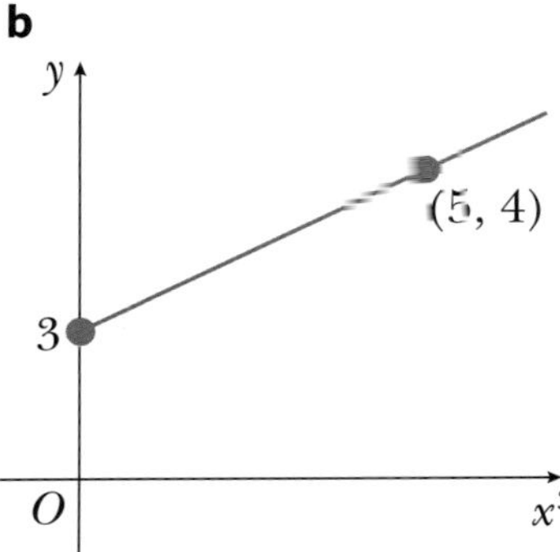

c

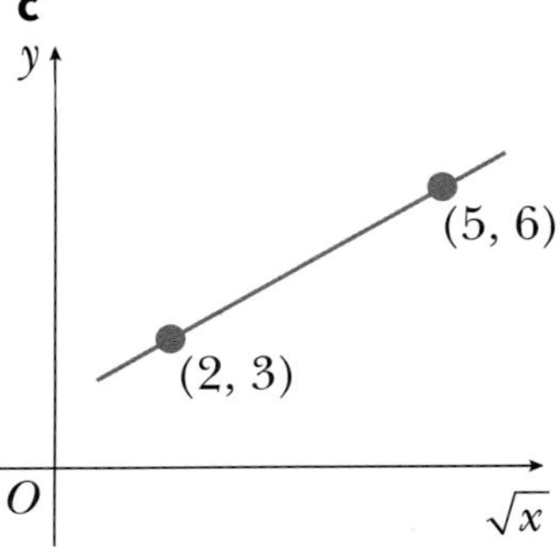

d

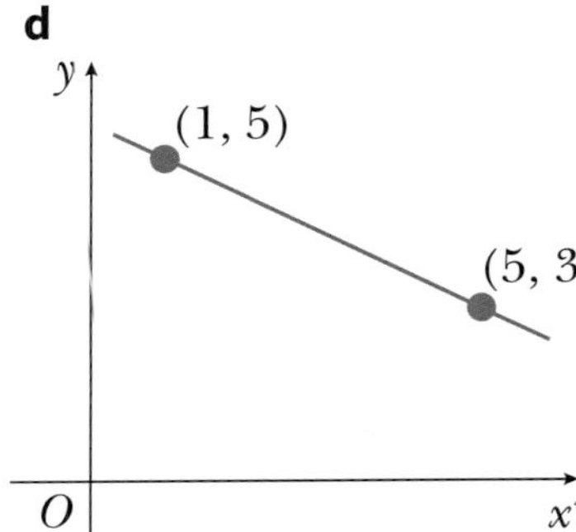

e

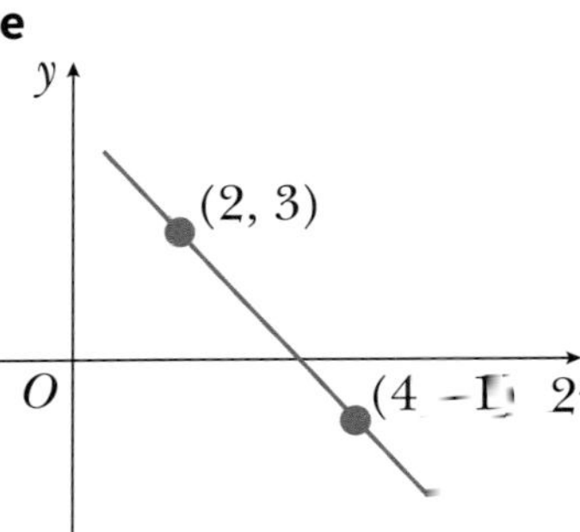

f

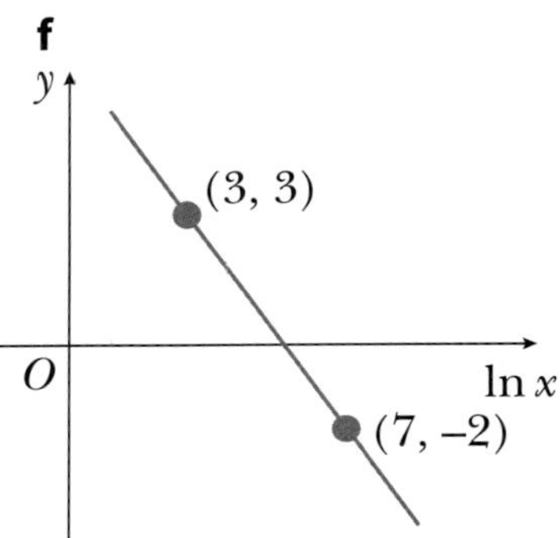

2 For each of the following relations

i express y in terms of x **ii** find the value of y when $x = 2$.

a

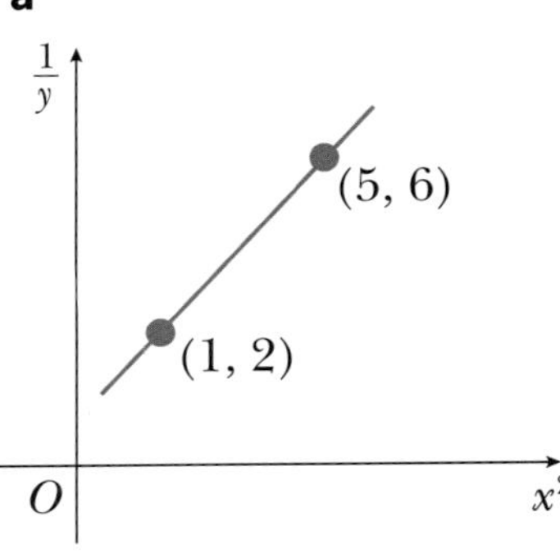

b

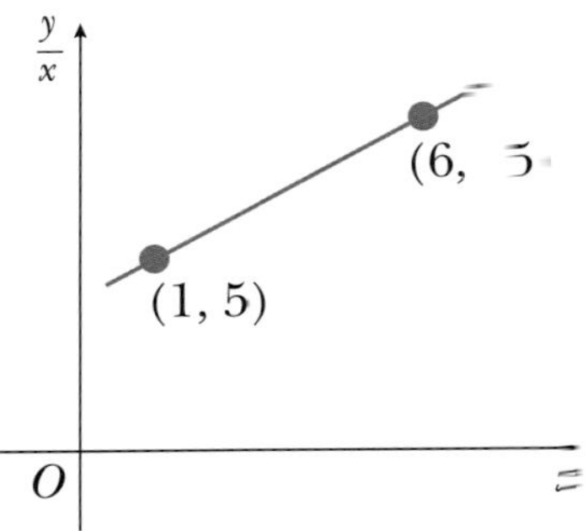

c

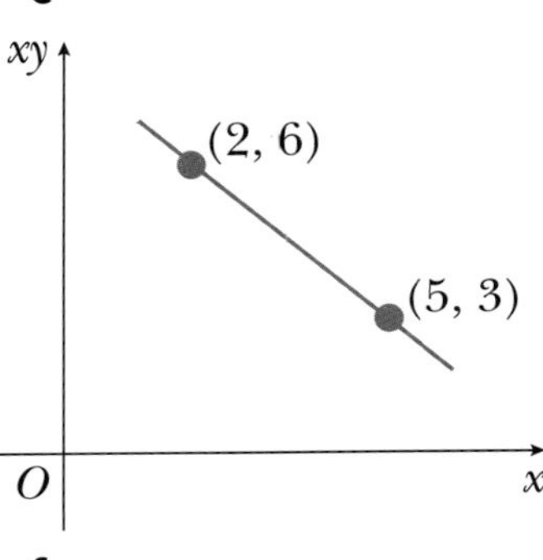

d

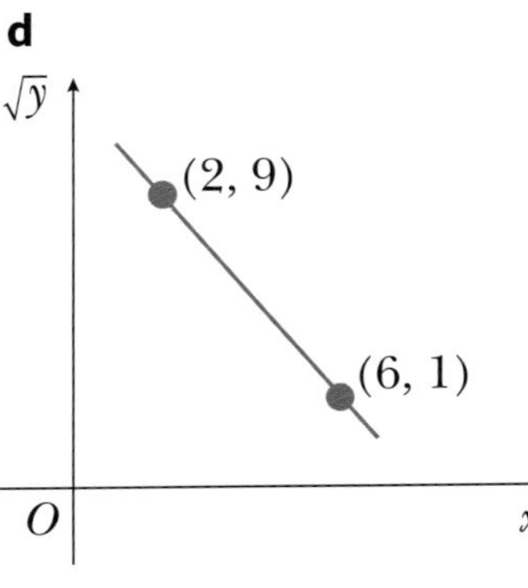

e

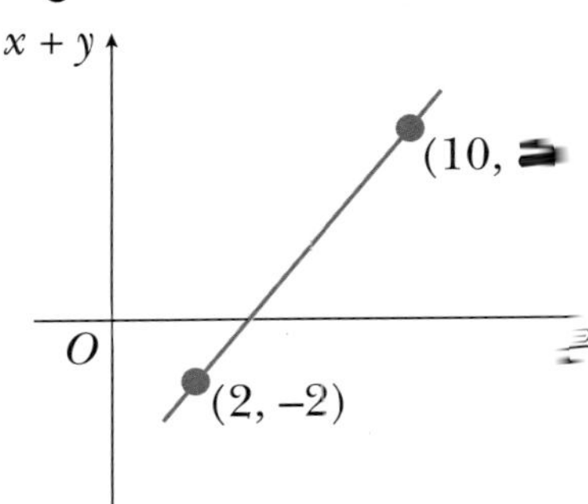

f

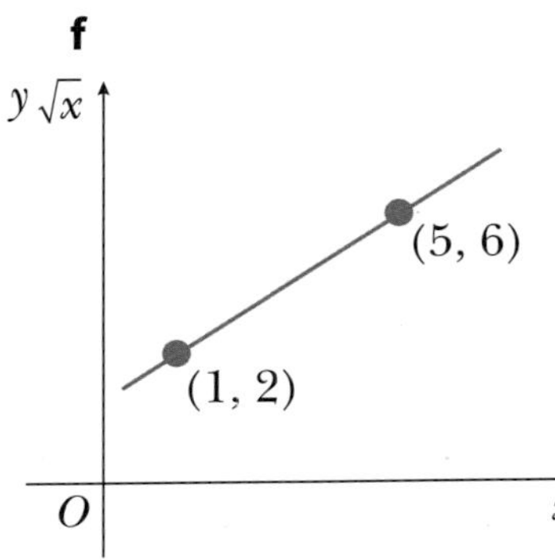

3 Variables x and y are related so that, when $\frac{y}{x^2}$ is plotted on the vertical axis and x^3 is plotted on the horizontal axis, a straight-line graph passing through (2, 12) and (6, 4) is obtained.

Express y in terms of x.

4 Variables x and y are related so that, when y^2 is plotted on the vertical axis and 2^x is plotted on the horizontal axis, a straight-line graph which passes through the point (8, 49) with gradient 3 is obtained.

a Express y^2 in terms of 2^x.

b Find the value of x when $y = 11$.

5 Variables x and y are related so that, when $\frac{y}{x}$ is plotted on the vertical axis and x is plotted on the horizontal axis, a straight-line graph passing through the points (2, 4) and (5, −2) is obtained.

a Express y in terms of x.

b Find the value of x and the value of y such that $\frac{y}{x} = 3$.

6 Variables x and y are related so that, when e^y is plotted on the vertical axis and x^2 is plotted on the horizontal axis, a straight-line graph passing through the points (3, 4) and (8, 9) is obtained.

a Express e^y in terms of x.

b Express y in terms of x.

7 Variables x and y are related so that, when $\lg y$ is plotted on the vertical axis and x is plotted on the horizontal axis, a straight-line graph passing through the points (6, 2) and (10, 8) is obtained.

a Express $\lg y$ in terms of x.

b Express y in terms of x, giving your answer in the form $y = a \times 10^{bx}$.

8 Variables x and y are related so that, when $\lg y$ is plotted on the vertical axis and $\lg x$ is plotted on the horizontal axis, a straight-line graph passing through the points (4, 8) and (8, 14) is obtained.

a Express y in terms of x, giving your answer in the form $y = a \times x^b$.

b Find the value of x when $y = 51.2$.

9 Variables x and y are related so that, when $\ln y$ is plotted on the vertical axis and $\ln x$ is plotted on the horizontal axis, a straight-line graph passing through the points (1, 2) and (4, 11) is obtained.

a Express $\ln y$ in terms of x.

b Express y in terms of x.

10 Variables x and y are such that, when $\ln y$ is plotted on the vertical axis and $\ln x$ is plotted on the horizontal axis, a straight-line graph passing through the points (2.5, 7.7) and (3.7, 5.3) is obtained.

a Find the value of $\ln y$ when $\ln x = 0$.

b Given that $y = a \times x^b$, find the value of a and the value of b.

7.7 Finding relationships from data

When experimental data is collected for two variables, it is useful if you can then establish the mathematical relationship connecting the two variables.

If the data forms a straight-line when a graph is plotted, it is easy to establish the connection using the equation $y = mx + c$.

It is more usual, however, for the data to lie on a curve and to be connected by a non-linear equation.

In this section, you will learn how to apply what you have just learnt in sections **7.5** and **7.6** to find the non-linear equation connecting two variables.

WORKED EXAMPLE 14

x	5	10	20	40	80
y	2593	1596	983	605	372

The table shows experimental values of the variables x and y.

a By plotting a suitable straight-line graph, show that x and y are related by the equation $y = k \times x^n$, where k and n are constants.

b Use your graph to estimate the value of k and the value of n.

Answers

a

$y = k \times x^n$ — take logs of both sides

$\lg y = \lg (k \times x^n)$ — use the multiplication law

$\lg y = \lg k + \lg x^n$ — use the power law

$\lg y = n \lg x + \lg k$

Now compare $\lg y = n \lg x + \lg k$ with $Y = mX + c$:

$$\lg y = n \lg x + \lg k$$
$$Y = m\,X + c$$

Hence the graph of $\lg y$ against $\lg x$ needs to be drawn where

- gradient $= n$
- intercept on vertical axis $= \lg k$.

Table of values is

$\lg x$	0.699	1.000	1.301	1.602	1.903
$\lg y$	3.414	3.203	2.993	2.782	2.571

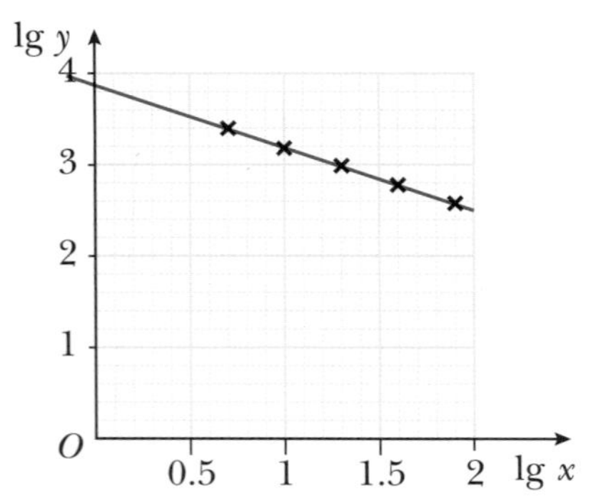

b The points form an approximate straight line, so x and y are related by the equation
$y = k \times x^n$.

$$n = \text{gradient}$$
$$\approx \frac{2.571 - 3.414}{1.903 - 0.699}$$
$$\approx -0.7$$
$$\lg k = \text{intercept on vertical axis}$$
$$\lg k \approx 3.9$$
$$k \approx 10^{3.9}$$
$$k \approx 7943$$

WORKED EXAMPLE 15

x	2	4	6	8	0
y	4.75	2.19	1.42	1.05	0.83

The table shows experimental values of the variables x and y.

The variables are known to be related by the equation $y = \frac{a + bx}{x^2}$, where a and b are constants.

a Draw the graph of x^2y against x.

b Use your graph to estimate the value of a and the value of b.

An alternate method for obtaining a straight-line graph for the equation $y = \frac{a + bx}{x^2}$ is to plot xy on the vertical axis and $\frac{1}{x}$ on the horizontal axis.

c Without drawing a second graph, estimate the gradient and the intercept on the vertical axis of this graph.

Answers

a First make a table of values for of x^2y and x:

x	2	4	6	8	10
x^2y	19	35.0	51.1	67.2	83

The graph of x^2y against x is:

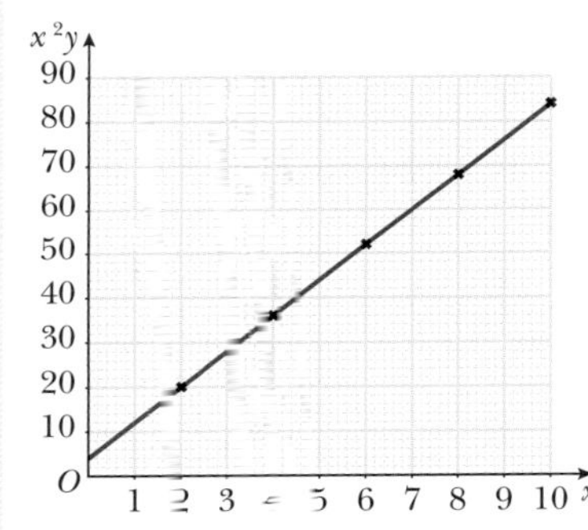

b Using $y = \frac{a + bx}{x^2}$

$x^2y = bx + a$

Now compare $x^2y = bx + a$ with $Y = mX + c$:

$$\underset{Y}{x^2y} = \underset{m}{b}\ \underset{X}{x} + \underset{c}{a}$$

Hence, b = gradient $= \frac{83 - 19}{10 - 2} = 8$ and a = y-intercept = 3

$a = 3$ and $b = 8$

c Using $y = \frac{a + bx}{x^2}$

$$xy = \frac{a + bx}{x}$$

$$xy = \frac{a}{x} + b$$

Now compare $xy = \frac{a}{x} + b$ with $Y = mX + c$:

$$\underset{Y}{xy} = \underset{m}{a} \times \underset{X}{\left(\frac{1}{x}\right)} + \underset{c}{b}$$

Gradient $= a = 3$ and intercept on vertical axis $= b = 8$.

Exercise 7.7

1

x	0.5	1.0	1.5	2.0	2.5
y	1.00	3.00	3.67	4.00	4.20

The table shows experimental values of the variables x and y.

a Copy and complete the following table.

x					
xy					

b Draw the graph of xy against x.

c Express y in terms of x.

d Find the value of x and the value of y for which $xy = 2$.

2

x	0.1	0.2	0.3	0.4	0.5
y	0.111	0.154	0.176	0.189	0.200

The table shows experimental values of the variables x and y.

a Copy and complete the following table.

$\frac{1}{x}$					
$\frac{1}{y}$					

b Draw the graph of $\frac{1}{y}$ against $\frac{1}{x}$.

c Express y in terms of x.

d Find the value of x when $y = 0.16$.

3

x	1	2	3	4	5
y	12.8	7.6	6.4	6.2	6.4

The table shows experimental values of the variables x and y.

a Draw the graph of xy against x^2.

b Use your graph to express y in terms of x.

c Find the value of x and the value of y for which $xy = 12.288$.

4 The mass, m grams, of a radioactive substance is given by the formula $m = m_0 e^{-kt}$, where t is the time in days after the mass was first recorded and m_0 and k are constants.

The table below shows experimental values of t and m.

t	10	20	30	40	50
m	40.9	33.5	27.4	22.5	18.4

a Draw the graph of $\ln m$ against t.

b Use your graph to estimate the value of m_0 and k.

c Estimate the value of m when $t = 27$.

5

x	10	100	1000	10 000
y	15	75	378	1893

The table shows experimental values of the variables x and y.

The variables are known to be related by the equation $y = kx^n$ where k and n are constants.

a Draw the graph of $\lg y$ against $\lg x$.

b Use your graph to estimate the value of k and n.

6

x	2	4	6	8	10
y	12.8	32.8	83.9	214.7	549.8

The table shows experimental values of the variables x and y.

The variables are known to be related by the equation $y = a \times b^x$ where a and b are constants.

a Draw the graph of $\lg y$ against x.

b Use your graph to estimate the value of a and the value of b.

7

x	2	4	6	8	10
y	4.9	13.3	36.2	98.3	267.1

The table shows experimental values of the variables x and y.

The variables are known to be related by the equation $y = a \times e^{nx}$ where a and n are constants.

a Draw the graph of $\ln y$ against x.

b Use your graph to estimate the value of a and the value of n.

8

x	2	4	6	8	10
y	30.0	44.7	66.7	99.5	148.4

The table shows experimental values of the variables x and y.

The variables are known to be related by the equation $y = e^{ax+b}$ where a and b are constants.

a Draw the graph of $\ln y$ against x.

b Use your graph to estimate the value of a and the value of b.

c Estimate the value of x when $y = 50$.

9

x	2	4	6	8	10
y	0.10	0.33	1.08	3.48	11.29

The table shows experimental values of the variables x and y.

The variables are known to be related by the equation $y = 10^a \times b^x$, where a and b are constants.

a Draw the graph of $\lg y$ against x.

b Use your graph to estimate the value of a and the value of b.

c Estimate the value of x when $y = 5$.

10

x	0.2	0.4	0.5	0.7	0.9
y	36	12	9	6	4.5

The table shows experimental values of the variables x and y.

The variables are known to be related by the equation $y = \dfrac{a}{x+b}$, where a and b are constants.

a Draw the graph of y against xy.

b Use your graph to estimate the value of a and the value of b.

An alternate method for obtaining a straight-line graph for the equation $y = \dfrac{a}{x+b}$ is to plot x on the vertical axis and $\dfrac{1}{y}$ on the horizontal axis.

c Without drawing a second graph, estimate the gradient and the intercept on the vertical axis of this graph.

11

x	2	5	15	25	60
y	11.5	5.54	2.30	1.53	0.76

The table shows experimental values of the variables x and y.

a Draw the graph of $\ln y$ against $\ln x$.

b Express y in terms of x.

An alternate method for obtaining the relationship between x and y is to plot $\lg y$ on the vertical axis and $\lg x$ on the horizontal axis.

c Without drawing a second graph, find the gradient and the intercept on the vertical axis of this graph.

Summary

Length of a line segment, gradient and midpoint

Length of $PQ = \sqrt{(x_2 - x_1)^2 + (y_2 - y_1)^2}$

Gradient of $PQ = \dfrac{y_2 - y_1}{x_2 - x_1}$

Midpoint of $PQ = \left(\dfrac{x_1 + x_2}{2}, \dfrac{y_1 + y_2}{2}\right)$

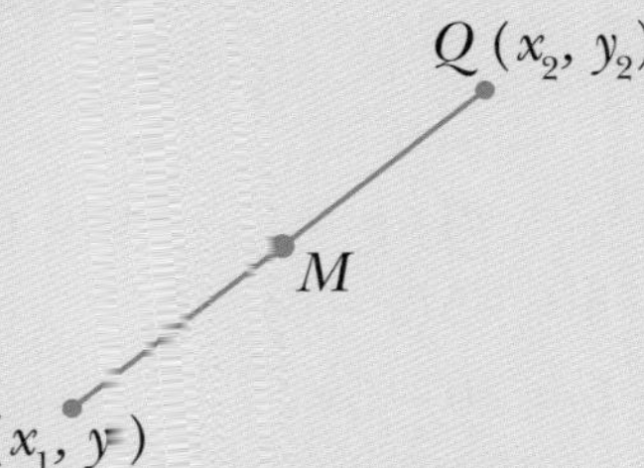

Parallel and perpendicular lines

If two lines are parallel then their gradients are equal.

If a line has a gradient of m, a line perpendicular to it has a gradient of $-\dfrac{1}{m}$.

If the gradients of the two perpendicular lines are m_1 and m_2, then $m_1 \times m_2 = -1$.

The equation of a straight line

$y = mx + c$ where m = the gradient and c = the y-intercept.

$y - y_1 = m(x - x_1)$ where m = the gradient and (x_1, y_1) is a known point on the line.

Non-linear equations

To convert a non-linear equation involving x and y into a linear equation, express the equation in the form $Y = mX + c$, where X and Y are expressions in x and/or y.

Examination questions

Worked example

Solutions to this question by accurate drawing will not be accepted.

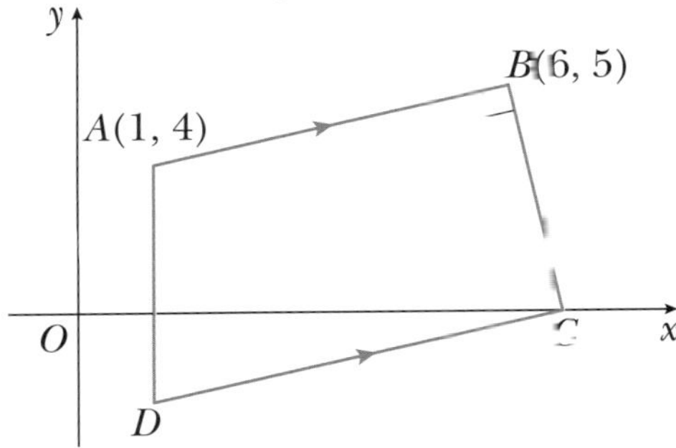

The diagram shows a quadrilateral $ABCD$ in which A is the point (1, 4), and B is the point (6, 5). Angle ABC is a right angle and the point C lies on the x-axis. The line AD is parallel to the y-axis and the line CD is parallel to BA. Find

a the equation of the line CD, [5]

b the area of the quadrilateral $ABCD$. [4]

Cambridge IGCSE Additional Mathematics 0606 Paper 21 Q10i,ii Nov 2010

Answers

a Gradient of $AB = \frac{5-4}{6-1} = \frac{1}{5}$ use $m_1 m_2 = -1$ to find gradient of BC

Gradient of $BC = -5$

Equation of BC: $y - y_1 = m(x - x_1)$ use $m = -5$, $x_1 = 6$ and $y_1 = 5$

$$y - 5 = -5(x - 6)$$
$$y - 5 = 30 - 5x$$
$$y = 35 - 5x$$

When $y = 0$, $0 = 35 - 5x$

$$x = 7$$

C is the point (7, 0)

Equation of CD: $y - y_1 = m(x - x_1)$ use $m = \frac{1}{5}$, $x_1 = 7$ and $y_1 = 0$

$$y - 0 = \frac{1}{5}(x - 7)$$

Equation of CD is $y = \frac{1}{5}(x - 7)$

b AD is parallel to the y-axis, hence the x-coordinate of D is 1.

Substituting $x = 1$ into the equation $y = \frac{1}{5}(x - 7)$ gives $y = -1.2$.

Use the 'shoestring' method with $A(1, 4)$, $B(6, 5)$, $C(7, 0)$ and $D(1, -1.2)$.

$$\text{Area of } ABCD = \frac{1}{2}\left| \begin{matrix} 1 & 6 & 7 & 1 & 1 \\ 4 & 5 & 0 & -1.2 & 4 \end{matrix} \right|$$

$$= \frac{1}{2}|5 + 0 + (-8.4) + 4 - 24 - 35 - 0 - (-1.2)|$$

$$= \frac{1}{2}|-57.2|$$

$$= 28.6 \text{ units}^2$$

Exercise 7.8

Exam exercise

1 The point P lies on the line joining $A(-2, 3)$ and $B(10, 19)$ such that $AP : PB = 1:3$.

a Show that the x-coordinate of P is 1 and find the y-coordinate of P. [2]

b Find the equation of the line through P which is perpendicular to AB. [3]

The line through P which is perpendicular to AB meets the y-axis at the point Q.

c Find the area of the triangle AQB. [3]

Cambridge IGCSE Additional Mathematics 0606 Paper 11 Q8 Nov 2014

2 The table shows values of variables V and p.

V	10	50	100	200
p	95.0	8.5	3.0	1.1

a By plotting a suitable straight line graph, show that V and p are related by the equation $p = kV^n$, where k and n are constants. [4]

Use your graph to find

b the value of n, [2]

c the value of p when $V = 35$. [2]

Cambridge IGCSE Additional Mathematics 0606 Paper 11 Q8i,ii,iii Jun 2014

3 **Solutions to this question by accurate drawing will not be accepted.**

The points $A(-3, 2)$ and $B(1, 4)$ are vertices of an isosceles triangle ABC, where angle $B = 90°$.

a Find the length of the line AB. [1]

b Find the equation of the line BC. [3]

c Find the coordinates of each of the two possible positions of C. [6]

Cambridge IGCSE Additional Mathematics 0606 Paper 11 Q10i,ii,iii Nov 2013

4 Variables x and y are such that $y = Ab^x$, where A and b are constants. The diagram shows the graph of $\ln y$ against x, passing through the points (2, 4) and (8, 10).

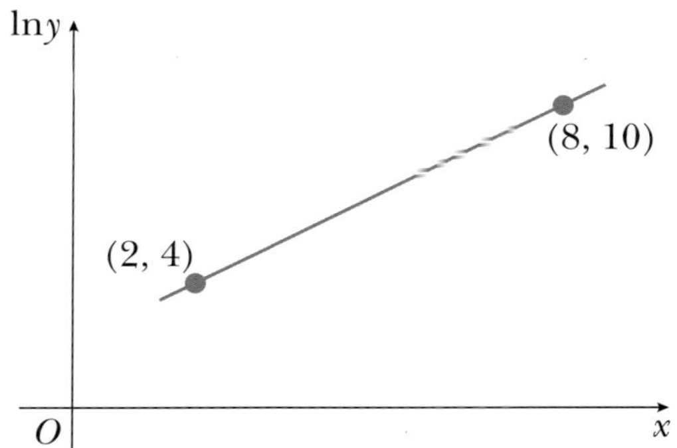

Find the value of A and of b. [5]

Cambridge IGCSE Additional Mathematics 0606 Paper 11 Q2 Jun 2013

5 **Solutions to this question by accurate drawing will not be accepted.**

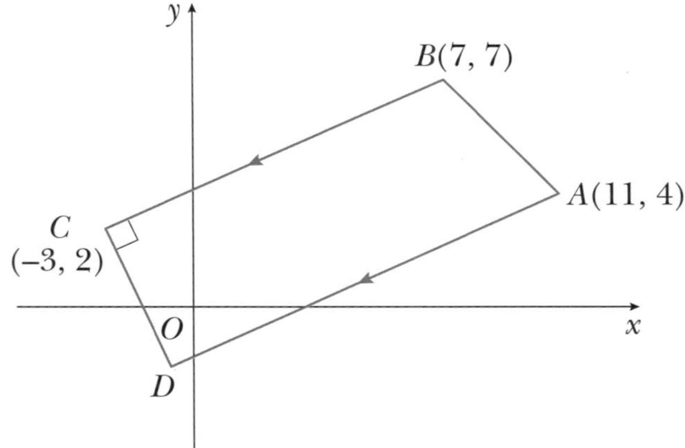

The diagram shows a trapezium $ABCD$ with vertices $A(11, 4)$, $B(7, 7)$, $C(-3, 2)$ and D.
The side AD is parallel to BC and the side CD is perpendicular to BC.
Find the area of the trapezium $ABCD$. [9]

Cambridge IGCSE Additional Mathematics 0606 Paper 21 Q10 Jun 2012

6 The table shows experimental values of two variables x and y.

x	1	2	3	4	5
y	3.40	2.92	2.93	3.10	3.34

It is known that x and y are related by the equation $y = \dfrac{a}{\sqrt{x}} + bx$, where a and b are constants.

a Complete the following table.

$x\sqrt{x}$					
$y\sqrt{x}$					

[1]

b On a grid plot $y\sqrt{x}$ against $x\sqrt{x}$ and draw a straight line graph. [2]

c Use your graph to estimate the value of a and of b. [3]

d Estimate the value of y when x is 1.5. [1]

Cambridge IGCSE Additional Mathematics 0606 Paper 21 Q9i-iv Nov 2011

7 The points A and B have coordinates $(-2, 15)$ and $(3, 5)$ respectively.
The perpendicular to the line AB at the point $A(-2, 15)$ crosses the y-axis at the point C.
Find the area of triangle ABC. [6]

Cambridge IGCSE Additional Mathematics 0606 Paper 11 Q7 Jun 2011

8 Variables x and y are such that, when $\ln y$ is plotted against $\ln x$, a straight line graph passing through the points (2, 5.8) and (6, 3.8) is obtained.

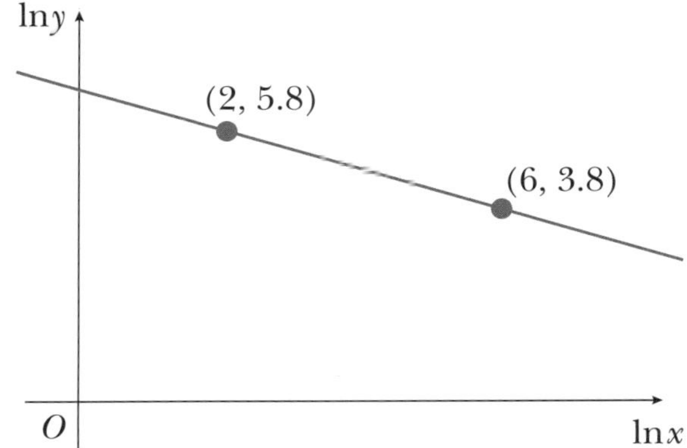

a Find the value of $\ln y$ when $\ln x = 0$. [2]

b Given that $y = Ax^b$, find the value of A and of b. [5]

Cambridge IGCSE Additional Mathematics 0606 Paper 11 Q8i,ii Nov 2010

9 **Solutions to this question by accurate drawing will not be accepted.**

The points A and B have coordinates (2, –1) and (6, 5) respectively.

i Find the equation of the perpendicular bisector of AB, giving your answer in the form $ax + by = c$, where a, b and c are integers. [4]

The point C has coordinates (10, –2).

ii Find the equation of the line through C which is parallel to AB. [2]

iii Calculate the length of BC. [2]

iv Show that triangle ABC is isosceles. [1]

Cambridge IGCSE Additional Mathematics 0606 Paper 22 Q8 Mar 2015

10 The curve $y = xy + x^2 - 4$ intersects the line $y = 3x - 1$ at the points A and B. Find the equation of the perpendicular bisector of the line AB. [8]

Cambridge IGCSE Additional Mathematics 0606 Paper 11 Q5 Jun 2015

11 **Solutions to this question by accurate drawing will not be accepted.**

Two points A and B have coordinates (–3, 2) and (5, 8) respectively.

i Find the coordinates of C, the point where the line AB cuts the y-axis. [3]

ii Find the coordinates of D, the mid-point of AB. [1]

iii Find the equation of the perpendicular bisector of AB. [2]

The perpendicular bisector of AB cuts the y-axis at the point E.

iv Find the coordinates of E. [1]

v Show that the area of triangle ABE is four times the area of triangle ECD. [3]

Cambridge IGCSE Additional Mathematics 0606 Paper 21 Q8 Nov 2015

Chapter 8
Circular measure

This section will show you how to:

- use radian measure
- solve problems involving the arc length and sector area of a circle.

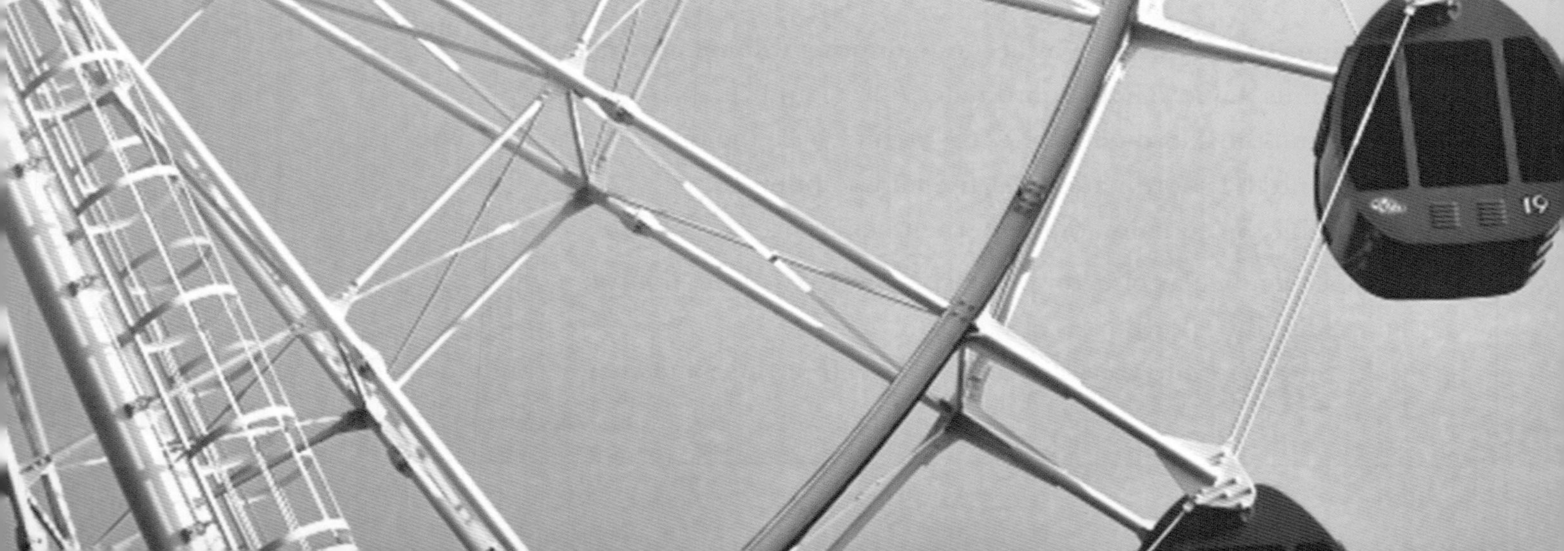

8.1 Circular measure

Have you ever wondered why there are 360 degrees in one complete revolution?

The original reason for choosing the degree as a unit of angular measure is actually unknown but there are a number of different theories:

- ancient astronomers claimed that the Sun advanced in its path by one degree each day and that a solar year consisted of 360 days
- the ancient Babylonians divided the circle into 6 equilateral triangles and then subdivided each angle at O into 60 further parts, resulting in 360 divisions in one complete revolution
- 360 has many factors which makes division of the circle so much easier.

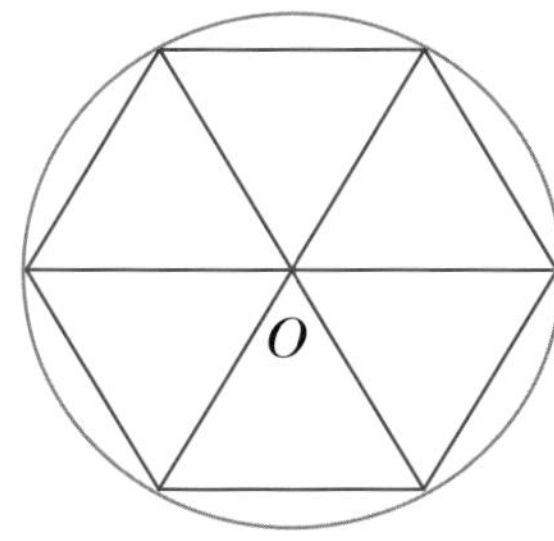

Degrees are not the only way in which you can measure angles. In this section you will learn how to use **radian** measure. This is sometimes referred to as the natural unit of angular measure and it is used extensively in mathematics because it can simplify many formulae and calculations.

In the diagram below, the magnitude of angle AOB is 1 radian (1 radian is written as 1 rad or 1^c).

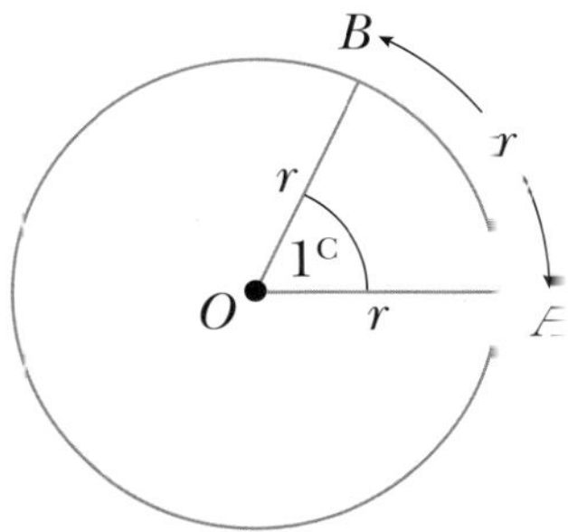

An arc equal in length to the radius of a circle subtends an angle of 1 radian at the centre.

It follows that the circumference (an arc of length $2\pi r$) subtends an angle of 2π radians at the centre.

$$2\pi \text{ radians} = 360°$$

$$\pi \text{ radians} = 180°$$

When an angle is written in terms of π, the radian symbol is usually omitted. Hence, $\pi = 180°$.

Converting from degrees to radians

Since $180° = \pi$, then $90° = \frac{\pi}{2}$, $45° = \frac{\pi}{4}$ etc.

Angles that are not simple fractions of 180° can be converted using the following rule:

> To change from degrees to radians, multiply by $\frac{\pi}{180}$.

Converting from radians to degrees

Since $\pi = 180°$, $\frac{\pi}{6} = 30°$, $\frac{\pi}{10} = 18°$ etc.

Angles that are not simple fractions of π can be converted using the following rule:

> To change from radians to degrees, multiply by $\frac{180}{\pi}$.

(It is useful to remember that 1 radian $= 1 \times \frac{180}{\pi} \approx 57°$.)

WORKED EXAMPLE 1

a Change 60° to radians, giving your answer in terms of π.

b Change $\frac{3\pi}{5}$ radians to degrees.

Answers

a **Method 1:**

$$180° = \pi \text{ radians}$$
$$\left(\frac{180}{3}\right)^\circ = \frac{\pi}{3} \text{ radians}$$
$$60° = \frac{\pi}{3} \text{ radians}$$

Method 2:

$$60° = \left(60 \times \frac{\pi}{180}\right) \text{ radians}$$
$$60° = \frac{\pi}{3} \text{ radians}$$

b **Method 1:**

$$\pi \text{ radians} = 180°$$
$$\frac{\pi}{5} \text{ radians} = 36°$$
$$\frac{3\pi}{5} \text{ radians} = 108°$$

Method 2:

$$\frac{3\pi}{5} \text{ radians} = \left(\frac{3\pi}{5} \times \frac{180}{\pi}\right)^\circ$$
$$\frac{3\pi}{5} \text{ radians} = 108°$$

Exercise 8.1

1 Change these angles to radians, in terms of π.

a $10°$ **b** $20°$ **c** $40°$ **d** $50°$ **e** $15°$

f $120°$ **g** $135°$ **h** $225°$ **i** $360°$ **j** $720°$

k $80°$ **l** $300°$ **m** $9°$ **n** $75°$ **o** $210°$

2 Change these angles to degrees.

a $\frac{\pi}{2}$ **b** $\frac{\pi}{6}$ **c** $\frac{\pi}{12}$ **d** $\frac{\pi}{9}$ **e** $\frac{2\pi}{3}$

f $\frac{4\pi}{5}$ **g** $\frac{7\pi}{10}$ **h** $\frac{5\pi}{12}$ **i** $\frac{3\pi}{20}$ **j** $\frac{9\pi}{10}$

k $\frac{6\pi}{5}$ **l** 3π **m** $\frac{7\pi}{4}$ **n** $\frac{8\pi}{3}$ **o** $\frac{9\pi}{2}$

3 Write each of these angles in radians correct to 3 sf.

a $32°$ **b** $55°$ **c** $84°$ **d** $128°$ **e** $247°$

4 Write each of these angles in degrees correct to 1 decimal place.

a 1.3 rad **b** 2.5 rad **c** 1.02 rad **d** 1.83 rad **e** 0.58 rad

5 Copy and complete the tables, giving your answers in terms of π.

a

Degrees	0	45	90	135	180	225	270	315	360
Radians	0				π				2π

b

Degrees	0	30	60	90	120	150	180	210	240	270	300	330	360
Radians	0						π						2π

6 Use your calculator to find

a sin 1.3 rad **b** tan 0.8 rad **c** sin 1.2 rad

d $\sin\frac{\pi}{2}$ **e** $\cos\frac{\pi}{3}$ **f** $\tan\frac{\pi}{4}$.

Note:
You do not need to change the angle to degrees. You should set the angle mode on your calculator to radians.

CHALLENGE Q

7 Anna is told the size of angle BAC in degrees and she is then asked to calculate the length of the line BC. She uses her calculator but forgets that her calculator is in radian mode. Luckily she still manages to obtain the correct answer. Given that angle BAC is between 10° and 15°, use graphing software to help you find the size of angle BAC in degrees correct to 2 decimal places.

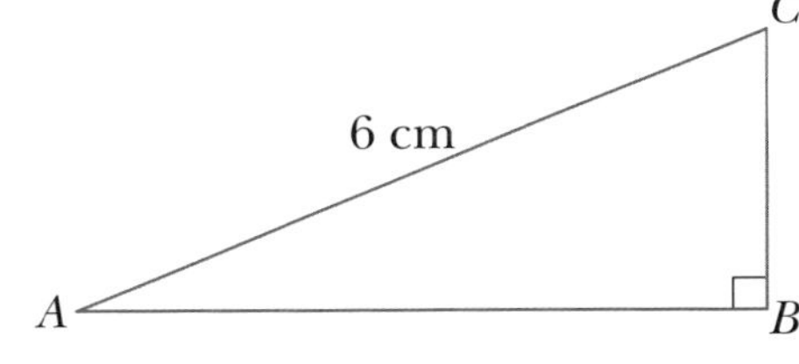

CLASS DISCUSSION

You should already be familiar with the following mathematical words that are used in circle questions.

chord | arc | sector | segment

Discuss and explain, with the aid of diagrams, the meaning of each of these words.

Explain what is meant by:

- minor arc and major arc
- minor sector and major sector
- minor segment and major segment.

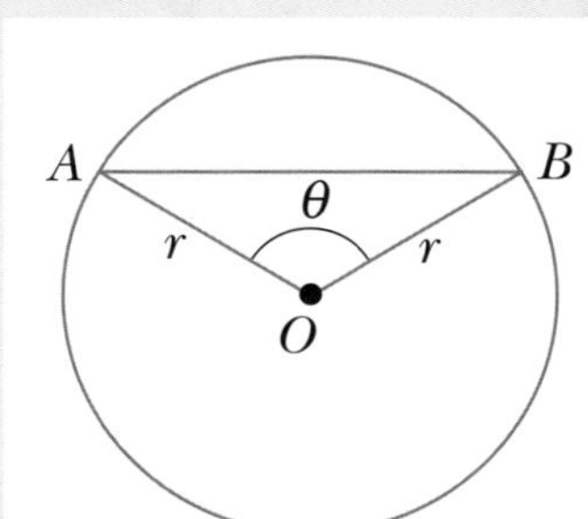

If you know the radius, r cm, and the angle θ (in degrees) at the centre of the circle, describe how you would find:

- arc length
- perimeter of sector
- perimeter of segment
- area of sector
- length of chord
- area of segment.

8.2 Length of an arc

From the definition of a radian, the arc that subtends an angle of 1 radian at the centre of the circle is of length r. Hence, if an arc subtends an angle of θ radians at the centre, the length of the arc is $r\theta$.

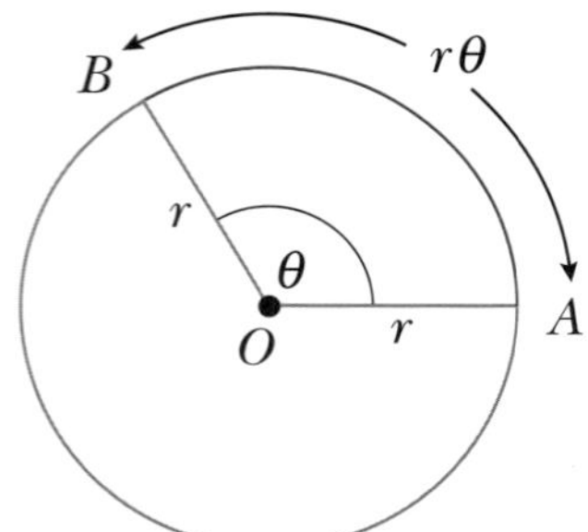

Arc length = $r\theta$

WORKED EXAMPLE 2

An arc subtends an angle of $\frac{\pi}{6}$ radians at the centre of a circle with radius 8 cm. Find the length of the arc in terms of π.

Answers

$$\text{Arc length} = r\theta$$
$$= 8 \times \frac{\pi}{6}$$
$$= \frac{4\pi}{3}\ \text{cm}$$

WORKED EXAMPLE 3

A sector has an angle of 2 radians and an arc length of 9.6 cm.
Find the radius of the sector.

Answers

Arc length $= r\theta$

$9.6 = r \times 2$

$r = 4.8\,\text{cm}$

WORKED EXAMPLE 4

The circle has radius 5 cm and centre O.

PQ is a tangent to the circle at the point P.

QRO is a straight line. Find

a angle POQ, in radians

b QR

c the perimeter of the shaded region.

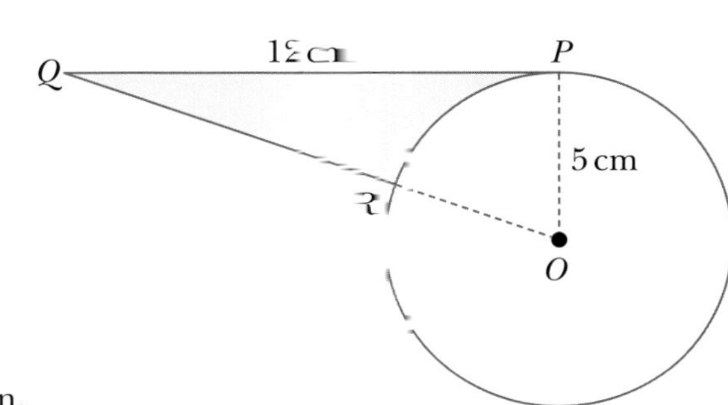

Answers

a $\tan POQ = \frac{12}{5}$ — triangle QPO is right-angled since PQ is a tangent

Angle $POQ = \tan^{-1}\left(\frac{12}{5}\right)$ — remember to have your calculator in radian mode

$= 1.176\ldots$

$= 1.18$ radians

b $OQ^2 = 12^2 + 5^2$ — using Pythagoras

$OQ^2 = 169$

$OQ = 13$

Hence $QR = 8\,\text{cm}$.

c Perimeter $= PQ + QR +$ arc PR — use arc $PR = r\theta$

$= 12 + 8 + (5 \times 1.176\ldots)$

$= 25.9\,\text{cm}$

Exercise 8.2

1 Find, in terms of π, the arc length of a sector of

a radius 6 cm and angle $\frac{\pi}{4}$

b radius 5 cm and angle $\frac{2\pi}{5}$

c radius 10 cm and angle $\frac{3\pi}{8}$

d radius 15 cm and angle $\frac{5\pi}{6}$.

2 Find the arc length of a sector of

a radius 8 cm and angle 1.2 radians **b** radius 2.5 cm and angle 0.8 radians.

3 Find, in radians, the angle of a sector of

a radius 4 cm and arc length 5 cm **b** radius 9 cm and arc length 13.5 cm.

4 Find the perimeter of each of these sectors.

a

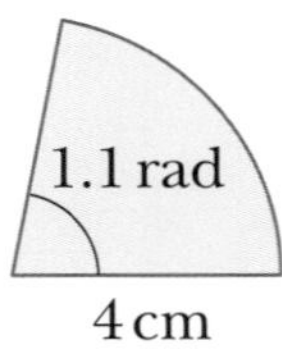

b

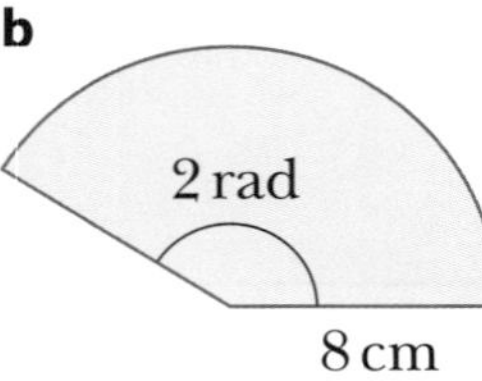

c

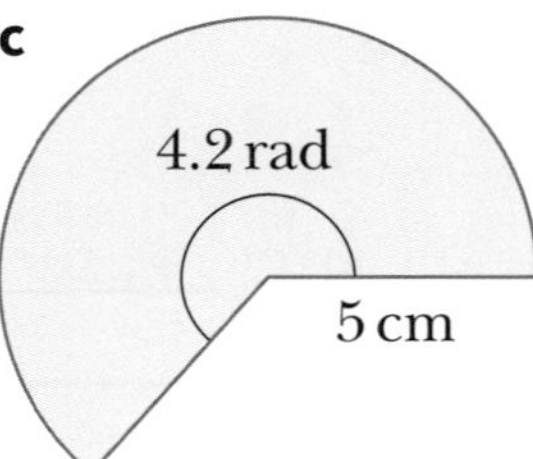

5 $ABCD$ is a rectangle with $AB = 6$ cm and $BC = 16$ cm.
O is the midpoint of BC.
$OAED$ is a sector of a circle, centre O. Find

a AO

b angle AOD, in radians

c the perimeter of the shaded region.

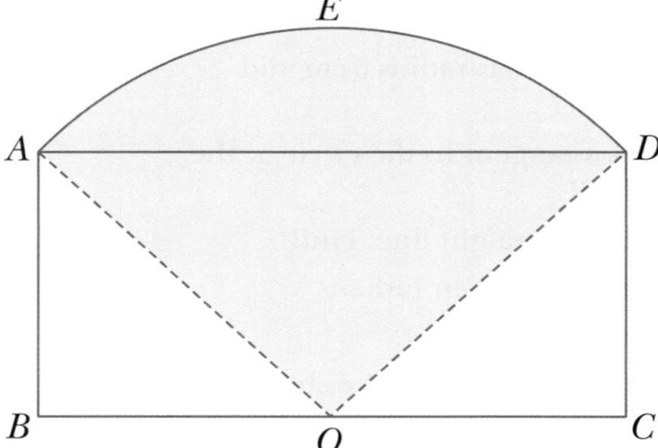

6 Find

a the length of arc AB

b the length of chord AB

c the perimeter of the shaded segment.

7 Triangle EFG is isosceles with $EG = FG = 16$ cm.
GH is an arc of a circle, centre F, with angle $HFG = 0.85$ radians. Find

a the length of arc GH

b the length of EF

c the perimeter of the shaded region.

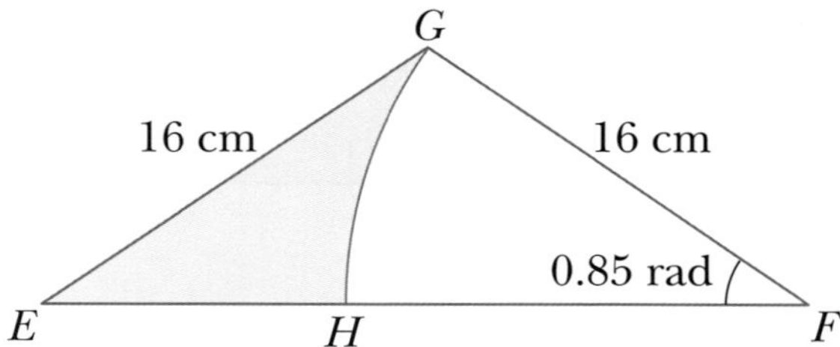

8.3 Area of a sector

To find the formula for the area of a sector you use the ratio:

$$\frac{\text{area of sector}}{\text{area of circle}} = \frac{\text{angle in the sector}}{\text{complete angle at the centre}}$$

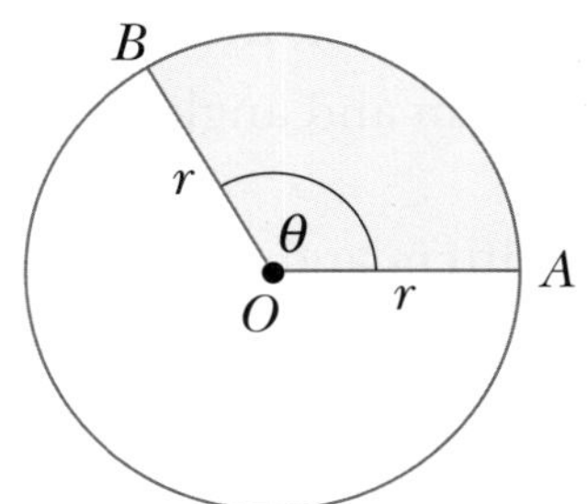

When θ is measured in radians, the ratio becomes

$$\frac{\text{area of sector}}{\pi r^2} = \frac{\theta}{2\pi}$$

$$\text{area of sector} = \frac{\theta}{2\pi} \times \pi r^2$$

$$\text{area of sector} = \frac{1}{2} r^2 \theta$$

WORKED EXAMPLE 5

Find the area of a sector of a circle with radius 6 cm and angle $\frac{2\pi}{3}$ radians.
Give your answer in terms of π.

Answers

$$\text{Area of sector} = \frac{1}{2} r^2 \theta$$

$$= \frac{1}{2} \times 6^2 \times \frac{2\pi}{3}$$

$$= 12\pi \text{ cm}^2$$

WORKED EXAMPLE 6

Calculate the area of the shaded segment correct to 3 sf.

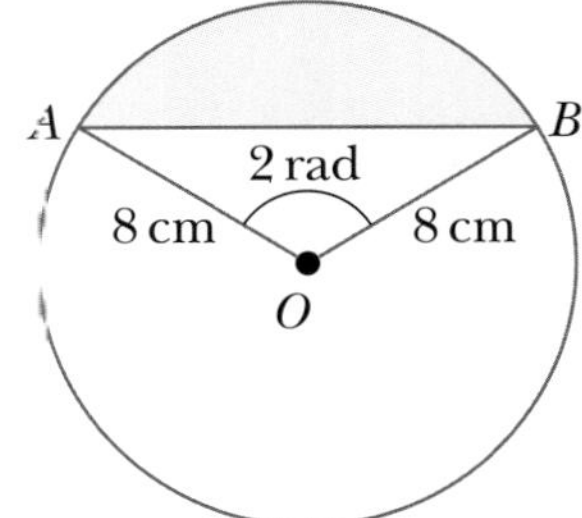

Answers

Area of triangle $AOB = \frac{1}{2} \times 8 \times 8 \times \sin(2^c)$ using area of triangle $= \frac{1}{2} ab \sin C$

$= 29.0975...$

$= 29.0975...$

Area of sector $AOB = \frac{1}{2} \times 8 \times 8 \times 2$ using area of sector $= \frac{1}{2} r^2 \theta$

$= 64$

Area of segment = area of sector AOB – area of triangle AOB

$= 64 - 29.0975...$

$= 34.9 \text{ cm}^2$

177

Exercise 8.3

1 Find, in terms of π, the area of a sector of

a radius 6 cm and angle $\frac{\pi}{3}$ **b** radius 15 cm and angle $\frac{3\pi}{5}$

c radius 10 cm and angle $\frac{7\pi}{10}$ **d** radius 9 cm and angle $\frac{5\pi}{6}$.

2 Find the area of a sector of

a radius 4 cm and angle 1.3 radians **b** radius 3.8 cm and angle 0.6 radians.

3 Find, in radians, the angle of a sector of

a radius 3 cm and area 5 cm^2 **b** radius 7 cm and area 30 cm^2.

4 *POQ* is the sector of a circle, centre *O*, radius 10 cm.
The length of arc *PQ* is 8 cm. Find

a angle *POQ*, in radians **b** the area of the sector *POQ*.

5 A sector of a circle, radius *r* cm, has a perimeter of 150 cm.
Find an expression, in terms of *r*, for the area of the sector.

6 *ABCD* is a rectangle with *AB* = 9 cm and *BC* = 18 cm.
O is the midpoint of *BC*.
OAED is a sector of a circle, centre *O*. Find

a *AO*

b angle *AOD*, in radians

c the area of the shaded region.

7 The circle has radius 12 cm and centre *O*.
PQ is a tangent to the circle at the point *P*.
QRO is a straight line. Find

a angle *POQ*, in radians

b the area of sector *POR*

c the area of the shaded region.

8 *AOB* is the sector of a circle, centre *O*, radius 8 cm.
AC is a tangent to the circle at the point *A*.
CBO is a straight line and the area of sector *AOB* is 32 cm^2.
Find

a angle *AOB*, in radians

b the area of triangle *AOC*

c the area of the shaded region.

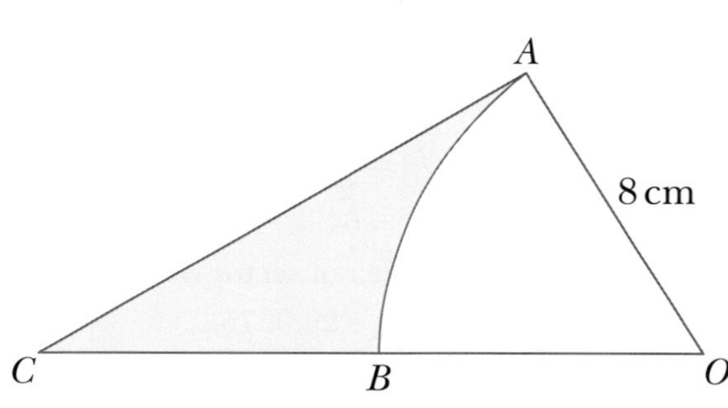

9 Triangle EFG is isosceles with $EG = FG = 9$ cm.
GH is an arc of a circle, centre F, with angle $HFG = 0.6$ radians. Find

a the area of sector of HFG

b the area of triangle EFG

c the area of the shaded region.

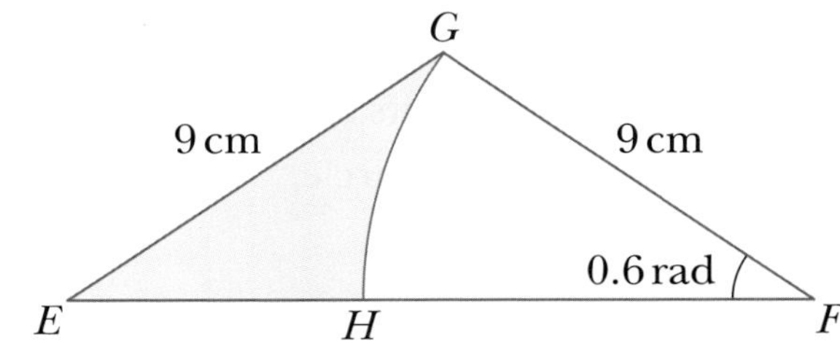

10 The diagram shows a circle, centre O, radius 12 cm
Angle $AOB = \theta$ radians.
Arc $AB = 9\pi$ cm.

a Show that $\theta = \dfrac{3\pi}{4}$.

b Find the area of the shaded region.

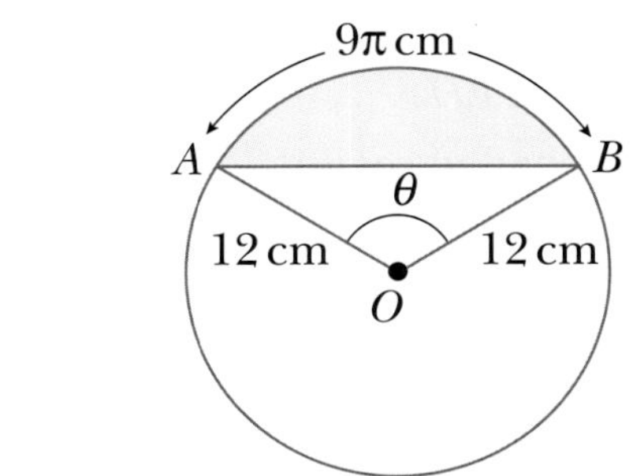

11 AOD is a sector of a circle, centre O, radius 4 cm.
BOC is a sector of a circle, centre O, radius 10 cm.
The shaded region has a perimeter of 18 cm. Find

a angle AOD, in radians

b the area of the shaded region.

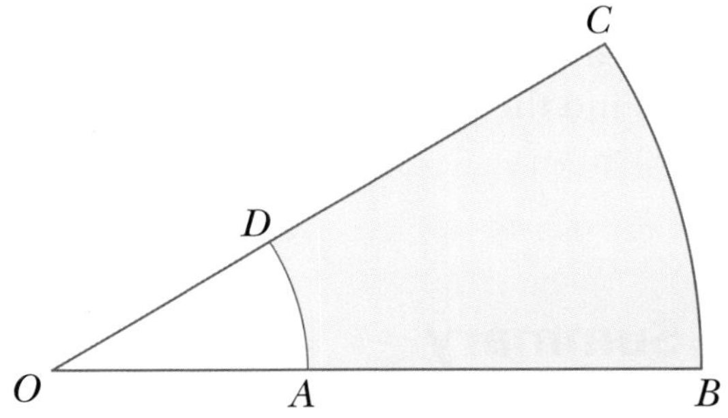

12 AOB is a sector of a circle, centre O, with radius 9 cm
Angle $COD = 0.5$ radians and angle ODC is a right angle.
$OC = 5$ cm. Find

a OD

b CD

c the perimeter of the shaded region

d the area of the shaded region.

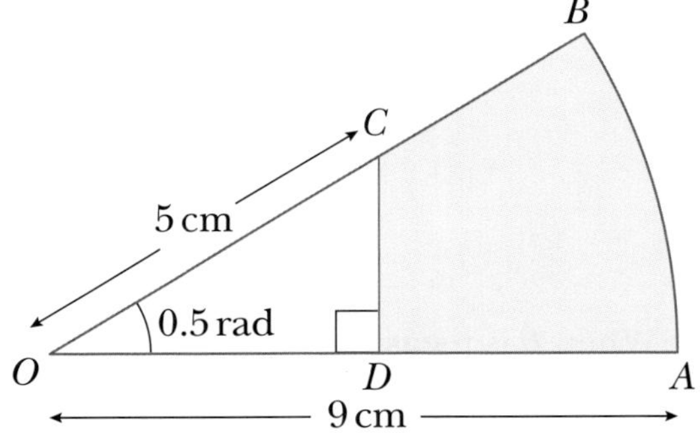

13 FOG is a sector of a circle, centre O, with angle $FOG = 1.2$ radians.

EOH is a sector of a circle, centre O, with radius 5 cm.

The shaded region has an area of $71.4\,\text{cm}^2$.

Find the perimeter of the shaded region.

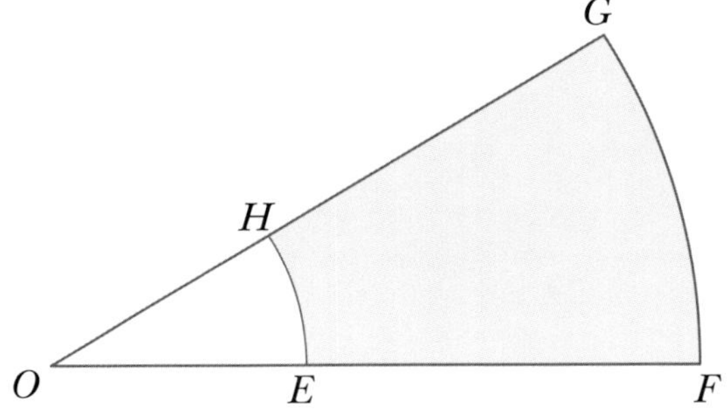

CHALLENGE Q

14 The diagram shows a semi-circle, centre O, radius 10 cm.

FH is the arc of a circle, centre E.

Find the area of

a triangle EOF

b sector FOG

c sector FEH

d the shaded region.

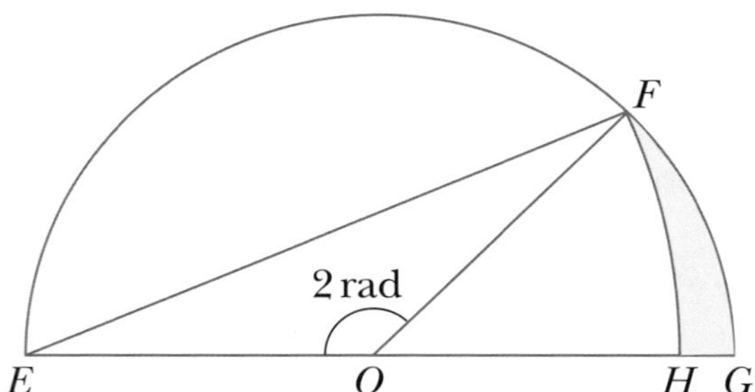

CHALLENGE Q

15 The diagram shows a circle inscribed inside a square of side length 10 cm. A quarter circle of radius 10 cm is drawn with the vertex of the square as its centre. Find the shaded area.

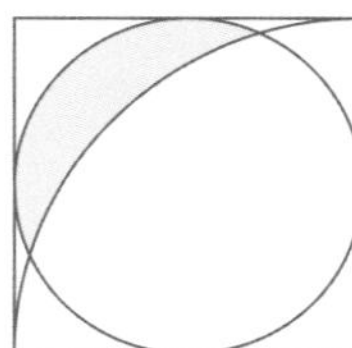

Summary

One radian (1^c) is the size of the angle subtended at the centre of a circle, radius r, by an arc of length r.

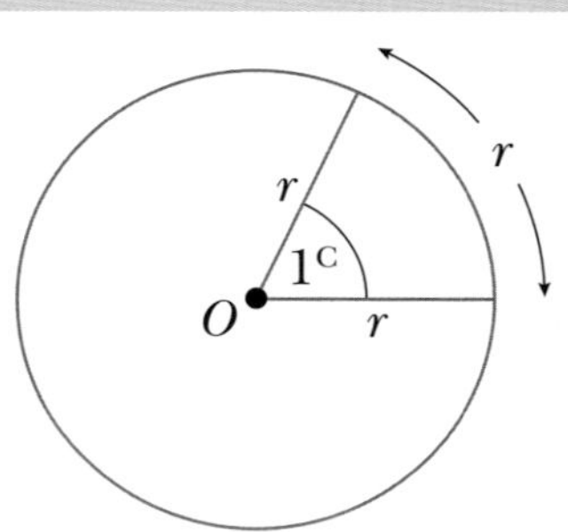

When θ is measured in radians:

- the length of arc $AB = r\theta$
- the area of sector $AOB = \frac{1}{2}r^2\theta$.

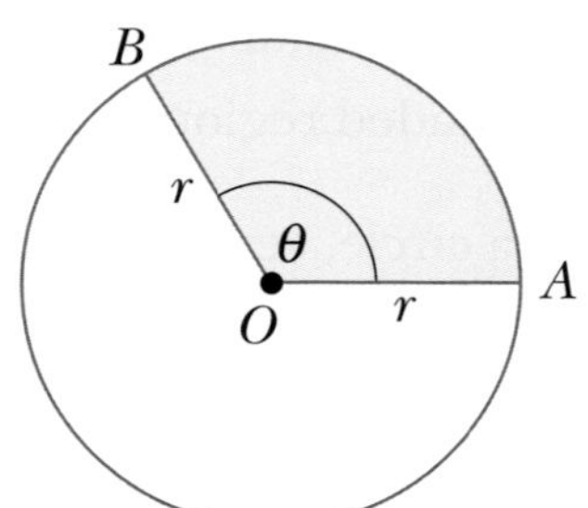

Examination questions

Worked example

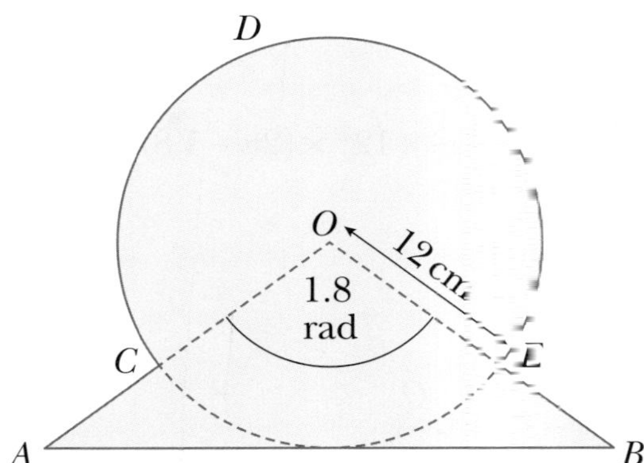

The diagram shows an isosceles triangle AOB and a sector $OCDEO$ of a circle with centre O.

The line AB is a tangent to the circle.

Angle $AOB = 1.8$ radians and the radius of the circle is 12 cm.

a Show that the distance $AC = 7.3$ cm to 1 decimal place. [2]

b Find the perimeter of the shaded region. [6]

c Find the area of the shaded region. [4]

Cambridge IGCSE Additional Mathematics 0606 Paper 21 Q11 Jun 2011

Answer

a $\cos 0.9 = \dfrac{12}{OA}$

$OA = \dfrac{12}{\cos 0.9} = 19.3047\ldots$

$AC = OA - 12 = 7.3047\ldots$

$= 7.3$ to 1 dp

b Perimeter = arc $CDE + EB + BA + AC$ — hence need to find arc CDE, EB and BA

arc CDE: arc $CDE = r\theta$ — where θ is the angle in the major sector $= 2\pi - 1.8$

$= 12 \times (2\pi - 1.8)$

$= 53.798\ldots$

EB: $\cos 0.9 = \dfrac{12}{OB}$ — using half of the isosceles triangle

$OB = \dfrac{12}{\cos 0.9} = 19.3047\ldots$

$EB = OB - OE = 19.3047 - 12 = 7.3047\ldots$

BA: $BA = 2 \times (OA \times \sin 0.9) = 30.24378\ldots$

Perimeter = arc $CDE + EB + BA + AC$

$= 53.798\ldots + 7.3047\ldots + 30.24378\ldots + 7.3047\ldots$

$= 98.7$ cm

c area of shaded region = area of triangle OAB + area of major sector CDE

$$= \frac{1}{2}ab\sin C + \frac{1}{2}r^2\theta$$

$$= \frac{1}{2}19.307^2 \times \sin 1.8 + \frac{1}{2} \times 12^2 \times (2\pi - 1.8)$$

$$= 504 \text{ cm}^2$$

Exercise 8.4

Exam Exercise

1

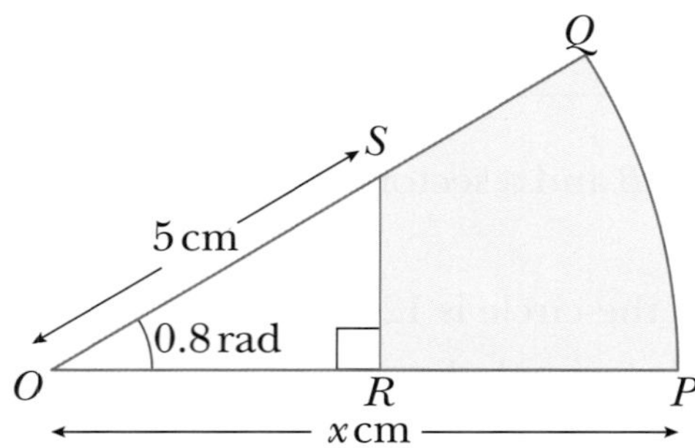

The diagram shows a sector OPQ of a circle with centre O and radius x cm.

Angle POQ is 0.8 radians. The point S lies on OQ such that $OS = 5$ cm.

The point R lies on OP such that angle ORS is a right angle.

Given that the area of triangle ORS is one-fifth of the area of sector OPQ, find

a the area of sector OPQ in terms of x and hence show that the value of x is 8.837 correct to 4 significant figures, [5]

b the perimeter of $PQSR$, [3]

c the area of $PQSR$. [2]

Cambridge IGCSE Additional Mathematics 0606 Paper 21 Q11a,b Nov 2014

2

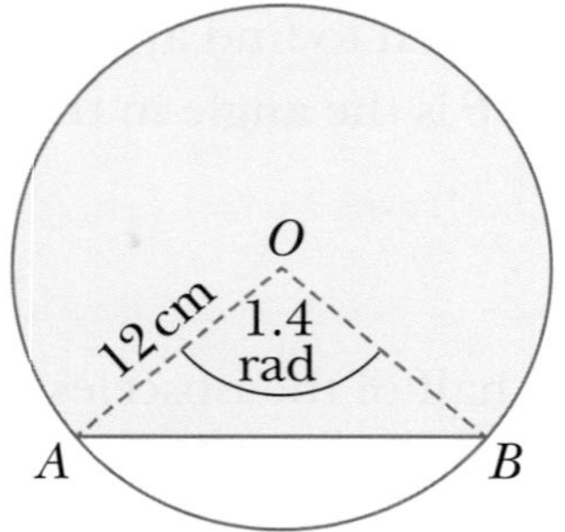

The diagram shows a circle with centre O and a chord AB.

The radius of the circle is 12 cm and angle AOB is 1.4 radians.

a Find the perimeter of the shaded region. [5]

b Find the area of the shaded region. [4]

Cambridge IGCSE Additional Mathematics 0606 Paper 21 Q10i,ii Nov 2013

3

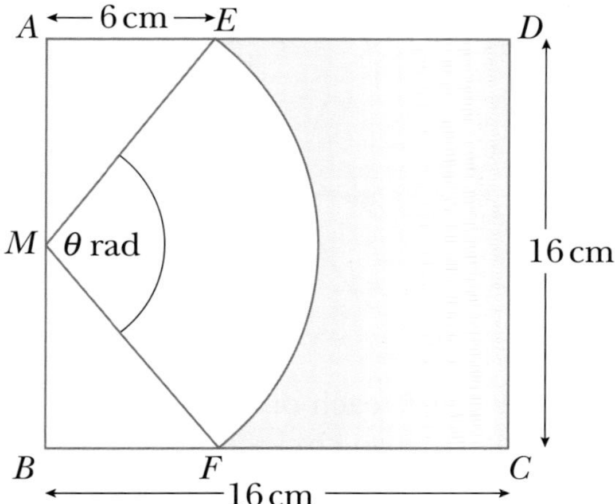

The diagram shows a square $ABCD$ of side 16 cm. M is the mid-point of AB.
The points E and F are on AD and BC respectively such that $AE = BF = 6$ cm.
EF is an arc of the circle centre M, such that angle EMF is θ radians.

a Show that $\theta = 1.855$ radians, correct to 3 decimal places. [2]

b Calculate the perimeter of the shaded region. [4]

c Calculate the area of the shaded region. [3]

Cambridge IGCSE Additional Mathematics 0606 Paper 11 Q8i,ii,iii Jun 2013

4

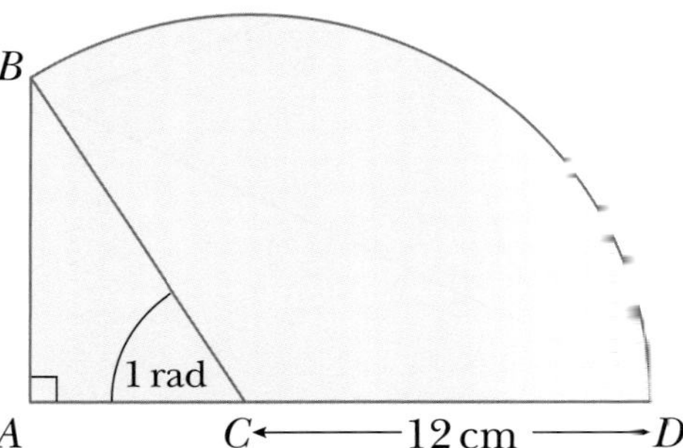

The diagram shows a right-angled triangle ABC and a sector $CBDC$ of a circle with centre C and radius 12 cm. Angle $ACB = 1$ radian and ACD is a straight line.

a Show that the length of AB is approximately 10.1 cm. [1]

b Find the perimeter of the shaded region. [5]

c Find the area of the shaded region. [4]

Cambridge IGCSE Additional Mathematics 0606 Paper 21 Q11i,ii,iii Jun 2012

5

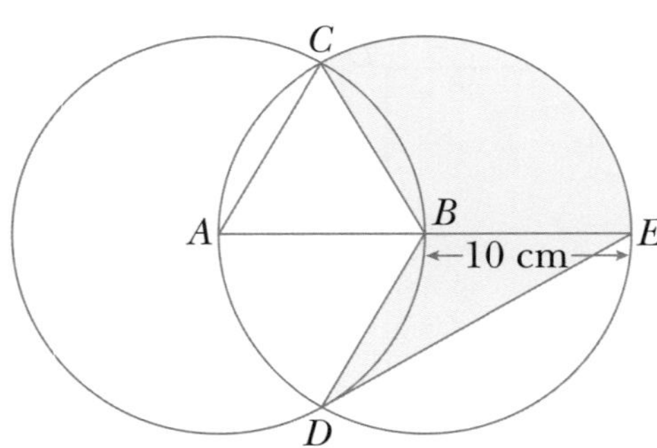

The diagram shows two circles, centres A and B, each of radius 10cm. The point B lies on the circumference of the circle with centre A. The two circles intersect at the points C and D. The point E lies on the circumference of the circle centre B such that ABE is a diameter.

i Explain why triangle ABC is equilateral. [1]

ii Write down, in terms of π, angle CBE. [1]

iii Find the perimeter of the shaded region. [5]

iv Find the area of the shaded region. [3]

Cambridge IGCSE Additional Mathematics 0606 Paper 11 Q10 Nov 2015

6

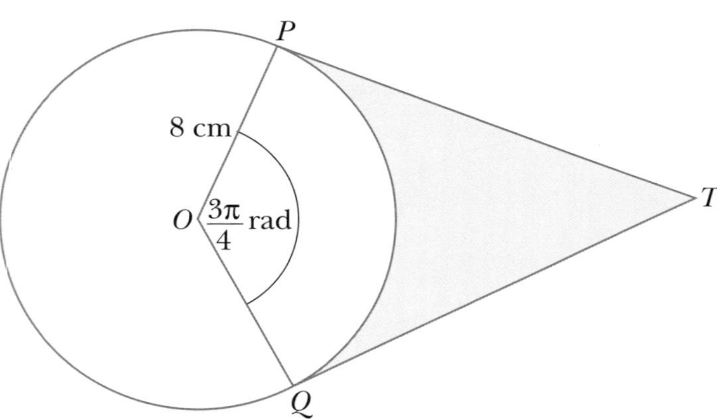

The diagram shows a circle, centre O, radius 8 cm. The points P and Q lie on the circle.

The lines PT and QT are tangents to the circle and angle $POQ = \dfrac{3\pi}{4}$ radians.

i Find the length of PT. [2]

ii Find the area of the shaded region. [3]

iii Find the perimeter of the shaded region. [2]

Cambridge IGCSE Additional Mathematics 0606 Paper 21 Q4 Jun 2015

7

The diagram shows a circle, centre O, radius r cm. Points A, B and C are such that A and B lie on the circle and the tangents at A and B meet at C. Angle $AOB = \theta$ radians.

i Given that the area of the major sector AOB is 7 times the area of the minor sector AOB, find the value of θ. [2]

ii Given also that the perimeter of the minor sector AOB is 20 cm, show that the value of r, correct to 2 decimal places, is 7.18. [2]

iii Using the values of θ and r from **parts i** and **ii**, find the perimeter of the shaded region ABC. [3]

iv Find the area of the shaded region ABC. [3]

Cambridge IGCSE Additional Mathematics 0606 Paper 12 Q9 Mar 2016

Chapter 9
Trigonometry

This section will show you how to:

- find the trigonometric ratios of angles of any magnitude
- determine the amplitude and period of trigonometric functions
- describe the relationship between trigonometric graphs
- sketch graphs of $y = |f(x)|$, where $f(x)$ is a trigonometric function
- draw and use the graphs of $y = a\sin bx + c$, $y = a\cos bx + c$, $y = a\tan bx + c$ where a is a positive integer, b is a simple fraction or integer and c is an integer
- use trigonometric relationships
- solve simple trigonometric equations
- prove simple trigonometric identities.

RECAP

You should already know the following trigonometric ratios

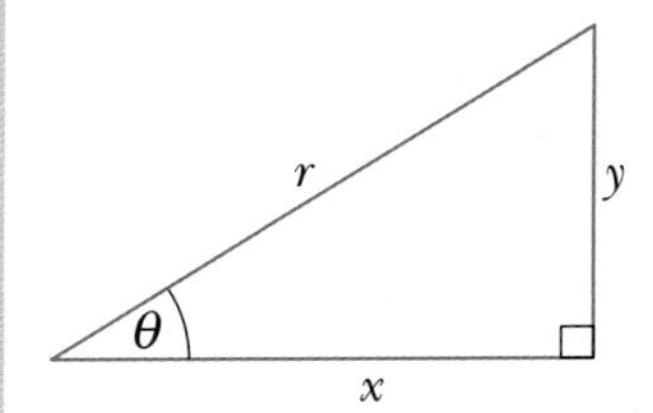

$$\sin\theta = \frac{\text{opposite}}{\text{hypotenuse}} \qquad \cos\theta = \frac{\text{adjacent}}{\text{hypotenuse}} \qquad \tan\theta = \frac{\text{opposite}}{\text{adjacent}}$$

$$\sin\theta = \frac{y}{r} \qquad \cos\theta = \frac{x}{r} \qquad \tan\theta = \frac{y}{x}$$

9.1 Angles between 0° and 90°

WORKED EXAMPLE 1

Given that $\sin\theta = \frac{2}{\sqrt{5}}$ and that θ is acute, find the exact values of

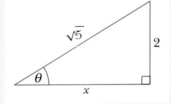

a $\sin^2\theta$ **b** $\cos\theta$ **c** $\tan\theta$ **d** $\frac{\sin\theta}{\tan\theta - \cos\theta}$.

Answers

a $\sin^2\theta = \sin\theta \times \sin\theta$ — $\sin^2\theta$ means $(\sin\theta)^2$

$$= \frac{2}{\sqrt{5}} \times \frac{2}{\sqrt{5}}$$

$$= \frac{4}{5}$$

b $\sin\theta = \frac{2}{\sqrt{5}}$

The right-angled triangle to represent θ is:

Using Pythagoras' theorem, $x = \sqrt{\left(\sqrt{5}\right)^2 - 2^2}$

$x = 1$

Hence, $\cos\theta = \frac{1}{\sqrt{5}} = \frac{\sqrt{5}}{5}$.

c $\tan\theta = \frac{2}{1} = 2$

d $\frac{\sin\theta}{\tan\theta - \cos\theta} = \frac{\frac{2}{\sqrt{5}}}{2 - \frac{1}{\sqrt{5}}}$ — multiply numerator and denominator by $\sqrt{5}$

$$= \frac{2}{2\sqrt{5} - 1}$$ — multiply numerator and denominator by $\left(2\sqrt{5} + 1\right)$

$$= \frac{2\left(2\sqrt{5} + 1\right)}{\left(2\sqrt{5} - 1\right)\left(2\sqrt{5} + 1\right)}$$

$$= \frac{2\left(2\sqrt{5} + 1\right)}{19}$$

$$= \frac{2 + 4\sqrt{5}}{19}$$

The sine, cosine and tangent of 30°, 45° and 60° (or $\frac{\pi}{6}$, $\frac{\pi}{4}$ and $\frac{\pi}{3}$) can be obtained exactly from the following two triangles:

Consider a right-angled isosceles triangle whose two equal sides are of length 1 unit.

The third side is found using Pythagoras' theorem: $\sqrt{1^2 + 1^2} = \sqrt{2}$

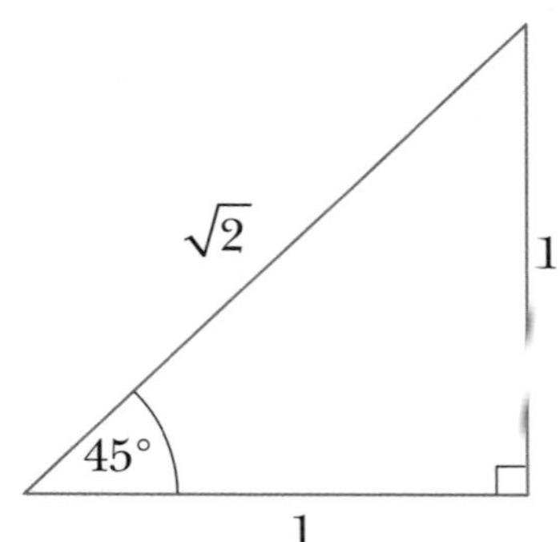

$\sin 45° = \frac{1}{\sqrt{2}}\left(= \frac{\sqrt{2}}{2}\right)$ $\quad \sin \frac{\pi}{4} = \frac{1}{\sqrt{2}}\left(= \frac{\sqrt{2}}{2}\right)$

$\cos 45° = \frac{1}{\sqrt{2}}\left(= \frac{\sqrt{2}}{2}\right)$ $\quad \cos \frac{\pi}{4} = \frac{1}{\sqrt{2}}\left(= \frac{\sqrt{2}}{2}\right)$

$\tan 45° = 1$ $\quad \tan \frac{\pi}{4} = 1$

Consider an equilateral triangle whose sides are of length 2 units.

The perpendicular bisector to the base splits the equilateral triangle into two congruent right-angled triangles.

The height of the triangle can be found using Pythagoras' theorem: $\sqrt{2^2 - 1^2} = \sqrt{3}$

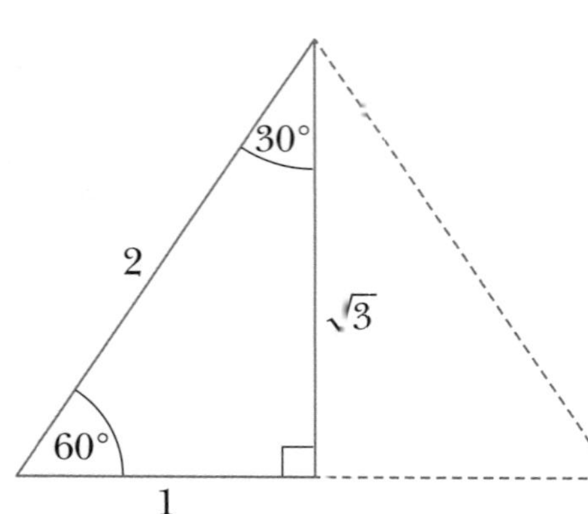

$\sin 60° = \frac{\sqrt{3}}{2}$ $\quad \sin \frac{\pi}{3} = \frac{\sqrt{3}}{2}$

$\cos 60° = \frac{1}{2}$ $\quad \cos \frac{\pi}{3} = \frac{1}{2}$

$\tan 60° = \sqrt{3}$ $\quad \tan \frac{\pi}{3} = \sqrt{3}$

$\sin 30° = \frac{1}{2}$ $\quad \sin \frac{\pi}{6} = \frac{1}{2}$

$\cos 30° = \frac{\sqrt{3}}{2}$ $\quad \cos \frac{\pi}{6} = \frac{\sqrt{3}}{2}$

$\tan 30° = \frac{1}{\sqrt{3}}\left(= \frac{\sqrt{3}}{3}\right)$ $\quad \tan \frac{\pi}{6} = \frac{1}{\sqrt{3}}\left(= \frac{\sqrt{3}}{3}\right)$

Note:
You do not need to learn these triangles and ratios for the examination, but you may find it useful to know them.

WORKED EXAMPLE 2

Find the exact value of

a $\sin 45° \sin 60°$ **b** $\cos^2 45°$ **c** $\dfrac{\tan\frac{\pi}{3} + \sin\frac{\pi}{4}}{1 - \cos\frac{\pi}{3}}$.

Answers

a $\sin 45° \sin 60° = \dfrac{1}{\sqrt{2}} \times \dfrac{\sqrt{3}}{2}$

$= \dfrac{\sqrt{3}}{2\sqrt{2}}$ rationalise the denominator

$= \dfrac{\sqrt{3} \times \sqrt{2}}{2\sqrt{2} \times \sqrt{2}}$

$= \dfrac{\sqrt{6}}{4}$

b $\cos^2 45° = \cos 45° \times \cos 45°$ $\cos^2 45°$ means $(\cos 45°)^2$

$= \dfrac{1}{\sqrt{2}} \times \dfrac{1}{\sqrt{2}}$

$= \dfrac{1}{2}$

c $\dfrac{\tan\frac{\pi}{3} + \sin\frac{\pi}{4}}{1 - \cos\frac{\pi}{3}} = \dfrac{\sqrt{3} + \frac{1}{\sqrt{2}}}{1 - \frac{1}{2}}$ the denominator simplifies to $\dfrac{1}{2}$

$= \left(\sqrt{3} + \dfrac{1}{\sqrt{2}}\right) \times 2$ expand brackets

$= 2\sqrt{3} + \dfrac{2}{\sqrt{2}}$ rationalise the denominator

$= 2\sqrt{3} + \sqrt{2}.$

Exercise 9.1

1 Given that $\tan\theta = \dfrac{2}{3}$ and that θ is acute, find the exact values of

a $\sin\theta$ **b** $\cos\theta$ **c** $\sin^2\theta$

d $\sin^2\theta + \cos^2\theta$ **e** $\dfrac{2 + \sin\theta}{3 - \cos\theta}$.

2 Given that $\sin\theta = \dfrac{\sqrt{2}}{5}$ and that θ is acute, find the exact values of

a $\cos\theta$ **b** $\tan\theta$ **c** $1 - \sin^2\theta$

d $\sin\theta + \cos\theta$ **e** $\dfrac{\cos\theta - \sin\theta}{\tan\theta}$.

3 Given that $\cos\theta = \dfrac{1}{7}$ and that θ is acute, find the exact values of

a $\sin\theta$ **b** $\tan\theta$ **c** $\tan\theta\cos\theta$

d $\sin^2\theta + \cos^2\theta$ **e** $\dfrac{\cos\theta - \tan\theta}{1 - \cos^2\theta}$.

4 Find the exact value of each of the following.

a $\tan 45° \cos 60°$ **b** $\tan^2 60°$ **c** $\dfrac{\tan 30°}{\cos 30°}$

d $\sin 45° + \cos 30°$ **e** $\dfrac{\cos^2 30°}{\cos 45° + \cos 60°}$ **f** $\dfrac{\tan 45° - \sin 30°}{1 + \sin^2 60°}$.

5 Find the exact value of each of the following.

a $\sin\dfrac{\pi}{4}\cos\dfrac{\pi}{3}$ **b** $\sin^2\dfrac{\pi}{4}$ **c** $\dfrac{\tan\dfrac{\pi}{6}}{\cos\dfrac{\pi}{4}}$

d $\dfrac{5 - \tan\dfrac{\pi}{3}}{\sin\dfrac{\pi}{3}}$ **e** $\dfrac{1}{\sin\dfrac{\pi}{6}} - \dfrac{1}{\cos\dfrac{\pi}{4}}$ **f** $\dfrac{\tan\dfrac{\pi}{4} - \sin\dfrac{\pi}{4}}{\tan\dfrac{\pi}{6}\sin\dfrac{\pi}{6}}$.

9.2 The general definition of an angle

You need to be able to use the three basic trigonometric functions for any angle.

To do this you need a general definition for an angle:

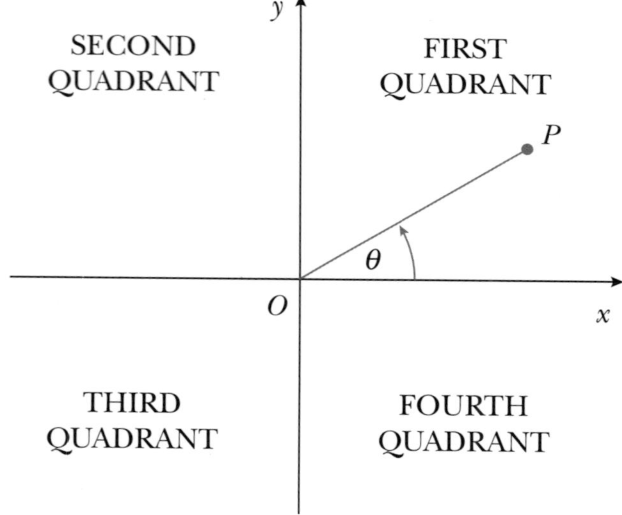

An angle is a measure of the rotation of a line OP about a fixed point O.

The angle is measured from the positive x-direction.

An anticlockwise rotation is taken as positive and a clockwise rotation is taken as negative.

The Cartesian plane is divided into four quadrants and the angle θ is said to be in the quadrant where OP lies. In the diagram above, θ is in the first quadrant.

WORKED EXAMPLE 3

Draw a diagram showing the quadrant in which the rotating line OP lies for each of the following angles. In each case find the acute angle that the line OP makes with the x-axis.

a $240°$ **b** $-70°$ **c** $490°$ **d** $\frac{2\pi}{3}$

Answers

a $240°$ is an anticlockwise rotation

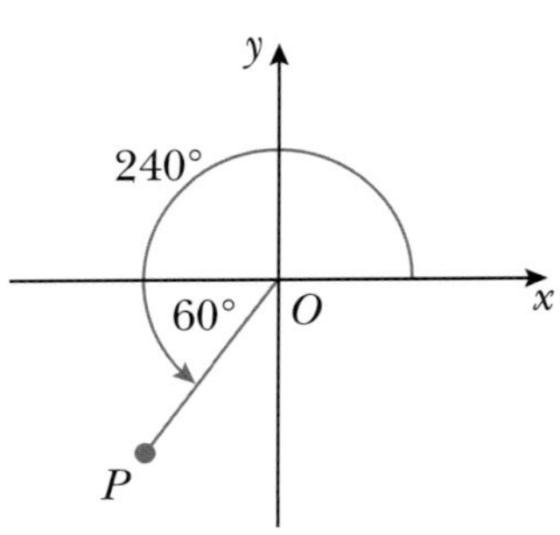

acute angle = $60°$

b $-70°$ is a clockwise rotation

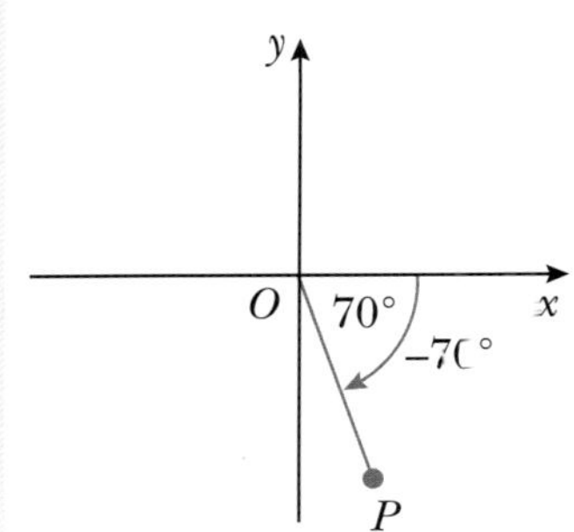

acute angle = $70°$

c $490°$ is an anticlockwise rotation
$490° = 360° + 130°$

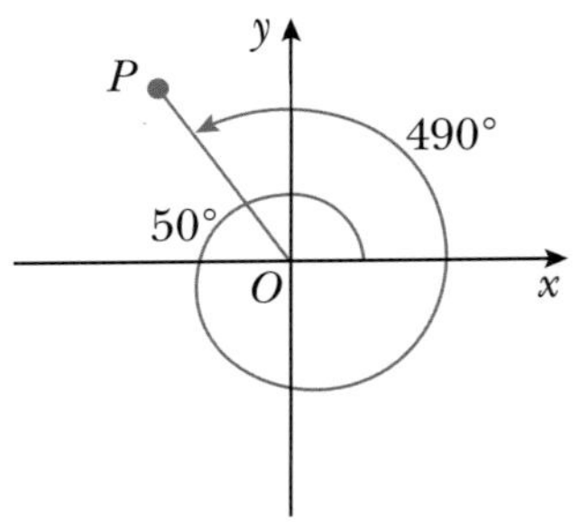

acute angle = $50°$

d $\frac{2\pi}{3}$ is an anticlockwise rotation

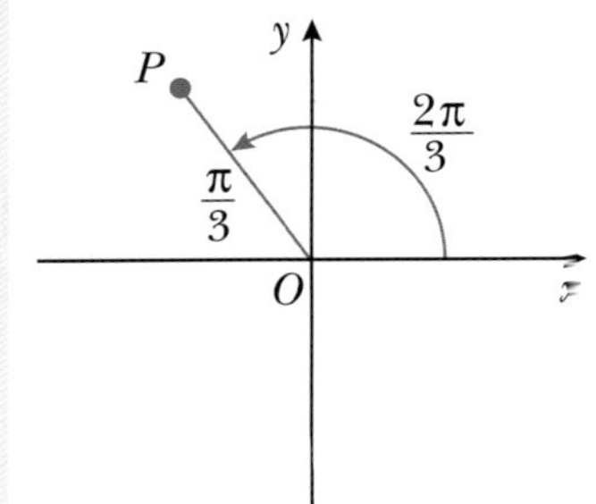

acute angle = $\frac{\pi}{3}$

Exercise 9.2

1 Draw a diagram showing the quadrant in which the rotating line OP lies for each of the following angles. In each question indicate clearly the direction of rotation and find the acute angle that the line OP makes with the x-axis.

a $110°$ **b** $-60°$ **c** $220°$ **d** $-135°$ **e** $-300°$

f $\frac{3\pi}{4}$ **g** $\frac{7\pi}{6}$ **h** $-\frac{5\pi}{3}$ **i** $\frac{13\pi}{9}$ **j** $-\frac{5\pi}{3}$

2 State the quadrant that OP lies in when the angle that OP makes with the positive x-axis is

a $110°$ **b** $300°$ **c** $-160°$ **d** $245°$ **e** $-500°$

f $\frac{\pi}{4}$ **g** $\frac{11\pi}{6}$ **h** $-\frac{5\pi}{6}$ **i** $\frac{13\pi}{6}$ **j** $\frac{9\pi}{4}$

9.3 Trigonometric ratios of general angles

In general, trigonometric ratios of any angle θ in any quadrant are defined as:

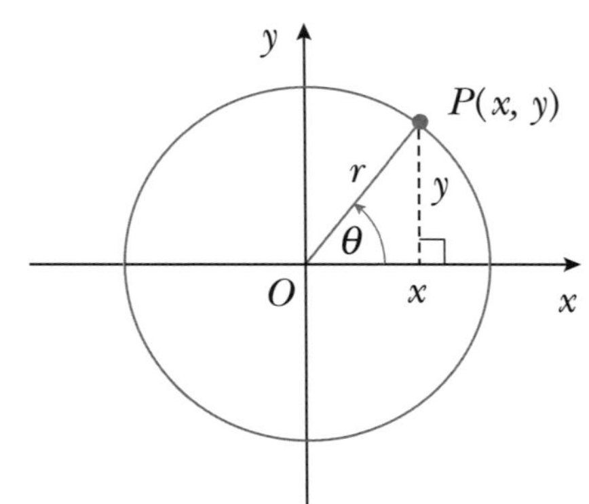

$$\sin\theta = \frac{y}{r}, \quad \cos\theta = \frac{x}{r}, \quad \tan\theta = \frac{y}{x}, \quad x \neq 0$$

where x and y are the coordinates of the point P

and r is the length of OP and $r = \sqrt{x^2 + y^2}$.

You need to know the signs of the three trigonometric ratios in the four quadrants.

In the first quadrant sin, cos and tan are positive. (Since x, y and r are all positive.)

By considering the sign of x and y you can find the sign of each of the three trigonometric ratios in the other three quadrants.

CLASS DISCUSSION

192

$\sin\theta = \frac{y}{r}$ By considering the sign of y in the second, third and fourth quadrants, determine the signs of the sine ratio in each of these quadrants.

$\cos\theta = \frac{x}{r}$ By considering the sign of x in the second, third and fourth quadrants, determine the signs of the cosine ratio in each of these quadrants.

$\tan\theta = \frac{y}{x}$ By considering the sign of x and y in the second, third and fourth quadrants, determine the signs of the tangent ratio in each of these quadrants. What happens to the tangent ratio when $x = 0$?

On a copy of the diagram, record which ratios are positive in each quadrant.

The first quadrant has been completed for you.

(All three ratios are positive in the first quadrant.)

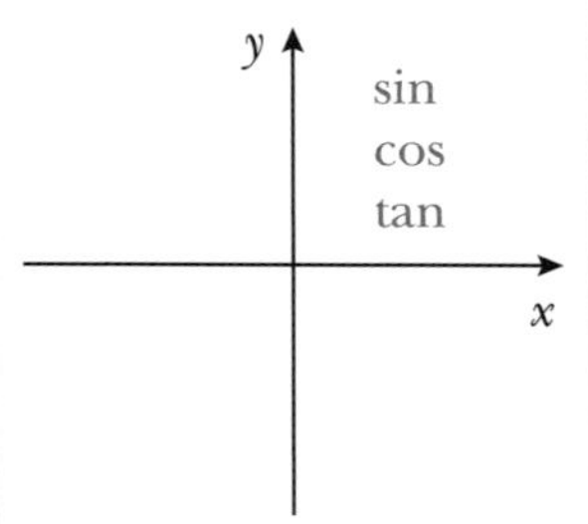

The results of the class discussion, can be summarised as:

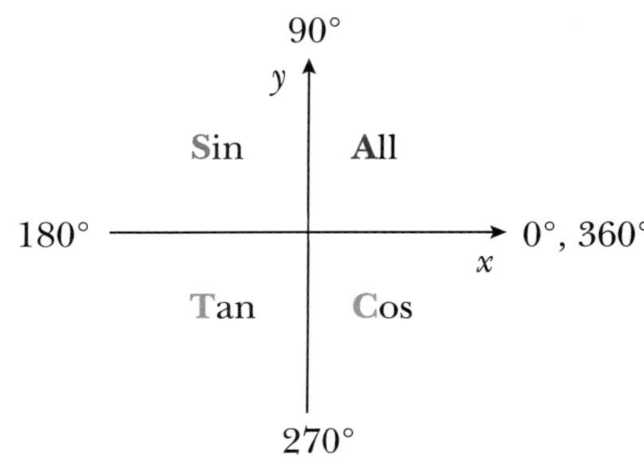

You can memorise this diagram using a mnemonic such as 'All Students Trust Cambridge'.

WORKED EXAMPLE 4

Express in terms of trigonometric ratios of acute angles.

a $\cos(-110°)$ **b** $\sin 125°$

Answers

a The acute angle made with the x-axis is 70°.
In the third quadrant only tan is positive, so cos is negative.
$\cos(-110°) = -\cos 70°$

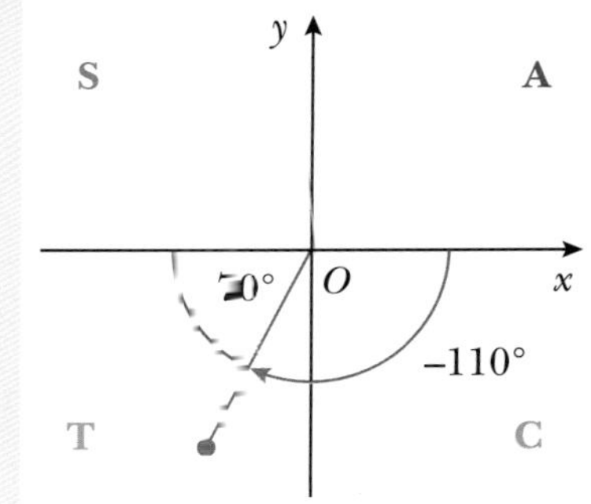

b The acute angle made with the x-axis is 55°.
In the second quadrant sin is positive.
$\sin 125° = \sin 55°$

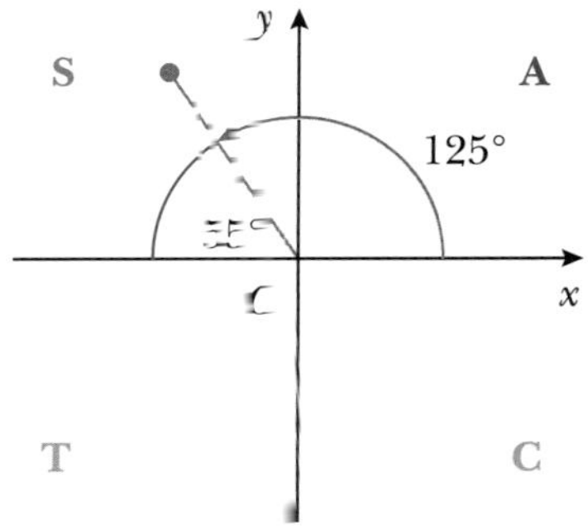

WORKED EXAMPLE 5

Given that $\sin\theta = -\frac{3}{5}$ and that $180° \leqslant \theta \leqslant 270°$, find the value of $\tan\theta$ and the value of $\cos\theta$.

Answers

θ is in the third quadrant.

tan is positive and cos is negative in this quadrant.

$x^2 + (-3)^2 = 5^2$

$x^2 = 25 - 9 = 16$

Since $x < 0$, $x = -4$

$\tan\theta = \frac{-3}{-4} = \frac{3}{4}$ and $\cos\theta = \frac{-4}{5} = -\frac{4}{5}$

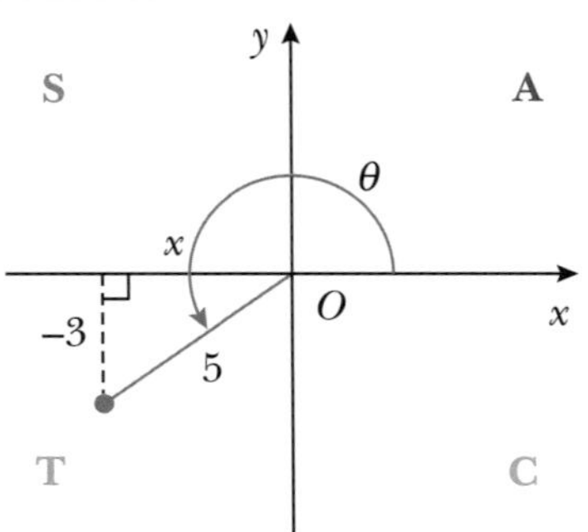

Exercise 9.3

1 Express the following as trigonometric ratios of acute angles.

a $\sin 220°$ **b** $\cos 325°$ **c** $\tan 140°$ **d** $\cos(-25°)$

e $\tan 600°$ **f** $\sin\frac{4\pi}{5}$ **g** $\tan\frac{7\pi}{4}$ **h** $\cos\left(-\frac{11\pi}{6}\right)$

i $\tan\frac{2\pi}{3}$ **j** $\sin\frac{9\pi}{4}$

2 Given that $\cos\theta = \frac{2}{5}$ and that $270° \leqslant \theta \leqslant 360°$, find the value of

a $\tan\theta$ **b** $\sin\theta$.

3 Given that $\tan\theta = -\sqrt{3}$ and that $90° \leqslant \theta \leqslant 180°$, find the value of

a $\sin\theta$ **b** $\cos\theta$.

4 Given that $\sin\theta = \frac{5}{13}$ and that θ is obtuse, find the value of

a $\cos\theta$ **b** $\tan\theta$.

5 Given that $\tan\theta = \frac{2}{3}$ and that θ is reflex find the value of

a $\sin\theta$ **b** $\cos\theta$.

6 Given that $\tan A = \frac{4}{3}$ and $\cos B = -\frac{1}{\sqrt{3}}$, where A and B are in the same quadrant, find the value of

a $\sin A$ **b** $\cos A$ **c** $\sin B$ **d** $\tan B$.

7 Given that $\sin A = -\frac{12}{13}$ and $\cos B = \frac{3}{5}$, where A and B are in the same quadrant, find the value of

a $\cos A$ **b** $\tan A$ **c** $\sin B$ **d** $\tan B$.

9.4 Graphs of trigonometric functions

CLASS DISCUSSION

Consider taking a ride on a Ferris wheel, with radius 50 metres, which rotates at a constant speed.

You enter the ride from a platform that is level with the centre of the wheel and the wheel turns in an anticlockwise direction.

Sketch the following two graphs and discuss their properties:

- a graph of your **vertical displacement from the centre of the wheel** plotted against **angle turned through**
- a graph of your **horizontal displacement from the centre of the wheel** plotted against **angle turned through**.

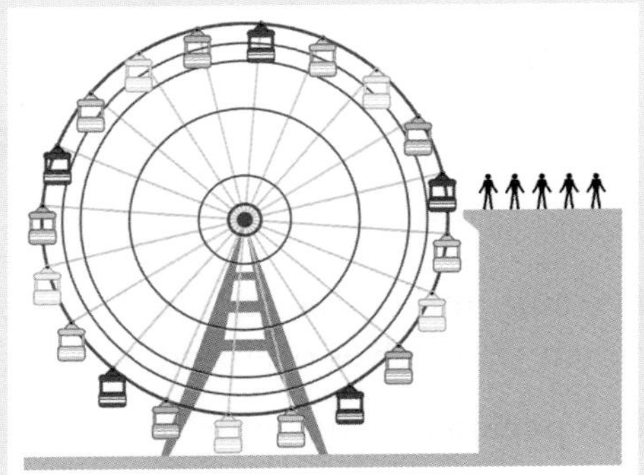

The graphs of $y = \sin x$ and $y = \cos x$

Suppose that OP makes an angle of x with the positive horizontal axis and that P moves around the unit circle, through one complete revolution. The coordinates of P will be $(\cos x, \sin x)$.

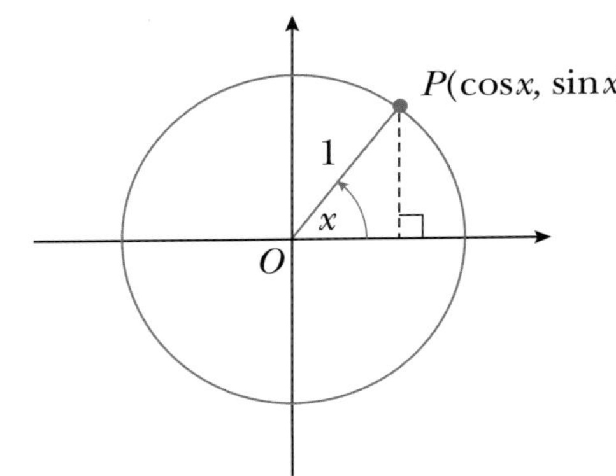

The height of P above the horizontal axis changes from $0 \to 1 \to 0 \to -1 \to 0$.

The graph of $\sin x$ against x for $0° \leqslant x \leqslant 360°$ is:

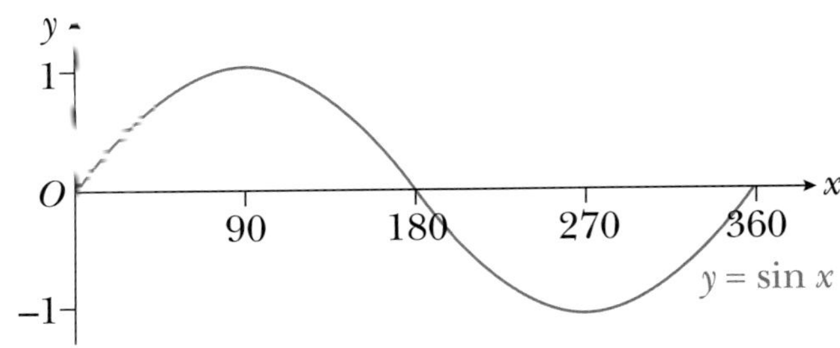

The distance of P from the vertical axis changes from $1 \to 0 \to -1 \to 0 \to 1$.

The graph of $\cos x$ against x for $0° \leqslant x \leqslant 360°$ is:

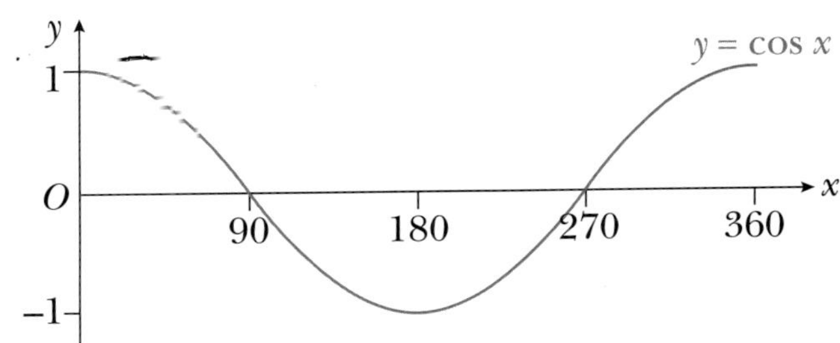

The graphs of $y = \sin x$ and $y = \cos x$ can be continued beyond $0° \leqslant x \leqslant 360°$:

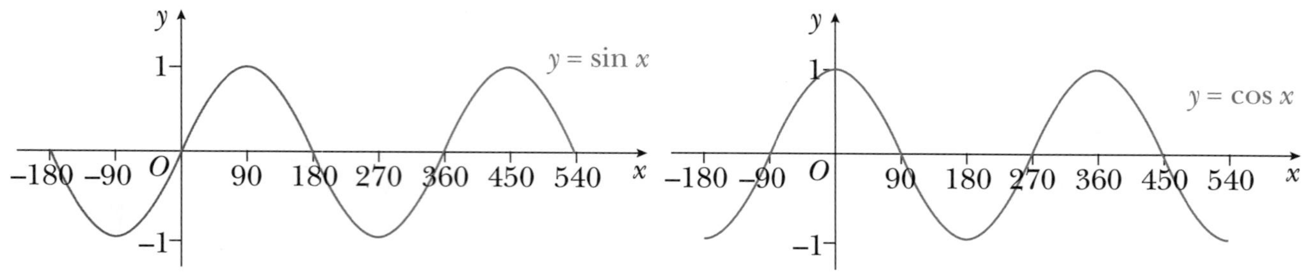

The sine and cosine functions are called **periodic functions** because they repeat themselves over and over again.

The **period** of a periodic function is defined as the length of one repetition or cycle.

The basic sine and cosine functions repeat every 360°.

We say they have a **period** of 360°. (Period = 2π, if working in radians.)

The **amplitude** of a periodic function is defined as the distance between a maximum (or minimum) point and the principal axis.

The basic sine and cosine functions have amplitude 1.

The graph of $y = \tan x$

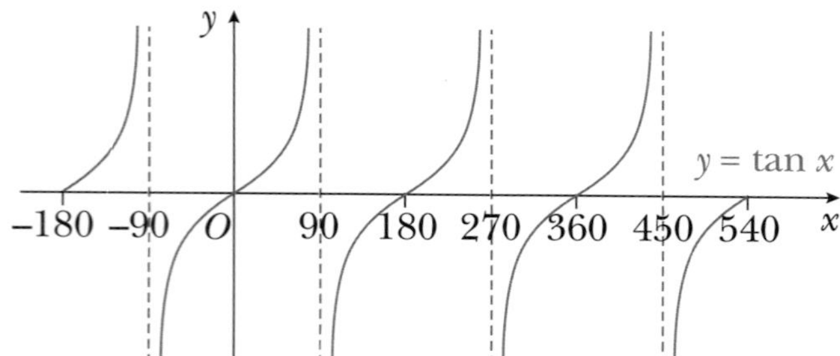

The tangent function behaves very differently to the sine and cosine functions.

The tangent function repeats its cycle every 180° so its period is 180°.

The red dashed lines at $x = \pm 90°$, $x = 270°$ and $x = 450°$ are asymptotes. The branches of the graph get closer and closer to the asymptotes without ever reaching them.

The tangent function does not have an amplitude.

The graphs of $y = a\sin bx + c$, $y = a\cos bx + c$ and $y = a\tan bx + c$

You have already learnt about the graphs of $y = \sin x$, $y = \cos x$ and $y = \tan x$.

In this section you will learn how to sketch the graphs of $y = a\sin bx + c$, $y = a\cos bx + c$ and $y = a\tan bx + c$ where a and b are positive integers and c is an integer.

You can use graphing software to observe how the values of a, b and c affect the trigonometric functions.

The graph of $y = a \sin x$

Using graphing software, the graphs of $y = \sin x$ and $y = 2\sin x$ are:

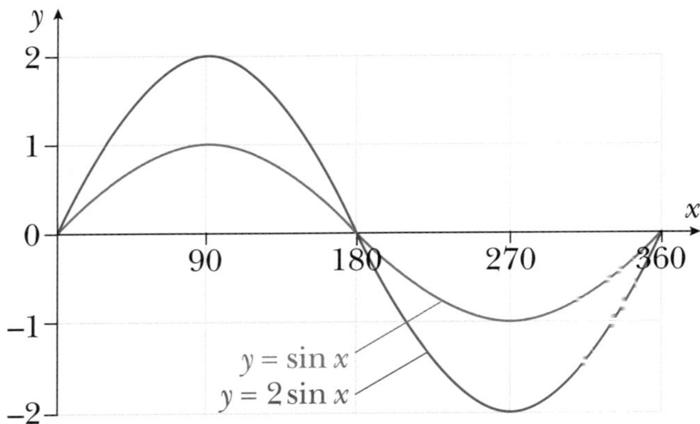

The graph of $y = 2\sin x$ is a stretch of the graph of $y = \sin x$.

It has been stretched from the x-axis with a stretch factor of 2.

The amplitude of $y = 2\sin x$ is 2 and the period is 360°.

Similarly, it can be shown that graph of $y = 3\sin x$ is a stretch of $y = \sin x$ from the x-axis with stretch factor 3. The amplitude of $y = 3\sin x$ is 3 and the period is 360°.

ACTIVITY

Use graphing software to confirm that:

- $y = 2 \cos x$ is a stretch of $y = \cos x$ from the x-axis with stretch factor 2
- $y = 3 \cos x$ is a stretch of $y = \cos x$ from the x-axis with stretch factor 3

and

- $y = 2 \tan x$ is a stretch of $y = \tan x$ from the x-axis with stretch factor 2
- $y = 3 \tan x$ is a stretch of $y = \tan x$ from the x-axis with stretch factor 3.

The graph of $y = \sin bx$

Using graphing software, the graphs of $y = \sin x$ and $y = \sin 2x$ are:

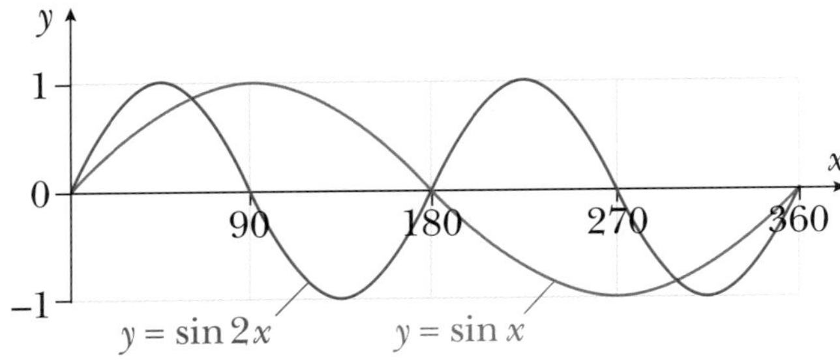

The graph of $y = \sin 2x$ is a stretch of the graph of $y = \sin x$.

It has been stretched from the y-axis with a stretch factor of $\frac{1}{2}$.

The amplitude of $y = \sin 2x$ is 1 and the period is 180°.

Similarly, the graph of $y = \sin 3x$ is a stretch, from the y-axis, of $y = \sin x$ with stretch factor $\frac{1}{3}$.

The amplitude of $y = \sin 3x$ is 1 and the period is 120°.

ACTIVITY

Use graphing software to confirm that:

- $y = \cos 2x$ is a stretch of $y = \cos x$ from the y-axis with stretch factor $\frac{1}{2}$
- $y = \cos 3x$ is a stretch of $y = \cos x$ from the y-axis with stretch factor $\frac{1}{3}$

and

- $y = \tan 2x$ is a stretch of $y = \tan x$ from the y-axis with stretch factor $\frac{1}{2}$
- $y = \tan 3x$ is a stretch of $y = \tan x$ from the y-axis with stretch factor $\frac{1}{3}$

The graph of $y = \sin x + c$

Using graphing software, the graphs of $y = \sin x$ and $y = \sin x + 1$ are:

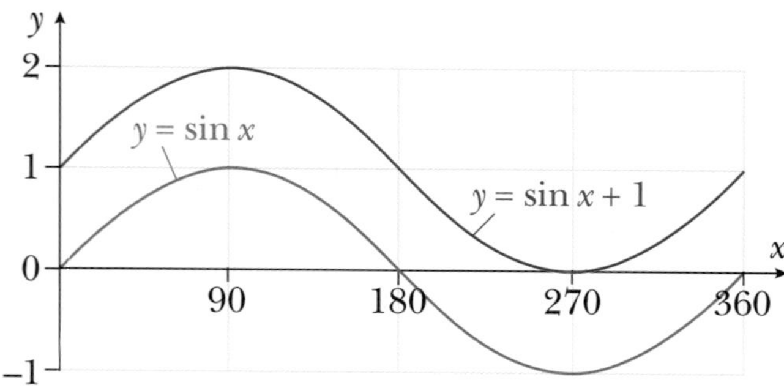

The graph of $y = \sin x + 1$ is a translation of the graph of $y = \sin x$.

It has been translated by the vector $\begin{pmatrix} 0 \\ 1 \end{pmatrix}$.

The amplitude of $y = \sin x + 1$ is 1 and the period is 360°.

Similarly, the graph of $y = \sin x + 2$ is a translation of $y = \sin x$ by the vector $\begin{pmatrix} 0 \\ 2 \end{pmatrix}$.

The amplitude of $y = \sin x + 2$ is 1 and the period is 360°.

ACTIVITY

Use graphing software to confirm that:

- $y = \cos x + 1$ is a translation of $y = \cos x$ by the vector $\begin{pmatrix} 0 \\ 1 \end{pmatrix}$
- $y = \cos x + 2$ is a translation of $y = \cos x$ by the vector $\begin{pmatrix} 0 \\ 2 \end{pmatrix}$
- $y = \cos x - 3$ is a translation of $y = \cos x$ by the vector $\begin{pmatrix} 0 \\ -3 \end{pmatrix}$

and

- $y = \tan x + 1$ is a translation of $y = \tan x$ by the vector $\begin{pmatrix} 0 \\ 1 \end{pmatrix}$
- $y = \tan x - 2$ is a translation of $y = \tan x$ by the vector $\begin{pmatrix} 0 \\ -2 \end{pmatrix}$

In conclusion,

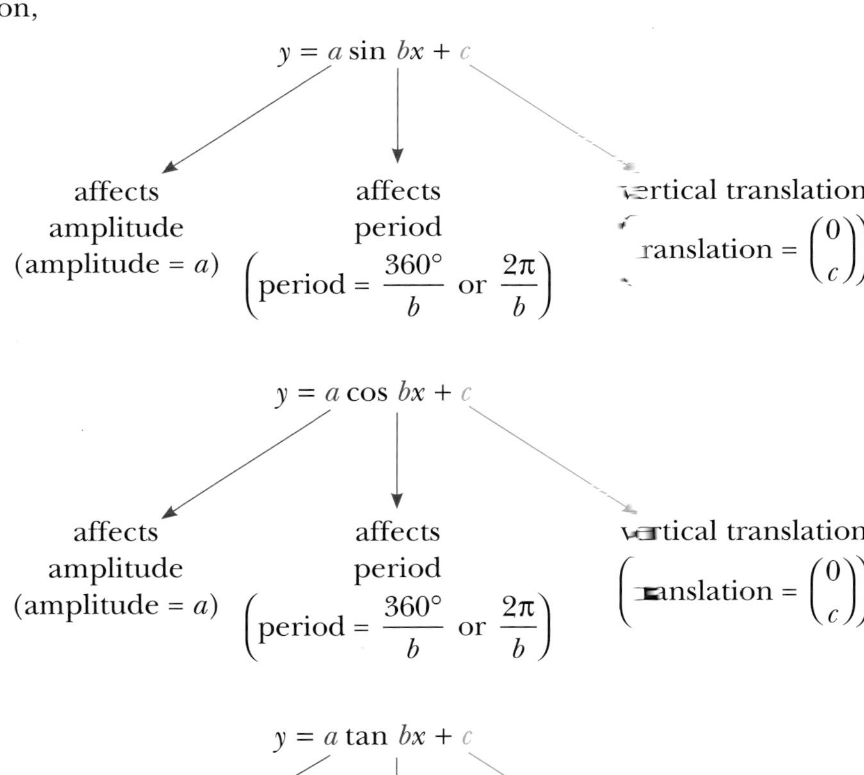

$y = a \tan bx + c$

stretches the graph
Note: there is no amplitude for a tangent function

affects period $\left(\text{period} = \frac{180°}{b} \text{ or } \frac{\pi}{b}\right)$

vertical translation $\left(\text{translation} = \begin{pmatrix} 0 \\ c \end{pmatrix}\right)$

Sketching trigonometric functions

The sketch graph of a trigonometric function, such as $y = 2\cos 3x - 1$ for $0° \leqslant x \leqslant 360°$, can be built up in steps.

Step 1: Start with a sketch of $y = \cos x$:

Period = 360°

Amplitude = 1

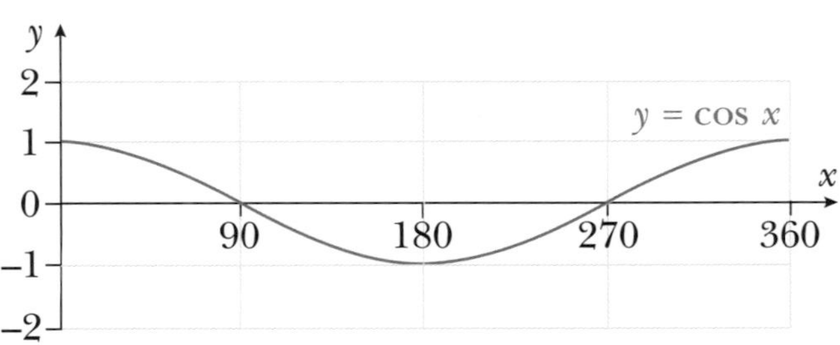

Step 2: Sketch the graph of $y = \cos 3x$:

Stretch $y = \cos x$ from the y-axis with stretch factor $\frac{1}{3}$.

Period $= \frac{360°}{3} = 120°$

Amplitude = 1

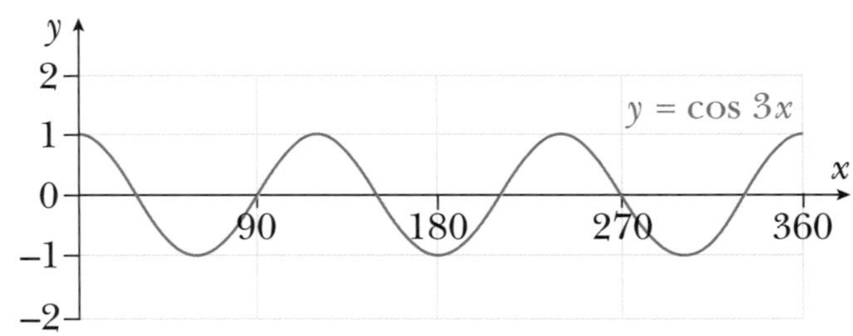

Step 3: Sketch the graph of $y = 2\cos 3x$:

Stretch $y = \cos 3x$ from the x-axis with stretch factor 2.

Period $= \frac{360°}{3} = 120°$

Amplitude = 2

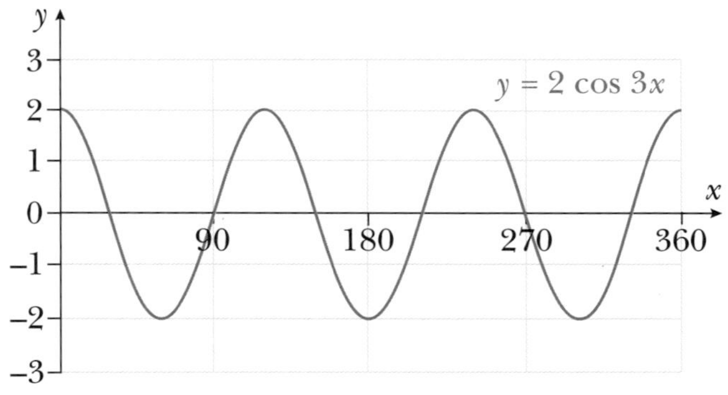

Step 4: Sketch the graph of $y = 2\cos 3x - 1$:

Translate $y = 2\cos 3x$ by $\begin{pmatrix} 0 \\ -1 \end{pmatrix}$.

Period $= \frac{360°}{3} = 120°$

Amplitude = 2

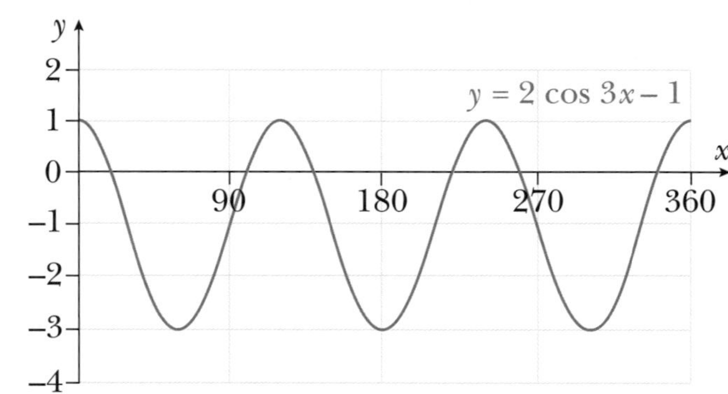

WORKED EXAMPLE 6

$f(x) = 3 \sin 2x$ for $0° \leqslant x \leqslant 360°$

a Write down the period of f.

b Write down the amplitude of f.

c Write down the coordinates of the maximum and minimum points on the curve $y = f(x)$.

d Sketch the graph of $y = f(x)$.

e Use your answer to **part d** to sketch the graph of $y = 3 \sin 2x + 1$.

Answers

a Period $= \frac{360°}{2} = 180°$

b Amplitude $= 3$

c $y = \sin x$ has its maximum and minimum points at:

$(90°, 1)$, $(270°, -1)$, $(450°, 1)$ and $(630°, -1)$

Hence, $f(x) = 3 \sin 2x$ has its maximum and minimum points at:

$(45°, 3)$, $(135°, -3)$, $(225°, 3)$ and $(315°, -3)$

d

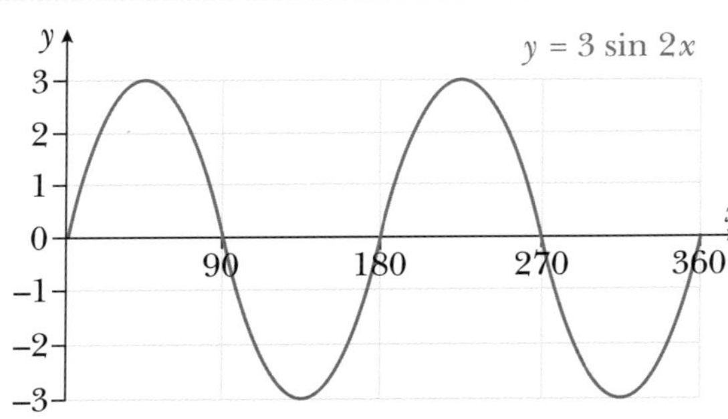

e $y = 3 \sin 2x + 1$ is a translation of the graph $y = 3 \sin 2x$ by the vector $\begin{pmatrix} 0 \\ 1 \end{pmatrix}$.

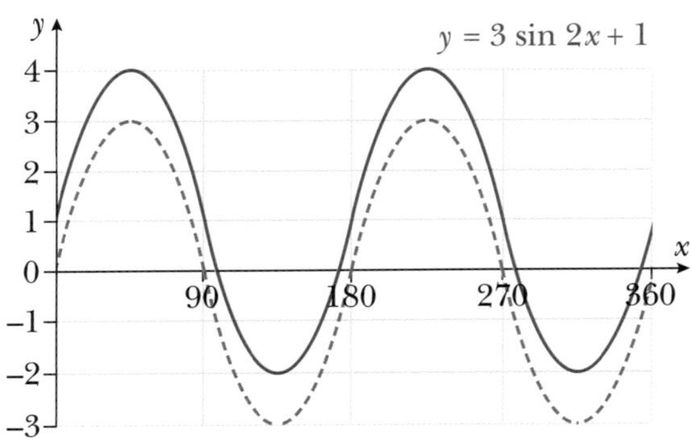

WORKED EXAMPLE 7

a On the same grid, sketch the graphs of $y = \sin 2x$ and $y = 1 + \cos 2x$ for $0° \leqslant x \leqslant 360°$.

b State the number of roots of the equation $\sin 2x = 1 + \cos 2x$ for $0° \leqslant x \leqslant 360°$.

Answers

a

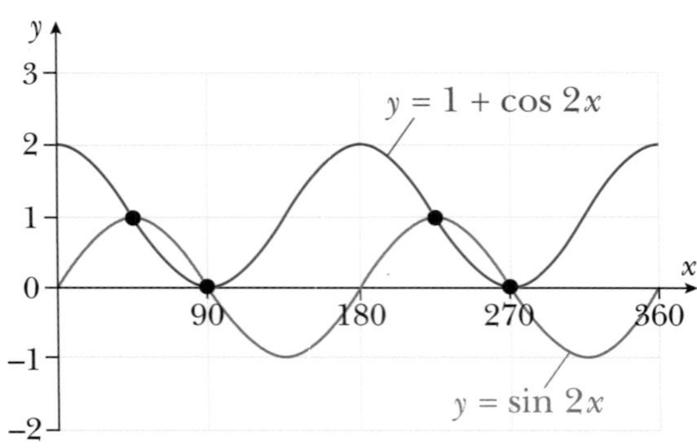

b The graphs of $y = \sin 2x$ and $y = 1 + \cos 2x$ intersect each other at 4 points in the interval.

Hence, the number of roots of $\sin 2x = 1 + \cos 2x$ is 4.

Exercise 9.4

1 **a** The following functions are defined for $0° \leqslant x \leqslant 360°$.

For each function, write down the amplitude, the period and the coordinates of the maximum and minimum points.

i $f(x) = 7\cos x$ **ii** $f(x) = 2\sin 2x$ **iii** $f(x) = 2\cos 3x$

iv $f(x) = 3\sin\frac{1}{2}x$ **v** $f(x) = 4\cos x + 1$ **vi** $f(x) = 5\sin 2x - 2$

b Sketch the graph of each function in **part a** and use graphing software to check your answers.

2 **a** The following functions are defined for $0 \leqslant x \leqslant 2\pi$.

For each function, write down the amplitude, the period and the coordinates of the maximum and minimum points.

i $f(x) = 4\sin x$ **ii** $f(x) = \cos 3x$ **iii** $f(x) = 2\sin 3x$

iv $f(x) = 3\cos\frac{1}{2}x$ **v** $f(x) = \sin 2x + 3$ **vi** $f(x) = 4\cos 2x - 1$

b Sketch the graph of each function in **part a** and use graphing software to check your answers.

3 The graph of $y = a + b\sin cx$, for $0 \leqslant x \leqslant \pi$, is shown above.

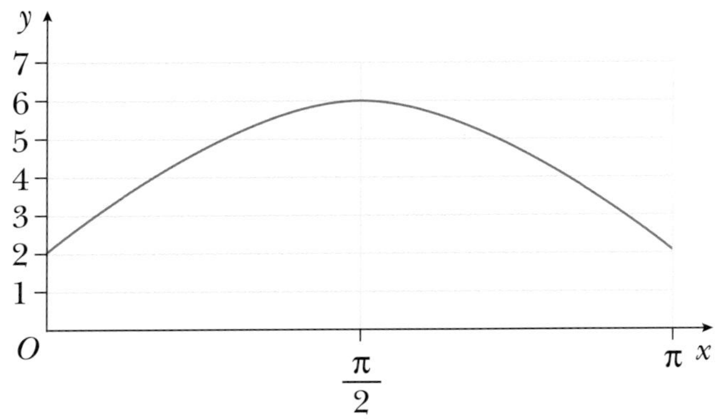

Write down the value of a, the value of b and the value of c.

4 Part of the graph of $y = a\sin bx + c$ is shown above.

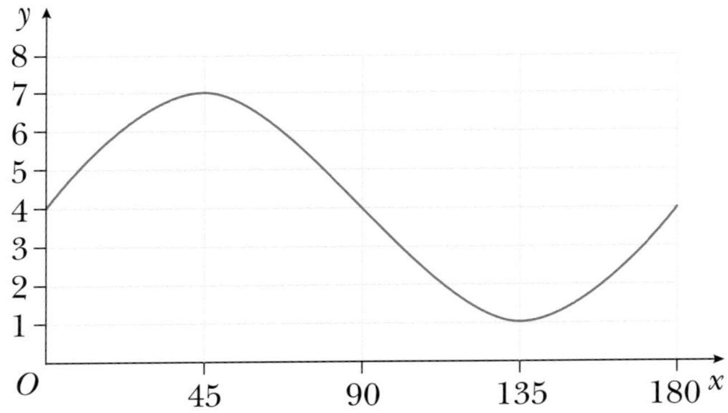

Write down the value of a, the value of b and the value of c.

5 The graph of $y = a + b\cos cx$, for $0° \leqslant x \leqslant 360°$, is shown above.

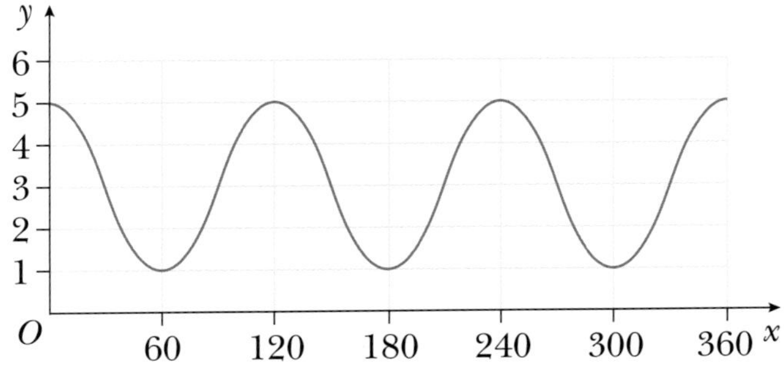

Write down the value of a, the value of b and the value of c.

6 **a** The following functions are defined for $0° \leqslant x \leqslant 360°$.

For each function, write down the period and the equations of the asymptotes.

i $f(x) = \tan 2x$ **ii** $f(x) = 3\tan\frac{1}{2}x$ **iii** $f(x) = 2\tan 3x + 1$

b Sketch the graph of each function and use graphing software to check your answers.

7 **a** The following functions are defined for $0 \leqslant x \leqslant 2\pi$.

For each function, write down the period and the equations of the asymptotes.

i $f(x) = \tan 4x$ **ii** $f(x) = 2\tan 3x$ **iii** $f(x) = 5\tan 2x - 3$

b Sketch the graph of each function and use graphing software to check your answers.

8 

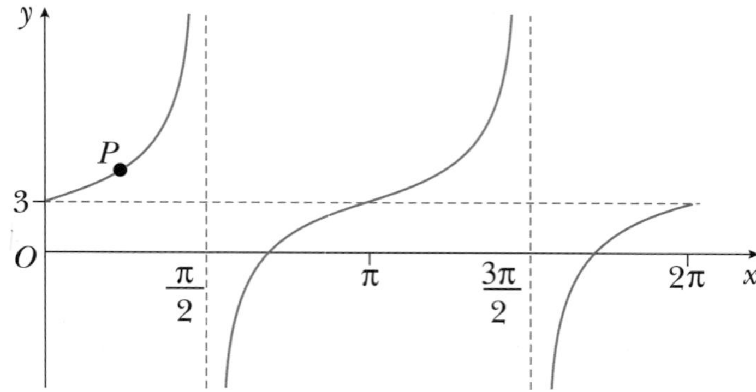

Part of the graph of $y = A\tan Bx + C$ is shown above.

The graph passes through the point $P\left(\frac{\pi}{4}, 4\right)$.

Find the value of A, the value of B and the value of C.

9 $f(x) = a + b\sin cx$

The maximum value of f is 13, the minimum value of f is 5 and the period is 60°.

Find the value of a, the value of b and the value of c.

10 $f(x) = A + 3\cos Bx$ for $0° \leqslant x \leqslant 360°$

The maximum value of f is 5 and the period is 72°.

a Write down the value of A and the value of B.

b Write down the amplitude of f.

c Sketch the graph of f.

11 $f(x) = A + B\sin Cx$ for $0° \leqslant x \leqslant 360°$

The amplitude of f is 3, the period is 90° and the minimum value of f is −2.

a Write down the value of A, the value of B and the value of C.

b Sketch the graph of f.

12 **a** On the same grid, sketch the graphs of $y = \sin x$ and $y = 1 + \sin 2x$ for $0° \leqslant x \leqslant 360°$.

b State the number of roots of the equation $\sin 2x - \sin x + 1 = 0$ for $0° \leqslant x \leqslant 360°$.

13 a On the same grid, sketch the graphs of $y = \sin x$ and $y = 1 + \cos 2x$ for $0° \leqslant x \leqslant 360°$.

b State the number of roots of the equation $\sin x = 1 + \cos 2x$ for $0° \leqslant x \leqslant 360°$.

14 a On the same grid, sketch the graphs of $y = 3\cos 2x$ and $y = 2 + \sin x$ for $0° \leqslant x \leqslant 360°$.

b State the number of roots of the equation $3\cos 2x = 2 + \sin x$ for $0° \leqslant x \leqslant 360°$.

9.5 Graphs of $y = |f(x)|$, where $f(x)$ is a trigonometric function

You have already learnt how to sketch graphs of $y = |f(x)|$ where f(x) is either linear or quadratic.

In this section you will learn how to sketch graphs of $y = |f(x)|$ where f(x) is a trigonometric function.

WORKED EXAMPLE 8

a Sketch the graph of $f(x) = |\sin x|$ for $0 \leqslant x \leqslant 2\pi$.

b State the range of the function f.

Answers

a Step 1: Sketch the graph of $y = \sin x$

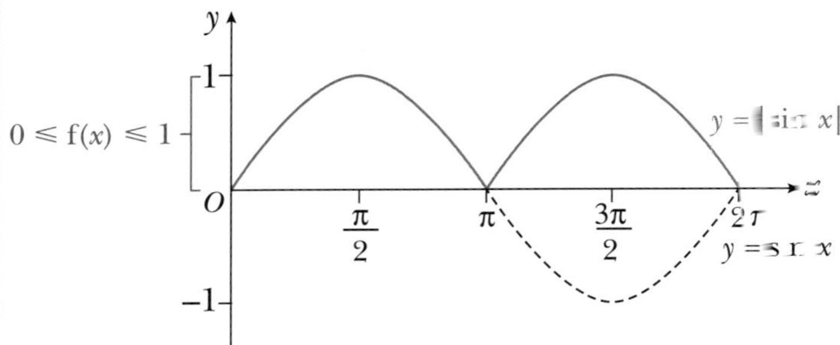

Step 2: Reflect in the x-axis the part of the curve $y = \sin x$ that is below the x-axis.

b The range of the function f is $0 \leqslant f(x) \leqslant 1$.

WORKED EXAMPLE 9

a On the same grid, sketch the graphs of $y = |\sin 2x|$ and $y = \cos x$ for $0° \leqslant x \leqslant 360°$.

b State the number of roots of the equation $|\sin 2x| = \cos x$ for $0° \leqslant x \leqslant 360°$.

Answers

a For $y = |\sin 2x|$ sketch the graph of $y = \sin 2x$ and then reflect in the x-axis the part of the curve $y = \sin 2x$ that is below the x-axis.

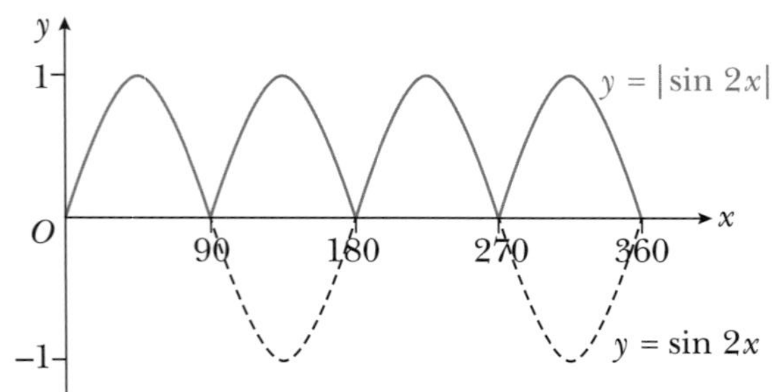

Hence, the graphs of $y = |\sin 2x|$ and $y = \cos x$ are:

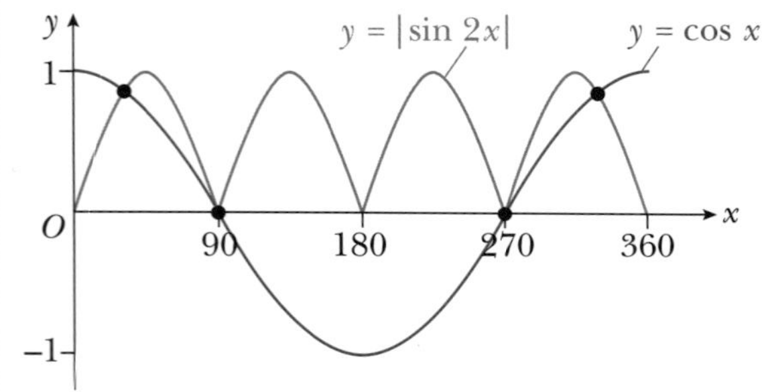

b The graphs of $y = |\sin 2x|$ and $y = \cos x$ intersect each other at 4 points in the interval.

Hence, the number of roots of $|\sin 2x| = \cos x$ is 4.

Exercise 9.5

Use graphing software to check your graphs in this exercise.

1 Sketch the graphs of each of the following functions, for $0° \leqslant x \leqslant 360°$, and state the range of each function.

a $f(x) = |\tan x|$ **b** $f(x) = |\cos 2x|$ **c** $f(x) = |3 \sin x|$

d $f(x) = \left|\sin \frac{1}{2}x\right|$ **e** $f(x) = \left|2 \cos \frac{1}{2}x\right|$ **f** $f(x) = |2 \sin 2x|$

g $f(x) = |\sin x - 2|$ **h** $f(x) = |5 \sin x + 1|$ **i** $f(x) = |4 \cos x - 3|$

2 **a** Sketch the graph of $y = 2 \sin x - 1$ for $0° \leqslant x \leqslant 180°$.

b Sketch the graph of $y = |2 \sin x - 1|$ for $0° \leqslant x \leqslant 180°$.

c Write down the number of solutions of the equation $|2 \sin x - 1| = 0.5$ for $0° \leqslant x \leqslant 180°$.

3 **a** Sketch the graph of $y = 2 + 5\cos x$ for $0° \leqslant x \leqslant 180°$.

b Sketch the graph of $y = |2 + 5\cos x|$ for $0° \leqslant x \leqslant 180°$.

c Write down the number of solutions of the equation $|2 + 5\cos x| = 1$ for $0° \leqslant x \leqslant 180°$.

4 **a** Sketch the graph of $y = 2 + 3\cos x$ for $0° \leqslant x \leqslant 180°$.

b Sketch the graph of $y = |2 + 3\cos x|$ for $0° \leqslant x \leqslant 180°$.

c Write down the number of solutions of the equation $|2 + 3\sin 2x| = 1$ for $0° \leqslant x \leqslant 180°$.

5 **a** On the same grid, sketch the graphs of $y = |\tan x|$ and $y = \cos x$ for $0° \leqslant x \leqslant 360°$.

b State the number of roots of the equation $|\tan x| = \cos x$ for $0° \leqslant x \leqslant 360°$.

6 **a** On the same grid, sketch the graphs of $y = |\sin 2x|$ and $y = \tan x$ for $0 \leqslant x \leqslant 2\pi$.

b State the number of roots of the equation $|\sin 2x| = \tan x$ for $0 \leqslant x \leqslant 2\pi$.

7 **a** On the same grid, sketch the graphs of $y = |0.5 + \sin x|$ and $y = \cos x$ for $0° \leqslant x \leqslant 360°$.

b State the number of roots of the equation $|0.5 + \sin x| = \cos x$ for $0° \leqslant x \leqslant 360°$.

8 **a** On the same grid, sketch the graphs of $y = |1 + 4\cos x|$ and $y = 2 + \cos x$ for $0° \leqslant x \leqslant 360°$.

b State the number of roots of the equation $|1 + 4\cos x| = 2 - \cos x$ for $0° \leqslant x \leqslant 360°$.

9 The equation $|3\cos x - 2| = k$, has 2 roots for the interval $0 \leqslant x \leqslant 2\pi$. Find the possible values of k.

CHALLENGE Q

10

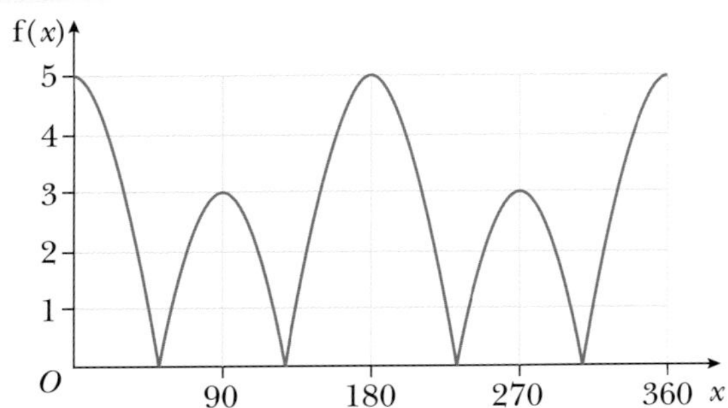

The diagram shows the graph of $f(x) = |a + b\cos cx|$, where a, b and c are positive integers.

Find the value of a, the value of b and the value of c.

9.6 Trigonometric equations

Consider the right-angled triangle:

$\sin\theta = \frac{y}{r} \qquad \cos\theta = \frac{x}{r} \qquad \tan\theta = \frac{y}{x}$

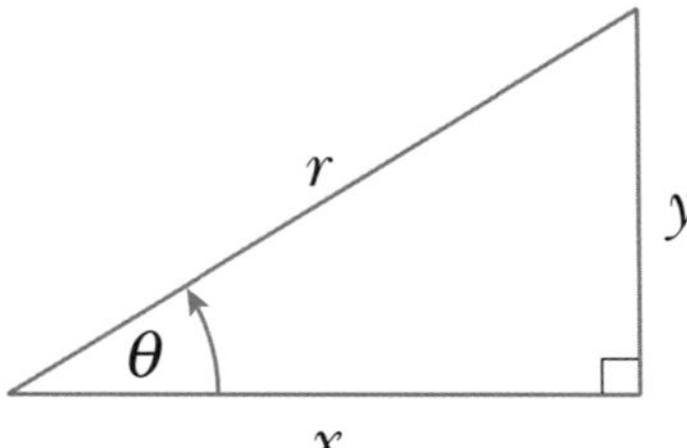

The following rules can be found from this triangle:

$\tan\theta = \frac{y}{x}$ divide numerator and denominator by r

$= \frac{\frac{y}{r}}{\frac{x}{r}}$ use $\frac{y}{r} = \sin\theta$ and $\frac{x}{r} = \cos\theta$

$$\tan\theta = \frac{\sin\theta}{\cos\theta}$$

$x^2 + y^2 = r^2$ divide both sides by r^2

$\left(\frac{x}{r}\right)^2 + \left(\frac{y}{r}\right)^2 = 1$ use $\frac{x}{r} = \cos\theta$ and $\frac{y}{r} = \sin\theta$

$$\cos^2\theta + \sin^2\theta = 1$$

These two important rules will be needed to solve some trigonometric equations later in this section.

Consider solving the equation: $\sin x = 0.5$

$x = \sin^{-1}(0.5)$

A calculator will give the answer: $x = 30°$

There are, however, many more values of x for which $\sin x = 0.5$.

Consider the graph of $y = \sin x$ for $-360° \leqslant x \leqslant 360°$:

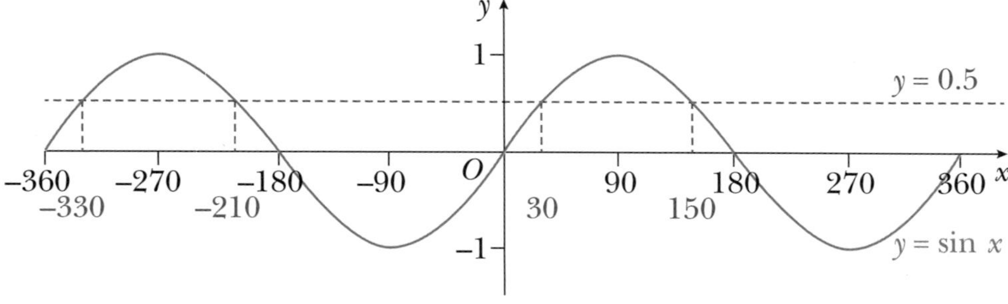

The sketch graph shows there are four values of x, between $-360°$ and $360°$, for which $\sin x = 0.5$.

You can use the calculator value of $x = 30°$, together with the symmetry of the curve to find the remaining answers.

Hence the solution of $\sin x = 0.5$ for $-360° \leqslant x \leqslant 360°$ is:

$$x = -330°, -210°, 30° \text{ or } 150°$$

WORKED EXAMPLE 10

Solve $\cos x = -0.4$ for $0° \leqslant x \leqslant 360°$.

Answers

$\cos x = -0.4$ — use a calculator to find $\cos^{-1}(-0.4)$ to 1 decimal place

$x = 113.6°$

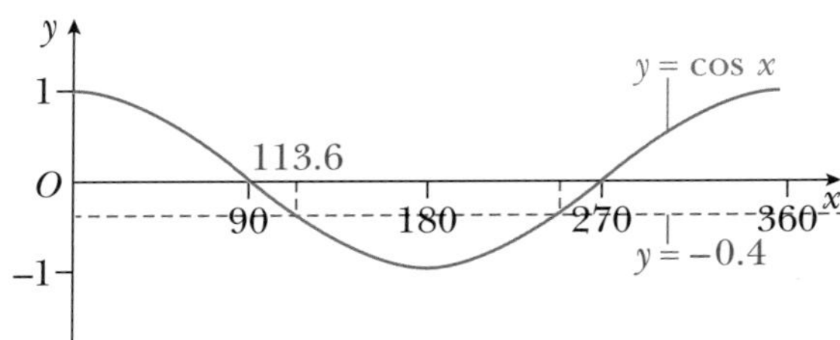

The sketch graph shows there are two values of x, between 0° and 360°, for which $\cos x = -0.4$.

Using the symmetry of the curve, the second value is $(360° - 113.6°) = 246.4°$.

Hence the solution of $\cos x = -0.4$ for $0° \leqslant x \leqslant 360°$ is

$$x = 113.6° \text{ or } 246.4°.$$

WORKED EXAMPLE 11

Solve $\tan 2A = -1.8$ for $0° \leqslant A \leqslant 180°$.

Answers

$\tan 2A = -1.8$ let $x = 2A$

$\tan x = -1.8$ use a calculator to find $\tan^{-1}(-1.8)$

$x = -60.95°$

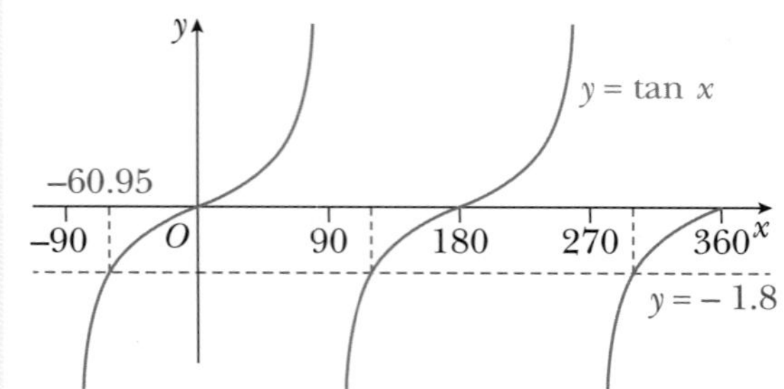

Using the symmetry of the curve:

$x = -60.95$ $\quad x = (-60.95 + 180) = 119.05$ $\quad x = (119.05 + 180) = 299.05$

Using $x = 2A$,

$2A = -60.95$, $A = -30.5$ $\quad 2A = 119.05$, $A = 59.5$ $\quad 2A = 299.05$, $A = 149.5$

Hence the solution of $\tan 2A = -1.8$ for $0° \leqslant x \leqslant 180°$ is
$A = 59.5°$ or $A = 149.5°$.

WORKED EXAMPLE 12

Solve $\sin\left(2A - \frac{\pi}{3}\right) = 0.6$ for $0 \leqslant A \leqslant \pi$.

Answers

$\sin\left(2A - \frac{\pi}{3}\right) = 0.6$ — let $x = 2A - \frac{\pi}{3}$

$\sin x = 0.6$ — use a calculator to find $\sin^{-1} 0.6$

$x = 0.6435$ radians

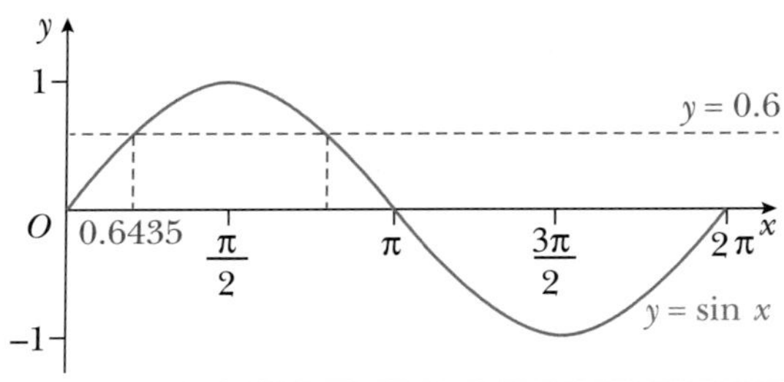

Using the symmetry of the curve:

$x = 0.6435$ $\qquad$ $x = \pi - 0.6435$
$\qquad\qquad\qquad\qquad = 2.498$

Using $\quad x = 2A - \frac{\pi}{3}$

$2A - \frac{\pi}{3} = 0.6435$ $\qquad$ $2A - \frac{\pi}{3} = 2.498$

$A = \frac{1}{2}\left(0.6435 + \frac{\pi}{3}\right)$ $\qquad$ $A = \frac{1}{2}\left(2.498 + \frac{\pi}{3}\right)$

$A = 0.845$ $\qquad$ $A = 1.77$

Hence the solution of $\sin\left(2A - \frac{\pi}{3}\right) = 0.6$ for $0 \leqslant A \leqslant \pi$ is

$A = 0.845$ or 1.77 radians.

WORKED EXAMPLE 13

Solve $\sin^2 x - 2\sin x\cos x = 0$ for $0° \leqslant x \leqslant 360°$.

Answers

$\sin^2 x - 2\sin x\cos x = 0$ factorise

$\sin x(\sin x - 2\cos x) = 0$

$\sin x = 0$ or $\sin x - 2\cos x = 0$

$x = 0°, 180°, 360°$ $\sin x = 2\cos x$

$\tan x = 2$

$x = 63.4$ or $180 + 63.4$

$x = 63.4°$ or $243.4°$

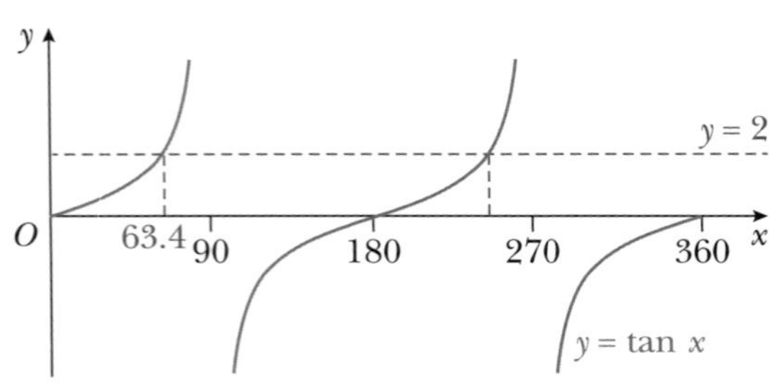

The solution of $\sin^2 x - 2\sin x\cos x = 0$ for $0° \leqslant x \leqslant 360°$ is

$x = 0°, 63.4°, 180°, 243.4°$ or $360°$.

WORKED EXAMPLE 14

Solve $1 + \cos x = 3\sin^2 x$ for $0° \leqslant x \leqslant 360°$.

Answers

$1 + \cos x = 3\sin^2 x$ use $\sin^2 x = 1 - \cos^2 x$

$1 + \cos x = 3(1 - \cos^2 x)$ expand brackets and collect terms

$3\cos^2 x + \cos x - 2 = 0$ factorise

$(3\cos x - 2)(\cos x + 1) = 0$

$3\cos x - 2 = 0$ or $\cos x + 1 = 0$

$\cos x = \frac{2}{3}$ $\cos x = -1$

$x = 48.2°$ or $360 - 48.2$ $x = 180°$

$x = 48.2°$ or $311.8°$

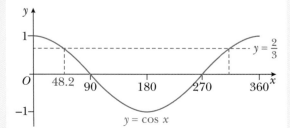

The solution of $1 + \cos x = 3\sin^2 x$ for $0° \leqslant x \leqslant 360°$ is

$x = 48.2°, 180°$ or $311.8°$.

Exercise 9.6

1 Solve each of these equations for $0° \leqslant x \leqslant 360°$.

a $\sin x = 0.3$ **b** $\cos x = 0.2$ **c** $\tan x = 2$ **d** $\sin x = -0.6$

e $\tan x = -1.4$ **f** $\sin x = -0.8$ **g** $4\sin x - 3 = 0$ **h** $2\cos x + 1 = 0$

2 Solve each of the these equations for $0 \leqslant x \leqslant 2\pi$.

a $\cos x = 0.5$ **b** $\tan x = 0.2$ **c** $\sin x = 2$ **d** $\tan x = -3$

e $\sin x = -0.75$ **f** $\cos x = -0.55$ **g** $4\sin x = 1$ **h** $5\sin x + 2 = 0$

3 Solve each of these equations for $0° \leqslant x \leqslant 180°$.

a $\sin 2x = 0.8$ **b** $\cos 2x = -0.6$ **c** $\tan 2x = 2$ **d** $\sin 2x = -0.6$

e $5\cos 2x = 4$ **f** $7\sin 2x = -2$ **g** $1 + 3\tan 2x = 0$ **h** $2 - 3\sin 2x = 0$

4 Solve each of these equations for the given domains.

a $\cos(x - 30°) = -0.5$ for $0° \leqslant x \leqslant 360°$.

b $6\sin(2x + 45°) = -5$ for $0° \leqslant x \leqslant 180°$.

c $2\cos\left(\dfrac{2x}{3}\right) + \sqrt{3} = 0$ for $0° \leqslant x \leqslant 540°$.

d $\cos\left(x + \dfrac{\pi}{6}\right) = -0.5$ for $0 < x < 2\pi$.

e $\sin(2x - 3) = 0.6$ for $0 < x < \pi$ radians.

f $\sqrt{2}\sin\left(\dfrac{x}{2} + \dfrac{\pi}{6}\right) = 1$ for $0 < x < 4\pi$ radians.

5 Solve each of these equations for $0° \leqslant x \leqslant 360°$.

a $4\sin x = \cos x$ **b** $3\sin x + 4\cos x = 0$

c $5\sin x - 3\cos x = 0$ **d** $5\cos 2x - 1\sin 2x = 0$

6 Solve $4\sin(2x - 0.4) - 5\cos(2x - 0.4) = 0$ for $0 \leqslant x \leqslant \pi$.

7 Solve each of these equations for $0° \leqslant x \leqslant 360°$.

a $\sin x \tan(x - 30°) = 0$ **b** $5\tan^2 x -$ [illegible] $\tan x = 0$

c $3\cos^2 x = \cos x$ **d** $\sin^2 x + \sin x \cos x = 0$

e $5\sin x \cos x = \cos x$ **f** $\sin x \tan x = \sin x$

8 Solve each of these equations for $0° \leqslant x \leqslant 360°$.

a $4\sin^2 x = 1$ **b** $25\tan^2 x =$ [illegible]

9 Solve each of these equations for $0° \leqslant x \leqslant 360°$.

a $\tan^2 x + 2\tan x - 3 = 0$ **b** $2\sin^2 x + \sin x - 1 = 0$

c $3\cos^2 x - 2\cos x - 1 = 0$ **d** $2\sin^2 x - \cos x - 1 = 0$

e $3\cos^2 x - 3 = \sin x$ **f** $\sin x + 5 = 6\cos^2 x$

g $2\cos^2 x - \sin^2 x - 2\sin x - 1 = 0$ **h** $1 + \tan x \cos x = 2\cos^2 x$

i $3\cos x = 8\tan x$

10 $f(x) = \sin x$ for $0 \leqslant x \leqslant \dfrac{\pi}{2}$ $g(x) = 2x - 1$ for $x \in \mathbb{R}$

Solve $gf(x) = 0.5$.

9.7 Trigonometric identities

$\sin^2 x + \cos^2 x = 1$ is called a **trigonometric identity** because it is true for all values of x.

In this section you will learn how to prove more complicated identities involving $\sin x$, $\cos x$ and $\tan x$.

When proving an identity, it is usual to start with the more complicated side of the identity and prove that it simplifies to the less complicated side. This is illustrated in the next example.

Note:
LHS means left-hand side and RHS means right-hand side.

WORKED EXAMPLE 15

Prove the identity $(1 + \sin x)^2 + (1 - \sin x)^2 + 2\cos^2 x = 4$.

Answers

$\text{LHS} = (1 + \sin x)^2 + (1 - \sin x)^2 + 2\cos^2 x$

$= (1 + \sin x)(1 + \sin x) + (1 - \sin x)(1 - \sin x) + 2\cos^2 x$ expand brackets

$= 1 + 2\sin x + \sin^2 x + 1 - 2\sin x + \sin^2 x + 2\cos^2 x$ collect like terms

$= 2 + 2\sin^2 x + 2\cos^2 x$

$= 2 + 2(\sin^2 x + \cos^2 x)$ use $\sin^2 x + \cos^2 x = 1$

$= 2 + 2 \times 1$

$= 4$

$= \text{RHS}$

WORKED EXAMPLE 16

Prove the identity $\frac{1}{\cos x} - \cos x = \sin x \tan x$.

Answers

$\text{LHS} = \frac{1}{\cos x} - \cos x$

$= \frac{1}{\cos x} - \frac{\cos^2 x}{\cos x}$

$= \frac{1 - \cos^2 x}{\cos x}$ use $1 - \cos^2 x = \sin^2 x$

$= \frac{\sin^2 x}{\cos x}$

$= \sin x \times \frac{\sin x}{\cos x}$ use $\frac{\sin x}{\cos x} = \tan x$

$= \sin x \tan x$

$= \text{RHS}$

CLASS DISCUSSION

Equivalent trigonometric expressions

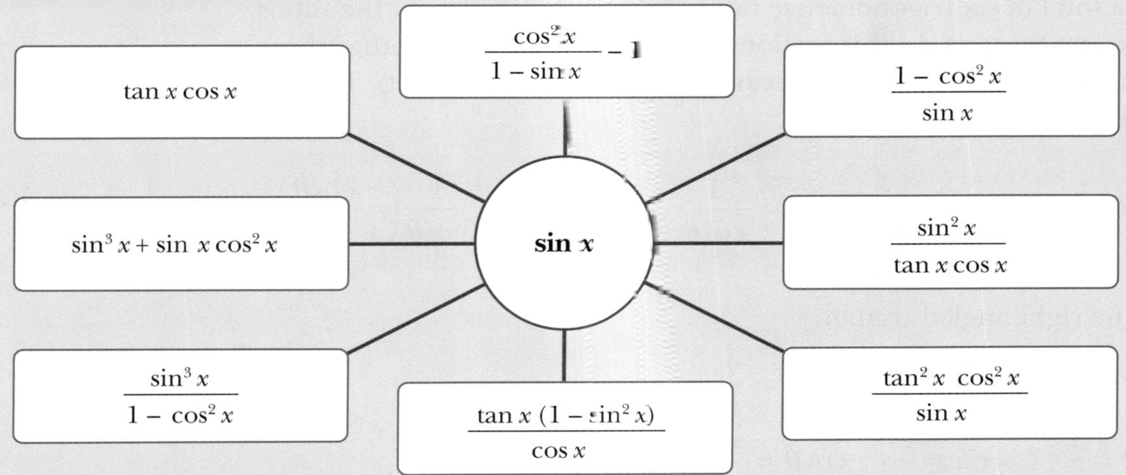

Discuss why each of the trigonometric expressions in the blue boxes simplify to sin *x*.

Create as many trigonometric expressions of your own which simplify to tan *x*.

(Your expressions must contain at least two different trigonometric ratios.)

Compare your answers with your classmates.

Exercise 9.7

1 Prove each of these identities.

a $\frac{\sin x}{\tan x} = \cos x$

b $\frac{\cos x \sin x}{\tan x} = 1 - \sin^2 x$

c $\frac{1-\sin^2 x}{\cos x} = \cos x$

d $\frac{\cos^2 x - \sin^2 x}{\cos x + \sin x} + \sin x = \cos x$

e $(\sin x + \cos x)^2 = 1 + 2\sin x \cos x$

f $\tan^2 x - \sin^2 x = \tan^2 x \sin^2 x$

2 Prove each of these identities.

a $\cos^2 x - \sin^2 x = 2\cos^2 x - 1$

b $\cos^2 x - \sin^2 x = 1 - 2\sin^2 x$

c $\cos^4 x + \sin^2 x \cos^2 x = \cos^2 x$

d $2(1+\cos x) - (1+\cos x)^2 = \sin^2 x$

e $2 - (\sin x + \cos x)^2 = (\sin x - \cos x)^2$

f $\cos^4 x + \sin^2 x = \sin^4 x + \cos^2 x$

3 Prove each of these identities.

a $\frac{\cos^2 x - \sin^2 x}{\cos x - \sin x} = \cos x + \sin x$

b $\frac{\sin x}{1+\cos x} + \frac{1+\cos x}{\sin x} = \frac{2}{\sin x}$

c $\frac{\cos^4 x - \sin^4 x}{\cos^2 x} = 1 - \tan^2 x$

d $\frac{\sin^2 x\left(1-\cos^2 x\right)}{\cos^2 x\left(1-\sin^2 x\right)} = \tan^4 x$

9.8 Further trigonometric equations

The cosecant, secant and cotangent ratios

There are a total of six trigonometric ratios. You have already met the ratios sine, cosine and tangent. In this section you will learn about the other three ratios, which are **cosecant** (cosec), **secant** (sec) and **cotangent** (cot). These three ratios are defined as:

$$\operatorname{cosec}\theta = \frac{1}{\sin\theta} \qquad \sec\theta = \frac{1}{\cos\theta} \qquad \cot\theta = \frac{1}{\tan\theta}\left(= \frac{\cos\theta}{\sin\theta}\right)$$

Consider the right-angled triangle:

$$\sin\theta = \frac{y}{r} \qquad \cos\theta = \frac{x}{r} \qquad \tan\theta = \frac{y}{x}$$

$$\operatorname{cosec}\theta = \frac{r}{y} \qquad \sec\theta = \frac{r}{x} \qquad \cot\theta = \frac{x}{y}$$

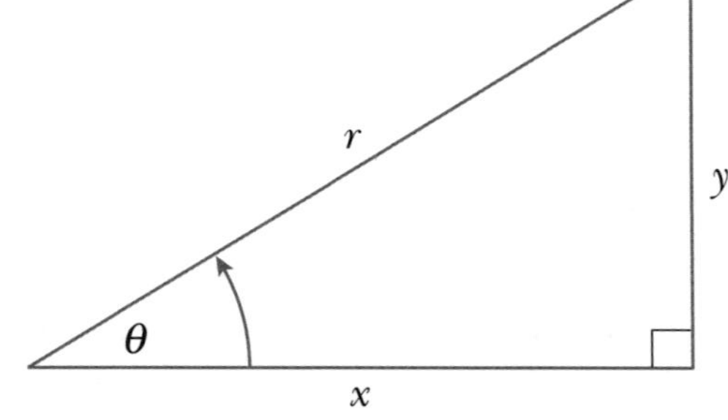

The following rules can be found from this triangle:

$x^2 + y^2 = r^2$ divide both sides by x^2

$1 + \left(\frac{y}{x}\right)^2 = \left(\frac{r}{x}\right)^2$ use $\frac{y}{x} = \tan\theta$ and $\frac{r}{x} = \sec\theta$

$$1 + \tan^2\theta = \sec^2\theta$$

$x^2 + y^2 = r^2$ divide both sides by y^2

$\left(\frac{x}{y}\right)^2 + 1 = \left(\frac{r}{y}\right)^2$ use $\frac{x}{y} = \cot\theta$ and $\frac{r}{y} = \operatorname{cosec}\theta$

$$\cot^2\theta + 1 = \operatorname{cosec}^2\theta$$

These important identities will be needed to solve trigonometric equations in this section.

WORKED EXAMPLE 17

Solve $2\operatorname{cosec}^2 x + \cot x - 8 = 0$ for $0° \leqslant x \leqslant 360°$.

Answers

$2\operatorname{cosec}^2 x + \cot x - 8 = 0$ — use $1 + \cot^2 x = \operatorname{cosec}^2 x$

$2\left(1 + \cot^2 x\right) + \cot x - 8 = 0$ — expand brackets and collect terms

$2\cot^2 x + \cot x - 6 = 0$ — factorise

$(2\cot x - 3)(\cot x + 2) = 0$

$2\cot x - 3 = 0$ or $\cot x + 2 = 0$

$\cot x = \dfrac{3}{2}$ $\qquad$ $\cot x = -2$

$\tan x = \dfrac{2}{3}$ $\qquad$ $\tan x = -\dfrac{1}{2}$

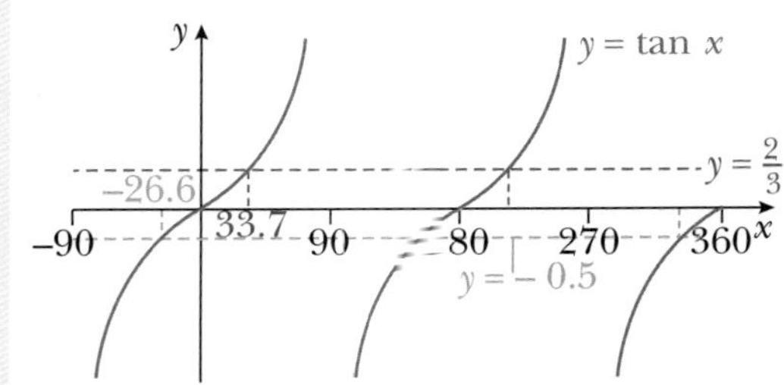

$x = 33.7$ or $33.7 + 180$ $\qquad$ $x = -26.6$ or $-26.6 + 180$ or $-26.6 + 360$

$x = 33.7°$ or $213.7°$ $\qquad$ $x = 153.4°$ or $333.4°$ (since $-26.6°$ is out of range)

The solution of $2\operatorname{cosec}^2 x + \cot x - 8 = 0$ for $0° \leqslant x \leqslant 360°$ is $x = 33.7°, 153.4°, 213.7°$ or $333.4°$.

Exercise 9.8

1 Solve each of these equations for $0° \leqslant x \leqslant 360°$.

a $\cot x = 0.3$ **b** $\sec x = 4$ **c** $\operatorname{cosec} x = -2$ **d** $3\sec x - 5 = 0$

2 Solve each of the these equations for $0 \leqslant x \leqslant 2\pi$.

a $\operatorname{cosec} x = 5$ **b** $\cot x = 0.8$ **c** $\sec x = -4$ **d** $2\cot x + 3 = 0$

3 Solve each of these equations for $0° \leqslant x \leqslant 180°$.

a $\sec 2x = 1.6$ **b** $\operatorname{cosec} 2x = 5$ **c** $\cot 2x = -1$ **d** $5\operatorname{cosec} 2x = -7$

4 Solve each of these equations for the given domains.

a $\sec(x - 30°) = 3$ for $0° \leqslant x \leqslant 360°$

b $\operatorname{cosec}(2x + 45°) = -5$ for $0° \leqslant x \leqslant 180°$

c $\cot\left(x + \dfrac{\pi}{3}\right) = 2$ for $0 < x < 2\pi$

d $3\sec(2x + 3) = 4$ for $0 < x < \pi$

5 Solve each of these equations for $0° \leqslant x \leqslant 360°$.

a $\sec^2 x = 4$ **b** $9\cot^2 x = 4$ **c** $16\cot^2 \dfrac{1}{2}x = 9$

6 Solve each of these equations for $0° \leqslant x \leqslant 360°$.

a $3\tan^2 x - \sec x - 1 = 0$ **b** $4\tan^2 x + 8\sec x = 1$

c $2\sec^2 x = 5\tan x + 5$ **d** $2\cot^2 x - 5\operatorname{cosec} x - 1 = 0$

e $6\cos x + 6\sec x = 13$ **f** $\cot x + 6\sin x - 2\cos x = 3$

g $3\cot x = 2\sin x$ **h** $12\sec x - 10\cos x - 9\tan x =$ [illegible]

9.9 Further trigonometric identities

In this section you will learn how to prove trigonometric identities that involve any of the six trigonometric ratios.

CLASS DISCUSSION

Odd one out

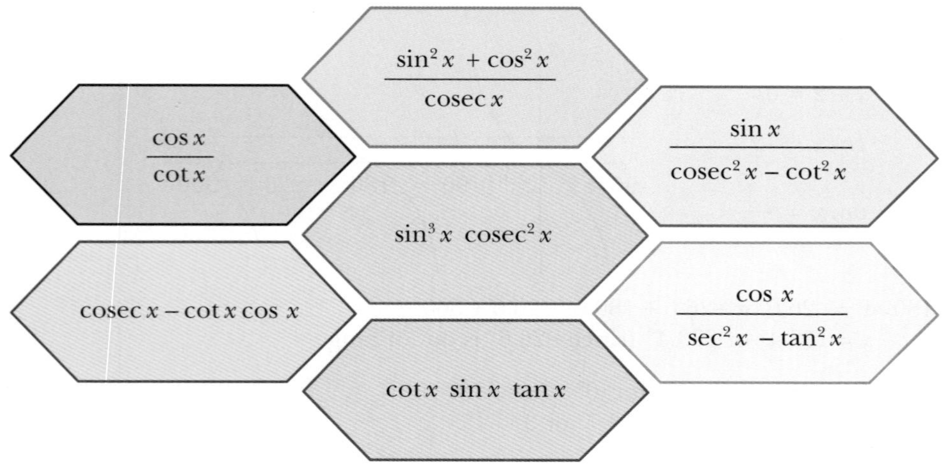

Find the trigonometric expression that does not match the other six expressions.
Create as many expressions of your own to match the 'odd one out'.
(Your expressions must contain at least two different trigonometric ratios.)
Compare your answers with your classmates.

WORKED EXAMPLE 18

Prove the identity $\dfrac{1 + \sec x}{\tan x + \sin x} = \operatorname{cosec} x$.

Answers

$\text{LHS} = \dfrac{1 + \sec x}{\tan x + \sin x}$ — use $\sec x = \dfrac{1}{\cos x}$ and $\tan x = \dfrac{\sin x}{\cos x}$

$= \dfrac{1 + \dfrac{1}{\cos x}}{\dfrac{\sin x}{\cos x} + \sin x}$ — multiply numerator and denominator by $\cos x$

$= \dfrac{\cos x + 1}{\sin x + \sin x \cos x}$ — factorise the denominator

$= \dfrac{\cos x + 1}{\sin x\,(\cos x + 1)}$ — divide numerator and denominator by $(\cos x + 1)$

$= \dfrac{1}{\sin x}$ — use $\operatorname{cosec} x = \dfrac{1}{\sin x}$

$= \operatorname{cosec} x$

$= \text{RHS}$

Exercise 9.9

1 Prove each of these identities.

a $\tan x + \cot x = \sec x \operatorname{cosec} x$

b $\sin x + \cos x \cot x = \operatorname{cosec} x$

c $\operatorname{cosec} x - \sin x = \cos x \cot x$

d $\sec x \operatorname{cosec} x - \cot x = \tan x$

2 Prove each of these identities.

a $(1 + \sec x)(\operatorname{cosec} x - \cot x) = \tan x$

b $(1 + \sec x)(1 - \cos x) = \sin x \tan x$

c $\tan^2 x - \sec^2 x + 2 = \operatorname{cosec}^2 x - \cot^2 x$

d $(\cot x + \tan x)(\cot x - \tan x) = \operatorname{cosec}^2 x - \sec^2 x$

3 Prove each of these identities.

a $\dfrac{1}{\tan x + \cot x} = \sin x \cos x$

b $\dfrac{\sin^2 x + \cos^2 x}{\cos^2 x} = \sec^2 x$

c $\dfrac{\sin^2 x \cos x + \cos^3 x}{\sin x} = \cot x$

d $\dfrac{1 - \cos^2 x}{\sec^2 x - 1} = 1 - \sin^2 x$

e $\dfrac{1 + \tan^2 x}{\tan x} = \sec x \operatorname{cosec} x$

f $\dfrac{\sin x}{1 - \cos^2 x} = \operatorname{cosec} x$

g $\dfrac{\sin x \tan^2 x}{1 + \tan^2 x} = \sin^3 x$

h $\dfrac{1 - \sec^2 x}{1 - \operatorname{cosec}^2 x} = \tan^4 x$

i $\dfrac{1 + \sin x}{1 - \sin x} = (\tan x + \sec x)^2$

j $\dfrac{\cos x \cot x}{\cos x + \cot x} = \sec x - \tan x$

4 Prove each of these identities.

a $\dfrac{\sin x}{\cos x} + \dfrac{\cos x}{\sin x} = \sec x \operatorname{cosec} x$

b $\dfrac{1}{1 - \sin x} - \dfrac{1}{1 + \sin x} = 2 \tan x \sec x$

c $\dfrac{1}{1 + \cos x} + \dfrac{1}{1 - \cos x} = 2 \operatorname{cosec}^2 x$

d $\dfrac{\cos x}{1 - \tan x} + \dfrac{\sin x}{1 - \cot x} = \sin x + \cos x$

e $\dfrac{\cos x}{1 + \sin x} + \dfrac{\cos x}{1 - \sin x} = 2 \sec x$

f $\dfrac{\cos x}{\operatorname{cosec} x + 1} + \dfrac{\cos x}{\operatorname{cosec} x - 1} = 2 \tan x$

5 Show that $(3 + 2\sin x)^2 + (3 - 2\sin x)^2 + 8\cos^2 x$ has a constant value for all x and state this value.

6 **a** Express $5\sin^2 x - 2\cos^2 x$ in the form $a + b\sin^2 x$.

b State the range of the function $f(x) = 5\sin^2 x - 2\cos^2 x$ for $0 \leqslant x \leqslant 2\pi$.

CHALLENGE Q

7 **a** Express $\sin^2\theta + 4\cos\theta + 2$ in the form $a - (\cos\theta - b)^2$.

b Hence state the maximum and minimum values of $\sin^2\theta + 4\cos\theta + 2$.

Summary

Positive and negative angles

Angles measured anticlockwise from the positive x-direction are positive.

Angles measured clockwise from the positive x-direction are negative.

Diagram showing where sin, cos and tan are positive

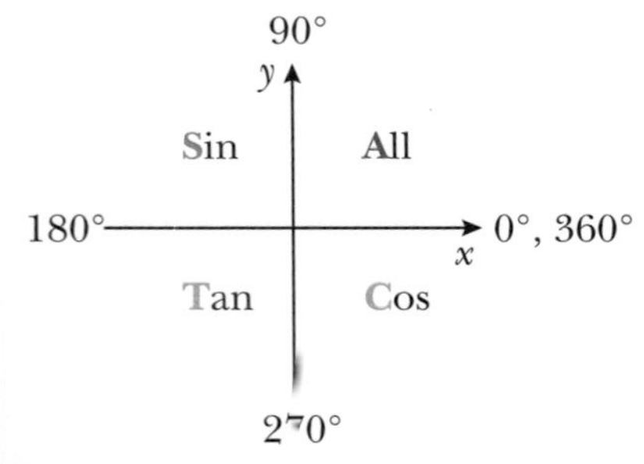

Useful mnemonic: 'All Students Trust Cambridge'

Cosecant, secant and cotangent

$\operatorname{cosec}\theta = \frac{1}{\sin\theta}$ $\qquad \sec\theta = \frac{1}{\cos\theta}$ $\qquad \cot\theta = \frac{1}{\tan\theta}$

Trigonometric identities

$$\tan x = \frac{\sin x}{\cos x}$$

$$\sin^2 x + \cos^2 x = 1$$

$$1 + \tan^2 x = \sec^2 x$$

$$1 + \cot^2 x = \operatorname{cosec}^2 x$$

Examination questions

Worked example

The diagram shows the graph of $y = a\sin(bx) + c$ for $0 \leqslant x \leqslant 2\pi$, where a, b and c are positive integers.

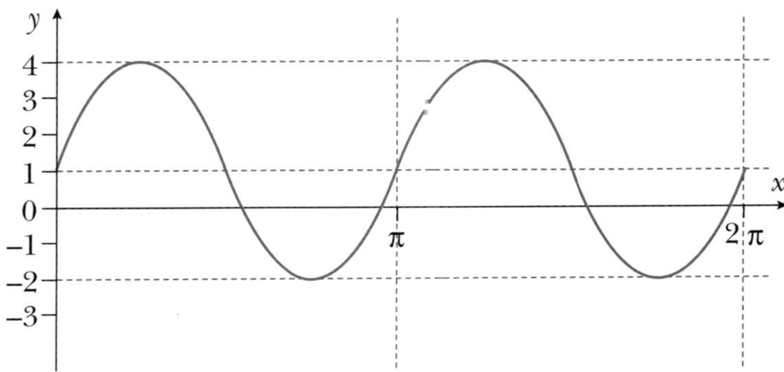

State the value of a, of b and of c. [3]

Cambridge IGCSE Additional Mathematics 0606 Paper 11 Q1 Nov 2013

Answer

$y = a\sin(bx) + c$

a = amplitude period $= \pi = \dfrac{2\pi}{b}$

$a = 3$ $b = 2$

The graph of $y = 3\sin 2x$ has been translated by the vector $\begin{pmatrix} 0 \\ 1 \end{pmatrix}$, hence $c = 1$.

$a = 3$, $b = 2$, $c = 1$

Exercise 9.10

Exam Exercise

1 **a** Sketch the curve $y = 3\cos 2x - 1$ for $0° \leqslant x \leqslant 180°$. [3]

b **i** State the amplitude of $1 - 4\sin 2x$. [1]

ii State the period of $5\tan 3x + 1$. [1]

Cambridge IGCSE Additional Mathematics 0606 Paper 11 Q2 Nov 2014

2 **a** Solve $2\cos 3x = \cot 3x$ for $0° \leqslant x \leqslant 90°$. [5]

b Solve $\sec\left(y + \dfrac{\pi}{2}\right) = -2$ for $0 \leqslant y \leqslant \pi$ radians. [4]

Cambridge IGCSE Additional Mathematics 0606 Paper 11 Q11a,b Nov 2014

3 **a** Prove that $\sec x \operatorname{cosec} x - \cot x = \tan x$. [4]

b Use the result from **part a** to solve the equation $\sec x \operatorname{cosec} x = 3\cot x$ for $0° < x < 360°$. [4]

Cambridge IGCSE Additional Mathematics 0606 Paper 21 Q10i,ii Nov 2014

4 Show that $\frac{1+\sin\theta}{\cos\theta} + \frac{\cos\theta}{1+\sin\theta} = 2\sec\theta$. [4]

Cambridge IGCSE Additional Mathematics 0606 Paper 21 Q12a,b Nov 2013

5 **a** Solve the equation $2\operatorname{cosec}x + \frac{7}{\cos x} = 0$ for $0° \leqslant x \leqslant 360°$. [4]

b Solve the equation $7\sin(2y-1) = 5$ for $0 \leqslant y \leqslant 5$ radians. [5]

Cambridge IGCSE Additional Mathematics 0606 Paper 11 Q1i,ii,iii Jun 2013

6 On a copy of the axes below sketch, for $0 \leqslant x \leqslant 2\pi$, the graph of

a $y = \cos x - 1$ [2]

b $y = \sin 2x$. [2]

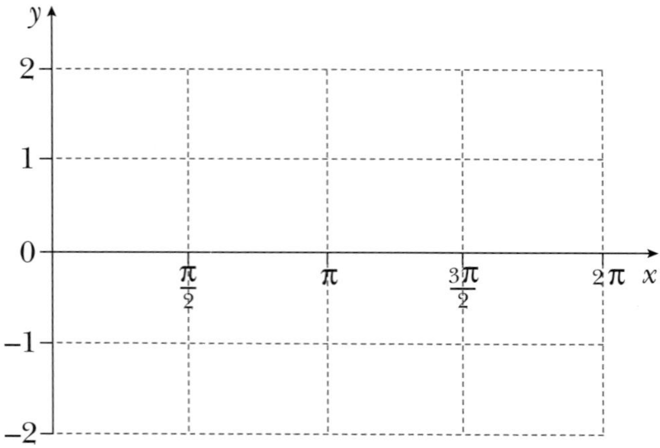

c State the number of solutions of the equation $\cos x - \sin 2x = 1$, for $0 \leqslant x \leqslant 2\pi$. [1]

Cambridge IGCSE Additional Mathematics 0606 Paper 11 Q1i,ii,iii Jun 2013

7 Prove that $\left(\frac{1+\sin\theta}{\cos\theta}\right)^2 + \left(\frac{1-\sin\theta}{\cos\theta}\right)^2 = 2 + 4\tan^2\theta$. [4]

Cambridge IGCSE Additional Mathematics 0606 Paper 21 Q1 Jun 2013

8 **a** Given that $15\cos^2\theta + 2\sin^2\theta = 7$, show that $\tan^2\theta = \frac{8}{5}$. [4]

b Solve $15\cos^2\theta + 2\sin^2\theta = 7$ for $0 \leqslant \theta \leqslant \pi$ radians. [3]

Cambridge IGCSE Additional Mathematics 0606 Paper 11 Q6i,ii Jun 2012

9

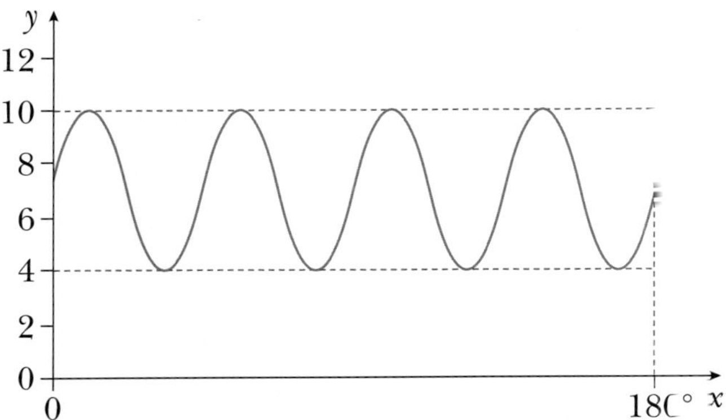

a The diagram shows a sketch of the curve $y = a\sin(bx) + c$ for $0° \leqslant x \leqslant 180°$.
Find the values of a, b and c. [3]

b Given that $f(x) = 5\cos 3x + 1$, for all x, state

i the period of f, [1]

ii the amplitude of f. [1]

Cambridge IGCSE Additional Mathematics 0606 Paper 21 Q3a,bi,ii Jun 2012

10 a Solve $4\sin x = \operatorname{cosec} x$ for $0° \leqslant x \leqslant 360°$. [3]

b Solve $\tan^2 3y - 2\sec 3y - 2 = 0$ for $0° \leqslant y \leqslant 180°$. [6]

c Solve $\tan\left(z - \frac{\pi}{3}\right) = \sqrt{3}$ for $0 \leqslant z \leqslant 2\pi$ radians. [3]

Cambridge IGCSE Additional Mathematics 0606 Paper 11 Q10 Jun 2015

11 Show that $\sqrt{\sec^2\theta - 1} + \sqrt{\operatorname{cosec}^2\theta - 1} = \sec\theta\operatorname{cosec}\theta$. [5]

Cambridge IGCSE Additional Mathematics 0606 Paper 11 Q3 Nov 2015

12 Solve the following equations.

i $4\sin 2x + 5\cos 2x = 0$ for $0° \leqslant x \leqslant 180°$ [3]

ii $\cot^2 y + 3\operatorname{cosec} y = 3$ for $0° \leqslant y \leqslant 360°$ [5]

iii $\cos\left(z + \frac{\pi}{4}\right) = -\frac{1}{2}$ for $0 \leqslant z \leqslant 2\pi$ radians, giving each answer as a multiple of π [4]

Cambridge IGCSE Additional Mathematics 0606 Paper 21 Q9 Nov 2015

Chapter 10
Permutations and combinations

This section will show you how to:

- find the number of arrangements of n distinct items
- find the number of permutations of r items from n distinct items
- find the number of combinations of r items from n distinct items
- solve problems using permutations and combinations.

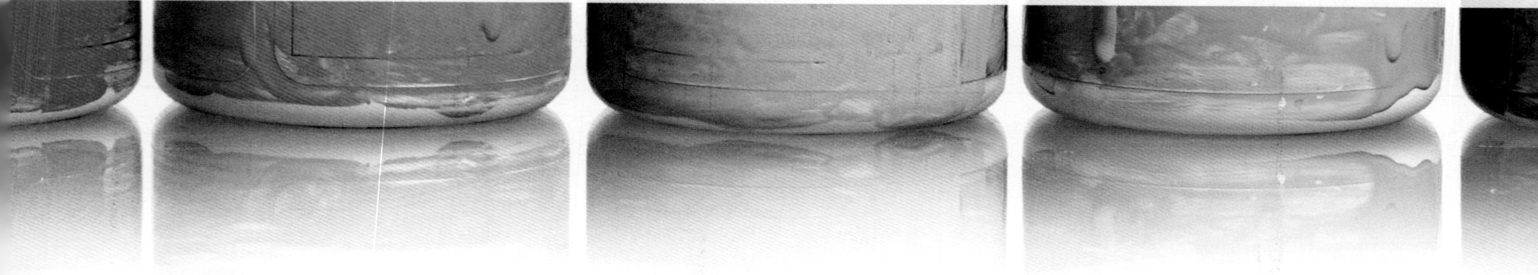

10.1 Factorial notation

$5 \times 4 \times 3 \times 2 \times 1$ is called 5 factorial and is written as $5!$

It is useful to remember that $n! = n \times (n-1)!$

For example $5! = 5 \times 4!$

WORKED EXAMPLE 1

Find the value of

a $\dfrac{8!}{5!}$ **b** $\dfrac{11!}{8!3!}$

Answers

a $\dfrac{8!}{5!} = \dfrac{8 \times 7 \times 6 \times \cancel{5} \times \cancel{4} \times \cancel{3} \times \cancel{2} \times \cancel{1}}{\cancel{5} \times \cancel{4} \times \cancel{3} \times \cancel{2} \times \cancel{1}}$

$= 8 \times 7 \times 6$

$= 336$

b $\dfrac{11!}{8!3!} = \dfrac{11 \times 10 \times 9 \times \cancel{8} \times \cancel{7} \times \cancel{6} \times \cancel{5} \times \cancel{4} \times \cancel{3} \times \cancel{2} \times \cancel{1}}{\cancel{8} \times \cancel{7} \times \cancel{6} \times \cancel{5} \times \cancel{4} \times \cancel{3} \times \cancel{2} \times \cancel{1} \times 3 \times 2 \times 1}$

$= \dfrac{990}{6}$

$= 165$

Exercise 10.1

1 Without using a calculator, find the value of each of the following. Use the $x!$ key on your calculator to check your answers.

a $7!$ **b** $\dfrac{4!}{2!}$ **c** $\dfrac{7!}{3!}$ **d** $\dfrac{8!}{5!}$

d $\dfrac{4!}{2!2!}$ **e** $\dfrac{6!}{3!2!}$ **f** $\dfrac{6!}{(3!)^2}$ **g** $\dfrac{5!}{3!} \times \dfrac{7!}{4!}$

2 Rewrite each of the following using factorial notation.

a 2×1 **b** $6 \times 5 \times 4 \times 3 \times 2 \times 1$ **c** $5 \times 4 \times 3$

d $17 \times 16 \times 15 \times 14$ **e** $\dfrac{10 \times 9 \times 8}{3 \times 2 \times 1}$ **f** $\dfrac{12 \times 11 \times 10 \times 9 \times 8}{4 \times 3 \times 2 \times 1}$

CHALLENGE Q

3 Rewrite each of the following using factorial notation.

a $n(n-1)(n-2)(n-3)$ **b** $n(n-1)(n-2)(n-3)(n-4)(n-5)$

c $\dfrac{n(n-1)(n-2)}{5 \times 4 \times 3 \times 2 \times 1}$ **d** $\dfrac{n(n-1)(n-2)(n-3)(n-4)}{3 \times 2 \times 1}$

10.2 Arrangements

CLASS DISCUSSION

These books are arranged in the order **BROG**. (**B**lue, **R**ed, **O**range, **G**reen).

The books could be arranged in the order **OGBR**.

Find the number of different ways that the 4 books can be arranged in a line.

You will need to be systematic.

How many ways are there of arranging five different books in a line?

To find the number of ways of arranging the letters A, B and C in a line you can use two methods.

Method 1

List all the possible arrangements.

These are: ABC ACB BAC BCA CAB and CBA.

There are 6 different arrangements.

Method 2

Consider filling 3 spaces.

□□□

The first space can be filled in **3** ways with either A or B or C.

For each of these **3** ways of filling the first space there are 2 ways of filling the second space.

There are $\mathbf{3} \times \mathbf{2}$ ways of filling the first and second spaces.

For each of the ways of filling the first and second spaces there is just **1** way of filling the third space.

There are $\mathbf{3} \times \mathbf{2} \times \mathbf{1}$ ways of filling the three spaces.

The number of arrangements $= 3 \times 2 \times 1 = 6$.

$3 \times 2 \times 1$ is called 3 factorial and can be written as 3!

In the class discussion, you should have found that there were 24 different ways of arranging the 4 books.

$4! = 4 \times 3 \times 2 \times 1 = 24$

The number of ways of arranging n distinct items in a line $= n!$.

WORKED EXAMPLE 2

a Find the number of different arrangements of these nine cards if there are no restrictions.

b Find the number of arrangements that begin with **GRAD**.

c Find the number of arrangements that begin with **G** and end with **S**.

Answers

a There are 9 different cards.
number of arrangements = 9! = 362 880

b The first four letters are **GRAD**, so there are now only 5 letters left to be arranged.
number of arrangements = 5! = 120

c The first and last letters are fixed, so there are now 7 letters to arrange between the **G** and the **S**.
number of arrangements = 7! = 5040

WORKED EXAMPLE 3

a Find the number of different arrangements of these seven objects if there are no restrictions.

b Find the number of arrangements where the squares and circles alternate.

c Find the number of arrangements where all the squares are together.

d Find the number of arrangements where the squares are together and the circles are together.

Answers

a There are 7 different objects.
number of arrangements = 7! = 5040

b If the squares and circles alternate, a possible arrangement is:

There are 4! different ways of arranging the four squares.
There are 3! different ways of arranging the three circles.
So the total number of possible arrangements = 4! × 3! = 24 × 6 = 144.

c If the squares are all together, a possible arrangement is:

The number of ways of arranging the 1 block of four squares and the 3 circles = 4!
There are 4! ways of arranging the four squares within the block of squares.
So the total number of possible arrangements = 4! × 4! = 24 × 24 = 576.

d If the squares are together and the circles are together, a possible arrangement is:

There are 4! × 3! ways of having the squares at the start and the circles at the end.
Another possible arrangement is:

There are 3! × 4! ways of having the circles at the start and the squares at the end.
total number of arrangements = 4! × 3! + 3! × 4! = 144 + 144 = 288

Exercise 10.2

1 Find the number of different arrangements

a 4 people sitting in a row on a bench

b 7 different books on a shelf.

2 Find the number of different arrangements of letters in each of the following words.

a TIGER **b** OLYMPICS **c** PAINTBRUSH

3 **a** Find the number of different four-digit numbers that can be formed using the digits 3, 5, 7 and 8 without repetition.

b How many of these four-digit numbers are

i even

ii greater than 8000?

4 A shelf holds 7 different books.

4 of the books are cookery books and 3 of the books are history books.

a Find the number of ways the books can be arranged if there are no restrictions.

b Find the number of ways the books can be arranged if the 4 cookery books are kept together.

5 Five-digit numbers are to be formed using the digits 2, 3, 4, 5 and 6. Each digit may only be used once in any number.

a Find how many different five-digit numbers can be formed.

How many of these five-digit numbers are

b even

c greater than 40 000

d even and greater than 40 000?

6 Three girls and two boys are to be seated in a row.

Find the number of different ways that this can be done if

a the girls and boys sit alternately

b a girl sits at each end of the row

c the girls sit together and the boys sit together.

7 **a** Find the number of different arrangements of the letters in the word ORANGE.

Find the number of these arrangements that

b begin with the letter O

c have the letter O at one end and the letter E at the other end.

8 **a** Find the number of different six-digit numbers which can be made using the digits 0, 1, 2, 3, 4 and 5 without repetition. Assume that a number cannot begin with 0.

b How many of the six-digit numbers in **part a** are even?

9 6 girls and 2 boys are to be seated in a row.
Find the number of ways that this can be done if the 2 boys must have exactly 4 girls seated between them.

10.3 Permutations

In the last section, you learnt that if you had three letters A, B and C and 3 spaces to fill, then the number of ways of filling the spaces was $3 \times 2 \times 1 = 3!$

Now consider having 8 letters A, B, C, D, E, F, G, H and 3 spaces to fill.

The first space can be filled in **8** ways.

For each of these **8** ways of filling the first space there are **7** ways of filling the second space.

There are $\mathbf{8} \times \mathbf{7}$ ways of filling the first and second spaces.

For each of the ways of filling the first and second spaces there are **6** ways of filling the third space.

There are $\mathbf{8} \times \mathbf{7} \times \mathbf{6}$ ways of filling the three spaces.

The number of different ways of arranging three letters chosen from eight letters $= 8 \times 7 \times 6 = 336$.

The different arrangements of the letters are called **permutations**.

The notation $^8P_3$ is used to represent the number of permutations of 3 items chosen from 8 items.

Note that $8 \times 7 \times 6$ can also be written as $\dfrac{8 \times 7 \times 6 \times 5 \times 4 \times 3 \times 2 \times 1}{5 \times 4 \times 3 \times 2 \times 1} = \dfrac{8!}{5!} = \dfrac{8!}{(8-3)!}$

So $^8P_3 = \dfrac{8!}{(8-3)!} = \dfrac{8!}{5!} = 336$.

The general rule for finding the number of **permutations** of r items from n distinct items is $^nP_r = \dfrac{n!}{(n-r)!}$.

Note:

- In permutations, **order matters**.
- By definition, $0! = 1$.

To explain why $0! = 1$, consider finding the number of permutations of 5 letters taken from 5 letters.

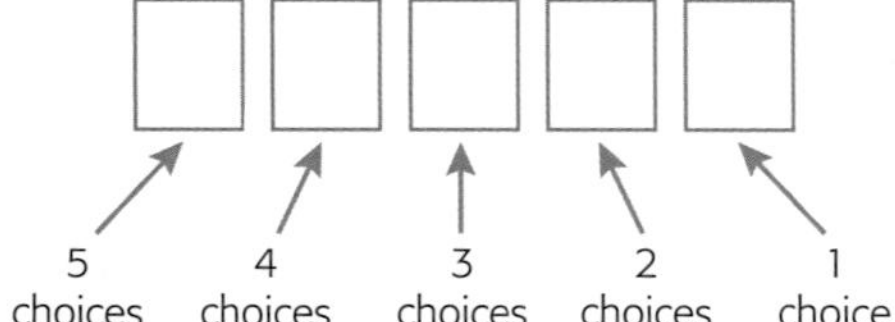

The number of ways of filling the 5 spaces with the 5 letters $= 5 \times 4 \times 3 \times 2 \times 1 = 120$.

But, ${}^5P_5 = \dfrac{5!}{(5-5)!} = \dfrac{5!}{0!} = \dfrac{120}{0!}$.

So $\dfrac{120}{0!} = 120$. Hence $0!$ must be equal to 1.

WORKED EXAMPLE 4

A security code consists of 3 letters selected from A, B, C, D, E, F followed by 2 digits selected from 5, 6, 7, 8, 9.

Find the number of possible security codes if no letter or number can be repeated.

Answers

Method 1

There are 6 letters and 5 digits to select from.

Number of arrangements of 3 letters from 6 letters $= {}^6P_3$

Number of arrangements of 2 digits from 5 digits $= {}^5P_2$

So number of possible security codes $= {}^6P_3 \times {}^5P_2 = 120 \times 20 = 2400$.

Method 2

There are 6 letters and 5 digits to select from.

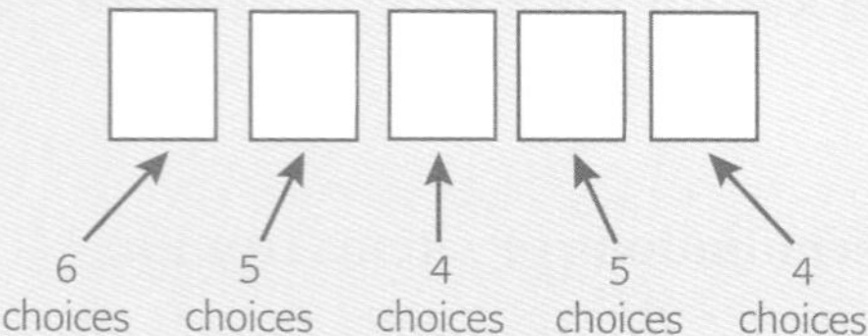

The first three spaces must be filled with three of the six letters.

There is a choice of 6 for the first space, 5 for the second space and 4 for the third space.

The last two spaces must be filled with two of the 5 digits.

There is a choice of 5 for the first space and 4 for the second space.

So number of possible security codes $= 6 \times 5 \times 4 \times 5 \times 4 = 2400$.

WORKED EXAMPLE 5

Find how many even numbers between 3000 and 4000 can be formed using the digits 1, 3, 5, 6, 7 and 9 if no number can be repeated.

Answers

Method 1

The first number must be a 3 and the last number must be a 6.

3	*	*	6

There are now two spaces to fill using two of the remaining four digits 1, 5, 7 and 9.

Number of ways of filling the remaining two spaces = $^4P_2 = \frac{4!}{(4-2)!} = \frac{4}{2} = 12$.

There are 12 different numbers that satisfy the conditions.

Method 2

Consider the number of choices for filling each of the four spaces.

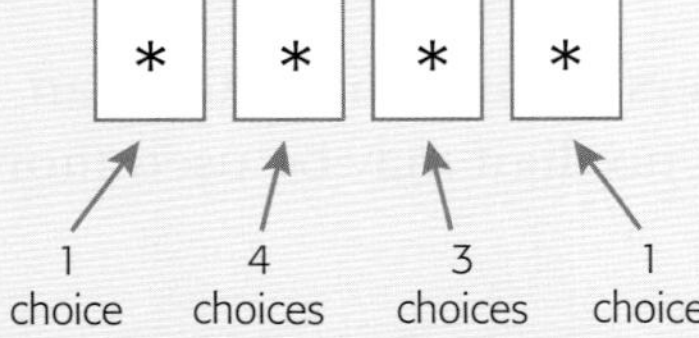

Number of ways of filling the four spaces = $1 \times 4 \times 3 \times 1$

There are 12 different numbers that satisfy the conditions.

Method 3

In this example it is not impractical to list all the possible permutations.

These are: 3156 3516 3176 3716 3196 3916

3576 3756 3196 3916 3796 3976

There are 12 different numbers that satisfy the conditions.

Exercise 10.3

1 Without using a calculator, find the value of each of the following.
Use the ^nP_r key on you calculator to check your answers.

a $^8P_5$ **b** $^6P_4$ **c** $^{11}P_8$ **d** $^7P_7$

2 Find the number of different ways that 4 books, chosen from 6 books be arranged on a shelf.

3 How many different five-digit numbers can be formed from the digits 1, 2, 3, 4, 5, 6, 7, 8, 9 if no digit can be repeated?

4 There are 8 competitors in a long jump competition.
In how many different ways can the first, second and third prizes be awarded?

5 Find how many different four-digit numbers greater than 4000 that can be formed using the digits 1, 2, 3, 4, 5, 6 and 7 if no digit can be used more than once.

6 Find how many even numbers between 5000 and 6000 can be formed from the digits 2, 4, 5, 7, 8, if no digit can be used more than once.

7 A four-digit number is formed using four of the eight digits 1, 2, 3, 4, 5, 6, 7 and 8. No digit can be used more than once.
Find how many different four-digit numbers can be formed if
   a there are no restrictions
   b the number is odd
   c the number is greater than 6000
   d the number is odd and greater than 6000.

8 Numbers are formed using the digits 3, 5, 6, 8 and 9.
No digit can be used more than once.
Find how many different
   a three-digit numbers can be formed
   b numbers using three or more digits can be formed.

9 Find how many different even four-digit numbers greater than 2000 can be formed using the digits 1, 2, 3, 4, 5, 6, 7, 8 if no digit may be used more than once.

CLASS DISCUSSION

You have already investigated the number of ways of arranging 4 different books in a line.

You are now going to consider the number of ways you can select 3 books from the 4 books where the order of selection does not matter.

If the order does not matter, then the selection **BRO** is the same as **OBR**.

Find the number of different ways of selecting 3 books from the 4 books.

A combination is a selection of some items where the order of selection does not matter.

So for **combinations order does not matter**.

Consider the set of 5 crayons.

To find the number of different ways of choosing 3 crayons from the set of 5 crayons you can use two methods.

Method 1
List all the possible selections.

So there are 10 different ways of choosing 3 crayons from 5.

Method 2

The number of combinations of 3 from 5 $= \frac{5!}{3!2!} = \frac{5 \times 4}{2!} = 10$

10.4 Combinations

The general rule for finding the number of **combinations** of r items from n distinct items is:

$$^{n}C_{r} = \frac{n!}{r!(n-r)!}$$

Note:

- In combinations, **order does not matter.**
- $^{n}C_{r}$ is read as 'n choose r'.
  So $^{5}C_{3}$ is read as '5 choose 3'.
- $^{n}C_{r}$ can also be written as $\binom{n}{r}$.
- $^{10}C_{3}$ is the same as $^{10}C_{7}$.
  So the number of ways of choosing 3 from 10 is the same as the number of ways of choosing 7 from 10. This is because when you choose a group of 3 from 10, you are automatically left with a group of 7

WORKED EXAMPLE 6

A team of 6 swimmers is to be selected from a group of 20 swimmers.
Find the number of different ways in which the team can be selected.

Answers

Number of ways of selecting the team $= {}^{20}C_{6} = \frac{20!}{6!14!} = 38\,760.$

WORKED EXAMPLE 7

A

B

The diagram shows 2 different tents A and B.

Tent A holds 3 people and tent B holds 4 people.

Find the number of ways in which 7 people can be assigned to the two tents.

Answers

Number of ways of choosing 3 people from 7 for tent A = ${}^7C_3 = 35$.

So, the number of ways of assigning the 7 people to the two tents = 35.

WORKED EXAMPLE 8

3 coats and 2 dresses are to be selected from 9 coats and 7 dresses.

Find the number of different selections that can be made.

Answers

Number of ways of choosing 3 coats from 9 coats = ${}^9C_3$.

Number of ways of choosing 2 dresses from 7 dresses = ${}^7C_2$.

So, the number of possible selections = ${}^9C_3 \times {}^7C_2 = 84 \times 21 = 1764$.

WORKED EXAMPLE 9

A quiz team of 5 students is to be selected from 6 boys and 4 girls.

Find the number of possible teams that can be selected in which there are more boys than girls.

Answers

If there are more boys than girls there could be:

5 boys 0 girls number of ways = ${}^6C_5 \times {}^4C_0 = 6 \times 1 = 6$

4 boys 1 girl number of ways = ${}^6C_4 \times {}^4C_1 = 15 \times 4 = 60$

3 boys 2 girls number of ways = ${}^6C_3 \times {}^4C_2 = 20 \times 6 = 120$

So, the total number of possible teams = $6 + 60 + 120 = 186$.

WORKED EXAMPLE 10

Sofia has to play 5 pieces of music for her music examination.
She has 13 pieces of music to choose from.
There are 7 pieces written by Chopin, 4 written by Mozart and 2 written by Bach.
Find the number of ways the 5 pieces can be chosen if

a there are no restrictions

b there must be 2 pieces by Chopin, 2 pieces by Mozart and 1 piece by Bach

c there must be at least one piece by each composer.

Answers

a Number of ways of choosing 5 from 13 = $^{13}C_5 = 1287$

b Number of ways of choosing 2 from 7 pieces by Chopin = $^7C_2$
Number of ways of choosing 2 from 4 pieces by Mozart = $^4C_2$
Number of ways of choosing 1 from 2 pieces by Bach = $^2C_1$
So, number of possible selections = $^7C_2 \times {}^4C_2 \times {}^2C_1 = 21 \times 6 \times 2 = 252$.

c If there is at least one piece by each composer there could be:

3 Chopin	1 Mozart	1 Bach	number of ways = $^7C_3 \times {}^4C_1 \times {}^2C_1 = 35 \times 4 \times 2 = 280$
1 Chopin	3 Mozart	1 Bach	number of ways = $^7C_1 \times {}^4C_3 \times {}^2C_1 = 7 \times 4 \times 2 = 56$
2 Chopin	2 Mozart	1 Bach	number of ways = $^7C_2 \times {}^4C_2 \times {}^2C_1 = 21 \times 6 \times 2 = 252$
2 Chopin	1 Mozart	2 Bach	number of ways = $^7C_2 \times {}^4C_1 \times {}^2C_2 = 21 \times 4 \times 1 = 84$
1 Chopin	2 Mozart	2 Bach	number of ways = $^7C_1 \times {}^4C_2 \times {}^2C_2 = 7 \times 6 \times 1 = 42$

So, total number of ways = 280 + 56 + 252 + 84 + 42 = 714.

Exercise 10.4

1 Without using a calculator find the value of each of the following, and then use the ^nC_r key on your calculator to check your answers.

a $^5C_1$ **b** $^6C_3$ **c** $^4C_4$ **d** $\binom{8}{4}$ **e** $\binom{5}{5}$ **f** $\binom{7}{4}$

2 Show that $^8C_3 = {}^8C_5$.

3 How many different ways are there of selecting

a 3 photographs from 10 photographs

b 5 books from 7 books

c a team of 11 footballers from 14 footballers?

4 How many different combinations of 3 letters can be chosen from the letters P, Q, R, S, T?

5 The diagram shows 2 different boxes, A and B.
8 different toys are to be placed in the boxes.
Find the number of ways in which the 8 toys can be placed in the boxes so that 5 toys are in box A and 3 toys are in box B.

A B

6 4 pencils and 3 pens are to be selected from a collection of 8 pencils and 5 pens.
Find the number of different selections that can be made.

7 Four of the letters of the word PAINTBRUSH are selected at random.
Find the number of different combinations if

a there is no restriction on the letters selected

b the letter T must be selected.

8 A test consists of 30 questions.
Each answer is either correct or incorrect.
Find the number of different ways in which it is possible to answer

a exactly 10 questions correctly

b exactly 25 questions correctly.

9 An athletics club has 10 long distance runners, 8 sprinters and 5 jumpers.
A team of 3 long distance runners, 5 sprinters and 2 jumpers is to be selected.
Find the number of ways in which the team can be selected.

10 A team of 5 members is to be chosen from 5 men and 3 women.
Find the number of different teams that can be chosen

a if there are no restrictions

b that consist of 3 men and 2 women

c that consist of no more than 1 woman.

11 A committee of 5 people is to be chosen from 6 women and 7 men.
Find the number of different committees that can be chosen

a if there are no restrictions

b if there are more men than women.

12 A committee of 6 people is to be chosen from 6 men and 7 women.
The committee must contain at least 1 man.
Find the number of different committees that can be formed.

13 A school committee of 5 people is to be selected from a group of 4 teachers and 7 students.
Find the number of different ways that the committee can be selected if

a there are no restrictions

b there must be at least 1 teacher and there must be more students than teachers.

14 A test consists of 10 different questions.

4 of the questions are on trigonometry and 6 questions are on algebra.

Students are asked to answer 8 questions.

a Find the number of ways in which students can select 8 questions if there are no restrictions.

b Find the number of these selections which contain at least 4 algebra questions.

15 Rafiu has a collection of 10 CDs.

4 of the CDs are classical, 3 are jazz and 3 are rock.

He selects 5 of the CDs from his collection.

Find the number of ways he can make his selection if

a there are no restrictions

b his selection must contain his favourite jazz CD

c his selection must contain at least 3 classical CDs.

16 In a group of 15 entertainers, there are 6 singers, 5 guitarists and 4 comedians.

A show is to be given by 6 of these entertainers.

In the show there must be at least 1 guitarist and 1 comedian.

There must also be more singers than guitarists.

Find the number of ways that the 6 entertainers can be selected.

Summary

Arrangements in a line

The number of ways of arranging n distinct items in a line is

$$n \times (n-1) \times (n-2) \times \ldots \times 3 \times 2 \times 1 = n!$$

Permutations

The number of **permutations** of r items from n distinct items is

$$^{n}\mathrm{P}_{r} = \frac{n!}{(n-r)!}.$$

In permutations, **order matters.**

Combinations

The number of **combinations** of r items from n distinct items is

$$^{n}\mathrm{C}_{r} = \binom{n}{r} = \frac{n!}{r!(n-r)!}.$$

In combinations, **order does not matter**.

Examination questions

Worked example

1 a i Find how many different 4-digit numbers can be formed using the digits 1, 2, 3, 4, 5 and 6 if no digit is repeated. [1]

ii How many of the 4-digit numbers found in **part i** are greater than 6000? [1]

iii How many of the 4-digit numbers found in **part i** are greater than 6000 and are odd? [1]

b A quiz team of 10 players is to be chosen from a class of 8 boys and 12 girls.

i Find the number of different teams that can be chosen if the team has to have equal numbers of girls and boys. [3]

ii Find the number of different teams that can be chosen if the team has to include the youngest and oldest boy and the youngest and oldest girl. [2]

Cambridge IGCSE Additional Mathematics 0606 Paper 11 Q10ai,ii,iii,bi,ii Nov 2014

Answers

1 a i Number of 4-digit numbers = ${}^6P_4 = 360$.

ii Method 1

The first number must be a 6.

6	*	*	*

There are now three spaces to fill using three of the remaining five digits 1, 2, 3, 4 and 5.

Number of ways of filling the remaining three spaces = ${}^5P_3 = \frac{5!}{(5-3)!} = \frac{5!}{2!} = 60.$

There are 60 different numbers that satisfy the conditions.

Method 2

Consider the number of choices for filling each of the four spaces.

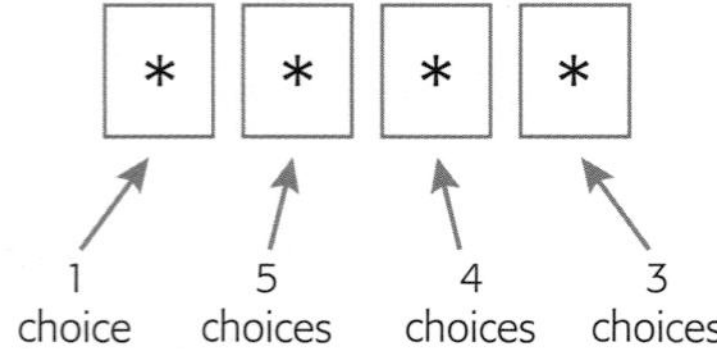

Number of ways of filling the four spaces = $1 \times 5 \times 4 \times 3$.

There are 60 different numbers that satisfy the conditions.

iii **Method 1**

The first number must be a 6.

6	*	*	*

The last number must be a 1, 3 or 5.

The middle two spaces must then be filled using two of the remaining four numbers.

Number of ways of filling the four spaces $= 1 \times {}^4P_2 \times 3 = 1 \times \dfrac{4!}{(4-2)!} \times 3 = 3 \times \dfrac{4!}{2!} = 36.$

There are 36 different numbers that satisfy the conditions.

Method 2

Consider the number of choices for filling each of the four spaces.

The first number must be a 6.

The last number must be a 1, 3 or 5.

When the first and last spaces have been filled there will be four numbers left to choose from.

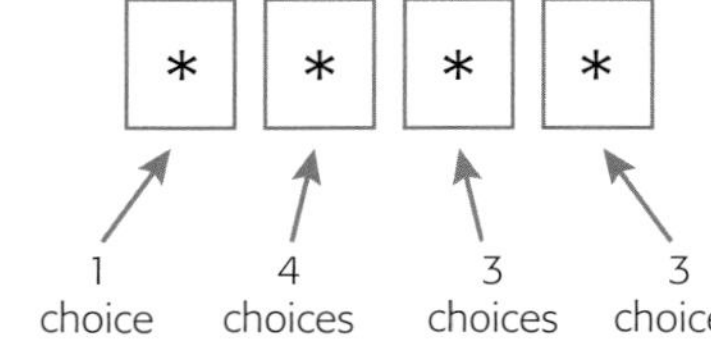

Number of ways of filling the four spaces $= 1 \times 4 \times 3 \times 3.$

There are 36 different numbers that satisfy the conditions.

b **i** There must be 5 boys and 5 girls.

Number of ways of choosing 5 boys from $8 = {}^8C_5$.

Number of ways of choosing 5 girls from $12 = {}^{12}C_5$.

Number of possible teams $= {}^8C_5 \times {}^{12}C_5 = 56 \times 792 = 44\,352.$

ii The team includes the youngest and oldest boy and the youngest and oldest girl.

There are now 6 places left to fill and 16 people left to choose from.

Number of ways of choosing 6 from $16 = {}^{16}C_6 = 8008.$

Number of possible teams = 8008.

Exercise 10.5

Exam Exercise

1 **a** How many even numbers less than 500 can be formed using the digits 1, 2, 3, 4 and 5?

Each digit may be used only once in any number. [4]

b A committee of 8 people is to be chosen from 7 men and 5 women.

Find the number of different committees that could be selected if

i the committee contains at least 3 men and at least 3 women, [4]

ii the oldest man or the oldest woman, but not both, must be included in the committee. [2]

Cambridge IGCSE Additional Mathematics 0606 Paper 11 Q10a,bi,ii Jun 2014

2 **a** An art gallery displays 10 paintings in a row.

Of these paintings, 5 are by Picasso, 4 by Monet and 1 by Turner.

i Find the number of different ways the paintings can be displayed if there are no restrictions. [1]

ii Find the number of different ways the paintings can be displayed if the paintings by each of the artists are kept together. [3]

b A committee of 4 senior students and 2 junior students is to be selected from a group of 6 senior students and 5 junior students.

i Calculate the number of different committees that can be selected. [3]

One of the 6 senior students is a cousin of one of the 5 junior students.

ii Calculate the number of different committees which can be selected if at most one of these cousins is included. [3]

Cambridge IGCSE Additional Mathematics 0606 Paper 21 Q9ai,ii,bi,ii Nov 2012

3 **a** Arrangements containing 5 different letters from the word AMPLITUDE are to be made.

Find

i the number of 5-letter arrangements if there are no restrictions, [1]

ii the number of 5-letter arrangements which start with the letter A and end with the letter E. [1]

b Tickets for a concert are given out randomly to a class containing 20 students.

No student is given more than one ticket. There are 15 tickets.

i Find the number of ways in which this can be done. [1]

There are 12 boys and 8 girls in the class. Find the number of different ways in which

ii 10 boys and 5 girls get tickets, [3]

iii all the boys get tickets. [1]

Cambridge IGCSE Additional Mathematics 0606 Paper 11 Q4ai,ii,bi,ii,iii Jun 2012

4 Six-digit numbers are to be formed using the digits 3, 4, 5, 6, 7 and 9.

Each digit may only be used once in any number.

a Find how many different six-digit numbers can be formed. [1]

Find how many of these six-digit numbers are

b even, [1]

c greater than 500 000, [1]

d even and greater than 500 000. [3]

Cambridge IGCSE Additional Mathematics 0606 Paper 11 Q4i-iv Nov 2011

5 **a** A shelf contains 8 different travel books, of which 5 are about Europe and 3 are about Africa.

i Find the number of different ways the books can be arranged if there are no restrictions. [2]

ii Find the number of different ways the books can be arranged if the 5 books about Europe are kept together. [2]

b 3 DVDs and 2 videotapes are to be selected from a collection of 7 DVDs and 5 videotapes. Calculate the number of different selections that could be made. [3]

Cambridge IGCSE Additional Mathematics 0606 Paper 21 Q6ai,ii,b Jun 2011

6 A 4-digit number is formed by using four of the seven digits 1, 3, 4, 5, 7, 8 and 9.

No digit can be used more than once in any number.

Find how many different 4-digit numbers can be formed if

a there are no restrictions, [2]

b the number is less than 4000, [2]

c the number is even and less than 4000. [2]

Cambridge IGCSE Additional Mathematics 0606 Paper 21 Q6i,ii,iii Nov 2010

7 **a** Jean has nine different flags.

i Find the number of different ways in which Jean can choose three flags from her nine flags. [1]

ii Jean has five flagpoles in a row. She puts one of her nine flags on each flagpole. Calculate the number of different five-flag arrangements she can make. [1]

b The six digits of the number 738925 are rearranged so that the resulting six-digit number is even. Find the number of different ways in which this can be done. [2]

Cambridge IGCSE Additional Mathematics 0606 Paper 22 Q2 Mar 2015

8 a A lock can be opened using only the number 4351. State whether this is a permutation or a combination of digits, giving a reason for your answer. [1]

b There are twenty numbered balls in a bag. Two of the balls are numbered 0, six are numbered 1, five are numbered 2 and seven are numbered 3, as shown in the table below.

Number on ball	0	1	2	3
Frequency	2	6	5	7

Four of these balls are chosen at random, without replacement. Calculate the number of ways this can be done so that

i the four balls all have the same number, [2]

ii the four balls all have different numbers, [2]

iii the four balls have numbers that total 3. [3]

Cambridge IGCSE Additional Mathematics 0606 Paper 21 Q5 Jun 2015

9 a 6 books are to be chosen at random from 8 different books.

i Find the number of different selections of 6 books that could be made. [1]

A clock is to be displayed on a shelf with 3 of the 8 different books on each side of it. Find the number of ways this can be done if

ii there are no restrictions on the choice of books, [1]

iii 3 of the 8 books are music books which have to be kept together. [2]

b A team of 6 tennis players is to be chosen from 10 tennis players consisting of 7 men and 3 women. Find the number of different teams that could be chosen if the team must include at least 1 woman. [3]

Cambridge IGCSE Additional Mathematics 0606 Paper 11 Q4 Nov 2015

10 a A 6-character password is to be chosen from the following 9 characters.

letters	A	B	E	F
numbers	5	8	9	
symbols	*	$		

Each character may be used only once in any password.

Find the number of different 6-character passwords that may be chosen if

i there are no restrictions, [1]

ii the password must consist of 2 letters, 2 numbers and 2 symbols, in that order, [2]

iii the password must start and finish with a symbol. [2]

b An examination consists of a section A, containing 10 short questions, and a section B, containing 5 long questions. Candidates are required to answer 6 questions from section A and 3 questions from section B. Find the number of different selections of questions that can be made if

i there are no further restrictions, [2]

ii candidates must answer the first 2 questions in section A and the first question in section B. [2]

Cambridge IGCSE Additional Mathematics 0606 Paper 12 Q5 Mar 2016

Chapter 11
Series

This section will show you how to:

- use the binomial theorem for expansion of $(a+b)^n$ for positive integral n
- use the general term $\binom{n}{r}a^{n-r}b^r$ for a binomial expansion
- recognise arithmetic and geometric progressions
- use the formula for the nth term and for the sum of the first n terms to solve problems involving arithmetic and geometric progressions
- use the condition for the convergence of a geometric progression, and the formula for the sum to infinity of a convergent geometric progression.

11.1 Pascal's triangle

The word 'binomial' means 'two terms'.

The word is used in algebra for expressions such as $x + 5$ and $2x - 3y$.

You should already know that $(a+b)^2 = (a+b)(a+b) = a^2 + 2ab + b^2$.

The expansion of $(a+b)^2$ can be used to expand $(a+b)^3$.

$$\begin{aligned}(a+b)^3 &= (a+b)(a+b)^2 \\ &= (a+b)(a^2+2ab+b^2) \\ &= a^3+2a^2b+ab^2+a^2b+2ab^2+b^3 \\ &= a^3+3a^2b+3ab^2+b^3\end{aligned}$$

Similarly it can be shown that $(a+b)^4 = a^4 + 4a^3b + 6a^2b^2 + 4ab^3 + b^4$.

Writing the expansions of $(a+b)^n$ out in order:

$$\begin{aligned}(a+b)^1 &= 1a + 1b \\ (a+b)^2 &= 1a^2 + 2ab + 1b^2 \\ (a+b)^3 &= 1a^3 + 3a^2b + 3ab^2 + 1b^3 \\ (a+b)^4 &= 1a^4 + 4a^3b + 6a^2b^2 + 4ab^3 + 1b^4\end{aligned}$$

If you look at the expansion of $(a+b)^4$, you should notice that the powers of a and b form a pattern.

- The first term is a^4 and then the power of a decreases by 1 whilst the power of b increases by 1 in each successive term.
- All of the terms have a total index of 4 (a^4, a^3b, a^2b^2, ab^3 and b^4).

There is a similar pattern in the other expansions.

The coefficients also form a pattern that is known as **Pascal's triangle**.

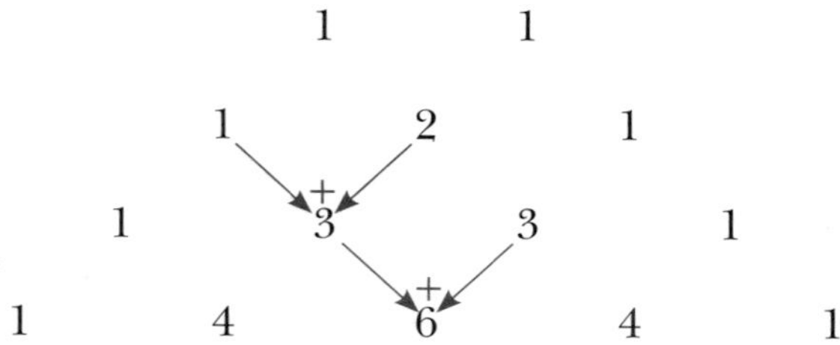

Note:

- Each row always starts and finishes with a 1.
- Each number is the sum of the two numbers in the row above it.

The next row would be:

1 5 10 10 5 1

This row can then be used to write down the expansion of $(a+b)^5$.

$$(a+b)^5 = 1a^5 + 5a^4b + 10a^3b^2 + 10a^2b^3 + 5ab^4 + 1b^5$$

CLASS DISCUSSION

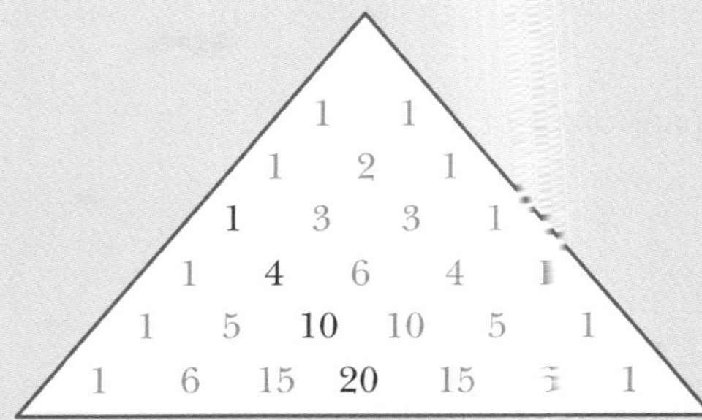

There are many number patterns in Pascal's triangle.

For example, the numbers 1, 4, 10 and 20 have been highlighted.

These numbers are called tetrahedral numbers.

Which other number patterns can you find in Pascal's triangle?

What do you notice if you find the total of each row in Pascal's triangle?

WORKED EXAMPLE 1

Use Pascal's triangle to find the expansion of

a $(2+5x)^3$ **b** $(2x-3)^4$

Answers

a $(2+5x)^3$

The index = 3 so use the third row in Pascal's triangle.

The third row of Pascal's triangle is 1, 3, 3 and 1.

$(2+5x)^3 = 1(2)^3 + 3(2)^2(5x) + 3(2)(5x)^2 + 1(5x)^3$ Use the expansion of $(a+b)^3$.

$= 8 + 60x + 150x^2 + 125x^3$

b $(2x-3)^4$

The index = 4 so use the fourth row in Pascal's triangle.

The fourth row of Pascal's triangle is 1, 4, 6, 4 and 1.

$(2x-3)^4 = 1(2x)^4 + 4(2x)^3(-3) + 6(2x)^2(-3)^2$ Use the expansion of $(a+b)^4$.

$+ 4(2x)(-3)^3 + 1(-3)^4$

$= 16x^4 - 96x^3 + 216x^2 - 216x^3 + 81$

WORKED EXAMPLE 2

a Expand $(2-x)^5$.

b Find the coefficient of x^3 in the expansion of $(1+3x)(2-x)^5$.

Answers

a $(2-x)^5$

The index = 5 so use the fifth row in Pascal's triangle.

The fifth row of Pascal's triangle is 1, 5, 10, 10, 5 and 1.

$$(2-x)^5 = 1(2)^5 + 5(2)^4(-x) + 10(2)^3(-x)^2 + 10(2)^2(-x)^3 + 5(2)(-x)^4 + 1(-x)^5$$
$$= 32 - 80x + 80x^2 - 40x^3 + 10x^4 - x^5$$

b $(1+3x)(2-x)^5 = (1+3x)(32 - 80x + 80x^2 - 40x^3 + 10x^4 - x^5)$

The term in x^3 comes from the products:

$(1+3x)(32 - 80x + 80x^2 - 40x^3 + 10x^4 - x^5)$

$1 \times (-40x^3) = -40x^3$ and $3x \times 80x^2 = 240x^3$

So the coefficient of x^3 is $-40 + 240 = 200$.

Exercise 11.1

1 Write down the sixth and seventh rows of Pascal's triangle.

2 Use Pascal's triangle to find the expansions of

a $(1+x)^3$ **b** $(1-x)^4$ **c** $(p+q)^4$ **d** $(2+x)^3$

e $(x+y)^5$ **f** $(y+4)^3$ **g** $(a-b)^3$ **h** $(2x+y)^4$

i $(x-2y)^3$ **j** $(3x-4)^4$ **k** $\left(x+\frac{2}{x}\right)^3$ **l** $\left(x^2-\frac{1}{2x^3}\right)^3$

3 Find the coefficient of x^3 in the expansions of

a $(x+4)^4$ **b** $(1+x)^5$ **c** $(3-x)^4$ **d** $(3+2x)^3$

e $(x-2)^5$ **f** $(2x+5)^4$ **g** $(4x-3)^5$ **h** $\left(3-\frac{1}{2}x\right)^4$

4 $(4+x)^5 + (4-x)^5 = A + Bx^2 + Cx^4$

Find the value of A, the value of B and the value of C.

5 Expand $(1+2x)(1+3x)^4$.

6 The coefficient of x in the expansion of $(2+ax)^3$ is 96.

Find the value of the constant a.

7 **a** Expand $(3+x)^4$.

b Use your answer to **part a** to express $\left(3+\sqrt{5}\right)^4$ in the form $a+b\sqrt{5}$.

8 **a** Expand $(1+x)^5$.

b Use your answer to **part a** to express

i $\left(1+\sqrt{3}\right)^5$ in the form $a+b\sqrt{3}$, **ii** $\left(1-\sqrt{3}\right)^5$ in the form $c+d\sqrt{3}$.

c Use your answers to **part b** to simplify $\left(1+\sqrt{3}\right)^5+\left(1-\sqrt{3}\right)^5$.

9 **a** Expand $\left(2-x^2\right)^4$.

b Find the coefficient of x^6 in the expansion of $\left(1+3x^2\right)\left(2-x^2\right)^4$.

10 Find the coefficient of x in the expansion $\left(x-\dfrac{3}{x}\right)^5$.

11 Find the term independent of x in the expansion of $\left(x^2-\dfrac{1}{2x}\right)^3$.

CHALLENGE Q

12 **a** Find the first three terms, in ascending powers of y, in the expansion of $(2+y)^5$.

b By replacing y with $3x-4x^2$, find the coefficient of x^2 in the expansion of $\left(2+3x-4x^2\right)^5$.

CHALLENGE Q

13 The coefficient of x^3 in the expansion of $(3+ax)^5$ is 12 times the coefficient of x^2 in the expansion of $\left(1+\dfrac{ax}{2}\right)^4$. Find the value of a.

CHALLENGE Q

14 **a** Given that $\left(x^2+\dfrac{4}{x}\right)^3-\left(x^2-\dfrac{4}{x}\right)^3=ax^3+\dfrac{b}{x^3}$, find the value of a and the value of b.

b Hence, without using a calculator, find the exact value of

$$\left(2+\frac{4}{\sqrt{2}}\right)^3-\left(2-\frac{4}{\sqrt{2}}\right)^3.$$

CHALLENGE Q

15 Given that $y=x+\dfrac{1}{x}$, express

a $x^3+\dfrac{1}{x^3}$ in terms of y

b $x^5+\dfrac{1}{x^5}$ in terms of y.

CLASS DISCUSSION

The stepping stone game

The rules are that you can move East ⟶ or South ↓ from any stone.

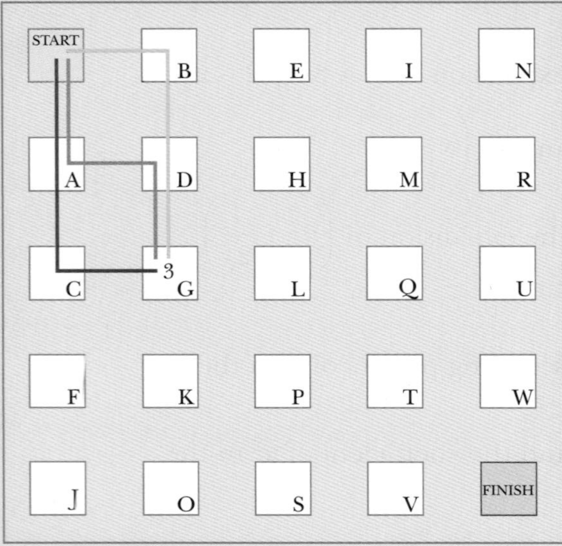

The diagram shows there are 3 routes from the START stone to stone G.

1 Find the number of routes from the START stone to each of the following stones.

a **i** A **ii** B

b **i** C **ii** D **iii** E

c **i** F **ii** G **iii** H **iv** I

What do you notice about your answers to **parts a**, **b** and **c**?

2 There are 6 routes from the START to stone L.

How could you have calculated that there are 6 routes without drawing or visualising them?

3 What do you have to do to find the number of routes to any stone?

4 How many routes are there from the START stone to the FINISH stone?

In the class discussion you should have found that the number of routes from the START stone to stone Q is 10.

To move from START to Q you must move East (E) 3 and South (S) 2, in any order.

Hence the number of routes is the same as the number of different combinations of 3 E's and 2 S's.

The combinations are:

EEESS EESES EESSE ESESE ESEES

ESSEE SSEEE SESEE SEESE SEEES

So the number of routes is 10.

This is the same as ${}^5C_3$ (or ${}^5C_2$).

11.2 The binomial theorem

Pascal's triangle can be used to expand $(a + b)^n$ for any positive integer n, but if n is large it can take a long time. Combinations can be used to help expand binomial expressions more quickly.

Using a calculator:

$^5C_0 = 1 \quad ^5C_1 = 5 \quad ^5C_2 = 10 \quad ^5C_3 = 10 \quad ^5C_4 = 5 \quad ^5C_5 = 1$

These numbers are the same as the numbers in the fifth row of Pascal's triangle.

So the expansion of $(a + b)^5$ is:

$$(a + b)^5 = {}^5C_0\, a^5 + {}^5C_1\, a^4 b + {}^5C_2\, a^3 b^2 + {}^5C_3\, a^2 b^3 + {}^5C_4\, ab^4 + {}^5C_5\, b^5$$

This can be written more generally as:

$$(a + b)^n = {}^nC_0\, a^n + {}^nC_1\, a^{n-1} b + {}^nC_2\, a^{n-2} b^2 + {}^nC_3\, a^{n-3} b^3 + \ldots + {}^nC_r\, a^{n-r} b^r + \ldots + {}^nC_n\, b^n$$

But $^nC_0 = 1$ and $^nC_n = 1$, so the formula simplifies to:

$$(a + b)^n = a^n + {}^nC_1\, a^{n-1} b + {}^nC_2\, a^{n-2} b^2 + {}^nC_3\, a^{n-3} b^3 + \ldots + {}^nC_r\, a^{n-r} b^r + \ldots + b^n$$

or

$$(a + b)^n = a^n + \binom{n}{1} a^{n-1} b + \binom{n}{2} a^{n-2} b^2 + \binom{n}{3} a^{n-3} b^3 + \ldots + \binom{n}{r} a^{n-r} b^r + \ldots + b^n$$

The formulae above are known as the **binomial theorem**.

WORKED EXAMPLE 3

Use the binomial theorem to expand $(3 + 4x)^5$.

Answers

$$\begin{aligned}(3 + 4x)^5 &= 3^5 + {}^5C_1\, 3^4(4x) + {}^5C_2\, 3^3(4x)^2 + {}^5C_3\, 3^2(4x)^3 + {}^5C_4\, 3(4x)^4 + (4x)^5 \\ &= 243 + 1620x + 4320x^2 + 5760x^3 + 3840x^4 + 1024x^5\end{aligned}$$

WORKED EXAMPLE 4

Find the coefficient of x^{20} in the expansion of $(2 - x)^{25}$.

Answers

$(2 - x)^{25} = 2^{25} + {}^{25}C_1\, 2^{24}(-x) + {}^{25}C_2\, 2^{23}(-x)^2 + \ldots + {}^{25}C_{20}\, 2^5(-x)^{20} + \ldots + (-x)^{25}$

The term containing x^{20} is $^{25}C_{20} \times 2^5 \times (-x)^{20}$.

$= 53\,130 \times 32 \times x^{20}$

$= 1\,700\,160x^{20}$

So the coefficient of x^{20} is 1 700 160.

Using the binomial theorem,

$$(1+x)^7 = 1^7 + {}^7C_1\, 1^6\, x + {}^7C_2\, 1^5\, x^2 + {}^7C_3\, 1^4\, x^3 + {}^7C_4\, 1^3 x^4 + \ldots$$
$$= 1 + {}^7C_1\, x + {}^7C_2\, x^2 + {}^7C_3\, x^3 + {}^7C_4\, x^4 + \ldots$$

But ${}^7C_1$, ${}^7C_2$, ${}^7C_3$ and ${}^7C_4$ can also be written as:

$${}^7C_1 = \frac{7!}{1!6!} = 7 \qquad {}^7C_2 = \frac{7!}{2!5!} = \frac{7\times 6}{2!} \qquad {}^7C_3 = \frac{7!}{3!4!} = \frac{7\times 6\times 5}{3!}$$

$${}^7C_4 = \frac{7!}{4!3!} = \frac{7\times 6\times 5\times 4}{4!}$$

So, $(1+x)^7 = 1 + 7x + \dfrac{7\times 6}{2!}x^2 + \dfrac{7\times 6\times 5}{3!}x^3 + \dfrac{7\times 6\times 5\times 4}{4!}x^4 + \ldots$

This leads to an alternative formula for binomial expansions:

$$(1+x)^n = 1 + nx + \frac{n(n-1)}{2!}x^2 + \frac{n(n-1)(n-2)}{3!}x^3 + \frac{n(n-1)(n-2)(n-3)}{4!}x^4 + \ldots$$

The following example illustrates how this alternative formula can be applied.

WORKED EXAMPLE 5

Find the first four terms of the binomial expansion to

a $(1+3y)^7$ **b** $(2-y)^6$

Answers

a $(1+3y)^7 = 1 + 7(3y) + \dfrac{7\times 6}{2!}(3y)^2 + \dfrac{7\times 6\times 5}{3!}(3y)^3 + \ldots$

$= 1 + 21y + 189y^2 + 945y^3 + \ldots$

Replace x by $3y$ and n by 7 in the formula.

b $(2-y)^6 = \left[2\left(1-\dfrac{y}{2}\right)\right]^6$

The formula is for $(1+x)^n$ so take out a factor of 2.

$= 2^6\left(1-\dfrac{y}{2}\right)^6$

$= 2^6\left[1 + 6\left(-\dfrac{y}{2}\right) + \dfrac{6\times 5}{2!}\left(-\dfrac{y}{2}\right)^2 + \dfrac{6\times 5\times 4}{3!}\left(-\dfrac{y}{2}\right)^3 + \ldots\right]$

Replace x by $\left(-\dfrac{y}{2}\right)$ and n by 6 in the formula.

$= 2^6\left[1 - 3y + \dfrac{15}{4}y^2 - \dfrac{5}{2}y^3 + \ldots\right]$

Multiply terms in brackets by 2^6.

$= 64 - 192y + 240y^2 - 160y^3 + \ldots$

Exercise 11.2

1 Write the following rows of Pascal's triangle using combination notation.

a row 3 **b** row 4 **c** row 5

2 Use the binomial theorem to find the expansions of

a $(1+x)^4$ **b** $(1-x)^5$ **c** $(1+2x)^{\text{[illegible]}}$ **d** $(3+x)^3$

e $(x+y)^4$ **f** $(2-x)^5$ **g** $(a-2b)^{\text{[illegible]}}$ **h** $(2x+3y)^4$

i $\left(\frac{1}{2}x-3\right)^4$ **j** $\left(1-\frac{x}{10}\right)^5$ **k** $\left(x-\frac{3}{x}\right)^{\text{[illegible]}}$ **l** $\left(x^2+\frac{1}{2x^2}\right)^6$.

3 Find the term in x^3 for each of the following expansions.

a $(2+x)^5$ **b** $(5+x)^8$ **c** $(1+2x)^6$ **d** $(3+2x)^5$

e $(1-x)^6$ **f** $(2-x)^9$ **g** $(10-3x)^{\text{[illegible]}}$ **h** $(4-5x)^{15}$.

4 Use the binomial theorem to find the first three terms in each of these expansions.

a $(1+x)^{10}$ **b** $(1+2x)^8$ **c** $(1-3x)^7$ **d** $(3+2x)^6$

e $(3-x)^9$ **f** $\left(2+\frac{1}{2}x\right)^8$ **g** $(5-x^2)^9$ **h** $(4x-5y)^{10}$.

5 **a** Write down, in ascending powers of x, the first 4 terms in the expansion of $(1+2x)^6$.

b Find the coefficient of x^3 in the expansions of $\left(1-\frac{x}{3}\right)(1+2x)^6$.

6 **a** Write down, in ascending powers of x, the first 4 terms in the expansion of $\left(1+\frac{x}{2}\right)^{13}$.

b Find the coefficient of x^3 in the expansions of $(1+3x)\left(1-\frac{x}{2}\right)^{13}$.

7 **a** Write down, in ascending powers of x, the first 4 terms in the expansion of $(1-3x)^{10}$.

b Find the coefficient of x^3 in the expansions of $(1-4x)(1-3x)^{10}$.

8 **a** Find, in ascending powers of x, the first 3 terms of the expansion of $(1+2x)^7$.

b Hence find the coefficient of x^2 in the expansion of $(1+2x)^7(1-3x+5x^2)$.

9 **a** Find, in ascending powers of x, the first 4 terms of the expansion of $(1+x)^7$.

b Hence find the coefficient of y^3 in the expansion of $(1+y-y^{\text{[illegible]}})^7$.

10 Find the coefficient of x in the binomial expansion of $\left(x-\frac{3}{x}\right)^{\text{[illegible]}}$.

11 Find the term independent of x in the binomial expansion of $\left(x+\frac{1}{2x^2}\right)^9$.

CHALLENGE Q

12 When $(1+ax)^n$ is expanded the coefficients of x^2 and x^3 are equal.

Find a in terms of n.

11.3 Arithmetic progressions

At IGCSE level you learnt that a number sequence is an ordered set of numbers that satisfy a rule and that the numbers in the sequence are called the terms of the sequence. A number sequence is also called a **progression**.

The sequence 5, 8, 11, 14, 17, ... is called an **arithmetic progression**. Each term differs from the term before by a constant. This constant is called the **common difference**.

The notation used for arithmetic progressions is:

a = first term d = common difference l = last term

The first five terms of an arithmetic progression whose first term is a and whose common difference is d are:

a	$a + d$	$a + 2d$	$a + 3d$	$a + 4d$
term 1	term 2	term 3	term 4	term 5

This leads to the formula:

$$n\text{th term} = a + (n - 1)d$$

WORKED EXAMPLE 6

Find the number of terms in the arithmetic progression −17, −14, −11, −8, ... , 58.

Answers

nth term $= a + (n - 1)d$ use $a = -17$, $d = 3$ and nth term $= 58$

$58 = -17 + 3(n - 1)$ solve

$n - 1 = 25$

$n = 26$

WORKED EXAMPLE 7

The fifth term of an arithmetic progression is 4.4 and the ninth term is 7.6. Find the first term and the common difference.

Answers

fifth term = 4.4 $\Rightarrow a + 4d = 4.4$ -------(1)

ninth term = 7.6 $\Rightarrow a + 8d = 7.6$ -------(2)

(2) − (1), gives $4d = 3.2$

$d = 0.8$

Substituting in (1) gives $a + 3.2 = 4.4$

$a = 1.2$

First term = 1.2, common difference = 0.8.

WORKED EXAMPLE 8

The nth term of an arithmetic progression is $11 - 3n$. Find the first term and the common difference.

Answers

First term $= 11 - 3(1) = 8$ substitute $n = 1$ into nth term $= 11 - 3n$

second term $= 11 - 3(2) = 5$ substitute $n = 2$ into nth term $= 11 - 3n$

Common difference = second term − first term = −3.

The sum of an arithmetic progression

When the terms in a sequence are added together the resulting sum is called a **series**.

CLASS DISCUSSION

$1 + 2 + 3 + 4 + \ldots + 97 + 98 + 99 + 100 = ?$

It is said that at the age of eight, the famous mathematician Carl Gauss was asked to find the sum of the numbers from 1 to 100. His teacher expected this task to keep him occupied for some time but Gauss surprised his teacher by writing down the correct answer after just a couple of seconds. His method involved adding the numbers in pairs: $1 + 100 = 101$, $2 + 99 = 101$, $3 + 98 = 101$, …

1 Can you complete his method to find the answer?

2 Use Gauss's method to find the sum of

a $2 + 4 + 6 + 8 + \ldots + 394 + 396 + 398 + 400$

b $3 + 6 + 9 + 12 + \ldots + 441 + 444 + 447 + 450$

c $17 + 24 + 31 + 38 + \ldots + 339 + 346 + 353 + 360$.

3 Use Gauss's method to find an expression, in terms of n, for the sum

$1 + 2 + 3 + 4 + \ldots + (n-3) + (n-2) + (n-1) + n$.

It can be shown that the sum of an arithmetic progression, S_n, can be written as:

$$S_n = \frac{n}{2}(a+l) \quad \text{or} \quad S_n = \frac{n}{2}[2a+(n-1)d]$$

Proof: $S_n = a + (a+d) + (a+2d) + \ldots + (l-2d) + (l-d) + l$

Reversing: $S_n = l + (l-d) + (l-2d) + \ldots + (a+2d) + (a+d) + a$

Adding: $2S_n = n(a+l) + (a+l) + (a+l) + \ldots + (a+l) + (a+l) + (a+l)$

$2S_n = n(a+l)$

$$S_n = \frac{n}{2}(a+l)$$

Using $l = a + (n-1)d$, gives $S_n = \frac{n}{2}[2a + (n-1)d]$

It is useful to remember the following rule that applies for all progressions:

nth term $= S_n - S_{n-1}$

WORKED EXAMPLE 9

In an arithmetic progression, the first term is 25, the 19th term is –38 and the last term is –87. Find the sum of all the terms in the progression.

Answers

nth term $= a + (n-1)d$ — use nth term $= -38$ when $n = 19$ and $a = 25$

$-38 = 25 + 18d$ — solve

$d = -3.5$

nth term $= a + (n-1)d$ — use nth term $= -87$ when $a = 25$ and $d = -3.5$

$-87 = 25 - 3.5(n-1)$ — solve

$n - 1 = 32$

$n = 33$

$S_n = \frac{n}{2}(a + l)$ — use $a = 25$, $l = -87$ and $n = 33$

$S_{33} = \frac{33}{2}(25 - 87)$

$= -1023$

WORKED EXAMPLE 10

The 12th term in an arithmetic progression is 8 and the sum of the first 13 terms is 78. Find the first term of the progression and the common difference.

Answers

nth term $= a + (n-1)d$ — use nth term $= 8$ when $n = 12$

$8 = a + 11d$ ------------ (1)

$S_n = \frac{n}{2}[2a + (n-1)d]$ — use $n = 13$ and $S_{13} = 78$

$78 = \frac{13}{2}(2a + 12d)$ — simplify

$6 = a + 6d$ -------------------- (2)

(1) – (2) gives $5d = 2$

$d = 0.4$

Substituting $d = 0.4$ in equation (1) gives $a = 3.6$.

First term = 3.6, common difference = 0.4.

WORKED EXAMPLE 11

The sum of the first n terms, S_n, of a particular arithmetic progression is given by $S_n = 5n^2 - 3n$.

a Find the first term and the common difference.

b Find an expression for the nth term.

Answers

a $S_1 = 5(1)^2 - 3(1) = 2 \quad \Rightarrow \quad$ first term = 2

$S_2 = 5(2)^2 - 3(2) = 14 \quad \Rightarrow \quad$ first term + second term = 14

second term = 14 − 2 = 12

First term = 2, common difference = 10.

b **Method 1:**

nth term $= a + (n-1)d$ use $a = 2$, $d = 10$

$= 2 + 10(n-1)$

$= 10n - 8$

Method 2:

nth term $= S_n - S_{n-1} = 5n^2 - 3n - [5(n-1)^2 - 3(n-1)]$

$= 5n^2 - 3n - (5n^2 - 10n + 5 - 3n + 3)$

$= 10n - 8$

Exercise 11.3

1 The first term in an arithmetic progression is a and the common difference is d.

Write down expressions, in terms of a and d, for the fifth term and the 14th term.

2 Find the sum of each of these arithmetic series.

a $2 + 9 + 16 + \ldots$ (15 terms)   **b** $20 + 11 + 2 + \ldots$ (20 terms)

c $8.5 + 10 + 11.5 + \ldots$ (30 terms)   **d** $-2x - 5x - 8x - \ldots$ (40 terms)

3 Find the number of terms and the sum of each of these arithmetic series.

a $23 + 27 + 31 \ldots + 159$ **b** $28 + 11 - 6 - \ldots -210$

4 The first term of an arithmetic progression is 2 and the sum of the first 12 terms is 618.

Find the common difference.

5 In an arithmetic progression, the first term is −13, the 20th term is 82 and the last term is 112.

a Find the common difference and the number of terms.

b Find the sum of the terms in this progression.

6 The first two terms in an arithmetic progression are 57 and 46. The last term is −207. Find the sum of all the terms in this progression.

7 The first two terms in an arithmetic progression are –2 and 5. The last term in the progression is the only number in the progression that is greater than 200. Find the sum of all the terms in the progression.

8 The first term of an arithmetic progression is 8 and the last term is 34. The sum of the first six terms is 58. Find the number of terms in this progression.

9 Find the sum of all the integers between 100 and 400 that are multiples of 6.

10 The first term of an arithmetic progression is 7 and the eleventh term is 32. The sum of all the terms in the progression is 2790. Find the number of terms in the progression.

11 Rafiu buys a boat for \$15 500. He pays for this boat by making monthly payments that are in arithmetic progression. The first payment that he makes is \$140 and the debt is fully repaid after 31 payments. Find the fifth payment.

12 The eighth term of an arithmetic progression is –10 and the sum of the first twenty terms is –350.

a Find the first term and the common difference.

b Given that the nth term of this progression is –97, find the value of n.

13 The sum of the first n terms, S_n, of a particular arithmetic progression is given by $S_n = 4n^2 + 2n$. Find the first term and the common difference.

14 The sum of the first n terms, S_n, of a particular arithmetic progression is given by $S_n = -3n^2 - 2n$. Find the first term and the common difference.

15 The sum of the first n terms, S_n, of a particular arithmetic progression is given by $S_n = \frac{n}{12}(4n + 5)$. Find an expression for the nth term.

16 A circle is divided into twelve sectors. The sizes of the angles of the sectors are in arithmetic progression. The angle of the largest sector is 6.5 times the angle of the smallest sector. Find the angle of the smallest sector.

17 An arithmetic sequence has first term a and common difference d. The sum of the first 25 terms is 15 times the sum of the first 4 terms.

a Find a in terms of d.

b Find the 55th term in terms of a.

18 The eighth term in an arithmetic progression is three times the third term. Show that the sum of the first eight terms is four times the sum of the first four terms.

CHALLENGE Q

19 The first term of an arithmetic progression is $\cos^2 x$ and the second term is 1.

a Write down an expression, in terms of $\cos x$, for the seventh term of this progression.

b Show that the sum of the first twenty terms of this progression is $20 + 170\sin^2 x$.

CHALLENGE Q

20 The sum of the digits in the number 56 is 11. $(5 + 6 = 11)$

a Show that the sum of the digits of the integers from 15 to 18 is 30.

b Find the sum of the digits of the integers from 1 to 100.

11.4 Geometric progressions

The sequence 7, 14, 28, 56, 112, … is called a **geometric progression**. Each term is double the preceding term. The constant multiple is called the **common ratio**.

Other examples of geometric progressions are:

Progression	Common ratio
$1, -2, 4, -8, 16, -32, \ldots$	-2
$81, 54, 36, 24, 16, 10\frac{2}{3}, \ldots$	$\frac{2}{3}$
$-8, 4, -2, 1, -\frac{1}{2}, \frac{1}{4}, \ldots$	$-\frac{1}{2}$

The notation used for a geometric progression is:

a = first term r = common ratio

The first five terms of a geometric progression whose first term is a and whose common ratio is r are:

a	ar	ar^2	ar^3	ar^4
term 1	term 2	term 3	term 4	term 5

This leads to the formula:

$$n\text{th term} = ar^{n-1}$$

WORKED EXAMPLE 12

The third term of a geometric progression is 144 and the common ratio is $\frac{3}{2}$. Find the seventh term and an expression for the nth term.

Answers

$n\text{th term} = ar^{n-1}$ use nth term = 144 when $n = 3$ and $r = \frac{3}{2}$

$$144 = a\left(\frac{3}{2}\right)^2$$

$$a = 64$$

$$\text{seventh term} = 64\left(\frac{3}{2}\right)^6 = 729$$

$$n\text{th term} = ar^{n-1} = 64\left(\frac{3}{2}\right)^{n-1}$$

WORKED EXAMPLE 13

The second and fourth terms in a geometric progression are 108 and 48 respectively. Given that all the terms are positive, find the first term and the common ratio. Hence, write down an expression for the nth term.

Answers

$108 = ar$ ---------(1) $\quad 48 = ar^3$----------(2)

(2) ÷ (1) gives $\dfrac{ar^3}{ar} = \dfrac{48}{108}$

$r^2 = \dfrac{4}{9}$

$r = \pm\dfrac{2}{3}$ $\quad$ all terms are positive $\Rightarrow r > 0$

$r = \dfrac{2}{3}$

Substituting $r = \dfrac{2}{3}$ into equation (1) gives $a = 162$.

First term = 162, common ratio $= \dfrac{2}{3}$, nth term $= 162\left(\dfrac{2}{3}\right)^{n-1}$.

WORKED EXAMPLE 14

The nth term of a geometric progression is $30\left(-\dfrac{1}{2}\right)^n$. Find the first term and the common ratio.

Answers

first term $= 30\left(-\dfrac{1}{2}\right)^1 = -15$

second term $= 30\left(-\dfrac{1}{2}\right)^2 = 7.5$

Common ratio $= \dfrac{\text{2nd term}}{\text{1st term}} = \dfrac{7.5}{-15} = -\dfrac{1}{2}$

First term = −15, common ratio $= -\dfrac{1}{2}$.

WORKED EXAMPLE 15

In the geometric sequence 2, 6, 18, 54, … which is the first term to exceed 1000000?

Answers

$n\text{th term} = ar^{n-1}$	use $a = 2$ and $r = 3$
$2 \times 3^{n-1} > 1000000$	divide by 2 and take logs
$\log_{10} 3^{n-1} > \log_{10} 500000$	use the power rule for logs
$(n-1)\log_{10} 3 > \log_{10} 500000$	divide both sides by $\log_{10} 3$

$$n - 1 > \frac{\log_{10} 500000}{\log_{10} 3}$$

$$n - 1 > 11.94\ldots$$

$$n > 12.94\ldots$$

The 13th term is the first to exceed 1000000.

CLASS DISCUSSION

In this class discussion you are not allowed to use a calculator.

1 Consider the sum of the first 10 terms, S_{10}, of a geometric progression with $a = 1$ and $r = 5$.

$S_{10} = 1 + 5 + 5^2 + 5^3 + \ldots + 5^7 + 5^8 + 5^9$

a Multiply both sides of the equation above by the common ratio, 5, and complete the following statement.

$5S_{10} = 5 + 5^2 + 5^{\cdots} + 5^{\cdots} + \ldots + 5^{\cdots} + 5^{\cdots} + 5^{\cdots}$

b What happens when you subtract the equation for S_{10} from the equation for $5S_{10}$?

c Can you find an alternative way of expressing the sum S_{10}?

2 Use the method from **question 1** to find an alternative way of expressing each of the following

a $3 + 3 \times 2 + 3 \times 2^2 + 3 \times 2^3 + \ldots$ (12 terms)

b $32 + 32 \times \frac{1}{2} + 32 \times \left(\frac{1}{2}\right)^2 + 32 \times \left(\frac{1}{2}\right)^3 + \ldots$ (15 terms)

c $27 - 18 + 12 - 8 + \ldots$ (20 terms)

It can be shown that the sum of a geometric progression, S_n, can be written as:

$$S_n = \frac{a(1 - r^n)}{1 - r} \quad \text{or} \quad S_n = \frac{a(r^n - 1)}{r - 1}$$

Note:
For these formulae, $r \neq 1$

Either formula can be used but it is usually easier to

- use the first formula when $-1 < r < 1$.
- use the second formula when $r > 1$ or when $r < -1$.

Proof:

$$S_n = a + ar + ar^2 + \ldots + ar^{n-3} + ar^{n-2} + ar^{n-1} \quad \text{-------------(1)}$$

$$r \times (1): \quad rS_n = ar + ar^2 + \ldots + ar^{n-3} + ar^{n-2} + ar^{n-1} + ar^n \quad \text{-------------(2)}$$

$$(2) - (1): \quad rS_n - S_n = ar^n - a$$

$$(r-1)S_n = a(r^n - 1)$$

$$S_n = \frac{a(r^n - 1)}{r - 1}$$

Multiplying numerator and denominator by –1 gives the alternative formula $S_n = \dfrac{a(1 - r^n)}{1 - r}$.

WORKED EXAMPLE 16

Find the sum of the first ten terms of the geometric series 2 + 6 + 18 + 54 + …

Answers

$S_n = \dfrac{a(r^n - 1)}{r - 1}$ — use $a = 2$, $r = 3$ and $n = 10$

$S_{12} = \dfrac{2(3^{10} - 1)}{3 - 1}$ — simplify

$= 59\,048$

WORKED EXAMPLE 17

The second term of a geometric progression is 9 less than the first term. The sum of the second and third terms is 30. Given that all the terms in the progression are positive, find the first term.

Answers

second term = first term –9

$ar = a - 9$ — rearrange to make a the subject

$a = \dfrac{9}{1 - r}$ ---------(1)

second term + third term = 30

$ar + ar^2 = 30$ — factorise

$ar(1 + r) = 30$ ---------(2)

(2) ÷ (1) gives $\dfrac{ar(1 + r)}{a} = \dfrac{30(1 - r)}{9}$ — simplify

$3r^2 + 13r - 10 = 0$ — factorise and solve

$(3r - 2)(r + 5) = 0$

$r = \dfrac{2}{3}$ or $r = -5$ — all terms are positive $\Rightarrow r > 0$

$r = \dfrac{2}{3}$

Substituting $r = \dfrac{2}{3}$ into (1) gives $a = 27$.

First term is 27.

Exercise 11.4

1 Identify whether the following sequences are geometric. If they are geometric, write down the common ratio and the eighth term.

a 1, 2, 4, 6, …

b –1, 4, –16, 64, …

c 81, 27, 9, 3, …

d $\frac{2}{11}, \frac{3}{11}, \frac{5}{11}, \frac{8}{11}, \ldots$

e 2, 0.4, 0.08, 0.16, …

f –5, 5, –5, 5, …

2 The first term in a geometric progression is a and the common ratio is r. Write down expressions, in terms of a and r, for the ninth term and the 20th term.

3 The third term of a geometric progression is 108 and the sixth term is –32. Find the common ratio and the first term.

4 The first term of a geometric progression is 75 and the third term is 27. Find the two possible values for the fourth term.

5 The second term of a geometric progression is 12 and the fourth term is 27. Given that all the terms are positive, find the common ratio and the first term.

6 The sixth and 13th terms of a geometric progression are $\frac{5}{2}$ and 320 respectively. Find the common ratio, the first term and the 10th term of this progression.

7 The sum of the second and third terms in a geometric progression is 30. The second term is 9 less than the first term. Given that all the terms in the progression are positive, find the first term.

8 Three consecutive terms of a geometric progression are x, $x + 6$ and $x + 9$. Find the value of x.

9 In the geometric sequence $\frac{1}{4}, \frac{1}{2}, 1, 2, 4, \ldots$ which is the first term to exceed 500000?

10 In the geometric sequence 256, 128, 64, 32, … which is the first term that is less than 0.001?

11 Find the sum of the first eight terms of each of these geometric series.

a 4 + 8 + 16 + 32 + …

b 729 + 243 + 81 + 27 + …

c 2 – 6 + 18 – 54 + …

d –5000 + 1000 – 200 + 40 – … …

12 The first four terms of a geometric progression are 1, 3, 9 and 27. Find the smallest number of terms that will give a sum greater than 2000000.

13 A ball is thrown vertically upwards from the ground. The ball rises to a height of 10m and then falls and bounces. After each bounce it rises to $\frac{4}{5}$ of the height of the previous bounce.

a Write down an expression, in terms of n, for the height that the ball rises after the nth impact with the ground.

b Find the total distance that the ball travels from the first throw to the fifth impact with the ground.

14 The third term of a geometric progression is nine times the first term. The sum of the first four terms is k times the first term. Find the possible values of k.

15 John competes in a 10 km race. He completes the first kilometre in 4 minutes. He reduces his speed in such a way that each kilometre takes him 1.05 times the time taken for the preceding kilometre. Find the total time, in minutes and seconds, John takes to complete the 10 km race.

Give your answer correct to the nearest second.

16 A geometric progression has first term a, common ratio r and sum to n terms, S_n.

Show that $\dfrac{S_{3n} - S_{2n}}{S_n} = r^{2n}$.

CHALLENGE Q

17 $1, 1, 3, \frac{1}{3}, 9, \frac{1}{9}, 27, \frac{1}{27}, 81, \frac{1}{81}, \ldots$

Show that the sum of the first $2n$ terms of this sequence is $\frac{1}{2}\left(3^n - 3^{1-n} + 2\right)$.

CHALLENGE Q

18 $S_n = 6 + 66 + 666 + 6666 + 66666 + \ldots$

Find the sum of the first n terms of this sequence.

11.5 Infinite geometric series

An infinite series is a series whose terms continue forever.

The geometric series where $a = 2$ and $r = \frac{1}{2}$ is $2 + 1 + \frac{1}{2} + \frac{1}{4} + \frac{1}{8} + \ldots$

For this series it can be shown that

$S_1 = 2,\ S_2 = 3,\ S_3 = 3\frac{1}{2},\ S_4 = 3\frac{3}{4},\ S_5 = 3\frac{7}{8}, \ldots.$

This suggests that the sum to infinity approaches the number 4.

The diagram of the 2 by 2 square is a visual representation of this series. If the pattern of rectangles inside the square is continued the total areas of the inside rectangles approaches the value 4.

This confirms that the sum to infinity of the series $2 + 1 + \frac{1}{2} + \frac{1}{4} + \frac{1}{8} + \ldots$ is 4.

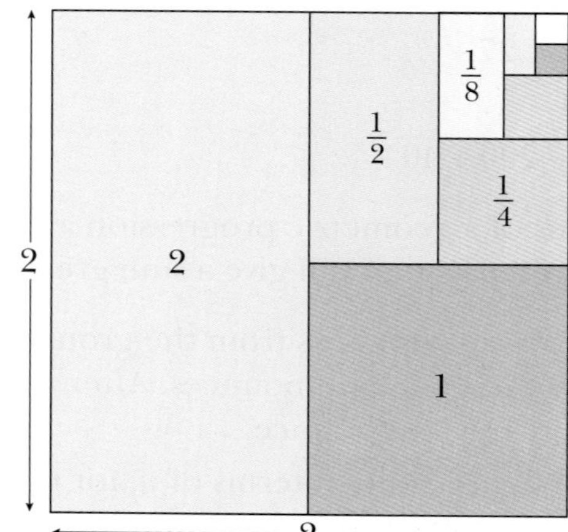

This is an example of a **convergent** series because the sum to infinity converges on a finite number.

CLASS DISCUSSION

1 Use a spreadsheet to investigate whether the sum of each of these infinite geometric series converge or diverge. If they converge, state their sum to infinity.

$a = \frac{2}{5}, r = 2$ | $a = -3, r = -\frac{1}{2}$ | $a = 5, r = \frac{2}{3}$ | $a = \frac{1}{2}, r = -5$

2 Find other convergent geometric series of your own. In each case find the sum to infinity.

3 Can you find a condition for r for which a geometric series is convergent?

Consider the geometric series $a + ar + ar^2 + ar^3 + \dots + ar^{n-1}$.

The sum, S_n, is given by the formula $S_n = \frac{a(1 - r^n)}{1 - r}$.

If $-1 < r < 1$, then as n gets larger and larger, r^n gets closer and closer to 0.

We say that as $n \to \infty$, $r^n \to 0$.

Hence, as $n \to \infty$, $\frac{a(1 - r^n)}{1 - r} \to \frac{a(1 - 0)}{1 - r} = \frac{a}{1 - r}$.

This gives the result

$$S_\infty = \frac{a}{1 - r} \quad \text{provided that } -1 < r < 1$$

Note:
This is not true when $r > 1$ or when $r = -1$

WORKED EXAMPLE 18

The first three terms of a geometric progression are 25, 15 and 9.

a Write down the common ratio.

b Find the sum to infinity.

Answers

a Common ratio $= \frac{\text{second term}}{\text{first term}} = \frac{15}{25} = \frac{3}{5}$

b $S_\infty = \frac{a}{1 - r}$ use $a = 25$ and $r = \frac{3}{5}$

$= \frac{25}{1 - \frac{3}{5}}$

$= 62.5$

WORKED EXAMPLE 19

A geometric progression has a common ratio of $-\frac{4}{5}$ and the sum of the first four terms is 164.

a Find the first term of the progression.

b Find the sum to infinity.

Answers

a $S_4 = \frac{a(1-r^4)}{1-r}$ — use $S_4 = 164$ and $r = -\frac{4}{5}$

$164 = \frac{a\left(1-\left(-\frac{4}{5}\right)^4\right)}{1-\left(-\frac{4}{5}\right)}$ — simplify

$164 = \frac{41}{125}a$ — solve

$a = 500$

b $S_\infty = \frac{a}{1-r}$ — use $a = 500$ and $r = -\frac{4}{5}$

$= \frac{500}{1-\left(-\frac{4}{5}\right)}$

$= 277\frac{7}{9}$

Exercise 11.5

1 Find the sum to infinity of each of the following geometric series.

a $3+1+\frac{1}{3}+\frac{1}{9}+\ldots$

b $1-\frac{1}{2}+\frac{1}{4}-\frac{1}{8}+\frac{1}{16}-\ldots$

c $8+\frac{8}{5}+\frac{8}{25}+\frac{8}{125}+\ldots$

d $-162+108-72+48-\ldots$

2 The first term of a geometric progression is 10 and the second term is 8. Find the sum to infinity.

3 The first term of a geometric progression is 300 and the fourth term is $-2\frac{2}{5}$. Find the common ratio and the sum to infinity.

4 The first four terms of a geometric progression are 1, 0.8^2, 0.8^4 and 0.8^6. Find the sum to infinity.

5 **a** Write the recurring decimal $0.\dot{4}\dot{2}$ as the sum of a geometric progression.

b Use your answer to **part a** to show that $0.\dot{4}\dot{2}$ can be written as $\frac{14}{33}$.

6 The first term of a geometric progression is –120 and the sum to infinity is –72. Find the common ratio and the sum of the first three terms.

7 The second term of a geometric progression is 6.5 and the sum to infinity is 26. Find the common ratio and the first term.

8 The second term of a geometric progression is -96 and the fifth term is $40\frac{1}{2}$.

a Find the common ratio and the first term.

b Find the sum to infinity.

9 The first three terms of a geometric progression are 175, k and 63. Given that all the terms in the progression are positive, find

a the value of k

b the sum to infinity.

10 The second term of a geometric progression is 18 and the fourth term is 1.62. Given that the common ratio is positive, find

a the common ratio and the first term

b the sum to infinity.

11 The first three terms of a geometric progression are $k+15$, k and $k-12$ respectively, find

a the value of k

b the sum to infinity.

12 The fourth term of a geometric progression is 48 and the sum to infinity is three times the first term. Find the first term.

13 A geometric progression has first term a and common ratio r. The sum of the first three terms is 62 and the sum to infinity is 62.5. Find the value of a and the value of r.

14 The first term of a geometric progression is 1 and the second term is $2\sin x$ where $-\frac{\pi}{2} < x < \frac{\pi}{2}$. Find the set of values of x for which this progression is convergent.

15 A ball is dropped from a height of 12 m. After each bounce it rises to $\frac{3}{4}$ of the height of the previous bounce. Find the total vertical distance that the ball travels.

CHALLENGE Q

16 Starting with an equilateral triangle, a Koch snowflake pattern can be constructed using the following steps:

Step 1: Divide each line segment into three equal segments.
Step 2: Draw an equilateral triangle, pointing outwards, which has the middle segment from step 1 as its base.
Step 3: Remove the line segments that were used as the base of the equilateral triangles in step 2.

These three steps are then repeated to produce the next pattern.

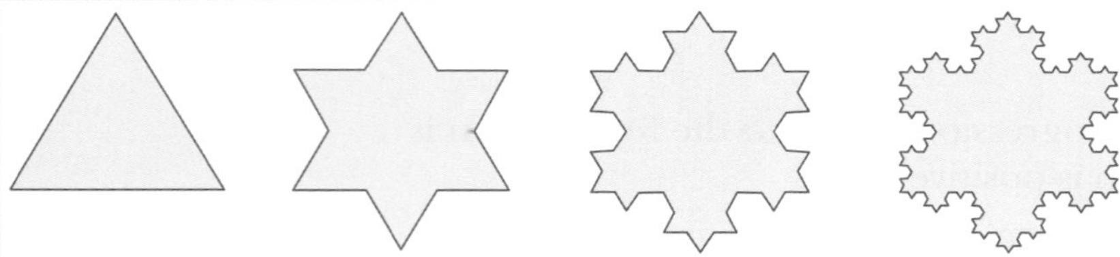

Pattern 1 Pattern 2 Pattern 3 Pattern 4

You are given that the triangle in **pattern 1** has side length x units.

a Find, in terms of x, expressions for the perimeter of each of patterns 1, 2, 3 and 4 and explain why this progression for the perimeter of the snowflake diverges to infinity.

b Show that the area of each of patterns 1, 2, 3 and 4 can be written as

Pattern	Area
1	$\frac{\sqrt{3}x^2}{4}$
2	$\frac{\sqrt{3}x^2}{4} + 3\frac{\sqrt{3}\left(\frac{x}{3}\right)^2}{4}$
3	$\frac{\sqrt{3}x^2}{4} + 3\frac{\sqrt{3}\left(\frac{x}{3}\right)^2}{4} + 12\frac{\sqrt{3}\left(\frac{x}{9}\right)^2}{4}$
4	$\frac{\sqrt{3}x^2}{4} + 3\frac{\sqrt{3}\left(\frac{x}{3}\right)^2}{4} + 12\frac{\sqrt{3}\left(\frac{x}{9}\right)^2}{4} + 48\frac{\sqrt{3}\left(\frac{x}{27}\right)^2}{4}$

Hence show that the progression for the area of the snowflake converges to $\frac{8}{5}$ times the area of the original triangle.

CHALLENGE Q

17 A circle of radius 1 unit is drawn touching the three edges of an equilateral triangle.

Three smaller circles are then drawn at each corner to touch the original circle and two edges of the triangle.

This process is then repeated an infinite number of times.

a Find the sum of the circumferences of all the circles.

b Find the sum of the areas of all the circles.

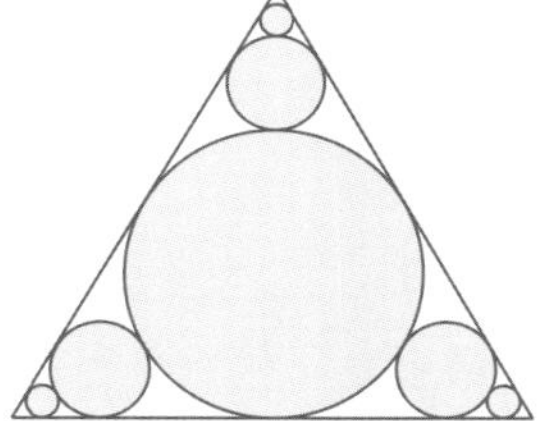

11.6 Further arithmetic and geometric series

Some problems may involve more than one progression.

CLASS DISCUSSION

$a, b, c, \ldots$

1 Given that a, b and c are in arithmetic progression, find an equation connecting a, b and c.

2 Given that a, b and c are in geometric progression, find an equation connecting a, b and c.

WORKED EXAMPLE 20

The first, second and third terms of an arithmetic series are x, y and x^2. The first, second and third terms of a geometric series are x, x^2 and y. Given that $x < 0$, find:

a the value of x and the value of y

b the sum to infinity of the geometric series

c the sum of the first 20 terms of the arithmetic series.

Answers

a Arithmetic series is: $x + y + x^2 + \ldots$ — use common differences

$$y - x = x^2 - y$$

$$2y = x^2 + x \text{ -----------(1)}$$

Geometric series is: $x + x^2 + y + \ldots$ — use common ratios

$$\frac{y}{x^2} = \frac{x^2}{x}$$

$$y = x^3 \text{ -----------------(2)}$$

(1) and (2) give $2x^3 = x^2 + x$ — divide by x (since $x \neq 0$) and rearrange

$$2x^2 - x - 1 = 0$$ — factorise and solve

$$(2x + 1)(x - 1) = 0$$

$$x = -\frac{1}{2} \text{ or } x = 1$$ — $x \neq 1$ since $x < 0$

Hence, $x = -\dfrac{1}{2}$ and $y = -\dfrac{1}{8}$.

b $S_\infty = \dfrac{a}{1-r}$ use $a = -\dfrac{1}{2}$ and $r = -\dfrac{1}{2}$

$S_\infty = \dfrac{-\frac{1}{2}}{1-\left(-\frac{1}{2}\right)} = -\dfrac{1}{3}$

c $S_n = \dfrac{n}{2}[2a + (n-1)d]$ use $n = 20$, $a = -\dfrac{1}{2}$, $d = y - x = \dfrac{3}{8}$

$S_{20} = \dfrac{20}{2}\left[-1 + 19\left(\dfrac{3}{8}\right)\right]$

$= 61.25$

Exercise 11.6

1 The first term of a progression is 8 and the second term is 12. Find the sum of the first six terms given that the progression is

a arithmetic **b** geometric.

2 The first term of a progression is 25 and the second term is 20.

a Given that the progression is geometric, find the sum to infinity.

b Given that the progression is arithmetic, find the number of terms in the progression if the sum of all the terms is –1550.

3 The first, second and third terms of a geometric progression are the first, fifth and 11th terms respectively of an arithmetic progression. Given that the first term in each progression is 48 and the common ratio of the geometric progression is r, where $r \neq 1$, find

a the value of r

b the sixth term of each progression.

4 A geometric progression has six terms. The first term is 486 and the common ratio is $\dfrac{2}{3}$. An arithmetic progression has 35 terms and common difference $\dfrac{3}{2}$. The sum of all the terms in the geometric progression is equal to the sum of all the terms in the arithmetic progression. Find the first term and the last term of the arithmetic progression.

5 The first, second and third terms of a geometric progression are the first, fifth and eighth terms respectively of an arithmetic progression. Given that the first term in each progression is 200 and the common ratio of the geometric progression is r, where $r \neq 1$, find

a the value of r

b the fourth term of each progression

c the sum to infinity of the geometric progression.

6 The first term of an arithmetic progression is 12 and the sum of the first 16 terms is 282.

a Find the common difference of this progression.

The first, fifth and nth term of this arithmetic progression are the first, second and third term respectively of a geometric progression.

b Find the common ratio of the geometric progression and the value of n.

7 The first two terms of a geometric progression are 80 and 64 respectively. The first three terms of this geometric progression are also the first, 11th and nth terms respectively of an arithmetic progression. Find the value of n.

8 The first two terms of a progression are $5x$ and x^2 respectively.

a For the case where the progression is arithmetic with a common difference of 24, find the two possible values of x and the corresponding values of the third term.

b For the case where the progression is geometric with a third term of $-\frac{8}{5}$, find the common ratio and the sum to infinity.

Summary

Binomial expansions

If n is a positive integer then $(a+b)^n$ can be expanded using the formula

$$(a+b)^n = a^n + {}^nC_1\, a^{n-1} b + {}^nC_2\, a^{n-2} b^2 + {}^nC_3\, a^{n-3} b^3 + \ldots + {}^nC_r\, a^{n-r} b^r + \ldots + b^n$$

or

$$(a+b)^n = a^n + \binom{n}{1} a^{n-1} b + \binom{n}{2} a^{n-2} b^2 + \binom{n}{3} a^{n-3} b^3 + \ldots + \binom{n}{r} a^{n-r} b^r + \ldots + b^n$$

and where ${}^nC_r = \binom{n}{r} = \frac{n!}{(n-r)!\,r!}$.

In particular,

$$(1+x)^n = 1 + nx + \frac{n(n-1)}{2!}x^2 + \frac{n(n-1)(n-2)}{3!}x^3 + \frac{n(n-1)(n-2)(n-3)}{4!}x^4 + \ldots + x^n.$$

Arithmetic series

For an arithmetic progression with first term a, common difference d and n terms:

- the kth term $= a + (k-1)d$
- the last term $= l = a + (n-1)d$
- the sum of the terms $= S_n = \frac{n}{2}(a+l) = \frac{n}{2}[2a + (n-1)d]$.

Geometric series

For a geometric progression with first term a, common ratio r and n terms:

- the kth term $= ar^{k-1}$
- the last term $= ar^{n-1}$
- the sum of the terms $= S_n = \dfrac{a(1-r^n)}{1-r} = \dfrac{a(r^n-1)}{r-1}$.

The condition for a geometric series to converge is $-1 < r < 1$.

When a geometric series converges, $S_\infty = \dfrac{a}{1-r}$.

Examination questions

Worked example

a Find the first 4 terms in the expansion of $(2 + x^2)^6$ in ascending powers of x. [3]

b Find the term independent of x in the expansion of $(2 + x^2)^6\left(1 - \dfrac{3}{x^2}\right)^2$. [3]

Cambridge IGCSE Additional Mathematics 0606 Paper 11 Q3i,ii Jun 2015

Answer

a Expanding $(2 + x^2)^6$ using the binomial theorem gives

$$2^6 + {}^6C_1\, 2^5 x^2 + {}^6C_2\, 2^4 (x^2)^2 + {}^6C_3\, 2^3 (x^2)^3 = 64 + 192x^2 + 240x^4 + 160x^6 \ldots$$

b $(2 + x^2)^6\left(1 - \dfrac{2}{x^2}\right)^2 = (64 + 192x^2 + 240x^4 + 160x^6 \ldots)\left(1 - \dfrac{6}{x^2} + \dfrac{9}{x^4}\right)$

Term independent of $x = (64 \times 1) + \left(192x^2 \times -\dfrac{6}{x^2}\right) + \left(240x^4 \times \dfrac{9}{x^4}\right)$

$= 64 - 1152 + 2160$

$= 1072$

Exercise 11.7

Exam Exercise

1 a Find the first four terms in the expansion of $(2 + x)^6$ in ascending powers of x. [3]

b Hence find the coefficient of x^3 in the expansion of $(1 + 3x)(1 - x)(2 + x)^6$. [4]

Cambridge IGCSE Additional Mathematics 0606 Paper 21 Q7i,ii Jun 2013

2 a Find the first 3 terms, in descending powers of x, in the expansion of $\left(x + \dfrac{2}{x^2}\right)^6$. [3]

b Hence find the term independent of x in the expansion of $\left(2 - \dfrac{4}{x^3}\right)\left(x + \dfrac{2}{x^2}\right)^6$. [2]

Cambridge IGCSE Additional Mathematics 0606 Paper 11 Q6i,ii Nov 2012

3 The coefficient of x^2 in the expansion of $\left(1+\frac{x}{5}\right)^n$, where n is a positive integer is $\frac{3}{5}$.

a Find the value of n. [4]

b Using this value of n, find the term independent of x in the expansion of

$$\left(1+\frac{x}{5}\right)^n\left(2-\frac{3}{x}\right)^2.$$ [4]

Cambridge IGCSE Additional Mathematics 0606 Paper 11 Q7i,ii Nov 2011

4 **a** Find the coefficient of x^3 in the expansion of $\left(1-\frac{x}{2}\right)^{12}$. [2]

b Find the coefficient of x^3 in the expansion of $(1+4x)\left(1-\frac{x}{2}\right)^{12}$. [3]

Cambridge IGCSE Additional Mathematics 0606 Paper 21 Q2i,ii Jun 2011

5 **a** Find, in ascending powers of x, the first 3 terms in the expansion of $(2-5x)^6$, giving your answer in the form $a+bx+cx^2$, where a, b and c are integers. [3]

b Find the coefficient of x in the expansion of $(2-5x)^6\left(1+\frac{x}{2}\right)^{10}$. [3]

Cambridge IGCSE Additional Mathematics 0606 Paper 11 Q6i,ii Nov 2010

6 **i** Write down, in ascending powers of x, the first 3 terms in the expansion of $(3+2x)^6$. Give each term in its simplest form. [3]

ii Hence find the coefficient of x^2 in the expansion of $(2-x)(3+2x)^6$. [2]

Cambridge IGCSE Additional Mathematics 0606 Paper 12 Q4 Mar 2015

7 **i** Find the first 4 terms in the expansion of $(2+x^2)^6$ in ascending powers of x. [3]

ii Find the term independent of x in the expansion of $(2+x^2)^6\left(1-\frac{3}{x^2}\right)^2$. [3]

Cambridge IGCSE Additional Mathematics 0606 Paper 11 Q3 Jun 2015

8 **a** **i** Use the Binomial Theorem to expand $(a+b)^4$, giving each term in its simplest form. [2]

ii Hence find the term independent of x in the expansion of $\left(2x+\frac{1}{5x}\right)^4$. [2]

b The coefficient of x^3 in the expansion of $\left(1+\frac{x}{2}\right)^n$ equals $\frac{5n}{12}$. Find the value of the positive integer n. [3]

Cambridge IGCSE Additional Mathematics 0606 Paper 21 Q8 Jun 2016

9 The first term of a geometric progression is 35 and the second term is -14.

a Find the fourth term. [3]

b Find the sum to infinity. [2]

Examination style question

10 The first three terms of a geometric progression are $2k + 6$, $k + 12$ and k respectively. All the terms in the progression are positive.

a Find value of k. [3]

b Find the sum to infinity. [2]

Examination style question

11 An arithmetic progression has first term a and common difference d. Give that the sum of the first 100 terms is 25 times the sum of the first 20 terms.

a Find d in terms of a. [3]

b Write down an expression, in terms of a, for the 50th term. [2]

Examination style question

12 The 15th term of an arithmetic progression is 3 and the sum of the first 8 terms is 194.

a Find the first term of the progression and the common difference. [4]

b Given that the nth term of the progression is -22, find the value of n. [2]

Examination style question

13 The second term of a geometric progression is -576 and the fifth term is 243. Find

a the common ratio [3]

b the first term [1]

c the sum to infinity. [2]

Examination style question

14 a The sixth term of an arithmetic progression is 35 and the sum of the first ten terms is 335. Find the eighth term. [4]

b A geometric progression has first term 8 and common ratio r. A second geometric progression has first term 10 and common ratio $\frac{1}{4}r$. The two progressions have the same sum to infinity, S. Find the values of r and the value of S. [3]

Examination style question

15 a The 10th term of an arithmetic progression is 4 and the sum of the first 7 terms is -28. Find the first term and the common difference. [4]

b The first term of a geometric progression is 40 and the fourth term is 5. Find the sum to infinity of the progression. [3]

Examination style question

16 a A geometric progression has first term a, common ratio r and sum to infinity S.

A second geometric progression has first term $3a$, common ratio $2r$ and sum to infinity $4S$. Find the value of r. [3]

b An arithmetic progression has first term -24. The nth term is -13.8 and the $(2n)$th term is -3. Find the value of n. [4]

Examination style question

Chapter 12
Differentiation 1

This section will show you how to:

- use the notations $f'(x)$, $f''(x)$, $\frac{dy}{dx}$, $\frac{d^2y}{dx^2}$, $\left[\frac{d}{dx}\left(\frac{dy}{dx}\right)\right]$
- use the derivative of x^n (for any rational n), together with constant multiples, sums and composite functions of these
- differentiate products and quotients of functions
- apply differentiation to gradients, tangents and normals, stationary points, connected rates of change, small increments and approximations and practical maxima and minima problems
- use the first and second derivative tests to discriminate between maxima and minima.

RECAP

You have learnt how to find the gradient of a straight line joining the two points (x_1, y_1) and (x_2, y_2) using the formula:

$$\text{Gradient} = \frac{y_2 - y_1}{x_2 - x_1}$$

You should also have learnt how to estimate the gradient of a curve at a particular point.

For example, to find the gradient of the curve $y = x^2$ at the point (1, 1):

Step 1: Draw the graph of $y = x^2$.

Step 2: Draw a tangent to the curve at the point (1, 1).

Step 3: Find the gradient of the tangent using $\frac{y_2 - y_1}{x_2 - x_1}$.

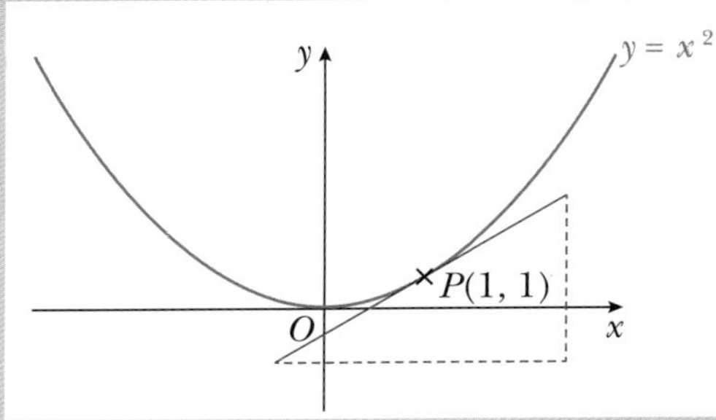

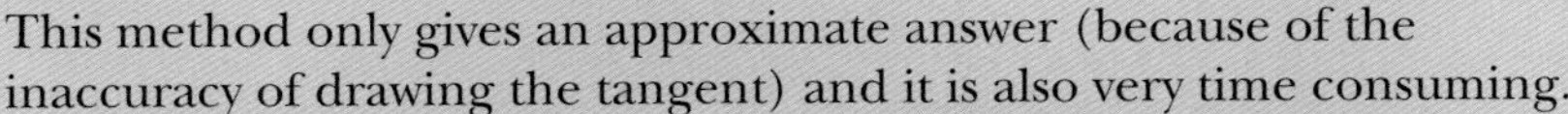

This method only gives an approximate answer (because of the inaccuracy of drawing the tangent) and it is also very time consuming.

In this chapter you will learn an accurate method for finding the gradient of a curve, which does not involve drawing the curve first. This accurate method is called **differentiation**.

12.1 The gradient function

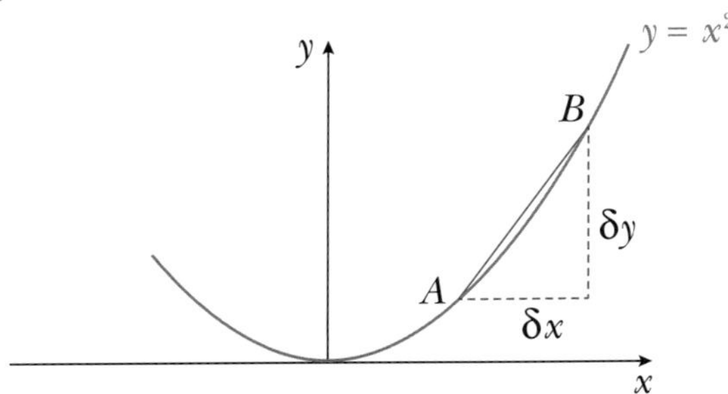

The diagram shows a point $A(x, y)$ on the curve $y = x^2$ and a point B which is close to the point A.

The coordinates of B are $(x + \delta x,\ y + \delta y)$ where δx is a small increase in the value of x and δy is a small increase in the value of y.

The coordinates of A and B can also be written as (x, x^2) and $\left(x + \delta x, (x + \delta x)^2\right)$.

$$\begin{aligned}
\text{gradient of chord } AB &= \frac{y_2 - y_1}{x_2 - x_1} \\
&= \frac{(x + \delta x)^2 - x^2}{(x + \delta x) - x} \\
&= \frac{x^2 + 2x\delta x + (\delta x)^2 - x^2}{\delta x} \\
&= \frac{2x\delta x + (\delta x)^2}{\delta x} \\
&= 2x + \delta x
\end{aligned}$$

As $B \to A$, $\delta x \to 0$ and the gradient of the chord $AB \to$ the gradient of the curve at A.

Hence, gradient of curve $= 2x$.

This process of finding the gradient of a curve at any point is called **differentiation** from first principles.

Notation

There are three different notations that can be used to describe the rule above.

1 If $y = x^2$, then $\frac{dy}{dx} = 2x$.

2 If $f(x) = x^2$, then $f'(x) = 2x$.

3 $\frac{d}{dx}(x^2) = 2x$.

$\frac{dy}{dx}$ is called the **derivative** of y with respect to x.

$f'(x)$ is called the **gradient function** of the curve $y = f(x)$.

$\frac{d}{dx}(x^2) = 2x$ means 'if you differentiate x^2 with respect to x, the result is $2x$'.

You do not need to be able to differentiate from first principles for the examination but you are expected to know the rules of differentiation.

Differentiation of power functions

The rule for differentiating power functions is:

$$\text{If } y = x^n, \text{ then } \frac{dy}{dx} = nx^{n-1}.$$

It is easier to remember this rule as:

'multiply by the power n and then subtract one from the power'

So for the earlier example where $y = x^2$,

$$\begin{aligned}\frac{dy}{dx} &= 2 \times x^{2-1} \\ &= 2x^1 \\ &= 2x.\end{aligned}$$

WORKED EXAMPLE 1

Differentiate with respect to *x*.

a x^5 **b** $\frac{1}{x^3}$ **c** $\sqrt{x}$ **d** 3

Answers

a $\frac{d}{dx}(x^5) = 5x^{5-1}$

$= 5x^4$

b $\frac{d}{dx}\left(\frac{1}{x^3}\right) = \frac{d}{dx}(x^{-3})$

$= -3x^{-3-1}$

$= -3x^{-4}$

$= -\frac{3}{x^4}$

c $\frac{d}{dx}(\sqrt{x}) = \frac{d}{dx}\left(x^{\frac{1}{2}}\right)$

$= \frac{1}{2}x^{\frac{1}{2}-1}$

$= \frac{1}{2}x^{-\frac{1}{2}}$

$= \frac{1}{2\sqrt{x}}$

d $\frac{d}{dx}(3) = \frac{d}{dx}(3x^0)$

$= 0x^{0-1}$

$= 0$

You need to know and be able to use the following two rules:

Scalar multiple rule:

$$\frac{d}{dx}\left[kf(x)\right] = k\frac{d}{dx}\left[f(x)\right]$$

Addition/subtraction rule:

$$\frac{d}{dx}\left[f(x) \pm g(x)\right] = \frac{d}{dx}\left[f(x)\right] \pm \frac{d}{dx}\left[g(x)\right]$$

WORKED EXAMPLE 2

Differentiate $2x^5 - 3x^2 + \frac{1}{2x^3} + \frac{5}{\sqrt{x}}$ with respect to x.

Answers

$$\frac{d}{dx}\left(2x^5 - 3x^2 + \frac{1}{2x^3} + \frac{5}{\sqrt{x}}\right) = \frac{d}{dx}\left(2x^5 - 3x^2 + \frac{1}{2}x^{-3} + 5x^{-\frac{1}{2}}\right)$$

$$= 2\frac{d}{dx}(x^5) - 3\frac{d}{dx}(x^2) + \frac{1}{2}\frac{d}{dx}(x^{-3}) + 5\frac{d}{dx}\left(x^{-\frac{1}{2}}\right)$$

$$= 2(5x^4) - 3(2x) + \frac{1}{2}(-3x^{-4}) + 5\left(-\frac{1}{2}x^{-\frac{3}{2}}\right)$$

$$= 10x^4 - 6x - \frac{3}{2}x^{-4} - \frac{5}{2}x^{-\frac{3}{2}}$$

WORKED EXAMPLE 3

Find the gradient of the curve $y = (3x + 2)(2x - 1)$ at the point $(-1, 3)$.

Answers

$y = (3x + 2)(2x - 1)$

$y = 6x^2 + x - 2$

$\frac{dy}{dx} = 12x + 1$

When $x = -1$, $\frac{dy}{dx} = 12(-1) + 1$

$= -11$

Gradient of curve at $(-1, 3)$ is -11.

Exercise 12.1

1 Differentiate with respect to x.

a x^4	**b** x^9	**c** x^{-3}	**d** x^{-6}	**e** $\frac{1}{x}$
f $\frac{1}{x^5}$	**g** $\sqrt{x}$	**h** $\sqrt{x^5}$	**i** $x^{-\frac{1}{5}}$	**j** $x^{\frac{1}{3}}$
k $\sqrt[3]{x^2}$	**l** $\frac{1}{\sqrt{x}}$	**m** x	**n** $x^{\frac{3}{2}}$	**o** $\sqrt[3]{x^5}$
p $x^2 \times x^4$	**q** $x^2 \times x$	**r** $\frac{x^4}{x^2}$	**s** $\frac{x}{\sqrt{x}}$	**t** $\frac{x\sqrt{x}}{x^3}$

2 Differentiate with respect to x.

a $2x^3 - 5x + 4$ **b** $8x^5 - 3x^2 - 2$ **c** $7 - 2x^3 + 4x$

d $3x^2 + \frac{2}{x} - \frac{1}{x^2}$ **e** $2x - \frac{1}{x} - \frac{1}{\sqrt{x}}$ **f** $\frac{x + 5}{\sqrt{x}}$

g $\frac{x^2 - 3}{x}$ **h** $\frac{5x^2 - \sqrt{x}}{x}$ **i** $\frac{x^2 - x - \text{[illegible]}}{\sqrt{x}}$

j $5x^2(x + 1)$ **k** $x^{-2}(2x - 5)$ **l** $\frac{1}{x}(x^2 - 2)$

m $(3x + 1)^2$ **n** $(1 - x^3)^2$ **o** $(2x - 1)(3x + 4)$

3 Find the value of $\frac{dy}{dx}$ at the given point on the curve.

a $y = 3x^2 - 4$ at the point $(1, -1)$

b $y = 4 - 2x^2$ at the point $(-1, 2)$

c $y = 2 + \frac{8}{x}$ at the point $(-2, -2)$

d $y = 5x^3 - 2x^2 - 3$ at the point $(0, -3)$

e $y = \frac{x + 5}{x}$ at the point $(5, 2)$

f $y = \frac{x - 3}{\sqrt{x}}$ at the point $(9, 2)$

4 Find the coordinates of the point on the curve $y = 2x^2 - x - 1$ at which the gradient is 7.

5 Find the gradient of the curve $y = \frac{x - 4}{x}$ at the point where the curve crosses the x-axis.

6 Find the gradient of the curve $y = x^3 - 2x^2 + 5x - 3$ at the point where the curve crosses the y-axis.

7 The curve $y = 2x^2 + 7x - 4$ and the line $y = 5$ meet at the points P and Q.

Find the gradient of the curve at the point P and at the point Q.

8 The curve $y = ax^2 + bx$ has gradient 8 when $x = 2$ and has gradient -10 when $x = -1$.

Find the value of a and the value of b.

9 The gradient of the curve $y = ax + \frac{b}{x}$ at the point (–1, –3) is –7.

Find the value of a and the value of b.

10 Find the coordinates of the points on this curve $y = \frac{x^3}{3} - \frac{5x^2}{2} + 6x - 1$ where the gradient is 2.

11 The curve $y = \frac{1}{3}x^3 - 2x^2 - 8x + 5$ and the line $y = x + 5$ meet at the points A, B and C.

a Find the coordinates of the points A, B and C.

b Find the gradient of the curve at the points A, B and C.

12 $y = 4x^3 + 3x^2 - 6x - 1$

a Find $\frac{dy}{dx}$.

b Find the range of values of x for which $\frac{dy}{dx} \geqslant 0$.

13 $y = x^3 + x^2 - 16x - 16$

a Find $\frac{dy}{dx}$.

b Find the range of values of x for which $\frac{dy}{dx} \leqslant 0$.

CHALLENGE Q

14 A curve has equation $y = x^5 - 5x^3 + 25x^2 + 145x + 10$. Show that the gradient of the curve is never negative.

12.2 The chain rule

To differentiate $y = (2x + 3)^8$, you could expand the brackets and then differentiate each term separately. This would take a long time to do. There is a more efficient method available that allows you to find the derivative without expanding:

Let $u = 2x + 3$, then $y = (2x + 3)^8$ becomes $y = u^8$.

The derivative of the composite function $y = (2x + 3)^8$ can then be found using the **chain rule**:

$$\frac{dy}{dx} = \frac{dy}{du} \times \frac{du}{dx}$$

WORKED EXAMPLE 4

Find the derivative of $y = (2x + 3)^8$.

Answers

$y = (2x + 3)^8$

Let $u = 2x + 3$ so $y = u^8$

$\frac{du}{dx} = 2$ and $\frac{dy}{du} = 8u^7$

Using $\frac{dy}{dx} = \frac{dy}{du} \times \frac{du}{dx}$

$= 8u^7 \times 2$

$= 8(2x + 3)^7 \times 2$

$= 16(2x + 3)^7$

With practice you will find that you can do this mentally:

Consider the 'inside' of $(2x + 3)^8$ to be $2x + 3$.

To differentiate $(2x + 3)^8$:

Step 1: Differentiate the 'outside' first: $8(2x + 3)^7$

Step 2: Then differentiate the 'inside': 2

Step 3: Multiply these two expressions: $16(2x + 3)^7$

WORKED EXAMPLE 5

Find the derivative of $y = \frac{2}{(5x^2 - 1)^4}$.

Answers

$y = \frac{2}{(5x^2 - 1)^4}$

Let $u = 5x^2 - 1$ so $y = 2u^{-4}$

$\frac{du}{dx} = 10x$ and $\frac{dy}{du} = -8u^{-5}$

Using $\frac{dy}{dx} = \frac{dy}{du} \times \frac{du}{dx}$

$= -8u^{-5} \times 10x$

$= -8(5x^2 - 1)^{-5} \times 10x$

$= \frac{-80x}{(5x^2 - 1)^5}$

Alternatively, to differentiate the expression mentally:

Write $\frac{2}{(5x^2 - 1)^4}$ as $2(5x^2 - 1)^{-4}$.

Step 1: Differentiate the 'outside' first: $-8(5x^2 - 1)^{-5}$

Step 2: Then differentiate the 'inside': $10x$

Step 3: Multiply the two expressions: $-80x(5x^2 - 1)^{-5} = \frac{-80x}{(5x^2 - 1)^5}$

Exercise 12.2

1 Differentiate with respect to x.

a $(x+2)^9$ **b** $(3x-1)^7$ **c** $(1-5x)^6$ **d** $\left(\frac{1}{2}x-7\right)^4$

e $\frac{(2x+1)^6}{3}$ **f** $2(x-4)^6$ **g** $6(5-x)^5$ **h** $\frac{1}{2}(2x+5)^8$

i $(x^2+2)^4$ **j** $(1-2x^2)^7$ **k** $(x^2-3x)^5$ **l** $\left(x^2+\frac{2}{x}\right)^4$

2 Differentiate with respect to x.

a $\frac{1}{(x+4)}$ **b** $\frac{3}{(2x-1)}$ **c** $\frac{5}{(2-3x)}$ **d** $\frac{16}{(2x^2-5)}$

e $\frac{4}{(x^2-2x)}$ **f** $\frac{1}{(x-1)^5}$ **g** $\frac{2}{(5x+1)^3}$ **h** $\frac{1}{2(3x-2)^4}$

3 Differentiate with respect to x.

a $\sqrt{x+2}$ **b** $\sqrt{5x-1}$ **c** $\sqrt{2x^2-3}$ **d** $\sqrt{x^3+2x}$

e $\sqrt[3]{3-2x}$ **f** $4\sqrt{2x-1}$ **g** $\frac{1}{\sqrt{3x-1}}$ **h** $\frac{3}{\sqrt[3]{2-5x}}$

4 Find the gradient of the curve $y=(2x-5)^4$ at the point (3, 1).

5 Find the gradient of the curve $y=\frac{8}{(x-2)^2}$ at the point where the curve crosses the y-axis.

6 Find the gradient of the curve $y=x+\frac{4}{x-5}$ at the points where the curve crosses the x-axis.

7 Find the coordinates of the point on the curve $y=\sqrt{(x^2-6x+13)}$ where the gradient is 0.

8 The curve $y=\frac{a}{\sqrt{bx+1}}$ passes through the point (1, 4) and has gradient $-\frac{3}{2}$ at this point.

Find the value of a and the value of b.

12.3 The product rule

Consider the function $y=x^2\left(x^5+1\right)$.

$$y=x^7+x^2$$

$$\frac{dy}{dx}=7x^6+2x$$

The function $y=x^2\left(x^5+1\right)$ can also be considered as the product of two separate functions $y=uv$ where $u=x^2$ and $v=x^5+1$.

To differentiate the product of two functions you can use the **product rule**:

$$\frac{d}{dx}(uv)=u\frac{dv}{dx}+v\frac{du}{dx}$$

It is easier to remember this rule as

'(first function × derivative of second function) + (second function × derivative of first function)'

So for $y = x^2(x^5+1)$, $$\frac{dy}{dx} = \underbrace{(x^2)}_{\text{first}}\underbrace{\frac{d}{dx}(x^5+1)}_{\text{differentiate second}} + \underbrace{(x^5+1)}_{\text{second}}\underbrace{\frac{d}{dx}(x^2)}_{\text{differentiate first}}$$

$$= (x^2)(5x^4) + (x^5+1)(2x)$$

$$= 5x^6 + 2x^6 + 2x$$

$$= 7x^6 + 2x$$

WORKED EXAMPLE 6

Find the derivative of $y = (5x+1)\sqrt{6x-1}$.

Answers

$$y = (5x+1)\sqrt{6x-1}$$

$$= (5x+1)(6x-1)^{\frac{1}{2}}$$

$$\frac{dy}{dx} = \underbrace{(5x+1)}_{\text{first}}\underbrace{\frac{d}{dx}\left[(6x-1)^{\frac{1}{2}}\right]}_{\text{differentiate second}} + \underbrace{\left[(6x-1)^{\frac{1}{2}}\right]}_{\text{second}}\underbrace{\frac{d}{dx}(5x+1)}_{\text{differentiate first}}$$

$$= (5x+1)\underbrace{\left[\frac{1}{2}(6x-1)^{-\frac{1}{2}}(6)\right]}_{\text{use the chain rule}} + \left(\sqrt{6x-1}\right)(5)$$

$$= \frac{3(5x+1)}{\sqrt{6x-1}} + 5\sqrt{6x-1}$$ write as a single fraction

$$= \frac{3(5x+1)+5(6x-1)}{\sqrt{6x-1}}$$ simplify the numerator

$$= \frac{45x-2}{\sqrt{6x-1}}$$

WORKED EXAMPLE 7

Find the x-coordinate of the points on the curve $y = (x+2)^2(2x-5)^3$ where the gradient is 0.

Answers

$$y = (x+2)^2(2x-5)^3$$

$$\frac{dy}{dx} = \underbrace{(x+2)^2}_{\text{first}} \underbrace{\frac{d}{dx}\left[(2x-5)^3\right]}_{\text{differentiate second}} + \underbrace{(2x-5)^3}_{\text{second}} \underbrace{\frac{d}{dx}\left[(x+2)^2\right]}_{\text{differentiate first}}$$

$$= (x+2)^2\underbrace{[3(2x-5)^2(2)]}_{\text{use the chain rule}} + (2x-5)^3\underbrace{[2(x+2)^1(1)]}_{\text{use the chain rule}}$$

$$= 6(x+2)^2(2x-5)^2 + 2(x+2)(2x-5)^3 \quad \text{factorise}$$

$$= 2(x+2)(2x-5)^2[3(x+2)+(2x-5)] \quad \text{simplify}$$

$$= 2(x+2)(2x-5)^2(5x+1)$$

$$\frac{dy}{dx} = 0 \text{ when } 2(x+2)(2x-5)^2(5x+1) = 0$$

$x+2=0$ $\quad$ $2x-5=0$ $\quad$ $5x+1=0$

$x=-2$ $\quad$ $x=2.5$ $\quad$ $x=-0.2$

Exercise 12.3

1 Use the product rule to differentiate each of the following with respect to x:

a $x(x+4)$ **b** $2x(3x+5)$ **c** $x(x+2)^3$

d $x^2(x-1)^3$ **e** $x\sqrt{x-5}$ **f** $(x+2)\sqrt{x}$

g $x^2\sqrt{x+3}$ **h** $\sqrt{x}(3-x^2)^3$ **i** $(2x+1)(x^2+5)$

j $(x+4)(x-3)^3$ **k** $(x-1)^2(x+2)^2$ **l** $(2x+1)^3(x-3)^4$

2 Find the gradient of the curve $y = x^2\sqrt{x+2}$ at the point (2, 8).

3 Find the gradient of the curve $y = (x-1)^3(x+3)^2$ at the point where $x = 2$.

4 Find the gradient of the curve $y = (x+2)(x-5)^2$ at the points where the curve meets the x-axis.

5 Find the x-coordinate of the points on the curve $y = (2x-3)^3(x+2)^4$ where the gradient is zero.

6 Find the x-coordinate of the point on the curve $y = (x+3)\sqrt{4-x}$ where the gradient is zero.

12.4 The quotient rule

The function $y = \dfrac{x^3 + 1}{(2x - 3)}$ can be differentiated by writing the function in the form $y = (x^3 + 1)(2x - 3)^{-1}$ and then by applying the product rule.

Alternatively, $y = \dfrac{x^3 + 1}{(2x - 3)}$ can be considered as the division (quotient) of two separate functions:

$$y = \frac{u}{v} \quad \text{where} \quad u = x^3 + 1 \quad \text{and} \quad v = 2x - 3.$$

To differentiate the quotient of two functions you can use the **quotient rule:**

$$\frac{\mathrm{d}}{\mathrm{d}x}\left(\frac{u}{v}\right) = \frac{v\dfrac{\mathrm{d}u}{\mathrm{d}x} - u\dfrac{\mathrm{d}v}{\mathrm{d}x}}{v^2}$$

It is easier to remember this rule as:

$$\frac{(\text{denominator} \times \text{derivative of numerator}) - (\text{numerator} \times \text{derivative of denominator})}{(\text{denominator})^2}$$

WORKED EXAMPLE 8

Use the quotient rule to find the derivative of $y = \dfrac{x^3 + 1}{(2x - 3)}$.

Answers

$$y = \frac{x^3 + 1}{(2x - 3)}$$

denominator, differentiate numerator, –, numerator, differentiate denominator

$$\frac{\mathrm{d}y}{\mathrm{d}x} = \frac{\overbrace{(2x - 3)}^{\text{denominator}} \times \overbrace{\frac{\mathrm{d}}{\mathrm{d}x}(x^3 + 1)}^{\text{differentiate numerator}} - \overbrace{(x^3 + 1)}^{\text{numerator}} \times \overbrace{\frac{\mathrm{d}}{\mathrm{d}x}(2x - 3)}^{\text{differentiate denominator}}}{\underbrace{(2x - 3)^2}_{\text{denominator squared}}}$$

$$= \frac{(2x - 3)(3x^2) - (x^3 + 1)(2)}{(2x - 3)^2}$$

$$= \frac{6x^3 - 9x^2 - 2x^3 - 2}{(2x - 3)^2}$$

$$= \frac{4x^3 - 9x^2 - 2}{(2x - 3)^2}$$

CLASS DISCUSSION

An alternative method for finding $\frac{dy}{dx}$ in worked example 8 is to express y in the form

$y = (x^3 + 1)(2x - 3)^{-1}$

and to then differentiate using the product rule.

Try this method and then discuss with your classmates which method you prefer.

WORKED EXAMPLE 9

Find the derivative of $y = \frac{(x+1)^2}{\sqrt{x+2}}$.

Answers

$$y = \frac{(x+1)^2}{\sqrt{x+2}}$$

$$\frac{dy}{dx} = \frac{\overbrace{\sqrt{x+2}}^{\text{denominator}} \times \overbrace{\frac{d}{dx}\left[(x+1)^2\right]}^{\text{differentiate numerator}} \; - \; \overbrace{(x+1)^2}^{\text{numerator}} \times \overbrace{\frac{d}{dx}\left[\sqrt{x+2}\right]}^{\text{differentiate denominator}}}{\underbrace{\left(\sqrt{x+2}\right)^2}_{\text{denominator squared}}}$$

$$= \frac{\left(\sqrt{x+2}\right)\left[2(x+1)^1(1)\right] - (x+1)^2\left[\frac{1}{2}(x+2)^{-\frac{1}{2}}(1)\right]}{x+2}$$

$$= \frac{2(x+1)\sqrt{x+2} - \frac{(x+1)^2}{2\sqrt{x+2}}}{x+2}$$ multiply numerator and denominator by $2\sqrt{x+2}$

$$= \frac{4(x+1)(x+2) - (x+1)^2}{2(x+2)\sqrt{x+2}}$$ factorise the numerator

$$= \frac{(x+1)\left[4(x+2) - (x+1)\right]}{2(x+2)^{\frac{3}{2}}}$$

$$= \frac{(x+1)(3x+7)}{2(x+2)^{\frac{3}{2}}}$$

Exercise 12.4

1 Use the quotient rule to differentiate each of the following with respect to x:

a $\dfrac{1+2x}{5-x}$ **b** $\dfrac{3x+2}{x+4}$ **c** $\dfrac{x-1}{3x+4}$ **d** $\dfrac{5x-2}{3-8x}$

e $\dfrac{x^2}{5x-2}$ **f** $\dfrac{x}{x^2-1}$ **g** $\dfrac{5}{3x-1}$ **h** $\dfrac{x+4}{x^2-2}$

2 Find the gradient of the curve $y = \dfrac{x+3}{x-1}$ at the point (2, 5).

3 Find the coordinates of the points on the curve $y = \dfrac{x^2}{2x-1}$ where $\dfrac{dy}{dx} = 0$.

4 Find the gradient of the curve $y = \dfrac{7x-2}{2x+3}$ at the point where the curve crosses the y-axis.

5 Differentiate with respect to x:

a $\dfrac{\sqrt{x}}{2x+1}$ **b** $\dfrac{x}{\sqrt{1-2x}}$ **c** $\dfrac{x^2}{\sqrt{x^2+2}}$ **d** $\dfrac{5\sqrt{x}}{3+x}$

6 Find the gradient of the curve $y = \dfrac{x-2}{\sqrt{x+5}}$ at the point $(-4, -6)$.

7 Find the coordinates of the point on the curve $y = \dfrac{2(x-5)}{\sqrt{x+1}}$ where the gradient is $\dfrac{5}{4}$.

CHALLENGE Q

8 The line $5x - 5y = 2$ intersects the curve $x^2y - 5x + y + 2 = 0$ at three points.

a Find the coordinates of the points of intersection.

b Find the gradient of the curve at each of the points of intersection.

12.5 Tangents and normals

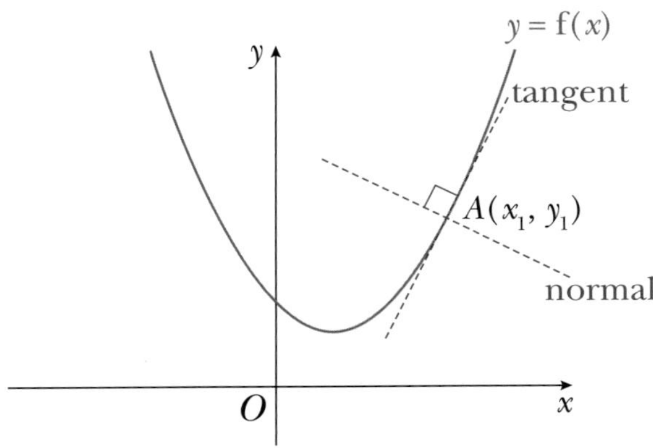

The line perpendicular to the tangent at the point A is called the **normal** at A.

If the value of $\frac{dy}{dx}$ at the point (x_1, y_1) is m, then the equation of the tangent is given by:

$$y - y_1 = m(x - x_1)$$

The normal at the point (x_1, y_1) is perpendicular to the tangent, so the gradient of the normal is $-\frac{1}{m}$ and the equation of the normal is given by:

$$y - y_1 = -\frac{1}{m}(x - x_1), \quad m \neq 0$$

WORKED EXAMPLE 10

Find the equation of the tangent and the normal to the curve $y = 3x^2 - x + \frac{8}{x}$ at the point where $x = 2$.

Answers

$$y = 3x^2 - x + 8x^{-1}$$

$$\frac{dy}{dx} = 6x - 1 - 8x^{-2}$$

When $x = 2$, $y = 3(2)^2 - (2) + 8(2)^{-1} = 14$

and $\quad \frac{dy}{dx} = 6(2) - 1 - 8(2)^{-2} = 9$

Tangent: passes through the point (2, 14) and gradient = 9

$$y - 14 = 9(x - 2)$$

$$y = 9x - 4$$

Normal: passes through the point (2, 14) and gradient $= -\frac{1}{9}$

$$y - 14 = -\frac{1}{9}(x - 2)$$

$$9y + x = 128$$

WORKED EXAMPLE 11

The normals to the curve $y = x^3 - 5x^2 + 3x + 1$, at the points $A(4, -3)$ and $B(1, 0)$, meet at the point C.

a Find the coordinates of C.

b Find the area of triangle ABC.

Answers

a $$\frac{dy}{dx} = 3x^2 - 10x + 3$$

When $x = 4$, $\frac{dy}{dx} = 3(4)^2 - 10(4) + 3 = 11$

When $x = 1$, $\frac{dy}{dx} = 3(1)^2 - 10(1) + 3 = -4$

Normal at A: passes through the point $(4, -3)$ and gradient $= -\frac{1}{11}$

$$y - (-3) = -\frac{1}{11}(x - 4)$$
$$11y = -x - 29 \text{ ----------(1)}$$

Normal at B: passes through the point $(1, 0)$ and gradient $= \frac{1}{4}$

$$y - 0 = \frac{1}{4}(x - 1)$$
$$4y = x - 1 \text{ ----------(2)}$$

Adding equations (1) and (2) gives $15y = -30$

$$y = -2$$

When $y = -2$, $11(-2) = -x - 29$

$$x = -7$$

Hence, C is the point $(-7, -2)$.

b

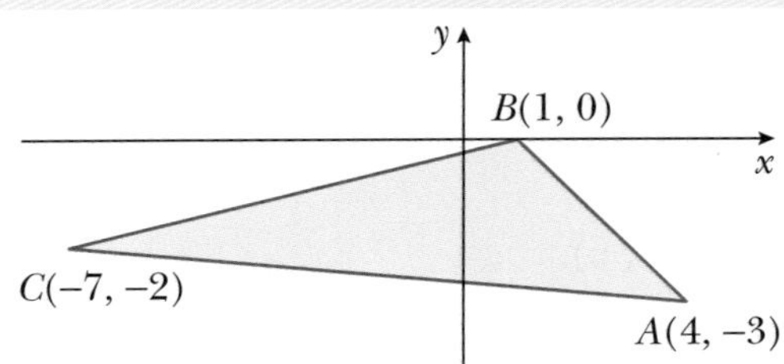

Area of triangle $ABC = \frac{1}{2}\left| \begin{matrix} 4 \\ -3 \end{matrix} \times \begin{matrix} 1 \\ 0 \end{matrix} \times \begin{matrix} -7 \\ -2 \end{matrix} \times \begin{matrix} 4 \\ -3 \end{matrix} \right|$

$= \frac{1}{2}|0 + (-2) + 21 - (-3) - 0 - (-8)|$

$= \frac{1}{2}|30|$

$= 15 \text{ units}^2$

Exercise 12.5

1 Find the equation of the tangent to the curve at the given value of x.

a $y = x^4 - 3$ at $x = 1$

b $y = x^2 + 3x + 2$ at $x = -2$

c $y = 2x^3 + 5x^2 - 1$ at $x = 1$

d $y = 5 + \frac{2}{x}$ at $x = -2$

e $y = (x-3)(2x-1)^2$ at $x = 2$

f $y = \frac{x}{x+1}$ at $x = -3$

2 Find the equation of the normal to the curve at the given value of x.

a $y = x^2 + 5x$ at $x = -1$

b $y = 3x^2 - 4x + 1$ at $x = 2$

c $y = 5x^4 - 7x^2 + 2x$ at $x = -1$

d $y = 4 - \frac{2}{x^2}$ at $x = -2$

e $y = 2x(x-3)^3$ at $x = 2$

f $y = \frac{x+2}{x-2}$ at $x = 6$

3 Find the equation of the tangent and the normal to the curve $y = 5x - \frac{3}{x}$ at the point where $x = 1$.

4 The normal to the curve $y = x^3 - 2x + 1$ at the point (2, 5) intersects the y-axis at the point P.

Find the coordinates of P.

5 Find the equation of the tangent and the normal to the curve $y = \frac{x-1}{\sqrt{x+4}}$ at the point where the curve intersects the y-axis.

6 The tangents to the curve $y = x^2 - 5x + 4$, at the points (1, 0) and (3, –2), meet at the point Q.

Find the coordinates of Q.

7 The tangent to the curve $y = 3x^2 - 10x - 8$ at the point P is parallel to the line $y = 2x - 5$.

Find the equation of the tangent at P.

8 A curve has equation $y = x^3 - x + 6$.

a Find the equation of the tangent to this curve at the point $P(-1, 6)$.

The tangent at the point Q is parallel to the tangent at P.

b Find the coordinates of Q.

c Find the equation of the normal at Q.

9 A curve has equation $y = 4 + (x-1)^4$.

The normal at the point $P(1, 4)$ and the normal at the point $Q(2, 5)$ intersect at the point R.

Find the coordinates of R.

10 A curve has equation $y = \left(2 - \sqrt{x}\right)^4$.

The normal at the point $P(1, 1)$ and the normal at the point $Q(9, 1)$ intersect at the point R.

a Find the coordinates of R.

b Find the area of triangle PQR.

11 A curve has equation $y = \sqrt{x}\,(x-2)^3$.

The tangent at the point $P\left(3, \sqrt{3}\right)$ and the normal at the point $Q(9, 1)$ intersect at the point R.

a Show that the equation of the tangent at the point $\left(3, \sqrt{3}\right)$ is $y = \dfrac{19\sqrt{3}}{6}x - \dfrac{17\sqrt{3}}{2}$.

b Find the equation of the normal at the point $Q(1, -$

12 The equation of a curve is $y = \dfrac{x^2}{x+2}$.

The tangent to the curve at the point where $x = -3$ meets the y-axis at M.

The normal to the curve at the point where $x = -3$ meets the x-axis at N.

Find the area of the triangle MNO, where O is the origin.

13 The equation of a curve is $y = \dfrac{x-3}{x+2}$.

The curve intersects the x-axis at the point P.

The normal to the curve at P meets the y-axis at the point Q.

Find the area of the triangle POQ, where O is the origin.

12.6 Small increments and approximations

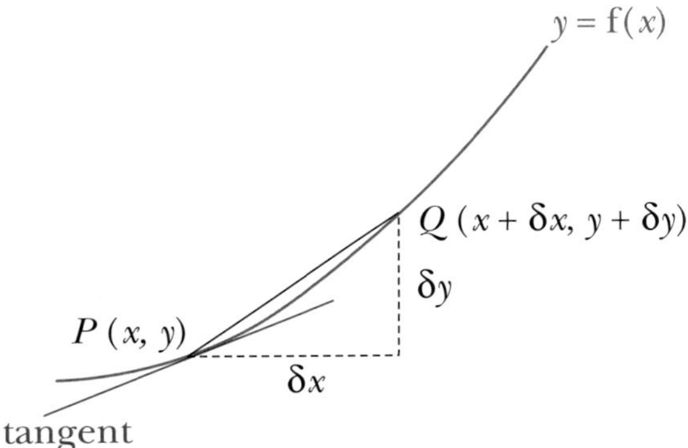

The diagram shows the tangent to the curve $y = f(x)$ at the point $P(x, y)$.

The gradient of the tangent at the point P is $\dfrac{dy}{dx}$.

The point $Q(x + \delta x, y + \delta y)$ is a point on the curve close to the point P.

The gradient of the chord PQ is $\dfrac{\delta y}{\delta x}$.

If P and Q are sufficiently close then:

$$\frac{\delta y}{\delta x} \approx \frac{dy}{dx}$$

WORKED EXAMPLE 12

Variables x and y are connected by the equation $y = x^3 + x^2$.
Find the approximate increase in y as x increases from 2 to 2.05.

Answers

$$y = x^3 + x^2$$

$$\frac{dy}{dx} = 3x^2 + 2x$$

When $x = 2$, $\frac{dy}{dx} = 3(2)^2 + 2(2) = 16$

Using $\frac{\delta y}{\delta x} \approx \frac{dy}{dx}$

$$\frac{\delta y}{0.05} \approx 16$$

$$\delta y \approx 16 \times 0.05$$

$$\delta y \approx 0.8$$

WORKED EXAMPLE 13

The volume, V cm^3, of a sphere with radius r cm is $V = \frac{4}{3}\pi r^3$.
Find, in terms of p, the approximate change in V as r increases from 10 to $10 + p$, where p is small.

Answers

$$V = \frac{4}{3}\pi r^3$$

$$\frac{dV}{dr} = 4\pi r^2$$

When $r = 10$, $\frac{dV}{dr} = 4\pi(10)^2 = 400\pi$

Using $\frac{\delta V}{\delta r} \approx \frac{dV}{dr}$

$$\frac{\delta V}{p} \approx 400\pi$$

$$\delta V \approx 400\pi p$$

Exercise 12.6

1 Variables x and y are connected by the equation $y = 2x^3 - 3x$.
Find the approximate change in y as x increases from 2 to 2.01.

2 Variables x and y are connected by the equation $y = 5x^2 - \frac{8}{x^3}$.
Find the approximate change in y as x increases from 1 to 1.02.

3 Variables x and y are connected by the equation $x^2y = 300$.
Find, in terms of p, the approximate change in y as x increases from 10 to $10 + p$, where p is small.

4 Variables x and y are connected by the equation $y = \left(\frac{1}{3}x - 2\right)^6$.
Find, in terms of p, the approximate change in y as x increases from 9 to $9 + p$, where p is small.

5 A curve has equation $y = (x + 1)(2x - 3)^4$.
Find, in terms of p, the approximate change in y as x increases from 2 to $2 + p$, where p is small.

6 A curve has equation $y = (x - 2)\sqrt{2x + 1}$.
Find, in terms of p, the approximate change in y as x increases from 4 to $4 + p$, where p is small.

7 The periodic time, T seconds, for a pendulum of length L m is
$T = 2\pi\sqrt{\frac{L}{10}}$.
Find the approximate increase in T as L increases from 40 to 41.

8

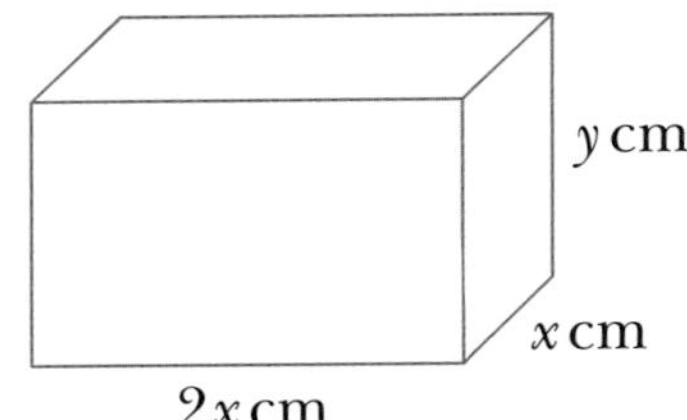

The volume of the solid cuboid is $360\,\text{cm}^3$ and the surface area is $A\,\text{cm}^2$.

a Express y in terms of x.

b Show that $A = 4x^2 + \frac{1080}{x}$.

c Find, in terms of p, the approximate change in A as x increases from 2 to $2 + p$, where p is small. State whether the change is an increase or decrease.

12.7 Rates of change

CLASS DISCUSSION

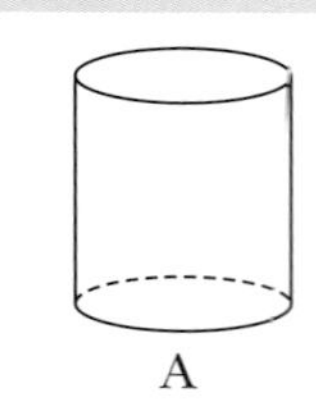

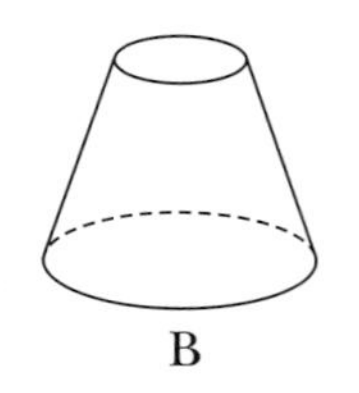

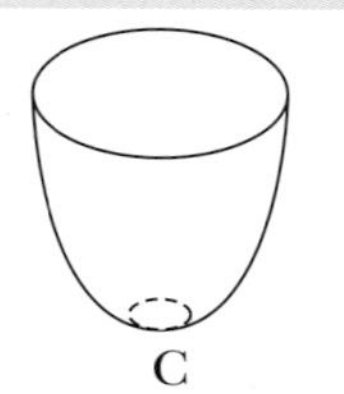

Consider pouring water at a constant rate of $10\,\text{cm}^3\,\text{s}^{-1}$ into each of these three large containers.

1 Discuss how the height of water in container A changes with time.

2 Discuss how the height of water in container B changes with time.

3 Discuss how the height of water in container C changes with time.

On copies of the axes below, sketch graphs to show how the height (h cm) varies with time (t seconds) for each container.

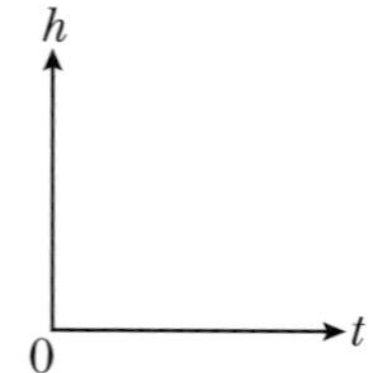

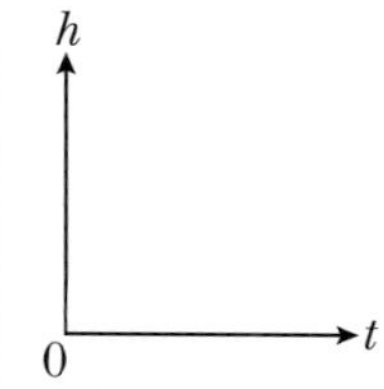

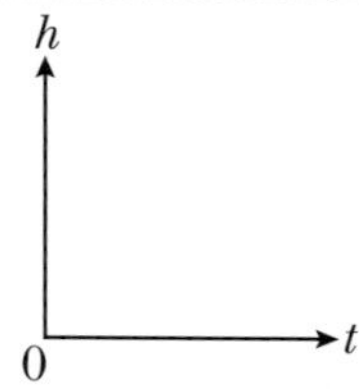

You already know that $\frac{dy}{dx}$ represents the rate of change of y with respect to x.

There are many situations where the rate of change of one quantity depends on the changing value of a second quantity.

In the class discussion, the **rate of change** of the height of water at a particular time, t, can be found by finding the value of $\frac{dh}{dt}$ at time t. (The gradient of the tangent at time t.)

WORKED EXAMPLE 14

Variables V and t are connected by the equation $V = 5t^2 - 8t + 3$.
Find the rate of change of V with respect to t when $t = 4$.

Answers

$V = 5t^2 - 8t + 3$

$\frac{dV}{dt} = 10t - 8$

When $t = 4$, $\frac{dV}{dt} = 10(4) - 8 = 32$

Connected rates of change

When two variables x and y both vary with a third variable t, the three variables can be connected using the chain rule:

$$\frac{dy}{dt} = \frac{dy}{dx} \times \frac{dx}{dt}$$

You may also need to use the rule that:

$$\frac{dx}{dy} = \frac{1}{\frac{dy}{dx}}$$

WORKED EXAMPLE 15

Variables x and y are connected by the equation $y = x^3 - 5x^2 + 15$.
Given that x increases at a rate of 0.1 units per second, find the rate of change of y when $x = 4$.

Answers

$y = x^3 - 5x^2 + 15$ and $\frac{dx}{dt} = 0.1$

$\frac{dy}{dx} = 3x^2 - 10x$

When $x = 4$, $\frac{dy}{dx} = 3(4)^2 - 10(4)$

$= 8$

Using the chain rule, $\frac{dy}{dt} = \frac{dy}{dx} \times \frac{dx}{dt}$

$= 8 \times 0.1$

$= 0.8$

Rate of change of y is 0.8 units per second.

WORKED EXAMPLE 16

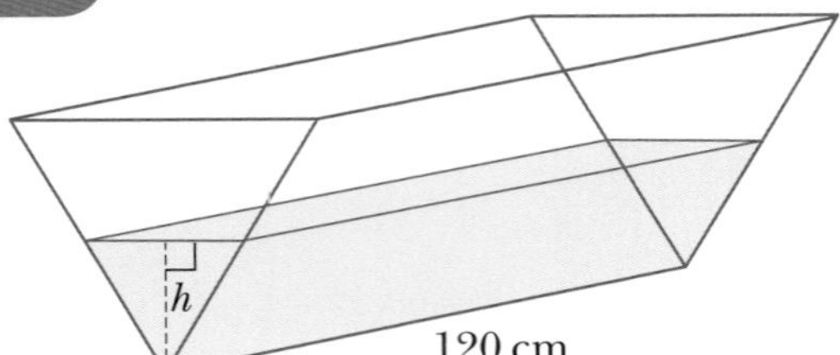

The diagram shows a water container in the shape of a triangular prism of length 120 cm.

The vertical cross-section is an equilateral triangle.

Water is poured into the container at a rate of $24\,\text{cm}^3\,\text{s}^{-1}$.

a Show that the volume of water in the container, $V\,\text{cm}^3$, is given by $V = 40\sqrt{3}\,h^2$, where h cm is the height of the water in the container.

b Find the rate of change of h when $h = 12$.

Answers

a Length of side of triangle $= \dfrac{h}{\sin 60°}$

$$= \frac{2\sqrt{3}h}{3}$$

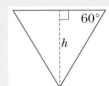

Area of triangle $= \dfrac{1}{2} \times \dfrac{2\sqrt{3}h}{3} \times h$

$$= \frac{\sqrt{3}h^2}{3}$$

V = area of triangle $\times$ 120

$$= \frac{\sqrt{3}h^2}{3} \times 120$$

$$= 40\sqrt{3}\,h^2$$

b $\dfrac{dV}{dh} = 80\sqrt{3}\,h$ and $\dfrac{dV}{dt} = 24$

When $h = 12$, $\dfrac{dV}{dh} = 80\sqrt{3}\,(12)$

$$= 960\sqrt{3}$$

Using the chain rule, $\dfrac{dh}{dt} = \dfrac{dh}{dV} \times \dfrac{dV}{dt}$

$$= \frac{1}{960\sqrt{3}} \times 24$$

$$= \frac{\sqrt{3}}{120}$$

Rate of change of h is $\dfrac{\sqrt{3}}{120}$ cm per second.

Exercise 12.7

1 Variables x and y are connected by the equation $y = x^2 - 5x$.

Given that x increases at a rate of 0.05 units per second, find the rate of change of y when $x = 4$.

2 Variables x and y are connected by the equation $y = x + \sqrt{x - 5}$.

Given that x increases at a rate of 0.1 units per second, find the rate of change of y when $x = 9$.

3 Variables x and y are connected by the equation $y = (x - 3)(x + 5)^3$.

Given that x increases at a rate of 0.2 units per second, find the rate of change of y when $x = -4$.

4 Variables x and y are connected by the equation $y = \dfrac{5}{2x - 1}$

Given that y increases at a rate of 0.1 units per second, find the rate of change of x when $x = -2$.

5 Variables x and y are connected by the equation $y = \dfrac{2x}{x^2 + 3}$.

Given that x increases at a rate of 2 units per second, find the rate of increase of y when $x = 1$.

6 Variables x and y are connected by the equation $y = \dfrac{2x - 5}{x - 1}$

Given that x increases at a rate of 0.02 units per second, find the rate of change of y when $y = 1$.

7 Variables x and y are connected by the equation $\dfrac{1}{y} = \dfrac{1}{8} - \dfrac{2}{x}$.

Given that x increases at a rate of 0.01 units per second, find the rate of change of y when $x = 8$.

8 A square has sides of length x cm and area A cm^2.

The area is increasing at a constant rate of 0.2 cm^2 s^{-1}.

Find the rate of increase of x when $A = 16$.

9 A cube has sides of length x cm and volume V cm^3.

The volume is increasing at a rate of 2 cm^3 s^{-1}.

Find the rate of increase of x when $V = 512$.

10 A sphere has radius r cm and volume V cm^3.

The radius is increasing at a rate of $\dfrac{1}{\pi}$ cm s^{-1}.

Find the rate of increase of the volume when $V = 972\pi$.

11 A solid metal cuboid has dimensions x cm by x cm by $5x$ cm.

The cuboid is heated and the volume increases at a rate of 0.5 cm^3 s^{-1}.

Find the rate of increase of x when $x = 4$.

12 A cone has base radius r cm and a fixed height 18 cm.

The radius of the base is increasing at a rate of 0.1 cm s^{-1}.

Find the rate of change of the volume when $r = 10$.

13 Water is poured into the conical container at a rate of $5\,\text{cm}^3\,\text{s}^{-1}$.
After t seconds, the volume of water in the container, $V\,\text{cm}^3$, is given by $V = \frac{1}{12}\pi h^3$, where h cm is the height of the water in the container.

a Find the rate of change of h when $h = 5$.

b Find the rate of change of h when $h = 10$.

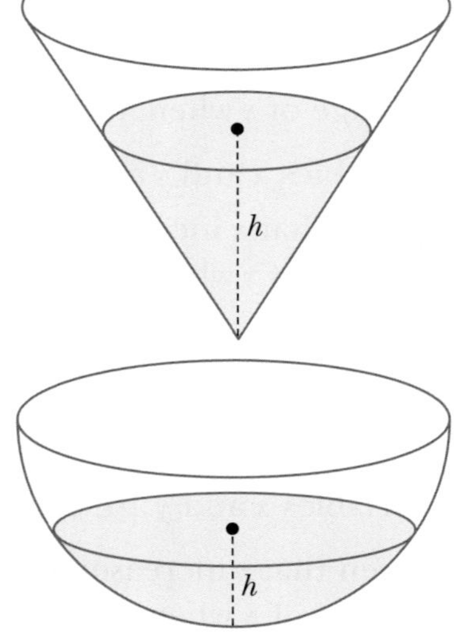

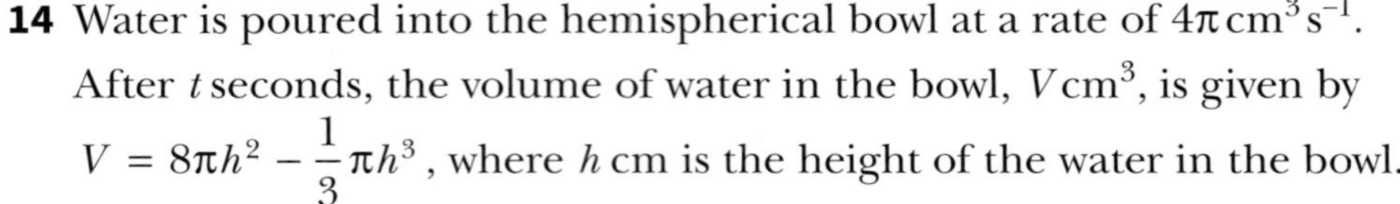

14 Water is poured into the hemispherical bowl at a rate of $4\pi\,\text{cm}^3\,\text{s}^{-1}$.
After t seconds, the volume of water in the bowl, $V\,\text{cm}^3$, is given by $V = 8\pi h^2 - \frac{1}{3}\pi h^3$, where h cm is the height of the water in the bowl.

a Find the rate of change of h when $h = 2$.

b Find the rate of change of h when $h = 4$.

12.8 Second derivatives

If you differentiate y with respect to x you obtain $\frac{dy}{dx}$.

$\frac{dy}{dx}$ is called the **first derivative** of y with respect to x.

If you differentiate $\frac{dy}{dx}$ with respect to x you obtain $\frac{d}{dx}\left(\frac{dy}{dx}\right)$ which can also be written as $\frac{d^2y}{dx^2}$.

$\frac{d^2y}{dx^2}$ is called the **second derivative** of y with respect to x.

So for $y = x^3 - 7x^2 + 2x + 1$ or $f(x) = x^3 - 7x^2 + 2x + 1$

$\frac{dy}{dx} = 3x^2 - 14x + 2$ or $f'(x) = 3x^2 - 14x + 2$

$\frac{d^2y}{dx^2} = 6x - 14$ or $f''(x) = 6x - 14$

WORKED EXAMPLE 17

Given that $y = 3x^2 - \frac{5}{x}$, find $\frac{d^2y}{dx^2}$.

Answers

$$y = 3x^2 - 5x^{-1}$$

$$\frac{dy}{dx} = 6x + 5x^{-2}$$

$$\frac{d^2y}{dx^2} = 6 - 10x^{-3}$$

$$= 6 - \frac{10}{x^3}$$

Exercise 12.8

1 Find $\dfrac{d^2y}{dx^2}$ for each of the following functions.

a $y = 5x^2 - 7x + 3$ **b** $y = 2x^3 + 3x^2 - 1$ **c** $y = 4 - \dfrac{3}{x^2}$

d $y = (4x+1)^5$ **e** $y = \sqrt{2x+1}$ **f** $y = \dfrac{4}{\sqrt{x+3}}$

2 Find $\dfrac{d^2y}{dx^2}$ for each of the following functions.

a $y = x(x-4)^3$ **b** $y = \dfrac{4x-1}{x^2}$ **c** $y = \dfrac{x+1}{x-3}$

d $y = \dfrac{x+2}{x^2-1}$ **e** $y = \dfrac{x^2}{x-5}$ **f** $y = \dfrac{2x+5}{3x-1}$

3 Given that $f(x) = x^3 - 7x^2 + 2x + 1$, find

a $f(1)$ **b** $f'(1)$ **c** $f''(1)$.

4 A curve has equation $y = 4x^3 + 3x^2 - 6x - 1$.

a Show that $\dfrac{dy}{dx} = 0$ when $x = -1$ and when $x = 0.5$.

b Find the value of $\dfrac{d^2y}{dx^2}$ when $x = -1$ and when $x = 0.5$

5 A curve has equation $y = 2x^3 - 15x^2 + 24x + 6$.

Copy and complete the table to show whether $\dfrac{dy}{dx}$ and $\dfrac{d^2y}{dx^2}$ are positive (+), negative (–) or zero (0) for the given values of x.

x	0	1	2	3	4	5
$\dfrac{dy}{dx}$						
$\dfrac{d^2y}{dx^2}$						

6 A curve has equation $y = 2x^3 + 3x^2 - 36x + 5$. Find the range of values of x for which both $\dfrac{dy}{dx}$ and $\dfrac{d^2y}{dx^2}$ are both positive.

7 Given that $y = x^2 - 2x + 5$, show that $4\dfrac{d^2y}{dx^2} + (x-1)\dfrac{dy}{dx} = 2y$.

CHALLENGE Q

8 Given that $y = 8\sqrt{x}$, show that $4x^2\dfrac{d^2y}{dx^2} + 4x\dfrac{dy}{dx} = y$.

12.9 Stationary points

Consider the graph of the function $y = f(x)$ shown below.

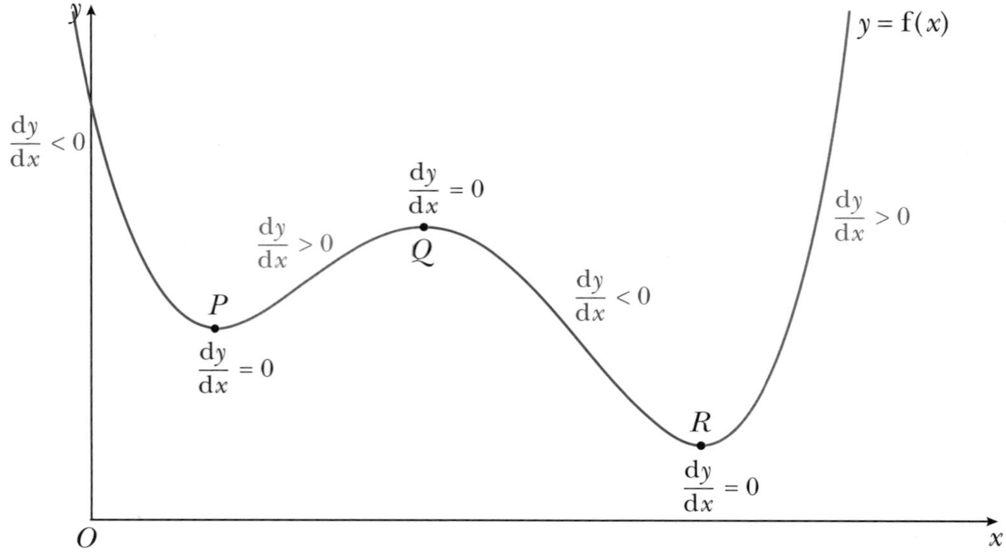

The red sections of the curve show where the gradient is negative (where $f(x)$ is a decreasing function) and the blue sections show where the gradient is positive (where $f(x)$ is an increasing function). The gradient of the curve is zero at the points P, Q and R.

A point where the gradient is zero is called a **stationary point** or a **turning point**.

Maximum points

The stationary point Q is called a **maximum point** because the value of y at this point is greater than the value of y at other points close to Q.

At a maximum point:

- $\frac{dy}{dx} = 0$
- the gradient is positive to the left of the maximum and negative to the right

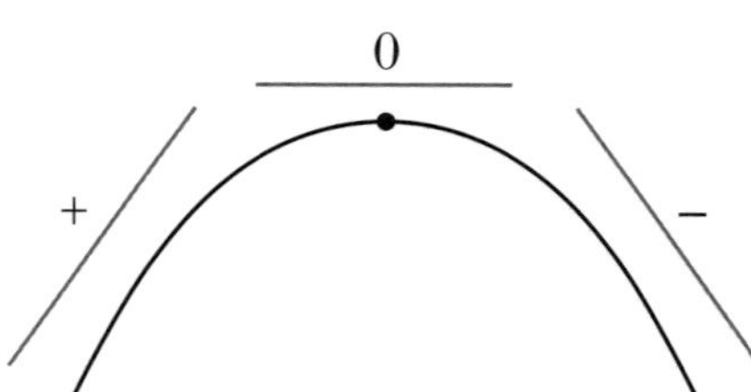

Minimum points

The stationary points P and R are called **minimum points**.

At a minimum point:

- $\frac{dy}{dx} = 0$
- the gradient is negative to the left of the minimum and positive to the right

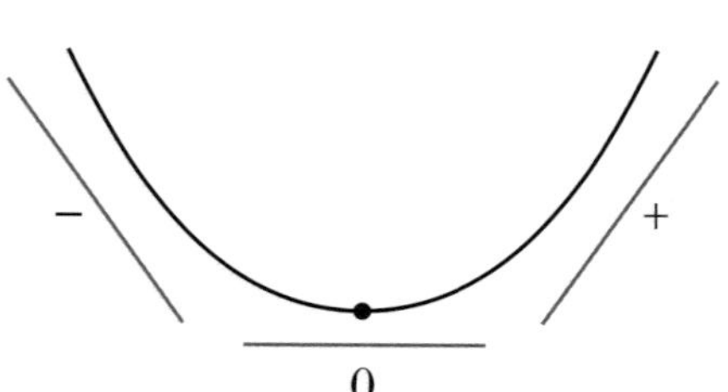

Stationary points of inflexion

There is a third type of stationary point (turning point) called a **point of inflexion**.

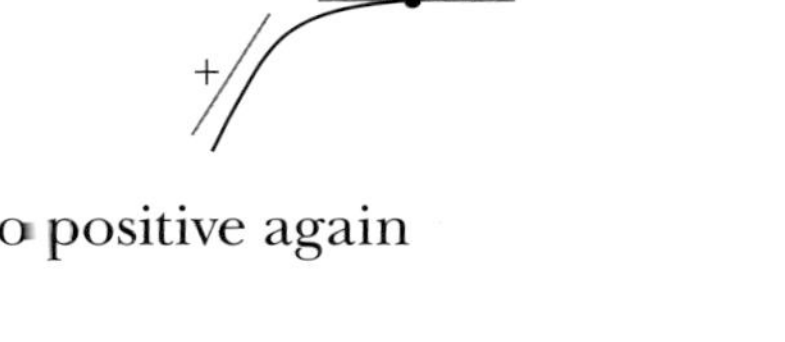

At a stationary point of inflexion:

- $\frac{dy}{dx} = 0$
- the gradient changes $\begin{cases} \text{from positive to zero and then to positive again} \\ \text{or} \\ \text{from negative to zero and then to negative again} \end{cases}$

You do not need to know about points of inflexion for the examination. They have been included here for completeness.

WORKED EXAMPLE 18

Find the coordinates of the stationary points on the curve $y = x^3 - 3x + 1$ and determine the nature of these points. Sketch the graph of $y = x^3 - 3x + 1$.

Answers

$y = x^3 - 3x + 1$

$\frac{dy}{dx} = 3x^2 - 3$

For stationary points, $\frac{dy}{dx} = 0.$

$$3x^2 - 3 = 0$$
$$x^2 - 1 = 0$$
$$(x + 1)(x - 1) = 0$$
$$x = -1 \text{ or } x = 1$$

When $x = -1$, $y = (-1)^3 - 3(-1) + 1 = 3$

When $x = 1$, $y = (1)^3 - 3(1) + 1 = -1$

The stationary points are $(-1, 3)$ and $(1, -1)$.

Now consider the gradient on either side of the points $(-1, 3)$ and $(1, -1)$:

x	−1.1	−1	−0.9
$\frac{dy}{dx}$	$3(-1.1)^2 - 3 =$ positive	0	$3(-0.9)^2 - 3 =$ negative
direction of tangent			
shape of curve			

x	0.9	1	1.1
$\frac{dy}{dx}$	$3(0.9)^2 - 3 =$ negative	0	$3(1.1)^2 - 3 =$ positive
direction of tangent			
shape of curve			

So (−1, 3) is a maximum point and (1, −1) is a minimum point.

The sketch graph of $y = x^3 - 3x + 1$ is:

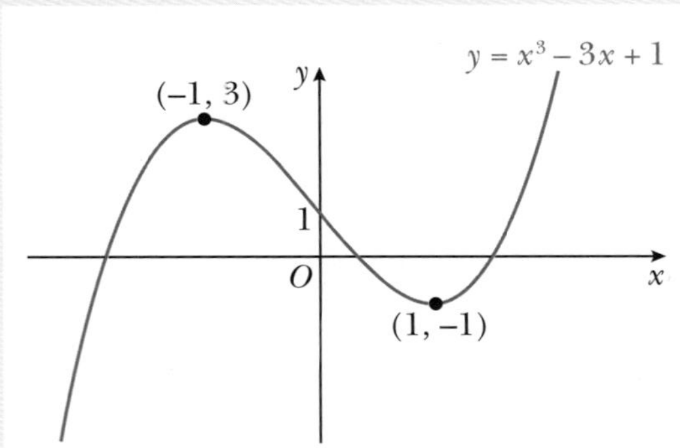

Second derivatives and stationary points

Consider moving from left to right along a curve, passing through a maximum point:

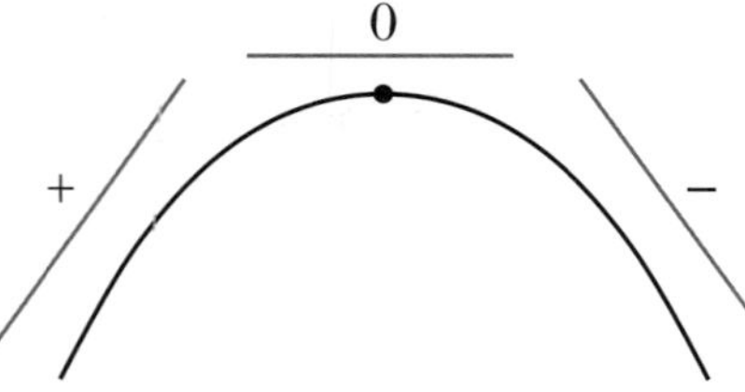

The gradient, $\frac{dy}{dx}$, starts as a positive value, decreases to zero at the maximum point and then decreases to a negative value.

Since $\frac{dy}{dx}$ decreases as x increases, then the rate of change of $\frac{dy}{dx}$ is negative.

[The rate of change of $\frac{dy}{dx}$ is written as $\frac{d}{dx}\left(\frac{dy}{dx}\right) = \frac{d^2y}{dx^2}$.]

This leads to the rule:

If $\frac{dy}{dx} = 0$ and $\frac{d^2y}{dx^2} < 0$, then the point is a maximum point.

Now, consider moving from left to right along a curve, passing through a minimum point:

The gradient, $\frac{dy}{dx}$, starts as a negative value, increases to zero at the minimum point and then increases to a positive value.

Since $\frac{dy}{dx}$ increases as x increases, then the rate of change of $\frac{dy}{dx}$ is positive.

This leads to the rule:

If $\frac{dy}{dx} = 0$ and $\frac{d^2y}{dx^2} > 0$, then the point is a minimum point.

WORKED EXAMPLE 19

Find the coordinates of the stationary points on the curve $y = 2x^3 - 15x^2 + 24x + 6$ and determine the nature of these points. Sketch the graph of $y = 2x^3 - 15x^2 + 24x + 6$.

Answers

$$y = 2x^3 - 15x^2 + 24x + 6$$

$$\frac{dy}{dx} = 6x^2 - 30x + 24$$

For stationary points, $\frac{dy}{dx} = 0$.

$$6x^2 - 30x + 24 = 0$$

$$x^2 - 5x + 4 = 0$$

$$(x - 1)(x - 4) = 0$$

$$x = 1 \text{ or } x = 4$$

When $x = 1$, $y = 2(1)^3 - 15(1)^2 + 24(1) + 6 = 17$

When $x = 4$, $y = 2(4)^3 - 15(4)^2 + 24(4) + 6 = -10$

The stationary points are $(1, 17)$ and $(4, -10)$.

$$\frac{d^2y}{dx^2} = 12x - 30$$

When $x = 1$, $\frac{d^2y}{dx^2} = -18$ which is < 0

When $x = 4$, $\frac{d^2y}{dx^2} = 18$ which is > 0

So $(1, 17)$ is a maximum point and $(4, -10)$ is a minimum point.

The sketch graph of $y = 2x^3 - 15x^2 + 24x + 6$ is:

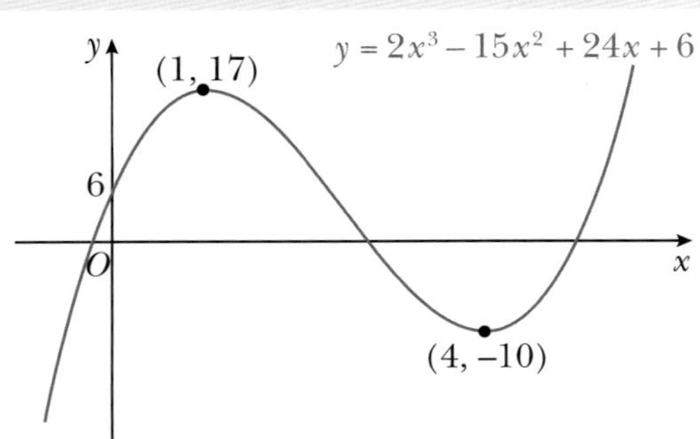

Exercise 12.9

1 Find the coordinates of the stationary points on each of the following curves and determine the nature of each of the stationary points.

a $y = x^2 - 12x + 8$ **b** $y = (5 + x)(1 - x)$

c $y = x^3 - 12x + 2$ **d** $y = x^3 + x^2 - 16x - 16$

e $y = x(3 - 4x - x^2)$ **f** $y = (x - 1)(x^2 - 6x + 2)$

2 Find the coordinates of the stationary points on each of the following curves and determine the nature of each of the stationary points.

a $y = \sqrt{x} + \dfrac{4}{\sqrt{x}}$ **b** $y = x^2 - \dfrac{2}{x}$ **c** $y = \dfrac{4}{x} + \sqrt{x}$

d $y = \dfrac{2x}{x^2 + 9}$ **e** $y = \dfrac{x^2}{x + 1}$ **f** $y = \dfrac{x^2 - 5x + 3}{x + 1}$

3 The equation of a curve is $y = \dfrac{2x + 5}{x + 1}$.

Find $\dfrac{dy}{dx}$ and hence explain why the curve has no turning points.

4 The curve $y = 2x^3 + ax^2 - 12x + 7$ has a maximum point at $x = -2$.

Find the value of a.

5 The curve $y = x^3 + ax + b$ has a stationary point at (1, 3).

a Find the value of a and the value of b.

b Determine the nature of the stationary point (1, 3).

c Find the coordinates of the other stationary point on the curve and determine the nature of this stationary point.

6 The curve $y = x^2 + \dfrac{a}{x} + b$ has a stationary point at (1, –1).

a Find the value of a and the value of b.

b Determine the nature of the stationary point (1, –1).

7 The curve $y = ax + \dfrac{b}{x^2}$ has a stationary point at (–1, –12).

a Find the value of a and the value of b.

b Determine the nature of the stationary point (–1, –12).

CHALLENGE Q

8 The curve $y = 2x^3 - 3x^2 + ax + b$ has a stationary point at the point (3, –77).

a Find the value of a and the value of b.

b Find the coordinates of the second stationary point on the curve.

c Determine the nature of the two stationary points.

d Find the coordinates of the point on the curve where the gradient is minimum and state the value of the minimum gradient.

12.10 Practical maximum and minimum problems

There are many problems for which you need to find the maximum or minimum value of a function, such as the maximum area that can be enclosed within a shape or the minimum amount of material that can be used to make a container.

WORKED EXAMPLE 20

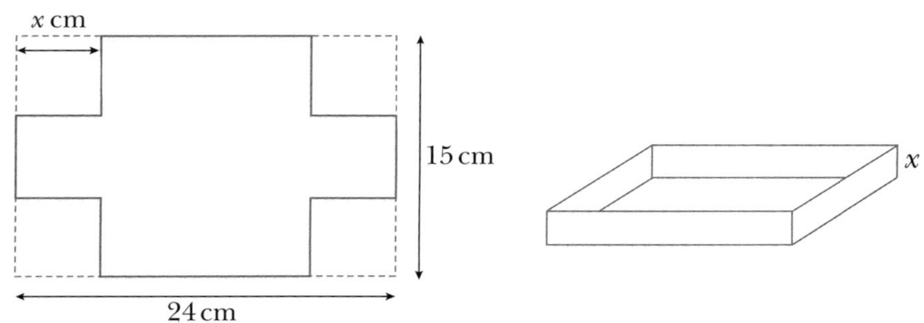

The diagram shows a 24 cm by 15 cm sheet of metal with a square of side x cm removed from each corner. The metal is then folded to make an open rectangular box of depth x cm and volume $V\text{ cm}^3$.

a Show that $V = 4x^3 - 78x^2 + 360x$.

b Find the stationary value of V and the value of x for which this occurs.

c Determine the nature of this stationary value.

Answers

a V = length × breadth × height

$= (24 - 2x)(15 - 2x)x$

$= \left(360 - 78x + 4x^2\right)x$

$= 4x^3 - 78x^2 + 360x$

b $\dfrac{dV}{dx} = 12x^2 - 156x + 360$

Stationary values occur when $\dfrac{dy}{dx} = 0$.

$$12x^2 - 156x + 360 = 0$$
$$x^2 - 13x + 30 = 0$$
$$(x - 10)(x - 3) = 0$$
$$x = 10 \text{ or } x = 3$$

The dimensions of the box must be positive so $x = 3$.

When $x = 3$, $V = 4(3)^3 - 78(3)^2 + 360(3) = 486$.

The stationary value of V is 486 and occurs when $x = 3$.

c $\dfrac{d^2V}{dx^2} = 24x - 156$

When $x = 3$, $\dfrac{d^2V}{dx^2} = 24(3) - 156 = -84$ which is < 0

The stationary value is a maximum value.

WORKED EXAMPLE 21

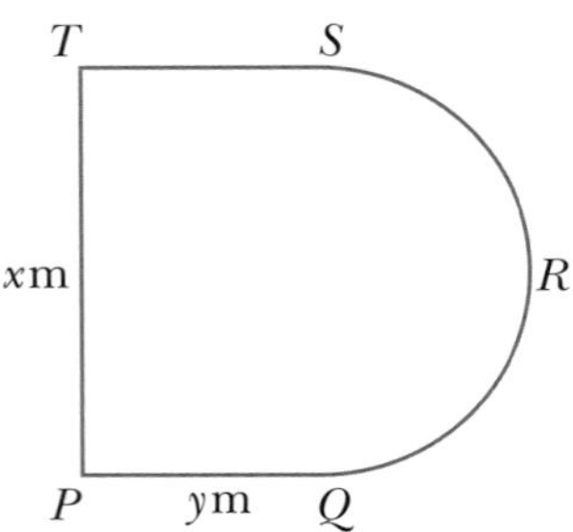

A piece of wire, of length 2 m, is bent to form the shape *PQRST*.
PQST is a rectangle and *QRS* is a semi-circle with diameter *SQ*.
$PT = x$ m and $PQ = ST = y$ m.
The total area enclosed by the shape is $A\,\text{m}^2$.

a Express y in terms of x.

b Show that $A = x - \frac{1}{2}x^2 - \frac{1}{8}\pi x^2$.

c Find $\frac{dA}{dx}$ and $\frac{d^2A}{dx^2}$.

d Find the value for x for which there is a stationary value of A.

e Determine the magnitude and nature of this stationary value.

Answers

a Perimeter = PQ + arc QRS + ST + TP

$$2 = y + \frac{1}{2} \times 2\pi\left(\frac{x}{2}\right) + y + x$$

$$2 = 2y + \frac{1}{2}\pi x + x$$

$$2y = 2 - x - \frac{1}{2}\pi x$$

$$y = 1 - \frac{1}{2}x - \frac{1}{4}\pi x$$

b A = area of rectangle + area of semi-circle

$$= xy + \frac{1}{2}\pi\left(\frac{x}{2}\right)^2$$

$$= x\left(1 - \frac{1}{2}x - \frac{1}{4}\pi x\right) + \frac{1}{8}\pi x^2$$

$$= x - \frac{1}{2}x^2 - \frac{1}{4}\pi x^2 + \frac{1}{8}\pi x^2$$

$$= x - \frac{1}{2}x^2 - \frac{1}{8}\pi x^2$$

c $\frac{dA}{dx} = 1 - x - \frac{1}{4}\pi x$

$\frac{d^2A}{dx^2} = -1 - \frac{1}{4}\pi$

d Stationary values occur when $\frac{dA}{dx} = 0$.

$$1 - x - \frac{1}{4}\pi x = 0$$
$$4 - 4x - \pi x = 0$$
$$x(4 + \pi) = 4$$

Stationary value occurs when $x = \frac{4}{(4+\pi)}$.

e When $x = \frac{4}{(4+\pi)}$, $A = \frac{4}{(4+\pi)} - \frac{1}{2}\left[\frac{4}{(4+\pi)}\right]^2 - \frac{1}{8}\pi\left[\frac{4}{(4+\pi)}\right]^2$

$$= \frac{4(4+\pi) - 8 - 2\pi}{(4+\pi)^2}$$
$$= \frac{8 + 2\pi}{(4+\pi)^2}$$
$$= \frac{2(4+\pi)}{(4+\pi)^2}$$
$$= \frac{2}{(4+\pi)}$$

When $x = \frac{4}{(4+\pi)}$, $\frac{d^2A}{dx^2} = -1 - \frac{1}{4}\pi$ which is < 0

The stationary value of A is $\frac{2}{(4+\pi)}$ m^2 and it is a maximum value

Exercise 12.10

1 The sum of two numbers x and y is 8.

a Express y in terms of x.

b **i** Given that $P = xy$, write down an expression for P in terms of x.

ii Find the maximum value of P.

c **i** Given that $S = x^2 + y^2$, write down an expression for S in terms of x.

ii Find the minimum value of S.

2 The diagram shows a rectangular garden with a fence on three of its sides and a wall on its fourth side. The total length of the fence is 100 m and the area enclosed is $A\,m^2$.

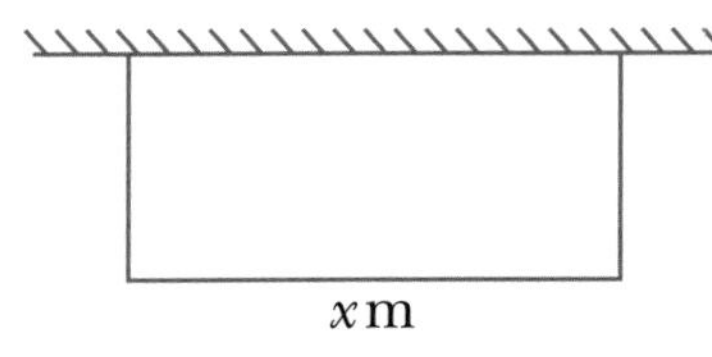

a Show that $A = \frac{1}{2}x(100 - x)$.

b Find the maximum area of the garden enclosed and the value of x for which this occurs.

3 The volume of the solid cuboid is $576\,cm^3$ and the surface area is $A\,cm^2$.

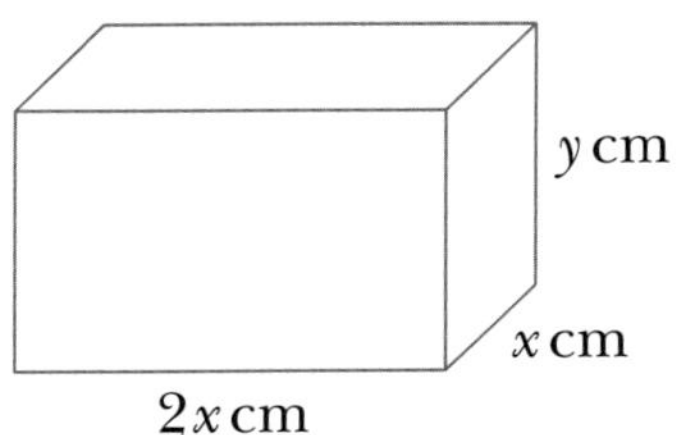

a Express y in terms of x.

b Show that $A = 4x^2 + \frac{1728}{x}$.

c Find the maximum value of A and state the dimensions of the cuboid for which this occurs.

4 A cuboid has a total surface area of $400\,\text{cm}^2$ and a volume of $V\,\text{cm}^3$.

The dimensions of the cuboid are $4x$ cm by x cm by h cm.

a Express h in terms of V and x.

b Show that $V = 160x - \dfrac{16}{5}x^3$.

c Find the value of x when V is a maximum.

5 A piece of wire, of length 60 cm, is bent to form a sector of a circle with radius r cm and sector angle θ radians. The total area enclosed by the shape is $A\,\text{cm}^2$.

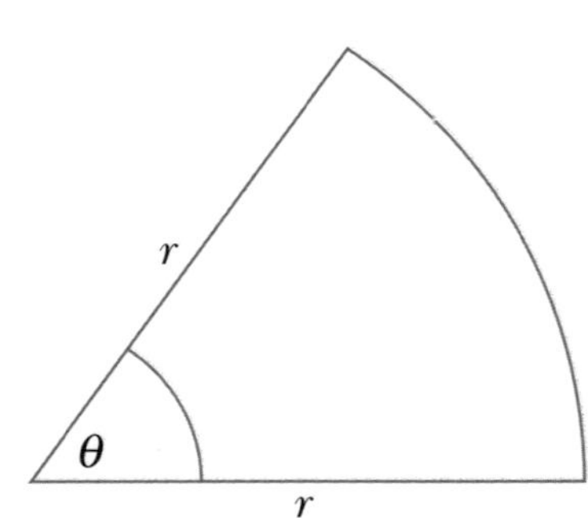

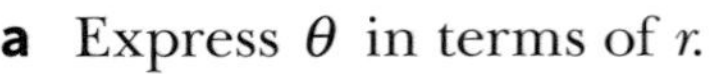

a Express θ in terms of r.

b Show that $A = 30r - r^2$.

c Find $\dfrac{dA}{dr}$ and $\dfrac{d^2A}{dr^2}$.

d Find the value for r for which there is a stationary value of A.

e Determine the magnitude and nature of this stationary value.

6 The diagram shows a window made from a rectangle with base $2r$ m and height h m and a semicircle of radius r m. The perimeter of the window is 6 m and the surface area is $A\,\text{m}^2$.

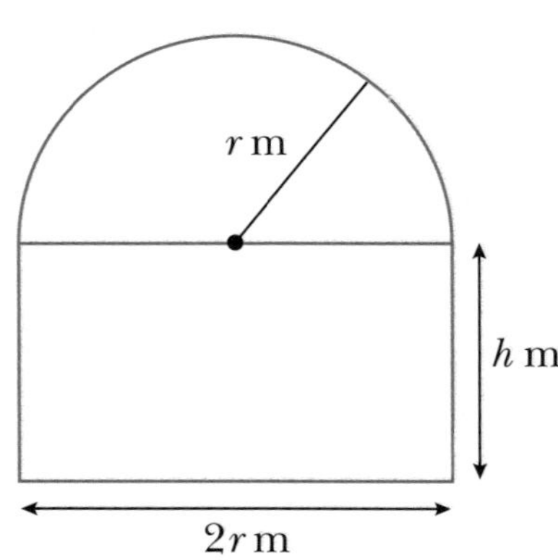

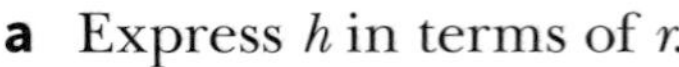

a Express h in terms of r.

b Show that $A = 6r - 2r^2 - \dfrac{1}{2}\pi r^2$.

c Find $\dfrac{dA}{dr}$ and $\dfrac{d^2A}{dr^2}$.

d Find the value for r for which there is a stationary value of A.

e Determine the magnitude and nature of this stationary value.

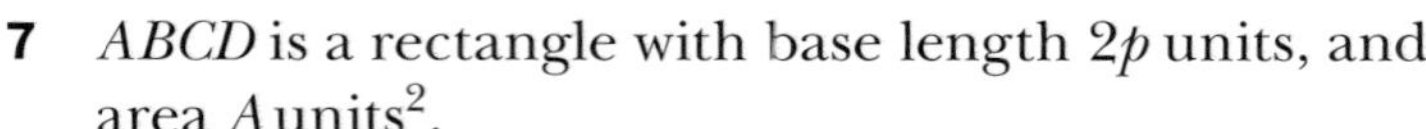

7 $ABCD$ is a rectangle with base length $2p$ units, and area A units^2.

The points A and B lie on the x-axis and the points C and D lie on the curve $y = 4 - x^2$.

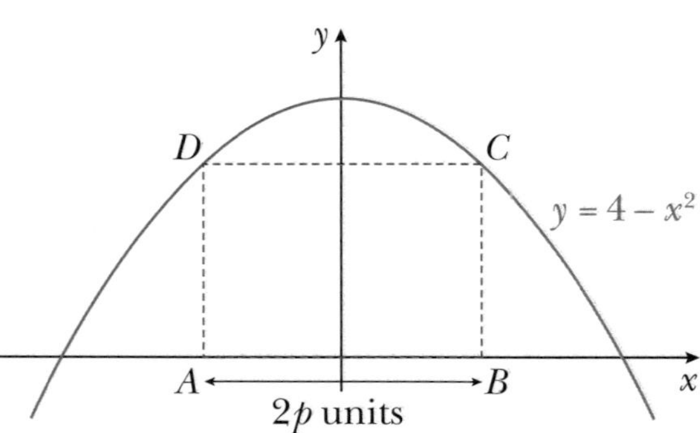

a Express BC in terms of p.

b Show that $A = 2p(4 - p^2)$.

c Find the value of p for which A has a stationary value.

d Find this stationary value and determine its nature.

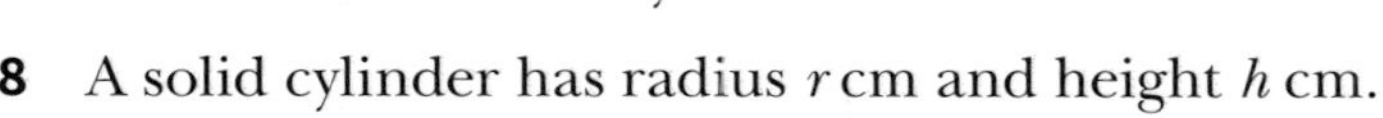

8 A solid cylinder has radius r cm and height h cm.

The volume of this cylinder is $250\pi\,\text{cm}^3$ and the surface area is $A\,\text{cm}^2$.

a Express h in terms of r.

b Show that $A = 2\pi r^2 + \dfrac{500\pi}{r}$.

c Find $\dfrac{dA}{dr}$ and $\dfrac{d^2A}{dr^2}$.

d Find the value for r for which there is a stationary value of A.

e Determine the magnitude and nature of this stationary value.

9 The diagram shows a solid formed by joining a hemisphere of radius r cm to a cylinder of radius r cm and height h cm. The surface area of the solid is 288π cm^2 and the volume is V cm^3.

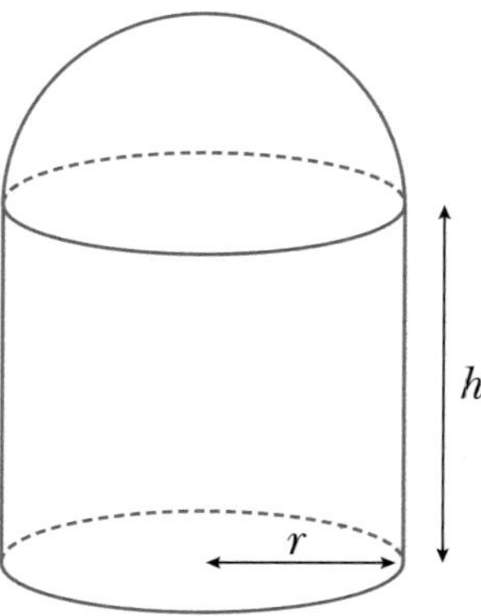

a Express h in terms of r.

b Show that $V = 144\pi r - \frac{5}{6}\pi r^3$.

c Find the exact value of r such that V is a maximum.

10 A piece of wire, of length 50 cm, is cut into two pieces.

One piece is bent to make a square of side x cm and the other is bent to make a circle of radius r cm. The total area enclosed by the two shapes is A cm^2.

a Express r in terms of x.

b Show that $A = \frac{(\pi + 4)x^2 - 100x + 625}{\pi}$.

c Find the stationary value of A and the value of x for which this occurs.

Give your answers correct to 3 sf.

11 The diagram shows a solid cylinder of radius r cm and height $2h$ cm cut from a solid sphere of radius 5 cm. The volume of the cylinder is V cm^3.

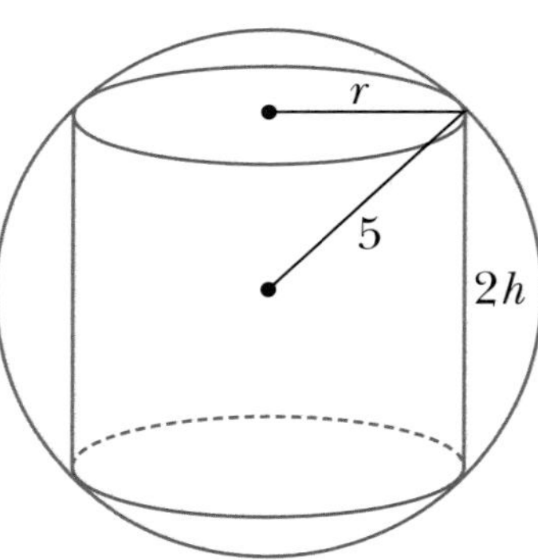

a Express r in terms of h.

b Show that $V = 2\pi h(25 - h^2)$.

c Find the value for h for which there is a stationary value of V.

d Determine the nature of this stationary value.

CHALLENGE Q

12 The diagram shows a hollow cone with base radius 12 cm and height 24 cm.

A solid cylinder stands on the base of the cone and the upper edge touches the inside of the cone.

The cylinder has base radius r cm, height h cm and volume V cm^3.

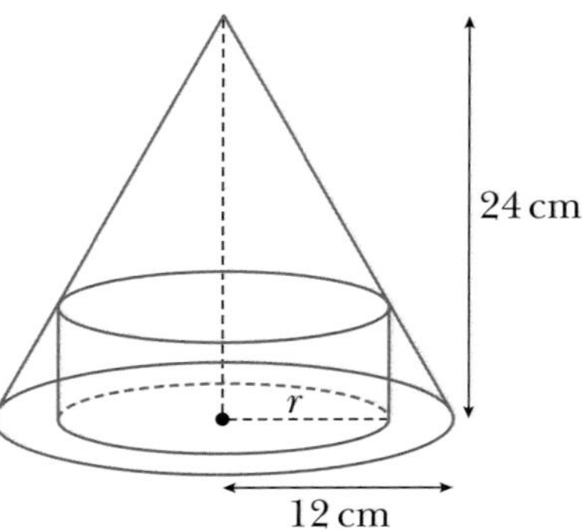

a Express h in terms of r.

b Show that $V = 2\pi r^2(12 - r)$.

c Find the volume of the largest cylinder which can stand inside the cone.

CHALLENGE Q

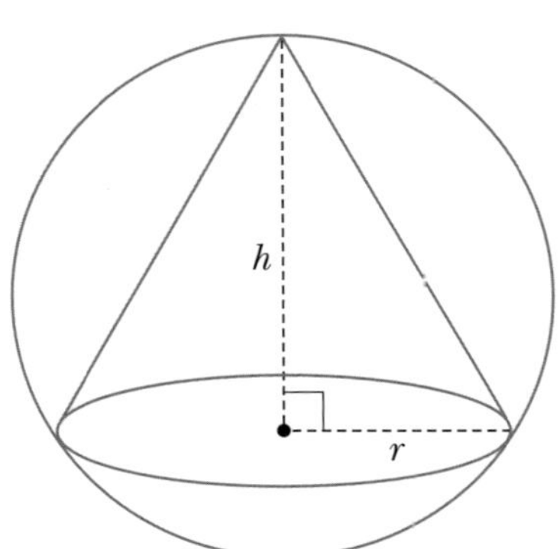

13 The diagram shows a right circular cone of base radius r cm and height h cm cut from a solid sphere of radius 10 cm. The volume of the cone is V cm^3.

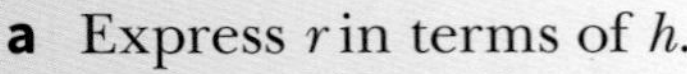

a Express r in terms of h.

b Show that $V = \frac{1}{3}\pi h^2(20 - h)$.

c Find the value for h for which there is a stationary value of V.

d Determine the magnitude and nature of this stationary value.

Summary

Rules of differentiation

Power rule: If $y = x^n$, then $\frac{dy}{dx} = nx^{n-1}$

Scalar multiple rule: $\frac{d}{dx}[kf(x)] = k\frac{d}{dx}[f(x)]$

Addition/subtraction rule: $\frac{d}{dx}[f(x) \pm g(x)] = \frac{d}{dx}[f(x)] \pm \frac{d}{dx}[g(x)]$

Chain rule: $\frac{dy}{dx} = \frac{dy}{du} \times \frac{du}{dx}$

Product rule: $\frac{d}{dx}(uv) = u\frac{dv}{dx} + v\frac{du}{dx}$

Quotient rule: $\frac{d}{dx}\left(\frac{u}{v}\right) = \frac{v\frac{du}{dx} - u\frac{dv}{dx}}{v^2}$

Tangents and normals

If the value of $\frac{dy}{dx}$ at the point (x_1, y_1) is m, then:

- the equation of the tangent is given by $y - y_1 = m(x - x_1)$
- the equation of the normal is given by $y - y_1 = -\frac{1}{m}(x - x_1)$

Small increments and approximations

If δx and δy are sufficiently small then $\frac{\delta y}{\delta x} \approx \frac{dy}{dx}$.

Stationary points

Stationary points (turning points) of a function $y = f(x)$ occur when $\frac{dy}{dx} = 0$.

First derivative test for maximum and minimum points

At a maximum point:

- $\frac{dy}{dx} = 0$
- the gradient is positive to the left of the maximum and negative to the right

At a minimum point:

- $\frac{dy}{dx} = 0$
- the gradient is negative to the left of the minimum and positive to the right

Second derivative test for maximum and minimum points

$$\text{If } \frac{dy}{dx} = 0 \text{ and } \begin{cases} \frac{d^2y}{dx^2} < 0, \text{ then the point is a maximum point} \\ \frac{d^2y}{dx^2} > 0, \text{ then the point is a minimum point} \end{cases}$$

Examination questions

Worked example

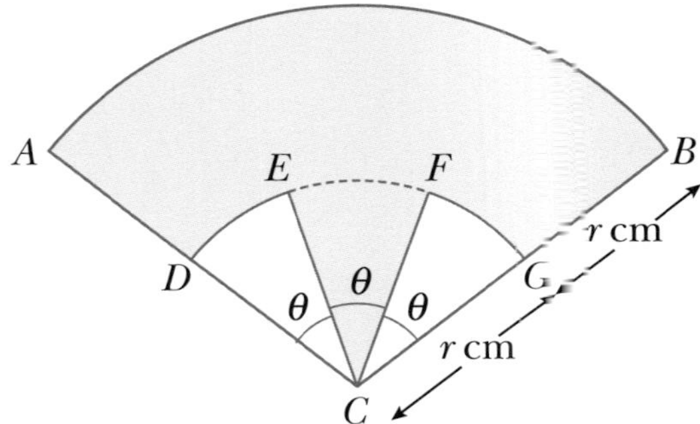

The figure shows a sector ABC of a circle centre C, radius $2r$ cm, where angle ACB is 3θ radians. The points D, E, F and G lie on an arc of a circle centre C, radius r cm. The points D and G are the mid-points of CA and CB respectively. Angles DCE and FCG are each θ radians. The area of the shaded region is $5\,\text{cm}^2$.

a By first expressing θ in terms of r, show that the perimeter, P cm, of the shaded region is given by $P = 4r + \frac{8}{r}$. [6]

b Given that r can vary, show that the stationary value of P can be written in the form $k\sqrt{2}$, where k is a constant to be found. [4]

c Determine the nature of this stationary value and find the value of θ for which it occurs. [2]

Cambridge IGCSE Additional Mathematics 0606 Paper 11 Q10(part) Nov 2011

Answers

a Area of sector ABC – (area of sector DCE + area of sector FCG) = 5

$$\frac{1}{2}(2r)^2(3\theta) - \left(\frac{1}{2}r^2\theta + \frac{1}{2}r^2\theta\right) = 5$$

$$6r^2\theta - r^2\theta = 5$$

$$5r^2\theta = 5$$

$$\theta = \frac{1}{r^2}$$

$$P = CE + \text{arc } ED + DA + \text{arc } AB + BG + \text{arc } GF + FC$$

$$= r + r\theta + r + (2r)(3\theta) + r + r\theta + r$$

$$= 4r + 8r\theta$$

$$= 4r + 8r \times \frac{1}{r^2}$$

$$= 4r + \frac{8}{r}$$

b $P = 4r + 8r^{-1}$

$$\frac{dP}{dr} = 4 - 8r^{-2}$$

Stationary values occur when $\frac{dP}{dr} = 0$.

$$4 - \frac{8}{r^2} = 0$$

$$r^2 = 2$$

$$r = \sqrt{2}$$

When $r = \sqrt{2}$, $P = 4\left(\sqrt{2}\right) + \frac{8}{\sqrt{2}} = 8\sqrt{2}$

Stationary value of P is $8\sqrt{2}$.

c When $r = \sqrt{2}$, $\theta = \frac{1}{\left(\sqrt{2}\right)^2} = \frac{1}{2}$

$$\frac{dP}{dr} = 4 - 8r^{-2}$$

$$\frac{d^2P}{dr^2} = 16r^{-3}$$

When $r = \sqrt{2}$, $\frac{d^2P}{dr^2} = \frac{16}{\left(\sqrt{2}\right)^3} = \text{positive}$

The stationary value is a minimum and occurs when $\theta = \frac{1}{2}$.

Exercise 12.11

Exam Exercise

1 Find the coordinates of the stationary point on the curve $y = x^2 + \dfrac{16}{x}$. [4]

Cambridge IGCSE Additional Mathematics 0606 Paper 11 Q1 Nov 2014

2 Given that $y = \dfrac{x^2}{2 + x^2}$, show that $\dfrac{dy}{dx} = \dfrac{kx}{(2 + x)^2}$, where k is a constant to be found. [3]

Cambridge IGCSE Additional Mathematics 0606 Paper 21 Q8i Nov 2014

3 Given that a curve has equation $y = \dfrac{1}{x} + 2\sqrt{x}$, where $x > 0$, find

a $\dfrac{dy}{dx}$, [2]

b $\dfrac{d^2y}{dx^2}$. [2]

Hence or otherwise, find

c the coordinates and nature of the stationary point on the curve. [4]

Cambridge IGCSE Additional Mathematics 0606 Paper 21 Q7i,ii,iii Jun 2014

4 A sector of a circle of radius r cm has an angle θ radians, where $\theta < \pi$. The perimeter of the sector is 30 cm.

a Show that the area, $A\,\text{cm}^2$, of the sector is given by $A = 15r - r^2$. [3]

b Given that r can vary, find the maximum area of the sector. [3]

Cambridge IGCSE Additional Mathematics 0606 Paper 21 Q8i,ii Jun 2014

5 a Given that $y = \left(\dfrac{1}{4}x - 5\right)^8$, find $\dfrac{dy}{dx}$. [2]

b Hence find the approximate change in y as x increases from 12 to $12 + p$, where p is small. [2]

Cambridge IGCSE Additional Mathematics 0606 Paper 21 Q3i,ii Nov 2013

6 Find the equation of the normal to the curve $y = \dfrac{x^2 + 8}{x - 2}$ at the point on the curve where $x = 4$. [6]

Cambridge IGCSE Additional Mathematics 0606 Paper 21 Q6 Jun 2013

7 a Find the equation of the tangent to the curve $y = x^3 + 2x^2 - 3x + 4$ at the point where the curve crosses the y-axis. [4]

b Find the coordinates of the point where the tangent meets the curve again. [3]

Cambridge IGCSE Additional Mathematics 0606 Paper 11 Q5i,ii Jun 2012

8 The normal to the curve $y = x^3 + 6x^2 - 34x + 44$ at the point $P(2, 8)$ cuts the x-axis at A and the y-axis at B. Show that the mid-point of the line AB lies on the line $4y = x + 9$. [8]

Cambridge IGCSE Additional Mathematics 0606 Paper 21 Q6 Nov 2012

9 Given that $f(x) = x^2 - \dfrac{648}{\sqrt{x}}$, find the value of x for which $f''(x) = 0$. [6]

Cambridge IGCSE Additional Mathematics 0606 Paper 21 Q7 Jun 2012

10

x cm

x cm

45 cm

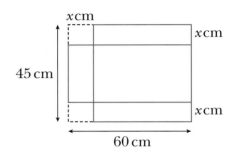

x cm

60 cm

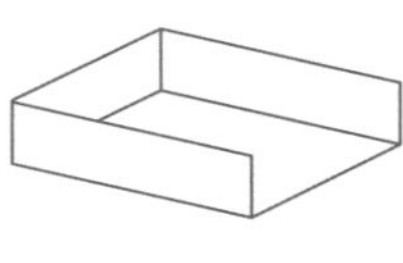

A rectangular sheet of metal measures 60 cm by 45 cm. A scoop is made by cutting out squares, of side x cm, from two corners of the sheet and folding the remainder as shown.

a Show that the volume, $V\text{cm}^3$ of the scoop is given by

$$V = 2700x - 165x^2 + 2x^3.$$ [2]

b Given that x can vary, find the value of x for which V has a stationary value. [4]

Cambridge IGCSE Additional Mathematics 0606 Paper 21 Q7i,ii Nov 2010

11

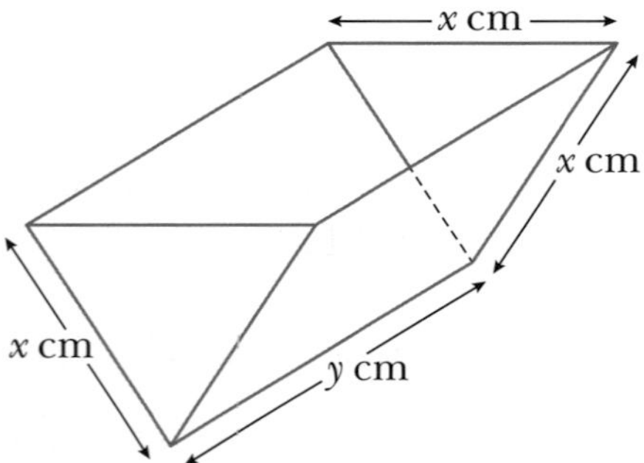

The diagram shows an empty container in the form of an open triangular prism. The triangular faces are equilateral with a side of $x$cm and the length of each rectangular face is $y$cm. The container is made from thin sheet metal. When full, the container holds $200\sqrt{3}\ \text{cm}^3$.

i Show that $A\text{cm}^2$, the total area of the thin sheet metal used, is given by

$$A = \frac{\sqrt{3}x^2}{2} + \frac{1600}{x}.$$ [5]

ii Given that x and y can vary, find the stationary value of A and determine its nature. [6]

Cambridge IGCSE Additional Mathematics 0606 Paper 12 Q9 Mar 2015

Chapter 13
Vectors

This section will show you how to:

- use vectors in any form, e.g. $\begin{pmatrix} a \\ b \end{pmatrix}$, $\overrightarrow{AB}$, $\mathbf{p}$, $a\mathbf{i} + b\mathbf{j}$
- use position vectors and unit vectors
- find the magnitude of a vector; add and subtract vectors and multiply vectors by scalars
- compose and resolve velocities.

RECAP

You should already be familiar with the following vector work:

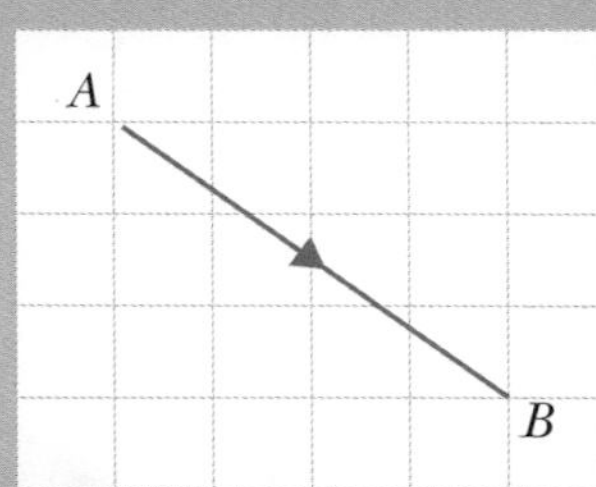

Quantities that have both magnitude and direction are called **vectors**.

Quantities that have only magnitude are called **scalars**.

$\overrightarrow{AB}$ means the displacement from the point A to the point B.

For the diagram, $\overrightarrow{AB} = \begin{pmatrix} 4 \\ -3 \end{pmatrix}$.

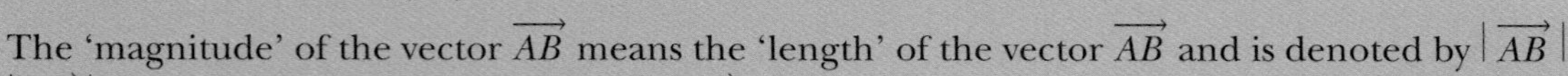

The 'magnitude' of the vector $\overrightarrow{AB}$ means the 'length' of the vector $\overrightarrow{AB}$ and is denoted by $|\overrightarrow{AB}|$.
$|\overrightarrow{AB}|$ is called the **modulus** of the vector $\overrightarrow{AB}$.

Using Pythagoras for the diagram, $|\overrightarrow{AB}| = \sqrt{(4)^2 + (-3)^2} = 5$.

Two vectors are said to be equal if they are the same length and are in the same direction.

The vector $-\mathbf{a}$ is the same length as the vector $\mathbf{a}$ but is in the opposite direction.

Addition and subtraction of vectors

The vector $\mathbf{a} + \mathbf{b}$ means the vector $\mathbf{a}$ followed by the vector $\mathbf{b}$.
The vector $\mathbf{a} - \mathbf{b}$ means the vector $\mathbf{a}$ followed by the vector $-\mathbf{b}$.
The resultant vector is often shown with a double arrow.
It is drawn from the starting point to the finishing point.

For example, if $\mathbf{a} = \begin{pmatrix} 2 \\ 3 \end{pmatrix}$ and $\mathbf{b} = \begin{pmatrix} 4 \\ 1 \end{pmatrix}$, then $\mathbf{a} + \mathbf{b}$ and $\mathbf{a} - \mathbf{b}$ can be shown on a vector diagram as:

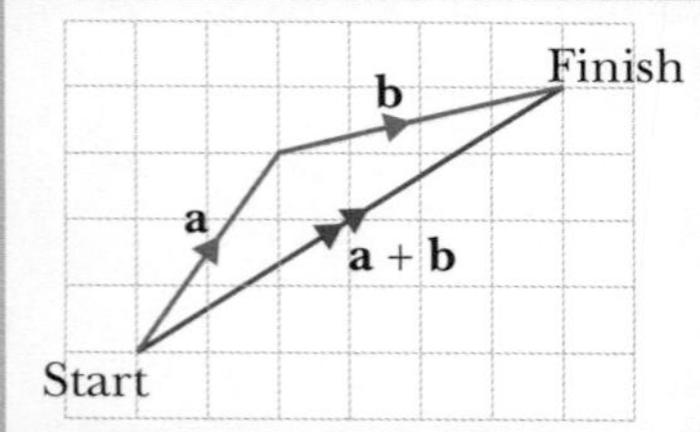

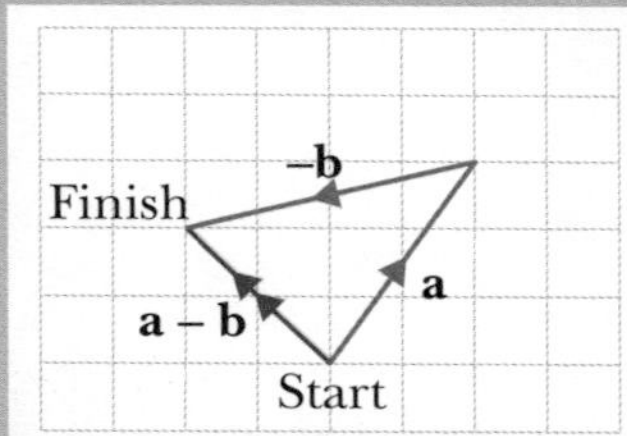

$\mathbf{a} + \mathbf{b}$ and $\mathbf{a} - \mathbf{b}$ can also be found as follows:

$\mathbf{a} + \mathbf{b} = \begin{pmatrix} 2 \\ 3 \end{pmatrix} + \begin{pmatrix} 4 \\ 1 \end{pmatrix} = \begin{pmatrix} 2+4 \\ 3+1 \end{pmatrix} = \begin{pmatrix} 6 \\ 4 \end{pmatrix}$ $\qquad$ $\mathbf{a} - \mathbf{b} = \begin{pmatrix} 2 \\ 3 \end{pmatrix} - \begin{pmatrix} 4 \\ 1 \end{pmatrix} = \begin{pmatrix} 2-4 \\ 3-1 \end{pmatrix} = \begin{pmatrix} -2 \\ 2 \end{pmatrix}$

Multiplication by a scalar

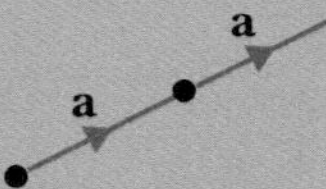

The vector $\mathbf{a} + \mathbf{a}$ can be written as $2\mathbf{a}$.

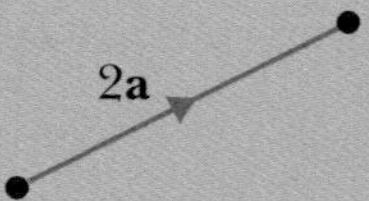

The vectors $\mathbf{a}$ and $2\mathbf{a}$ are examples of parallel vectors.
Two vectors are parallel if one vector can be written as a multiple of the other vector.
For example:

$\begin{pmatrix} -1 \\ 3 \end{pmatrix}$ and $\begin{pmatrix} -5 \\ 15 \end{pmatrix}$ are parallel and in the same direction because $\begin{pmatrix} -5 \\ 15 \end{pmatrix} = 5\begin{pmatrix} -1 \\ 3 \end{pmatrix}$.

$\begin{pmatrix} 2 \\ -4 \end{pmatrix}$ and $\begin{pmatrix} -6 \\ 12 \end{pmatrix}$ are parallel and in opposite directions because $\begin{pmatrix} -6 \\ 12 \end{pmatrix} = -3\begin{pmatrix} 2 \\ -4 \end{pmatrix}$.

Collinear points

If $\overrightarrow{AB} = k\overrightarrow{AC}$ then the points A, B and C are **collinear**.
(This is because the lines AB and AC must be parallel and the point A lies on both lines.)

13.1 Further vector notation

The vector $\overrightarrow{AB}$ in the diagram can be written in component form as $\begin{pmatrix} 4 \\ 3 \end{pmatrix}$.

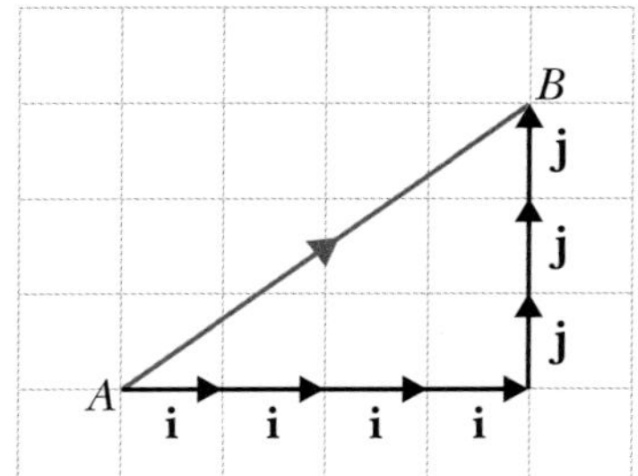

$\overrightarrow{AB}$ can also be written as $4\mathbf{i} + 3\mathbf{j}$, where:

i is a vector of length 1 unit in the positive x-direction

and **j** is a vector of length 1 unit in the positive y-direction.

Note:
A vector of length 1 unit is called a **unit vector**.

WORKED EXAMPLE 1

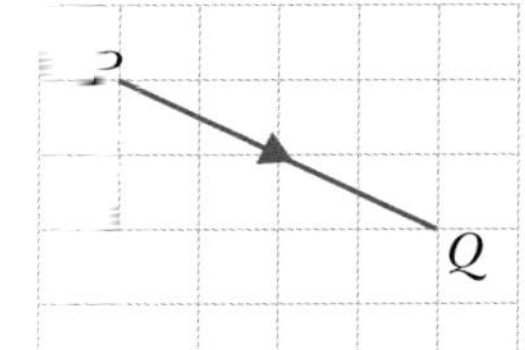

a Write $\overrightarrow{PQ}$ in the form $a\mathbf{i} + b\mathbf{j}$.
b Find $\left|\overrightarrow{PQ}\right|$.

Answers

a $\overrightarrow{PQ} = 4\mathbf{i} - 2\mathbf{j}$
b Using Pythagoras, $\left|\overrightarrow{PQ}\right| = \sqrt{(4)^2 + (-2)^2} = \sqrt{20} = 2\sqrt{5}$.

You could be asked to find the unit vector in the direction of a given vector.

The method is outline in the following example.

WORKED EXAMPLE 2

$\overrightarrow{EF} = 4\mathbf{i} + 3\mathbf{j}$
Find the unit vector in the direction of the vector $\overrightarrow{EF}$.

Answers

First find the length of the vector $\overrightarrow{EF}$:

$EF^2 = 4^2 + 3^2$ using Pythagoras

$EF = 5$

Hence the unit vector in the direction of $\overrightarrow{EF}$ is:

$\frac{1}{5}(4\mathbf{i} + 3\mathbf{j})$

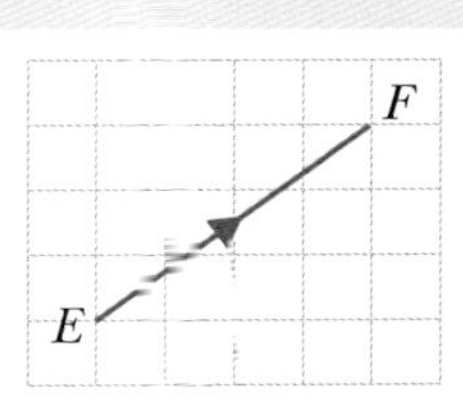

WORKED EXAMPLE 3

$\mathbf{a} = -2\mathbf{i} + 3\mathbf{j}$, $\mathbf{b} = 4\mathbf{i} - \mathbf{j}$ and $\mathbf{c} = -22\mathbf{i} + 18\mathbf{j}$.

Find λ and μ such that $\lambda\mathbf{a} + \mu\mathbf{b} = \mathbf{c}$.

Answers

$\lambda\mathbf{a} + \mu\mathbf{b} = \mathbf{c}$

$\lambda(-2\mathbf{i} + 3\mathbf{j}) + \mu(4\mathbf{i} - \mathbf{j}) = -22\mathbf{i} + 18\mathbf{j}$

Equating the **i**'s gives

$-2\lambda + 4\mu = -22$

$-\lambda + 2\mu = -11$ -------------(1)

Equating the **j**'s gives

$3\lambda - \mu = 18$

$6\lambda - 2\mu = 36$ -------------(2)

Adding equations (1) and (2) gives

$5\lambda = 25$

$\lambda = 5$

Substituting for λ in equation (1) gives

$-5 + 2\mu = -11$

$2\mu = -6$

$\mu = -3$

So $\lambda = 5$, $\mu = -3$.

Exercise 13.1

1 Write each vector in the form $a\mathbf{i} + b\mathbf{j}$.

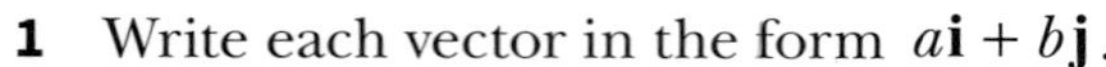

a $\overrightarrow{AB}$ **b** $\overrightarrow{AC}$ **c** $\overrightarrow{AD}$

d $\overrightarrow{AE}$ **e** $\overrightarrow{BE}$ **f** $\overrightarrow{DE}$

g $\overrightarrow{EA}$ **h** $\overrightarrow{DB}$ **i** $\overrightarrow{DC}$

2 Find the magnitude of each of these vectors.

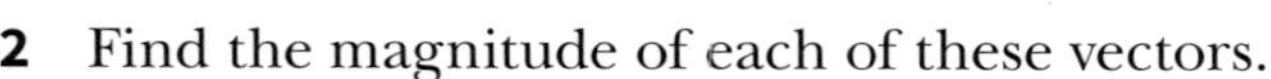

a $-2\mathbf{i}$ **b** $4\mathbf{i} + 3\mathbf{j}$ **c** $5\mathbf{i} - 12\mathbf{j}$ **d** $-8\mathbf{i} - 6\mathbf{j}$

e $7\mathbf{i} + 24\mathbf{j}$ **f** $15\mathbf{i} - 8\mathbf{j}$ **g** $-4\mathbf{i} + 4\mathbf{j}$ **h** $5\mathbf{i} - 10\mathbf{j}$

3 The vector $\overrightarrow{AB}$ has a magnitude of 20 units and is parallel to the vector $4\mathbf{i} + 3\mathbf{j}$.

Find $\overrightarrow{AB}$.

4 The vector $\overrightarrow{PQ}$ has a magnitude of 39 units and is parallel to the vector $12\mathbf{i} - 5\mathbf{j}$.

Find $\overrightarrow{PQ}$.

5 Find the unit vector in the direction of each of these vectors.

a $6\mathbf{i} + 8\mathbf{j}$ **b** $5\mathbf{i} + 12\mathbf{j}$ **c** $-4\mathbf{i} - 3\mathbf{j}$ **d** $8\mathbf{i} - 15\mathbf{j}$ **e** $3\mathbf{i} + 3\mathbf{j}$

6 $\mathbf{p} = 8\mathbf{i} - 6\mathbf{j}$, $\mathbf{q} = -2\mathbf{i} + 3\mathbf{j}$ and $\mathbf{r} = 10\mathbf{i}$

Find

a $2\mathbf{q}$ **b** $2\mathbf{p} + \mathbf{q}$ **c** $\frac{1}{2}\mathbf{p} - 3\mathbf{r}$ **d** $\frac{1}{2}\mathbf{r} - \mathbf{p} - \mathbf{q}$.

7 $\mathbf{p} = 9\mathbf{i} + 12\mathbf{j}$, $\mathbf{q} = 3\mathbf{i} - 3\mathbf{j}$ and $\mathbf{r} = 7\mathbf{i} + \mathbf{j}$

Find

a $|\mathbf{p} + \mathbf{q}|$ **b** $|\mathbf{p} + \mathbf{q} + \mathbf{r}|$.

8 $\mathbf{p} = 7\mathbf{i} - 2\mathbf{j}$ and $\mathbf{q} = \mathbf{i} + \mu\mathbf{j}$.

Find λ and μ such that $\lambda\mathbf{p} + \mathbf{q} = 36\mathbf{i} - 13\mathbf{j}$.

9 $\mathbf{a} = 5\mathbf{i} - 6\mathbf{j}$, $\mathbf{b} = -\mathbf{i} + 2\mathbf{j}$ and $\mathbf{c} = -13\mathbf{i} + 18\mathbf{j}$.

Find λ and μ such that $\lambda\mathbf{a} + \mu\mathbf{b} = \mathbf{c}$.

13.2 Position vectors

The position vector of a point P relative to an origin, O, means the displacement of the point P from O.

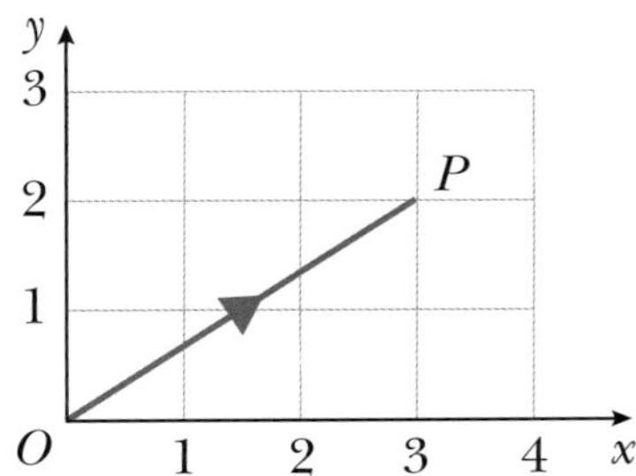

For this diagram, the position vector of P is

$\overrightarrow{OP} = \begin{pmatrix} 3 \\ 2 \end{pmatrix}$ or $\overrightarrow{OP} = 3\mathbf{i} + 2\mathbf{j}$

Now consider two points A and B with position vectors $\mathbf{a}$ and $\mathbf{b}$.

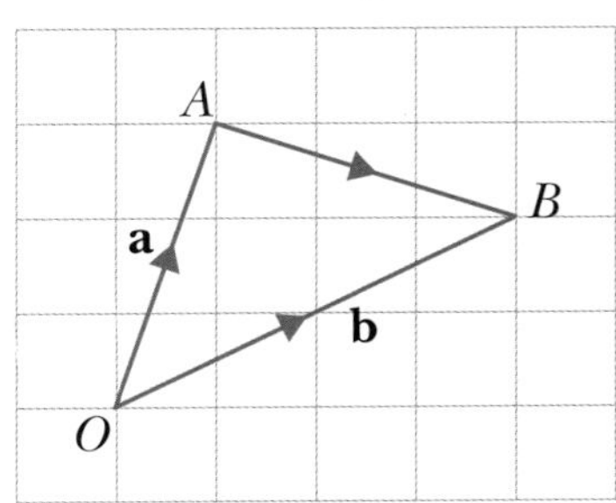

$\overrightarrow{AB}$ means the position vector of B relative to A.

$$\overrightarrow{AB} = \overrightarrow{AO} + \overrightarrow{OB}$$
$$= -\overrightarrow{OA} + \overrightarrow{OB}$$

Hence:

$$\overrightarrow{AB} = \overrightarrow{OB} - \overrightarrow{OA} \quad \text{or} \quad \overrightarrow{AB} = \mathbf{b} - \mathbf{a}$$

WORKED EXAMPLE 4

Relative to an origin O, the position vector of P is $4\mathbf{i} + 5\mathbf{j}$ and the position vector of Q is $10\mathbf{i} - 3\mathbf{j}$.

a Find $\overrightarrow{PQ}$.

The point R lies on PQ such that $\overrightarrow{PR} = \frac{1}{4}\overrightarrow{PQ}$.

b Find the position vector of R.

Answers

a $\overrightarrow{PQ} = \overrightarrow{OQ} - \overrightarrow{OP}$ — $\overrightarrow{OQ} = 10\mathbf{i} - 3\mathbf{j}$ and $\overrightarrow{OP} = 4\mathbf{i} + 5\mathbf{j}$

$= (10\mathbf{i} - 3\mathbf{j}) - (4\mathbf{i} + 5\mathbf{j})$ — collect **i**'s and **j**'s

$\overrightarrow{PQ} = 6\mathbf{i} - 8\mathbf{j}$

b $\overrightarrow{PR} = \frac{1}{4}\overrightarrow{PQ}$

$= \frac{1}{4}(6\mathbf{i} - 8\mathbf{j})$

$= 1.5\mathbf{i} - 2\mathbf{j}$

$\overrightarrow{OR} = \overrightarrow{OP} + \overrightarrow{PR}$

$= (4\mathbf{i} + 5\mathbf{j}) + (1.5\mathbf{i} - 2\mathbf{j})$

$\overrightarrow{OR} = 5.5\mathbf{i} + 3\mathbf{j}$

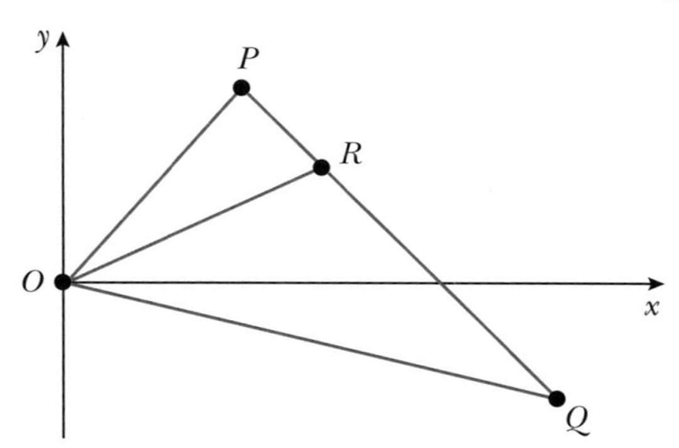

WORKED EXAMPLE 5

Relative to an origin O, the position vectors of points A, B and C are $-2\mathbf{i} + 5\mathbf{j}$, $10\mathbf{i} - \mathbf{j}$ and $\lambda(2\mathbf{i} + \mathbf{j})$ respectively. Given that C lies on the line AB, find the value of λ.

Answers

$\overrightarrow{AB} = \overrightarrow{OB} - \overrightarrow{OA}$ — $\overrightarrow{OB} = 10\mathbf{i} - \mathbf{j}$ and $\overrightarrow{OA} = -2\mathbf{i} + 5\mathbf{j}$

$= (10\mathbf{i} - \mathbf{j}) - (-2\mathbf{i} + 5\mathbf{j})$ — collect **i**'s and **j**'s

$= 12\mathbf{i} - 6\mathbf{j}$

If C lies on the line AB, then $\overrightarrow{AC} = k\overrightarrow{AB}$.

$\overrightarrow{AC} = \overrightarrow{OC} - \overrightarrow{OA}$ — $\overrightarrow{OC} = \lambda(2\mathbf{i} + \mathbf{j})$ and $\overrightarrow{OA} = -2\mathbf{i} + 5\mathbf{j}$

$= \lambda(2\mathbf{i} + \mathbf{j}) - (-2\mathbf{i} + 5\mathbf{j})$ — collect **i**'s and **j**'s

$= (2\lambda + 2)\mathbf{i} - (5 - \lambda)\mathbf{j}$

$k\overrightarrow{AB} = k(12\mathbf{i} - 6\mathbf{j})$

$= 12k\mathbf{i} - 6k\mathbf{j}$

Hence, $(2\lambda + 2)\mathbf{i} - (5 - \lambda)\mathbf{j} = 12k\mathbf{i} - 6k\mathbf{j}$

Equating the **i**'s gives: $2\lambda + 2 = 12k$ ---------------(1)

Equating the **j**'s gives: $5 - \lambda = 6k$ — multiply both sides by 2

$10 - 2\lambda = 12k$ ---------------(2)

Using equation (1) and equation (2) gives

$2\lambda + 2 = 10 - 2\lambda$

$4\lambda = 8$

$\lambda = 2$

Exercise 13.2

1 Find $\overrightarrow{AB}$, in the form $a\mathbf{i} + b\mathbf{j}$, for each of the following

a $A(4, 7)$ and $B(3, 4)$

b $A(0, 6)$ and $B(2,$ [illegible]$)$

c $A(3, -3)$ and $B(6, -2)$

d $A(7, 0)$ and $B(-5,$ [illegible]$)$

e $A(-4, -2)$ and $B(-3, 5)$

f $A(5, -6)$ and $B(-1\ -7)$.

2 **a** O is the origin, P is the point $(1, 5)$ and $\overrightarrow{PQ} = \begin{pmatrix} 3 \\ 5 \end{pmatrix}$. Find $\overrightarrow{OQ}$.

b O is the origin, E is the point $(-3, 4)$ and $\overrightarrow{EF} = \begin{pmatrix} -2 \\ 7 \end{pmatrix}$.
Find the position vector of F.

c O is the origin, M is the point $(4, -2)$ and $\overrightarrow{NM} = \begin{pmatrix} 3 \\ -5 \end{pmatrix}$.
Find the position vector of N.

3 The vector $\overrightarrow{OA}$ has a magnitude of 25 units and is parallel to the vector $-3\mathbf{i} + 4\mathbf{j}$.

The vector $\overrightarrow{OB}$ has a magnitude of 26 units and is parallel to the vector $12\mathbf{i} + 5\mathbf{j}$.

Find:

a $\overrightarrow{OA}$ **b** $\overrightarrow{OB}$ **c** $\overrightarrow{AB}$ **d** $|\overrightarrow{AB}|$.

4 Relative to an origin O, the position vector of A is $-7\mathbf{i} -$ [illegible] and the position vector of B is $9\mathbf{i} + 5\mathbf{j}$.

The point C lies on AB such that $\overrightarrow{AC} = 3\overrightarrow{CB}$.

a Find $\overrightarrow{AB}$.

b Find the unit vector in the direction of $\overrightarrow{AB}$.

c Find the position vector of C.

5 Relative to an origin O, the position vector of P is $-2\mathbf{i} - 4\mathbf{j}$ and the position vector of Q is $8\mathbf{i} + 20\mathbf{j}$.

a Find $\overrightarrow{PQ}$.

b Find $|\overrightarrow{PQ}|$.

c Find the unit vector in the direction of $\overrightarrow{PQ}$.

d Find the position vector of M, the midpoint of PQ.

6 Relative to an origin O, the position vector of A is $4\mathbf{i} - 2\mathbf{j}$ and the position vector of B is $\lambda\mathbf{i} + 2\mathbf{j}$.

The unit vector in the direction of $\overrightarrow{AB}$ is $0.3\mathbf{i} + 0.4\mathbf{j}$. Find the value of λ.

7 Relative to an origin O, the position vector of A is $\begin{pmatrix} -10 \\ 10 \end{pmatrix}$ and the position vectors of B is $\begin{pmatrix} 10 \\ -11 \end{pmatrix}$.

a Find $\overrightarrow{AB}$.

The points A, B and C lie on a straight line such that $\overrightarrow{AC} =$ [illegible] $\overrightarrow{AB}$.

b Find the position vector of the point C.

8 Relative to an origin O, the position vector of A is $\begin{pmatrix} 21 \\ -20 \end{pmatrix}$ and the position vectors of B is $\begin{pmatrix} 24 \\ 18 \end{pmatrix}$.

a Find:

i $|\overrightarrow{OA}|$ **ii** $|\overrightarrow{OB}|$ **iii** $|\overrightarrow{AB}|$.

The points A, B and C lie on a straight line such that $\overrightarrow{AC} = \overrightarrow{CB}$.

b Find the position vector of the point C.

9 Relative to an origin O, the position vector of A is $3\mathbf{i} - 2\mathbf{j}$ and the position vector of B is $15\mathbf{i} + 7\mathbf{j}$.

a Find $\overrightarrow{AB}$.

The point C lies on AB such that $\overrightarrow{AC} = \frac{1}{3}\overrightarrow{AB}$.

b Find the position vector of C.

10 Relative to an origin O, the position vector of A is $6\mathbf{i} + 6\mathbf{j}$ and the position vector of B is $12\mathbf{i} - 2\mathbf{j}$.

a Find $\overrightarrow{AB}$.

The point C lies on AB such that $\overrightarrow{AC} = \frac{3}{4}\overrightarrow{AB}$.

b Find the position vector of C.

11 Relative to an origin O, the position vector of A is $\begin{pmatrix} 3 \\ 4 \end{pmatrix}$ and the position vector of B is $\begin{pmatrix} 5 \\ 5 \end{pmatrix}$.

The points A, B and C are such that $\overrightarrow{BC} = 2\overrightarrow{AB}$. Find the position vector of C.

12 Relative to an origin O, the position vectors of points A, B and C are $-5\mathbf{i} - 11\mathbf{j}$, $23\mathbf{i} - 4\mathbf{j}$ and $\lambda(\mathbf{i} - 3\mathbf{j})$ respectively.
Given that C lies on the line AB, find the value of λ.

13 Relative to an origin O, the position vectors of A, B and C are $-2\mathbf{i} + 7\mathbf{j}$, $2\mathbf{i} - \mathbf{j}$ and $6\mathbf{i} + \lambda\mathbf{j}$ respectively.

a Find the value of λ when $AC = 17$.

b Find the value of λ when ABC is a straight line.

c Find the value of λ when ABC is a right-angle.

14 Relative to an origin O, the position vector of A is $-6\mathbf{i} + 4\mathbf{j}$ and the position vector of B is $18\mathbf{i} + 6\mathbf{j}$. C lies on the y-axis and $\overrightarrow{OC} = \overrightarrow{OA} + \lambda\overrightarrow{OB}$.
Find $\overrightarrow{OC}$.

15 Relative to an origin O, the position vector of P is $8\mathbf{i} + 3\mathbf{j}$ and the position vector of Q is $-12\mathbf{i} - 7\mathbf{j}$. R lies on the x-axis and $\overrightarrow{OR} = \overrightarrow{OP} + \mu\overrightarrow{OQ}$.
Find $\overrightarrow{OR}$.

CHALLENGE Q

16 Relative to an origin O, the position vectors of points P, Q and R are $-6\mathbf{i} + 8\mathbf{j}$, $-4\mathbf{i} + 2\mathbf{j}$ and $5\mathbf{i} + 5\mathbf{j}$ respectively.

a Find the magnitude of:

i $\overrightarrow{PQ}$ **ii** $\overrightarrow{PR}$ **iii** $\overrightarrow{QR}$.

b Show that angle PQR is 90°.

c If $\overrightarrow{OP} = \lambda\overrightarrow{OQ} + \mu\overrightarrow{OR}$, find the value of λ and the value of μ.

13.3 Vector geometry

WORKED EXAMPLE 6

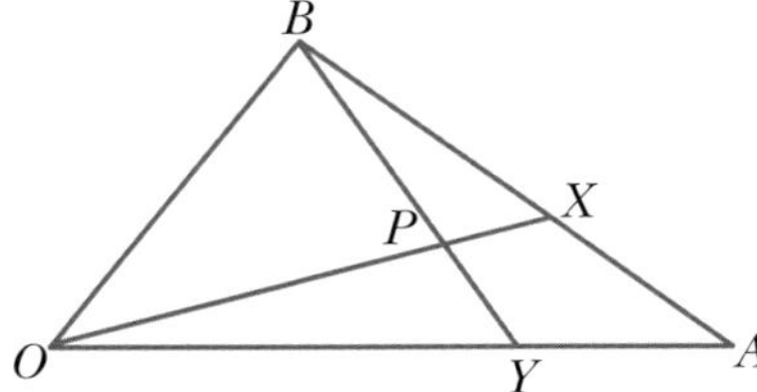

$\overrightarrow{OA} = \mathbf{a}$, $\overrightarrow{OB} = \mathbf{b}$, $\overrightarrow{BX} = \frac{3}{5}\overrightarrow{BA}$ and $\overrightarrow{OY} = \frac{3}{4}\overrightarrow{OA}$.

a Find in terms of **a** and **b**:

i $\overrightarrow{BA}$ **ii** $\overrightarrow{BX}$ **iii** $\overrightarrow{OX}$ **iv** $\overrightarrow{BY}$

b Given that $\overrightarrow{OP} = \lambda\overrightarrow{OX}$, find $\overrightarrow{OP}$ in terms of λ, **a** and **b**.

c Given that $\overrightarrow{BP} = \mu\overrightarrow{BY}$, find $\overrightarrow{OP}$ in terms of μ, **a** and **b**.

d Find the value of λ and the value of μ.

Answers

a i $\overrightarrow{BA} = \overrightarrow{OA} - \overrightarrow{OB} = \mathbf{a} - \mathbf{b}$

ii $\overrightarrow{BX} = \frac{3}{5}\overrightarrow{BA} = \frac{3}{5}(\mathbf{a} - \mathbf{b})$

iii $\overrightarrow{OX} = \overrightarrow{OB} + \overrightarrow{BX} = \mathbf{b} + \frac{3}{5}(\mathbf{a} - \mathbf{b}) = \frac{3}{5}\mathbf{a} + \frac{2}{5}\mathbf{b}$

iv $\overrightarrow{BY} = \overrightarrow{BO} + \overrightarrow{OY} = -\mathbf{b} + \frac{3}{4}\overrightarrow{OA} = \frac{3}{4}\mathbf{a} - \mathbf{b}$

b $\overrightarrow{OP} = \lambda\overrightarrow{OX}$

$= \lambda\left(\frac{3}{5}\mathbf{a} + \frac{2}{5}\mathbf{b}\right)$

$= \frac{3\lambda}{5}\mathbf{a} + \frac{2\lambda}{5}\mathbf{b}$

c $\overrightarrow{OP} = \overrightarrow{OB} + \overrightarrow{BP}$

$= \mathbf{b} + \mu\overrightarrow{BY}$

$= \mathbf{b} + \mu\left(\frac{3}{4}\mathbf{a} - \mathbf{b}\right)$

$= \frac{3\mu}{4}\mathbf{a} + (1 - \mu)\mathbf{b}$

d Equating the coefficients of **a** for $\overrightarrow{OP}$ gives:

$\frac{3\lambda}{5} = \frac{3\mu}{4}$ divide both sides by 3

$\frac{\lambda}{5} = \frac{\mu}{4}$ multiply both sides by 20

$4\lambda = 5\mu$ ----------------(1)

Equating the coefficients of **b** for $\overrightarrow{OP}$ gives:

$\frac{2\lambda}{5} = 1 - \mu$ multiply both sides by 5

$2\lambda = 5 - 5\mu$ ----------(2)

Adding equation (1) and equation (2) gives:

$6\lambda = 5$

$\lambda = \frac{5}{6}$

Substituting $\lambda = \frac{5}{6}$ in equation (1) gives $\mu = \frac{2}{3}$.

Hence, $\lambda = \frac{5}{6}$ and $\mu = \frac{2}{3}$.

WORKED EXAMPLE 7

$\overrightarrow{OA} = 3\mathbf{a}$, $\overrightarrow{OB} = 4\mathbf{b}$ and M is the midpoint of OB.

$OP : PA = 4 : 3$ and $\overrightarrow{BX} = \lambda\overrightarrow{BP}$.

a Find in terms of **a** and **b**:

i $\overrightarrow{AB}$ **ii** $\overrightarrow{MA}$.

b Find in terms of λ, **a** and **b**:

i $\overrightarrow{BX}$ **ii** $\overrightarrow{MX}$.

c If M, X and A are collinear, find the value of λ.

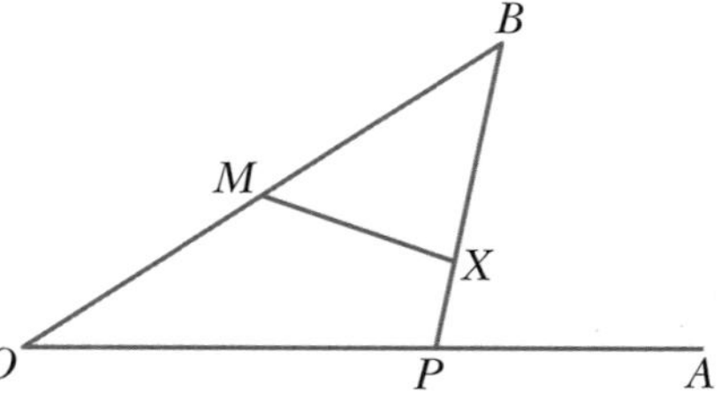

Answers

a i $\overrightarrow{AB} = \overrightarrow{AO} + \overrightarrow{OB}$

$= -3\mathbf{a} + 4\mathbf{b}$

ii $\overrightarrow{MA} = \overrightarrow{MO} + \overrightarrow{OA}$

$= -2\mathbf{b} + 3\mathbf{a}$

$= 3\mathbf{a} - 2\mathbf{b}$

b **i** $\overrightarrow{BX} = \lambda\overrightarrow{BP}$

$= \lambda(\overrightarrow{BO} + \overrightarrow{OP})$

$= \lambda\left(-4\mathbf{b} + \frac{4}{7}\overrightarrow{OA}\right)$ use $\overrightarrow{OA} = 3\mathbf{a}$

$= \frac{12\lambda}{7}\mathbf{a} - 4\lambda\mathbf{b}$

ii $\overrightarrow{MX} = \overrightarrow{MB} + \overrightarrow{BX}$ use $\overrightarrow{BX} = \frac{12\lambda}{7}\mathbf{a} - 4\lambda\mathbf{b}$

$= 2\mathbf{b} + \frac{12\lambda}{7}\mathbf{a} - 4\lambda\mathbf{b}$ collect **a**'s and **b**'s

$= \frac{12\lambda}{7}\mathbf{a} + (2 - 4\lambda)\mathbf{b}$

c If M, X and A are collinear, then $\overrightarrow{MX} = k\overrightarrow{MA}$.

$\frac{12\lambda}{7}\mathbf{a} + (2 - 4\lambda)\mathbf{b} = k(3\mathbf{a} - 2\mathbf{b})$

Equating the coefficients of **a** gives:

$3k = \frac{12\lambda}{7}$ divide both sides by 3

$k = \frac{4\lambda}{7}$ ----------------(1)

Equating the coefficients of **b** gives:

$-2k = 2 - 4\lambda$ divide both sides by -2

$k = 2\lambda - 1$ ----------(2)

Using equation (1) and equation (2) gives:

$2\lambda - 1 = \frac{4\lambda}{7}$

$14\lambda - 7 = 4\lambda$

$10\lambda = 7$

$\lambda = 0.7$

Exercise 13.3

1 $\overrightarrow{OA} = \mathbf{a}$, $\overrightarrow{OB} = \mathbf{b}$.

R is the midpoint of OA and $\overrightarrow{OP} = 3\overrightarrow{OB}$.

$\overrightarrow{AQ} = \lambda\overrightarrow{AB}$ and $\overrightarrow{RQ} = \mu\overrightarrow{RP}$.

a Find $\overrightarrow{OQ}$ in terms of λ, **a** and **b**.

b Find $\overrightarrow{OQ}$ in terms of μ, **a** and **b**.

c Find the value of λ and the value of μ.

2 $\overrightarrow{AB} = 5\mathbf{a}$, $\overrightarrow{DC} = 3\mathbf{a}$ and $\overrightarrow{CB} = \mathbf{b}$.

$\overrightarrow{AX} = \lambda\overrightarrow{AC}$ and $\overrightarrow{DX} = \mu\overrightarrow{DB}$.

a Find in terms of **a** and **b**, **i** $\overrightarrow{AD}$, **ii** $\overrightarrow{DB}$.

b Find in terms of λ, μ, **a** and/or **b**, **i** $\overrightarrow{AX}$, **ii** $\overrightarrow{DX}$.

c Find the value of λ and the value of μ.

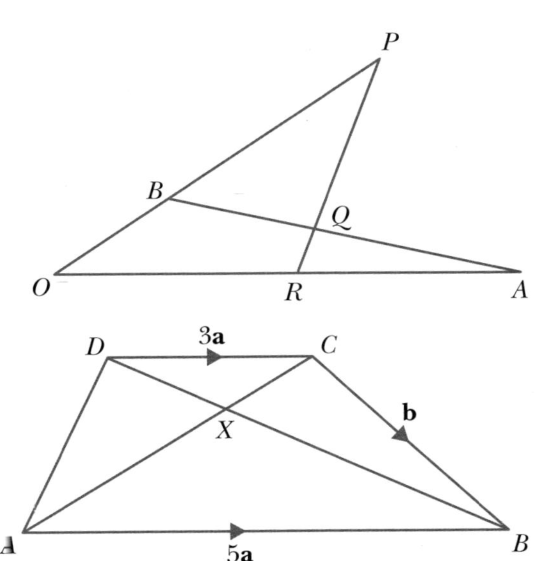

3 $\overrightarrow{OP} = \mathbf{a}$, $\overrightarrow{PY} = 2\mathbf{b}$, and $\overrightarrow{OQ} = 3\mathbf{b}$.

$\overrightarrow{OX} = \lambda\overrightarrow{OY}$ and $\overrightarrow{QX} = \mu\overrightarrow{QP}$.

a Find $\overrightarrow{OX}$ in terms of λ, $\mathbf{a}$ and $\mathbf{b}$,

b Find $\overrightarrow{OX}$ in terms of μ, $\mathbf{a}$ and $\mathbf{b}$,

c Find the value of λ and the value of μ.

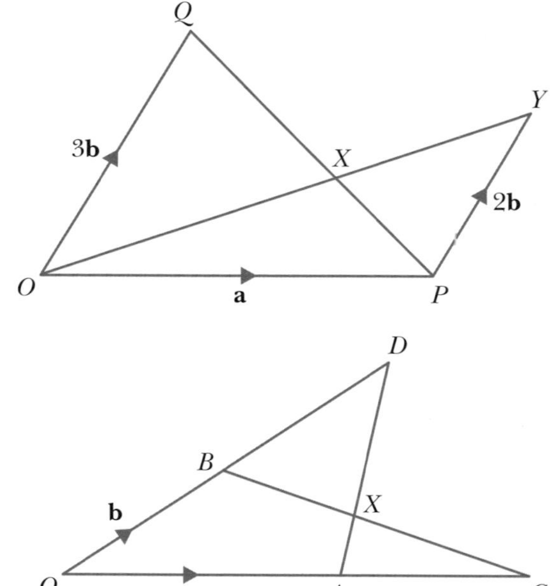

4 $\overrightarrow{OA} = \mathbf{a}$, $\overrightarrow{OB} = \mathbf{b}$.

B is the midpoint of OD and $\overrightarrow{AC} = \frac{2}{3}\overrightarrow{OA}$.

$\overrightarrow{AX} = \lambda\overrightarrow{AD}$ and $\overrightarrow{BX} = \mu\overrightarrow{BC}$.

a Find $\overrightarrow{OX}$ in terms of λ, $\mathbf{a}$ and $\mathbf{b}$.

b Find $\overrightarrow{OX}$ in terms of μ, $\mathbf{a}$ and $\mathbf{b}$.

c Find the value of λ and the value of μ.

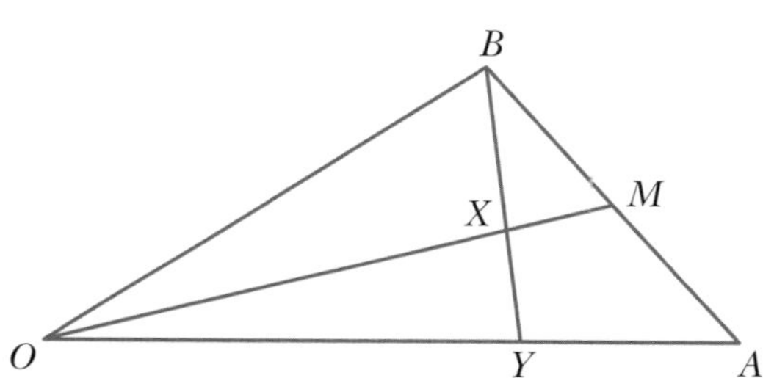

5 $\overrightarrow{OA} = \mathbf{a}$, $\overrightarrow{OB} = \mathbf{b}$.

M is the midpoint of AB and $\overrightarrow{OY} = \frac{3}{4}\overrightarrow{OA}$.

$\overrightarrow{OX} = \lambda\overrightarrow{OM}$ and $\overrightarrow{BX} = \mu\overrightarrow{BY}$.

a Find in terms of $\mathbf{a}$ and $\mathbf{b}$,

i $\overrightarrow{AB}$ **ii** $\overrightarrow{OM}$.

b Find $\overrightarrow{OX}$ in terms of λ, $\mathbf{a}$ and $\mathbf{b}$.

c Find $\overrightarrow{OX}$ in terms of μ, $\mathbf{a}$ and $\mathbf{b}$.

d Find the value of λ and the value of μ.

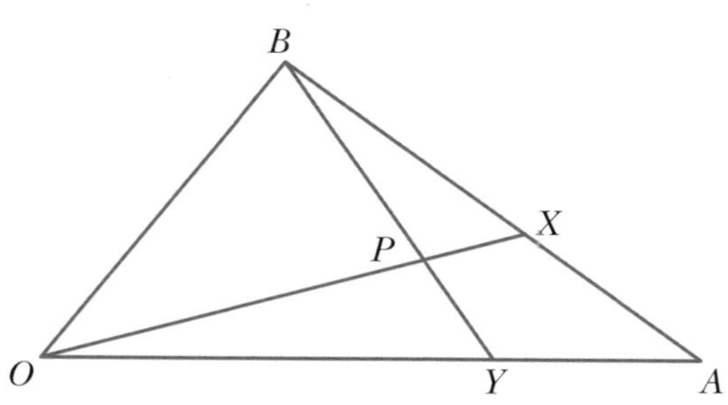

6 $\overrightarrow{OA} = \mathbf{a}$, $\overrightarrow{OB} = \mathbf{b}$, $\overrightarrow{BX} = \frac{3}{5}\overrightarrow{BA}$ and $\overrightarrow{OY} = \frac{5}{7}\overrightarrow{OA}$.

$\overrightarrow{OP} = \lambda\overrightarrow{OX}$ and $\overrightarrow{BP} = \mu\overrightarrow{BY}$.

a Find $\overrightarrow{OP}$ in terms of λ, $\mathbf{a}$ and $\mathbf{b}$.

b Find $\overrightarrow{OP}$ in terms of μ, $\mathbf{a}$ and $\mathbf{b}$.

c Find the value of λ and the value of μ.

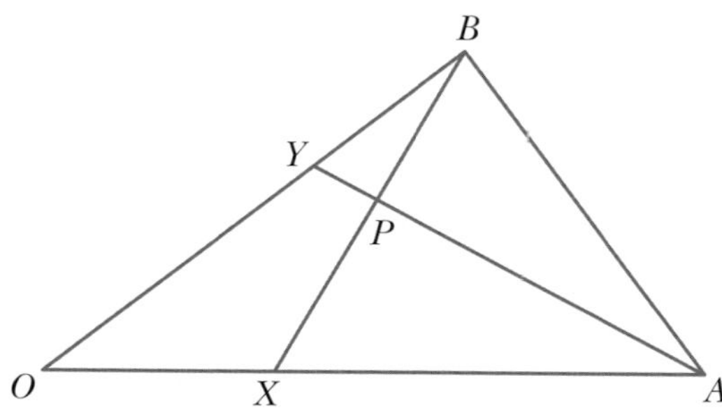

7 $\overrightarrow{OA} = \mathbf{a}$, $\overrightarrow{OB} = \mathbf{b}$ and O is the origin.

$\overrightarrow{OX} = \lambda\overrightarrow{OA}$ and $\overrightarrow{OY} = \mu\overrightarrow{OB}$.

a **i** Find $\overrightarrow{BX}$ in terms of λ, $\mathbf{a}$ and $\mathbf{b}$.

ii Find $\overrightarrow{AY}$ in terms of μ, $\mathbf{a}$ and $\mathbf{b}$.

b $5\overrightarrow{BP} = 2\overrightarrow{BX}$ and $\overrightarrow{AY} = 4\overrightarrow{PY}$.

i Find $\overrightarrow{OP}$ in terms of λ, $\mathbf{a}$ and $\mathbf{b}$.

ii Find $\overrightarrow{OP}$ in terms of μ, $\mathbf{a}$ and $\mathbf{b}$.

iii Find the value of λ and the value of μ.

B
Y
P
O
X
A

8 O, A, B and C are four points such that
$\overrightarrow{OA} = 7\mathbf{a} - 5\mathbf{b}$, $\overrightarrow{OB} = 2\mathbf{a} + 5\mathbf{b}$ and $\overrightarrow{OC} = -2\mathbf{a} + 13\mathbf{b}$.

a Find **i** $\overrightarrow{AC}$ **ii** $\overrightarrow{AB}$.

b Use your answers to **part a** to explain why B lies on the line AC.

CHALLENGE Q

9 $\overrightarrow{OA} = \mathbf{a}$ and $\overrightarrow{OB} = \mathbf{b}$.
$OA : AE = 1 : 3$ and $AB : BC = 1 : 2$.
$OB = BD$

a Find, in terms of **a** and/or **b**,
i $\overrightarrow{OE}$ **ii** $\overrightarrow{OD}$ **iii** $\overrightarrow{OC}$.

b Find, in terms of **a** and/or **b**,
i $\overrightarrow{CE}$ **ii** $\overrightarrow{CD}$ **iii** $\overrightarrow{DE}$.

c Use your answers to **part b** to explain why C, D and E are collinear.

d Find the ratio $CD : DE$.

13.4 Constant velocity problems

If an object moves with a constant velocity, **v**, where $\mathbf{v} = (4\mathbf{i} - 2\mathbf{j})\ \text{m s}^{-1}$, the velocity can be represented on a diagram as:

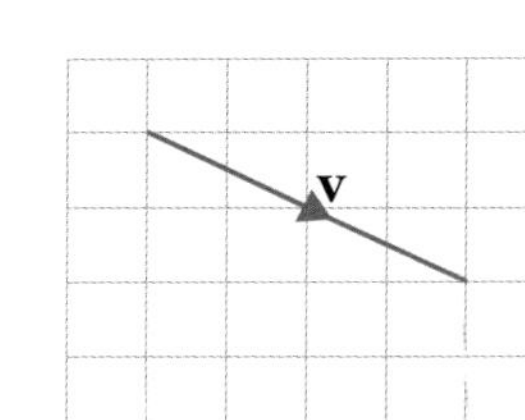

Velocity is a quantity that has both magnitude and direction.

The magnitude of the velocity is the speed.

If $\mathbf{v} = (4\mathbf{i} - 2\mathbf{j})\ \text{m s}^{-1}$ then,

$$\begin{aligned}\text{speed} &= \sqrt{(4)^2 + (-2)^2}\\ &= \sqrt{20}\\ &= 2\sqrt{5}\ \text{m s}^{-1}.\end{aligned}$$

You should already know the formula for an object moving with constant speed:

$$\text{speed} = \frac{\text{distance travelled}}{\text{time taken}}$$

Similarly, the formula for an object moving with constant velocity is:

$$\text{velocity} = \frac{\text{displacement}}{\text{time taken}}$$

Splitting a velocity into its components

The velocity of a particle travelling north-east at $4\sqrt{2}\,\text{m s}^{-1}$ can be written in the form $(a\mathbf{i} + b\mathbf{j})\,\text{m s}^{-1}$:

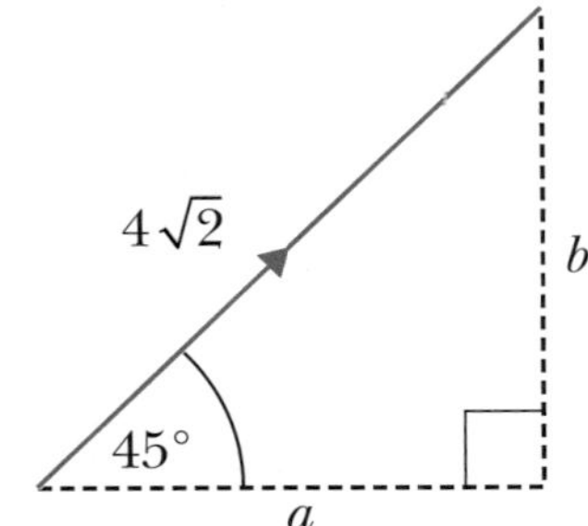

$\cos 45° = \dfrac{a}{4\sqrt{2}}$ and $\sin 45° = \dfrac{b}{4\sqrt{2}}$

$a = 4\sqrt{2} \times \cos 45°$ $\quad b = 4\sqrt{2} \times \sin 45°$

$a = 4$ $\quad b = 4$

Hence the velocity vector is $(4\mathbf{i} + 4\mathbf{j})\,\text{m s}^{-1}$.

The velocity of a particle travelling on a bearing of 120° at $20\,\text{m s}^{-1}$ can be written in the form $(x\mathbf{i} + y\mathbf{j})\,\text{m s}^{-1}$:

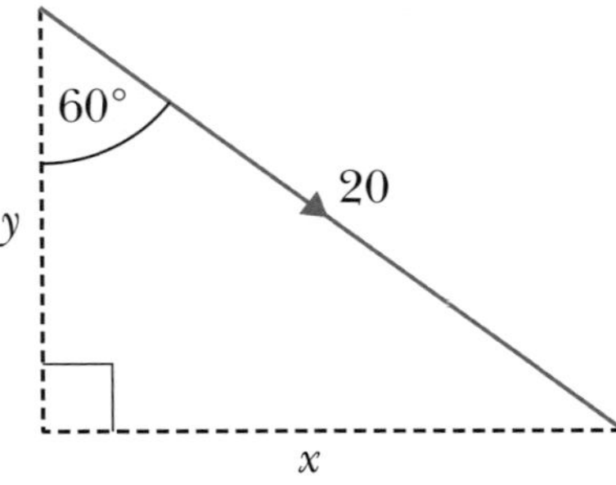

$\sin 60° = \dfrac{x}{20}$ and $\cos 60° = \dfrac{y}{20}$

$x = 20 \times \sin 60°$ $\quad y = 20 \times \cos 60°$

$x = 10\sqrt{3}$ $\quad y = 10$

Hence the velocity vector is $(10\sqrt{3}\mathbf{i} - 10\mathbf{j})\,\text{m s}^{-1}$.

WORKED EXAMPLE 8

An object travels at a constant velocity from point A to point B.
$\overrightarrow{AB} = (32\mathbf{i} - 24\mathbf{j})$ m and the time taken is 4 s. Find:

a the velocity **b** the speed.

Answers

a velocity $= \dfrac{\text{displacement}}{\text{time taken}} = \dfrac{32\mathbf{i} - 24\mathbf{j}}{4} = (8\mathbf{i} - 6\mathbf{j})\,\text{m s}^{-1}$

b speed $= \sqrt{(8)^2 + (-6)^2} = 10\,\text{m s}^{-1}$

Consider a boat sailing with velocity $\begin{pmatrix} 3 \\ -2 \end{pmatrix}$ km h^{-1}.

At 12 00 hours the boat is at the point A with position vector $\begin{pmatrix} 3 \\ 13 \end{pmatrix}$ km relative to an origin O.

The diagram shows the positions of the boat at 12 00 hours, 1 pm, 2 pm, 3 pm, 4 pm …

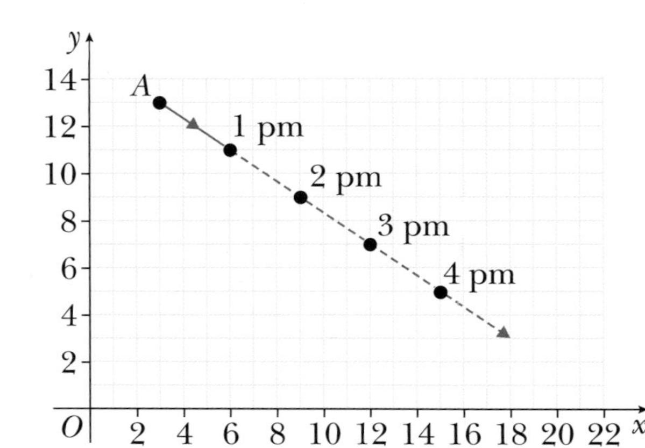

The position at 1 pm $= \begin{pmatrix} 3 \\ 13 \end{pmatrix} + 1\begin{pmatrix} 3 \\ -2 \end{pmatrix} = \begin{pmatrix} 6 \\ 11 \end{pmatrix}$

The position at 2 pm $= \begin{pmatrix} 3 \\ 13 \end{pmatrix} + 2\begin{pmatrix} 3 \\ -2 \end{pmatrix} = \begin{pmatrix} 9 \\ 9 \end{pmatrix}$

The position at 3 pm $= \begin{pmatrix} 3 \\ 13 \end{pmatrix} + 3\begin{pmatrix} 3 \\ -2 \end{pmatrix} = \begin{pmatrix} 12 \\ 7 \end{pmatrix}$

The position at 4 pm $= \begin{pmatrix} 3 \\ 13 \end{pmatrix} + 4\begin{pmatrix} 3 \\ -2 \end{pmatrix} = \begin{pmatrix} 15 \\ 5 \end{pmatrix}$

Hence the position vector, **r**, of the boat t hours after 12 00 hours is given by the expression:

$$\mathrm{r} = \begin{pmatrix} 3 \\ 13 \end{pmatrix} + t\begin{pmatrix} 3 \\ -2 \end{pmatrix}.$$

This leads to the general rule:

If an object has initial position **a** and moves with a constant velocity **v**, the position vector **r**, at time t, is given by the formula: $\mathbf{r} = \mathbf{a} + t\mathbf{v}$.

Exercise 13.4

1 **a** Displacement $= (21\mathbf{i} + 54\mathbf{j})$ m, time taken = 6 seconds. Find the velocity.

b Velocity $= (5\mathbf{i} - 6\mathbf{j})\,\mathrm{m\,s^{-1}}$, time taken = 6 seconds. Find the displacement.

c Velocity $= (-4\mathbf{i} + 4\mathbf{j})\,\mathrm{km\,h^{-1}}$, displacement $= (-50\mathbf{i} + 50\mathbf{j})$ km.
Find the time taken.

2 A car travels from a point A with position vector $(60\mathbf{i} - 40\mathbf{j})$ km to a point B with position vector $(-50\mathbf{i} + 18\mathbf{j})$ km.
The car travels with constant velocity and takes 5 hours to complete the journey.
Find the velocity vector.

3 A helicopter flies from a point P with position vector $(50\mathbf{i} - 100\mathbf{j})$ km to a point Q.
The helicopter flies with a constant velocity of $(30\mathbf{i} - 40\mathbf{j})\,\mathrm{km\,h^{-1}}$ and takes 2.5 hours to complete the journey. Find the position vector of the point Q.

4 **a** A car travels north-east with a speed of $18\sqrt{2}\ \mathrm{km\,h^{-1}}$.
Find the velocity vector of the car.

b A boat sails on a bearing of 030° with a speed of $20\,\mathrm{km\,h^{-1}}$.
Find the velocity vector of the boat.

c A plane flies on a bearing of 240° with a speed of $100\,\mathrm{m\,s^{-1}}$.
Find the velocity vector of the plane.

5 A particle starts at a point P with position vector $(-80\mathbf{i} + 60\mathbf{j})$ m relative to an origin O.
The particle travels with velocity $(12\mathbf{i} - 16\mathbf{j})\,\mathrm{m\,s^{-1}}$.

a Find the speed of the particle.

b Find the position vector of the particle after

i 1 second **ii** 2 seconds **iii** 3 seconds.

c Find the position vector of the particle t seconds after leaving P.

6 At 12 00 hours, a ship leaves a point Q with position vector $(10\mathbf{i} + 38\mathbf{j})$ km relative to an origin O. The ship travels with velocity $(6\mathbf{i} - 8\mathbf{j})\,\text{km h}^{-1}$.

- **a** Find the speed of the ship.
- **b** Find the position vector of the ship at 3 pm.
- **c** Find the position vector of the ship t hours after leaving Q.
- **d** Find the time when the ship is at the point with position vector $(61\mathbf{i} - 30\mathbf{j})$ km.

7 At 12 00 hours, a tanker sails from a point P with position vector $(5\mathbf{i} + 12\mathbf{j})$ km relative to an origin O. The tanker sails south-east with a speed of $12\sqrt{2}\,\text{km h}^{-1}$.

- **a** Find the velocity vector of the tanker.
- **b** Find the position vector of the tanker at
  - **i** 14 00 hours **ii** 12 45 hours.
- **c** Find the position vector of the tanker t hours after leaving P.

8 At 12 00 hours, a boat sails from a point P.

The position vector, $\mathbf{r}$ km, of the boat relative to an origin O, t hours after 12 00 is given by $\mathbf{r} = \begin{pmatrix} 10 \\ 6 \end{pmatrix} + t\begin{pmatrix} 5 \\ 12 \end{pmatrix}$.

- **a** Write down the position vector of the point P.
- **b** Write down the velocity vector of the boat.
- **c** Find the speed of the boat.
- **d** Find the distance of the boat from P after 4 hours.

9 At 15 00 hours, a submarine departs from point A and travels a distance of 120 km to a point B.

The position vector, $\mathbf{r}$ km, of the submarine relative to an origin O, t hours after 15 00 is given by $\mathbf{r} = \begin{pmatrix} 15 + 8t \\ 20 + 6t \end{pmatrix}$.

- **a** Write down the position vector of the point A.
- **b** Write down the velocity vector of the submarine.
- **c** Find the position vector of the point B.

10 At 12 00 hours two boats, A and B, have position vectors $(-10\mathbf{i} + 40\mathbf{j})$ km and $(70\mathbf{i} + 10\mathbf{j})$ km and are moving with velocities $(20\mathbf{i} + 10\mathbf{j})\,\text{km h}^{-1}$ and $(-10\mathbf{i} + 30\mathbf{j})\,\text{km h}^{-1}$ respectively.

- **a** Find the position vectors of A and B at 15 00 hours.
- **b** Find the distance between A and B at 15 00 hours.

11 At time $t = 0$, boat P leaves the origin and travels with velocity $(3\mathbf{i} + 4\mathbf{j})\,\text{km h}^{-1}$.

Also at time $t = 0$, boat Q leaves the point with position vector $(-10\mathbf{i} + 17\mathbf{j})$ km and travels with velocity $(5\mathbf{i} + 2\mathbf{j})\,\text{km h}^{-1}$.

- **a** Write down the position vectors of boats A and B after 2 hours.
- **b** Find the distance between boats P and Q when $t = 2$.

Summary

Position vectors

$\overrightarrow{AB}$ means the position vector of B relative to A.

$\overrightarrow{AB} = \overrightarrow{OB} - \overrightarrow{OA}$ or $\overrightarrow{AB} = \mathbf{b} - \mathbf{a}$

If an object has initial position $\mathbf{a}$ and moves with a constant velocity $\mathbf{v}$, the position vector $\mathbf{r}$, at time t, is given by the formula: $\mathbf{r} = \mathbf{a} + t\mathbf{v}$.

Velocity

$$\text{Velocity} = \frac{\text{displacement}}{\text{time taken}}$$

Examination questions

Worked example

In this question $\begin{pmatrix}1\\0\end{pmatrix}$ is a unit vector due east and $\begin{pmatrix}0\\1\end{pmatrix}$ is a unit vector due north.

At 12:00 a coastguard, at point O, observes a ship with position vector $\begin{pmatrix}16\\12\end{pmatrix}$ km relative to O. The ship is moving at a steady speed of $10\,\text{km}\,\text{h}^{-1}$ on a bearing of 330°.

a Find the value of p such that $\begin{pmatrix}-5\\p\end{pmatrix}$ $\text{km}\,\text{h}^{-1}$ represents the velocity of the ship. [2]

b Write down, in terms of t, the position vector of the ship, relative to O, t hours after 12 00. [2]

c Find the time when the ship is due north of O. [2]

d Find the distance of the ship from O at this time. [2]

Cambridge IGCSE Additional Mathematics 0606 Paper 21 Q7i-iv Nov 2012

331

Answers

a $\cos 60° = \dfrac{x}{10}$ and $\sin 60° = \dfrac{y}{10}$

$x = 10 \times \cos 60°$ $\qquad y = 10 \times \sin 60°$

$x = 5$ $\qquad y = 5\sqrt{3}$

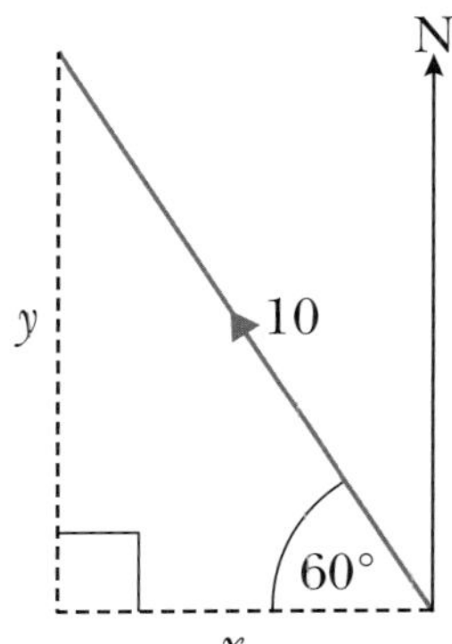

The velocity vector of the ship is $\begin{pmatrix}-5\\5\sqrt{3}\end{pmatrix}$ $\text{m}\,\text{s}^{-1}$.

Hence, $p = 5\sqrt{3}$.

b $\mathbf{r} = \begin{pmatrix} 16 \\ 12 \end{pmatrix} + t\begin{pmatrix} -5 \\ 5\sqrt{3} \end{pmatrix} = \begin{pmatrix} 16 - 5t \\ 12 + 5\sqrt{3}t \end{pmatrix}$

c $\mathbf{r} = \begin{pmatrix} 16 - 5t \\ 12 + 5\sqrt{3}t \end{pmatrix}$

Ship is due north of O when

$16 - 5t = 0$

$t = 3.2$

Time $= 15\ 12$

d When $t = 3.2$, $\mathbf{r} = \begin{pmatrix} 16 - 5 \times 3.2 \\ 12 + 5\sqrt{3} \times 3.2 \end{pmatrix} = \begin{pmatrix} 0 \\ 12 + 16\sqrt{3} \end{pmatrix}$

Distance of ship from $O = 12 + 16\sqrt{3} = 39.7$ km to 3 sf.

Exercise 13.5

Exam Exercise

1 Relative to an origin O, the position vectors of the points A and B are $2\mathbf{i} - 3\mathbf{j}$ and $11\mathbf{i} + 42\mathbf{j}$ respectively.

a Write down an expression for $\overrightarrow{AB}$. [2]

The point C lies on AB such that $\overrightarrow{AC} = \frac{1}{3}\overrightarrow{AB}$.

b Find the length of $\overrightarrow{OC}$. [4]

The point D lies on $\overrightarrow{OA}$ such that $\overrightarrow{DC}$ is parallel to $\overrightarrow{OB}$.

c Find the position vector of D. [2]

Cambridge IGCSE Additional Mathematics 0606 Paper 21 Q8i,ii,iii Jun 2012

2

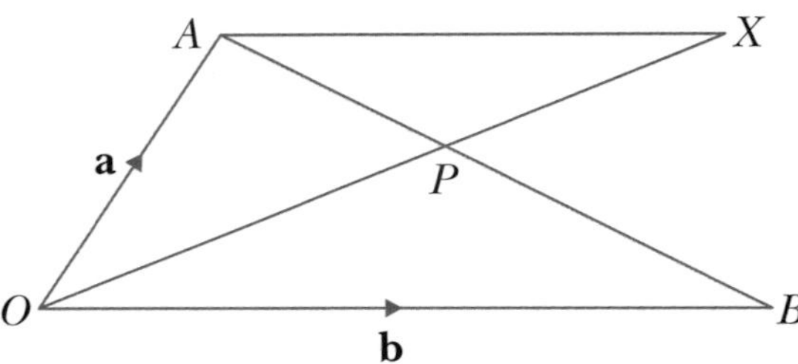

In the diagram $\overrightarrow{OA} = \mathbf{a}$, $\overrightarrow{OB} = \mathbf{b}$ and $\overrightarrow{AP} = \frac{2}{5}\overrightarrow{AB}$.

a Given that $\overrightarrow{OX} = \mu\overrightarrow{OP}$, where μ is a constant, express $\overrightarrow{OX}$ in terms of μ, **a** and **b**. [3]

b Given also that $\overrightarrow{AX} = \lambda\overrightarrow{OB}$, where λ is a constant, use a vector method to find the value of μ and of λ. [5]

Cambridge IGCSE Additional Mathematics 0606 Paper 21 Q8i,ii Nov 2011

3 Relative to an origin O, the position vectors of the points A and B are $\mathbf{i} - 4\mathbf{j}$ and $7\mathbf{i} + 20\mathbf{j}$ respectively. The point C lies on AB and is such that $\overrightarrow{AC} = \frac{2}{3}\overrightarrow{AB}$. Find the position vector of C and the magnitude of this vector. [5]

Cambridge IGCSE Additional Mathematics 0606 Paper 21 Q3 Jun 2011

4 The position vectors of the points A and B relative to an origin O are $-2\mathbf{i} + 17\mathbf{j}$ and $6\mathbf{i} + 2\mathbf{j}$ respectively.

i Find the vector $\overrightarrow{AB}$. [1]

ii Find the unit vector in the direction of $\overrightarrow{AB}$. [2]

iii The position vector of the point C relative to the origin O is such that $\overrightarrow{OC} = \overrightarrow{OA} + m\overrightarrow{OB}$, where m is a constant. Given that C lies on the x-axis, find the vector $\overrightarrow{OC}$. [3]

Cambridge IGCSE Additional Mathematics 0606 Paper 22 Q5 Mar 2015

5 a The four points O, A, B and C are such that $\overrightarrow{OA} = 5\mathbf{a}$, $\overrightarrow{OB} = 15\mathbf{b}$, $\overrightarrow{OC} = 24\mathbf{b} - 3\mathbf{a}$.

Show that B lies on the line AC. [3]

b Relative to an origin O, the position vector of the point P is $\mathbf{i} - 4\mathbf{j}$ and the position vector of the point Q is $3\mathbf{i} + 7\mathbf{j}$. Find

i $|\overrightarrow{PQ}|$, [2]

ii the unit vector in the direction $\overrightarrow{PQ}$, [1]

iii the position vector of M, the mid-point of PQ. [2]

Cambridge IGCSE Additional Mathematics 0606 Paper 21 Q7 Jun 2015

6 Relative to an origin O, points A, B and C have position vectors $\begin{pmatrix} 5 \\ 4 \end{pmatrix}$, $\begin{pmatrix} -10 \\ 12 \end{pmatrix}$ and $\begin{pmatrix} 6 \\ -18 \end{pmatrix}$ respectively. All distances are measured in kilometres. A man drives at a constant speed directly from A to B in 20 minutes.

i Calculate the speed in km h^{-1} at which the man drives from A to B. [3]

He now drives directly from B to C at the same speed.

ii Find how long it takes him to drive from B to C. [3]

Cambridge IGCSE Additional Mathematics 0606 Paper 21 Q3 Nov 2015

7

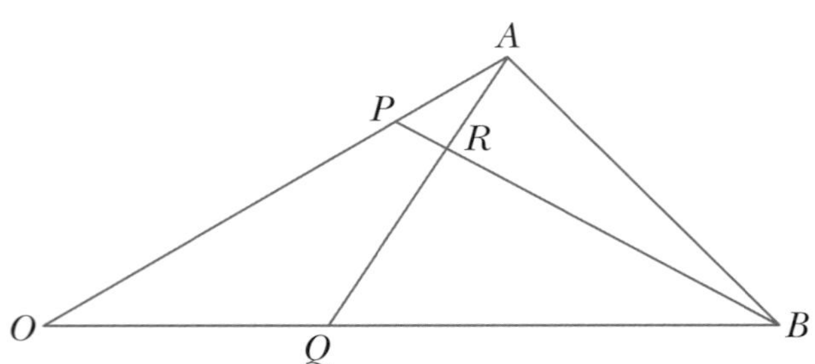

The position vectors of points A and B relative to an origin O are **a** and **b** respectively. The point P is such that $\overrightarrow{OP} = \mu\overrightarrow{OA}$. The point Q is such that $\overrightarrow{OQ} = \lambda\overrightarrow{OB}$. The lines AQ and BP intersect at the point R.

i Express $\overrightarrow{AQ}$ in terms of λ, **a** and **b**. [1]

ii Express $\overrightarrow{BP}$ in terms of μ, **a** and **b**. [1]

It is given that $3\overrightarrow{AR} = \overrightarrow{AQ}$ and $8\overrightarrow{BR} = 7\overrightarrow{BP}$.

iii Express $\overrightarrow{OR}$ in terms of λ, **a** and **b**. [2]

iv Express $\overrightarrow{OR}$ in terms of μ, **a** and **b**. [2]

v Hence find the value of μ and of λ. [3]

Cambridge IGCSE Additional Mathematics 0606 Paper 11 Q12 Nov 2014

8

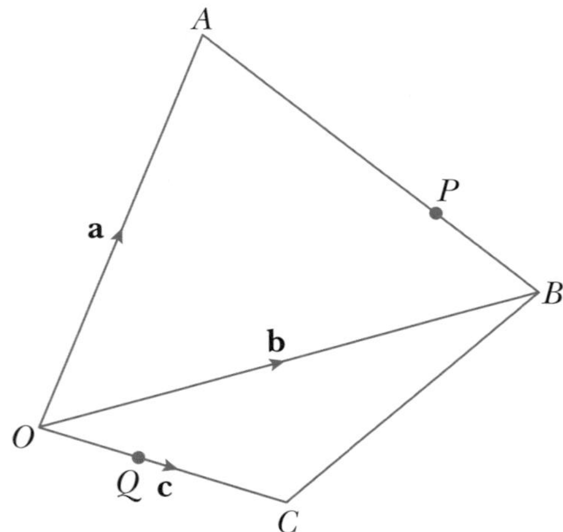

The figure shows points A, B and C with position vectors **a**, **b** and **c** respectively, relative to an origin O. The point P lies on AB such that $AP : AB = 3 : 4$. The point Q lies on OC such that $OQ : QC = 2 : 3$.

i Express $\overrightarrow{AP}$ in terms of **a** and **b** and hence show that $\overrightarrow{OP} = \frac{1}{4}(\mathrm{a} + 3\mathbf{b})$. [3]

ii Find $\overrightarrow{PQ}$ in terms of **a**, **b** and **c**. [3]

iii Given that $5\overrightarrow{PQ} = 6\overrightarrow{BC}$, find **c** in terms of **a** and **b**. [2]

Cambridge IGCSE Additional Mathematics 0606 Paper 11 Q9 Jun 2013

9 **a** The vectors **p** and **q** are such that $\mathbf{p} = 11\mathbf{i} - 24\mathbf{j}$ and $\mathbf{q} = 2\mathbf{i} + \alpha\mathbf{j}$.

i Find the value of each of the constants α and β such that $\mathbf{p} + 2\mathbf{q} = (\alpha + \beta)\mathbf{i} - 20\mathbf{j}$. [3]

ii Using the values of α and β found in **part i**, find the unit vector in the direction $\mathbf{p} + 2\mathbf{q}$. [2]

b

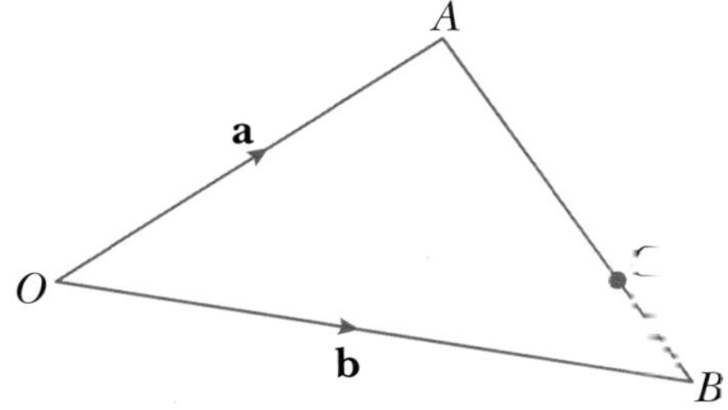

The points A and B have position vectors **a** and **b** with respect to an origin O. The point C lies on AB and is such that $AB : AC = 1 : \lambda$. Find an expression for $\overrightarrow{OC}$ in terms of **a**, **b** and λ. [3]

c The points S and T have position vectors **s** and **t** with respect to an origin O.

The points O, S and T do not lie in a straight line. Given that the vector $2\mathbf{s} + \mu\mathbf{t}$ is parallel to the vector $(\mu + 3)\mathbf{s} + 9\mathbf{t}$ where μ is a positive constant, find the value of μ. [3]

Cambridge IGCSE Additional Mathematics 0606 Paper 22 Q10 Mar 2016

Chapter 14
Differentiation 2

This section will show you how to:

- differentiate $\sin x$, $\cos x$, $\tan x$, e^x and $\ln x$ together with constant multiples, sums and composite functions of these.

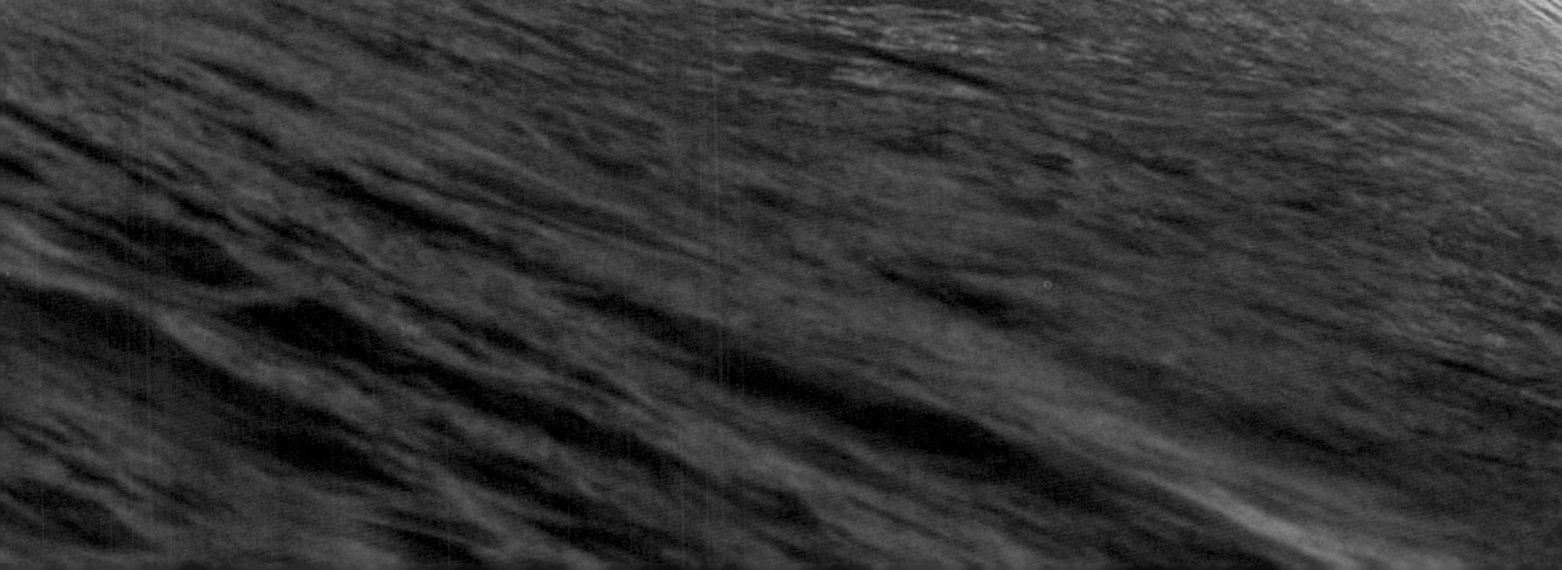

RECAP

In Chapter 12 you learnt that if $y = x^2$, then $\frac{dy}{dx} = 2x$.

This can also be written as: if $f(x) = x^2$, then $f'(x) = 2x$.

Graphing software can be used to show the function $f(x) = x^2$ and its gradient (derived) function $f'(x)$.

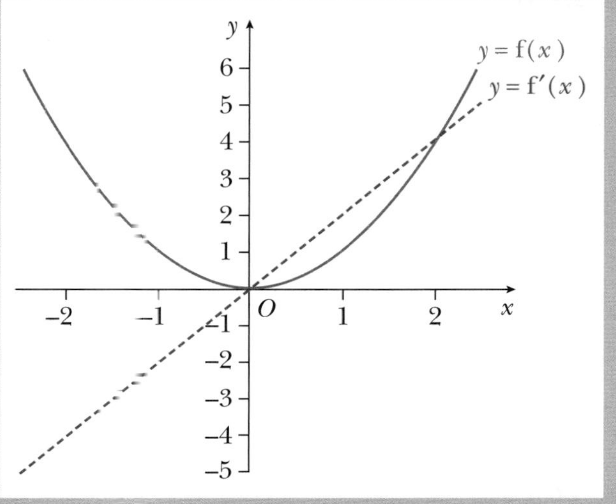

14.1 Derivatives of exponential functions

CLASS DISCUSSION

Graphing software has been used to draw the graphs of $y = 2^x$ and $y = 3^x$ together with their gradient (derived) functions.

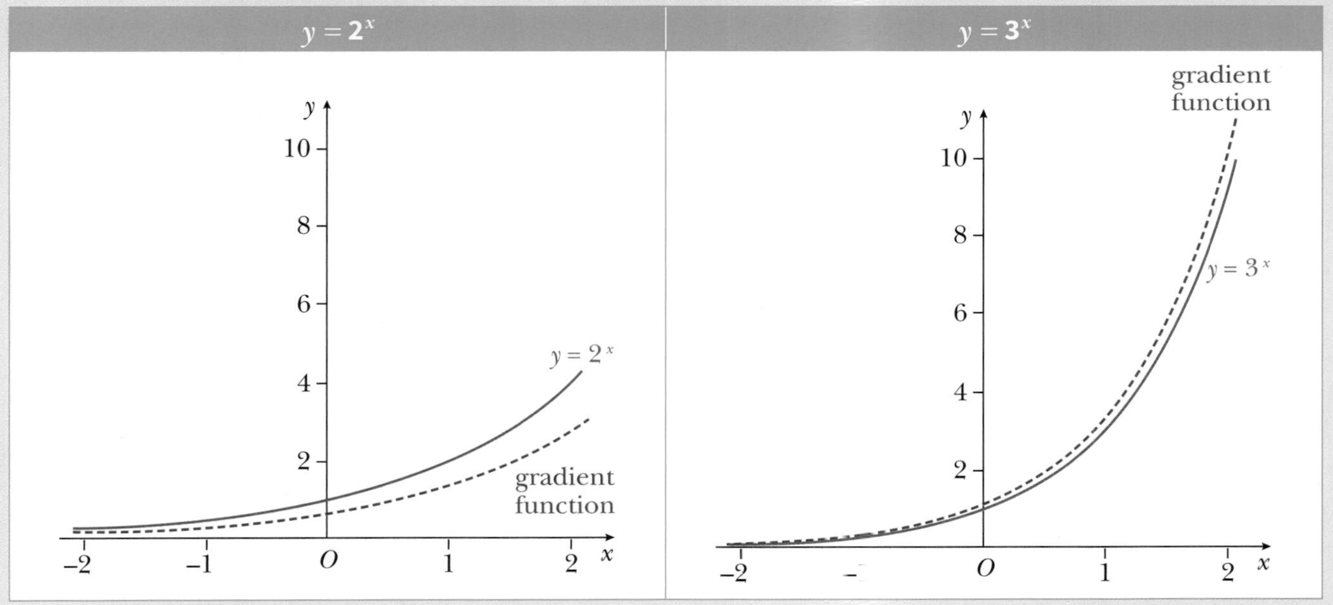

Discuss with your classmates what conclusions can be made from these two graphs.

In Chapter 6 you learnt about the exponential function $y = e^x$ where $e \approx 2.718$.

This function has the very special property that the gradient function is identical to the original function. This leads to the rule:

$$\frac{d}{dx}(e^x) = e^x$$

The derivative of $e^{f(x)}$

Consider the function $y = e^{f(x)}$.

Let $\quad y = e^u \quad$ where $\quad u = f(x)$

$$\frac{dy}{du} = e^u \qquad \frac{du}{dx} = f'(x)$$

Using the chain rule:
$$\begin{aligned}\frac{dy}{dx} &= \frac{dy}{du} \times \frac{du}{dx}\\ &= e^u \times f'(x)\\ &= f'(x) \times e^{f(x)}\end{aligned}$$

$$\frac{d}{dx}\left[e^{f(x)}\right] = f'(x) \times e^{f(x)}$$

In particular:

$$\frac{d}{dx}\left[e^{ax+b}\right] = a \times e^{ax+b}$$

WORKED EXAMPLE 1

Differentiate with respect to x.

a e^{5x} **b** e^{x^2-3x} **c** x^2e^{-3x} **d** $\dfrac{e^{2x}}{x}$

Answers

a $\dfrac{d}{dx}\left(e^{5x}\right) = \underbrace{5}_{\text{differentiate index}} \times \underbrace{e^{5x}}_{\text{original function}} = 5e^{5x}$

b $\dfrac{d}{dx}\left(e^{x^2-3x}\right) = \underbrace{(2x-3)}_{\text{differentiate index}} \times \underbrace{e^{x^2-3x}}_{\text{original function}} = (2x-3)e^{x^2-3x}$

c $\dfrac{d}{dx}\left(x^2e^{-3x}\right) = x^2 \times \dfrac{d}{dx}\left(e^{-3x}\right) + e^{-3x} \times \dfrac{d}{dx}\left(x^2\right)$ product rule

$= x^2 \times \left(-3e^{-3x}\right) + e^{-3x} \times 2x$

$= -3x^2e^{-3x} + 2xe^{-3x}$

$= x\,e^{-3x}(2-3x)$

d $\dfrac{d}{dx}\left(\dfrac{e^{2x}}{x}\right) = \dfrac{x \times \dfrac{d}{dx}\left(e^{2x}\right) - e^{2x} \times \dfrac{d}{dx}(x)}{x^2}$ quotient rule

$= \dfrac{x \times 2e^{2x} - e^{2x} \times 1}{x^2}$

$= \dfrac{e^{2x}(2x-1)}{x^2}$

WORKED EXAMPLE 2

A curve has equation $y = \left(e^{2x} + e^{3x}\right)^5$.

Find the value of $\dfrac{dy}{dx}$ when $x = 0$.

Answers

$y = \left(e^{2x} + e^{3x}\right)^5$

$\dfrac{dy}{dx} = 5\left(e^{2x} + e^{3x}\right)^4 \times \left(2e^{2x} + 3e^{3x}\right)$ chain rule

When $x = 0$, $\dfrac{dy}{dx} = 5\left(e^0 + e^0\right)^4 \times \left(2e^0 + 3e^0\right)$

$= 5 \times 2^4 \times 5$

$= 400$

CLASS DISCUSSION

By writing 2 as $e^{\ln 2}$ find an expression for $\frac{d}{dx}(2^x)$.

Discuss with your classmates whether you can find similar expressions for $\frac{d}{dx}(3^x)$ and $\frac{d}{dx}(4^x)$.

Exercise 14.1

1 Differentiate with respect to x.

a e^{7x} **b** e^{3x} **c** $3e^{5x}$

d $2e^{-4x}$ **e** $6e^{-\frac{x}{2}}$ **f** e^{3x+1}

g e^{x^2+1} **h** $5x - 3e^{\sqrt{x}}$ **i** $2 + \frac{1}{e^{3x}}$

j $2(3 - e^{2x})$ **k** $\frac{e^x + e^{-x}}{2}$ **l** $5\left(x^2 + e^{x^2}\right)$

2 Differentiate with respect to x.

a xe^x **b** x^2e^{2x} **c** $3xe^{-x}$

d $\sqrt{x}\, e^x$ **e** $\frac{e^x}{x}$ **f** $\frac{e^{2x}}{\sqrt{x}}$

g $\frac{e^x + 1}{e^x - 1}$ **h** $xe^{2x} - \frac{e^{2x}}{2}$ **i** $\frac{x^2e^x - 5}{e^x + 1}$

3 Find the equation of the tangent to

a $y = \frac{5}{e^{2x} + 3}$ at $x = 0$

b $y = \sqrt{e^{2x} + 1}$ at $x = \ln 5$

c $y = x^2(1 + e^x)$ at $x = 1$.

4 A curve has equation $y = 5e^{2x} - 4x - 3$.

The tangent to the curve at the point (0, 2) meets the x-axis at the point A.

Find the coordinates of A.

5 A curve has equation $y = xe^x$.

a Find, in terms of e, the coordinates of the stationary point on this curve and determine its nature.

b Find, in terms of e, the equation of the normal to the curve at the point $P(1, e)$.

c The normal at P meets the x-axis at A and the y-axis at B. Find, in terms of e, the area of triangle OAB, where O is the origin.

14.2 Derivatives of logarithmic functions

CLASS DISCUSSION

Graphing software has been used to draw the graph of $y = \ln x$ together with its gradient (derived) function.

The gradient function passes through the points $\left(\frac{1}{2}, 2\right)$, $(1, 1)$, $\left(2, \frac{1}{2}\right)$ and $\left(5, \frac{1}{5}\right)$.

Discuss with your classmates what conclusions you can make about the gradient function.

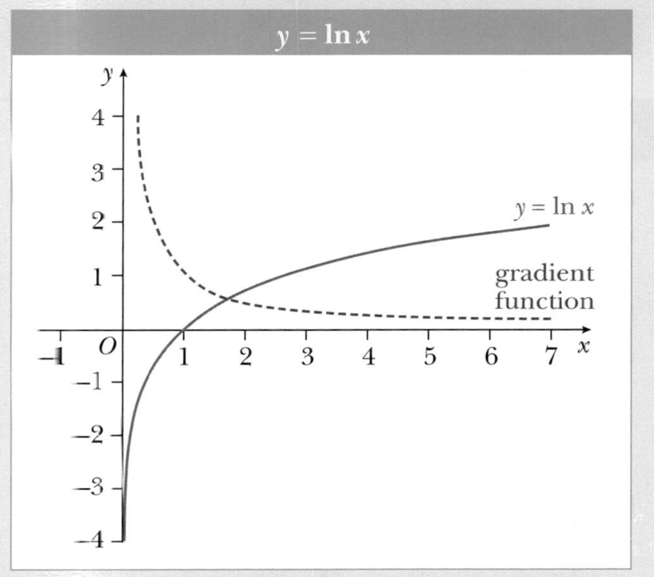

From the class discussion you should have concluded that

$$\frac{d}{dx}(\ln x) = \frac{1}{x}$$

The derivative of $\ln f(x)$

Consider the function $y = \ln f(x)$.

Let $y = \ln u$ where $u = f(x)$.

$$\frac{dy}{du} = \frac{1}{u} \qquad \frac{du}{dx} = f'(x)$$

Using the chain rule:
$$\frac{dy}{dx} = \frac{dy}{du} \times \frac{du}{dx}$$
$$= \frac{1}{u} \times f'(x)$$
$$= \frac{f'(x)}{f(x)}$$

$$\frac{d}{dx}\left[\ln f(x)\right] = \frac{f'(x)}{f(x)}$$

In particular:

$$\frac{d}{dx}[\ln(ax+b)] = \frac{a}{ax+b}$$

WORKED EXAMPLE 3

Differentiate with respect to x.

a $\ln 8x$ **b** $\ln(5x-7)$ **c** $\ln(2x^2+5)$ **d** $\ln\sqrt{x-10}$

Answers

a $\frac{d}{dx}(\ln 8x) = \frac{8}{8x}$ ← 'inside' differentiated; ← 'inside'

$= \frac{1}{x}$

b $\frac{d}{dx}[\ln(5x-7)] = \frac{5}{5x-7}$ ← 'inside' differentiated; ← 'inside'

c $\frac{d}{dx}[\ln(2x^2+5)] = \frac{4x}{2x^2+5}$ ← 'inside' differentiated; ← 'inside'

d **Method 1:** $\frac{d}{dx}[\ln\sqrt{x-10}\,] = \frac{\frac{1}{2}(x-10)^{-\frac{1}{2}}(1)}{\sqrt{x-10}}$ ← 'inside' differentiated; ← 'inside'

$= \frac{1}{2(x-10)}$

Method 2: using the rules of logarithms before differentiating.

$\frac{d}{dx}[\ln\sqrt{x-10}\,] = \frac{d}{dx}\left[\ln(x-10)^{\frac{1}{2}}\right]$ use $\ln a^m = m\ln a$

$= \frac{d}{dx}\left[\frac{1}{2}\ln(x-10)\right]$

$= \frac{1}{2}\times\frac{d}{dx}[\ln(x-10)]$

$= \frac{1}{2}\times\frac{1}{x-10}$ ← 'inside' differentiated; ← 'inside'

$= \frac{1}{2(x-10)}$

WORKED EXAMPLE 4

Differentiate with respect to x.

a $5x^6 \ln 2x$ **b** $\dfrac{\ln x}{3x}$

Answers

a $\dfrac{d}{dx}(5x^6 \ln 2x) = 5x^6 \times \dfrac{d}{dx}(\ln 2x) + \ln 2x \times \dfrac{d}{dx}(5x^6)$ product rule

$= 5x^6 \times \dfrac{2}{2x} + \ln 2x \times 30x^5$

$= 5x^5 + 30x^5 \ln 2x$

b $\dfrac{d}{dx}\left(\dfrac{\ln x}{3x}\right) = \dfrac{3x \times \dfrac{d}{dx}(\ln x) - \ln x \times \dfrac{d}{dx}(3x)}{(3x)^2}$ quotient rule

$= \dfrac{3x \times \dfrac{1}{x} - \ln x \times 3}{9x^2}$

$= \dfrac{1 - \ln x}{3x^2}$

WORKED EXAMPLE 5

A curve has equation $y = 3x \sin x + \dfrac{\pi}{6}$.

a Show that $y = \dfrac{1}{2}\ln(2x-1) - \ln(x^2+1)$.

b Hence, find the value of $\dfrac{dy}{dx}$ when $x = 1$.

Answers

a $y = \ln\left[\dfrac{\sqrt{2x-1}}{x^2+1}\right]$ use $\log_a\left(\dfrac{x}{y}\right) = \log_a x - \log_a y$

$= \ln(2x-1)^{\frac{1}{2}} - \ln(x^2+1)$ use $\log_a (x)^m = m \log_a x$

$= \dfrac{1}{2}\ln(2x-1) - \ln(x^2+1)$

b $\dfrac{dy}{dx} = \dfrac{d}{dx}\left[\dfrac{1}{2}\ln(2x-1)\right] - \dfrac{d}{dx}\left[\ln(x^2+1)\right]$

$= \dfrac{1}{2} \times \dfrac{d}{dx}[\ln(2x-1)] - \dfrac{d}{dx}\left[\ln(x^2+1)\right]$

$= \dfrac{1}{2} \times \dfrac{2}{2x-1} - \dfrac{2x}{x^2+1}$

$= \dfrac{1}{2x-1} - \dfrac{2x}{x^2+1}$

$= \dfrac{x^2+1-2x(2x-1)}{(2x-1)(x^2+1)}$

$= \dfrac{-3x^2+2x+1}{(2x-1)(x^2+1)}$

When $x = 1$, $\dfrac{dy}{dx} = 0$.

WORKED EXAMPLE 6

A curve has equation $y = \log_2(5x - 2)$.

a Show that $y = \frac{1}{\ln 2}[\ln(5x - 2)]$.

b Hence, find the value of $\frac{dy}{dx}$ when $x = 2$.

Answers

a $y = \log_2(5x - 2)$ use $\log_b a = \frac{\log_c a}{\log_c b}$

$= \frac{\ln(5x - 2)}{\ln 2}$

$= \frac{1}{\ln 2}[\ln(5x - 2)]$

b $\frac{dy}{dx} = \frac{1}{\ln 2} \times \frac{d}{dx}[\ln(5x - 2)]$

$= \frac{1}{\ln 2} \times \frac{5}{5x - 2}$

$= \frac{5}{(5x - 2)\ln 2}$

When $x = 2$, $\frac{dy}{dx} = \frac{5}{8\ln 2}$.

Exercise 14.2

1 Differentiate with respect to x.

a $\ln 5x$ **b** $\ln 12x$ **c** $\ln(2x + 3)$

d $2 + \ln(1 - x^2)$ **e** $\ln(3x + 1)^2$ **f** $\ln\sqrt{x + 2}$

g $\ln(2 - 5x)^4$ **h** $2x + \ln\left(\frac{4}{x}\right)$ **i** $5 - \ln\frac{3}{(2 - 3x)}$

j $\ln(\ln x)$ **k** $\ln\left(\sqrt{x} + 1\right)^2$ **l** $\ln(x^2 + \ln x)$

2 Differentiate with respect to x.

a $x\ln x$ **b** $2x^2\ln x$ **c** $(x - 1)\ln x$

d $5x\ln x^2$ **e** $x^2\ln(\ln x)$ **f** $\frac{\ln 2x}{x}$

g $\frac{4}{\ln x}$ **h** $\frac{\ln(2x + 1)}{x^2}$ **i** $\frac{\ln(x^3 - 1)}{2x + 3}$

3 A curve has equation $y = x^2\ln 3x$.

Find the value of $\frac{dy}{dx}$ and $\frac{d^2y}{dx^2}$ at the point where $x = 2$.

4 Use the laws of logarithms to help differentiate these expressions with respect to x.

a $\ln\sqrt{3x+1}$ **b** $\ln\dfrac{1}{(2x-5)}$ **c** $\ln\left[x(x-5)^4\right]$

d $\ln\left(\dfrac{2x+1}{x-1}\right)$ **e** $\ln\left(\dfrac{2-x}{x^2}\right)$ **f** $\ln\left[\dfrac{x(x+1)}{x+2}\right]$

g $\ln\left[\dfrac{2x+3}{(x-5)(x+1)}\right]$ **h** $\ln\left[\dfrac{2}{(x+3)^2(x-1)}\right]$ **i** $\ln\left[\dfrac{(x+1)(2x-3)}{x(x-1)}\right]$

5 Find $\dfrac{dy}{dx}$ for each of the following.

a $y = \log_3 x$

b $y = \log_2 x^2$

c $y = \log_4 (5x-1)$

Note:
Use change of base of logarithms before differentiating.

6 Find $\dfrac{dy}{dx}$ for each of the following.

a $e^y = 4x^2 - 1$

b $e^y = 5x^3 - 2x$

c $e^y = (x+3)(x-4)$

Note:
Take the natural logarithm of both sides of the equation before differentiating.

7 A curve has equation $x = \dfrac{1}{2}\left[e^{y(3x+7)} + 1\right]$.

Find the value of $\dfrac{dy}{dx}$ when $x = 1$.

14.3 Derivatives of trigonometric functions

CLASS DISCUSSION

Graphing software has been used to draw the graphs of $y = \sin x$ and $y = \cos x$ together with their gradient (derived) functions.

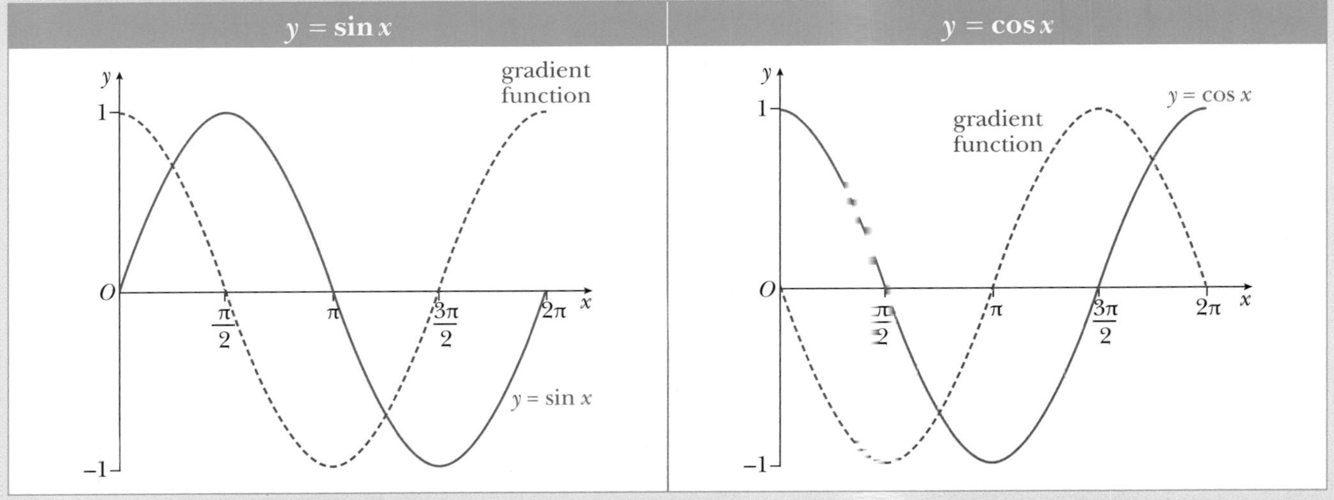

Discuss with your classmates what conclusions you can make from these two graphs.

From the class discussion you should have concluded that if x is measured in radians then:

$$\frac{\mathrm{d}}{\mathrm{d}x}(\sin x) = \cos x$$

$$\frac{\mathrm{d}}{\mathrm{d}x}(\cos x) = -\sin x$$

The derivative of $\tan x$ can be found using these two results together with the quotient rule.

$$\frac{\mathrm{d}}{\mathrm{d}x}(\tan x) = \frac{\mathrm{d}}{\mathrm{d}x}\left(\frac{\sin x}{\cos x}\right) \qquad \text{use the quotient rule}$$

$$= \frac{\cos x \times \frac{\mathrm{d}}{\mathrm{d}x}(\sin x) - \sin x \times \frac{\mathrm{d}}{\mathrm{d}x}(\cos x)}{(\cos x)^2}$$

$$= \frac{\cos x \times \cos x - \sin x \times (-\sin x)}{\cos^2 x}$$

$$= \frac{\cos^2 x + \sin^2 x}{\cos^2 x} \qquad \text{use } \cos^2 x + \sin^2 x = 1$$

$$= \frac{1}{\cos^2 x} \qquad \text{use } \frac{1}{\cos x} = \sec x$$

$$= \sec^2 x$$

$$\frac{\mathrm{d}}{\mathrm{d}x}(\tan x) = \sec^2 x$$

WORKED EXAMPLE 7

Differentiate with respect to x.

a $7\cos x$ **b** $x^2 \sin x$ **c** $\frac{3\tan x}{x}$ **d** $(5 - 3\cos x)^8$

Answers

a $\frac{d}{dx}(7\cos x) = 7\frac{d}{dx}(\cos x)$
$= -7\sin x$

b $\frac{d}{dx}(x^2 \sin x) = x^2 \times \frac{d}{dx}(\sin x) + \sin x \times \frac{d}{dx}(x^2)$ product rule
$= x^2 \cos x + 2x \sin x$

c $\frac{d}{dx}\left(\frac{3\tan x}{x}\right) = \frac{x \times \frac{d}{dx}(3\tan x) - 3\tan x \times \frac{d}{dx}(x)}{x^2}$ quotient rule

$= \frac{x \times 3\sec^2 x - 3\tan x \times 1}{x^2}$

$= \frac{3x\sec^2 x - 3\tan x}{x^2}$

d $\frac{d}{dx}\left[(5 - 3\cos x)^8\right] = 8(5 - 3\cos x)^7 \times 3\sin x$ chain rule
$= 24\sin x(5 - 3\cos x)^7$

Derivatives of sin (ax + b), cos (ax + b) and tan (ax + b)

Consider the function $y = \sin(ax + b)$ where x is measured in radians.

Let $y = \sin u$ where $u = ax + b$.

$\frac{dy}{du} = \cos u$ $\frac{du}{dx} = a$

Using the chain rule: $\frac{dy}{dx} = \frac{dy}{du} \times \frac{du}{dx}$
$= \cos u \times a$
$= a\cos(ax + b)$

$$\frac{d}{dx}[\sin(ax + b)] = a\cos(ax + b)$$

Similarly, it can be shown that:

$$\frac{d}{dx}[\cos(ax + b)] = -a\sin(ax + b)$$

$$\frac{d}{dx}[\tan(ax + b)] = a\sec^2(ax + b)$$

Note:
It is important to remember that, in calculus, all angles are measured in radians unless a question tells you otherwise.

WORKED EXAMPLE 8

Differentiate with respect to x.

a $5\sin\left(\frac{\pi}{3} - 2x\right)$ **b** $x\cos 3x$ **c** $\dfrac{x^2}{\sin\left(2x + \frac{\pi}{4}\right)}$ **d** $(1 + 3\tan 2x)^5$

Answers

a $$\frac{d}{dx}\left[5\sin\left(\frac{\pi}{3} - 2x\right)\right] = 5\frac{d}{dx}\left[\sin\left(\frac{\pi}{3} - 2x\right)\right]$$
$$= 5 \times \cos\left(\frac{\pi}{3} - 2x\right) \times (-2)$$
$$= -10\cos\left(\frac{\pi}{3} - 2x\right)$$

b $$\frac{d}{dx}(x\cos 3x) = x \times \frac{d}{dx}(\cos 3x) + \cos 3x \times \frac{d}{dx}(x)$$ product rule
$$= x \times (-3\sin 3x) + \cos 3x \times (1)$$
$$= \cos 3x - 3x\sin 3x$$

c $$\frac{d}{dx}\left[\frac{x^2}{\sin\left(2x + \frac{\pi}{4}\right)}\right] = \frac{\sin\left(2x + \frac{\pi}{4}\right) \times \frac{d}{dx}(x^2) - x^2 \times \frac{d}{dx}\left[\sin\left(2x + \frac{\pi}{4}\right)\right]}{\left[\sin\left(2x + \frac{\pi}{4}\right)\right]^2}$$ quotient rule
$$= \frac{\sin\left(2x + \frac{\pi}{4}\right) \times (2x) - x^2 \times \left[2\cos\left(2x + \frac{\pi}{4}\right)\right]}{\sin^2\left(2x + \frac{\pi}{4}\right)}$$
$$= \frac{2x\sin\left(2x + \frac{\pi}{4}\right) - 2x^2\cos\left(2x + \frac{\pi}{4}\right)}{\sin^2\left(2x + \frac{\pi}{4}\right)}$$

d $$\frac{d}{dx}\left[(1 + 3\tan 2x)^5\right] = 5(1 + 3\tan 2x)^4 \times 6\sec^2 2x$$ chain rule
$$= 30\sec^2 2x(1 + 3\tan 2x)^4$$

Exercise 14.3

1 Differentiate with respect to x.

a $2 + \sin x$ **b** $2\sin x + 3\cos x$ **c** $2\cos x - \tan x$

d $3\sin 2x$ **e** $4\tan 5x$ **f** $2\cos 3x - \sin 2x$

g $\tan(3x + 2)$ **h** $\sin\left(2x + \frac{\pi}{3}\right)$ **i** $2\cos\left(3x - \frac{\pi}{6}\right)$

2 Differentiate with respect to x.

a $\sin^3 x$ **b** $5\cos^2(3x)$ **c** $\sin^2 x - 2\cos x$

d $(3 - \cos x)^4$ **e** $2\sin^3\left(2x + \frac{\pi}{6}\right)$ **f** $3\cos^4 x + 2\tan^2\left(2x - \frac{\pi}{4}\right)$

3 Differentiate with respect to x.

a $x \sin x$ **b** $2\sin 2x \cos 3x$ **c** $x^2 \tan x$

d $x\tan^3\left(\frac{x}{2}\right)$ **e** $\frac{5}{\cos 3x}$ **f** $\frac{x}{\cos x}$

g $\frac{\tan x}{x}$ **h** $\frac{\sin x}{2 + \cos x}$ **i** $\frac{\sin x}{3x - 1}$

j $\frac{1}{\sin^3 2x}$ **k** $\frac{3x}{\sin 2x}$ **l** $\frac{\sin x + \cos x}{\sin x - \cos x}$

4 Differentiate with respect to x.

a $e^{\cos x}$ **b** $e^{\cos 5x}$ **c** $e^{\tan x}$

d $e^{(\sin x + \cos x)}$ **e** $e^x \sin x$ **f** $e^x \cos \frac{1}{2}x$

g $e^x(\cos x + \sin x)$ **h** $x^2 e^{\cos x}$ **i** $\ln(\sin x)$

j $x^2 \ln(\cos x)$ **k** $\frac{\sin 3x}{e^{2x-1}}$ **l** $\frac{x \sin x}{e^x}$

5 Find the gradient of the tangent to

a $y = 2x\cos 3x$ when $x = \frac{\pi}{3}$ **b** $y = \frac{2 - \cos x}{3\tan x}$ when $x = \frac{\pi}{4}$.

6 **a** By writing $\sec x$ as $\frac{1}{\cos x}$, find $\frac{d}{dx}(\sec x)$.

b By writing $\operatorname{cosec} x$ as $\frac{1}{\sin x}$, find $\frac{d}{dx}(\operatorname{cosec} x)$.

c By writing $\cot x$ as $\frac{\cos x}{\sin x}$, find $\frac{d}{dx}(\cot x)$.

7 Find $\frac{dy}{dx}$ for each of the following.

a $e^y = \sin 3x$ **b** $e^y = 3\cos 2x$

Note:
Take the natural logarithm of both sides of the equation before differentiating.

CHALLENGE Q

8 A curve has equation $y = A\sin x + B\sin 2x$.

The curve passes through the point $P\left(\frac{\pi}{2}, 3\right)$ and has a gradient of $\frac{3\sqrt{2}}{2}$ when $x = \frac{\pi}{4}$.

Find the value of A and the value of B.

CHALLENGE Q

9 A curve has equation $y = A\sin x + B\cos 2x$.

The curve has a gradient of $5\sqrt{3}$ when $x = \frac{\pi}{6}$ and has a gradient of $6 + 2\sqrt{2}$ when $x = \frac{\pi}{4}$.

Find the value of A and the value of B.

14.4 Further applications of differentiation

You need to be able to answer questions that involve the differentiation of exponential, logarithmic and trigonometric functions.

WORKED EXAMPLE 9

A curve has equation $y = 3x\sin x + \frac{\pi}{6}$.

The curve passes through the point $P\left(\frac{\pi}{2}, a\right)$.

a Find the value of a.

b Find the equation of the normal to the curve at P.

Answers

a When $x = \frac{\pi}{2}$, $y = 3 \times \frac{\pi}{2} \times \sin\left(\frac{\pi}{2}\right) + \frac{\pi}{6}$

$$y = \frac{3\pi}{2} + \frac{\pi}{6} = \frac{5\pi}{3}$$

Hence, $a = \frac{5\pi}{3}$.

b $y = 3x\sin x + \frac{\pi}{6}$

$$\frac{dy}{dx} = 3x\cos x + 3\sin x$$

When $x = \frac{\pi}{2}$, $\frac{dy}{dx} = 3\left(\frac{\pi}{2}\right)\cos\left(\frac{\pi}{2}\right) + 3\sin\left(\frac{\pi}{2}\right) = 3$

Normal: passes through the point $\left(\frac{\pi}{2}, \frac{5\pi}{3}\right)$ and gradient $= -\frac{1}{3}$

$$y - \frac{5\pi}{3} = -\frac{1}{3}\left(x - \frac{\pi}{2}\right)$$

$$y - \frac{5\pi}{3} = -\frac{1}{3}x + \frac{\pi}{6}$$

$$y = -\frac{1}{3}x + \frac{11\pi}{6}$$

WORKED EXAMPLE 10

A curve has equation $y = x^2 \ln x$.

Find the approximate increase in y as x increases from e to e + p, where p is small.

Answers

$$y = x^2 \ln x$$

$$\frac{dy}{dx} = x^2 \times \frac{1}{x} + \ln x \times 2x \qquad \text{product rule}$$

$$= x + 2x \ln x$$

When $x = \mathrm{e}$, $\frac{dy}{dx} = \mathrm{e} + 2\mathrm{e} \ln \mathrm{e}$

$$= 3\mathrm{e}$$

Using $\frac{\delta y}{\delta x} \approx \frac{dy}{dx}$

$$\frac{\delta y}{p} \approx 3\mathrm{e}$$

$$\delta y \approx 3\mathrm{e}p$$

WORKED EXAMPLE 11

Variables x and y are connected by the equation $y = \frac{\ln x}{2x + 5}$.

Given that y increases at a rate of 0.1 units per second, find the rate of change of x when $x = 2$.

Answers

$$y = \frac{\ln x}{2x + 5} \quad \text{and} \quad \frac{dy}{dt} = 0.1$$

$$\frac{dy}{dx} = \frac{(2x + 5)\frac{1}{x} - 2 \ln x}{(2x + 5)^2} \qquad \text{quotient rule}$$

$$= \frac{(2x + 5) - 2x \ln x}{x(2x + 5)^2}$$

When $x = 2$, $\frac{dy}{dx} = \frac{(4 + 5) - 4 \ln 2}{2(4 + 5)^2}$

$$= \frac{9 - 4 \ln 2}{162}$$

Using the chain rule, $\frac{dx}{dt} = \frac{dx}{dy} \times \frac{dy}{dt}$

$$= \frac{162}{9 - 4 \ln 2} \times 0.1$$

$$= 2.6014\ldots$$

Rate of change of x is 2.60 units per second correct to 3 sf.

WORKED EXAMPLE 12

A curve has equation $y = e^{-x}(2\sin 2x - 3\cos 2x)$ for $0 < x < \frac{\pi}{2}$ radians.

Find the x-coordinate of the stationary point on the curve and determine the nature of this point.

Answers

$$y = e^{-x}(2\sin 2x - 3\cos 2x)$$

$$\frac{dy}{dx} = e^{-x}(4\cos 2x + 6\sin 2x) - e^{-x}(2\sin 2x - 3\cos 2x) \quad \text{product rule}$$

$$= e^{-x}(7\cos 2x + 4\sin 2x)$$

Stationary points occur when $\frac{dy}{dx} = 0$.

$$e^{-x}(7\cos 2x + 4\sin 2x) = 0$$

$$7\cos 2x + 4\sin 2x = 0 \quad \text{or} \quad e^{-x} = 0$$

$$\tan 2x = -\frac{7}{4} \qquad \text{no solution}$$

$$2x = 2.0899$$

$$x = 1.045$$

There are other values of x for which $\tan 2x = -\frac{7}{4}$ but they are outside the range $0 < x < \frac{\pi}{2}$.

$$\frac{d^2y}{dx^2} = e^{-x}(-14\sin 2x + 8\cos 2x) - e^{-x}(7\cos 2x + 4\sin 2x)$$

$$= e^{-x}(\cos 2x - 18\sin 2x)$$

When $x = 1.045$, $\frac{d^2y}{dx^2} < 0$.

Hence the stationary point is a maximum point.

WORKED EXAMPLE 13

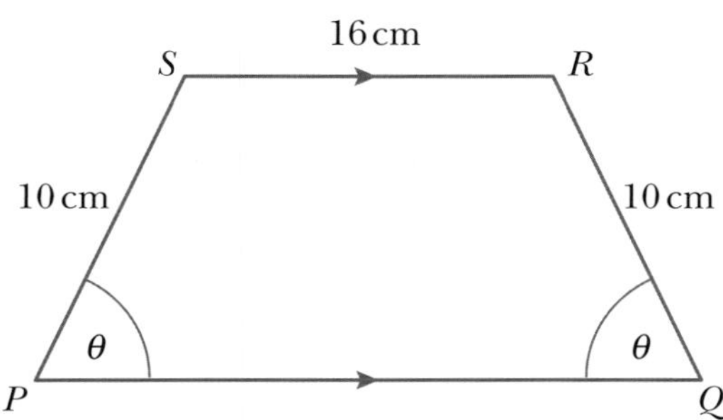

The diagram shows an isosceles trapezium $PQRS$ with area $A\,\text{cm}^2$.
Angle SPQ = angle $PQR = \theta$ radians.
$PS = QR = 10$ cm and $SR = 16$ cm.

a Show that $A = 160\sin\theta + 100\sin\theta\cos\theta$.
b Find the value of θ for which A has a stationary value.
c Determine the nature of this stationary value.

Answers

a $A = \frac{1}{2}(a+b)\,h$ — use $h = 10\sin\theta$

$= \frac{1}{2}(PQ + SR) \times 10\sin\theta$ — use $PQ = 10\cos\theta + 16 + 10\cos\theta = 16 + 20\cos\theta$

$= \frac{1}{2}[(16 + 20\cos\theta) + 16] \times 10\sin\theta$

$= 5\sin\theta(32 + 20\cos\theta)$

$= 160\sin\theta + 100\sin\theta\cos\theta$

b $\frac{dA}{dx} = 160\cos\theta + [100\sin\theta(-\sin\theta) + 100\cos^2\theta]$ — use the product rule on $100\sin\theta\cos\theta$

$= 160\cos\theta - 100\sin^2\theta + 100\cos^2\theta$ — use $\sin^2\theta = 1 - \cos^2\theta$

$= 160\cos\theta - 100(1 - \cos^2\theta) + 100\cos^2\theta$

$= 200\cos^2\theta + 160\cos\theta - 100$

Stationary values occur when $\frac{dA}{dx} = 0$.

$200\cos^2\theta + 160\cos\theta - 100 = 0$

$10\cos^2\theta + 8\cos\theta - 5 = 0$ — use the quadratic formula

$\cos\theta = 0.412$ or $\cos\theta = -1.212$

$\theta = 1.146$ radians   no solution

c $\frac{d^2A}{dx^2} = -400\cos\theta\sin\theta - 160\sin\theta$

When $\theta = 1.146$, $\frac{d^2A}{dx^2} < 0$.

Hence the stationary value is a maximum value.

Exercise 14.4

1 A curve has equation $y = 3\sin\left(2x + \frac{\pi}{2}\right)$.

Find the equation of the normal to the curve at the point on the curve where $x = \frac{\pi}{4}$.

2 A curve has equation $y = x \sin 2x$ for $0 \leqslant x \leqslant \pi$ radians.

a Find the equation of the normal to the curve at the point $P\left(\frac{\pi}{4}, \frac{\pi}{4}\right)$.

b The normal at P intersects the x-axis at Q and the y-axis at R.

Find the coordinates of Q and R.

c Find the area of triangle OQR where O is the origin.

3 A curve has equation $y = e^{\frac{1}{2}x} + 1$.

The curve crosses the y-axis at P.

The normal to the curve at P meets the x-axis at Q.

Find the coordinates of Q.

4 A curve has equation $y = 5 - e^{2x}$.

The curve crosses the x-axis at A and the y-axis at B.

a Find the coordinates of A and B.

b The normal to the curve at B meets the x-axis at the point C.

Find the coordinates of C.

5 A curve has equation $y = xe^x$.

The tangent to the curve at the point $P(1, e)$ meets the y-axis at the point A.

The normal to the curve at P meets the x-axis at the point B.

Find the area of triangle OAB, where O is the origin.

6 Variables x and y are connected by the equation $y = \sin 2x$.

Find the approximate increase in y as x increases from $\frac{\pi}{8}$ to $\frac{\pi}{8} + p$, where p is small.

7 Variables x and y are connected by the equation $y = 3 + \ln(2x - 5)$

Find the approximate change in y as x increases from 4 to $4 + p$, where p is small.

8 Variables x and y are connected by the equation $y = \frac{\ln x}{x^2 + 3}$.

Find the approximate change in y as x increases from 1 to $1 + p$, where p is small.

9 Variables x and y are connected by the equation $y = 3 + 2x - 5e^{-x}$.

Find the approximate change in y as x increases from $\ln 2$ to $\ln 2 + p$, where p is small.

10 A curve has equation $y = \frac{\ln(x^2 - 2)}{x^2 - 2}$.

Find the approximate change in y as x increases from $\sqrt{3}$ to $\sqrt{3} + p$, where p is small.

11 Find the coordinates of the stationary points on these curves and determine their nature.

a $y = xe^{\frac{x}{2}}$ **b** $y = x^2e^{2x}$ **c** $y = e^x - 7x - 2$

d $y = 5e^{2x} - 10x - 1$ **e** $y = (x^2 - 8)e^{-x}$ **f** $y = x^2 \ln x$

g $y = \dfrac{\ln x}{x^2}$ **h** $y = \dfrac{\ln(x^2 + 1)}{x^2 + 1}$

12 Find the coordinates of the stationary points on these curves and determine their nature.

a $y = 4 \sin x + 3 \cos x$ for $0 \leqslant x \leqslant \dfrac{\pi}{2}$

b $y = 6 \cos \dfrac{x}{2} + 8 \sin \dfrac{x}{2}$ for $0 \leqslant x \leqslant 2\pi$

c $y = 5 \sin\left(2x + \dfrac{\pi}{2}\right)$ for $-\dfrac{\pi}{6} \leqslant x \leqslant \dfrac{5\pi}{6}$

d $y = \dfrac{e^x}{\sin x}$ for $0 < x < \pi$

e $y = 2 \sin x \cos x + 2 \cos x$ for $0 \leqslant x \leqslant \pi$

13 A curve has equation $y = Ae^{2x} + Be^{-2x}$.

The gradient of the tangent at the point (0, 10) is –12.

a Find the value of A and the value of B.

b Find the coordinates of the turning point on the curve and determine its nature.

14 A curve has equation $y = x \ln x$.

The curve crosses the x-axis at the point A and has a minimum point at B.

Find the coordinates of A and the coordinates of B.

15 A curve has equation $y = x^2e^x$.

The curve has a minimum point at P and a maximum point at Q.

a Find the coordinates of P and the coordinates of Q.

b The tangent to the curve at the point A (1, e) meets the x-axis at the point B.

The normal to the curve at the point A (1, e) meets the y-axis at the point C.

Find the coordinates of B and the coordinates of C.

c Find the area of triangle ABC.

16 The diagram shows a semi-circle with diameter EF of length 12 cm.

Angle $GEF = \theta$ radians and the shaded region has an area of $A\,\text{cm}^2$.

a Show that $A = 36\theta + 18\sin 2\theta$.

b Given that θ is increasing at a rate of 0.05 radians per second, find the rate of change of A when $\theta = \frac{\pi}{6}$ radians.

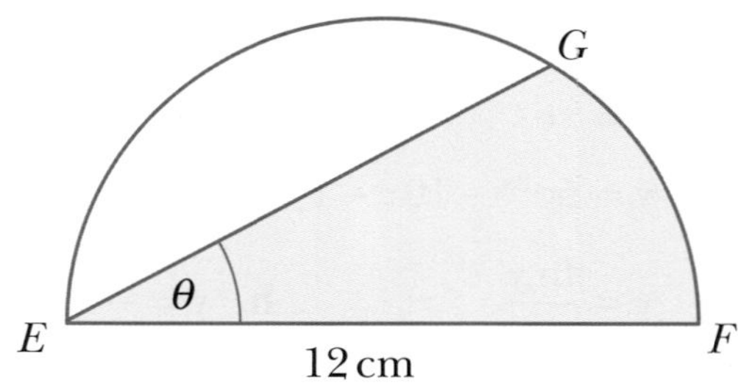

CHALLENGE Q

17 The diagram shows an isosceles triangle PQR inscribed in a circle, centre O, radius r cm.

$PR = QR$ and angle $ORP = \theta$ radians.

Triangle PQR has an area of $A\,\text{cm}^2$.

a Show that $A = r^2 \sin 2\theta + r^2 \sin 2\theta \cos 2\theta$.

b Find the value of θ for which A has a stationary value and determine the nature of this stationary value.

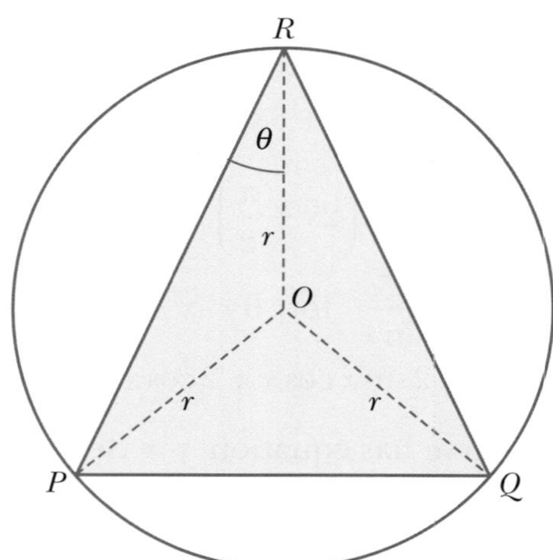

Summary

Exponential functions

$\frac{d}{dx}(e^x) = e^x$ $\qquad$ $\frac{d}{dx}\left[e^{ax+b}\right] = ae^{ax+b}$ $\qquad$ $\frac{d}{dx}\left[e^{f(x)}\right] = f'(x) \times e^{f(x)}$

Logarithmic functions

$\frac{d}{dx}(\ln x) = \frac{1}{x}$ $\qquad$ $\frac{d}{dx}[\ln(ax+b)] = \frac{a}{ax+b}$ $\qquad$ $\frac{d}{dx}\left[\ln\left(f(x)\right)\right] = \frac{f'(x)}{f(x)}$

Trigonometric functions

$\frac{d}{dx}(\sin x) = \cos x$ $\qquad$ $\frac{d}{dx}\left[\sin(ax+b)\right] = a\cos(ax+b)$

$\frac{d}{dx}(\cos x) = -\sin x$ $\qquad$ $\frac{d}{dx}\left[\cos(ax+b)\right] = -\,a\sin(ax+b)$

$\frac{d}{dx}(\tan x) = \sec^2 x$ $\qquad$ $\frac{d}{dx}\left[\tan(ax+b)\right] = a\sec^2(ax+b)$

Examination questions

Worked example

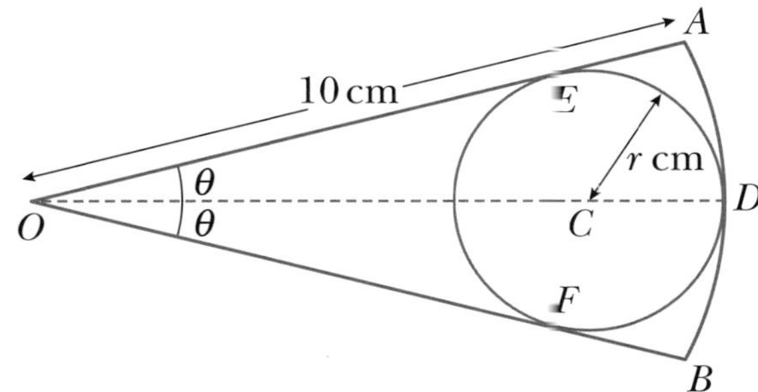

The figure shows a sector OAB of a circle, centre O, radius 10 cm. Angle $AOB = 2\theta$ radians where $0 < \theta < \frac{\pi}{2}$. A circle centre C, radius r cm, touches the arc AB at the point D. The lines OA and OB are tangents to the circle at the points E and F respectively.

a Write down, in terms of r, the length of OC. [1]

b Hence show that $r = \frac{10\sin\theta}{1+\sin\theta}$. [2]

c Given that θ can vary, find $\frac{dr}{d\theta}$ when $r = \frac{10}{3}$. [6]

d Given that r is increasing at $2\,\text{cm s}^{-1}$, find the rate at which θ is increasing when $\theta = \frac{\pi}{6}$. [3]

Cambridge IGCSE Additional Mathematics 0606 Paper 11 Q10(part) Nov 2011

Answers

a $OC = OD - CD$

$OC = 10 - r$

b Using triangle OCE:

$$\sin\theta = \frac{r}{OC}$$ use $OC = 10 - r$

$$\sin\theta = \frac{r}{10-r}$$ multiply both sides by $(10 - r)$

$$r = 10\sin\theta - r\sin\theta$$ collect terms involving r

$$r + r\sin\theta = 10\sin\theta$$ factorise

$$r(1+\sin\theta) = 10\sin\theta$$ divide both sides by $(1 + \sin\theta)$

$$r = \frac{10\sin\theta}{1+\sin\theta}$$

c $r = \dfrac{10\sin\theta}{1+\sin\theta}$ use the quotient rule

$$\frac{dr}{d\theta} = \frac{(1+\sin\theta)10\cos\theta - 10\sin\theta\cos\theta}{(1+\sin\theta)^2}$$

$$\frac{dr}{d\theta} = \frac{10\cos\theta}{(1+\sin\theta)^2} \text{ -----------------(1)}$$

When $r = \dfrac{10}{3}$, $\dfrac{10}{3} = \dfrac{10\sin\theta}{1+\sin\theta}$

$$30\sin\theta = 10 + 10\sin\theta$$

$$20\sin\theta = 10$$

$$\sin\theta = \frac{1}{2}$$

If $\sin\theta = \dfrac{1}{2}$, then $\cos\theta = \dfrac{\sqrt{3}}{2}$.

Substituting in equation (1) gives: $\dfrac{dr}{d\theta} = \dfrac{10\times\dfrac{\sqrt{3}}{2}}{\left(1+\dfrac{1}{2}\right)^2} = \dfrac{20\sqrt{3}}{9}$

d When $\theta = \dfrac{\pi}{6}$, $\sin\theta = \dfrac{1}{2}$, $\cos\theta = \dfrac{\sqrt{3}}{2}$ and $\dfrac{dr}{d\theta} = \dfrac{20\sqrt{3}}{9}$.

Using the chain rule: $\dfrac{d\theta}{dt} = \dfrac{d\theta}{dr}\times\dfrac{dr}{dt}$

$$= \frac{9}{20\sqrt{3}}\times 2$$

$$= \frac{9}{10\sqrt{3}}$$

$$= \frac{3\sqrt{3}}{10}$$

Exercise 14.5

Exam Exercise

1 **a** Find the equation of the tangent to the curve $y = x^3 - \ln x$ at the point on the curve where $x = 1$. [4]

b Show that the tangent bisects the line joining the points (–2, 16) and (12, 2). [2]

Cambridge IGCSE Additional Mathematics 0606 Paper 11 Q5i,ii Nov 2014

2 Find $\dfrac{dy}{dx}$ when

a $y = \cos 2x \sin\left(\dfrac{x}{3}\right)$, [4]

b $y = \dfrac{\tan x}{1+\ln x}$. [4]

Cambridge IGCSE Additional Mathematics 0606 Paper 21 Q10i,11 Jun 2014

3 Variables x and y are related by the equation $y = 10 - 4\sin^2 x$, where $0 \leqslant x \leqslant \dfrac{\pi}{2}$.
Given that x is increasing at a rate of 0.2 radians per second, find the corresponding rate of change of y when $y = 8$. [6]

Cambridge IGCSE Additional Mathematics 0606 Paper 21 Q3 Jun 2013

4 Given that $y = \dfrac{x^2}{\cos 4x}$, find

a $\dfrac{dy}{dx}$, [3]

b the approximate change in y when x increases from $\dfrac{\pi}{4}$ to $\dfrac{\pi}{4} + p$, where p is small. [2]

Cambridge IGCSE Additional Mathematics 0606 Paper 11 Q5i,ii Nov 2012

5 Variables x and y are such that $y = e^{2x} + e^{-2x}$.

a Find $\dfrac{dy}{dx}$. [2]

b By using the substitution $u = e^{2x}$, find the value of y when $\dfrac{dy}{dx} = 3$. [4]

c Given that x is decreasing at the rate of 0.5 units s^{-1}, find the corresponding rate of change of y when $x = 1$. [3]

Cambridge IGCSE Additional Mathematics 0606 Paper 11 Q10i,ii,iii Jun 2012

6

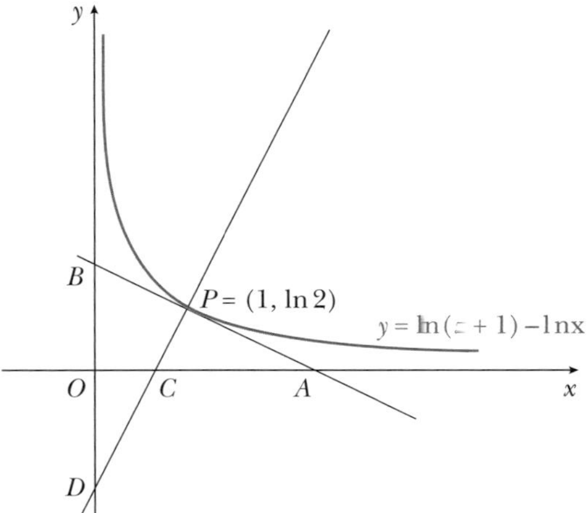

The diagram shows part of the curve $y = \ln(x+1) - \ln x$. The tangent to the curve at the point $P(1, \ln 2)$ meets the x-axis at A and the y-axis at B. The normal to the curve at P meets the x-axis at C and the y-axis at D.

a Find, in terms of $\ln 2$, the coordinates of A, B, C and D. [8]

b Given that $\dfrac{\text{Area of triangle } BPD}{\text{Area of triangle } APC} = \dfrac{1}{k}$, express k in terms of $\ln 2$. [3]

Cambridge IGCSE Additional Mathematics 0606 Paper 21 Q12(part) Nov 2011

7 A curve has equation $y = 2x\sin x + \dfrac{\pi}{3}$. The curve passes through the point $P\left(\dfrac{\pi}{2}, a\right)$.

a Find, in terms of π, the value of a. [1]

b Using your value of a, find the equation of the normal to the curve at P. [5]

Cambridge IGCSE Additional Mathematics 0606 Paper 11 Q5i,ii Nov 2010

8 **i** Given that $y = \dfrac{\tan 2x}{x}$, find $\dfrac{dy}{dx}$. [3]

ii Hence find the equation of the normal to the curve $y = \dfrac{\tan 2x}{x}$ at the point where $x = \dfrac{\pi}{8}$. [3]

Cambridge IGCSE Additional Mathematics 0606 Paper 12 Q6 Mar 2015

9 The point A, where $x = 0$, lies on the curve $y = \dfrac{\ln(4x^2 + 3)}{x - 1}$. The normal to the curve at A meets the x-axis at the point B.

i Find the equation of this normal. [7]

ii Find the area of the triangle AOB, where O is the origin. [2]

Cambridge IGCSE Additional Mathematics 0606 Paper 11 Q7 Jun 2015

10 Variables x and y are such that $y = (x - 3)\ln(2x^2 + 1)$.

i Find the value of $\dfrac{dy}{dx}$ when $x = 2$. [4]

ii Hence find the approximate change in y when x changes from 2 to 2.03. [2]

Cambridge IGCSE Additional Mathematics 0606 Paper 11 Q5 Nov 2015

11 A curve has equation $y = \dfrac{x}{x^2 + 1}$.

i Find the coordinates of the stationary points on the curve. [5]

ii Show that $\dfrac{d^2y}{dx^2} = \dfrac{px^3 + qx}{(x^2 + 1)^3}$, where p and q are integers to be found, and determine the nature of the stationary points of the curve. [5]

Cambridge IGCSE Additional Mathematics 0606 Paper 22 Q11 Mar 2016

12

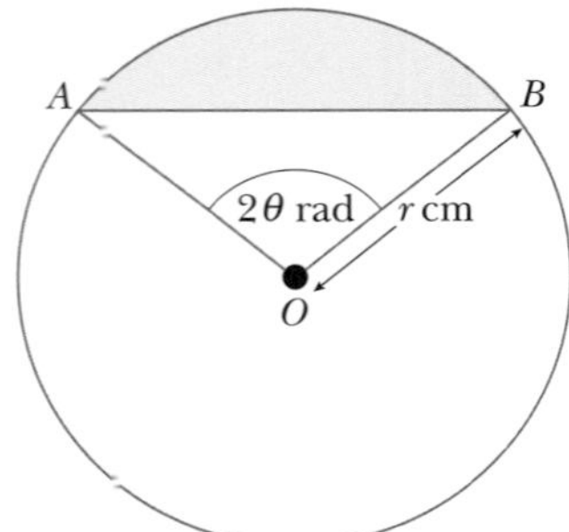

The diagram shows a circle, centre O, radius r cm. The points A and B lie on the circle such that angle $AOB = 2\theta$ radians.

i Find, in terms of r and θ, an expression for the length of the chord AB. [1]

ii Given that the perimeter of the shaded region is 20 cm, show that $r = \dfrac{10}{\theta + \sin\theta}$. [2]

iii Given that r and θ can vary, find the value of $\dfrac{dr}{d\theta}$ when $\theta = \dfrac{\pi}{6}$. [4]

iv Given that r is increasing at the rate of 15 cm s^{-1}, find the corresponding rate of change of θ when $\theta = \dfrac{\pi}{6}$. [3]

Cambridge IGCSE Additional Mathematics 0606 Paper 11 Q11 Jun 2016

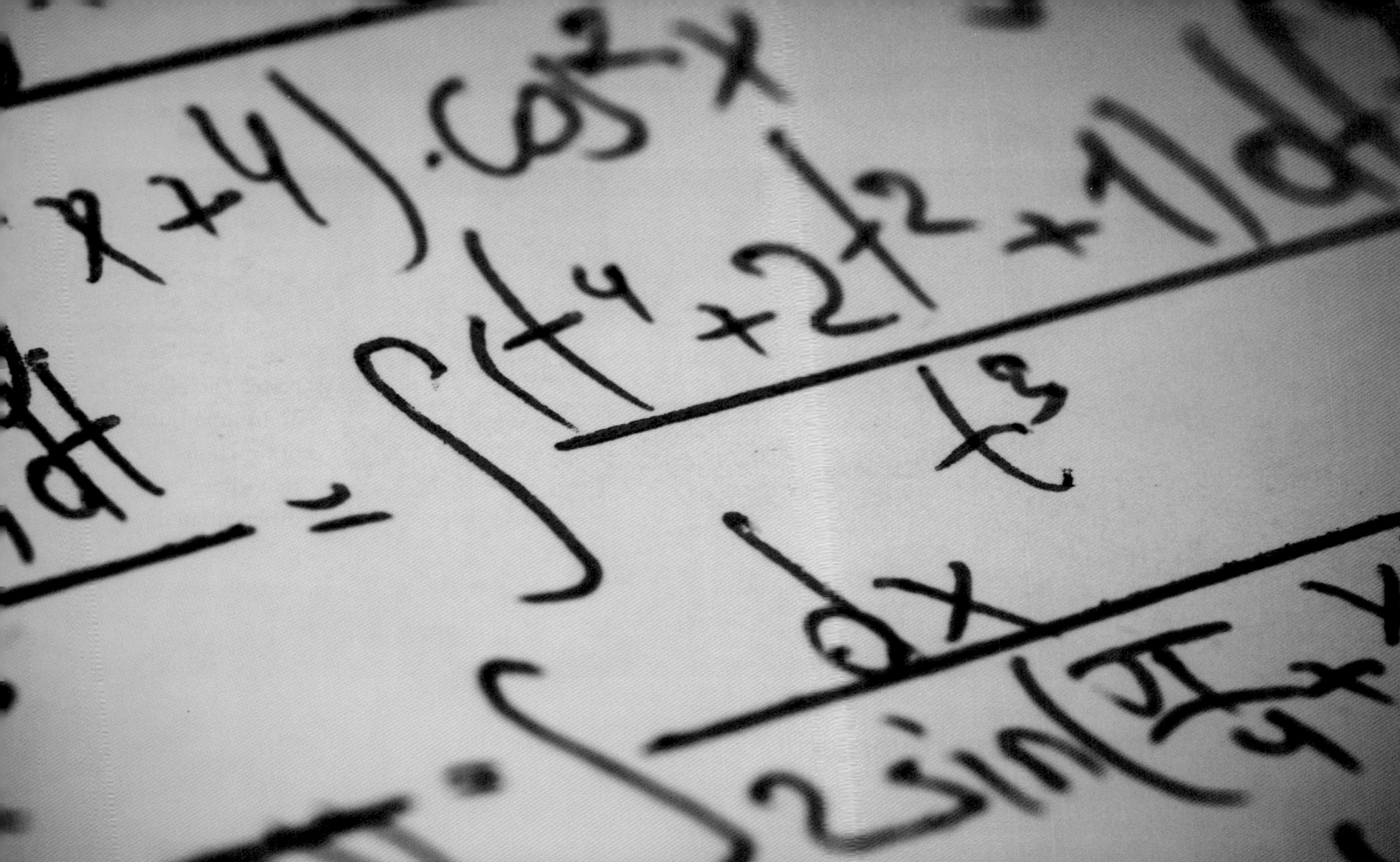

Chapter 15
Integration

This section will show you how to:

- use integration as the reverse process of differentiation
- integrate sums of terms in powers of x, including $\frac{1}{x}$ and $\frac{1}{ax+b}$
- integrate functions of the form $(ax+b)^n$, e^{ax+b}, $\sin(ax+b)$, $\cos(ax+b)$
- evaluate definite integrals and apply integration to the evaluation of plane areas

RECAP

In Chapter 12, you learnt about the process of obtaining $\frac{dy}{dx}$ when you know y. This process was called differentiation.

You learnt the rule for differentiating power functions: If $y = x^n$, then $\frac{dy}{dx} = nx^{n-1}$.

Applying this rule to functions of the form $y = x^2 + c$ you obtain:

$$\left.\begin{aligned} y &= x^2 + 5.3 \\ y &= x^2 + 2 \\ y &= x^2 \\ y &= x^2 - 3 \end{aligned}\right\} \frac{dy}{dx} = 2x$$

Note: There are an infinite number of functions that when differentiated give $2x$.

In this chapter you will learn about the reverse process of obtaining y when you know $\frac{dy}{dx}$. This reverse process is called **integration**.

15.1 Differentiation reversed

CLASS DISCUSSION

Find $\frac{dy}{dx}$ for each of the following functions.

$$y = \frac{1}{4}x^4 + 3$$

$$y = \frac{1}{7}x^7 - 0.8$$

$$y = \frac{1}{3}x^3 + 4$$

$$y = \frac{1}{-2}x^{-2} + 1$$

$$y = \frac{1}{\left(\frac{1}{2}\right)}x^{\frac{1}{2}} - 7$$

Discuss your results with your classmates and try to find a rule for obtaining y if $\frac{dy}{dx} = x^n$. Describe your rule in words.

From the class discussion you should have concluded that:

If $\frac{dy}{dx} = x^n$ then $y = \frac{1}{n+1}x^{n+1} + c$, where c is an arbitrary constant and $n \neq -1$.

It is easier to remember this rule as:

'increase the power n by 1 to get the new power, then divide by the new power'.

WORKED EXAMPLE 1

Find y in terms of x for each of the following.

a $\dfrac{dy}{dx} = x^4$ **b** $\dfrac{dy}{dx} = \sqrt{x}$ **c** $\dfrac{dy}{dx} = \dfrac{1}{x^3}$

Answers

a $\dfrac{dy}{dx} = x^4$

$$y = \frac{1}{4+1}x^{4+1} + c$$
$$= \frac{1}{5}x^5 + c$$

b $\dfrac{dy}{dx} = x^{\frac{1}{2}}$

$$y = \frac{1}{\frac{1}{2}+1}x^{\frac{1}{2}+1} + c$$
$$= \frac{2}{3}x^{\frac{3}{2}} + c$$
$$= \frac{2}{3}\sqrt{x^3} + c$$

c $\dfrac{dy}{dx} = x^{-3}$

$$y = \frac{1}{-3+1}x^{-3+1} + c$$
$$= -\frac{1}{2}x^{-2} + c$$
$$= -\frac{1}{2x^2} + c$$

WORKED EXAMPLE 2

Find y in terms of x for each of the following.

a $\dfrac{dy}{dx} = 6x^2 - \dfrac{5}{x^2} + 4x$ **b** $\dfrac{dy}{dx} = 8x^3 - \dfrac{4}{3x^5} - 2$ **c** $\dfrac{dy}{dx} = \dfrac{(x-2)(x+5)}{\sqrt{x}}$

Answers

a $\dfrac{dy}{dx} = 6x^2 - 5x^{-2} + 4x^1$ write in index form ready for integration

$$y = \frac{6}{3}x^3 - \frac{5}{(-1)}x^{-1} + \frac{4}{2}x^2 + c$$
$$= 2x^3 + 5x^{-1} + 2x^2 + c$$
$$= 2x^3 + \frac{5}{x} + 2x^2 + c$$

b $\dfrac{dy}{dx} = 8x^3 - \dfrac{4}{3}x^{-5} - 2x^0$ write in index form ready for integration

$$y = \frac{8}{4}x^4 - \frac{4}{3(-4)}x^{-4} - \frac{2}{1}x^1 + c$$
$$= 2x^4 + \frac{1}{3}x^{-4} - 2x + c$$
$$= 2x^4 + \frac{1}{3x^4} - 2x + c$$

c $\dfrac{dy}{dx} = \dfrac{x^2 + 3x - 10}{\sqrt{x}}$

$$= x^{\frac{3}{2}} + 3x^{\frac{1}{2}} - 10x^{-\frac{1}{2}}$$ write in index form ready for integration

$$y = \frac{1}{\frac{5}{2}}x^{\frac{5}{2}} + \frac{3}{\frac{3}{2}}x^{\frac{3}{2}} - \frac{10}{\frac{1}{2}}x^{\frac{1}{2}} + c$$
$$= \frac{2}{5}x^{\frac{5}{2}} + 2x^{\frac{3}{2}} - 20x^{\frac{1}{2}} + c$$

WORKED EXAMPLE 3

A curve is such that $\frac{dy}{dx} = (1 - x)(3x - 2)$ and (2, 8) is a point on the curve.

Find the equation of the curve.

Answers

$\frac{dy}{dx} = (1 - x)(3x - 2)$ expand brackets

$= -3x^2 + 5x - 2$

$= -3x^2 + 5x^1 - 2x^0$ write in index form ready for integration

$y = -x^3 + \frac{5}{2}x^2 - 2x + c$

When $x = 2,\ y = 8$

$8 = -(2)^3 + \frac{5}{2}(2)^2 - 2(2) + c$

$8 = -8 + 10 - 4 + c$

$c = 10$

The equation of the curve is $y = -x^3 + \frac{5}{2}x^2 - 2x + 10$.

Exercise 15.1

1 Find y in terms of x for each of the following.

a $\frac{dy}{dx} = 12x^4$ **b** $\frac{dy}{dx} = 5x^8$ **c** $\frac{dy}{dx} = 7x^3$

d $\frac{dy}{dx} = \frac{4}{x^3}$ **e** $\frac{dy}{dx} = \frac{1}{2x^2}$ **f** $\frac{dy}{dx} = \frac{3}{\sqrt{x}}$

2 Find y in terms of x for each of the following.

a $\frac{dy}{dx} = 7x^6 + 2x^4 + 3$ **b** $\frac{dy}{dx} = 2x^5 - 3x^3 + 5x$

c $\frac{dy}{dx} = \frac{3}{x^4} - \frac{15}{x^2} + x$ **d** $\frac{dy}{dx} = \frac{18}{x^{10}} + \frac{6}{x^7} - 2$

3 Find y in terms of x for each of the following.

a $\frac{dy}{dx} = 3x(x - 2)$ **b** $\frac{dy}{dx} = x^2(4x^2 - 3)$

c $\frac{dy}{dx} = \left(x + 2\sqrt{x}\right)^2$ **d** $\frac{dy}{dx} = x(x - 3)(x + 4)$

e $\frac{dy}{dx} = \frac{x^5 - 3x}{2x^3}$ **f** $\frac{dy}{dx} = \frac{(2x - 3)(x - 1)}{x^4}$

g $\frac{dy}{dx} = \frac{x^5 - 4x^2 + 1}{2x^2}$ **h** $\frac{dy}{dx} = \frac{(3x + 5)(x - 2)}{\sqrt{x}}$

4 A curve is such that $\frac{dy}{dx} = 3x^2 - 4x + 1$.
Given that the curve passes through the point (0, 5) find the equation of the curve.

5 A curve is such that $\frac{dy}{dx} = 6x(x - 1)$.
Given that the curve passes through the point (1, –5) find the equation of the curve.

6 A curve is such that $\frac{dy}{dx} = \frac{2x^3 + 6}{x^2}$.
Given that the curve passes through the point (–1, 10), find the equation of the curve.

7 A curve is such that $\frac{dy}{dx} = \frac{\left(2 - \sqrt{x}\right)^2}{\sqrt{x}}$.
Given that the curve passes through the point (9, 14), find the equation of the curve.

8 A curve is such that $\frac{dy}{dx} = kx^2 - 2x$ where k is a constant.
Given that the curve passes through the points (1, 6) and (–2, –15) find the equation of the curve.

9 A curve is such that $\frac{d^2y}{dx^2} = 12x - 12$.
The gradient of the curve at the point (2, 9) is 8.

a Express y in terms of x.

b Show that the gradient of the curve is never less than 2.

10 A curve is such that $\frac{dy}{dx} = kx - 5$ where k is a constant.
The gradient of the normal to the curve at the point (2, –1) is $-\frac{1}{3}$.
Find the equation of the curve.

15.2 Indefinite integrals

The special symbol $\int$ is used to denote integration.

When you need to integrate x^2, for example, you write

$$\int x^2 \, dx = \frac{1}{3}x^3 + c.$$

$\int x^2 \, dx$ is called the **indefinite integral** of x^2 with respect to x.

It is called 'indefinite' because it has infinitely many solutions.

Using this notation the rule for integrating powers of x can be written as:

$$\int x^n \, dx = \frac{1}{n+1}x^{n+1} + c, \text{ where } c \text{ is a constant and } n \neq -$$

This section provides you with practice at using this new notation together with the following rules:

$$\int kf(x)\ dx = k\int f(x)\ dx, \text{ where } k \text{ is a constant}$$

$$\int [f(x) \pm g(x)]\ dx = \int f(x)\ dx \pm \int g(x)\ dx$$

WORKED EXAMPLE 4

Find: **a** $\int x^2(10x^2 - 8x + 3)\ dx$ **b** $\int \frac{x^4 - 2}{x\sqrt{x}}\ dx$

Answers

a $\int x^2(10x^2 - 8x + 3)\ dx = \int (10x^4 - 8x^3 + 3x^2)\ dx$

$$= \frac{10x^5}{5} - \frac{8x^4}{4} + \frac{3x^3}{3} + c$$

$$= 2x^5 - 2x^4 + x^3 + c$$

b $\int \frac{x^4 - 2}{x\sqrt{x}}\ dx = \int \frac{x^4 - 2}{x^{\frac{3}{2}}}\ dx$

$$= \int \left(x^{\frac{5}{2}} - 2x^{-\frac{3}{2}}\right) dx$$

$$= \frac{1}{\left(\frac{7}{2}\right)}x^{\frac{7}{2}} - \frac{2}{\left(-\frac{1}{2}\right)}x^{-\frac{1}{2}} + c$$

$$= \frac{2}{7}x^{\frac{7}{2}} + 4x^{-\frac{1}{2}} + c$$

$$= \frac{2}{7}x^3\sqrt{x} + \frac{4}{\sqrt{x}} + c$$

Exercise 15.2

1 Find each of the following.

a $\int 4x^7\ dx$ **b** $\int 12x^5\ dx$ **c** $\int 2x^{-3}\ dx$

d $\int \frac{4}{x^2}\ dx$ **e** $\int \frac{3}{\sqrt{x}}\ dx$ **f** $\int \frac{6}{x^2\sqrt{x}}\ dx$

2 Find each of the following.

a $\int (x + 2)(x + 5)\ dx$ **b** $\int (x - 1)(2x + 3)\ dx$ **c** $\int (x - 5)^2\ dx$

d $\int (\sqrt{x} + 3)^2\ dx$ **e** $\int x(x - 1)^2\ dx$ **f** $\int \sqrt[3]{x}(x - 4)\ dx$

3 Find each of the following.

a $\int \frac{x^2 - 5}{x^2}\, dx$ **b** $\int \frac{x^4 - 8}{2x^3}\, dx$ **c** $\int \frac{(x+1)^5}{3x^4}\, dx$

d $\int \frac{4x^2 - 3\sqrt{x}}{x}\, dx$ **e** $\int \frac{x^5 + 5}{x^3\sqrt{x}}\, dx$ **f** $\int \left(\sqrt{x} + \frac{3}{x^2\sqrt{x}}\right)^2 dx$

15.3 Integration of functions of the form $(ax + b)^n$

In Chapter 12 you learnt that:

$$\frac{d}{dx}\left[\frac{1}{2 \times 8}(2x+5)^8\right] = (2x+5)^7$$

Hence $\int (2x+5)^7\, dx = \frac{1}{2 \times 8}(2x+5)^8 + c.$

This leads to the general rule:

$$\int (ax+b)^n\, dx = \frac{1}{a(n+1)}(ax+b)^{n+1} + c,\ n \neq -1 \text{ and } a \neq 0$$

WORKED EXAMPLE 5

Find

a $\int (3x-8)^5\, dx$ **b** $\int \frac{8}{(4x+1)^3}\, dx$ **c** $\int \frac{12}{\sqrt{2x-7}}\, dx.$

Answers

a $\int (3x-8)^5\, dx = \frac{1}{3(5+1)}(3x-8)^{5+1} + c$

$= \frac{1}{18}(3x-8)^6 + c$

b $\int \frac{8}{(4x+1)^3}\, dx = 8\int (4x+1)^{-3}\, dx$

$= \frac{8}{4(-3+1)}(4x+1)^{-3+1} + c$

$= -(4x+1)^{-2} + c$

$= -\frac{1}{(4x+1)^2} + c$

c $\int \frac{12}{\sqrt{2x-7}}\, dx = 12\int (2x-7)^{-\frac{1}{2}}\, dx$

$= \frac{12}{2\left(-\frac{1}{2}+1\right)}(2x-7)^{-\frac{1}{2}+1} + c$

$= 12\sqrt{2x-7} + c$

Exercise 15.3

1 Find:

a $\int (x+2)^9\,\mathrm{d}x$ **b** $\int (2x-5)^6\,\mathrm{d}x$ **c** $\int 2(3x+2)^9\,\mathrm{d}x$

d $\int 3(2-3x)^4\,\mathrm{d}x$ **e** $\int (7x+2)^{\frac{1}{3}}\,\mathrm{d}x$ **f** $\int \sqrt{(3x-1)^3}\,\mathrm{d}x$

g $\int \frac{6}{\sqrt{x+1}}\,\mathrm{d}x$ **h** $\int \left(\frac{2}{5x+3}\right)^3\mathrm{d}x$ **i** $\int \frac{3}{2(3-2x)^4}\,\mathrm{d}x$

2 A curve is such that $\frac{\mathrm{d}y}{\mathrm{d}x} = (4x+1)^4$.
Given that the curve passes through the point (0, –1.95) find the equation of the curve.

3 A curve is such that $\frac{\mathrm{d}y}{\mathrm{d}x} = \sqrt{2x+1}$.
Given that the curve passes through the point (4, 11) find the equation of the curve.

4 A curve is such that $\frac{\mathrm{d}y}{\mathrm{d}x} = \frac{1}{\sqrt{10-x}}$.
Given that the curve passes through the point (6, 1), find the equation of the curve.

5 A curve is such that $\frac{\mathrm{d}y}{\mathrm{d}x} = k(2x-3)^3$ where k is a constant.
The gradient of the normal to the curve at the point (2, 2) is $-\frac{1}{8}$.
Find the equation of the curve.

6 A curve is such that $\frac{\mathrm{d}y}{\mathrm{d}x} = 2(kx-1)^5$ where k is a constant.
Given that the curve passes through the points (0, 1) and (1, 8) find the equation of the curve.

15.4 Integration of exponential functions

In Chapter 15, you learnt the following rules for differentiating exponential functions:

$$\frac{\mathrm{d}}{\mathrm{d}x}\left(\mathrm{e}^x\right) = \mathrm{e}^x \qquad \frac{\mathrm{d}}{\mathrm{d}x}\left(\mathrm{e}^{ax+b}\right) = a\mathrm{e}^{ax+b}$$

Since integration is the reverse process of differentiation, the rules for integrating exponential functions are:

$$\int \mathrm{e}^x\,\mathrm{d}x = \mathrm{e}^x + c \qquad \int \mathrm{e}^{ax+b}\,\mathrm{d}x = \frac{1}{a}\mathrm{e}^{ax+b} + c$$

WORKED EXAMPLE 6

Find

a $\int e^{2x}\,dx$ **b** $\int e^{-7x}\,dx$ **c** $\int e^{6x-5}\,dx$.

Answers

a $\int e^{2x}\,dx = \frac{1}{2}e^{2x} + c$

b $\int e^{-7x}\,dx = \frac{1}{-7}e^{-7x} + c$

$= -\frac{1}{7}e^{-7x} + c$

c $\int e^{6x-5}\,dx = \frac{1}{6}e^{6x-5} + c$

Exercise 15.4

1 Find:

a $\int e^{5x}\,dx$ **b** $\int e^{9x}\,dx$ **c** $\int e^{\frac{1}{2}x}\,dx$

d $\int e^{-2x}\,dx$ **e** $\int 4e^{x}\,dx$ **f** $\int 2e^{4x}\,dx$

g $\int e^{7x+4}\,dx$ **h** $\int e^{5-2x}\,dx$ **i** $\int \frac{1}{3}e^{6x-1}\,dx$

2 Find:

a $\int e^{x}\left(5 - e^{2x}\right)dx$ **b** $\int \left(e^{2x} + 1\right)^2 dx$ **c** $\int \left(3e^{x} + e^{-x}\right)^2 dx$

d $\int \frac{e^{2x} + 4}{e^{x}}\,dx$ **e** $\int \frac{5e^{3x} - e^{2x}}{2e^{x}}\,dx$ **f** $\int \frac{\left(e^{4x} - 2e^{x}\right)^2}{e^{3x}}\,dx$

3 Find:

a $\int \left(2e^{x} + \frac{1}{\sqrt{x}}\right)dx$ **b** $\int \left(x^2 - 3e^{2x+1}\right)dx$ **c** $\int \frac{3x^2e^{2x} - 4e^{x}}{12x^2e^{x}}\,dx$

4 A curve is such that $\frac{dy}{dx} = 2e^{2x} + e^{-x}$.
Given that the curve passes through the point (0, 4), find the equation of the curve.

5 A curve is such that $\frac{dy}{dx} = ke^{2-x} + 4x$, where k is a constant.
At the point (2, 10) the gradient of the curve is 1.

a Find the value of k.

b Find the equation of the curve.

6 A curve is such that $\frac{d^2y}{dx^2} = 8e^{-2x}$.

Given that $\frac{dy}{dx} = 2$ when $x = 0$ and that the curve passes through the point $\left(1, \frac{2}{e^2}\right)$, find the equation of the curve.

7 The point $P\left(\frac{3}{2}, 5\right)$ lies on the curve for which $\frac{dy}{dx} = 2e^{3-2x}$.

The point $Q(1, k)$ also lies on the curve.

a Find the value of k.

The normals to the curve at the points P and Q intersect at the point R.

b Find the coordinates of R.

15.5 Integration of sine and cosine functions

In Chapter 14, you learnt how to differentiate sine and cosine functions:

$$\frac{d}{dx}(\sin x) = \cos x \qquad \frac{d}{dx}[\sin(ax+b)] = a\cos(ax+b)$$

$$\frac{d}{dx}(\cos x) = -\sin x \qquad \frac{d}{dx}[\cos(ax+b)] = -a\sin(ax+b)$$

Since integration is the reverse process of differentiation, the rules for integrating sine and cosine functions are:

$$\int \cos x \, dx = \sin x + c \qquad \int [\cos(ax+b)] \, dx = \frac{1}{a}\sin(ax+b) + c$$

$$\int \sin x \, dx = -\cos x + c \qquad \int [\sin(ax+b)] \, dx = -\frac{1}{a}\cos(ax+b) + c$$

Note:
It is important to remember that the formulae for differentiating and integrating these trigonometric functions only apply when x is measured in radians.

WORKED EXAMPLE 7

Find:

a $\int \sin 2x \, dx$ **b** $\int \cos 5x \, dx$ **c** $\int 3\sin\frac{x}{2} \, dx$

Answers

a $\int \sin 2x \, dx = -\frac{1}{2}\cos 2x + c$

b $\int \cos 5x \, dx = \frac{1}{5}\sin 5x + c$

c $\int 3\sin\frac{x}{2} \, dx = 3\int \sin\frac{x}{2} \, dx$

$= 3 \times \left(-2\cos\frac{x}{2}\right) + c$

$= -6\cos\frac{x}{2} + c$

WORKED EXAMPLE 8

Find:

a $\int (3\cos 2x + 5\sin 3x)\,dx$ **b** $\int [x^2 + 2\cos(5x - 1)]\,dx$

Answers

a $\int (3\cos 2x + 5\sin 3x)\,dx = 3\int \cos 2x\,dx + 5\int \sin 3x\,dx$

$$= 3 \times \left(\frac{1}{2}\sin 2x\right) + 5 \times \left(-\frac{1}{3}\cos 3x\right)$$

$$= \frac{3}{2}\sin 2x - \frac{5}{3}\cos 3x + c$$

b $\int [x^2 + 2\cos(5x - 1)]\,dx = \int x^2\,dx + 2\int \cos(5x - 1)\,dx$

$$= \frac{1}{3}x^3 + 2 \times \left[\frac{1}{5}\sin(5x - 1)\right] + c$$

$$= \frac{1}{3}x^3 + \frac{2}{5}\sin(5x - 1) + c$$

Exercise 15.5

1 Find

a $\int \sin 4x\,dx$ **b** $\int \cos 2x\,dx$ **c** $\int \sin\frac{x}{3}\,dx$

d $\int 2\cos 2x\,dx$ **e** $\int 6\sin 3x\,dx$ **f** $\int 3\cos(2x -$ [illegible]$)\,dx$

g $\int 5\sin(2 - 3x)\,dx$ **h** $\int 2\cos(2x - 7)\,dx$ **i** $\int 4\sin(1 - 5x)\,dx$

2 Find

a $\int (1 - \sin x)\,dx$ **b** $\int \left(\sqrt{x} - 2\cos 3x\right)\,dx$

c $\int \left(3\cos 2x - \pi\sin\frac{5x}{2}\right)\,dx$ **d** $\int \left(\frac{1}{x^2} - \cos\frac{3x}{2}\right)\,dx$

e $\int \left(e^{2x} - 5\sin 2x\right)\,dx$ **f** $\int \left(\frac{2}{\sqrt{x}} + \sin\frac{x}{2}\right)\,dx$

3 A curve is such that $\frac{dy}{dx} = \cos x - \sin x$.
Given that the curve passes through the point $\left(\frac{\pi}{2}, 3\right)$, find the equation of the curve.

4 A curve is such that $\frac{dy}{dx} = 1 - 4\cos 2x$.
Given that the curve passes through the point $\left(\frac{\pi}{4}, 1\right)$, find the equation of the curve.

5 A curve is such that $\frac{dy}{dx} = 4x - 6\sin 2x$.
Given that the curve passes through the point $(0, -2)$, find the equation of the curve.

6 A curve is such that $\frac{d^2y}{dx^2} = 45\cos 3x + 2\sin x$.

Given that $\frac{dy}{dx} = -2$ when $x = 0$ and that the curve passes through the point $(\pi, -1)$, find the equation of the curve.

7 A curve is such that $\frac{dy}{dx} = k\cos 3x - 4$, where k is a constant.

At the point $(\pi, 2)$ the gradient of the curve is -10.

a Find the value of k.

b Find the equation of the curve.

8 The point $\left(\frac{\pi}{2}, 5\right)$ lies on the curve for which $\frac{dy}{dx} = 4\sin\left(2x - \frac{\pi}{2}\right)$.

a Find the equation of the curve.

b Find the equation of the normal to the curve at the point where $x = \frac{\pi}{3}$.

9 The point $P\left(\frac{\pi}{3}, 3\right)$ lies on the curve for which $\frac{dy}{dx} = 3\cos\left(3x - \frac{\pi}{2}\right)$.

The point $Q\left(\frac{\pi}{2}, k\right)$ also lies on the curve.

a Find the value of k.

The tangents to the curve at the points P and Q intersect at the point R.

b Find the coordinates of R.

15.6 Integration of functions of the form $\frac{1}{x}$ and $\frac{1}{ax+b}$

In Chapter 14, you learnt the following rules for differentiating logarithmic functions:

$$\frac{d}{dx}(\ln x) = \frac{1}{x}, \quad x > 0 \qquad\qquad \frac{d}{dx}[\ln(ax+b)] = \frac{a}{ax+b}, \quad ax + b > 0$$

It is important to remember that $\ln x$ is only defined for $x > 0$.

Since integration is the reverse process of differentiation, the rules for integration are:

$$\int \frac{1}{x}\,dx = \ln x + c, \quad x > 0 \qquad\qquad \int \frac{1}{ax+b}\,dx = \frac{1}{a}\ln(ax+b) + c, \quad ax + b > 0$$

WORKED EXAMPLE 9

Find each of these integrals and state the values of x for which the integral is valid.

a $\int \frac{5}{x}\,dx$ **b** $\int \frac{6}{2x+5}\,dx$ **c** $\int \frac{8}{3-4x}\,dx$

Answers

a $\int \frac{5}{x}\,dx = 5\int \frac{1}{x}\,dx$

$= 5\ln x + c,\ x > 0$

b $\int \frac{6}{2x+5}\,dx = 6\int \frac{1}{2x+5}\,dx$

$= 6\left(\frac{1}{2}\right)\ln(2x+5) + c$ valid for $2x + 5 > 0$

$= 3\ln(2x+5) + c,\ x > -\frac{5}{2}$

c $\int \frac{8}{3-4x}\,dx = 8\int \frac{1}{3-4x}\,dx$

$= 8\left(\frac{1}{-4}\right)\ln(3-4x) + c$ valid for $3 - 4x > 0$

$= -2\ln(3-4x) + c,\ x < \frac{3}{4}$

CLASS DISCUSSION

Nicola is asked to find $\int x^{-1}dx$.

She tries to use the formula $\int x^n dx = \frac{1}{n+1}x^{n+1} + c$ to obtain her answer.

Nicola is also asked to find $\int (5x+2)^{-1}\,dx$.

She tries to use the formula $\int (ax+b)^n\,dx = \frac{1}{a(n+1)}(ax+b)^{n+1} - c$ to obtain her answer.

Discuss with your classmates why Nicola's methods do not work.

CLASS DISCUSSION

Raju and Sara are asked to find $\int \frac{1}{2(3x-1)}\,dx$.

Raju writes: $\int \frac{1}{2(3x-1)}\,dx = \int \frac{1}{6x-2}\,dx$

$= \frac{1}{6}\ln(6x-2) + c$

Sara writes: $\int \frac{1}{2(3x-1)}\,dx = \frac{1}{2}\int \frac{1}{3x-1}\,dx$

$= \left(\frac{1}{2}\right)\left(\frac{1}{3}\right)\ln(3x-1) + c$

$= \frac{1}{6}\ln(3x-1) + c$

Decide who is correct and discuss the reasons for your decision with your classmates.

Exercise 15.6

1 Find:

a $\int \frac{8}{x}\,dx$ **b** $\int \frac{5}{x}\,dx$ **c** $\int \frac{1}{2x}\,dx$

d $\int \frac{5}{3x}\,dx$ **e** $\int \frac{1}{3x+2}\,dx$ **f** $\int \frac{1}{1-8x}\,dx$

g $\int \frac{7}{2x-1}\,dx$ **h** $\int \frac{4}{2-3x}\,dx$ **i** $\int \frac{5}{2(5x-1)}\,dx$

2 Find:

a $\int \left(7x+1+\frac{2}{x}\right)dx$ **b** $\int \left(1+\frac{2}{x}\right)^2 dx$ **c** $\int \left(5-\frac{3}{x}\right)^2 dx$

d $\int \frac{x+1}{x}\,dx$ **e** $\int \frac{3-5x^3}{2x^4}\,dx$ **f** $\int \left(3x-\frac{2}{x^2}\right)^2 dx$

g $\int \frac{5x+2\sqrt{x}}{x^2}\,dx$ **h** $\int \frac{x^3-\sqrt{x}}{x\sqrt{x}}\,dx$ **i** $\int \frac{5xe^{4x}-2e^x}{10xe^x}\,dx$

3 A curve is such that $\frac{dy}{dx} = \frac{5}{2x-1}$ for $x > 0.5$.
Given that the curve passes through the point (1, 3), find the equation of the curve.

4 A curve is such that $\frac{dy}{dx} = 2x + \frac{5}{x}$ for $x > 0$.
Given that the curve passes through the point (e, e^2), find the equation of the curve.

5 A curve is such that $\frac{dy}{dx} = \frac{1}{x+e}$ for $x > -e$.
Given that the curve passes through the point $(e, 2 + \ln 2)$, find the equation of the curve.

CHALLENGE Q

6 The point $P(1, -2)$ lies on the curve for which $\frac{dy}{dx} = 3 - \frac{2}{x}$.
The point $Q(2, k)$ also lies on the curve.

a Find the value of k.

The tangents to the curve at the points P and Q intersect at the point R.

b Find the coordinates of R.

15.7 Further indefinite integration

This section uses the concept that integration is the reverse process of differentiation to help integrate complicated expressions.

$$\text{If } \frac{d}{dx}[F(x)] = f(x), \text{ then } \int f(x)\, dx = F(x) + c$$

WORKED EXAMPLE 10

Show that $\frac{d}{dx}\left(\frac{x^2+1}{\sqrt{4x-3}}\right) = \frac{2(3x^2-3x-1)}{\sqrt{(4x-3)^3}}$.

Hence find $\int \frac{3x^2-3x-1}{\sqrt{(4x-3)^3}}\, dx$.

Answers

Let $y = \frac{x^2+1}{\sqrt{4x-3}}$

$$\frac{dy}{dx} = \frac{(\sqrt{4x-3})2x - (x^2+1)\left[\frac{1}{2}(4x-3)^{-\frac{1}{2}}(4)\right]}{4x-3} \qquad \text{quotient rule}$$

$$= \frac{2x\sqrt{4x-3} - \frac{2(x^2+1)}{\sqrt{4x-3}}}{4x-3} \qquad \text{multiply numerator and denominator by } \sqrt{4x-3}$$

$$= \frac{2x(4x-3) - 2(x^2+1)}{(4x-3)\sqrt{4x-3}}$$

$$= \frac{2(4x^2-3x-x^2-1)}{\sqrt{(4x-3)^3}}$$

$$= \frac{2(3x^2-3x-1)}{\sqrt{(4x-3)^3}}$$

$$\int \frac{3x^2-3x-1}{\sqrt{(4x-3)^3}}\, dx = \frac{1}{2}\int \frac{2(3x^2-3x-1)}{\sqrt{(4x-3)^3}}\, dx$$

$$= \frac{x^2+1}{2\sqrt{4x-3}} + c$$

WORKED EXAMPLE 11

Differentiate $x \sin x$ with respect to x.

Hence find $\int x \cos x \, dx$.

Answers

Let $y = x \sin x$

$$\frac{dy}{dx} = (x)(\cos x) + (\sin x)(1) \quad \text{product rule}$$

$$= x \cos x + \sin x$$

Hence $\int (x \cos x + \sin x) \, dx = x \sin x$

$$\int x \cos x \, dx + \int \sin x \, dx = x \sin x$$

$$\int x \cos x \, dx = x \sin x - \int \sin x \, dx$$

$$\int x \cos x \, dx = x \sin x + \cos x + c$$

WORKED EXAMPLE 12

Differentiate $x^3\sqrt{2x-1}$ with respect to x.

Hence find $\int \frac{7x^3 - 3x^2 + 5}{\sqrt{2x-1}} \, dx$.

Answers

Let $y = x^3\sqrt{2x-1}$

$$\frac{dy}{dx} = (x^3)\left[\frac{1}{2} \times 2 \times (2x-1)^{-\frac{1}{2}}\right] + \sqrt{2x-1} \times (3x^2) \quad \text{product rule}$$

$$= \frac{x^3}{\sqrt{2x-1}} + 3x^2\sqrt{2x-1}$$

$$= \frac{x^3 + 3x^2(2x-1)}{\sqrt{2x-1}}$$

$$= \frac{7x^3 - 3x^2}{\sqrt{2x-1}}$$

$$\int \frac{7x^3 - 3x^2 + 5}{\sqrt{2x-1}} \, dx = \int \frac{7x^3 - 3x^2}{\sqrt{2x-1}} \, dx + \int \frac{5}{\sqrt{2x-1}} \, dx$$

$$= \int \frac{7x^3 - 3x^2}{\sqrt{2x-1}} \, dx + 5\int (2x-1)^{-\frac{1}{2}} \, dx$$

$$= x^3\sqrt{2x-1} + \frac{5}{2 \times \frac{1}{2}}(2x-1)^{\frac{1}{2}} + c$$

$$= x^3\sqrt{2x-1} + 5\sqrt{2x-1} + c$$

$$= (x^3 + 5)\sqrt{2x-1} + c$$

Exercise 15.7

1 a Given that $y = \frac{x+5}{\sqrt{2x-1}}$, show that $\frac{dy}{dx} = \frac{x-6}{\sqrt{(2x-1)^3}}$.

b Hence find $\int \frac{x-6}{\sqrt{(2x-1)^3}}\,dx$.

2 a Differentiate $(3x^2-1)^5$ with respect to x.

b Hence find $\int x(3x^2-1)^4\,dx$.

3 a Differentiate $x\ln x$ with respect to x.

b Hence find $\int \ln x\,dx$.

4 a Show that $\frac{d}{dx}\left(\frac{\ln x}{x}\right) = \frac{1-\ln x}{x^2}$.

b Hence find $\int \left(\frac{\ln x}{x^3}\right)dx$.

5 a Given that $y = x\sqrt{x^2-4}$, find $\frac{dy}{dx}$.

b Hence find $\int \frac{x^2-2}{\sqrt{x^2-4}}\,dx$.

6 a Given that $y = 3(x+1)\sqrt{x-5}$, show that $\frac{dy}{dx} = \frac{9(x-3)}{2\sqrt{x-5}}$.

b Hence find $\int \frac{(x-3)}{\sqrt{x-5}}\,dx$.

7 a Find $\frac{d}{dx}\left(xe^{2x} - \frac{e^{2x}}{2}\right)$.

b Hence find $\int xe^{2x}\,dx$.

8 a Show that $\frac{d}{dx}\left(\frac{\sin x}{1-\cos x}\right)$ can be written in the form $\frac{k}{\cos x - 1}$, and state the value of k.

b Hence find $\int \frac{5}{\cos x - 1}\,dx$.

9 a Given that $y = (x+8)\sqrt{x-4}$, show that $\frac{dy}{dx} = \frac{kx}{\sqrt{x-4}}$, and state the value of k.

b Hence find $\int \frac{x}{\sqrt{x-4}}\,dx$.

10 a Given that $y = \frac{1}{x^2-7}$, show that $\frac{dy}{dx} = \frac{kx}{(x^2-7)^2}$, and state the value of k.

b Hence find $\int \frac{4x}{(x^2-7)^2}\,dx$.

11 a Find $\frac{d}{dx}(2x^3\ln x)$.

b Hence find $\int x^2\ln x\,dx$.

12 a Differentiate $x\cos x$ with respect to x.

b Hence find $\int x\sin x\ \mathrm{d}x$.

13 a Given that $y = \mathrm{e}^{2x}(\sin 2x + \cos 2x)$, show that $\frac{\mathrm{d}y}{\mathrm{d}x} = 4\mathrm{e}^{2x}\cos 2x$.

b Hence find $\int \mathrm{e}^{2x}\cos 2x\ \mathrm{d}x$.

CHALLENGE Q

14 a Find $\frac{\mathrm{d}}{\mathrm{d}x}\left(x^2\sqrt{2x-7}\right)$.

b Hence find $\int \frac{5x^2 - 14x + 3}{\sqrt{2x-7}}\ \mathrm{d}x$.

15.8 Definite integration

You have learnt about indefinite integrals such as

$$\int x^2\ \mathrm{d}x = \frac{1}{3}x^3 + c$$

where c is an arbitrary constant.

$\int x^2\ \mathrm{d}x$ is called the **indefinite integral** of x^2 with respect to x.

It is called 'indefinite' because it has infinitely many solutions.

You can integrate a function between two defined limits.

The integral of the function x^2 with respect to x between the limits $x = 1$ and $x = 4$ is written as: $\int_1^4 x^2\ \mathrm{d}x$

The method for evaluating this integral is

$$\int_1^4 x^2\ \mathrm{d}x = \left[\frac{1}{3}x^3 + c\right]_1^4$$

$$= \left(\frac{1}{3}\times 4^3 + c\right) - \left(\frac{1}{3}\times 1^3 + c\right)$$

$$= 21$$

Note that the c's cancel out, so the process can be simplified to:

$$\int_1^4 x^2\ \mathrm{d}x = \left[\frac{1}{3}x^3\right]_1^4$$

$$= \left(\frac{1}{3}\times 4^3\right) - \left(\frac{1}{3}\times 1^3\right)$$

$$= 21$$

$\int_1^4 x^2\ \mathrm{d}x$ is called the **definite integral** of x^2 with respect to x.

It is called 'definite' because there is only one solution.

Hence, the evaluation of a definite integral can be written as:

$$\int_a^b \mathrm{f}(x)\ \mathrm{d}x = \left[\mathrm{F}(x)\right]_a^b = \mathrm{F}(b) - \mathrm{F}(a)$$

The following rules for definite integrals may also be used.

$$\int_a^b k\mathrm{f}(x)\,\mathrm{d}x = k\int_a^b \mathrm{f}(x)\,\mathrm{d}x, \text{ where } k \text{ is a constant}$$

$$\int_a^b \left[\mathrm{f}(x) \pm \mathrm{g}(x)\right]\mathrm{d}x = \int_a^b \mathrm{f}(x)\,\mathrm{d}x \pm \int_a^b \mathrm{g}(x)\,\mathrm{d}x$$

WORKED EXAMPLE 13

Evaluate: **a** $\displaystyle\int_1^2 \frac{x^5+3}{x^2}\,\mathrm{d}x$ **b** $\displaystyle\int_0^5 \sqrt{3x+1}\,\mathrm{d}x$ **c** $\displaystyle\int_{-1}^1 \frac{10}{(3-2x)^2}\,\mathrm{d}x$

Answers

a $\displaystyle\int_1^2 \frac{x^5+3}{x^2}\,\mathrm{d}x = \int_1^2 \left(x^3+3x^{-2}\right)\mathrm{d}x$

$$= \left[\frac{1}{4}x^4 + \frac{3}{-1}x^{-1}\right]_1^2$$

$$= \left(\frac{1}{4}(2)^4 - 3(2)^{-1}\right) - \left(\frac{1}{4}(1)^4 - 3(1)^{-1}\right)$$

$$= \left(4 - \frac{3}{2}\right) - \left(\frac{1}{4} - 3\right)$$

$$= 5\frac{1}{4}$$

b $\displaystyle\int_0^5 \sqrt{3x+1}\,\mathrm{d}x = \int_0^5 (3x+1)^{\frac{1}{2}}\,\mathrm{d}x$

$$= \left[\frac{1}{(3)\left(\frac{3}{2}\right)}(3x+1)^{\frac{3}{2}}\right]_0^5$$

$$= \left[\frac{2}{9}(3x+1)^{\frac{3}{2}}\right]_0^5$$

$$= \left(\frac{2}{9} \times 16^{\frac{3}{2}}\right) - \left(\frac{2}{9} \times 1^{\frac{3}{2}}\right)$$

$$= \left(\frac{128}{9}\right) - \left(\frac{2}{9}\right)$$

$$= 14$$

c $\displaystyle\int_{-1}^1 \frac{10}{(3-2x)^2}\,\mathrm{d}x = \int_{-1}^1 10(3-2x)^{-2}\,\mathrm{d}x$

$$= \left[\frac{10}{(-2)(-1)}(3-2x)^{-1}\right]_{-1}^1$$

$$= \left[\frac{5}{3-2x}\right]_{-1}^1$$

$$= \left(\frac{5}{1}\right) - \left(\frac{5}{5}\right)$$

$$= 4$$

WORKED EXAMPLE 14

Evaluate:

a $\int_1^2 4e^{2x-3}\,dx$ **b** $\int_0^{\frac{\pi}{4}} (3\cos 2x + 5)\,dx$

Answers

a $\int_1^2 4e^{2x-3}\,dx = \left[\frac{4}{2}e^{2x-3}\right]_1^2$

$= (2e^1) - (2e^{-1})$

$= 2e - \frac{2}{e}$

$= \frac{2e^2 - 2}{e}$

b $\int_0^{\frac{\pi}{4}} (5 + 3\cos 2x)\,dx = \left[5x + \frac{3}{2}\sin 2x\right]_0^{\frac{\pi}{4}}$

$= \left(\frac{5\pi}{4} + \frac{3}{2}\sin\frac{\pi}{2}\right) - \left(0 + \frac{3}{2}\sin 0\right)$

$= \left(\frac{5\pi}{4} + \frac{3}{2}\right) - (0 + 0)$

$= \frac{5\pi + 6}{4}$

In Section 15.10 you will learn why the modulus signs are included in the following integration formulae:

$$\int \frac{1}{x}\,dx = \ln|x| + c \qquad \int \frac{1}{ax+b}\,dx = \frac{1}{a}\ln|ax+b| + c$$

Note: It is normal practice to only include the modulus sign when finding definite integrals.

The next two worked examples show how these formulae are used in definite integrals.

WORKED EXAMPLE 15

Find the value of $\int_2^3 \frac{8}{2x+1}\,dx$.

Answers

$\int_2^3 \frac{8}{2x+1}\,dx = \left[\frac{8}{2}\ln|2x+1|\right]_2^3$ substitute limits

$= (4\ln|7|) - (4\ln|5|)$ simplify

$= 4(\ln 7 - \ln 5)$

$= 4\ln\frac{7}{5}$

WORKED EXAMPLE 16

Find the value of $\int_3^5 \frac{9}{2-3x}\,dx$.

Answers

$$\int_3^5 \frac{9}{2-3x}\,dx = \left[\frac{9}{-3}\ln|2-3x|\right]_3^5 \qquad \text{substitute limits}$$
$$= (-3\ln|-13|) - (-3\ln|-7|) \qquad \text{simplify}$$
$$= -3\ln 13 + 3\ln 7$$
$$= 3(\ln 7 - \ln 13)$$
$$= 3\ln\frac{7}{13}$$

Exercise 15.8

1 Evaluate.

a $\int_1^2 7x^6\,dx$ **b** $\int_1^2 \frac{4}{x^3}\,dx$ **c** $\int_1^3 (5x+2)\,dx$

d $\int_0^3 (x^2+2)\,dx$ **e** $\int_{-1}^2 (5x^2-3x)\,dx$ **f** $\int_1^4 \left(2+\frac{2}{x^2}\right)dx$

g $\int_2^4 \left(x^2-3-\frac{1}{x^2}\right)dx$ **h** $\int_1^3 \left(\frac{2x^2-1}{x^5}\right)dx$ **i** $\int_{-3}^{-2} (2x-1)(3x-5)\,dx$

j $\int_1^4 \sqrt{x}(x+3)\,dx$ **k** $\int_1^2 \frac{(5-x)(2+x)}{x^4}\,dx$ **l** $\int_1^4 \left(2\sqrt{x}-\frac{2}{\sqrt{x}}\right)dx$

2 Evaluate.

a $\int_1^2 (2x+1)^3\,dx$ **b** $\int_0^6 \sqrt{2x+4}\,dx$ **c** $\int_0^3 \sqrt{(x+1)^3}\,dx$

d $\int_{-1}^2 \frac{12}{(x+4)^3}\,dx$ **e** $\int_{-1}^1 \frac{2}{(3x+5)^2}\,dx$ **f** $\int_{-4}^0 \frac{6}{\sqrt{4-3x}}\,dx$

3 Evaluate.

a $\int_0^1 e^{2x}\,dx$ **b** $\int_0^{\frac{1}{4}} e^{4x}\,dx$ **c** $\int_0^2 5e^{-2x}\,dx$

d $\int_0^{\frac{1}{3}} e^{1-3x}\,dx$ **e** $\int_0^1 \frac{5}{e^{2x-1}}\,dx$ **f** $\int_0^1 (e^x+1)^2\,dx$

g $\int_0^1 (e^x+e^{2x})^2\,dx$ **h** $\int_0^1 \left(3e^x-\frac{2}{e^x}\right)^2 dx$ **i** $\int_0^2 \frac{3+8e^{2x}}{2e^x}\,dx$

381

4 Evaluate.

a $\int_0^{\pi} \sin x \, dx$ **b** $\int_0^{\frac{\pi}{2}} (3 + \cos 2x) \, dx$ **c** $\int_0^{\frac{\pi}{3}} \sin\left(2x - \frac{\pi}{6}\right) dx$

d $\int_{\frac{\pi}{6}}^{\frac{\pi}{3}} (2\cos x - \sin 2x) \, dx$ **e** $\int_0^{\frac{\pi}{4}} (2x - \sin 2x) \, dx$ **f** $\int_{\frac{\pi}{4}}^{\frac{\pi}{2}} (\sin 3x - \cos 2x) \, dx$

5 Evaluate.

a $\int_1^5 \frac{2}{3x+1} \, dx$ **b** $\int_{-1}^4 \frac{1}{2x+3} \, dx$ **c** $\int_2^8 \frac{3}{2x-1} \, dx$

d $\int_{-2}^{-1} \frac{5}{2x+1} \, dx$ **e** $\int_1^4 \frac{2}{1-3x} \, dx$ **f** $\int_{-3}^{-2} \frac{4}{3-2x} \, dx$

6 Evaluate.

a $\int_2^4 \left(1 + \frac{2}{3x-1}\right)$ **b** $\int_1^3 \left(\frac{2}{x} - \frac{1}{2x+1}\right) dx$ **c** $\int_0^1 \left(3 + \frac{1}{5-2x} - 2x\right) dx$

7 Given that $\int_1^k \frac{2}{3x-1} \, dx = \frac{2}{3}\ln 7$, find the value of k.

8 **a** Given that $\frac{4x}{2x+3} = 2 + \frac{A}{2x+3}$, find the value of the constant A.

b Hence show that $\int_0^1 \frac{4x}{2x+3} \, dx = 2 - 3\ln\frac{5}{3}$.

9 **a** Find the quotient and remainder when $4x^2 + 4x$ is divided by $2x + 1$.

b Hence show that $\int_0^1 \frac{4x^2 + 4x}{2x+1} \, dx = 2 - \frac{1}{2}\ln 3$.

CHALLENGE Q

10 Find the value of $\int_1^2 \frac{6x^2 - 8x}{2x-1} \, dx$.

15.9 Further definite integration

This section uses the concept that integration is the reverse process of differentiation to help evaluate complicated definite integrals.

WORKED EXAMPLE 17

Given that $y = \dfrac{3x}{\sqrt{x^2+5}}$, find $\dfrac{dy}{dx}$.

Hence evaluate $\displaystyle\int_0^2 \frac{3}{\sqrt{(x^2+5)^3}}\,dx$.

Answers

$$y = \frac{3x}{\sqrt{x^2+5}}$$

$$\frac{dy}{dx} = \frac{\left(\sqrt{x^2+5}\right)(3) - (3x)\left[\frac{1}{2}(x^2+5)^{-\frac{1}{2}}(2x)\right]}{x^2+5}$$ quotient rule

$$= \frac{3\sqrt{x^2+5} - \dfrac{3x^2}{\sqrt{x^2+5}}}{x^2+5}$$ multiply numerator and denominator by $\sqrt{x^2+5}$

$$= \frac{3(x^2+5) - 3x^2}{(x^2+5)\sqrt{x^2+5}}$$

$$= \frac{15}{\sqrt{(x^2+5)^3}}$$

$$\int_0^2 \frac{3}{\sqrt{(x^2+5)^3}}\,dx = \frac{1}{5}\int_0^2 \frac{15}{\sqrt{(x^2+5)^3}}\,dx$$

$$= \frac{1}{5}\left[\frac{3x}{\sqrt{x^2+5}}\right]_0^2$$

$$= \frac{1}{5}\left[\left(\frac{6}{\sqrt{4+5}}\right) - \left(\frac{0}{\sqrt{0+5}}\right)\right]$$

$$= \frac{2}{5}$$

WORKED EXAMPLE 18

Given that $y = x\cos 2x$, find $\dfrac{dy}{dx}$.

Hence evaluate $\displaystyle\int_0^{\frac{\pi}{6}} 2x\sin 2x\,dx$.

Answers

Let $y = x\cos 2x$

$$\frac{dy}{dx} = (x)\times(-2\sin 2x) + (\cos 2x)\times(1) \qquad \text{product rule}$$

$$= \cos 2x - 2x\sin 2x$$

$$\int_0^{\frac{\pi}{6}} (\cos 2x - 2x\sin 2x)\,dx = [x\cos 2x]_0^{\frac{\pi}{6}}$$

$$\int_0^{\frac{\pi}{6}} \cos 2x\,dx - \int_0^{\frac{\pi}{6}} 2x\sin 2x\,dx = \left(\frac{\pi}{6}\times\cos\frac{\pi}{3}\right) - (0\times\cos 0)$$

$$\left[\frac{1}{2}\sin 2x\right]_0^{\frac{\pi}{6}} - \int_0^{\frac{\pi}{6}} 2x\sin 2x\,dx = \frac{\pi}{12}$$

$$\int_0^{\frac{\pi}{6}} 2x\sin 2x\,dx = \left[\frac{1}{2}\sin 2x\right]_0^{\frac{\pi}{6}} - \frac{\pi}{12}$$

$$= \left(\frac{1}{2}\sin\frac{\pi}{3}\right) - \left(\frac{1}{2}\sin 0\right) - \frac{\pi}{12}$$

$$= \frac{\sqrt{3}}{4} - \frac{\pi}{12}$$

$$= \frac{3\sqrt{3} - \pi}{12}$$

Exercise 15.9

1 **a** Given that $y = (x+1)\sqrt{2x-1}$, find $\dfrac{dy}{dx}$.

b Hence evaluate $\displaystyle\int_1^5 \frac{x}{\sqrt{2x-1}}\,dx$.

2 **a** Given that $y = x\sqrt{3x^2+4}$, find $\dfrac{dy}{dx}$.

b Hence evaluate $\displaystyle\int_0^2 \frac{3x^2+2}{\sqrt{3x^2+4}}\,dx$.

3 **a** Given that $y = \dfrac{1}{x^2+5}$, find $\dfrac{dy}{dx}$.

b Hence evaluate $\displaystyle\int_1^2 \frac{4x}{(x^2+5)^2}\,dx$.

4 **a** Given that $y = \dfrac{x+2}{\sqrt{3x+4}}$, find $\dfrac{dy}{dx}$.

b Hence evaluate $\displaystyle\int_0^4 \frac{6x+4}{\sqrt{(3x+4)^3}}\,dx$.

5 **a** Show that $\dfrac{d}{dx}\left(\dfrac{x}{\cos x}\right) = \dfrac{\cos x + x\sin x}{\cos^2 x}$.

b Hence evaluate $\displaystyle\int_0^{\frac{\pi}{4}} \frac{\cos x + x\sin x}{5\cos^2 x}\,dx$.

CHALLENGE Q

6 **a** Find $\frac{d}{dx}(x \sin x)$. **b** Hence evaluate $\int_0^{\frac{\pi}{2}} x \cos x \, dx$.

CHALLENGE Q

7 **a** Find $\frac{d}{dx}(x^2 \ln x)$. **b** Hence evaluate $\int_1^{e} 4x \ln x \, dx$.

CHALLENGE Q

8 **a** Given that $y = x \sin 3x$, find $\frac{dy}{dx}$. **b** Hence evaluate $\int_0^{\frac{\pi}{6}} x \cos 3x \, dx$.

15.10 Area under a curve

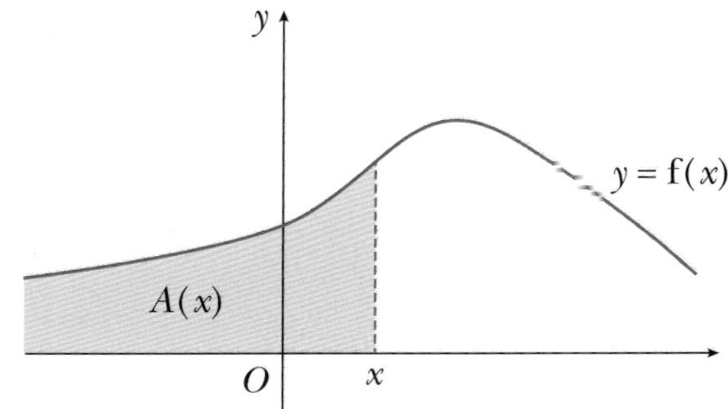

If you define the area under the curve $y = f(x)$ to the left of x as $A(x)$, then as x increases then $A(x)$ also increases.

Now consider a small increase in x, say δx, which results in a small increase, δA, in area.

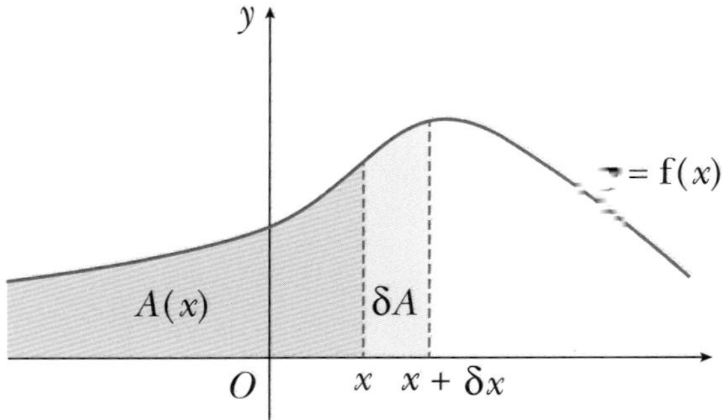

δA = area to the left of $(x + \delta x)$ – area to the left of x

$\delta A = A(x + \delta x) - A(x)$

Now consider the area δA which is approximately a rectangle.

$\delta A \approx y \delta x$

so $\frac{\delta A}{\delta x} \approx y$

y δA δx

As $\delta x \to 0$, then $\dfrac{\delta A}{\delta x} \to \dfrac{dA}{dx}$, hence $\dfrac{dA}{dx} = y$.

If $\dfrac{dA}{dx} = y$, then $A = \displaystyle\int y \, dx$.

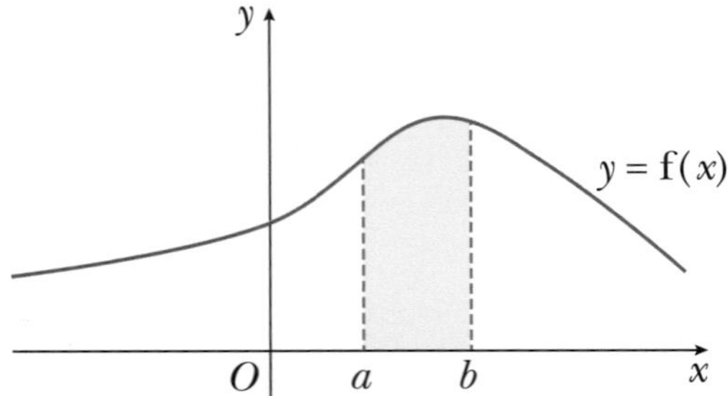

Hence the area of the region bounded by the curve $y = f(x)$, the lines $x = a$ and $x = b$ and the x-axis is given by the definite integral.

$$\text{Area} = \int_a^b f(x)\,dx, \text{ where } f(x) \geqslant 0$$

WORKED EXAMPLE 19

Find the area of the shaded region.

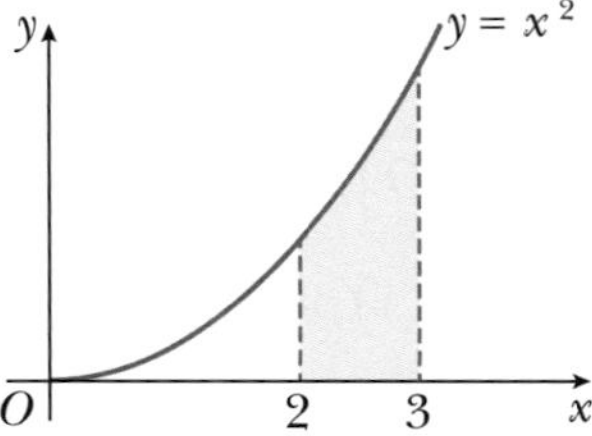

Answers

$$\text{Area} = \int_2^3 x^2\,dx$$

$$= \left[\frac{1}{3}x^3\right]_2^3$$

$$= \left(\frac{27}{3}\right) - \left(\frac{8}{3}\right)$$

$$= 6\frac{1}{3} \text{ units}^2$$

WORKED EXAMPLE 20

Find the area of the shaded region.

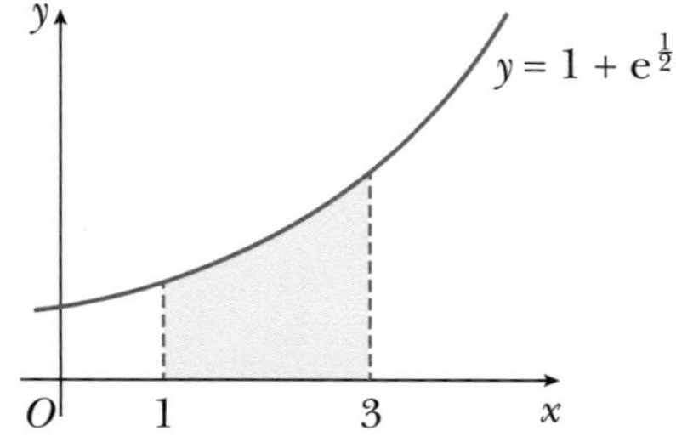

Answers

$$\text{Area} = \int_1^3 \left(1 + e^{\frac{1}{2}x}\right) dx$$

$$= \left[x + \frac{1}{\frac{1}{2}} e^{\frac{1}{2}x}\right]_1^3$$

$$= \left[x + 2e^{\frac{1}{2}x}\right]_1^3$$

$$= \left(3 + 2e^{\frac{3}{2}}\right) - \left(1 + 2e^{\frac{1}{2}}\right)$$

$$= 2 + 2e^{\frac{3}{2}} - 2e^{\frac{1}{2}}$$

$$= 2\left[1 + \sqrt{e}\,(e - 1)\right]$$

$$\approx 7.67 \text{ units}^2$$

In the examples so far, the required area has been above the x-axis.

If the required area between $y = f(x)$ and the x-axis lies below the x-axis, then $\int_a^b f(x)\,dx$ will be a negative value.

Hence, for a region that lies below the x-axis, the area is given as $\left|\int_a^b f(x)\,dx\right|$.

WORKED EXAMPLE 21

Find the area of the shaded region.

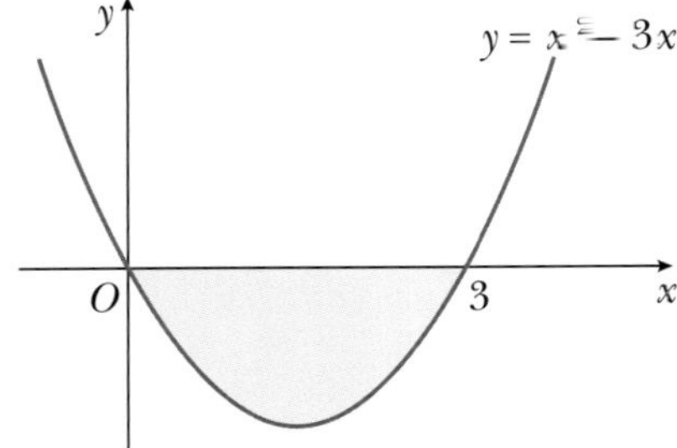

Answers

$$\int_0^3 (x^2 - 3x)\,dx = \left[\frac{1}{3}x^3 - \frac{3}{2}x^2\right]_0^3$$

$$= \left(9 - \frac{27}{2}\right) - (0 - 0)$$

$$= -4.5$$

Area is 4.5 units^2.

The required region could consist of a section above the x-axis and a section below the x-axis.

If this happens you must evaluate each area separately.

This is illustrated in the following example.

WORKED EXAMPLE 22

Find the total area of the shaded regions.

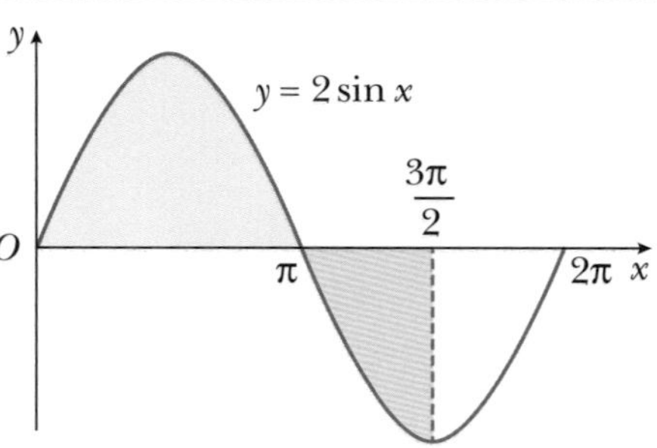

Answers

$$\int_0^{\pi} 2\sin x \, dx = [-2\cos x]_0^{\pi}$$
$$= (-2\cos\pi) - (-2\cos 0)$$
$$= (2) - (-2)$$
$$= 4$$

$$\int_{\pi}^{\frac{3\pi}{2}} 2\sin x \, dx = [-2\cos x]_{\pi}^{\frac{3\pi}{2}}$$
$$= \left(-2\cos\frac{3\pi}{2}\right) - (-2\cos\pi)$$
$$= (0) - (2)$$
$$= -2$$

Hence, the total area of the shaded regions = 4 + 2 = 6 units^2.

In Section 15.8 you were given the formula $\int \frac{1}{x} dx = \ln|x| + c$.

The use of the modus symbols in this formula can be explained by considering the symmetry properties of the graph of $y = \frac{1}{x}$.

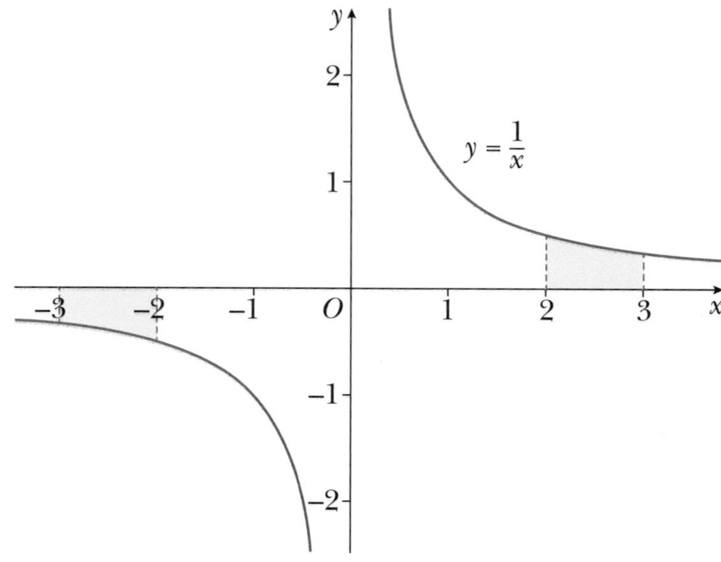

The shaded areas that represent the integrals $\int_2^3 \frac{1}{x}\,dx$ and $\int_{-3}^{-2} \frac{1}{x}\,dx$ are equal in magnitude.

However, one of the areas is below the x-axis, which suggests that $\int_{-3}^{-2} \frac{1}{x}\,dx = -\int_2^3 \frac{1}{x}\,dx$.

Evaluating $\int_2^3 \frac{1}{x}\,dx$ gives:

$$\int_2^3 \frac{1}{x}\,dx = [\ln x]_2^3 = \ln 3 - \ln 2 = \ln\frac{3}{2}$$

This implies that $\int_{-3}^{-2} \frac{1}{x}\,dx = -\ln\frac{3}{2} = \ln\frac{2}{3}$.

If you try using integration to find the value of $\int_{-3}^{-2} \frac{1}{x}\,dx$ you obtain

$$\int_{-3}^{-2} \frac{1}{x}\,dx = [\ln x]_{-3}^{-2} = \ln(-2) - \ln(-3) = \ln\frac{2}{3}$$

There is, however, a problem with this calculation in that $\ln x$ is only defined for $x > 0$ so $\ln(-2)$ and $\ln(-3)$ do not actually exist.

Hence for $x < 0$, we say that $\int \frac{1}{x}\,dx = \ln|x| + c$.

Exercise 15.10

1 Find the area of each shaded region.

a

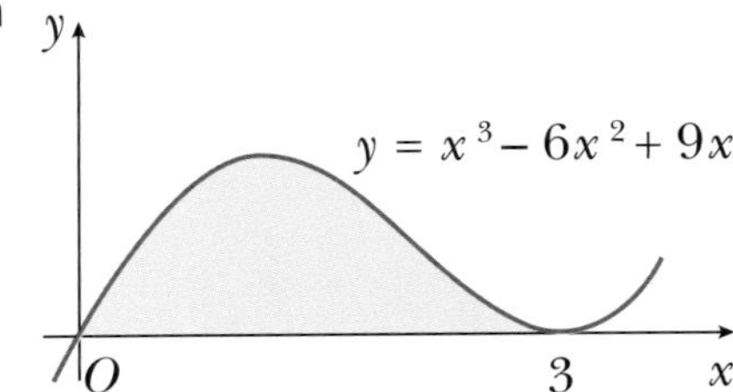

b

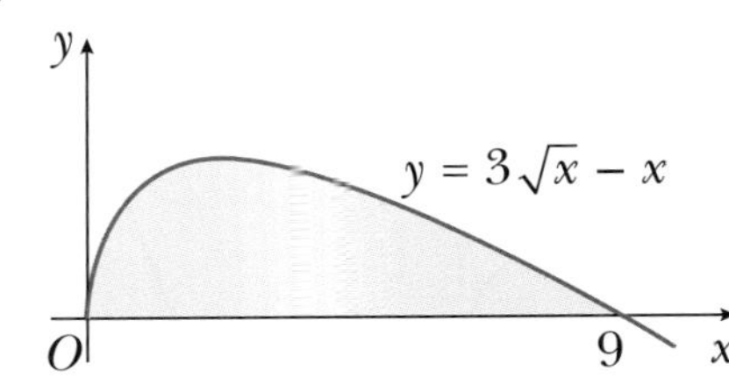

c

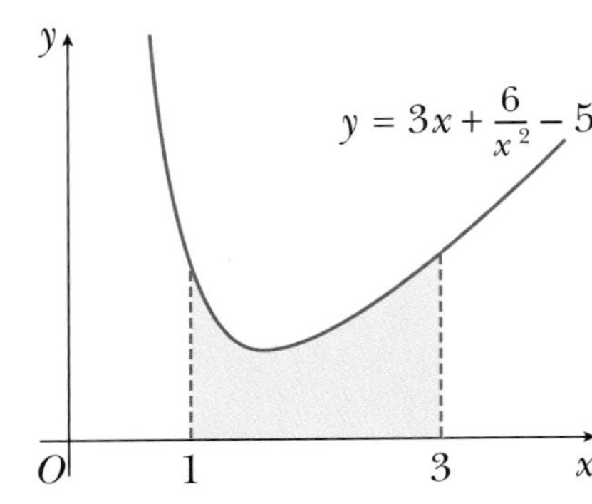

d

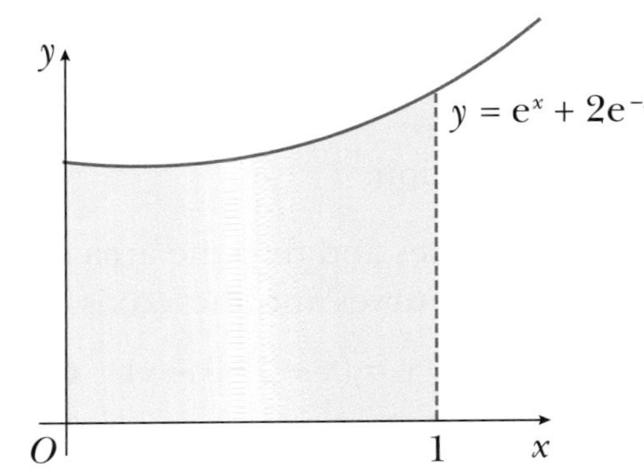

e

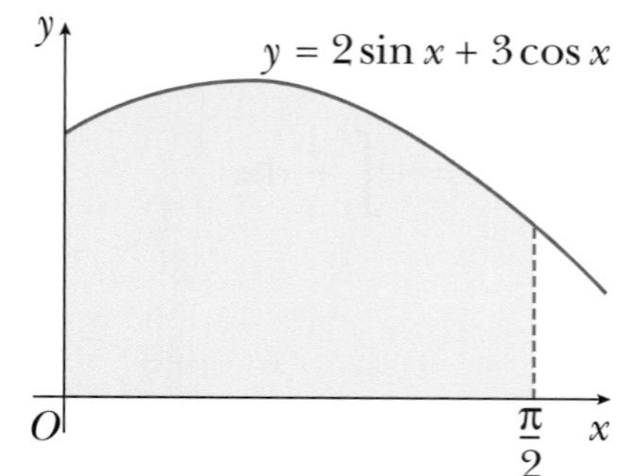

f

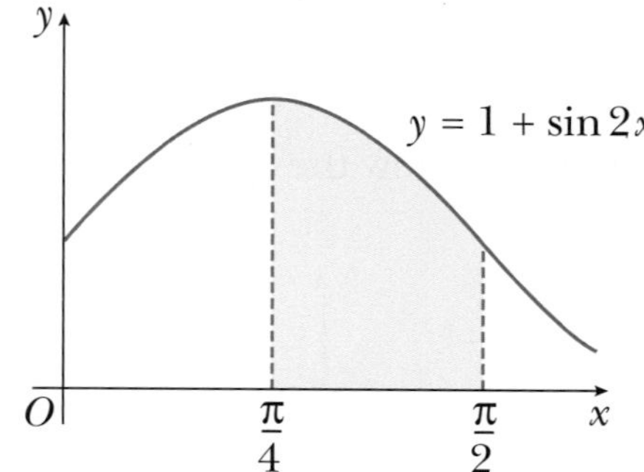

2 Find the area of each shaded region.

a

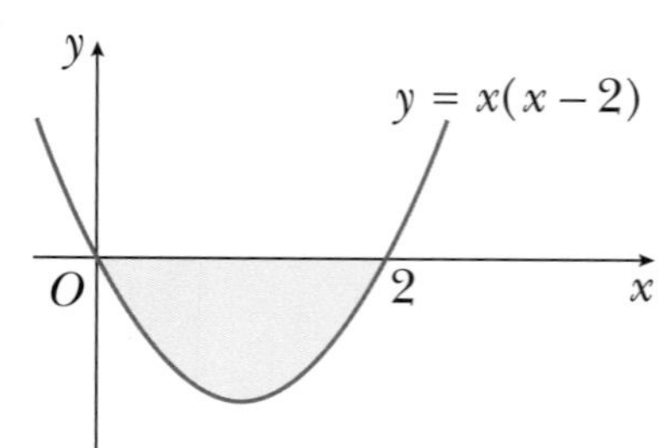

b

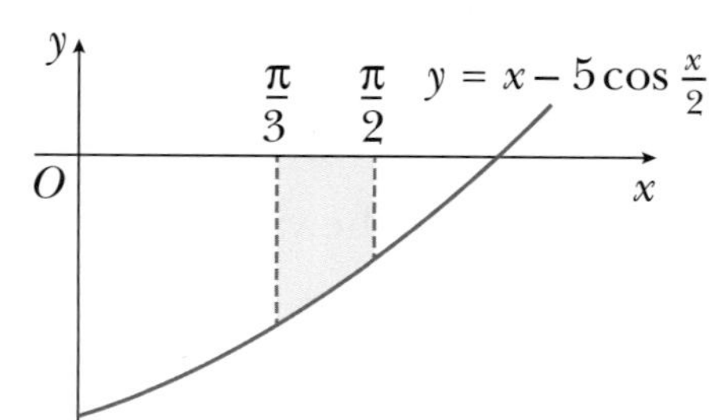

c

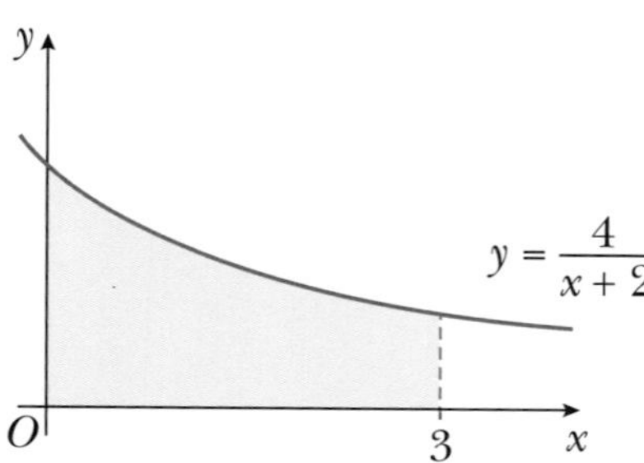

d

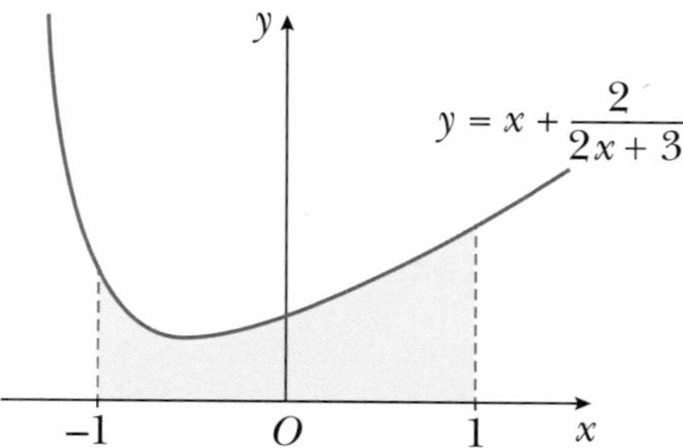

3

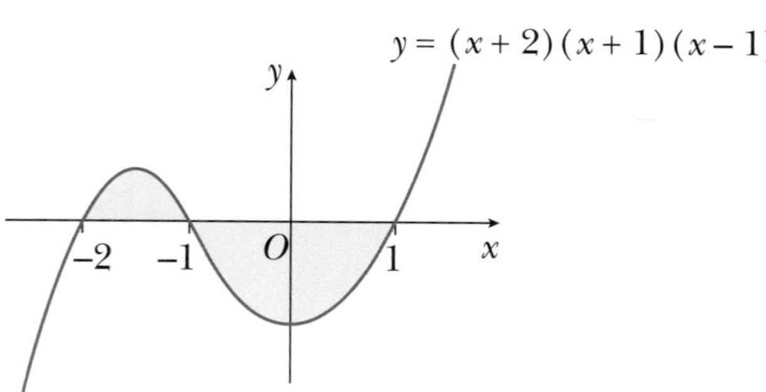

Find the total shaded region.

4 Sketch the following curves and find the area of the finite region or regions bounded by the curves and the x-axis.

a $y = x(x + 1)$ **b** $y = (x + 2)(3 - x)$ **c** $y = x(x^2 - 4)$

d $y = x(x - 2)(x + 4)$ **e** $y = x(x - 1)(x - 5)$ **f** $y = x^2(4 - x)$

5 Find the area enclosed by the curve $y = \frac{6}{\sqrt{x}}$, the x-axis and the lines $x = 4$ and $x = 9$.

6 **a** Find the area of the region enclosed by the curve $y = \frac{12}{x^2}$, the x-axis and the lines $x = 1$ and $x = 4$.

b The line $x = p$ divides the region in **part a** into two equal parts.

Find the value of p.

7 **a** Show that $\frac{d}{dx}\left(xe^x - e^x\right) = xe^x$.

b Use your result from **part a** to evaluate the area of the shaded region.

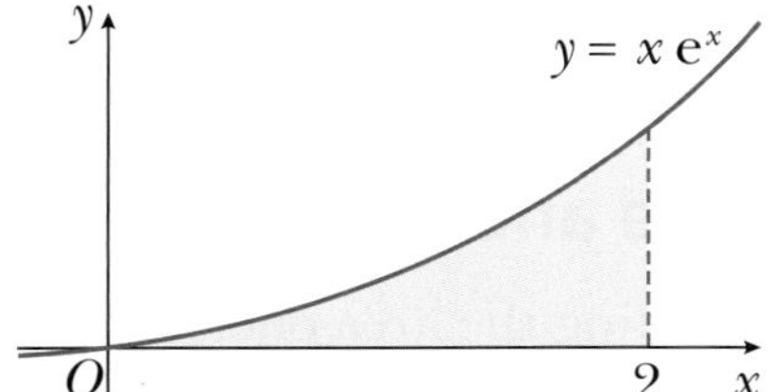

CHALLENGE Q

8

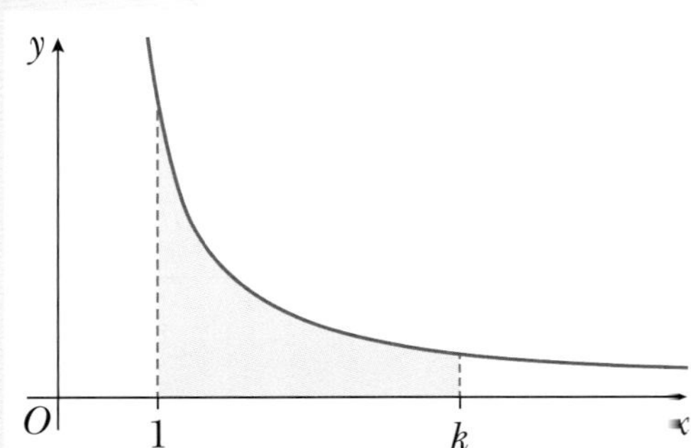

The diagram shows part of the curve $y = \frac{4}{2x-1}$. Given that the shaded region has area 8, find the exact value of k.

CHALLENGE Q

9 **a** Show that $\frac{d}{dx}(x \ln x) = 1 + \ln x$.

b Use your result from **part a** to evaluate the area of the shaded region.

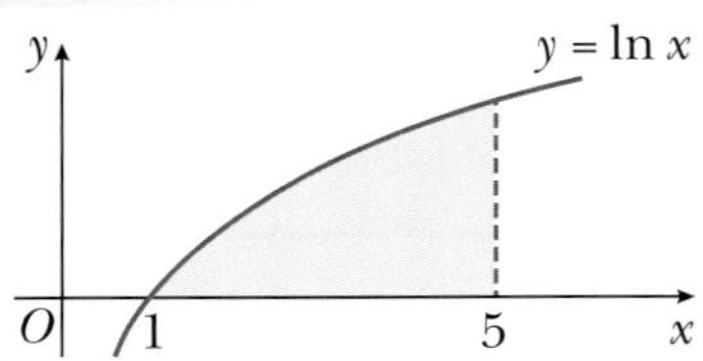

CHALLENGE Q

10 a Show that $\frac{d}{dx}(x\cos x) = \cos x - x\sin x$.

b Use your result from **part a** to evaluate the area of the shaded region.

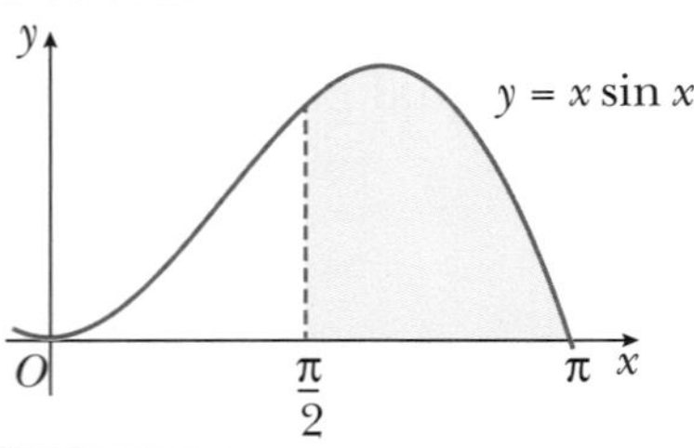

15.11 Area of regions bounded by a line and a curve

The following example shows a possible method for finding the area enclosed by a curve and a straight line.

WORKED EXAMPLE 23

The curve $y = 2\sqrt{x}$ intersects the line $y = x$ at the point (4, 4). Find the area of the shaded region bounded by the curve and the line.

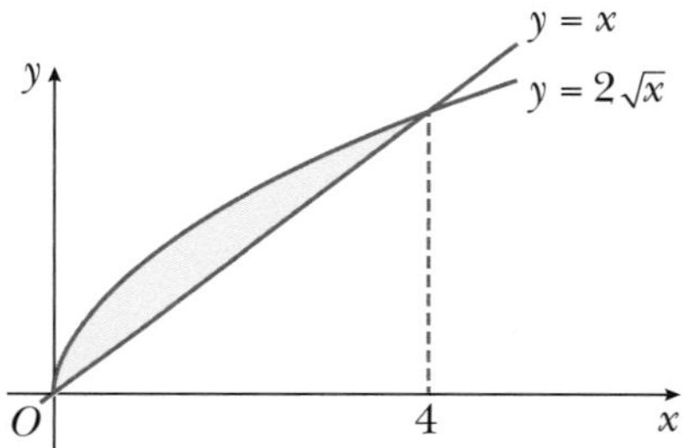

Answers

Area = area under curve − area of triangle

$$= \int_0^4 2\sqrt{x}\, dx - \frac{1}{2} \times 4 \times 4$$

$$= \int_0^4 2x^{\frac{1}{2}}\, dx - 8$$

$$= \left[\frac{2}{\frac{3}{2}} x^{\frac{3}{2}}\right]_0^4 - 8$$

$$= \left(\frac{4}{3} \times 4^{\frac{3}{2}}\right) - \left(\frac{4}{3} \times 0^{\frac{3}{2}}\right) - 8$$

$$= 2\frac{2}{3}\ \text{units}^2$$

There is an alternative method for finding the shaded area in the previous example.

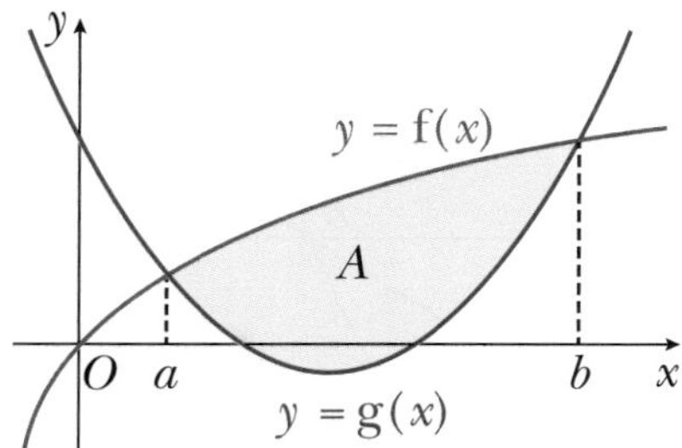

If two functions f(x) and g(x) intersect at $x = a$ and $x = b$, then the area, A, enclosed between the two curves is given by:

$$A = \int_a^b f(x)\,dx - \int_a^b g(x)\,dx$$

So for the area enclosed by $y = 2\sqrt{x}$ and $y = x$:

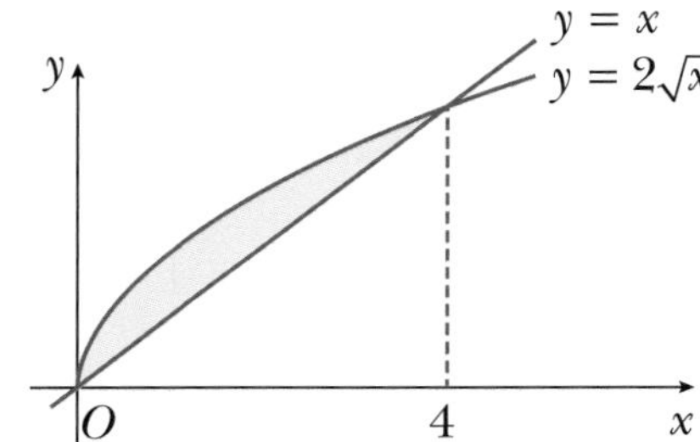

using $f(x) = 2\sqrt{x}$ and $g(x) = x$

$$\begin{aligned}
\text{area} &= \int_0^4 f(x)\,dx - \int_0^4 g(x)\,dx \\
&= \int_0^4 2\sqrt{x}\,dx - \int_0^4 x\,dx \\
&= \int_0^4 \left(2\sqrt{x} - x\right) dx \\
&= \left[\frac{2}{\frac{3}{2}}x^{\frac{3}{2}} - \frac{1}{2}x^2\right]_0^4 \\
&= \left(\frac{4}{3} \times 4^{\frac{3}{2}} - \frac{1}{2} \times 4^2\right) - \left(\frac{4}{3} \times 0^{\frac{3}{2}} - \frac{1}{2} \times 0^2\right) \\
&= 2\frac{2}{3} \text{ units}^2
\end{aligned}$$

This alternative method is the easiest method to use in this next example.

WORKED EXAMPLE 24

The curve $y = x^2 - 4$ intersects the x-axis at the points A and B and intersects the line $y = x - 2$ at the points B and C.

a Find the coordinates of A, B and C.

b Find the area of the shaded region bounded by the curve and the line.

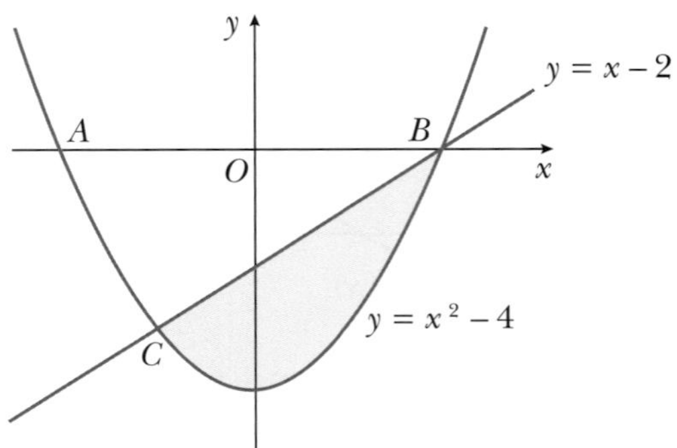

Answers

a When $y = 0$, $x^2 - 4 = 0$

$$x = \pm 2$$

A is the point $(-2, 0)$ and B is the point $(2, 0)$

For intersection of curve and line:

$$x^2 - 4 = x - 2$$

$$x^2 - x - 2 = 0$$

$$(x + 1)(x - 2) = 0$$

$$x = -1 \text{ or } x = 2$$

When $x = -1$, $y = -3$

C is the point $(-1, -3)$

b Area $= \int_{-1}^{2} (x - 2)\,dx - \int_{-1}^{2} (x^2 - 4)\,dx$

$$= \int_{-1}^{2} (x - 2 - x^2 + 4)\,dx = \int_{-1}^{2} (x + 2 - x^2)\,dx$$

$$= \left[\frac{1}{2}x^2 + 2x - \frac{1}{3}x^3\right]_{-1}^{2}$$

$$= \left(2 + 4 - \frac{8}{3}\right) - \left(\frac{1}{2} - 2 + \frac{1}{3}\right)$$

$$= 4.5 \text{ units}^2$$

CLASS DISCUSSION

Discuss with your classmates how you could find the shaded area, A, enclosed by the curve $y = x(8 - x)$ the line $y = 3x$ and the x-axis.

Can you find more than one method?

Calculate the area using each of your different methods.

Discuss with your classmates which method you preferred.

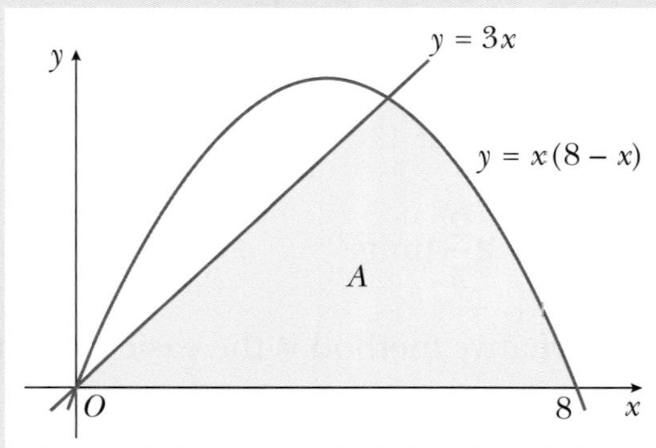

Exercise 15.11

1 Find the area of the region enclosed by the curve $y = 1 + \cos x$ and the line $y = 1$.

2 Find the area of the region bounded by the curve $y = 2 + 3x - x^2$, the line $x = 2$ and the line $y = 2$.

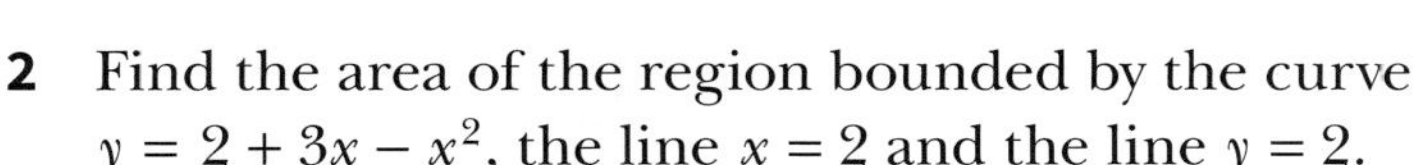

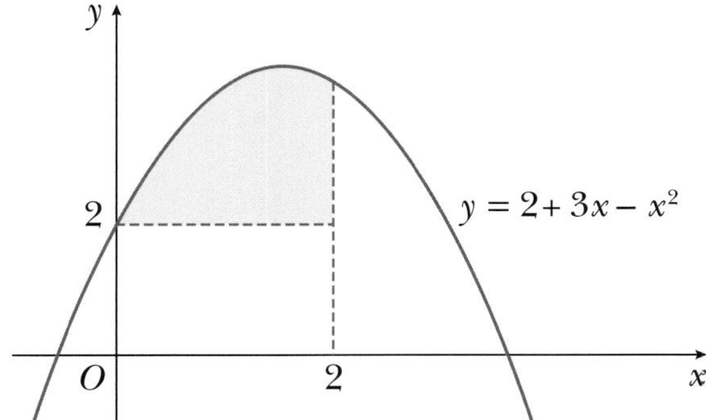

3 Find the area of the region bounded by the curve $y = 3x^2 + 2$, the line $y = 14$ and the y-axis.

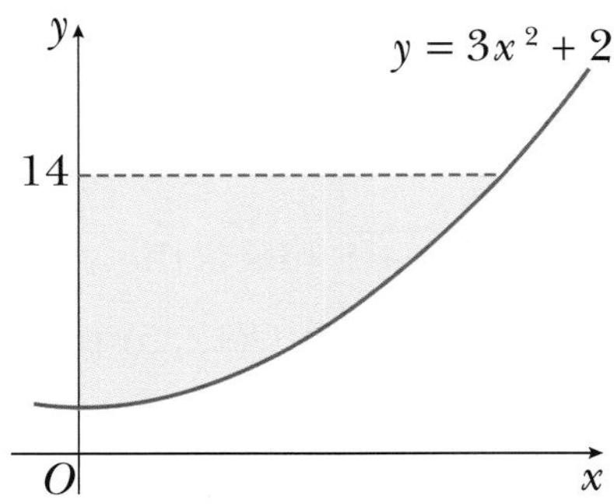

4 Find the area of the shaded region.

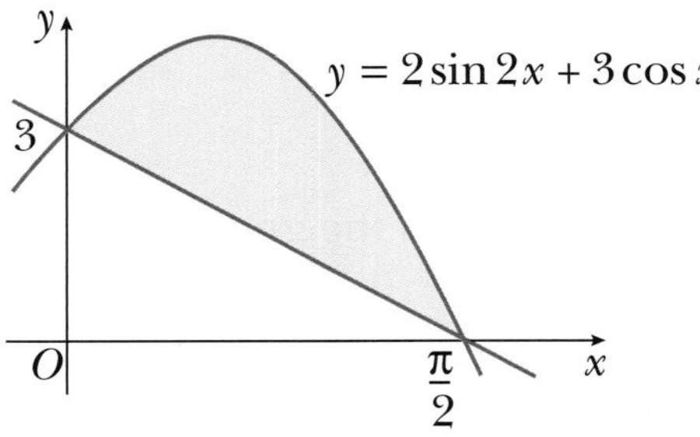

5 Sketch the following curves and lines and find the area enclosed between their graphs.

a $y = x^2 + 1$ and $y = 5$

b $y = x^2 - 2x + 3$ and $x + y = 9$

c $y = \sqrt{x}$ and $y = \frac{1}{2}x$

d $y = 4x - x^2$ and $2x + y = 0$

e $y = (x - 1)(x - 5)$ and $y = x - 1$

6 Sketch the following pairs of curves and find the area enclosed between their graphs for $x \geqslant 0$.

a $y = x^2$ and $y = x(2 - x)$

b $y = x^3$ and $y = 4x - 3x^2$

7 Find the shaded area enclosed by the curve $y = 3\sqrt{x}$ the line $y = 10 - x$ and the x-axis.

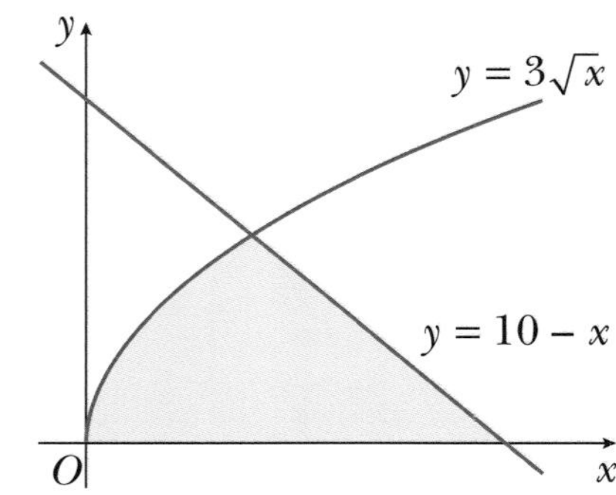

8 The tangent to the curve $y = 6x - x^2$ at the point (2, 8) cuts the x-axis at the point P.

a Find the coordinates of P.

b Find the area of the shaded region.

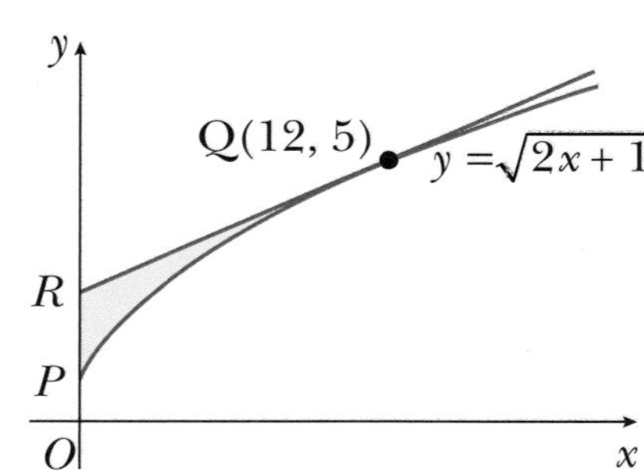

9 The curve $y = \sqrt{2x + 1}$ meets the y-axis at the point P.

The tangent at the point $Q(12, 5)$ to this curve meets the y-axis at the point R.

Find the area of the shaded region PQR.

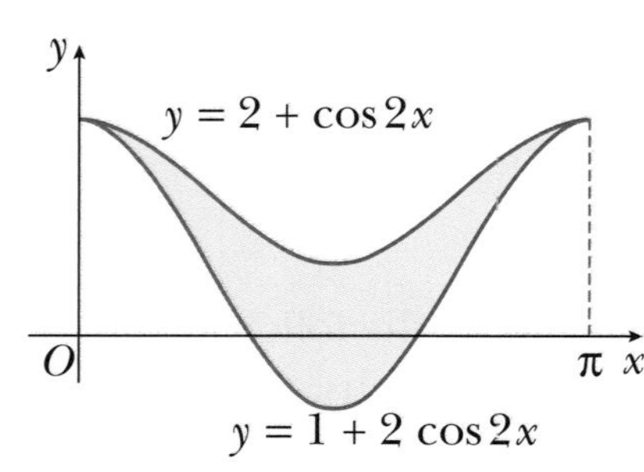

10 The diagram shows the graphs of $y = 2 + \cos 2x$ and $y = 1 + 2\cos 2x$ for $0 \leqslant x \leqslant \pi$.

Find the area of the shaded region.

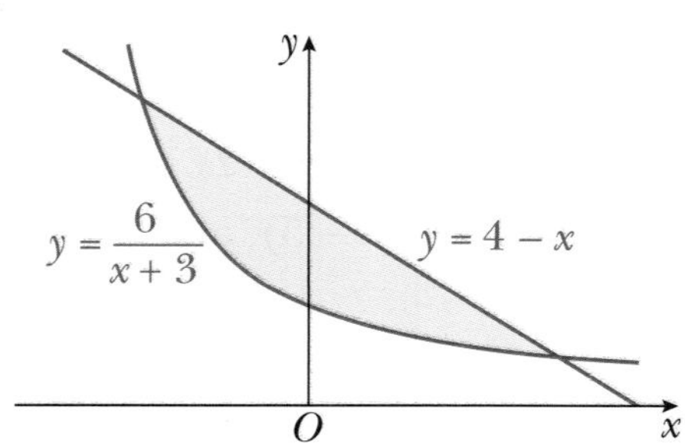

CHALLENGE Q

11 The diagram shows the graphs of $y = \dfrac{6}{x + 3}$ and $y = 4 - x$.

Find the area of the shaded region.

Summary

Integration as the reverse of differentiation

If $\frac{d}{dx}\left[F(x)\right] = f(x)$, then $\int f(x)\ dx = F(x) + c$.

Integration formulae

$$\int x^n\ dx = \frac{1}{n+1}x^{n+1} + c, \text{ where } c \text{ is a constant and } n \neq -1$$

$$\int (ax+b)^n\ dx = \frac{1}{a(n+1)}(ax+b)^{n+1} + c,\ n \neq -1 \text{ and } a \neq 0$$

$$\int e^x\ dx = e^x + c \qquad \int e^{ax+b}\ dx = \frac{1}{a}e^{ax+b} + c$$

$$\int \cos x\ dx = \sin x + c \qquad \int \left[\cos(ax+b)\right] dx = \frac{1}{a}\sin(ax+b) + c$$

$$\int \sin x\ dx = -\cos x + c \qquad \int \left[\sin(ax+b)\right] dx = -\frac{1}{a}\cos(ax+b) + c$$

$$\int \frac{1}{x} dx = \ln x + c,\ x > 0 \qquad \int \frac{1}{ax+b} dx = \frac{1}{a}\ln(ax+b) + c,\ ax+b > 0$$

$$\int \frac{1}{x} dx = \ln|x| + c \qquad \int \frac{1}{ax+b} dx = \frac{1}{a}\ln|ax+b| + c$$

Rules for indefinite integration

$$\int kf(x)\ dx = k\int f(x)\ dx, \text{ where } k \text{ is a constant}$$

$$\int \left[f(x) \pm g(x)\right] dx = \int f(x)\ dx \pm \int g(x)\ dx$$

Rules for definite integration

If $\int f(x)\ dx = F(x) + c$, then $\int_a^b f(x)\ dx = \left[F(x)\right]_a^b = F(b) - F(a)$.

$$\int_a^b kf(x)\ dx = k\int_a^b f(x)\ dx, \text{ where } k \text{ is a constant}$$

$$\int_a^b \left[f(x) \pm g(x)\right] dx = \int_a^b f(x)\ dx \pm \int_a^b g(x)\ dx$$

Area under a curve

The area, A, bounded by the curve $y = f(x)$, the x-axis and the lines $x = a$ and $x = b$ is given by the formula

$$A = \int_a^b f(x)\ dx \text{ if } f(x) \geqslant 0.$$

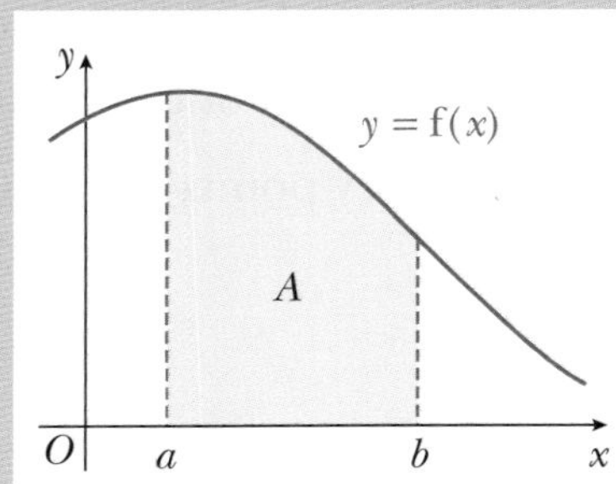

Area bounded by the graphs of two functions

If two functions f(x) and g(x) intersect at $x = a$ and $x = b$, then the area, A, enclosed between the two curves is given by the formula:

$$A = \int_a^b f(x)\,dx - \int_a^b g(x)\,dx.$$

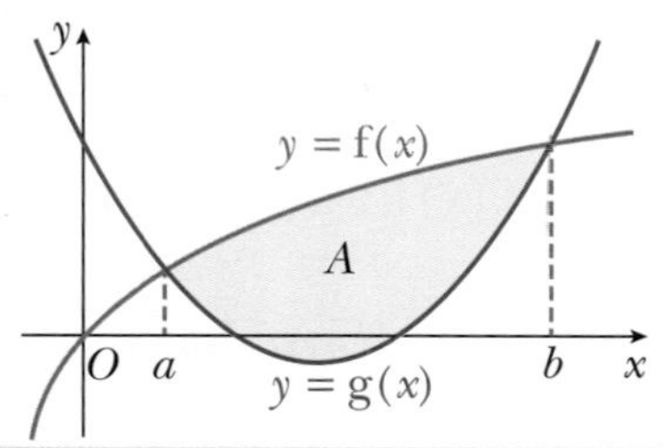

Examination questions

Worked example

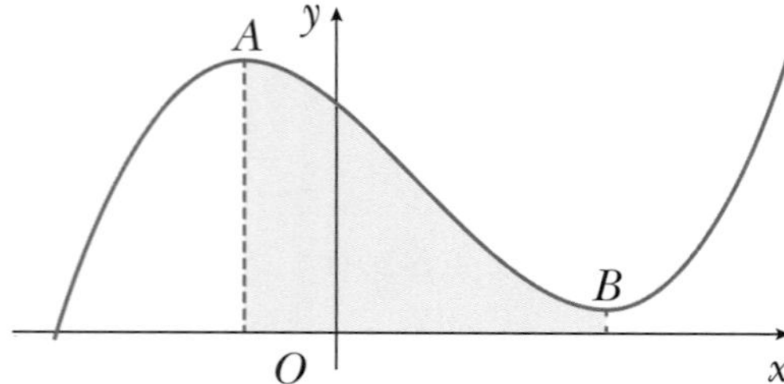

The diagram shows part of a curve such that $\frac{dy}{dx} = 3x^2 - 6x - 9$.

Points A and B are stationary points of the curve and lines from A and B are drawn perpendicular to the x-axis. Given that the curve passes through the point (0, 30), find

a the equation of the curve, [4]

b the x-coordinates of A and B, [3]

c the area of the shaded region. [4]

Cambridge IGCSE Additional Mathematics 0606 Paper 11 Q12(part) Nov 2012

Answers

a $\frac{dy}{dx} = 3x^2 - 6x - 9$

$y = x^3 - 3x^2 - 9x + c$

Using $x = 0$, $y = 30$ gives $c = 30$.

The equation of the curve is $y = x^3 - 3x^2 - 9x + 30$.

b Stationary points occur when $\frac{dy}{dx} = 0$

$$3x^2 - 6x - 9 = 0$$

$$x^2 - 2x - 3 = 0$$

$$(x + 1)(x - 3) = 0$$

$$x = -1 \text{ or } x = 3$$

The x-coordinate of A is -1 and the x-coordinate of B is 3.

c Area $= \int_{-1}^{3} y \, dx$

$$= \int_{-1}^{3} \left(x^3 - 3x^2 - 9x + 30\right) dx$$

$$= \left[\frac{x^4}{4} - x^3 - \frac{9x^2}{2} + 30x\right]_{-1}^{3}$$

$$= \left(\frac{(3)^4}{4} - (3)^3 - \frac{9(3)^2}{2} + 30(3)\right) - \left(\frac{(-1)^4}{4} - (-1)^3 - \frac{9(-1)^2}{2} + 30(-1)\right)$$

$$= 76$$

Area of shaded region is 76 units^2.

Exercise 15.12

Exam Exercise

1 **a** Given that $y = e^{x^2}$, find $\frac{dy}{dx}$. [2]

b Use your answer to part **a** to find $\int x e^{x^2} dx$. [2]

c Hence evaluate $\int_0^2 x e^{x^2} dx$. [2]

Cambridge IGCSE Additional Mathematics 0606 Paper 11 Q5i,ii,iii Jun 2014

2 A curve is such that $\frac{dy}{dx} = 4x + \frac{1}{(x+1)^2}$ for $x > 0$. The curve passes through the point $\left(\frac{1}{2}, \frac{5}{6}\right)$.

a Find the equation of the curve. [4]

b Find the equation of the normal to the curve at the point where $x = 1$. [4]

Cambridge IGCSE Additional Mathematics 0606 Paper 11 Q7i,ii Jun 2014

3 **a** Find $\int \left(1 - \frac{6}{x^2}\right) dx$. [2]

b Hence find the value of the positive constant k for which $\int_k^{3k} \left(1 - \frac{6}{x^2}\right) dx = 2$. [4]

Cambridge IGCSE Additional Mathematics 0606 Paper 11 Q5i,ii Jun 2013

4 The diagram shows part of the curve of $y = 9x^2 - x^3$, which meets the x-axis at the origin O and at the point A. The line $y - 2x + 18 = 0$ passes through A and meets the y-axis at the point B.

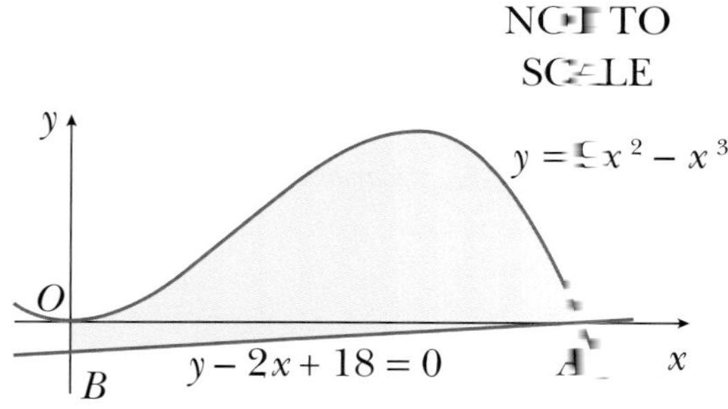

a Show that, for $x \geqslant 0$, $9x^2 - x^3 \leqslant 108$. [4]

b Find the area of the shaded region bounded by the curve, the line AB and the y-axis. [6]

Cambridge IGCSE Additional Mathematics 0606 Paper 11 Q11(part) Jun 2012

5 The diagram shows part of the curve $y = 2\sin 3x$. The normal to the curve $y = 2\sin 3x$ at the point where $x = \frac{\pi}{9}$ meets the y-axis at the point P.

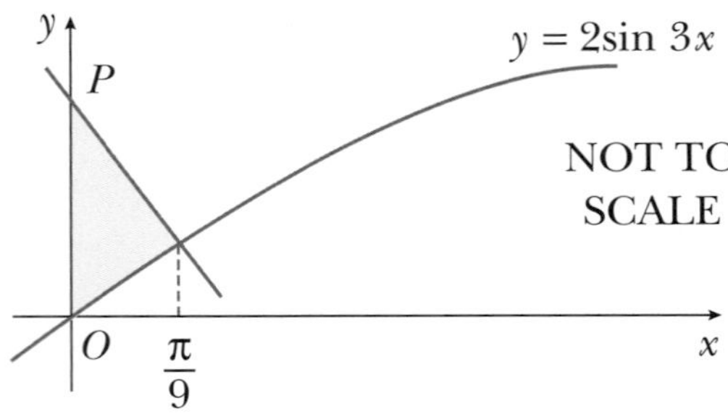

a Find the coordinates of P. [5]

b Find the area of the shaded region bounded by the curve, the normal and the y-axis. [5]

Cambridge IGCSE Additional Mathematics 0606 Paper 11 Q11(part) Jun 2012

6 Find the exact value of $\int_1^2 \left(5 + \frac{8}{4x - 3}\right) dx$, giving your answer in the form $\ln(ae^b)$, where a and b are integers. [5]

Examination style question

7 **a** Find the value of the constant A such that $\frac{6x - 5}{2x - 3} = 3 + \frac{A}{2x - 3}$. [2]

b Hence show that $\int_3^5 \frac{6x - 5}{2x - 3} dx = 6 + 2\ln\frac{7}{3}$. [5]

Examination style question

8 **a** Differentiate $4x^3\ln(2x + 1)$ with respect to x. [3]

b **i** Given that $y = \frac{2x}{\sqrt{x + 2}}$, show that $\frac{dy}{dx} = \frac{x + 4}{\left(\sqrt{x + 2}\right)^3}$. [4]

ii Hence find $\int \frac{5x + 20}{\left(\sqrt{x + 2}\right)^3} dx$. [2]

iii Hence evaluate $\int_2^7 \frac{5x + 20}{\left(\sqrt{x + 2}\right)^3} dx$. [2]

Cambridge IGCSE Additional Mathematics 0606 Paper 11 Q9 Nov 2013

9 **Do not use a calculator in this question.**

i Show that $\frac{d}{dx}\left(\frac{e^{4x}}{4} - xe^{4x}\right) = pxe^{4x}$, where p is an integer to be found. [4]

ii Hence find the exact value of $\int_0^{\ln 2} xe^{4x}\,dx$, giving your answer in the form $a\ln 2 + \frac{b}{c}$, where a, b and c are integers to be found. [4]

Cambridge IGCSE Additional Mathematics 0606 Paper 11 Q5 Jun 2016

10 **i** Find $\int \left(3x - x^{\frac{3}{2}}\right) dx$. [2]

The diagram shows part of the curve $y = 3x - x^{\frac{3}{2}}$ and the lines $y = 3x$ and $2y = 27 - 3x$. The curve and the line $y = 3x$ meet the x-axis at O and the curve and the line $2y = 27 - 3x$ meet the x-axis at A.

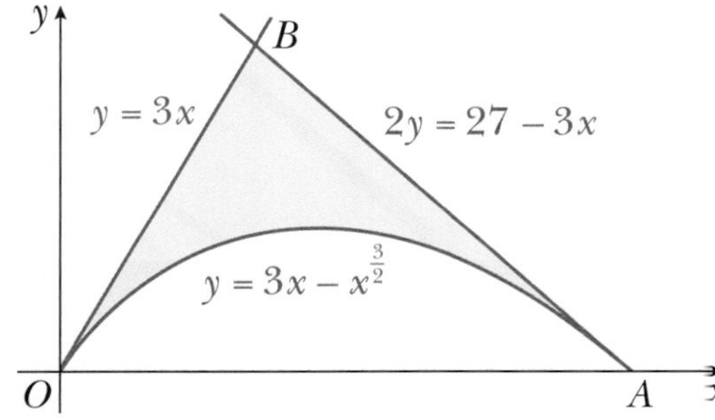

ii Find the coordinates of A. [1]

iii Verify that the coordinates of B are $(3, 9)$. [1]

iv Find the area of the shaded region. [4]

Cambridge IGCSE Additional Mathematics 0606 Paper 21 Q11 Jun 2016

Chapter 16
Kinematics

This section will show you how to:

- apply differentiation to kinematics problems that involve displacement, velocity and acceleration of a particle moving in a straight line with variable or constant acceleration, and the use of x-t and v-t graphs.

RECAP

You should already know about distance-time graphs and speed–time graphs.

Distance-time graphs can be used to find out how the distance changes with time.

- The gradient of a distance-time graph represents the speed.

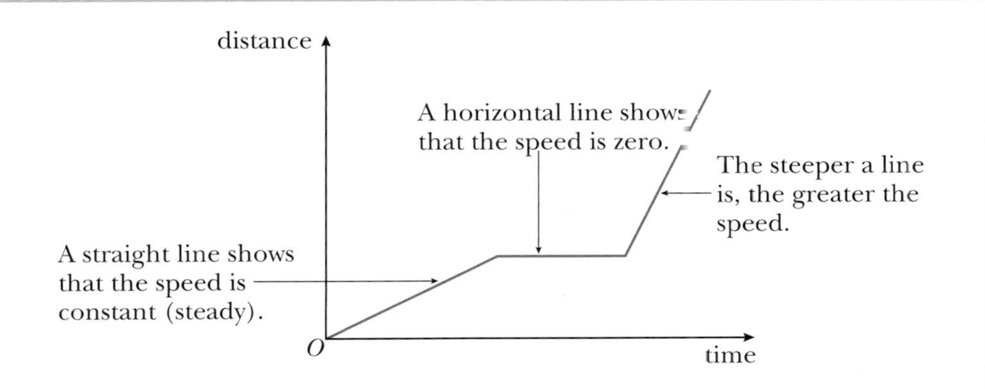

Speed-time graphs can be used to find out how the speed changes with time.

- The gradient of a speed-time graph represents the acceleration.
- The area under a speed-time graph represents the distance travelled.

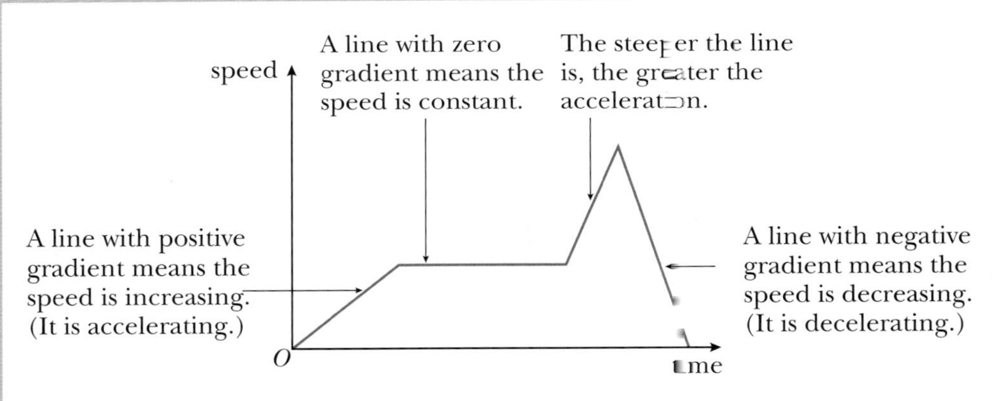

Distance and speed are examples of **scalar** quantities.
(Scalar quantities have magnitude but no direction.)

In this chapter you will learn about displacement, velocity and acceleration.

Displacement, velocity and acceleration are examples of **vector** quantities.
(Vector quantities have magnitude and direction.)

16.1 Applications of differentiation in kinematics

Displacement

Consider a particle, P, travelling along a straight line such that its displacement, s metres, from a fixed point O, t seconds after passing through O, is given by $s = 4t - t^2$.

The graph of s against t for $0 \leqslant t \leqslant 5$ is:

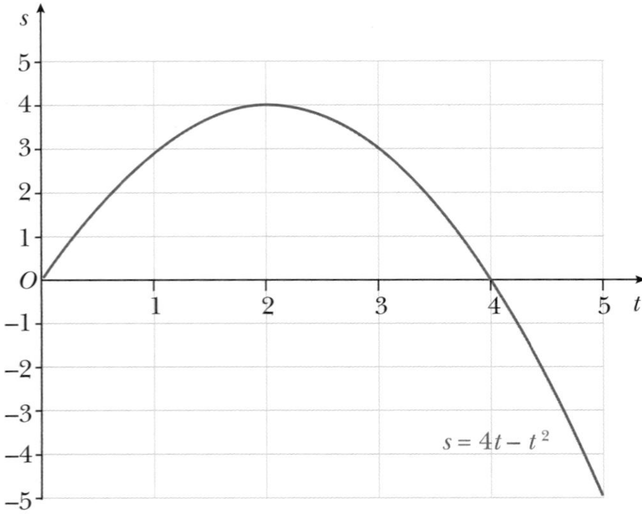

404

This can be represented on a motion diagram as:

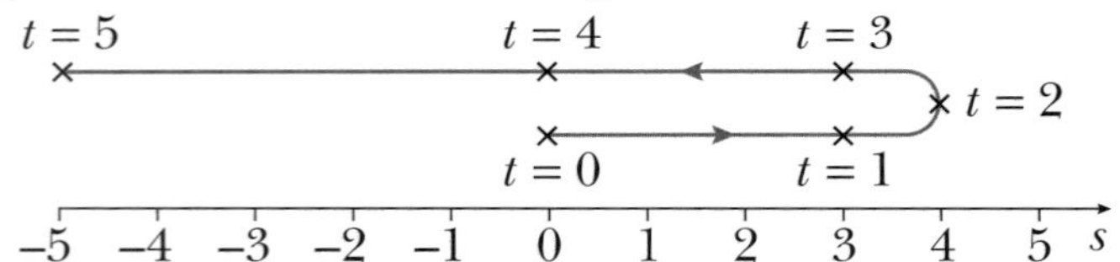

At time $t = 2$, the displacement of the particle from O is 4 m.

When $t = 2$ the particle stops instantaneously and reverses its direction of motion.

At time $t = 3$, the **displacement** is 3 m and the total distance travelled is $4 + (4 - 3) = 5$ m.

At time $t = 4$, the displacement is 0 m and the total distance travelled is $4 + 4 = 8$ m.

At time $t = 5$, the displacement is -5 m and the total distance travelled is $4 + 9 = 13$ m.

Velocity and acceleration

If a particle moves in a straight line, with displacement function $s(t)$, then the rate of change of displacement with respect to time, $\frac{ds}{dt}$, is the **velocity**, v, of the particle at time t.

$$v = \frac{ds}{dt}$$

If the velocity function is $v(t)$, then the rate of change of velocity with respect to time, $\frac{dv}{dt}$, is the **acceleration**, a, of the particle at time t.

$$a = \frac{dv}{dt} = \frac{d^2s}{dt^2}$$

CLASS DISCUSSION

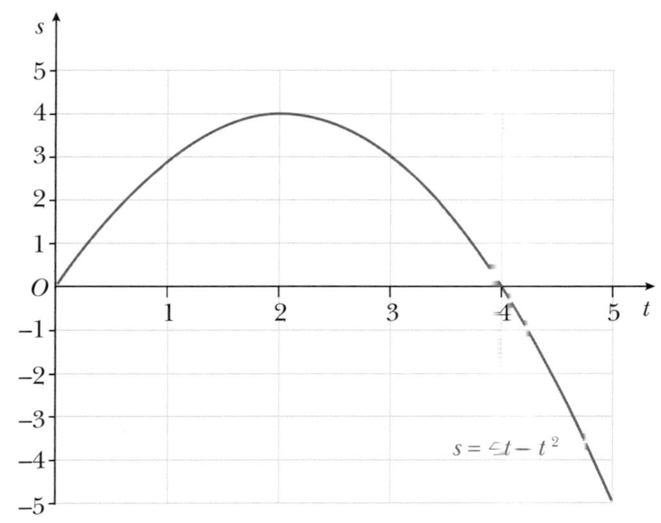

Earlier in this chapter you considered this displacement-time graph for the first 5 seconds of the motion of a particle P. The displacement of the particle, s metres, from a fixed point O, t seconds after passing through O, was given by $s = 4t - t^2$.

Working in small groups, complete the following tasks.

1 Find an expression, in terms of t, for the velocity, $v\,\text{m}\,\text{s}^{-1}$, of this particle.

2 Draw the graph of v against t for $0 \leqslant t \leqslant 5$.

3 State the values of t for which v is

a positive **b** zero **c** negative.

4 What can you say about the direction of motion of the particle when v is

a positive **b** zero **c** negative?

5 Find the acceleration, $a\,\text{m}\,\text{s}^{-2}$, of this particle and interpret your answer.

Now, discuss your conclusions with the whole class.

It is important that you are able to interpret the signs for displacements, velocities and accelerations.

These interpretations for a particle P relative to a fixed point O are summarised in the following tables.

Signs for displacement s

$s < 0$	$s = 0$	$s > 0$
P is to the left of O	P is at O	P is to the right of O

Signs for velocity v

$v < 0$	$v = 0$	$v > 0$
P is moving to the left	P is instantaneously at rest	P is moving to the right

Signs for acceleration a

$a < 0$	$a = 0$	$a > 0$
velocity is decreasing	velocity could be maximum or minimum or constant	velocity is increasing

WORKED EXAMPLE 1

A particle moves in a straight line so that, t seconds after passing a fixed point O, its displacement, s metres, from O is given by $s = t^3 - 12t^2 + 45t$.

a Find the velocity when $t = 2$.

b Find the acceleration when $t = 4$.

c Find the values of t when the particle is instantaneously at rest.

d Find the distance of the particle from O when $t = 7$.

e Find the total distance travelled by the particle during the first 7 seconds.

Answers

a $s = t^3 - 12t^2 + 45t$

$$v = \frac{ds}{dt} = 3t^2 - 24t + 45$$

When $t = 2$, $v = 3(2)^2 - 24(2) + 45 = 9$

The velocity is $9\,\text{m s}^{-1}$ when $t = 2$.

b $v = 3t^2 - 24t + 45$

$$a = \frac{dv}{dt} = 6t - 24$$

When $t = 4$, $a = 6(4) - 24 = 0$

The acceleration is $0\,\text{m s}^{-2}$ when $t = 4$.

c The particle is at instantaneous rest when $v = 0$.

$$3t^2 - 24t + 45 = 0$$
$$t^2 - 8t + 15 = 0$$
$$(t-3)(t-5) = 0$$
$$t = 3 \text{ or } t = 5$$

The particle is at instantaneous rest when $t = 3$ and $t = 5$.

d When $t = 7$, $s = (7)^3 - 12(7)^2 + 45(7) = 70$.

The particle is 70 m from O when $t = 7$.

e When $t = 0$, $s = 0$.

Critical values are when $t = 3$ and $t = 5$.

When $t = 3$, $s = (3)^3 - 12(3)^2 + 45(3) = 54$.

When $t = 5$, $s = (5)^3 - 12(5)^2 + 45(5) = 50$.

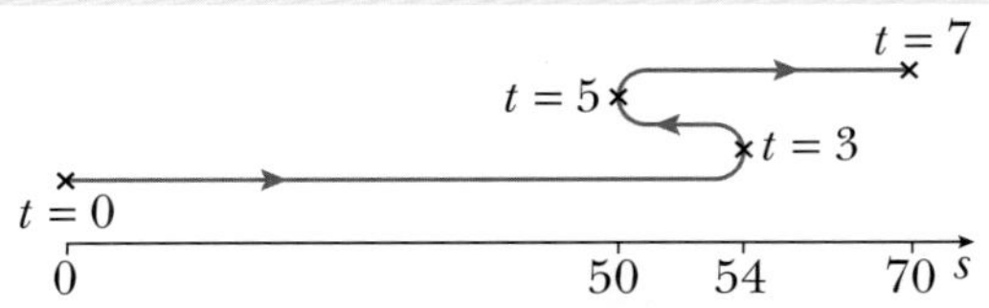

Total distance travelled = $54 + (54 - 50) + (70 - 50) = 78$ m.

WORKED EXAMPLE 2

A particle moves in a straight line so that the displacement, s metres, from a fixed point O, is given by $s = \ln(2t + 5)$, where t is the time in seconds after passing a point X on the line.

a Find OX.

b Find the velocity when $t = 10$.

c Find the distance travelled during the third second.

d Find the acceleration of the particle when $t = 2.5$.

Answers

a When $t = 0$, $s = \ln[2(0) + 5] = \ln 5$ — the particle is at X at time $t = 0$

$OX = \ln 5 \approx 1.61$ m

b $s = \ln(2t + 5)$

$$v = \frac{ds}{dt} = \frac{2}{2t+5}$$

When $t = 10$, $v = \dfrac{2}{2(10) + 5} = 0.08$

The velocity is $0.08\,\text{m s}^{-1}$.

c Since $v > 0$ for all values of t, there is no change in the direction of motion of the particle.

The third second is from $t = 2$ to $t = 3$.

When $t = 2$, $s = \ln[2(2) + 5] = \ln 9$.

When $t = 3$, $s = \ln[2(3) + 5] = \ln 11$.

$t = 0$ $t = 2$ $t = 3$

0 $\ln 5$ $\ln 9$ $\ln 11$ s

Distance travelled during the third second $= \ln 11 - \ln 9 = \ln\frac{11}{9} \approx 0.201\,\text{m}$.

d $v = \dfrac{2}{2t + 5} = 2(2t + 5)^{-1}$

$a = \dfrac{\mathrm{d}v}{\mathrm{d}t} = -2(2t + 5)^{-2} \times 2 = -\dfrac{4}{(2t + 5)^2}$

When $t = 2.5$, $a = -\dfrac{4}{[2(2.5) + 5]^2} = -0.04$

The acceleration is $-0.04\,\text{m}\,\text{s}^{-2}$.

WORKED EXAMPLE 3

A particle moves in a straight line such that its displacement, s metres, from a fixed point O on the line at time t seconds is given by $s = 20\left[e^{-2t} - e^{-3t}\right]$.

a Find value of t when the particle is instantaneously at rest.

b Find the displacement of the particle from O when $t = 1$.

c Find the total distance travelled during the first second of its motion.

Answers

a $s = 20\left[e^{-2t} - e^{-3t}\right]$

$v = \dfrac{\mathrm{d}s}{\mathrm{d}t} = 20\left[-2e^{-2t} + 3e^{-3t}\right]$

$v = 0$ when $-2e^{-2t} + 3e^{-3t} = 0$

$2e^{-2t} = 3e^{-3t}$

$e^{t} = \dfrac{3}{2}$

$t = \ln\dfrac{3}{2}$

It is instantaneously at rest when $t = \ln\dfrac{3}{2} = 0.405\,\text{s}$.

b When $t = 1$, $s = 20\left[e^{-2(1)} - e^{-3(1)}\right] \approx 1.711$.

Displacement from O is $1.71\,\text{m}$.

c When $t = 0$, $s = 0$.

Critical value is when $t = \ln\frac{3}{2}$.

When $t = \ln\frac{3}{2}$, $s = 20\left[e^{-2\left(\ln\frac{3}{2}\right)} - e^{-3\left(\ln\frac{3}{2}\right)}\right] \approx 2.963$.

$t = 1$ $\quad$ $t = \ln\frac{3}{2}$

$t = 0$

0 $\quad$ 1.711 $\quad$ 2.963 $\quad$ s

Total distance travelled = 2.963 + (2.963 − 1.711) ≈ 4.21 m.

WORKED EXAMPLE 4

A particle travels in a straight line so that, t seconds after passing through a fixed point O, its velocity v m s^{-1}, is given by $v = 5\cos\left(\frac{t}{2}\right)$.

a Find the value of t when the particle first comes to instantaneous rest.

b Find the acceleration of the particle when $t = \frac{\pi}{3}$.

Answers

a The particle is at rest when $v = 0$.

$$5\cos\left(\frac{t}{2}\right) = 0$$

$$\cos\left(\frac{t}{2}\right) = 0$$

$$\frac{t}{2} = \frac{\pi}{2}$$

$$t = \pi$$

It is at instantaneous rest when $t = \pi$.

b $v = 5\cos\left(\frac{t}{2}\right)$

$$a = \frac{dv}{dt} = -\frac{5}{2}\sin\left(\frac{t}{2}\right)$$

When $t = \frac{\pi}{3}$, $a = -\frac{5}{2}\sin\left(\frac{\pi}{6}\right) = -1.25$

When $t = \frac{\pi}{3}$ the acceleration is -1.25 m s^{-2}.

Exercise 16.1

1 A particle, moving in a straight line, passes through a fixed point O. Its velocity $v\,\mathrm{m\,s^{-1}}$, t seconds after passing through O, is given by $v = \dfrac{50}{(3t+2)^2}$.

a Find the velocity of the particle as it passes through O.

b Find the value of t when the velocity is $0.125\,\mathrm{m\,s^{-1}}$.

c Find the acceleration of the particle when $t = 1$.

2 A particle, moving in a straight line, passes through a fixed point O. Its velocity $v\,\mathrm{m\,s^{-1}}$, t seconds after passing through O, is given by $v = 6e^{2t} - 2t$.

a Find the initial velocity of the particle.

b Find the initial acceleration of the particle.

3 A particle starts from rest and moves in a straight line so that t seconds after passing through a fixed point O, its velocity $v\,\mathrm{m\,s^{-1}}$, is given by $v = 5\left(1 - e^{-t}\right)$.

a Find the velocity of the particle when $t = \ln 100$.

b State the value which v approaches as t becomes very large.

c Find the acceleration of the particle when $v = 4$.

d Sketch the velocity-time graph for the motion of the particle.

4 A particle moves in a straight line such that its displacement, s metres, from a fixed point O on the line at time t seconds is given by $s = 9\left[\ln(3t+2)\right]$.

a Find the value of t when the displacement of the particle from O is 36 m.

b Find the velocity of the particle when $t = 1$.

c Show that the particle is decelerating for all values of t.

5 A particle moves in a straight line so that, t seconds after passing through a fixed point O, its displacement, s metres, from O is given by $s = \ln(1+2t)$.

a Find the value of t when the velocity of the particle is $0.4\,\mathrm{m\,s^{-1}}$.

b Find the distance travelled by the particle during the third second.

c Find the acceleration of the particle when $t = 1.5$.

6 A particle travels in a straight line so that, t seconds after passing through a fixed point O, its velocity $v\,\mathrm{m\,s^{-1}}$, is given by $v = 8\cos\left(\dfrac{t}{4}\right)$.

a Find the value of t when the velocity of the particle first equals $4\,\mathrm{m\,s^{-1}}$.

b Find the acceleration of the particle when $t = 5$.

7 A particle, moving in a straight line, passes through a fixed point O. Its velocity $v\,\mathrm{m\,s^{-1}}$, t seconds after passing through O, is given by $v = \cos 3t + \sin 3t$.

a Find the value of t when the particle is first instantaneously at rest.

b Find the acceleration of the particle when $t = \pi$.

8 A particle starts from rest and moves in a straight line so that, t seconds after leaving a fixed point O, its displacement, s metres, is given by $s = 2 - 2\cos 2t$.

a Find an expression for the velocity and the acceleration of the particle in terms of t.

b Find the time when the particle first comes to rest and its distance from O at this instant.

9 A particle moves in a straight line such that its displacement s metres, from a fixed point O on the line at time t seconds is given by $s = 50\left[e^{-2t} - e^{-4t}\right]$.

a Find the time when the particle is instantaneously at rest.

b Find the displacement of the particle from O when $t = 2$.

c Find the total distance travelled during the first 2 seconds of its motion.

10 A particle moves in a straight line so that its displacement from a fixed point O, is given by $s = 2t + 2\cos 2t$, where t is the time in seconds after the motion begins.

a Find the initial position of the particle.

b Find an expression for the velocity and the acceleration of the particle in terms of t.

c Find the time when the particle first comes to rest and its distance from O at this instant.

d Find the time when the acceleration of the particle is zero for the first time and its distance from O at this instant.

11 A particle, moving in a straight line, passes through a fixed point O. Its velocity $v\,\mathrm{m\,s^{-1}}$, t seconds after passing through O, is given by $v = k\cos 4t$, where k is a positive constant.

a Find the value of t when the particle is first instantaneously at rest.

b Find an expression for the acceleration, a, of the particle t seconds after passing through O.

c Given that the acceleration of the particle is $10\,\mathrm{m\,s^{-2}}$ when $t = \frac{7\pi}{24}$, find the value of k.

CHALLENGE Q

12 A particle moves in a straight line such that its displacement, s metres, from a fixed point O at a time t seconds, is given by

$s = 2t$ for $0 \leqslant t \leqslant 4$,

$s = 8 + 2\ln(t - 3)$ for $t > 4$.

a Find the initial velocity of the particle.

b Find the velocity of the particle when **i** $t = 2$ **ii** $t = 6$.

c Find the acceleration of the particle when **i** $t = 2$ **ii** $t = 6$.

d Sketch the displacement-time graph for the motion of the particle.

e Find the distance travelled by the particle in the 8th second.

CHALLENGE Q

13 A particle moves in a straight line so that the displacement, s metres, from a fixed point O, is given by $s = 2t^3 - 17t^2 + 40t - 2$, where t is the time in seconds after passing a point X on the line.

a Find the distance OX.

b Find the value of t when the particle is first at rest.

c Find the values of t for which the velocity is positive.

d Find the values of t for which the velocity is negative.

16.2 Applications of integration in kinematics

In the last section you learnt that when a particle moves in a straight line where the displacement from a fixed point O on the line is s, then:

$$v = \frac{ds}{dt}$$

and
$$a = \frac{dv}{dt} = \frac{d^2s}{dt^2}$$

Conversely, if a particle moves in a straight line where the acceleration of the particle is a, then:

$$v = \int a \, dt \quad \text{and} \quad s = \int v \, dt$$

In this section you will solve problems that involve both differentiation and integration.

The following diagram should help you remember when to differentiate and when to integrate.

displacement (s)

$v = \dfrac{ds}{dt}$ $\qquad$ $s = \int v\,dt$

velocity (v)

$a = \dfrac{dv}{dt} = \dfrac{d^2s}{dt^2}$ $\qquad$ $v = \int a\,dt$

acceleration (a)

WORKED EXAMPLE 5

A particle moving in a straight line passes a fixed point O with velocity $8\,\mathrm{m\,s^{-1}}$. Its acceleration $a\,\mathrm{m\,s^{-2}}$, t seconds after passing through O is given by $a = 2t + 1$.

a Find the velocity when $t = 3$.

b Find the displacement from O when $t = 3$.

Answers

a $a = 2t + 1$

$$v = \int a\,dt$$

$$= \int (2t + 1)\,dt$$

$$= t^2 + t + c$$

Using $v = 8$ when $t = 0$, gives $c = 8$

$$v = t^2 + t + 8$$

When $t = 3$, $v = (3)^2 + (3) + 8 = 20$

The particle's velocity when $t = 3$ is $20\,\mathrm{m\,s^{-1}}$.

b $v = t^2 + t + 8$

$$s = \int v\,dt$$

$$= \int (t^2 + t + 8)\,dt$$

$$= \frac{1}{3}t^3 + \frac{1}{2}t^2 + 8t + c$$

Using $s = 0$ when $t = 0$, gives $c = 0$

$$s = \frac{1}{3}t^3 + \frac{1}{2}t^2 + 8t$$

When $t = 3$, $s = \frac{1}{3}(3)^3 + \frac{1}{2}(3)^2 + 8(3) = 37.5$

Its displacement when $t = 3$ is $37.5\,\mathrm{m}$.

WORKED EXAMPLE 6

A particle, moving in a straight line, passes through a fixed point O.
Its velocity $v\,\mathrm{m\,s^{-1}}$, t seconds after passing through O, is given by $v = 6\mathrm{e}^{3t} + 2t$.

a Find the acceleration of the particle when $t = 1$.

b Find an expression for the displacement of the particle from O.

c Find the total distance travelled by the particle in the first 2 seconds of its motion.

Answers

a $v = 6\mathrm{e}^{3t} + 2t$

$$a = \frac{\mathrm{d}v}{\mathrm{d}t} = 18\mathrm{e}^{3t} + 2$$

When $t = 1$, $a = 18\mathrm{e}^{3(1)} + 2 \approx 364$

Its acceleration when $t = 1$ is $364\,\mathrm{m\,s^{-2}}$.

b $v = 6\mathrm{e}^{3t} + 2t$

$$s = \int v\,\mathrm{d}t$$
$$= \int \left(6\mathrm{e}^{3t} + 2t\right)\mathrm{d}t$$
$$= 2\mathrm{e}^{3t} + t^2 + c$$

Using $s = 0$ when $t = 0$, gives $c = -2$

The displacement, s metres, is given by $s = 2\mathrm{e}^{3t} + t^2 - 2$.

c Since $v > 0$ for all values of t, there is no change in the direction of motion of the particle.

When $t = 0$, $s = 0$

When $t = 2$, $s = 2\mathrm{e}^{3(2)} + (2)^2 - 2 = 2\mathrm{e}^6 + 2$

Distance travelled during the first 2 seconds $= 2\mathrm{e}^6 + 2 \approx 809\,\mathrm{m}$.

Alternative method

Since there is no change in direction of motion:

$$s = \int v\,\mathrm{d}t$$
$$= \int_0^2 \left(6\mathrm{e}^{3t} + 2t\right)\mathrm{d}t$$
$$= \left[2\mathrm{e}^{3t} + t^2\right]_0^2$$
$$= \left(2\mathrm{e}^6 + 4\right) - \left(2\mathrm{e}^0 + 0\right)$$
$$= 2\mathrm{e}^6 + 2$$
$$\approx 809\,\mathrm{m}$$

Note:
This alternative method can only be used when there has been no change in direction of motion during the relevant time interval.

WORKED EXAMPLE 7

A particle starts from rest and moves in a straight line so that, t seconds after leaving a fixed point O, its velocity, $v\,\text{m s}^{-1}$, is given by $v = 4 + 8\cos 2t$.

a Find the range of values of the velocity.

b Find the range of values of the acceleration.

c Find the value of t when the particle first comes to instantaneous rest.

d Find the distance travelled during the time interval $0 \leqslant t \leqslant \frac{\pi}{2}$.

Answers

a $v = 4 + 8\cos 2t$ and $-1 \leqslant \cos 2t \leqslant 1$

$v_{min} = 4 + 8(-1) = -4$ and $v_{max} = 4 + 8(1) = 12$

Hence, $-4 \leqslant v \leqslant 12$.

b $v = 4 + 8\cos 2t$

$a = \frac{dv}{dt} = -16\sin 2t$ and $-1 \leqslant \sin 2t \leqslant 1$

$a_{min} = -16(1) = -16$ and $a_{max} = -16(-1) = 16$

Hence, $-16 \leqslant a \leqslant 16$.

c When $v = 0$, $4 + 8\cos 2t = 0$

$$\cos 2t = -\frac{1}{2}$$

$$2t = \frac{2\pi}{3}$$

$$t = \frac{\pi}{3}$$

The particle first comes to rest when $t = \frac{\pi}{3}$.

d $s = \int v\,dt$

$= \int (4 + 8\cos 2t)\,dt$

$= 4t + 4\sin 2t + c$

Using $s = 0$ when $t = 0$, gives $c = 0$

$s = 4t + 4\sin 2t$

Particle changes direction when $t = \frac{\pi}{3}$.

When $t = \frac{\pi}{3}$, $s = 4\left(\frac{\pi}{3}\right) + 4\sin\left(\frac{2\pi}{3}\right) \approx 7.6529$

When $t = \frac{\pi}{2}$, $s = 4\left(\frac{\pi}{2}\right) + 4\sin(\pi) = 2\pi \approx 6.2832$

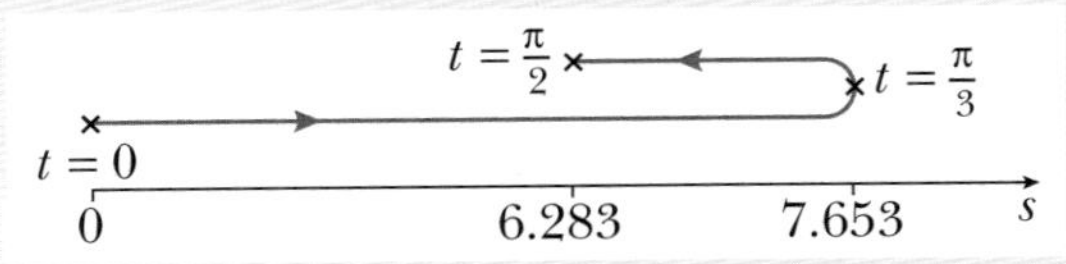

$t = \frac{\pi}{2}$ $t = \frac{\pi}{3}$
$t = 0$
0 6.283 7.653 s

Total distance travelled $= 7.653 + (7.653 - 6.283) \approx 9.02\,\text{m}$.

Exercise 16.2

1 A particle, moving in a straight line, passes through a fixed point O.

Its velocity $v\,\text{m s}^{-1}$, t seconds after passing through O, is given by $v = 10t - t^2$.

a Find the velocity of the particle when the acceleration is $6\,\text{m s}^{-2}$.

b Find the time taken before the particle returns to O.

c Find the distance travelled by the particle in the 2nd second.

d Find the distance travelled by the particle before it comes to instantaneous rest.

e Find the distance travelled by the particle in the first 12 seconds.

2 A particle, moving in a straight line, passes through a fixed point O.

Its velocity $v\,\text{m s}^{-1}$, t seconds after passing through O, is given by $v = \dfrac{32}{(t+2)^2}$.

a Find the acceleration of the particle when $t = 2$.

b Find an expression for the displacement of the particle from O.

c Find the distance travelled by the particle in the 3rd second.

3 A particle, moving in a straight line, passes through a fixed point O.

Its velocity $v\,\text{m s}^{-1}$, t seconds after passing through O, is given by $v = 4e^{2t} + 2t$.

a Find the acceleration of the particle when $t = 1$.

b Find an expression for the displacement of the particle from O.

c Find the total distance travelled by the particle in the first 2 seconds of its motion. Give your answer correct to the nearest metre.

4 A particle, moving in a straight line, passes through a fixed point O.

Its velocity $v\,\text{m s}^{-1}$, t seconds after passing through O, is given by

$v = t + 2\cos\left(\dfrac{t}{3}\right)$.

Find the displacement of the particle from O when $t = \dfrac{3\pi}{2}$ and its acceleration at this instant.

5 A particle, moving in a straight line, passes through a fixed point O.

Its velocity $v\,\text{m s}^{-1}$, t seconds after passing through O, is given by $v = 4e^{2t} + 6e^{-3t}$.

a Show that the velocity is never zero.

b Find the acceleration when $t = \ln 2$.

c Find, to the nearest metre, the displacement of the particle from O when $t = 2$.

6 A particle moves in a straight line, so that, t seconds after leaving a fixed point O, its velocity, $v\ \mathrm{m\,s^{-1}}$, is given by $v = pt^2 + qt - 12$, where p and q are constants.

When $t = 2$ the acceleration of the particle is $18\ \mathrm{m\,s^{-2}}$.

When $t = 4$ the displacement of the particle from O is 32 m.

Find the value of p and the value of q.

7 A particle moving in a straight line passes a fixed point O with velocity $10\ \mathrm{m\,s^{-1}}$.

Its acceleration $a\ \mathrm{m\,s^{-2}}$, t seconds after passing through O is given by $a = 3 - 2t$.

a Find the value of t when the particle is instantaneously at rest.

b Sketch the velocity-time graph for the motion of the particle.

c Find the total distance travelled in the first 7 seconds of its motion. Give your answer correct to 3 sf.

8 A particle moving in a straight line passes a fixed point O with velocity $18\ \mathrm{m\,s^{-1}}$.

Its acceleration $a\ \mathrm{m\,s^{-2}}$, t seconds after passing through O is given by $a = 3t - 12$.

a Find the values of t when the particle is instantaneously at rest.

b Find the distance the particle travels in the 4th second.

c Find the total distance travelled in the first 10 seconds of its motion.

9 A particle starts from rest and moves in a straight line so that t seconds after leaving a fixed point O, its velocity, $v\ \mathrm{m\,s^{-1}}$, is given by $v = 3 + 6\cos 2t$.

a Find the range of values for the acceleration.

b Find the distance travelled by the particle before it first comes to instantaneous rest. Give your answer correct to 3 sf.

10 A particle starts from rest at a fixed point O and moves in a straight line towards a point A. The velocity, $v\ \mathrm{m\,s^{-1}}$, of the particle, t seconds after leaving O, is given by $v = 8 - 8e^{-2t}$.

a Find the acceleration of the particle when $t = \ln 5$.

b Given that the particle reaches A when $t = 2$ find the distance OA. Give your answer correct to 3 sf.

11 A particle travels in a straight line so that, t seconds after passing through a fixed point O, its speed, $v\ \mathrm{m\,s^{-1}}$, is given by $v = 2\cos\left(\frac{t}{2}\right) - 1$.

a Find the value of t when the particle first comes to instantaneous rest at the point P.

b Find the total distance travelled from $t = 0$ to $t = 2\pi$.

CHALLENGE Q

12 A particle moves in a straight line so that t seconds after passing through a fixed point O, its acceleration, $a\,\text{m}\,\text{s}^{-2}$, is given by $a = pt + q$, where p and q are constants.

The particle passes through O with velocity $3\,\text{m}\,\text{s}^{-1}$ and acceleration $-2\,\text{m}\,\text{s}^{-2}$.

The particle first comes to instantaneous rest when $t = 2$.

a Find the value of p and the value of q.

b Find an expression, in terms of t, for the displacement of the particle.

c Find the second value of t for which the particle is at instantaneous rest.

d Find the distance travelled during the 4th second.

CHALLENGE Q

13 A particle starts from a point O and moves in a straight line so that its displacement, s cm, from O at time t seconds is given by $s = 2t\sin\dfrac{\pi t}{3}$.

a Find expressions for the velocity, v, and the acceleration, a, of the particle at time t seconds.

b Show that $18(vt - s) = t^2(9a + \pi^2 s)$.

Summary

The relationships between displacement, velocity and acceleration are:

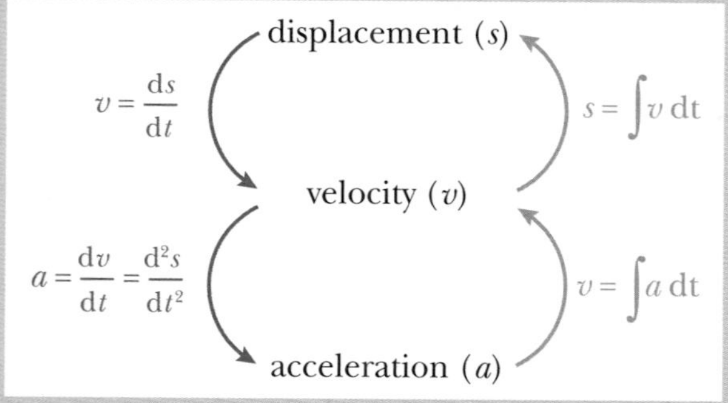

displacement (s)

$v = \dfrac{ds}{dt}$ $\quad s = \int v\,dt$

velocity (v)

$a = \dfrac{dv}{dt} = \dfrac{d^2s}{dt^2}$ $\quad v = \int a\,dt$

acceleration (a)

A particle is at instantaneous rest when $v = 0$.

Examination questions

Worked example

A particle travels in a straight line so that, t s after passing through a fixed point O, its velocity, $v\ \text{cm s}^{-1}$, is given by $v = 4e^{2t} - 24t$.

a Find the velocity of the particle as it passes through O. [1]

b Find the distance travelled by the particle in the third second. [4]

c Find an expression for the acceleration of the particle and hence find the stationary value of the velocity. [5]

Cambridge IGCSE Additional Mathematics 0606 Paper 21 Q11(part) Nov 2012

Answer

a When $t = 0$, $v = 4e^{(2\times 0)} - 24(0) = 4$.

The velocity of the particle as it passes through O is $4\ \text{cm s}^{-1}$.

b The third second is from $t = 2$ to $t = 3$.

$v \geqslant 0$ for $2 \leqslant t \leqslant 3$, hence there is no change in direction of motion in this time interval.

$$\begin{aligned}\text{Distance travelled} &= \int_2^3 v\,dt \\ &= \int_2^3 (4e^{2t} - 24t)\,dt \\ &= \left[2e^{2t} - 12t^2\right]_2^3 \\ &= (2e^6 - 108) - (2e^4 - 48) \\ &= 2e^6 - 2e^4 - 60\end{aligned}$$

Distance travelled in third second ≈ 638 m.

c
$$\begin{aligned}\text{Acceleration} &= \frac{d}{dt}(v) \\ &= \frac{d}{dt}(4e^{2t} - 24t) \\ &= 8e^{2t} - 24\end{aligned}$$

Acceleration is $(8e^{2t} - 24)\ \text{cm s}^{-2}$.

Stationary values of v occur when $\frac{dv}{dt} = 0$.

$$\begin{aligned}8e^{2t} - 24 &= 0 \\ e^{2t} &= 3 \\ 2t &= \ln 3 \\ t &= \frac{1}{2}\ln 3\end{aligned}$$

When $t = \frac{1}{2}\ln 3$, $v = 4e^{\ln 3} - 12\ln 3 = 12 - 12\ln 3$

Stationary value of velocity is $12(1 - \ln 3)\ \text{cm s}^{-1}$.

Exercise 16.3

Exam Exercise

1

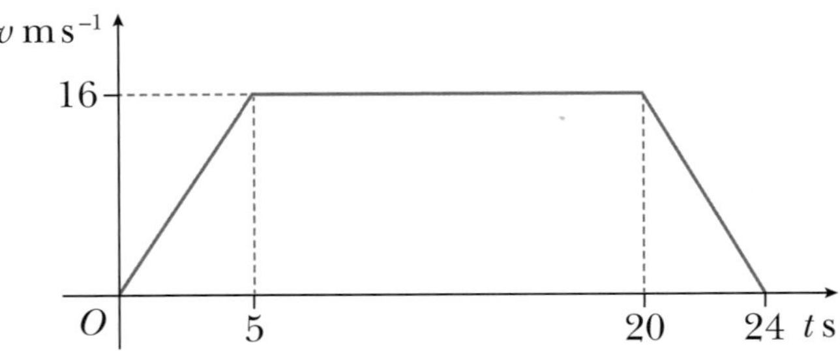

The velocity-time graph represents the motion of a particle moving in a straight line.

a Find the acceleration during the first 5 seconds. [1]

b Find the length of time for which the particle is travelling with constant velocity. [1]

c Find the total distance travelled by the particle. [3]

Cambridge IGCSE Additional Mathematics 0606 Paper 21 Q2i,ii,iii Jun 2013

2 A particle moves in a straight line so that, t s after passing through a fixed point O, its velocity, v m s^{-1}, is given by $v = 2t - 11 + \dfrac{6}{t+1}$. Find the acceleration of the particle when it is at instantaneous rest. [7]

Cambridge IGCSE Additional Mathematics 0606 Paper 21 Q9 Jun 2012

3 A particle moves in a straight line such that its displacement, x m, from a fixed point O at time t s, is given by $x = 3 + \sin 2t$, where $t \geqslant 0$.

a Find the velocity of the particle when $t = 0$. [2]

b Find the value of t when the particle is first at rest. [2]

c Find the distance travelled by the particle before it first comes to rest. [2]

d Find the acceleration of the particle when $t = \dfrac{3\pi}{4}$. [2]

Cambridge IGCSE Additional Mathematics 0606 Paper 11 Q5i-iv Nov 2011

4 A body moves in a straight line so that, t s after passing through a fixed point O, its displacement from O is s m. The velocity v m s^{-1} is such that $v = 5\cos 4t$.

a Write down the velocity of the body as it passes through O. [1]

b Find the value of t when the acceleration of the body is first equal to 10 m s^{-2}. [4]

c Find the value of s when $t = 5$. [4]

Cambridge IGCSE Additional Mathematics 0606 Paper 11 Q9i,ii,ii Jun 2011

5 A particle P is projected from the origin O so that it moves in a straight line. At time t seconds after projection, the velocity of the particle, $v\,\text{m s}^{-1}$, is given by $v = 2t^2 - 14t + 12$.

i Find the time at which P first comes to instantaneous rest. [2]

ii Find an expression for the displacement of P from O at time t seconds. [3]

iii Find the acceleration of P when $t = 3$. [2]

Cambridge IGCSE Additional Mathematics 0606 Paper 21 Q6 Jun 2015

6 **a** A particle P moves in a straight line. Starting from rest, P moves with constant acceleration for 30 seconds after which it moves with constant velocity, $k\,\text{m s}^{-1}$, for 90 seconds. P then moves with constant deceleration until it comes to rest; the magnitude of the deceleration is twice the magnitude of the initial acceleration.

i Use the information to complete the velocity-time graph. [2]

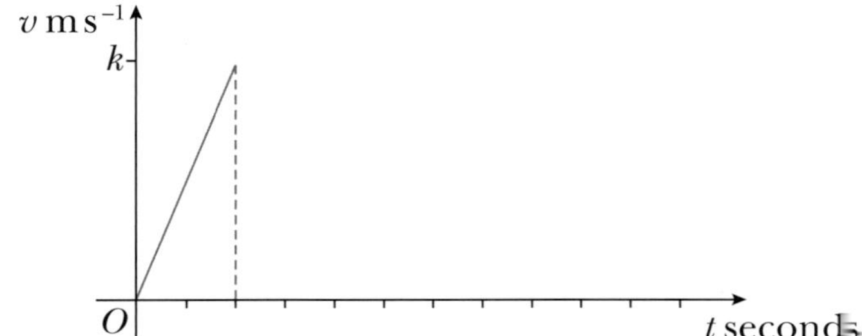

ii Given that the particle travels 450 metres while it is accelerating, find the value of k and the acceleration of the particle. [4]

b A body Q moves in a straight line such that, t seconds after passing a fixed point, its acceleration, $a\,\text{m s}^{-2}$, is given by $a = 3t^2 + 6$. When $t = 0$, the velocity of the body is $5\,\text{m s}^{-1}$. Find the velocity when $t = 3$. [5]

Cambridge IGCSE Additional Mathematics 0606 Paper 22 Q11 Mar 2015

7 A particle is moving in a straight line such that its velocity, $v\,\text{m s}^{-1}$, t seconds after passing a fixed point O is $v = \text{e}^{2t} - 6\text{e}^{-2t} - 1$.

i Find an expression for the displacement, s m, from O of the particle after t seconds. [3]

ii Using the substitution $u = \text{e}^{2t}$, or otherwise, find the time when the particle is at rest. [3]

iii Find the acceleration at this time. [2]

Cambridge IGCSE Additional Mathematics 0606 Paper 21 Q10 Nov 2015

8 A particle P is projected from the origin O so that it moves in a straight line. At time t seconds after projection, the velocity of the particle, $v\,\text{m s}^{-1}$, is given by $v = 9t^2 - 63t + 90$.

i Show that P first comes to instantaneous rest when $t = 2$. [2]

ii Find the acceleration of P when $t = 3.5$. [2]

iii Find an expression for the displacement of P from O at time t seconds. [3]

iv Find the distance travelled by P

a in the first 2 seconds, [2]

b in the first 3 seconds. [2]

Cambridge IGCSE Additional Mathematics 0606 Paper 22 Q12 Mar 2016

Answers

Chapter 1

Exercise 1.1

1 one-one **2** many-one

3 one-one **4** one-one

5 one-one **6** one-one

7 one-one **8** one-many

Exercise 1.2

1 1, 2, 3, 4, 5, 6 and 7

2 **a** $-7 \leqslant f(x) \leqslant 2$

b $2 \leqslant f(x) \leqslant 17$

c $-1 \leqslant f(x) \leqslant 9$

d $0 \leqslant f(x) \leqslant 9$

e $\frac{1}{8} \leqslant f(x) \leqslant 8$

f $\frac{1}{5} \leqslant f(x) \leqslant 1$

3 $g(x) \geqslant 2$ **4** $f(x) \geqslant -4$

5 $f(x) \geqslant 5$ **6** $f(x) \geqslant -5$

7 $f(x) \leqslant 10$ **8** $f(x) \geqslant 3$

Exercise 1.3

1 9 **2** 51 **3** 675 **4** 1

5 67

6 **a** hk **b** kh

7 $x = -\frac{1}{3}$

8 $x = -\frac{2}{3}$ or $x = 4$

9 $x = \pm\frac{3}{4}$

10 $x = 2.5$

11 $x = 5$

12 $x = 3$ or $x = 4$

13 **a** fg **b** gf **c** g^2 **d** f^2

Exercise 1.4

1 **a** $-2\frac{2}{3}, 4$ **b** $-2, -7$

c 0.8, 1.6 **d** $-23, 25$

e $-5, -2$ **f** $-0.5, 7.5$

g 16, 24 **h** $-5, 3\frac{8}{9}$

i $1\frac{2}{3}, 5$

2 **a** $-4\frac{5}{6}, -1.9$ **b** $-0.8, 0$

c $-5.6, 4$ **d** 0.75, 3.5

e 6.5 **f** $x = 3\frac{1}{3}$

3 **a** $-2, 2$ **b** $-3, 3$

c $-3, -1, 2$ **d** 0, 4, 6

e $-2, 1, 3$ **f** $-2, -1, 0, 3$

g 0.5, 1 **h** $-1, 2$

i 0, 2, 6

4 **a** $(-4, 0), (3, 7), (5, 9)$

b (0, 0), (1, 1), (2, 2)

c (1, 3), (2.5, 7.5)

Exercise 1.5

1 **a** ∨ shape, vertex at $(-1, 0)$, y-intercept 1

b ∨ shape, vertex at (1.5, 0), y-intercept 3

c ∨ shape, vertex at (5, 0), y-intercept 5

d ∨ shape, vertex at $(-6, 0)$, y-intercept 3

e ∨ shape, vertex at (5, 0), y-intercept 10

f ∨ shape, vertex at (18, 0), y-intercept 6

2 **a**

x	-2	-1	0	1	2	3	4
y	7	6	5	4	3	4	5

b

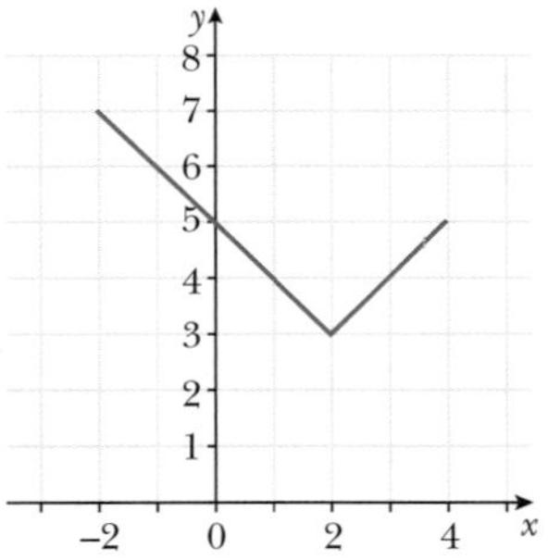

3 **a** ∨ shape, vertex at (0, 1)

b ∨ shape, vertex at $(0, -3)$

c ∧ shape, vertex at (0, 2)

d ∨ shape, vertex at (3, 1), y-intercept 4

e ∨ shape, vertex at $(-3, -3)$, y-intercept 3

4 **a** $-3 \leqslant f(x) \leqslant 11$

b $0 \leqslant g(x) \leqslant 11$

c $-3 \leqslant h(x) \leqslant 5$

5 $-5 \leqslant f(x) \leqslant 5$, $0 \leqslant g(x) \leqslant 5$, $-5 \leqslant h(x) \leqslant 3$

6 **a** ∨ shape, vertex at $(-2, 0)$, y-intercept 4

b straight line through $(-5, 0)$, (0, 5)

c $-3, 1$

7 **a** ∨ shape, vertex at $(3, -3)$, y-intercept 3

b $-3 \leqslant f(x) \leqslant 7$

c 0.5, 5.5

8 **a** ∨ shape, vertex at $\left(\frac{4}{3}, 0\right)$, y-intercept 4

b straight line through $(-2, -4)$, (5, 10)

c 0.8, 4

9 a

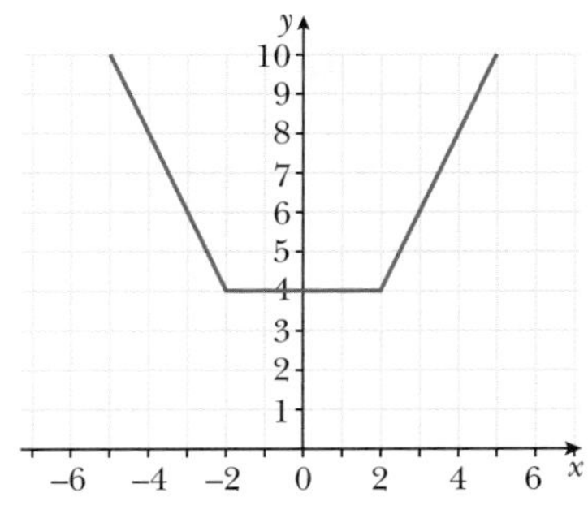

b −3, 3

Exercise 1.6

1 $f^{-1}(x) = \sqrt{x+7} - 5$

2 $f^{-1}(x) = \dfrac{6-2x}{x}$

3 $f^{-1}(x) = \dfrac{3+\sqrt{x-1}}{2}$

4 $f^{-1}(x) = (8-x)^2 + 3$

5 $f^{-1}(x) = \dfrac{x+3}{5}$, $g^{-1}(x) = \dfrac{2x-7}{x}$

6 a $f^{-1}(x) = \sqrt{x+5} - 2$ b 20

7 a $f^{-1}(x) = 4 + \sqrt{x-5}$ b 294

8 a $g^{-1}(x) = \dfrac{x+3}{x-2}$ b 3.25

9 a $f^{-1}(x) = 2(x-2)$

b no solution

10 0 **11** −2, 3.5

12 $f^{-1}(x) \geqslant 0$ **13** $f^{-1}g^{-1}$

14 f, h

15 a $x \geqslant 2$ b $g(x) \geqslant 0$

16 a $f^{-1}(x) = \dfrac{x+k}{3}$, $g^{-1}(x) = \dfrac{x+14}{5-x}$

b 13 c x

17 a $f^{-1}g$ b $g^{-1}f$

c gf^{-1} d $f^{-1}g^{-1}$

Exercise 1.7

1

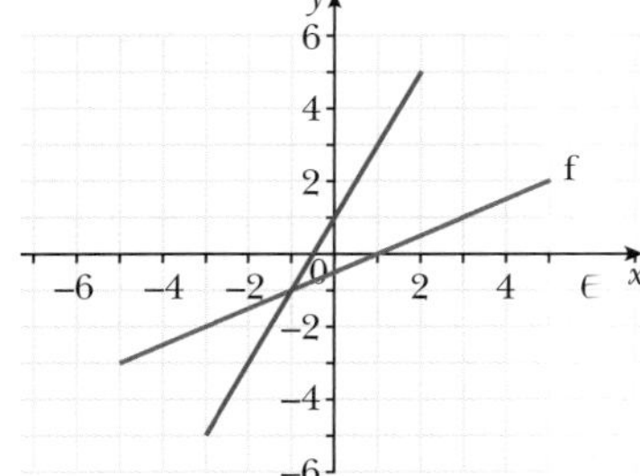

2

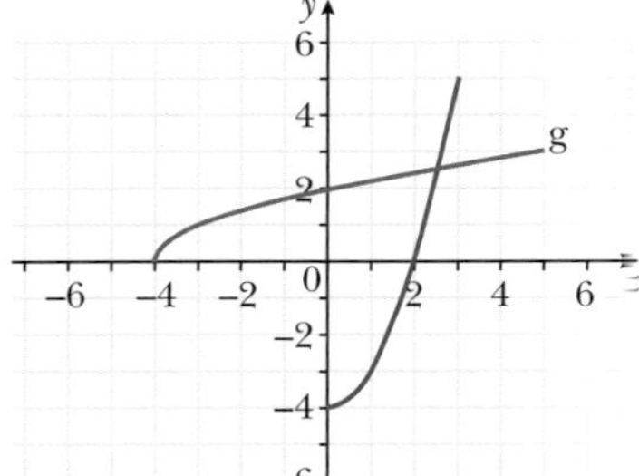

3

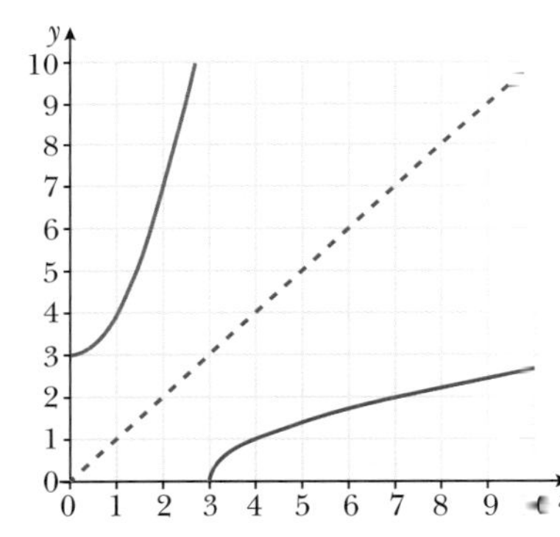

4

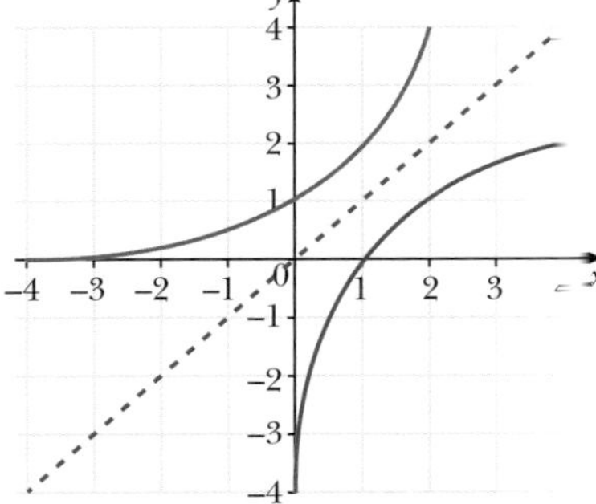

5

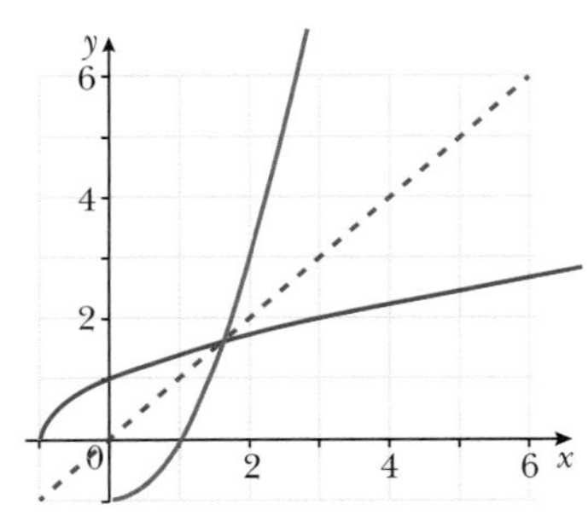

6

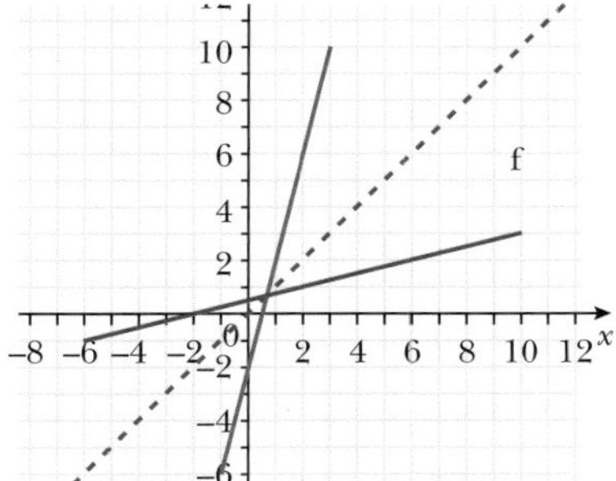

7 a f is a one-one function

b $f^{-1}(x) = \sqrt{3-x} - 1$

c

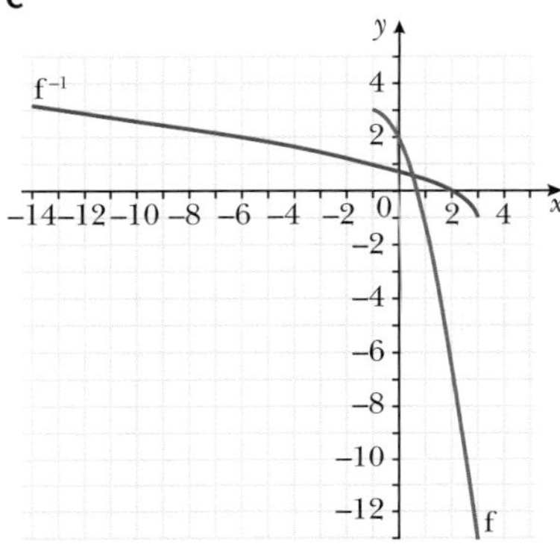

8 a $f^{-1}(x) = \dfrac{2x+7}{x-2}$

b The curve is symmetrical about the line $y = x$

Exercise 1.8

1 6.5, −4

2 a V shape, vertex at (−0.6, 0), y-intercept 3

b −0.2, −1

3 a V shape, vertex at (2.5, 0), y-intercept 5

b 1, 4

4 a $-1 \leqslant f(x) \leqslant 299$ b $x \geqslant 0$

5 a $\dfrac{1}{3}$

b $f^{-1}(x) = (x+3)^2 + 1$

c $g^{-1}(x) = \dfrac{3x-2}{2x-1}$

6 a $0.2 \leqslant g(x) \leqslant 1$

b $g^{-1}(x) = \dfrac{1+x}{2x}$

c $0.2 \leqslant x \leqslant 1$

d 1.25

7 **a** 33

b **i** kh **ii** h^2

iii $h^{-1}k^{-1}$ *or* $(kh)^{-1}$

8 **i** $2 - \sqrt{5} < f(x) \leqslant 2$

ii $f^{-1}(x) = (2 - x)^2 - 5$
domain $2 - \sqrt{5} < x \leqslant 2$
range $-5 \leqslant f^{-1}(x) < 0$

iii $x = -4$

9 **a** **i** $2(x - 2)^2 - 3$ **ii** $x \geqslant 2$

b **i** $g(x) \geqslant 4$, $h^{-1}(x) \geqslant 0$

ii

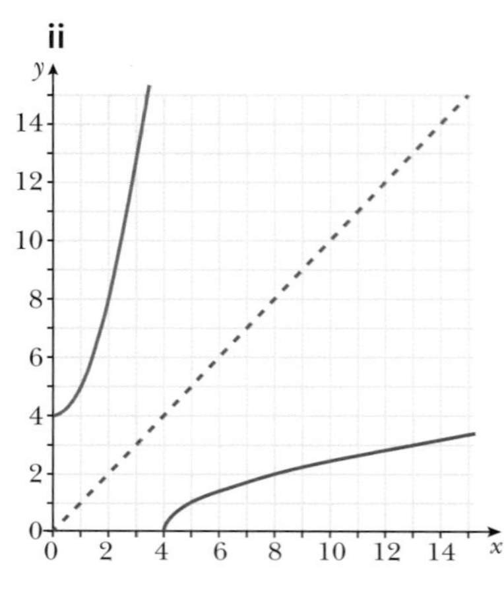

iii 8.5

10 **i**

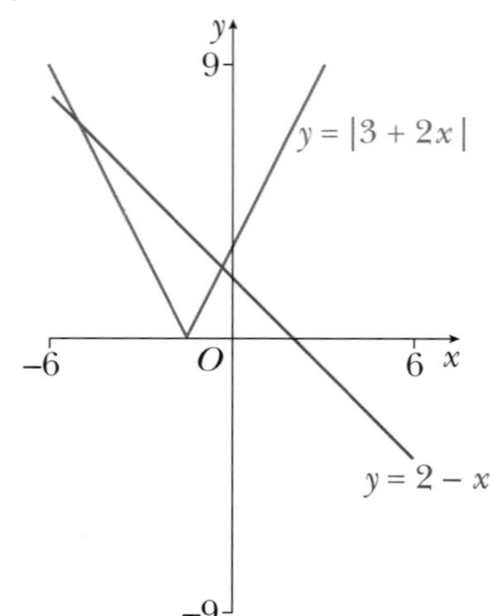

ii $-\frac{1}{3}, -5$

Chapter 2

Exercise 2.1

1 $x = 3, y = 9$ and $x = -2, y = 4$

2 $x = -1, y = -7$ and $x = 4, y = -2$

3 $x = -3, y = -4$ and $x = 4, y = 3$

4 $x = 1, y = 4$ and $x = -2, y = -2$

5 $x = 0.5, y = 0.5$ and $x = 0, y = 1$

6 $x = -1, y = -3$ and $x = 2, y = 1$

7 $x = 1.5, y = 4$ and $x = 2, y = 3$

8 $x = 3, y = 1$ and $x = 9, y = 7$

9 $x = 1.8, y = 2.6$ and $x = 1, y = 3$

10 $x = -1, y = -2$ and $x = 1, y = 2$

11 $x = 1, y = 2$ and $x = 2, y = 1$

12 $x = 1, y = 2$ and $x = 4, y = -4$

13 $x = 1, y = -\frac{1}{3}$ and $x = -\frac{1}{2}, y = \frac{1}{6}$

14 $x = 3, y = 1$ and $x = 1, y = 3$

15 $x = -1, y = -3$ and $x = 1, y = 3$

16 $x = 0, y = -0.5$ and $x = -1$, $y = -1$

17 $x = -1, y = 2$ and $x = 7\frac{1}{2}, y = -1.4$

18 $x = -1.5, y = -8$ and $x = 4, y = 3$

19 $(-0.2, 1.4)$ and $(1, -1)$

20 **a** $x + y = 11$, $xy = 21.25$

b $x = 2.5, y = 8.5$ and $x = 8.5$, $y = 2.5$

21 17 cm and 23 cm

22 $6\sqrt{5}$ or 13.4 to 3 sf

23 $(0.5, 0)$

24 $5\sqrt{2}$ or 7.07 to 3 sf

25 $(2, 2)$

26 $y = -2x - 1$

Exercise 2.2

1 **a** min $(2.5, -12.25)$, axis crossing points $(-1, 0)$, $(6, 0)$, $(0, -6)$

b min $(0.5, -20.25)$, axis crossing points $(-4, 0)$, $(5, 0)$, $(0, -20)$

c min $(-2, -25)$, axis crossing points $(-7, 0)$, $(3, 0)$, $(0, -21)$

d min $(-1.5, -30.25)$, axis crossing points $(-7, 0)$, $(4, 0)$, $(0, -28)$

e min $(-2, -3)$, axis crossing points $\left(-2 - \sqrt{3}, 0\right)$, $\left(-2 + \sqrt{3}, 0\right)$, $(0, 1)$

f max $(1, 16)$, axis crossing points $(-3, 0)$, $(5, 0)$, $(0, 15)$

2 **a** $(x - 4)^2 - 16$

b $(x - 5)^2 - 25$

c $(x - 2.5)^2 - 6.25$

d $(x - 1.5)^2 - 2.25$

e $(x + 2)^2 - 4$

f $(x + 3.5)^2 - 12.25$

g $(x + 4.5)^2 - 20.25$

h $(x + 1.5)^2 - 2.25$

3 **a** $(x - 4)^2 - 1$

b $(x - 5)^2 - 30$

c $(x - 3)^2 - 7$

d $(x - 1.5)^2 + 1.75$

e $(x + 3)^2 - 4$

f $(x + 3)^2 + 0$

g $(x + 2)^2 - 21$

h $(x + 2.5)^2 - 0.25$

4 **a** $2(x - 2)^2 - 5$

b $2(x - 3)^2 - 17$

c $3(x - 2)^2 - 7$

d $2(x - 0.75)^2 + 0.875$

e $2(x + 1)^2 - 1$

f $2(x + 1.75)^2 - 9.125$

g $2(x - 0.75)^2 + 3.875$

h $3\left(x - \frac{1}{6}\right)^2 + 5\frac{11}{12}$

5 **a** $9 - (x - 3)^2$

b $25 - (x - 5)^2$

c $2.25 - (x - 1.5)^2$

d $16 - (x - 4)^2$

6 a $6-(x+1)^2$

b $12-(x+2)^2$

c $16.25-(x+2.5)^2$

d $9.25-(x+1.5)^2$

7 a $13.5-2(x+1.5)^2$

b $3-2(x+1)^2$

c $15-2(x-2)^2$

d $4\frac{1}{12}-3\left(x-\frac{5}{6}\right)^2$

8 a $4\left(x+\frac{1}{4}\right)^2+4.75$

b No, since $4.75>0$

9 a $2(x-2)^2-7$ b $(2,-7)$

10 a $-5.25,\ 0.5$ b $x \geq 0.5$

11 a $11\frac{1}{8}-2\left(x+1\frac{3}{4}\right)^2$

b $x \leq 11\frac{1}{8}$

12 a $18.5-2(x-1.5)^2$

b $(1.5, 18.5)$

c $\cap$ shaped curve, vertex $=(1.5, 18.5)$

13 a $13.25-(x-2.5)^2$

b $(2.5, 13.25)$, maximum

c $-7 \leqslant f(x) \leqslant 13.25$

d No, it is not a one-one function.

14 a $2(x-2)^2-5$ b $x \geqslant 2$

15 -0.75

16 a $5-(x-2)^2$

b $(2, 5)$ maximum

c One-one function, $f^{-1}(x)=2+\sqrt{5-x}$

Exercise 2.3

1 a

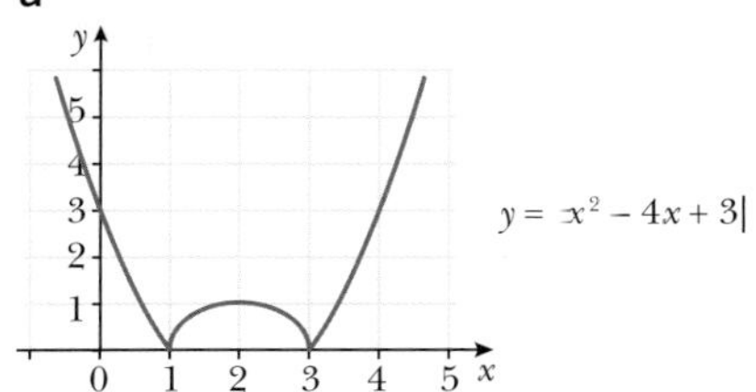

b

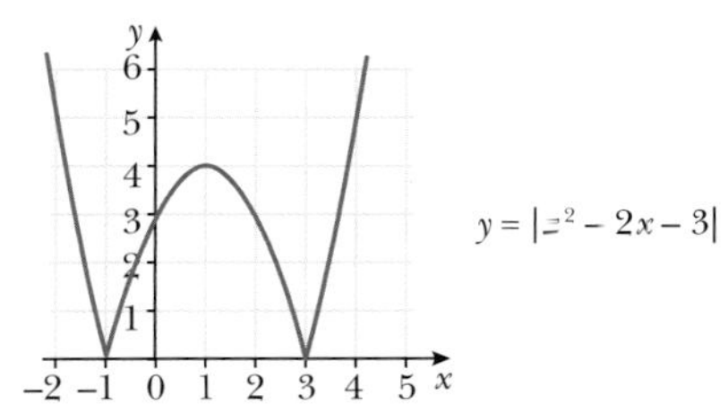

c

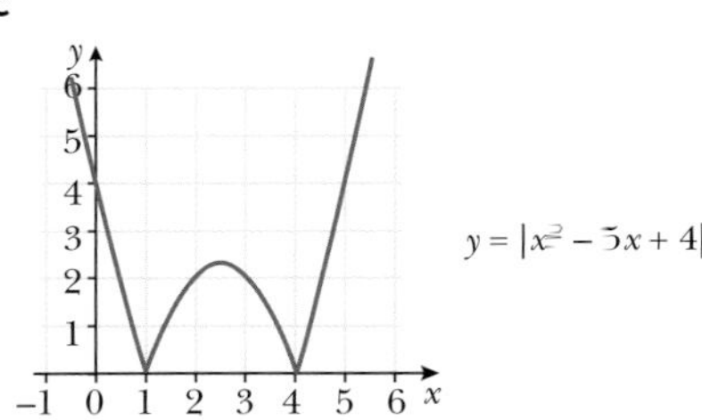

d

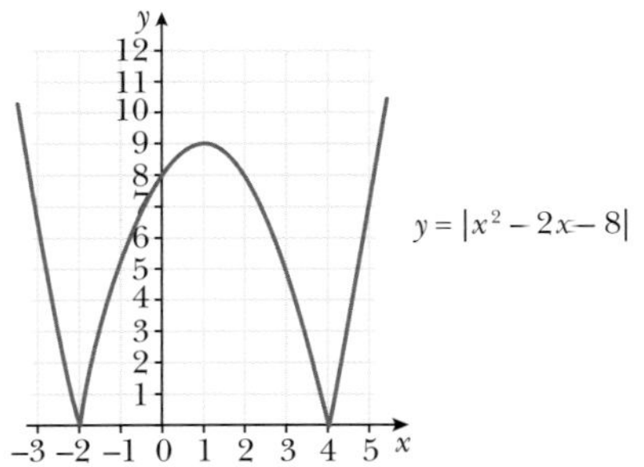

e

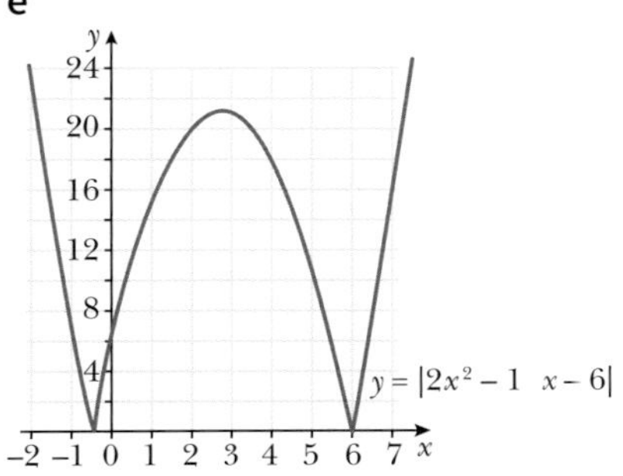

f

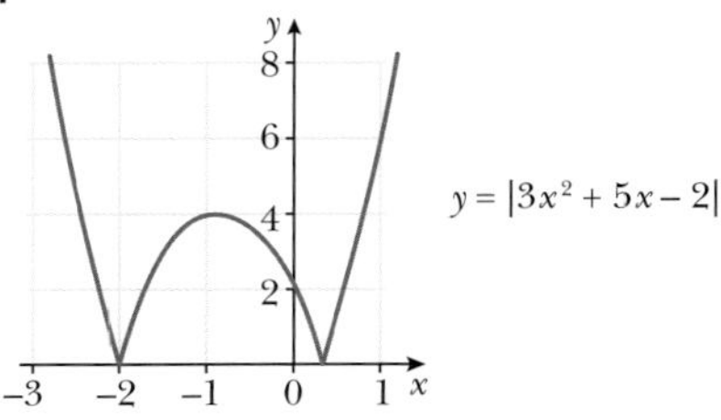

2 a $5-(x+2)^2$

b $\cap$ shaped curve, vertex $=(-2, 5)$

c

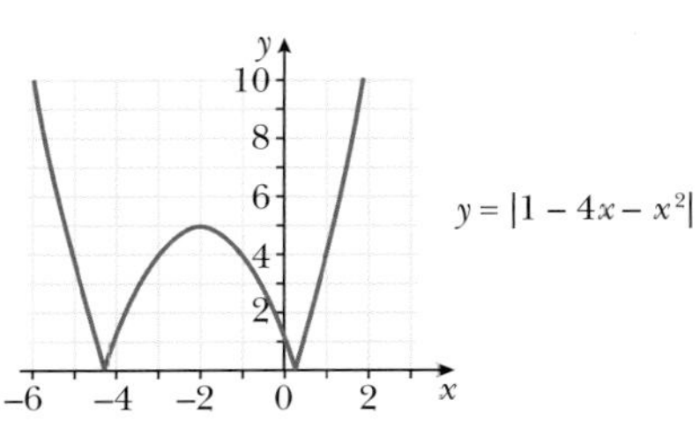

3 a $2(x+0.25)^2-3.125$

b

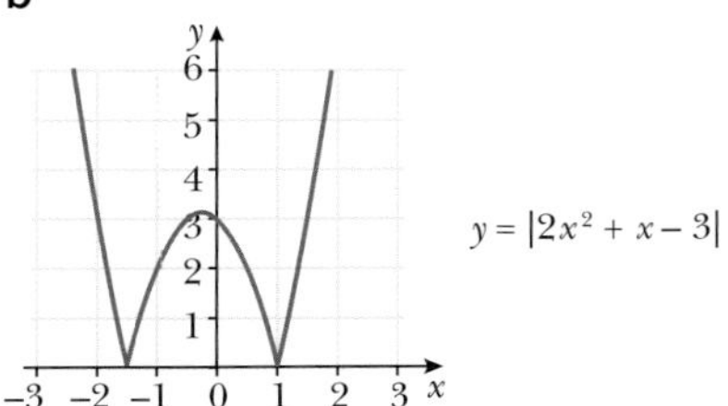

4 a $(3, 16)$

b

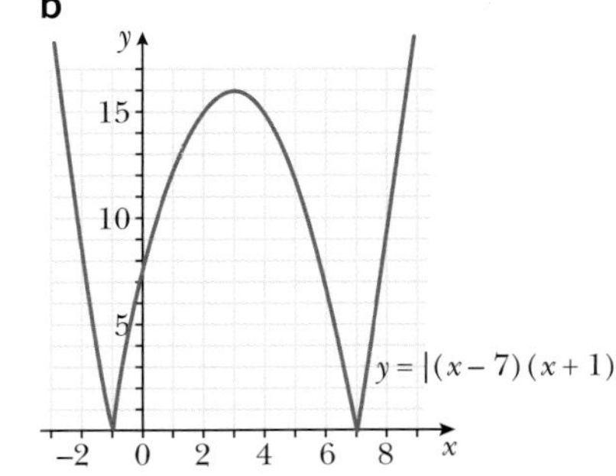

c $0<k<16$

5 a $(-3, 4)$ b $k>4$

6 a $(5.5, 6.25)$ b 6.25

7 a $-4, 4$ b $-2, 0, 2$

c $-1, 2, 3, 6$ d $-6, 4$

e $\frac{5-\sqrt{33}}{2}, 1, 4, \frac{5+\sqrt{33}}{2}$

f $-4, -2, -1, 1$

g $-1-\sqrt{10}, -1, -1+\sqrt{10}$

h $\frac{1+\sqrt{7}}{2}, \frac{-1+\sqrt{7}}{2}$

i $-1, 3$

8 a $(-1, 0), (2, 3), (4, 5)$

b $(-2, 1), (-1, 1.5), (2, 3), (5, 4.5)$

c $(1, 2), (2, 4)$

Exercise 2.4

1 a $x < -3, x > 4$

b $1 < x < 5$

c $x \leqslant -7, x \geqslant 3$

d $0 < x < 5$

e $-0.5 < x < 4$

f $-1 \leqslant x \leqslant 3$

g $-1.5 < x < 5$

h $-\infty < x < \infty$

i $x = 3$

2 a $-7 < x < 2$

b $x \leqslant -3, x \geqslant 2$

c $4 \leqslant x \leqslant 5$

d $x < -8, x > 6$

e $-2.5 \leqslant x \leqslant 3$

f $x < -1, x > -0.8$

3 a $-6 < x < 3$

b $x < 5, x > 7$

c $x \leqslant 0.5, x \geqslant 1$

d $-3 < x < 2$

e $x < -4, x > 1$

f $-0.5 < x < 0.6$

4 a $3 < x < 5$

b $1 < x \leqslant 6$

c $0.5 < x < 1$

d $3 < x < 5$

e $x < -2, x \geqslant 3$

5 a $-5 < x < 3$

b $0 < x < 2, 6 < x < 8$

c $0 < x < 2, 4 < x < 6$

6 $-1\frac{1}{3} < x < 2$

Exercise 2.5

1 a two equal roots

b two distinct roots

c two distinct roots

d no roots

e two distinct roots

f two equal roots

g no roots

h two distinct roots

2 $k = \pm 6$

3 $k < 0.5$

4 $k > \frac{1}{3}$

5 $0, -\frac{8}{9}$

6 $k > -1.5$

7 $k > 3\frac{2}{3}$

8 $k = -10, k = 14$

9 $k = 1, k = 4$

Exercise 2.6

1 $k = -3, k = 5$

2 $k = -7, k = -3$

3 $c = \pm 4$

4 $k < 1, k > 5$

5 a $k = \pm 10$

b $(-2, 6), (2, -6)$

6 $k > -5$

7 $k \geqslant 0.75$

8 $-11 < m < 1$

9 $m = -2, m = -6$

Exercise 2.7

1 $3 < k < 4$

2 $-1 < x < 0$

3 a $2\left(x - \frac{1}{4}\right)^2 + \frac{47}{8}$

b $\frac{47}{8}$ when $x = \frac{1}{4}$

4 $k < -\frac{5}{2}$

5 $-6 < x < 1$

6 $-2, -18$

7 a $a = 20, b = -4, (4, 20)$

b ∩ shaped curve, vertex $= (4, 20)$, y-intercept $= (0, 4)$

8 $k = c + 9$

9 $k < -6, k > 10$

10 a $a = -12, b = -4$ b -4

11 $m < 2, m > 14$

12 a

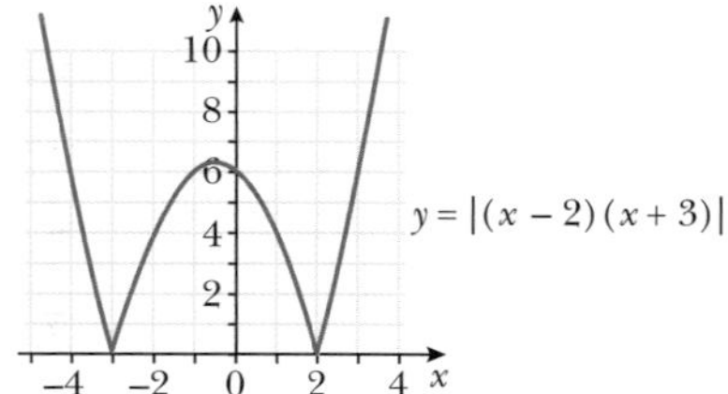

b $\left(-\frac{1}{2}, \frac{25}{4}\right)$

c $k > \frac{25}{4}$

13 i -27

ii $\frac{9}{8}$

14 $k < 2$

15 a $-5 \leqslant x \leqslant \frac{1}{4}$

b i $(x + 4)^2 - 25$

ii $25, -4$

iii

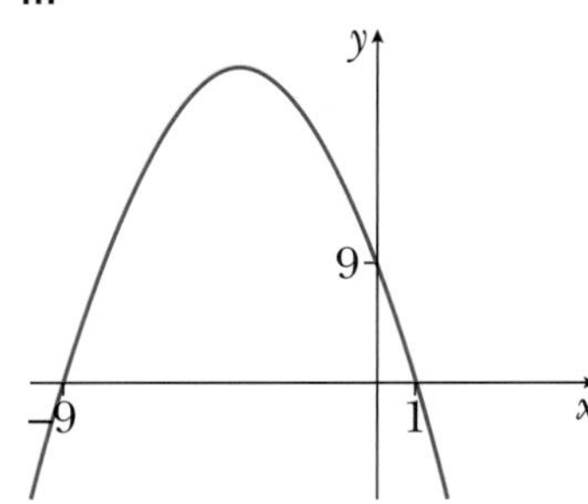

Chapter 3

Exercise 3.1

1 a x^{15} b x^{16} c x^{-3}
d x^5 e x^{-2} f x^{-15}
g x^2 h x^2 i $15x^6y^4$
j $5x^3y^{-2}$ k $16x^{12}y^6$ l $6x^6y^{-3}$

2 a x^4 b x^5 c x^4
d $\frac{9}{4}x^{-4}y^{-1}$

3 a $a = 1,\ b = 3,\ c = 5$

4 a $a = -\frac{7}{2},\ b = 1$

5 $x = \frac{3}{5},\ y = -1$

6 $x = 5,\ y = 8$

7 $x(1 + x)^{\frac{1}{2}}$

Exercise 3.2

1 a $\frac{1}{5}$ b 3
c −3 or 2 d $-\frac{1}{2}$ or 5

2 a 4 b 2 c 5
d 1 e −1 f −3
g −4 h ±4

3 a 6 b −1 c −7
d −10 e $-4\frac{2}{3}$ f $-\frac{4}{5}$
g −3 h $4\frac{1}{3}$ i $\frac{5}{16}$
j 1 or 3 k −1 or 4
l −0.5 or 2

4 a 0.8 b 1.5 c $-\frac{5}{3}$
d 8

5 a 0 b 3 c 0.4
d $\frac{1}{7}$

6 a −1 b 3 c −1.5

7 a $x = \frac{11}{6},\ y = -\frac{1}{3}$
b $x = \frac{3}{4},\ y = \frac{1}{4}$
c $x = \frac{7}{6},\ y = \frac{3}{2}$

8 a $-\frac{1}{2}$ or 4 b 2

9 a $-\frac{5}{4}$ or 3 b 1

10 a $-\frac{1}{3}$ or 3 b 9

Exercise 3.3

1 a $10\sqrt{5}$ b $5\sqrt{10}$
c $9\sqrt{11}$ d $5\sqrt{3}$

2 a $5\sqrt{5} + 4\sqrt{3}$
b $4\sqrt{5} + 5\sqrt{3}$
c $12\sqrt{5} + 5\sqrt{3}$
d $20\sqrt{5} + 27\sqrt{3}$

3 a $2 + 13\sqrt{7}$
b $10 + 35\sqrt{7}$
c $2 + (2n - 1)\sqrt{7}$

4 a $\sqrt{33}$ b $11 + \sqrt{35}$

5 $x = 5 - 3\sqrt{2},\ y = 8 + 4\sqrt{2},$
$z = 12 - 7\sqrt{2}.$

6 a $1 + \sqrt{2}$ b $3 + 2\sqrt{2}$

Exercise 3.4

1 a 6 b 12 c $\sqrt{30}$
d 2 e 13 f $5\sqrt{5}$
g $15\sqrt{6}$ h $14\sqrt{35}$

2 a 2 b $\sqrt{2}$ c 2
d $\frac{1}{2}$ e $\frac{1}{3}$ f $\sqrt{5}$
g 3 h $\frac{2}{5}$ i $\frac{\sqrt{5}}{9}$
j $\sqrt{2}$ k 6 l $\sqrt{5}$

3 a $2\sqrt{2}$ b $2\sqrt{3}$ c $2\sqrt{5}$
d $2\sqrt{7}$ e $5\sqrt{2}$ f $6\sqrt{2}$
g $3\sqrt{2}$ h $4\sqrt{2}$ i $4\sqrt{5}$
j $3\sqrt{10}$ k $3\sqrt{7}$ l $3\sqrt{11}$
m $2\sqrt{11}$ n $5\sqrt{5}$ o $3\sqrt{13}$
p $10\sqrt{2}$ q $5\sqrt{3}$ r $10\sqrt{30}$
s $\sqrt{5}$ t $\sqrt{3}$ u $2\sqrt{5}$
v $10\sqrt{2}$ w $2\sqrt{10}$ x $4\sqrt{3}$
y 35

4 a $9\sqrt{3}$ b $3\sqrt{3}$ c $5\sqrt{5}$
d $7\sqrt{3}$ e 0 f $9\sqrt{5}$
g $2\sqrt{5}$ h $-3\sqrt{5}$ i $6\sqrt{7}$
j $8\sqrt{2}$ k $10\sqrt{2}$ l 0
m $20\sqrt{5}$ n $8\sqrt{3}$ o $6\sqrt{2}$

5 a $2 + 3\sqrt{2}$ b 12
c $-4 + 5\sqrt{2}$ d $9 + 5\sqrt{3}$
e $3 - \sqrt{3}$ f 20
g 1 h $-2 + 4\sqrt{3}$
i $12 + 5\sqrt{5}$ j 7
k 13 l −4
m 4 n $17 + 3\sqrt{35}$
o $23 + 16\sqrt{2}$

6 a $9 + 4\sqrt{5}$ b $28 - 10\sqrt{3}$
c $91 + 40\sqrt{3}$ d $5 + 2\sqrt{6}$

7 $(10 + 12\sqrt{2})\ \text{cm}^2$

8 a 293 b $a = 9,\ b = 10$
c $p = 45,\ q = 2$

9 $(11 + 7\sqrt{2})\ \text{cm}^3$

10 $\sqrt{2}$

11 a $a = 4,\ b = 2$ b $c = 9,\ d = 2$

Exercise 3.5

1 a $\frac{\sqrt{5}}{5}$ b $\frac{3\sqrt{2}}{2}$ c $3\sqrt{3}$
d $\frac{\sqrt{3}}{3}$ e $\frac{4\sqrt{5}}{5}$ f $4\sqrt{3}$

g $\frac{2\sqrt{3}}{3}$ h $\frac{5\sqrt{2}}{2}$ i $\frac{3\sqrt{2}}{4}$

j $\frac{1}{4}$ k $\frac{\sqrt{5}}{5}$ l $\frac{\sqrt{13}}{13}$

m $\frac{5\sqrt{2}}{4}$ n $\frac{7\sqrt{3}}{6}$ o $\frac{5+\sqrt{5}}{5}$

p $\frac{3-\sqrt{3}}{3}$ q $\frac{-2+3\sqrt{2}}{2}$

r $-1+2\sqrt{7}$

2 a $-1+\sqrt{2}$ b $\frac{3-\sqrt{5}}{4}$

c $\frac{3-\sqrt{7}}{2}$ d $3+\sqrt{5}$

e $-10+5\sqrt{5}$ f $\frac{-7-2\sqrt{7}}{3}$

g $4+2\sqrt{3}$ h $\frac{15+10\sqrt{3}}{3}$

i $\frac{2\sqrt{3}+\sqrt{2}}{10}$ j $4\sqrt{7}+4\sqrt{5}$

3 a $7-4\sqrt{3}$ b $\frac{5+4\sqrt{2}}{7}$

c $\frac{5+3\sqrt{2}}{7}$ d $\frac{9-2\sqrt{14}}{5}$

e $2+\sqrt{5}$ f $\frac{14-\sqrt{187}}{3}$

g $\frac{-5+\sqrt{21}}{2}$ h $\frac{30+\sqrt{851}}{7}$

4 a $\sqrt{3}$ b $\frac{3\sqrt{7}-\sqrt{2}}{5}$

c $\frac{12+\sqrt{3}}{13}$

5 $(2\sqrt{5}-\sqrt{2})$ cm

6 $(4-\sqrt{5})$ cm

7 $7-2\sqrt{3}$ cm

8 a $\frac{1+5\sqrt{2}}{7}$ b $\frac{15+14\sqrt{2}}{2}$

9 $\frac{23-4\sqrt{7}}{30}$

10 $6-4\sqrt{2}$

Exercise 3.6

1 a $\frac{6+\sqrt{15}}{7}$ b $\frac{\sqrt{10}+2\sqrt{5}}{5}$

c $\frac{\sqrt{85}+2\sqrt{15}}{5}$

2 a $1+\sqrt{2}, 3-2\sqrt{2}$

b $2+\sqrt{6}, 3-\sqrt{6}$

c $2+\sqrt{5}, -3\sqrt{5}$

d $3+\sqrt{7}, 5-2\sqrt{7}$

e $3-\sqrt{2}, 5+\sqrt{2}$

3 a $\frac{100}{9}$ b $\frac{1}{9}$

c no solution d 5

e 19.5 f 2

g 15 h $2\sqrt{2}$

i 20

4 a 1 b 3 c 3

d −3 e 1 f 5

g 4 h no solution

i 4 j 0 or 1 j 0 or 2

5 a −3 or 1 b 9 c 0 or 4

d 0 e 3 f −4.5

6 $\frac{7+2\sqrt{6}}{5}$

7 $\frac{2+\sqrt{2}}{2}$

Exercise 3.7

1 2 or 3

2 $x=3, y=-0.5$

3 −4.5

4 $a=-3, 2$ $b=-18, 12$

5 $6-3\sqrt{3}$

6 $17\sqrt{5}+1$

7 a i $45-12\sqrt{10}+8$
$=53-12\sqrt{10}$

ii $-3\sqrt{5}+2\sqrt{2}$

b $-1+\sqrt{6}$

8 $7+3\sqrt{5}$

9 $a=-\frac{13}{6}, b=0, c=1$

10 $p=-27, q=23$

Chapter 4

Exercise 4.1

1 a $3x^4+2x^3+3x^2$

b $9x^4+2x^3+7x^2-2$

c $3x^4-4x^3-3$

d $6x^7+3x^6+4x^5+5x^4-2x^3+x^2-1$

2 a $8x^4-4x^3+2x^2+3x-2$

b $3x^4+8x^3+4x^2-3x-2$

c $3x^5+5x^4-3x^3+7x^2+8x-20$

d $3x^5+12x^4+13x^3+3x^2-4$

e $x^4-10x^3+29x^2-20x+4$

f $27x^3-27x^2+9x-1$

3 a $3x^2+x-7$

b $2x^3+17x^2+21x-4$

c $2x^5+5x^4-8x^3-x^2-19x$

4 a x^3+7x^2+x-4

b $4x^4-4x^3-15x^2+8x+16$

c $8x^4-8x^3-32x^2+17x+32$

d $4x^4-4x^3-5x^2+3x-2$

Exercise 4.2

1 a $x^2+2x-48$

b x^2+x-1

c $x^2-15x+25$

d x^2+2x+1

e x^2+4x-5

f x^2-9

2 a $3x^2+2x-1$

b $2x^2+3x-2$

c $3x^2-5x-10$

d $3x^2+4$

3 a $3x^2-4$

b $2x^2-x+5$

c $x-4$

d $x+3$

4 a $x^3 - x^2 + x - 1$

b $x^2 + 2x + 4$

Exercise 4.3

2 a 29

b 546

c 12

3 $b = -2 - 2a$

4 a $a = 0,\ b = -19$

b $a = 2,\ b = 38$

c $a = -12,\ b = -7$

5 $-66, 18$

6 $a = 13.5,\ b = 5.5$

7 a $p = 1,\ q = 9$

8 b 0, 1, 3

Exercise 4.4

1 b $(2x-1)(x+1)(x-1)$

2 a $(x-2)(x^2+4x+5)$

b $(x+4)(x+2)(x-2)$

c $x(2x+3)(x-6)$

d $(x-7)(x+1)(x-2)$

e $(2x+1)(x-3)(x-4)$

f $(x-2)(x+3)(3x-1)$

g $(2x-1)(2x+1)(x-2)$

h $(2x-1)(x-3)(x+5)$

3 a $-5, 1, 7$ b $1, 2, 3$

c $-4, -2, \frac{1}{3}$ d $-4, 1, 1.5$

e $-2, 0.5, 3$ f $-4, -\frac{1}{2}, 1$

g $-2, -1.5, 0.5$ h $-4, 2.5, 3$

4 a $1, -3 \pm \sqrt{7}$

b $-3, -\frac{5}{2} \pm \frac{1}{2}\sqrt{37}$

c $2, -2 \pm \sqrt{3}$

d $1.5, 1, 4$

5 $-0.5, -2 \pm \sqrt{13}$

6 $-5.54, -3, 0.54$

7 b 2

8 a $x^3 - 4x^2 - 7x + 10$

b $x^3 + 3x^2 - 18x - 40$

c $x^3 + x^2 - 6x$

9 a $2x^3 - 11x^2 + 10x + 8$

b $2x^3 - 7x^2 + 7x - 2$

c $2x^3 - 9x^2 - 8x + 15$

10 $x^3 + x^2 - 7x - 3$

11 $2x^3 - 9x^2 + 6x - 1$

12 b $2, \frac{1 \pm \sqrt{33}}{8}$

Exercise 4.5

1 a 5 b -1

c 76 d 2

2 a 5 b 57

c 11

3 $a = 4,\ b = 0$

4 $a = -6,\ b = -6$

5 a $a = -8,\ b = 15$

b $3, \frac{-1+\sqrt{21}}{2}, \frac{-1-\sqrt{21}}{2}$

6 a $a = -9,\ b = 2$

b 5

7 $b = 2$

8 $a = 6,\ b = -3$

9 a $b = 12 - 2a$

b $a = 5,\ b = 2$

10 a 5 b -72

11 a $a = -8,\ b = -5$

b -30

12 32

13 b $3, \frac{-7+\sqrt{13}}{6}, \frac{-7-\sqrt{13}}{6}$

14 a 3 b -5

15 $a = 2,\ b = -5,\ c = 7$

16 b $-3, 6$

Exercise 4.6

1 b $(x-2)(x-4)(3x+4)$

2 $a = -2,\ b = 2.5$

3 b $b^2 - 4ac = -11$

4 a -17 b 71

5 $(x+1)(x-7)(2x+1)$

6 $a = 7,\ b = -6$

7 i $a = 6,\ b = 2$

ii $(2x-1)(3x^2+5x-2)$

iii $(2x-1)(3x-1)(x+2)$

Chapter 5

Exercise 5.1

1 a $1, \frac{1}{3}$ b $-\frac{1}{2}$

c $-1, \frac{7}{3}$ d $-1, 0$

e $-\frac{1}{3}, \frac{3}{5}$ f $-\frac{6}{5}, -\frac{2}{7}$

g $-\frac{3}{5}, 7$ h $\frac{7}{4}$

i $-\frac{14}{3}, -\frac{6}{7}$

2 $x = \frac{13}{2},\ y = \frac{3}{2}$

3 $x = -\frac{7}{3}$ or $x = -\frac{5}{3}$

4 a $x = \pm 2,\ x = \pm 4$

c $f(x) \geqslant -1$

5 $x = -2,\ x = \frac{10}{3}$

6 $x = 0,\ y = 5$ or $x = 2,\ y = 3$

7 $x = 4,\ y = -\frac{5}{2}$

Exercise 5.2

1 $4 < x < 8$

2 **a**

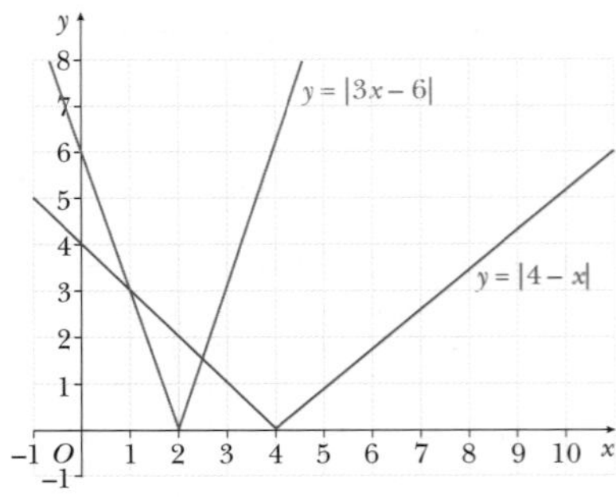

b $x \leqslant 1$ or $x \geqslant \frac{5}{2}$

3 **a** $x < -1$ or $x > 4$

b $-1 \leqslant x \leqslant \frac{13}{5}$

c $2 < x < \frac{10}{3}$

d $x < 2$ or $x > 5$

e $x < -3$ or $x > \frac{7}{3}$

f $-1 \leqslant x \leqslant 6$

4 **a** $\frac{4}{3} \leqslant x \leqslant 2$

b $x > \frac{2}{3}$ **c** $x \geqslant \frac{1}{4}$

5 **a** $x \leqslant -1$ or $x \geqslant \frac{1}{5}$

b $x > -\frac{1}{2}$

c $\frac{1}{2} < x < 1$

d $x < -1$ or $x > -\frac{3}{5}$

e $-1 \leqslant x \leqslant 3$ **f** $-3 < x < 1$

6 **a** $x > \frac{3}{2}$ **b** $x \leqslant -\frac{3}{2}$

c $x \leqslant -2$ or $x \geqslant -\frac{3}{2}$

d $-6 \leqslant x \leqslant 0$

e $-14 < x < 2$

f $x \leqslant -\frac{1}{2}$ or $x \geqslant 3$

7 **a** $-7 < x < 1$

b $\frac{2}{5} < x < 4$

c $x \leqslant -2$ or $x \geqslant \frac{1}{4}$

8 $x \geqslant \frac{k}{2}$

9 $x < \frac{k}{5}$ or $x > \frac{7k}{3}$

10 $-\frac{4}{3} \leqslant x \leqslant \frac{4}{3}$

Exercise 5.3

1 $A(-1, 0)$, $B(2, 0)$, $C(3, 0)$, $D(0, 6)$

2 **a** shaped curve, axis intercepts $(-3, 0)$, $(2, 0)$, $(4, 0)$, $(0, 24)$

b shaped curve, axis intercepts $(-2, 0)$, $(-1, 0)$, $(3, 0)$, $(0, 6)$

c shaped curve, axis intercepts $(-2, 0)$, $\left(-\frac{1}{2}, 0\right)$, $(2, 0)$, $(0, -4)$

d shaped curve, axis intercepts $(-2, 0)$, $(1, 0)$, $\left(\frac{3}{2}, 0\right)$, $(0, -6)$

3 $A\left(\frac{7}{2}, 0\right)$, $B(0, 14)$

4 **a** shaped curve, axisintercepts $(-2, 0)$ and $(0, 0)$ where $(0, 0)$ is a minimum point

b shaped curve, axis intercepts $\left(\frac{5}{2}, 0\right)$ and $(0, 0)$ where $(0, 0)$ is a minimum point

c shaped curve, axis intercepts $(-1, 0)$, $(2, 0)$, $(0, -2)$ where $(-1, 0)$ is a maximum point

d shaped curve, axis intercepts $(2, 0)$, $\left(\frac{10}{3}, 0\right)$, $(0, 40)$ where $(2, 0)$ is a minimum point

5 **a**

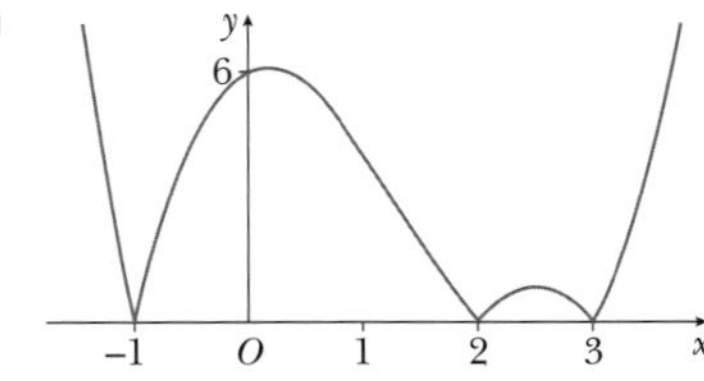

b

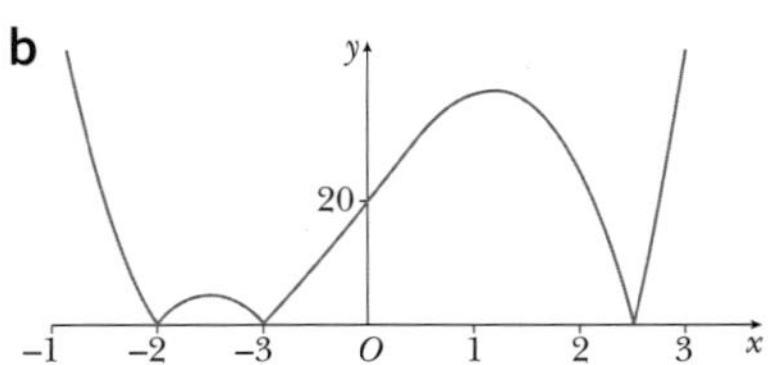

c

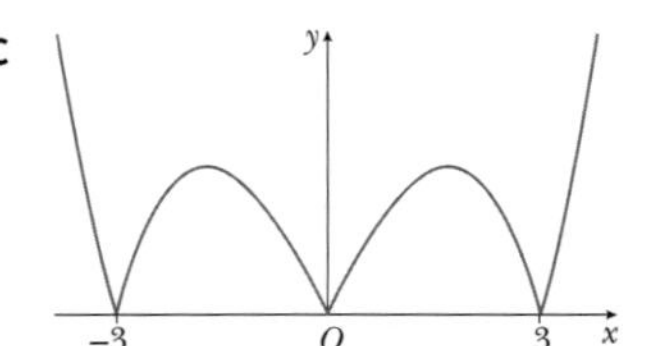

d

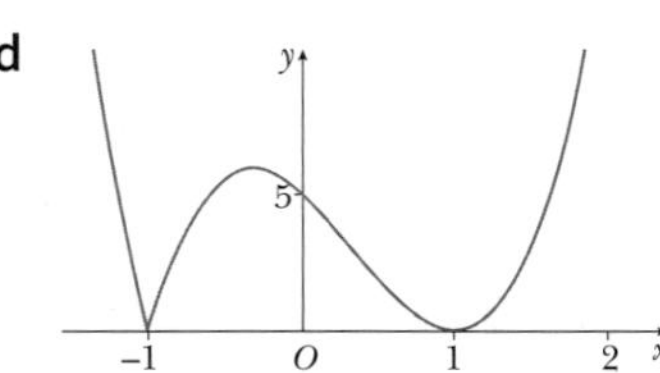

6 **a** shaped curve, axis intercepts $(-3, 0)$, $(0, 0)$, $(3, 0)$

b shaped curve, axis intercepts $(-3, 0)$, $(-2, 0)$, $(1, 0)$, $(0, -6)$

c shaped curve, axis intercepts $(-4, 0)$, $\left(\frac{1}{2}, 0\right)$, $(3, 0)$, $(0, 12)$

d shaped curve, axis intercepts $(-3, 0)$, $\left(-\frac{5}{2}, 0\right)$, $(4, 0)$, $(0, -60)$

7 **a**

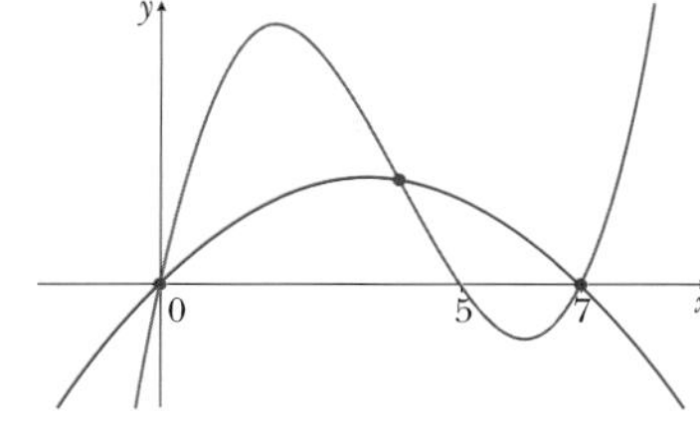

b (0, 0), (4, 12), (7, 0)

8 **a**

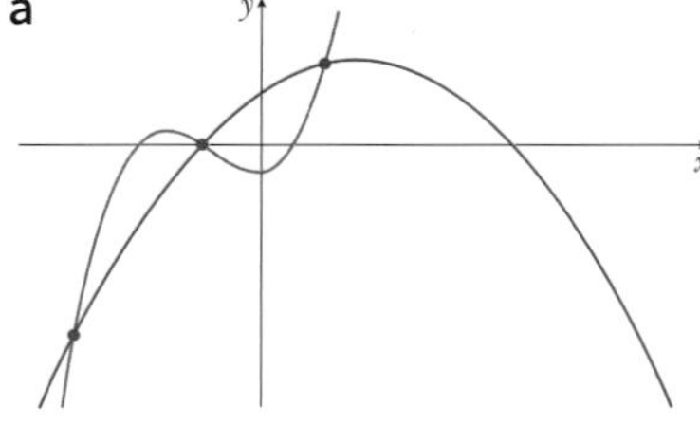

blue curve axis intercepts:
(–2, 0), (–1, 0), $\left(\frac{1}{2}, 0\right)$, (0, –2)
red curve axis intercepts:,
(–1, 0), (4, 0), (0, 4)

b (–3, –14), (–1, 0), (1, 6)

9 $a = 1$, $b = 2$ and $k = -2$

10 $a = -1$, $b = 1$, $c = 2$, $k = 3$

Exercise 5.4

1 **a** $x \leqslant -1$ or $0 \leqslant x \leqslant 2$

b $x \geqslant 2.1$

c $x \leqslant -1.4$ or $1 \leqslant x \leqslant 1.4$

2 **a** $x \leqslant 2$

b $x \geqslant -2$

c $-1.9 \leqslant x \leqslant 0.3$ or $x \geqslant 1.5$

3 **a** $x \geqslant 2.5$

b $-1 \leqslant x \leqslant 1$ or $x \geqslant 2$

c $x < -0.8$ or $0.6 \leqslant x \leqslant 2.2$

Exercise 5.5

1 **a** ±2, ±1 **b** $\pm\sqrt{2}$

c ±4, ±2 **d** $\pm\sqrt{2}$

e $\pm\sqrt{7}$ **f** ±3

g $\pm\sqrt{2}, \pm\frac{\sqrt{3}}{2}$ **h** $\pm\sqrt{\frac{2}{3}}$

i –1, 2

2 **a** ±0.356, ±2.81 **b** ±2.3

c ±1.16 **d** –1.11, 1.42

e 1.26, –0.693 **f** ±1.4

3 **a** 4, 25 **b** 16

c 9 **d** 25

e $\frac{9}{16}, \frac{9}{4}$ **f** $\frac{25}{9}$

g $\frac{1}{4}$, 16 **h** $\frac{1}{9}$, 2

i $\frac{1}{4}$, 16

4 $\frac{27}{8}$, 8

5 **a** $5\sqrt{x} = x + 4$ **b** (1, 1) (16, 4)

6 **a** 1, 2 **b** 0, 2

c –1, 2 **d** –2, 3

e –1

7 –2

8 1, 2

9 –4, –3, 0, 1

Exercise 5.6

1 $x = \frac{8}{5}$ or $x = 2$

2 $x < -3$ or $x > 4$

3 $\frac{4}{5} < x < 2$

4 $\frac{1}{2} < x < 1$

5 $x \geqslant -\frac{1}{2}$

6 $-6 < x < -\frac{2}{3}$

7 $x > -\frac{k}{2}$

8 **a** –1, 27

a –1, 3

9 shaped curve, axis intercepts (0, 0), $\left(\frac{3}{2}, 0\right)$, 1, 0)

10 shaped curve, axis intercepts (–1, 0) $\left(\frac{1}{2}, 0\right)$, (3, 0), (0, 6)

11 $x < -0.8$ or $0.55 < x < 2.25$

12 **a** shaped curve, axis intercepts (–2, 0), (1, 0), (4, 0), (0, 8)

b

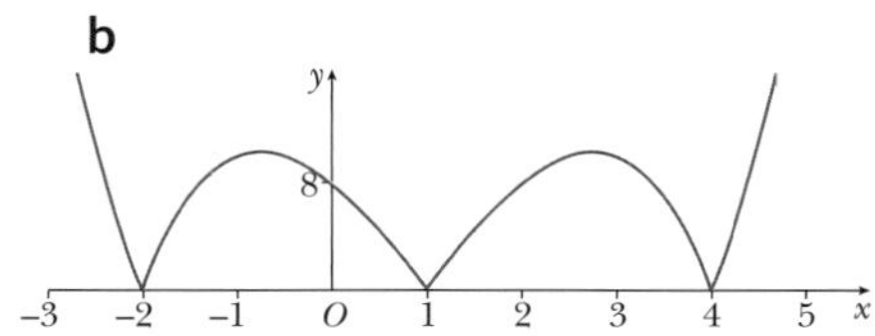

13 **a** $x(x - 2)(x + 3)$

b shaped curve, axis crossing points(–3, 0), (0, 0), (2, 0)

14 **a**

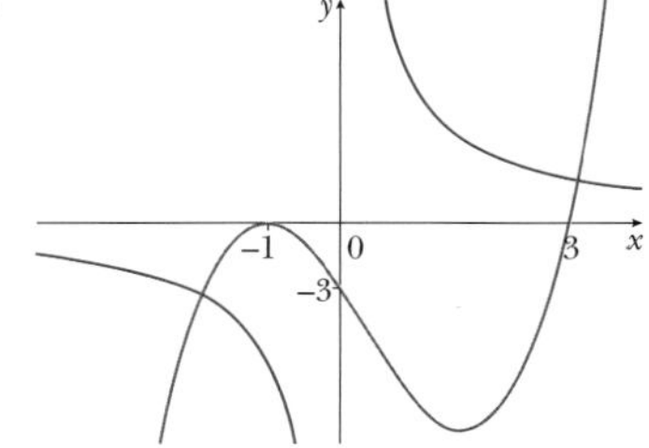

b 2

15 **a** $(x + 4)(2x - 1)(x - 3)$

b shaped curve, axis intercepts(–4, 0), $\left(\frac{1}{2}, 0\right)$, (3, 0), (0, 12)

16 **a**

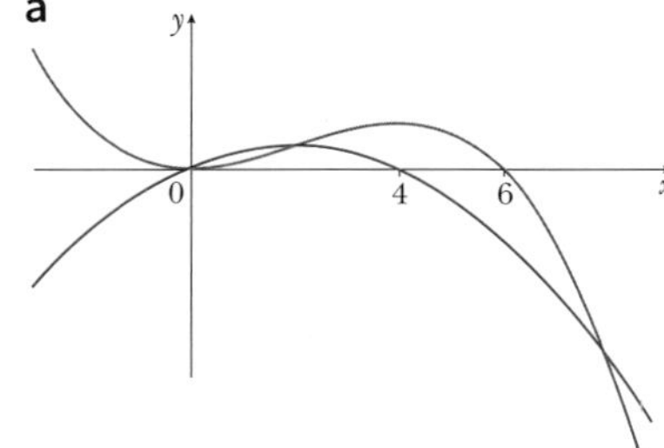

b (0, 0), (2, 16), (8, –128)

Chapter 6

Exercise 6.1

1 **a** lg 1000 = 3

b lg 100 = 2

c $\lg 1000000 = 6$

d $x = \lg 2$

e $x = \lg 15$

f $x = \lg 0.06$

2 a 1.88 b 2.48

c 2.86 d 1.19

e −1.70 f −2.30

3 a $10^5 = 10000$

b $10^1 = 1$ c $10^{-3} = \frac{1}{1000}$

d $x = 10^{7.5}$ e $x = 10^{1.7}$

f $x = 10^{-0.8}$

4 a 126000 b 1450

c 145 d 0.501

e 0.0316 f 0.00145

5 a 4 b −2

c 0.5 d $\frac{1}{3}$

e 1.5 f 2.5

Exercise 6.2

1 a $\log_4 64 = 3$

b $\log_2 32 = 5$

c $\log_5 125 = 3$

d $\log_6 36 = 2$

e $\log_2 \frac{1}{32} = -5$

f $\log_3 \frac{1}{81} = -4$

g $\log_a b = 2$

h $\log_x 4 = y$

i $\log_a c = b$

2 a $2^2 = 4$ b $2^6 = 64$

c $5^0 = 1$ d $3^2 = 9$

e $36^{\frac{1}{2}} = 6$ f $8^{\frac{1}{3}} = 2$

g $x^0 = 1$ h $x^y = 8$

i $a^c = b$

3 a 16 b 9

c 625 d $\sqrt{3}$

e 12 f 3 g 17

h 4 i −41

4 a 2 b 4 c 3

d −2 e 5 f 3.5

g 2.5 h −1.5 i 0.5

j −0.5 k $\frac{1}{3}$ l −0.5

5 a 2 b $\frac{1}{3}$ c 1.5

d −2 e −6 f 3.5

g $\frac{2}{3}$ h $\frac{7}{6}$

6 a 8 b 625

Exercise 6.3

1 a $\log_2 15$ b $\log_3 6$

c $\log_5 64$ d $\log_7 2$

e $\log_3 20$ f $\log_7 \left(\frac{1}{2}\right)$

g $\log_4 12$ h $\lg \frac{1}{20}$

i $\log_4 6.4$

2 a 3 b 2 c 1

d 1 e 1.5 f −2

3 a $\log_5 36$ b $\log_2 \frac{4}{3}$

4 a $2^4, 2^{-2}$ b −2

5 a 2 b 3 c −3

d −1

6 a 5^u b $u - 2$

c $1 + \frac{1}{2}u$ d $\frac{3}{2}u - 3$

7 a $1 + x$ b $2 - x$

c $x + 2y$ d 4^{x+y}

8 a −8 b −5.5

c 13 d 34

9 a 8 b 20

c 14 d 0

Exercise 6.4

1 a 5 b 7.5 c 25

d 77

2 a 12 b 8 c 10

d 3 e 0.7 f 7.5

3 a 2, 8 b 5 c 6

d 4 e 3 f $\frac{1}{4}, \frac{3}{2}$

g 5 h 20

4 a 16 b 4 c $\frac{2}{3}$

d $\sqrt{3}$

5 a 5, 25 b $\frac{1}{125}$, 3125

c $\frac{1}{125}$, 15625 d $\frac{1}{512}$, 16

6 a $x = 4,\ y = 16$

b $x = 20,\ y = 10$

c $x = 4,\ y = 12$

d $x = 40,\ y = 16$

e $a = 6.25,\ b = 2.5$

f $x = 1.25,\ y = 2.5$

7 b $\lg x = 8,\ \lg y = 2$

Exercise 6.5

1 a 6.13 b 2.73 c 0.861

d 2.41 e 2.65 f 1.66

g 6.90 h 5.19 i 1.15

j −13.4 k 0.641 l 0.262

2 b 10 c 3.32

3 a 0.415 b 2.42 c 2.46

d 1.63 e 1.03

4 −0.751, 1.38

5 a 0, 1.46

b 1.40 c 2.32 d 0.683

6 0.683, 1.21

7 a 1.58

b 0.257, 0.829

c 0.631, 1.26

d 0.792, 0.161

8 a 2.32 b 1.16

c 0.631, 1.26

d 0.431, 1.43

9 a 0.6 b −0.189

10 a 1.26 b 2.81

c ±1.89 d ±2.81

11 $x < \dfrac{\log_{10} 3}{\log_{10} 2}$

Exercise 6.6

1 a 3.32 b 3.18

c 1.29 d −3.08

2 a $\dfrac{1}{u}$ b $\dfrac{2}{u}$

c $\dfrac{1}{2u}$ d $\dfrac{3}{2u}$

3 a $\dfrac{1}{x}$ b $1 + x$

c $2x$ d $4 + 2x$

4 a 4 b 0.4

5 $\dfrac{1}{3}$

6 a 23 b 23

7 a $\dfrac{1}{2}\log_2 x$

b 256

8 a 16 b 9

c 1.59 d 1.87

9 a $\dfrac{1}{\log_3 x}$ b 3, 9

10 a $\dfrac{1}{27}$, 27 b 5

c $\dfrac{1}{256}$, 4 d 16, 64

e $\dfrac{1}{2}$, 512 f 25

11 a $\dfrac{1}{2}\log_2 x$ b $\dfrac{1}{3}\log_2 y$

c $x = 32$, $y = 2$

12 $x = 6.75$, $y = 13.5$

Exercise 6.7

1 a 7.39 b 4.48 c 1.22

d 0.0498

2 a 1.39 b 0.742 c −0.357

d −0.942

3 a 5 b 8 c [illegible]

d −2

4 a 7 b 2.5 c [illegible]

d 0.05

5 a 4.25 b 1.67 c 1.77

d 1.30

6 a $\ln 7$ b $\ln 3$

c $\dfrac{1}{2}(5 + \ln 3)$ d $\dfrac{1}{3}(1 + 3\ln 2)$

7 a 20.1 b 0.135 c [illegible]100

d 12.5

8 a 3.49 b −2.15 c [illegible].262

9 a $3 + e^2$ b $\dfrac{1}{2}(1 + \ln 7)$

c $2\ln 2$ d $\dfrac{1}{2}\ln$ [illegible]

e $2\ln 2$, $\ln 5$ f $\ln 2$, $\ln 3$

10 a 1.79 b 0, 1.39

c −3.69, 4.38

11 a $x = \dfrac{1}{e^2}$, $y = \dfrac{1}{e}$

b $x = \ln 0.6$, $y = \ln 0.1$[illegible]

12 0.822

13 0, 0.4

14 $\pm\sqrt{2}$, $\dfrac{1}{2}\ln 5$

Exercise 6.8

1 a 409 600 b 16.61

2 a 43 000 b 2091

3 a 0.0462 b 724

4 a 500 b 82.6

c 2.31

5 a \$250 000 b 0.112[illegible]

c 6.18

6 a $\dfrac{4}{3}$

b $\dfrac{81}{80}$, A_0 represents the area of the patch at the start of the measurements

c 6.72

Exercise 6.10

1 a asymptote: $y = -4$, y-intercept: $(0, -2)$ x-intercept: $(\ln 2, 0)$

b asymptote: $y = 6$, y-intercept: $(0, 9)$

c asymptote: $y = 2$, y-intercept: $(0, 7)$

d asymptote: $y = 6$, y-intercept: $(0, 8)$

e asymptote: $y = -1$, y-intercept: $(0, 2)$ x-intercept: $(\ln 3, 0)$

f asymptote: $y = 4$, y-intercept: $(0, 2)$ x-intercept: $(-\ln 2, 0)$

g asymptote: $y = 1$, y-intercept: $(0, 5)$

h asymptote: $y = 8$, y-intercept: $(0, 10)$

i asymptote: $y = 2$, y-intercept: $(0, 1)$ x-intercept: $\left(\dfrac{1}{4}\ln 2, 0\right)$

2 a asymptote: $x = -2$, x-intercept: $(-1.5, 0)$ y-intercept: $(0, \ln 4)$

b asymptote: $x = 2$, x-intercept: $\left(2\dfrac{1}{3}, 0\right)$

c asymptote: $x = 4$, x-intercept: $(3.5, 0)$ y-intercept: $(0, \ln 8)$

d asymptote: $x = -1$, x-intercept: $(-0.5, 0)$ y-intercept: $(0, 2\ln 2)$

e asymptote: $x = 2$, x-intercept: $(2.5, 0)$

f asymptote: $x = 1.5$, x-intercept: $\left(1\frac{2}{3}, 0\right)$

Exercise 6.11

1 a $f^{-1}(x) = \ln(x-4)$, $x > 4$

b $f^{-1}(x) = \ln(x+2)$, $x > -2$

c $f^{-1}(x) = \ln\left(\frac{x+1}{5}\right)$, $x > -1$

d $f^{-1}(x) = \frac{1}{2}\ln\left(\frac{x-1}{3}\right)$, $x > 1$

e $f^{-1}(x) = \frac{1}{2}\ln\left(\frac{x-3}{5}\right)$, $x > 3$

f $f^{-1}(x) = -\frac{1}{3}\ln\left(\frac{x-5}{4}\right)$, $x > 5$

g $f^{-1}(x) = \ln(2-x)$, $x < 2$

h $f^{-1}(x) = -\frac{1}{2}\ln\left(\frac{5-x}{2}\right)$, $x < 5$

2 a $f^{-1}(x) = e^x - 1$

b $f^{-1}(x) = e^x + 3$

c $f^{-1}(x) = e^{0.5x} - 2$

d $f^{-1}(x) = \frac{1}{2}(e^{0.5x} - 1)$

e $f^{-1}(x) = \frac{1}{2}\left(e^{\frac{1}{3}x} + 5\right)$

f $f^{-1}(x) = \frac{1}{3}(e^{-0.2x} + 1)$

3 a $f(x) > 1$

b $f^{-1}(x) = \frac{1}{2}\ln(x-1)$

c $x > 1$ d x

4 a i $5x$ ii $x + \ln 5$.

b $\sqrt{5}$

5 a i x^3 ii $3x$

b $\frac{1}{2}\ln 2$

6 a $(2x+1)^2$

b $x = \ln 2$

Exercise 6.12

1 a $5y^2 - 7y + 2 = 0$

b $0, -0.569$

2 $x = 5.8$, $y = 2.2$

3 a $g^{-1}(x) = \ln\left(\frac{x+2}{4}\right)$

b $x = 1$

4 a 10 b -5 c $\frac{1}{7}$

5 a 2 b 4, 6

6 3.14

7 $\lg \frac{ab^3}{1000}$

8 -0.569

9 a 70 b 39.7 c 17.0

10 a $\frac{1}{3}\log_3 x$

b $y = 125a$

11 i -2 ii $-n$

iii $y = 5$ iv $x = 10$

12 a i

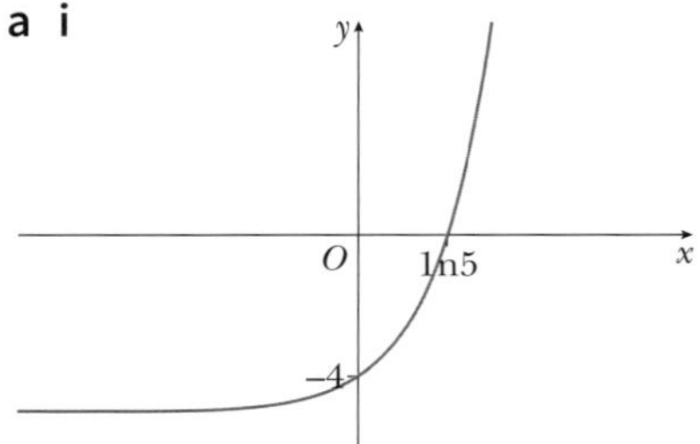

ii $k \leqslant -5$

b $\frac{5}{2}\log_a 2$ c $x = 36$

13 a $p = 5$, $q = 2$ b $x = 4$

Chapter 7

Exercise 7.1

1 a 3 b 4 c 10

d 13 e 5 f 25

g $\sqrt{74}$ h $\sqrt{13}$ i $12\sqrt{2}$

2 a $2\sqrt{5}$, $3\sqrt{5}$, $\sqrt{65}$; right-angled

b $2\sqrt{13}$, 10, $4\sqrt{10}$; not right-angled

c $4\sqrt{5}$, $3\sqrt{5}$, $5\sqrt{5}$; right-angled

4 5 and -5

5 1 and 3

6 a $(6, 4)$ b $(6.5, 7)$

c $(3, 8)$ d $(0.5, 1.5)$

e $(-4.5, -2.5)$

f $(3a, b)$

7 $a = 18$, $b = -8$

8 a $(0, 4.5)$ b $(1, 1)$

9 1

10 $A(-5, 2)$, $B(9, 4)$, $C(-3, 6)$

Exercise 7.2

1 a -2 b -3 c 0

d $3\frac{1}{3}$ e $\frac{1}{3}$ f $-\frac{3}{4}$

2 a $-\frac{1}{3}$ b 2 c $-\frac{5}{2}$

d $-\frac{4}{5}$ d $\frac{2}{5}$

3 a $\frac{2}{3}$ b $-\frac{3}{2}$

4 $(-3, -1)$

6 a $-\frac{3}{5}$, $-\frac{1}{2}$

b not collinear

7 5

8 1, 2

9 $(11, 0)$

Exercise 7.3

1 a $y = 3x - 13$

b $y = -4x + 7$

c $y = -\frac{1}{2}x + 1$

2 a $2y = 5x - 11$

b $3x + 2y = 9$

c $x + 2y = 1$

3 a $y = 2x - 10$

b $x + 2y = -8$

c $2y = 3x - 15$

d $x + 4y = 0$

4 a $4x - 5y = -17$

b $(0, 3.4)$

c 3.4 units^2

5 a $y = -2x$

b $3x + 4y = 2$

c $5x + 7y = -26$

6 a $P\left(1\frac{1}{2}, 0\right)$, $Q\left(0, 2\frac{1}{4}\right)$

b $\frac{3\sqrt{13}}{4}$

c 1.6875 units^2

7 a $(3, 2)$

b $3y = 2x + 5$

8 a $(5, 6)$ b $k = 8$

9 a $y = -2x + 13$

b $(6, 1)$

c $6\sqrt{5}$, $3\sqrt{5}$

d 45 units^2

10 a i $2x + 3y = 14$,

ii $y = \frac{1}{2}x$

b $(4, 2)$

Exercise 7.4

1 a 27.5 units^2

b 22 units^2

2 a 54.5 units^2

b 76 units^2

3 a $k = -9$

b 50 units^2

4 a $(-1, 1.5)$, $(2, -4.5)$

c 22.5 units^2

5 a $(4, 5)$, $(0, -3)$

b 20 units^2

6 a $(0, -7)$

b 60 units^2

7 a $(7.5, 9)$

b 38.25 units^2

8 a $(2, 2)$, $(4, -2)$, $(0, 6)$

b 40 units^2

9 a $(5.5, 1)$

b $(6, 7)$

c 116 units^2

Exercise 7.5

1 a $y = ax^2 + b$, $Y = y$, $X = x^2$, $m = a$, $c = b$

b $yx = ax^2 + b$, $Y = xy$, $X = x^2$, $m = a, c = b$

c $\frac{y}{x} = ax - b$, $Y = \frac{y}{x}$, $X = x$, $m = a, c = -b$

d $x = -b\frac{x}{y} + a$, $Y = x, X = \frac{x}{y}$, $m = -b$, $c = a$

e $y\sqrt{x} = ax + b$, $Y = y\sqrt{x}$ $X = x, m = a, c = b$

f $x^2y = bx^2 + a$, $Y = x^2y$, $X = x^2, m = b$, $c = a$

g $\frac{x}{y} = ax + b$, $Y = \frac{x}{y}$, $X = x, m = a$, $c = b$

h $\frac{\sqrt{x}}{y} = ax - b$, $Y = \frac{\sqrt{x}}{y}$, $X = x, m = a, c = -b$

2 a $\lg y = ax + b$, $Y = \lg y$, $X = x$, $m = a$, $c = b$

b $\ln y = ax - b$, $Y = \ln y$, $X = x$, $m = a, c = -b$

c $\lg y = b\lg x + \lg a$, $Y = \lg y$, $X = \lg x, m = b, c = \lg a$

d $\lg y = x\lg b + \lg a$, $Y = \lg y$, $X = x, m = \lg b$, $c = \lg a$

e $\ln y = -\frac{a}{b}\ln x + \frac{2}{b}, Y = \ln y$, $X = \ln x, m = -\frac{a}{b}$, $c = \frac{2}{b}$

f $\lg x = -y\lg a + \lg b$, $Y = \lg x$, $X = y, m = -\lg a$, $c = \lg b$

g $x^2 = -by + \ln a$, $Y = x^2$, $X = y, m = -b$, $c = \ln a$

h $\ln y = bx + \ln a$, $Y = \ln y$, $X = x, m = b$, $c = \ln a$

Exercise 7.6

1 a $y = 2x$

b $y = \frac{1}{5}x^3 + 3$

c $y = \sqrt{x} + 1$

d $y = -\frac{1}{2}x^4 + \frac{11}{2}$

e $y = -2 \times 2^x + 7$

f $y = -\frac{5}{4}\ln x + \frac{27}{4}$

2 a ii $y = \frac{1}{x^2 - 1}$ ii $\frac{1}{3}$

b ii $y = 2x^2 + 3x$ ii 14

c ii $y = \frac{8}{x} - 1$ ii 3

d ii $y = \left(13 - 2x^2\right)^2$ ii 25

e ii $y = \frac{5}{4}x^2 - x - \frac{9}{2}$ ii $-\frac{3}{2}$

f ii $y = x^{0.5} - x^{-0.5}$

ii $\frac{3\sqrt{2}}{2}$

3 $y = -2x^5 + 16x^2$

4 a $y^2 = 3\left(2^x\right) + 25$ b 5

5 a $y = -2x^2 + 8x$

b $x = 2.5$, $y = 7.5$

6 a $e^y = x^2 + 1$

b $y = \ln\left(x^2 + 1\right)$

7 a $\lg y = \frac{3}{2}x - 7$

b $y = 10^{-7} \times 10^{\frac{3}{2}x}$

8 **a** $y = 100x^{\frac{3}{2}}$

b 0.64

9 **a** $\ln y = 3\ln x - 1$

b $y = \frac{x^3}{e}$

10 **a** 12.7

b $a = e^{12.7}$, $b = -2$

Exercise 7.7

1 **a**

x	0.5	1.0	1.5	2.0	2.5
xy	0.5	3	5.51	8	10.5

c $y = 5 - \frac{2}{x}$

d $x = 0.8,\ y = 2.5$

2 **a**

$\frac{1}{x}$	10	5	3.33	2.5	2
$\frac{1}{y}$	9.01	6.49	5.68	5.29	5

c $y = \frac{2x}{1+8x}$ **d** 0.22

3 **b** $y = 0.8x + \frac{12}{x}$

c $x = 0.6,\ y = 20.48$

4 **b** $m_0 = 50$, $k = 0.02$

c 29.1

5 **b** $k = 3$, $k = 0.7$

6 **b** $a = 5,\ b = 1.6$

7 **b** $a = 1.8,\ n = 0.5$

8 **b** $a = 0.2,\ b = 3$ **c** 4.56

9 **b** $a = -1.5,\ b = 1.8$ **c** 8.61

10 **b** $a = 3.6,\ b = -0.1$

c gradient = 3.6, intercept = 0.1

11 **b** $y = e^3 \times x^{-0.8}$

c gradient = −0.8, intercept = 3

Exercise 7.8

1 **a** $y = 7$ **b** $3x + 4y = 31$

c 12.5

2 **b** allow − 1.4 to − 1.6

c allow 13 to 16

3 **a** $2\sqrt{5}$ **b** $y = -2x + 6$

c $(3, 0), (-1, 8)$

4 $A = e^2$, $b = e$

5 55

6 **a**

$x\sqrt{x}$	1	2.83	5.20	8	11.18
$y\sqrt{x}$	3.40	4.13	5.07	6.20	7.47

c $a = 3,\ b = 0.4$

d 3.05

7 12.5

8 **a** 6.8

b $A = 898,\ b = -0.5$

9 **i** $2x + 3y = 14$

ii $y + 2 = \frac{3}{2}(x - 10)$

iii $\sqrt{65}$

10 $x + 3y = 2$

11 **i** (0, 3.5) **ii** (3, 5)

iii $2x + y = 11$ **iv** (0, 11)

Chapter 8

Exercise 8.1

1 **a** $\frac{\pi}{18}$ **b** $\frac{\pi}{9}$ **c** $\frac{2\pi}{9}$

d $\frac{5\pi}{18}$ **e** $\frac{\pi}{12}$ **f** $\frac{2\pi}{3}$

g $\frac{3\pi}{4}$ **h** $\frac{5\pi}{4}$ **i** 2π

j 4π **k** $\frac{4\pi}{9}$ **l** $\frac{5\pi}{3}$

m $\frac{\pi}{20}$ **n** $\frac{5\pi}{12}$ **o** $\frac{7\pi}{6}$

2 **a** 90° **b** 30° **c** 15°

d 20° **e** 120° **f** 144°

g 126° **h** 75° **i** 27°

j 162° **k** 216° **l** 540°

m 315° **n** 480° **o** 810°

3 **a** 0.559 **b** 0.960 **c** 1.47

d 2.15 **e** 4.31

4 **a** 74.5° **b** 143.2° **c** 59°

d 104.9° **e** 33.2°

5 **a**

Degrees	0	45	90	135	180
Radians	0	$\frac{\pi}{4}$	$\frac{\pi}{2}$	$\frac{3\pi}{4}$	π

Degrees	225	270	315	360
Radians	$\frac{5\pi}{4}$	$\frac{3\pi}{2}$	$\frac{7\pi}{4}$	2π

b

Degrees	0	30	60	90	120
Radians	0	$\frac{\pi}{6}$	$\frac{\pi}{3}$	$\frac{\pi}{2}$	$\frac{2\pi}{3}$

Degrees	150	180	210	240	270
Radians	$\frac{5\pi}{6}$	π	$\frac{7\pi}{6}$	$\frac{4\pi}{3}$	$\frac{3\pi}{2}$

Degrees	300	330	360
Radians	$\frac{5\pi}{3}$	$\frac{11\pi}{6}$	2π

6 **a** 0.964 **b** 1.03 **c** 0.932

d 1 **e** 0.5 **f** 1

7 12.79°

Exercise 8.2

1 **a** $\frac{3\pi}{2}$ cm **b** 2π cm

c $\frac{15\pi}{4}$ cm **d** 15π cm

2 **a** 9.6 cm **b** 2 cm

3 **a** 1.25 rad **b** 1.5 rad

4 **a** 12.4 cm **b** 32 cm

c 31 cm

5 **a** 10 cm **b** 1.85 rad

c 38.5 cm

6 **a** 23 cm **b** 18.3 cm

c 41.3 cm

7 **a** 13.6 cm **b** 21.1 cm

c 34.7 cm

Exercise 8.3

1 **a** $6\pi\ \text{cm}^2$ **b** $\frac{135}{2}\pi\ \text{cm}^2$

c $35\pi\ \text{cm}^2$ **d** $\frac{135}{4}\pi\ \text{cm}^2$

2 **a** $10.4\,\text{cm}^2$ **b** $4.332\,\text{cm}^2$

3 **a** 1.11 rad **b** 1.22 rad

4 **a** 0.8 rad **b** $40\,\text{cm}^2$

5 $r(75 - r)$

6 **a** $9\sqrt{2}$ cm

b $\frac{\pi}{2}$

c $\frac{81}{2}\pi\ \text{cm}^2$

7 **a** 1.24 rad **b** $89.3\,\text{cm}^2$

c $121\,\text{cm}^2$

8 **a** 1 rad **b** $49.8\,\text{cm}^2$

c $17.8\,\text{cm}^2$

9 **a** $24.3\,\text{cm}^2$ **b** $37.7\,\text{cm}^2$

c $13.4\,\text{cm}^2$

10 **b** $54\pi - 36\sqrt{2}$

11 **a** $\frac{3}{7}$ rad **b** $18\,\text{cm}^2$

12 **a** 4.39 cm **b** 2.40 cm

c 15.5 cm **d** $15.0\,\text{cm}^2$

13 34.4 cm

14 **a** $45.5\,\text{cm}^2$ **b** $57.1\,\text{cm}^2$

c $80.8\,\text{cm}^2$ **d** $21.7\,\text{cm}^2$

15 $14.6\ \text{cm}^2$

Exercise 8.4

1 **a** $0.4x^2$ **b** 19.8 or 19.9

c 24.95 to 25

2 **a** 74.1 **b** 422 or 423

3 **b** 54.6 or 54.5 or 54.55

c 115.25 or 115.3 or 115

4 **a** 54.3 **c** 187

5 **i** all sides are equal to the radii of the circles, which are also equal

ii $\frac{2\pi}{3}$ **iii** 58.2 or 58.3

iv 148

6 **i** 19.3 **ii** 79.1 **iii** 57.3

7 **i** $\frac{\pi}{4}$ **iii** 11.6

iv $1.08 \leqslant \text{Area} \leqslant 1.11$

Chapter 9

Exercise 9.1

1 **a** $\frac{2\sqrt{13}}{13}$ **b** $\frac{3\sqrt{13}}{13}$

c $\frac{4}{13}$ **d** 1

e $\frac{7 + \sqrt{13}}{9}$

2 **a** $\frac{\sqrt{23}}{5}$ **b** $\frac{\sqrt{46}}{23}$

c $\frac{23}{25}$ **d** $\frac{\sqrt{2} + \sqrt{23}}{5}$

e $\frac{23\sqrt{2} - 2\sqrt{23}}{10}$

3 **a** $\frac{4\sqrt{3}}{7}$ **b** $4\sqrt{3}$

c $\frac{4\sqrt{3}}{7}$ **d** 1

e $\frac{7 - 196\sqrt{3}}{48}$

4 **a** $\frac{1}{2}$ **b** 3 **c** $\frac{2}{3}$

d $\frac{\sqrt{3} + \sqrt{2}}{2}$ **e** $\frac{2}{7}$

5 **a** $\frac{\sqrt{2}}{4}$ **b** $\frac{1}{2}$

c $\frac{\sqrt{6}}{3}$ **d** $\frac{-6 + 10\sqrt{3}}{3}$

e $2 - \sqrt{2}$ **f** $2\sqrt{3} - \sqrt{6}$

Exercise 9.2

1 **a**

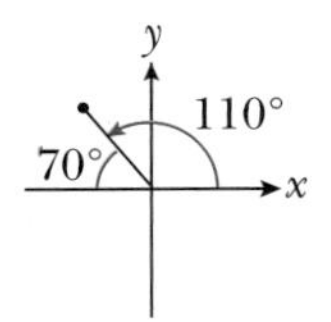

b

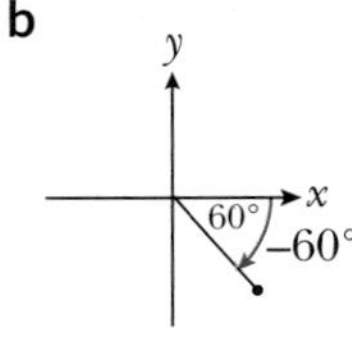

c

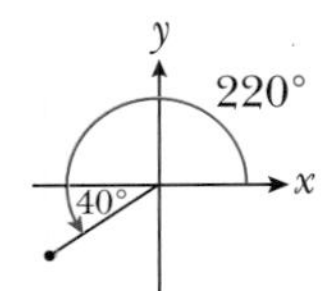

d

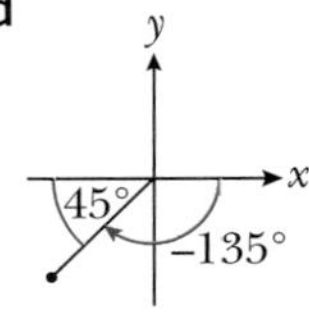

e

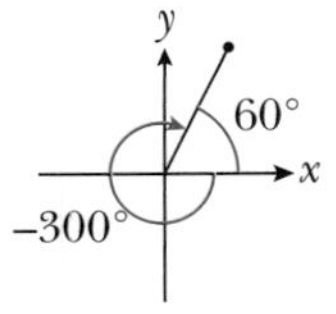

f

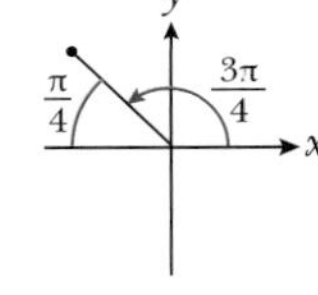

g

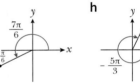

h

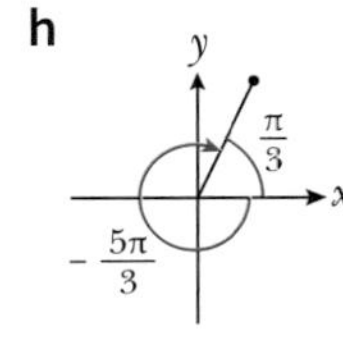

i **j**

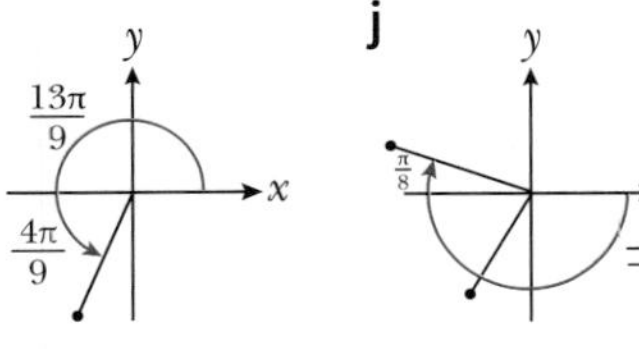

2 **a** second **b** fourth **c** third

d third **e** third **f** first

g fourth **h** third **i** first

j first

Exercise 9.3

1 **a** $-\sin 40°$ **b** $\cos 35°$

c $-\tan 40°$ **d** $\cos 25°$

e $\tan 60°$ **f** $\sin\frac{\pi}{5}$

g $-\tan\frac{\pi}{4}$ **h** $\cos\frac{\pi}{6}$

i $-\tan\frac{\pi}{3}$ **j** $\sin\frac{\pi}{4}$

2 **a** $-\frac{\sqrt{21}}{2}$ **b** $-\frac{\sqrt{21}}{5}$

3 **a** $\frac{\sqrt{3}}{2}$ **b** $-\frac{1}{2}$

4 **a** $-\frac{12}{13}$ **b** $-\frac{5}{12}$

5 **a** $-\frac{2\sqrt{13}}{13}$ **b** $-\frac{3\sqrt{13}}{13}$

6 **a** $-\frac{4}{5}$ **b** $-\frac{3}{5}$

c $-\frac{\sqrt{6}}{3}$ **d** $\sqrt{2}$

7 **a** $\frac{5}{13}$ **b** $-\frac{12}{5}$

c $-\frac{4}{5}$ **d** $-\frac{4}{3}$

Exercise 9.4

1 **a** **i** amplitude = 7, period = 360°, (0, 7), (180, −7), (360, 7)

ii amplitude = 2, period = 180°, (45, 2), (135, −2), (225, 2), (315, −2)

iii amplitude = 2, period = 120°, (0, 2), (60, −2), (120, 2), (180, −2), (240, 2), (300, −2), (360, 2)

iv amplitude = 3, period = 720°, (180, 3)

v amplitude = 4, period = 360°, (0, 5), (180, −3), (360, 5)

vi amplitude = 5, period = 180°, (45, 3), (135, −7), (225, 3), (315, −7)

2 **a** **i** amplitude = 4, period $= 2\pi, \left(\frac{\pi}{2}, 4\right), \left(\frac{3\pi}{2}, -4\right)$

ii amplitude = 1, period $= \frac{2\pi}{3}, (0, 1), \left(\frac{\pi}{3}, -1\right), \left(\frac{2\pi}{3}, 1\right), (\pi, -1), \left(\frac{4\pi}{3}, 1\right), \left(\frac{5\pi}{3}, -1\right), (2\pi, 1)$

iii amplitude = 2, period $= \frac{2\pi}{3}, \left(\frac{\pi}{6}, 2\right), \left(\frac{\pi}{2}, -2\right), \left(\frac{5\pi}{6}, 2\right), \left(\frac{7\pi}{6}, -2\right), \left(\frac{3\pi}{2}, 2\right), \left(\frac{11\pi}{6}, -2\right)$

iv amplitude = 3, period = 4π (0, 3), (2π, −3)

v amplitude = 1, period = π, $\left(\frac{\pi}{4}, 4\right), \left(\frac{3\pi}{4}, 2\right), \left(\frac{5\pi}{4}, 4\right), \left(\frac{7\pi}{4}, 2\right)$

vi amplitude = 4, period = π, $(0, 3), \left(\frac{\pi}{2}, -5\right), (\pi, 3), \left(\frac{3\pi}{2}, -5\right), (2\pi, 3)$

3 $a = 2, b = 4, c = 1$

4 $a = 3, b = 2, c = 4$

5 $a = 3, b = 2, c = 3$

6 **a** **i** period = 90°, $x = 45°$, $x = 135°$, $x = 225°$, $x = 315°$

ii period = 360°, $x = 180°$

iii period = 60°, $x = 30°$, $x = 90°$, $x = 150°$, $x = 210°$, $x = 270°$, $x = 330°$

7 **a** **i** period $= \frac{\pi}{4}$, $x = \frac{\pi}{8},\ x = \frac{3\pi}{8},\ x = \frac{5\pi}{8},\ x = \frac{7\pi}{8},\ x = \frac{9\pi}{8},\ x = \frac{11\pi}{8},\ x = \frac{13\pi}{8},\ x = \frac{15\pi}{8}$

ii period $= \frac{\pi}{3}$, $x = \frac{\pi}{6},\ x = \frac{\pi}{2},\ x = \frac{5\pi}{6},\ x = \frac{7\pi}{6},\ x = \frac{3\pi}{2},\ x = \frac{11\pi}{6}$

iii period $= \frac{\pi}{2}$, $x = \frac{\pi}{4},\ x = \frac{3\pi}{4},\ x = \frac{5\pi}{4},\ x = \frac{7\pi}{4}$

8 $a = 2, b = 1, c = 3$

9 $a = 9, b = 4, c = 6$

10 **a** $A = 2, B = 5$

b 3

c

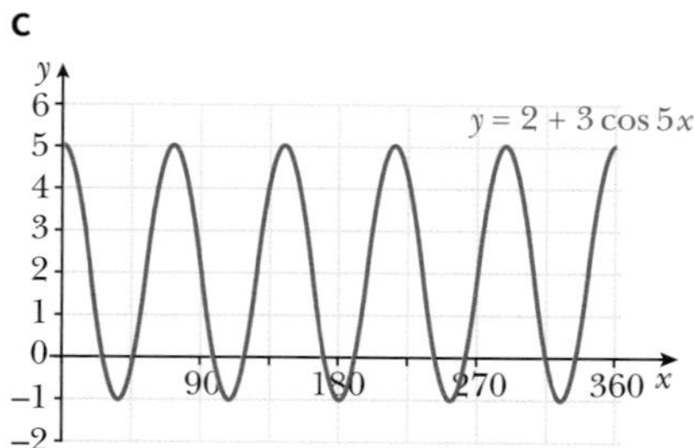

11 **a** $A = 1, B = 3, C = 4$

b

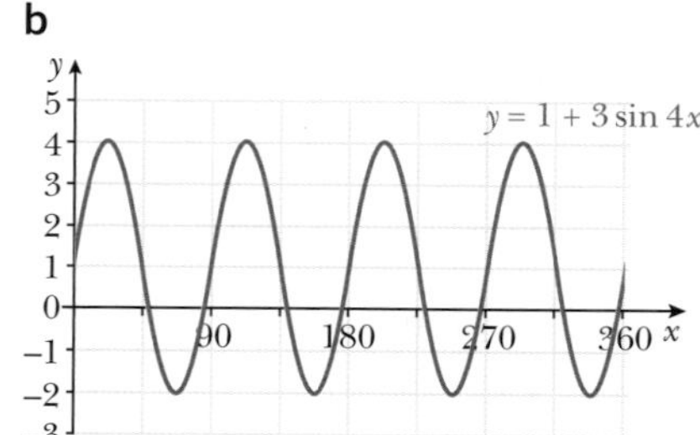

12 **b** 2

13 **b** 2

14 **b** 4

Exercise 9.5

1 **a** $f(x) \geqslant 0$

b $0 \leqslant f(x) \leqslant 1$

c $0 \leqslant f(x) \leqslant 3$

d $0 \leqslant f(x) \leqslant 1$

e $0 \leqslant f(x) \leqslant 2$

f $0 \leqslant f(x) \leqslant 2$

g $1 \leqslant f(x) \leqslant 3$

h $0 \leqslant f(x) \leqslant 6$

i $0 \leqslant f(x) \leqslant 7$

2 c 4 **3** c 2

4 c 3 **5** b 2

6 b 5 **7** b 2

8 b 4

9 $1 < k < 5$

10 $a = 1, b = 4, c = 2$

Exercise 9.6

1 a $17.5°, 162.5°$

b $41.4°, 318.6°$

c $63.4°, 243.4°$

d $216.9°, 323.1°$

e $125.5°, 305.5°$

f $233.1°, 306.9°$

g $48.6°, 131.4°$

h $120°, 240°$

2 a $\frac{\pi}{3}, \frac{5\pi}{3}$

b $0.197, 3.34$

c no solutions

d $1.89, 5.03$

e $3.99, 5.44$

f $2.15, 4.13$

g $0.253, 2.89$

h $3.55, 5.87$

3 a $26.6°, 63.4°$

b $63.4°, 116.6°$

c $31.7°, 121.7°$

d $108.4°, 161.6°$

e $18.4°, 161.6°$

f $98.3°, 171.7°$

g $80.8°, 170.8°$

h $20.9°, 69.1°$

4 a $150°, 270°$

b $95.7°, 129.3°$

c $225°, 315°$

d $\frac{\pi}{2}, \frac{7\pi}{6}$

e $1.82, 2.75$

f $\frac{\pi}{6}, \frac{7\pi}{6}$

5 a $14.0°, 194.0°$

b $126.9°, 306.9°$

c $31.0°, 211.0°$

d $25.7°, 115.7°, 205.7°, 295.7°$

6 $0.648, 2.22$

7 a $0°, 30°, 180°, 210°, 360°$

b $0°, 38.7°, 180°, 218.7°, 360°$

c $70.5°, 90°, 270°, 289.5°$

d $0°, 135°, 180°, 315°, 360°$

e $11.5°, 90°, 168.5°, 270°$

f $0°, 45°, 180°, 225°, 360°$

8 a $30°, 150°, 210°, 330°$

b $31.0°, 149.0°, 211.0°, 329.0°$

9 a $45°, 108.4°, 225°, 288.4°$

b $30°, 150°, 270°$

c $0°, 109.5°, 250.5°, 360°$

d $60°, 180°, 300°$

e $0°, 180°, 199.5°, 340.5°, 360°$

f $19.5°, 160.5°, 210°, 330°$

g $19.5°, 160.5°, 270°$

h $30°, 150°, 270°$

i $19.5°, 160.5°$

10 0.848

Exercise 9.8

1 a $73.3°, 253.3°$

b $75.5°, 284.5°$

c $210°, 330°$

d $53.1°, 306.9°$

2 a $0.201, 2.94$

b $0.896, 4.04$

c $1.82, 4.46$

d $2.55, 5.70$

3 a $25.7°, 154.3°$

b $5.8°, 84.2°$

c $67.5°, 157.5°$

d $112.8°, 157.2°$

4 a $100.5°, 319.5°$

b $73.3°, 151.7°$

d $2.56, 5.70$

e $1.28, 2.00$

5 a $60°, 120°, 240°, 300°$

b $56.3°, 123.7°, 263.3°, 303.7°$

c $106.3°, 253.7°$

6 a $41.4°, 180°, 318.6°$

b $113.6°, 246.4°,$

c $71.6°, 153.4°, 251.6°, 333.4°$

d $19.5°, 160.5°$

e $48.2°, 311.8°$

f $18.4°, 30°, 150°, 198.4°$

g $60°, 300°$

h $23.6°, 30°, 150°, 156.4°$

Exercise 9.9

5 26

6 a $-2+7\sin^2 x$

b $-2 \leqslant f(x) \leqslant 5$

7 a $7-(\cos\theta-2)^2$

b $6, -2$

Exercise 9.10

1 b i 4

ii $60°$

2 a $10°, 50°$

b $\frac{\pi}{6}, \frac{5\pi}{6}$

3 b $54.7°, 125.3°, 234.7°, 305.3°$

5 a $164.1°, 344.1°$

b $0.898, 1.67, 4.04, 4.81$

6 c 3

8 b 0.902, 2.24

9 a $a = 3, b = 8, c = 7$

b i 120°

ii 5

10 a 30°, 150°, 210°, 330°.

b 60°, 180°, 23.5°, 96.5°, 143.5°

c $\frac{2\pi}{3}, \frac{5\pi}{3}$

12 i 64.3°, 154.3°

ii 90°, 194.5°, 345.5°

iii $\frac{5\pi}{12}, \frac{13\pi}{12}$

Chapter 10

Exercise 10.1

1 a 5040 b 12 c 840
d 336 d 6 e 60
f 20 g 4200

2 a 2! b 6! c $\frac{5!}{2!}$
d $\frac{17!}{13!}$ e $\frac{10!}{7!3!}$ f $\frac{12!}{7!4!}$

3 a $\frac{n!}{(n-4)!}$ b $\frac{n!}{(n-6)!}$
c $\frac{n!}{(n-3)!5!}$ d $\frac{n!}{(n-5)!3!}$

Exercise 10.2

1 a 24 b 5040

2 a 120 b 40 320
c 3 628 800

3 a 24
b i 6 ii 6

4 a 5040 b 576

5 a 120 b 72 c 72
d 42

6 a 12 b 36 c 24

7 a 720 b 120 c 48

8 a 600 b 312

9 288

Exercise 10.3

1 a 6720 b 360
c 6 652 800 d 5040

2 360

3 15 120

4 336

5 480

6 18

7 a 1680 b 840 c 630
d 330

8 a 60 b 300

9 720

Exercise 10.4

1 a 5 b 20 c 1
d 70 e 1 f 35

2 $\frac{8!}{3!5!} = \frac{8!}{5!3!}$

3 a 120 b 21 c 364

4 10

5 56

6 700

7 a 210 b 84

8 a 30 045 015 b 142 506

9 67 200

10 a 16 b 30 c 16

11 a 1287 b 756

12 1709

13 a 462 b 350

14 a 45 b 45

15 a 252 b 126 c 66

16 2000

Exercise 10.5

1 a 28
b i 420 ii 240

2 a i 3628800 ii 17280
b i 150 ii 110

3 a i 15 120 ii 210
b i 15 504 ii 3696
iii 56

4 a 720 b 240 c 480
d 168

5 a i 40320 ii 2880
b 350

6 a 840 b 240 c 80

7 a i 84

ii 15120

b 240

8 a permutation because the order matters

b i 55 ii 420 iii 70

9 a i 28 ii 20160 iii 720

b 203

10 a i 60480 ii 144 iii 1680

b i 2100 ii 420

Chapter 11

Exercise 11.1

1 1, 6, 15, 20, 15, 6, 1

1, 7, 21, 35, 35, 21, 7, 1

2 a $1 + 3x + 3x^2 + x^3$

b $1 - 4x + 6x^2 - 4x^3 + x^4$

c $p^4 + 4p^3q + 6p^2q^2 + 4pq^3 + q^4$

d $8 + 12x + 6x^2 + x^3$

e $x^5 + 5x^4y + 10x^3y^2 + 10x^2y^3 + 5xy^4 + y^5$

f $y^3 + 12y^2 + 48y + 64$

g $a^3 - 3a^2b + 3ab^2 - b^3$

h $16x^4 + 32x^3y + 24x^2y^2 + 8xy^3 + y^4$

i $x^3 - 6x^2y + 12xy^2 - 8y^3$

j $81x^4 - 432x^3 + 864x^2 - 768x + 256$

k $x^3 + 6x + \frac{12}{x} + \frac{8}{x^3}$

l $x^6 - \frac{3}{2}x + \frac{3}{4}x^{-4} - \frac{1}{8}x^{-9}$

3 a 16 b 10 c –12

d 8 e 40 f 160

g 5760 h $-\frac{3}{2}$

4 $A = 2048,\ B = 1280,\ C = 40$

5 $1 + 14x + 74x^2 + 216x^3 + 297x^4 + 162x^5$

6 $a = 8$

7 a $81 + 108x + 54x^2 + 12x^3 + x^4$

b $376 + 168\sqrt{5}$

8 a $1 + 5x + 10x^2 + 10x^3 + 5x^4 + x^5$

b i $76 + 44\sqrt{3}$

ii $76 - 44\sqrt{3}$

c 152

9 a $16 - 32x^2 + 24x^4 - 8x^6 + x^8$

b 64

10 90

11 $\frac{3}{4}$

12 a $32 + 80y + 80y^2$

b 400

13 $\frac{1}{5}$

14 a $a = 24,\ b = 128$

b $80\sqrt{2}$

15 a $y^3 - 3y$

b $y^5 - 5y^3 + 5y$

Exercise 11.2

1 a ${}^3C_0\ \ {}^3C_1\ \ {}^3C_2\ \ {}^3C_3$

b ${}^4C_0\ \ {}^4C_1\ \ {}^4C_2\ \ {}^4C_3\ \ {}^4C_4$

c ${}^5C_0\ \ {}^5C_1\ \ {}^5C_2\ \ {}^5C_3\ \ {}^5C_4\ \ {}^5C_5$

2 a $1 + 4x + 6x^2 + 4x^3 + x^4$

b $1 - 5x + 10x^2 - 10x^3 + 5x^4 - x^5$

c $1 + 8x + 24x^2 + 32x^3 + 16x^4$

d $27 + 27x + 9x^2 + x^3$

e $x^4 + 4x^3y + 6x^2y^2 + 4xy^3 + y^4$

f $32 - 80x + 80x^2 - 40x^3 - 10x^4 - x^5$

g $a^4 - 8a^3b + 24a^2b^2 - 32ab^3 + 16b^4$

h $16x^4 + 96x^3y + 216x^2y^2 + 216xy^3 + 81y^4$

i $\frac{1}{16}x^4 - \frac{3}{2}x^3 + \frac{27}{2}x^2 - 54x + 81$

j $1 - \frac{x}{2} + \frac{x^2}{10} - \frac{x^3}{100} + \frac{x^4}{2000} - \frac{x^5}{100\,000}$

k $x^5 - 15x^3 + 90x - \frac{270}{x} - \frac{405}{x^3} - \frac{243}{x^5}$

l $x^{12} + 3x^8 + \frac{15}{4}x^4 + \frac{5}{2} + \frac{15}{16x^4} + \frac{3}{16x^8} + \frac{1}{64x^{12}}$

3 a $40x^3$ b $175\,000x^3$

c $160x^3$ d $720x^3$

e $-20x^3$ f $-5376x^3$

g $-9\,450\,000x^3$

h $-954\,204\,160\,000x^3$

4 a $1 + 10x + 45x^2$

b $1 + 16x + 112x^2$

c $1 - 21x + 189x^2$

d $729 + 2916x + 4860x^2$

e $19683 - 59049x + 78732x^2$

f $256 + 512x + 448x^2$

g $1953125 - 3\,515\,625x^2 + 2\,812\,500x^4$

h $1048\,576x^{10} - 13\,107\,200x^9y + 73\,728\,000x^8y^2$

5 a $1 + 12x + 60x^2 + 160x^3$

b 140

6 a $1 + \frac{13}{2}x + \frac{39}{2}x^2 + \frac{143}{4}x^3$

b $\frac{377}{4}$

7 a $1 - 30x + 405x^2 - 3240x^3$

b –4860

8 a $1 + 14x + 84x^2$

b 47

9 a $1 + 7x + 21x^2 + 35x^3$

b 7

10 –945

11 $\frac{21}{2}$

12 $a = \frac{3}{n-2}$

Exercise 11.3

1 $a + 4d,\ a + 13d$

2 a 765 b –1310

c 907.5 d $-2420x$

3 a 35, 3185

b 15, –1365

4 9

5 a 5, 26 b 1287

6 –1875

7 2985

8 40

9 12 450

10 45

11 \$236

12 a 11, –3 b 37

13 6, 8

14 –5, –6

15 $\frac{1}{12}(8n + 1)$

16 8°

17 a $a = 6d$

b $10a$

19 a $6 - 5\cos^2 x$

20 b 901

Exercise 11.4

1 **a** not geometric

b –4, 16 384

c $\frac{1}{3}, \frac{1}{27}$

d not geometric

e not geometric

f –1, 5

2 ar^8, ar^{19}

3 $-\frac{2}{3}$, 243

4 ±16.2

5 $\frac{3}{2}$, 8

6 2, $\frac{5}{64}$, 40

7 27

8 –12

9 22nd

10 19

11 **a** 1020 **b** $1093\frac{1}{3}$

c –3280 **d** –4166.656

12 14

13 **a** $10\left(\frac{4}{5}\right)^n$

b 67.232 m

14 40, –20

15 50 minutes 19 seconds

18 $\frac{2(10^{n+1} - 10 - 9n)}{27}$

Exercise 11.5

1 **a** 4.5 **b** $\frac{2}{3}$

c 10 **d** –97.2

2 50

3 $-\frac{1}{5}$, 250

4 $2\frac{7}{9}$

5 **a**

$0.\dot{4}\dot{2} = \frac{42}{100} + \frac{42}{10000} + \frac{42}{1000000} + \ldots$

6 $-\frac{2}{3}, -93\frac{1}{3}$

7 0.5, 13

8 **a** –0.75, 128

b $73\frac{1}{7}$

9 **a** 105

b 437.5

10 **a** $\frac{3}{10}$, 60

b $85\frac{5}{7}$

11 **a** 60

b 375

12 162

13 $a = 50,\ r = \frac{1}{5}$

14 $-\frac{\pi}{6} < x < \frac{\pi}{6}$

15 84 m

16 **a** $3x, 4x, \frac{16}{3}x, \frac{64}{9}x$

common ratio > 1

17 **a** 5π

b $\frac{11\pi}{8}$

Exercise 11.6

1 **a** 108 **b** 166.25

2 **a** 125 **b** 31

3 **a** 1.5

b 364.5, 78

4 12.5, 63.5

5 **a** $\frac{3}{4}$ **b** 84.375, 162.5

c 800

6 **a** 0.75 **b** $\frac{5}{4}$, $n = 10$

7 19

8 **a**

$x = -3$ or 8, 3rd term = 33 or 88

b $-\frac{2}{5}, -7\frac{1}{7}$

Exercise 11.7

1 **a** $64 + 192x + 240x^2 + 160x^3$

b 64

2 **a** $x^6 + 12x^3 + 60$ **b** 72

3 **a** $n = 6$ **b** –5

4 **a** –27.5 **b** 38.5

5 **a** $64 - 960x + 6000x^2$ **b** –640

6 **i** $729 + 2916x + 4860x^2$

ii 6804

7 **i** $64 + 192x^2 + 240x^4 + 160x^6$

ii 1072

8 **a** **i** $a^4 + 4a^3b + 6a^2b^2 + 4ab^3 + b^4$

ii $\frac{24}{25}$

b $n = 6$

9 **a** –2.24 **b** 25

10 **a** 24 **b** 162

11 **a** $d = 2a$ **b** $99a$

12 **a** $a = 38,\ d = -2.5$ **b** $n = 25$

13 **a** $-\frac{3}{4}$ **b** 768 **c** $438\frac{6}{7}$

14 **a** 41 **b** $r = \frac{1}{4},\ S = 10\frac{2}{3}$

15 **a** $a = -8,\ d = \frac{4}{3}$ **b** 80

16 **a** $\frac{1}{5}$ **b** 18

Chapter 12

Exercise 12.1

1 **a** $4x^3$ **b** $9x^8$ **c** $-3x^{-4}$

d $-6x^{-7}$ **e** $-x^{-2}$ **f** $-5x^{-6}$

g $\frac{1}{2}x^{-\frac{1}{2}}$ **h** $\frac{5}{2}x^{\frac{3}{2}}$ **i** $-\frac{1}{5}x^{-\frac{6}{5}}$

j $\frac{1}{3}x^{-\frac{2}{3}}$ **k** $\frac{2}{3}x^{-\frac{1}{3}}$ **l** $-\frac{1}{2}x^{-\frac{3}{2}}$

m 1 **n** $\frac{3}{2}x^{\frac{1}{2}}$ **o** $\frac{5}{3}x^{\frac{2}{3}}$

p $6x^5$ **q** $3x^2$ **r** $2x$

s $\frac{1}{2}x^{-\frac{1}{2}}$ **t** $-\frac{3}{2}x^{-\frac{5}{2}}$

2 a $6x^2-5$

b $40x^4-6x$

c $-6x^2+4$

d $6x-2x^{-2}+2x^{-3}$

e $2+x^{-2}+\frac{1}{2}x^{-\frac{3}{2}}$

f $\frac{1}{2}x^{-\frac{1}{2}}-\frac{5}{2}x^{-\frac{3}{2}}$

g $1+3x^{-2}$

h $5+\frac{1}{2}x^{-\frac{3}{2}}$

i $\frac{3}{2}x^{\frac{1}{2}}-\frac{1}{2}x^{-\frac{1}{2}}+\frac{1}{2}x^{-\frac{3}{2}}$

j $15x^2+10x$ k $-2x^{-2}+10x^{-3}$

l $1+2x^{-2}$ m $18x+6$

n $-6x^2+6x^5$ o $12x+5$

3 a 6 b 4 c −2

d 0 e −0.2 f $\frac{2}{9}$

4 (2, 5)

5 0.25

6 5

7 −11, 11

8 $a=3$, $b=-4$

9 $a=-2$, $b=5$

10 $\left(1, 2\frac{5}{6}\right), \left(4, 4\frac{1}{3}\right)$

11 a $(-3, 2), (0, 5), (9, 14)$

b 13, −8, 37

12 a $12x^2+6x-6$

b $x \leqslant -1$ and $x \geqslant 0.5$

13 a $3x^2+2x-16$

b $-\frac{8}{3} \leqslant x \leqslant 2$

14 $\frac{dy}{dx}=5\left[(x^2-2)^2+(x+5)^2\right]>0$

Exercise 12.2

1 a $9(x+2)^8$

b $21(3x-1)^6$

c $-30(1-5x)^5$

d $2\left(\frac{1}{2}x-7\right)^3$

e $4(2x+1)^5$

f $12(x-4)^5$

g $-30(5-x)^4$

h $8(2x+5)^7$

i $8x(x^2+2)^3$

j $-28x(1-2x^2)^6$

k $5(2x-3)(x^2-3x)^4$

l $8\left(x-\frac{1}{x^2}\right)\left(x^2+\frac{2}{x}\right)^3$

2 a $-\frac{1}{(x+4)^2}$

b $-\frac{6}{(2x-1)^2}$

c $\frac{15}{(2-3x)^2}$

d $-\frac{64x}{(2x^2-5)^2}$

e $-\frac{8(x-1)}{(x^2-2x)^2}$

f $\frac{5}{(x-1)^6}$

g $-\frac{30}{(5x+1)^4}$

h $-\frac{6}{(3x-2)^5}$

3 a $\frac{1}{2\sqrt{x+2}}$

b $\frac{5}{2\sqrt{5x-1}}$

c $\frac{2x}{\sqrt{2x^2-3}}$

d $-\frac{3x^2+2}{2\sqrt{x^3+2x}}$

e $-\frac{2}{3(3-2x)^{\frac{2}{3}}}$

f $\frac{4}{\sqrt{2x-1}}$

g $-\frac{3}{2(3x-1)^{\frac{3}{2}}}$

h $\frac{5}{(2-5x)^{\frac{4}{3}}}$

4 8

5 2

6 0.75, −3

7 (3, 2)

8 $a=8$, $b=3$

Exercise 12.3

1 a $2x+4$

b $12x+10$

c $(x+2)^2(4x+2)$

d $x(x-1)^2(5x-2)$

e $\frac{3x-10}{2\sqrt{x-5}}$

f $\frac{3x+2}{2\sqrt{x}}$

g $\frac{5x^2+12x}{2\sqrt{x+3}}$

h $\frac{(3-x^2)^2(13x^2-3)}{2\sqrt{x}}$

i $2(3x^2+x+5)$

j $(4x+9)(x-3)^2$

k $2(x-1)(x+2)(2x+1)$

l $14(x-1)(x-3)^3(2x+1)^2$

2 9 3 85

4 49, 0 5 −2, 0, 1.5

6 $1\frac{2}{3}$

Exercise 12.4

1 a $\frac{11}{(5-x)^2}$ b $\frac{10}{(x+4)^2}$

c $\frac{7}{(3x+4)^2}$ d $-\frac{1}{(3-8x)^2}$

e $\frac{x(5x-4)}{(5x-2)^2}$ f $-\frac{x^2+1}{(x^2-1)^2}$

g $-\frac{15}{(3x-1)^2}$ h $-\frac{x^2+8x+2}{(x^2-2)^2}$

2 -4

3 (0, 0), (1, 1)

4 $\frac{25}{9}$

5 a $\frac{1-2x}{2\sqrt{x}(2x+1)^2}$

b $\frac{1-x}{(1-2x)^{\frac{3}{2}}}$

c $\frac{x(x^2+4)}{(x^2+2)^{\frac{3}{2}}}$

d $\frac{-5(x-3)}{2\sqrt{x}(x+3)^2}$

6 4

7 (3, −2)

8 a (−2, −2.4), (0.4, 0), (2, 1.6)

b $-\frac{23}{25}, \frac{125}{29}, -\frac{7}{25}$

Exercise 12.5

1 a $y = 4x - 6$

b $y = -x - 2$

c $y = 16x - 10$

d $y = -\frac{1}{2}x + 3$

e $y = -3x - 3$

f $y = \frac{1}{4}x + 2\frac{1}{4}$

2 a $y = -\frac{1}{3}x - 4\frac{1}{3}$

b $y = -\frac{1}{8}x + 5\frac{1}{4}$

c $y = \frac{1}{4}x - 3\frac{3}{4}$

d $y = 2x + 7.5$

e $y = -0.1x - 3.8$

f $y = 4x - 22$

3 $y = 8x - 6$, $y = -\frac{1}{8}x + \frac{17}{8}$

4 (0, 5.2)

5 $y = \frac{9}{16}x - \frac{1}{2}$, $y = -\frac{16}{9}x - \frac{1}{2}$

6 (2, −3)

7 $y = 2x - 20$

8 a $y = x + 8$

b (1, 6)

c $y = -\frac{1}{2}x + \frac{13}{2}$

9 (1, 5.25)

10 a (7, 4)

b 12 units^2

11 b $y = -0.4x - 0.6$

12 216 units^2

13 22.5 units^2

Exercise 12.6

1 0.21 2 0.68

3 $-0.8p$ 4 $2p$

5 $25p$ 6 $\frac{11}{3}p$

7 $\frac{\pi}{20}$

8 a $y = \frac{180}{x^2}$

c $-254p$, decrease

Exercise 12.7

1 0.15 units per second

2 0.125 units per second

3 −4 units per second

4 −0.25 units per second

5 0.5 units per second

6 $\frac{1}{150}$ units per second

7 −0.08 units per second

8 0.025 cm s^{-1}

9 $\frac{1}{96}$ cm s^{-1}

10 324 cm^3 s^{-1}

11 $\frac{1}{480}$ cm s^{-1}

12 12π cm^3 s^{-1}

13 a $\frac{4}{5\pi}$ cm s^{-1} b $\frac{1}{5\pi}$ cm s^{-1}

14 a $\frac{1}{7}$ cm s^{-1} b $\frac{1}{12}$ cm s^{-1}

Exercise 12.8

1 a 10 b $12x + 6$

c $-\frac{18}{x^4}$ d $320(4x+1)^3$

e $-\frac{1}{(2x+1)^{\frac{3}{2}}}$ f $\frac{3}{(x+3)^{\frac{5}{2}}}$

2 a $12(x-4)(x-2)$

b $\frac{8x-6}{x^4}$

c $\frac{8}{(x-3)^3}$

d $\frac{2(x^3+6x^2+3x+2)}{(x^2-1)^3}$

e $y = \frac{50}{(x-5)^3}$

f $y = \frac{102}{(3x-1)^3}$

3 a −3 b −9 c −8

4 b −18, 18

5

x	0	1	2	3	4	5
$\frac{dy}{dx}$	+	0	−	−	0	+
$\frac{d^2y}{dx^2}$	−	−	−	+	+	+

6 $x > 2$

Exercise 12.9

1 a (6, −28) minimum

b (−2, 9) maximum

c (−2, 18) maximum, (2, −14) minimum

d $\left(-2\frac{2}{3}, 14\frac{22}{27}\right)$ maximum, (2, −36) minimum

e (−3, −18) minimum, $\left(\frac{1}{3}, \frac{14}{27}\right)$ maximum

f $\left(\frac{2}{3}, \frac{14}{27}\right)$ maximum, (4, –18) minimum

2 **a** (4, 4) minimum

b (–1, 3) minimum

c (4, 3) minimum

d $\left(-3, -\frac{1}{3}\right)$ minimum, $\left(3, \frac{1}{3}\right)$ maximum

e (–2, –4) maximum, (0, 0) minimum

f (–4, –13) maximum, (2, –1) minimum

3 $\frac{dy}{dx} = -\frac{3}{(x+1)^2}$, numerator of $\frac{dy}{dx}$ is never zero

4 $a = 3$

5 **a** $a = -3$, $b = 5$

b minimum

c (–1, 7), maximum

6 **a** $a = 2$, $b = -4$

b minimum

7 **a** $a = 8$, $b = -4$

b maximum

8 **a** $a = -36$, $b = 4$

b (–2, 48)

c (–2, 48) = maximum, (3, –77) = minimum

d (0.5, –14.5), –37.5

Exercise 12.10

1 **a** $y = 8 - x$

b **i** $P = 8x - x^2$

ii 16

c **i** $S = x^2 + (8 - x)^2$

ii 32

2 **b** $A = 1250$, $x = 50$

3 **a** $y = \frac{288}{x^2}$

c $A = 432$, 12 cm by 6 cm by 8 cm

4 **a** $h = \frac{V}{4x^2}$

c $\frac{5\sqrt{6}}{3}$

5 **a** $\theta = \frac{60}{r} - 2$

c $30 - 2r$, -2

d 15

e 225, maximum

6 **a** $h = 3 - \frac{1}{2}r(\pi + 2)$

c $6 - 4r - \pi r$, $-4 - \pi$

d $\frac{6}{4 + \pi}$

e $\frac{18}{4 + \pi}$, maximum

7 **a** $BC = 4 - p^2$

c $\frac{2\sqrt{3}}{3}$

d $\frac{32\sqrt{3}}{9}$, maximum

8 **a** $h = \frac{250}{r^2}$

c $4\pi r - \frac{500\pi}{r^2}$, $4\pi + \frac{1000\pi}{r^3}$

d 5

e 150π, minimum

9 **a** $h = \frac{144}{r} - \frac{3}{2}r$

c $\frac{12\sqrt{10}}{5}$

10 **a** $r = \frac{25 - 2x}{\pi}$

c $A = 87.5$, $x = 7.00$

11 **a** $r = \sqrt{25 - h^2}$

c $\frac{5\sqrt{3}}{3}$

d maximum

12 **a** $h = 24 - 2r$

c 512π

13 **a** $r = \sqrt{20h - h^2}$

c $13\frac{1}{3}$

d $\frac{32000}{81}\pi$, maximum

Exercise 12.11

1 (2, 12)

2 $k = 4$

3 **a** $-\frac{1}{x^2} + \frac{1}{\sqrt{x}}$

b $\frac{2}{x^3} - \frac{1}{2x^{\frac{3}{2}}}$

c (1, 3), minimum

4 **b** 56.25 cm^2

5 **a** $2\left(\frac{1}{4}x - 5\right)^7$

b $-256p$

6 $y = \frac{1}{2}x + 10$

7 **a** $y = -3x + 4$

b (–2, 10)

9 $x = 9$

10 **b** $x = 10$

11 **ii** $A = 246$, minimum

Chapter 13

Exercise 13.1

1 **a** $\mathbf{i} - 3\mathbf{j}$ **b** $3\mathbf{i} - 2\mathbf{j}$ **c** $4\mathbf{i} - \mathbf{j}$

d $2\mathbf{i}$ **e** $\mathbf{i} + 3\mathbf{j}$ **f** $-2\mathbf{i} + \mathbf{j}$

g $-2\mathbf{i}$ **h** $-3\mathbf{i} - 2\mathbf{j}$ **i** $-\mathbf{i} - \mathbf{j}$

2 **a** 2 **b** 5 **c** 13

d 10 **e** 25 **f** 17

g $4\sqrt{2}$ **h** $5\sqrt{5}$

3 $16\mathbf{i} + 12\mathbf{j}$

4 $36\mathbf{i} - 15\mathbf{j}$

5 **a** $\frac{1}{5}(3\mathbf{i} + 4\mathbf{j})$

b $\frac{1}{13}(5\mathbf{i} + 12\mathbf{j})$

c $-\frac{1}{5}(4\mathbf{i}+3\mathbf{j})$

d $\frac{1}{17}(8\mathbf{i}-15\mathbf{j})$

e $\frac{\sqrt{2}}{2}(\mathbf{i}+\mathbf{j})$

6 a $4\mathbf{i}$ b $14\mathbf{i}-9\mathbf{j}$

c $-26\mathbf{i}-3\mathbf{j}$ d $-\mathbf{i}+3\mathbf{j}$

7 a 15 b $\sqrt{461}$

8 $\mu=-3,\ \lambda=5$

9 $\mu=3,\ \lambda=-2$

Exercise 13.2

1 a $-\mathbf{i}-3\mathbf{j}$ b $2\mathbf{i}-10\mathbf{j}$

c $3\mathbf{i}+\mathbf{j}$ d $-12\mathbf{i}+3\mathbf{j}$

e $\mathbf{i}+7\mathbf{j}$ f $-6\mathbf{i}-\mathbf{j}$

2 a $\begin{pmatrix}4\\10\end{pmatrix}$ b $\begin{pmatrix}-5\\11\end{pmatrix}$

c $\begin{pmatrix}1\\3\end{pmatrix}$

3 a $-15\mathbf{i}+20\mathbf{j}$ b $24\mathbf{i}+10\mathbf{j}$

c $15\mathbf{i}+\mathbf{j}$ d $\sqrt{226}$

4 a $16\mathbf{i}+12\mathbf{j}$ b $\frac{1}{5}(4\mathbf{i}+3\mathbf{j})$

c $5\mathbf{i}+2\mathbf{j}$

5 a $10\mathbf{i}+24\mathbf{j}$ b 26

c $\frac{1}{13}(5\mathbf{i}+12\mathbf{j})$ d $3\mathbf{i}+8\mathbf{j}$

6 7

7 a $\begin{pmatrix}20\\-21\end{pmatrix}$ b $\begin{pmatrix}30\\-32\end{pmatrix}$

8 a i 29

ii 30

iii 38.1

b $\begin{pmatrix}22.5\\-1\end{pmatrix}$

9 a $12\mathbf{i}+9\mathbf{j}$ b $7\mathbf{i}+\mathbf{j}$

10 a $6\mathbf{i}-8\mathbf{j}$ b $7.5\,\mathbf{i}+4\mathbf{j}$

11 $\begin{pmatrix}9\\7\end{pmatrix}$

12 3

13 a 22 or −8 b −9

c 1

14 $6\mathbf{j}$

15 $\frac{20}{7}\mathbf{i}$

16 a i $2\sqrt{10}$

ii $\sqrt{130}$

iii $3\sqrt{10}$

c $\lambda=\frac{7}{3},\ \mu=\frac{2}{3}$

Exercise 13.3

1 a $(1-\lambda)\mathbf{a}+\lambda\mathbf{b}$

b $\left(\frac{1}{2}-\frac{1}{2}\mu\right)\mathbf{a}+3\mu\mathbf{b}$

c $\lambda=\frac{3}{5},\ \mu=\frac{1}{5}$

2 a i $2\mathbf{a}-\mathbf{b}$

ii $3\mathbf{a}+\mathbf{b}$

b i $\lambda(5\mathbf{a}-\mathbf{b})$

ii $\mu(3\mathbf{a}+\mathbf{b})$

c $\lambda=\frac{5}{8},\ \mu=\frac{3}{8}$

3 a $\lambda(\mathbf{a}+2\mathbf{b})$

b $\mu\mathbf{a}+(3-3\mu)\mathbf{b}$

c $\lambda=\frac{3}{5},\ \mu=\frac{3}{5}$

4 a $(1-\lambda)\mathbf{a}+2\lambda\mathbf{b}$

b $\frac{5}{3}\mu\mathbf{a}+(1-\mu)\mathbf{b}$

c $\lambda=\frac{2}{7},\ \mu=\frac{3}{7}$

5 a i $-\mathbf{a}+\mathbf{b}$

ii $\frac{1}{2}\mathbf{a}+\frac{1}{2}\mathbf{b}$

b $\frac{1}{2}\lambda\mathbf{a}+\frac{1}{2}\lambda\mathbf{b}$

c $\frac{3}{4}\mu\mathbf{a}+(1-\mu)\mathbf{b}$

d $\lambda=\frac{6}{7},\ \mu=\frac{4}{7}$

6 a $\frac{3}{5}\lambda\mathbf{a}+\frac{2}{5}\lambda\mathbf{b}$

b $\frac{5}{7}\mu\mathbf{a}+(1-\mu)\mathbf{b}$

c $\lambda=\frac{25}{31},\ \mu=\frac{21}{31}$

7 a i $\lambda\mathbf{a}-\mathbf{b}$

ii $-\mathbf{a}+\mu\mathbf{b}$

b i $\frac{2}{5}\lambda\mathbf{a}+\frac{3}{5}\lambda\mathbf{b}$

ii $\frac{1}{4}\mathbf{a}+\frac{3}{4}\mu\mathbf{b}$

iii $\lambda=\frac{5}{8},\ \mu=\frac{4}{5}$

8 a i $-9\mathbf{a}+18\mathbf{b}$

ii $-5\mathbf{a}+10\mathbf{b}$

b $\overrightarrow{AC}=\frac{9}{5}\overrightarrow{AB}$, so AB and AC are parallel and A lies on both lines

9 a i $4\mathbf{a}$

ii $2\mathbf{b}$

iii $-2\mathbf{a}+3\mathbf{b}$

b i $6\mathbf{a}-3\mathbf{b}$

ii $2\mathbf{a}-\mathbf{b}$

iii $4\mathbf{a}-2\mathbf{b}$

b $\overrightarrow{CE}=3\overrightarrow{CD}$, so CE and CD are parallel and C lies on both lines

d 1 : 2

Exercise 13.4

1 a $(3.5\mathbf{i}+9\mathbf{j})\ \text{m s}^{-1}$

b $(30\mathbf{i}-36\mathbf{j})\ \text{m}$

c 12.5 hours

2 $(-22\mathbf{i}+11.6\mathbf{j})\ \text{km h}^{-1}$

3 $125\mathbf{i}$ km

4 a $(18\mathbf{i}+18\mathbf{j})\ \text{km h}^{-1}$

b $(10\mathbf{i}+10\sqrt{3}\mathbf{j})\ \text{km h}^{-1}$

c $(-50\sqrt{3}\mathbf{i}-50\mathbf{j})\ \text{m s}^{-1}$

5 a $20\ \text{m s}^{-1}$

b i $(-68\mathbf{i}+44\mathbf{j})\ \text{m}$

ii $(-56\mathbf{i}+28\mathbf{j})\ \text{m}$

iii $(-44\mathbf{i} + 12\mathbf{j})\,\text{m}$

c $\mathbf{r} = \begin{pmatrix} -80 \\ 60 \end{pmatrix} + t\begin{pmatrix} 12 \\ -16 \end{pmatrix}$

6 a $10\,\text{km h}^{-1}$

b $(28\mathbf{i} + 14\mathbf{j})$ km

c $\mathbf{r} = \begin{pmatrix} 10 \\ 38 \end{pmatrix} + t\begin{pmatrix} 6 \\ -8 \end{pmatrix}$

d 2030

7 a $(12\mathbf{i} - 12\mathbf{j})\,\text{km h}^{-1}$

b i $(29\mathbf{i} - 12\mathbf{j})$ km

ii $(14\mathbf{i} + 3\mathbf{j})$ km

c $\mathbf{r} = \begin{pmatrix} 5 \\ 12 \end{pmatrix} + t\begin{pmatrix} 12 \\ -12 \end{pmatrix}$

8 a $(10\mathbf{i} + 6\mathbf{j})$ km

b $(5\mathbf{i} + 12\mathbf{j})\,\text{km h}^{-1}$

c $13\,\text{km h}^{-1}$

d 52

9 a $(15\mathbf{i} + 20\mathbf{j})$ km

b $(8\mathbf{i} + 6\mathbf{j})\,\text{km h}^{-1}$

c $(111\mathbf{i} + 92\mathbf{j})$ km

10 a $(50\mathbf{i} + 70\mathbf{j})$ km, $(40\mathbf{i} + 100\mathbf{j})$ km

b 31.6 km

11 a $(6\mathbf{i} + 8\mathbf{j})$ km, $21\mathbf{j}$ km

b 14.3 km

Exercise 13.5

1 a $9\mathbf{i} + 45\mathbf{j}$

b 13

c $\frac{4}{3}\mathbf{i} - 2\mathbf{j}$

2 a $\mu\left(\frac{3}{5}\mathbf{a} + \frac{2}{5}\mathbf{b}\right)$

b $\mu = \frac{5}{3}, \lambda = \frac{2}{3}$

3 $(5\mathbf{i} + 12\mathbf{j})$ km, 13 km

4 i $8\mathbf{i} - 15\mathbf{j}$ ii $\frac{1}{17}(8\mathbf{i} - 15\mathbf{j})$

iii $-53\mathbf{i}$

5 a $5\sqrt{5}$ b $\frac{1}{5\sqrt{5}}(2\mathbf{i} + 11\mathbf{j})$

c $2\mathbf{i} + 1.5\mathbf{j}$

6 i $51\,\text{km h}^{-1}$

ii 40 minutes

7 i $\lambda\mathbf{b} - \mathbf{a}$

ii $\mu\mathbf{a} - \mathbf{b}$

iii $\frac{2}{3}\mathbf{a} + \frac{1}{3}\lambda\mathbf{b}$

iv $\frac{1}{8}\mathbf{b} + \frac{7}{8}\mu\mathbf{a}$

v $\mu = \frac{16}{21}, \lambda = \frac{3}{8}$

8 i $\overrightarrow{AP} = \frac{3}{4}(\mathbf{b} - \mathbf{a})$

ii $\overrightarrow{PQ} = -\frac{1}{4}\mathbf{a} - \frac{3}{4}\mathbf{b} + \frac{2}{5}\mathbf{c}$

iii $\mathbf{c} = \frac{1}{16}(9\mathbf{b} - 5\mathbf{a})$

9 a i $\alpha = 2, \beta = 13$

ii $\frac{1}{5}(3\mathbf{i} - 4\mathbf{j})$

b $\overrightarrow{OC} = (1 - \lambda)\mathbf{a} + \lambda\mathbf{b}$

c $\mu = 3$

Chapter 14

Exercise 14.1

1 a $7\mathrm{e}^{7x}$ b $3\mathrm{e}^{3x}$

c $15\mathrm{e}^{5x}$ d $-8\mathrm{e}^{-4x}$

e $-3\mathrm{e}^{-\frac{x}{2}}$ f $3\mathrm{e}^{3x+1}$

g $2x\mathrm{e}^{x^2+1}$ h $5 - \frac{3\mathrm{e}^{\sqrt{x}}}{2\sqrt{x}}$

i $-3\mathrm{e}^{-3x}$ j $-4\mathrm{e}^{2x}$

k $\frac{\mathrm{e}^x - \mathrm{e}^{-x}}{2}$ l $10x\left(1 + \mathrm{e}^{\;\;2}\right)$

2 a $x\mathrm{e}^x + \mathrm{e}^x$

b $2x^2\mathrm{e}^{2x} + 2x\mathrm{e}^{2x}$

c $-3x\mathrm{e}^{-x} + 3\mathrm{e}^{-x}$

d $\sqrt{x}\,\mathrm{e}^x + \frac{\mathrm{e}^x}{2\sqrt{x}}$

e $\frac{x\mathrm{e}^x - \mathrm{e}^x}{x^2}$

f $\frac{\mathrm{e}^{2x}(4x - 1)}{2x^{\frac{3}{2}}}$

g $-\frac{2\mathrm{e}^x}{(\mathrm{e}^x - 1)^2}$

h $2x\mathrm{e}^{2x}$

i $\frac{\mathrm{e}^x(x^2 + 2x\mathrm{e}^x + 2x + 5)}{(\mathrm{e}^x + 1)^2}$

3 a $5x + 8y = 10$

b $5x - 6y + 15\ln 5 = 0$

c $y = 3\mathrm{e}x + 2x - 2\mathrm{e} - 1$

4 $A\left(-\frac{1}{3}, 0\right)$

5 a $\left(-1, -\frac{1}{\mathrm{e}}\right)$, minimum

b $y - \mathrm{e} = -\frac{1}{2\mathrm{e}}(x - 1)$

c $\frac{(2\mathrm{e}^2 + 1)^2}{4\mathrm{e}}$

Exercise 14.2

1 a $\frac{1}{x}$ b $\frac{1}{x}$

c $\frac{2}{2x + 3}$ d $\frac{2x}{x^2 - 1}$

e $\frac{6}{3x + 1}$ f $\frac{1}{2x + 4}$

g $\frac{20}{5x - 2}$ h $2 - \frac{1}{x}$

i $\frac{3}{3x - 2}$ j $\frac{1}{x \ln x}$

k $\frac{1}{(\sqrt{x} + 1)\sqrt{x}}$ l $\frac{2x^2 + 1}{x(x^2 + \ln x)}$

2 a $1 + \ln x$ b $2x + 4x\ln x$

c $1 - \frac{1}{x} + \ln x$ d $10 + 5\ln x^2$

e $\frac{x}{\ln x} + 2x\ln(\ln x)$

f $\frac{1-\ln 2x}{x^2}$ g $-\frac{4}{x(\ln x)^2}$

h $\frac{2}{x^2(2x+1)}-\frac{2\ln(2x+1)}{x^3}$

i $\frac{3x^2(2x+3)-2(x^3-1)\ln(x^3-1)}{(2x+3)^2(x^3-1)}$

3 $2+4\ln 6,\ 3+2\ln 6$

4 a $\frac{3}{6x+2}$

b $\frac{2}{5-2x}$

c $\frac{5(x-1)}{x(x-5)}$

d $\frac{-3}{(2x+1)(x-1)}$

e $\frac{x-4}{x(2-x)}$

f $\frac{x^2+4x+2}{x(x+1)(x+2)}$

g $\frac{2-6x-2x^2}{(x-5)(x+1)(2x+3)}$

h $\frac{-3x-1}{(x+3)(x-1)}$

i $\frac{-x^2+6x-3}{x(x-1)(x+1)(2x-3)}$

5 a $\frac{1}{x\ \ln 3}$

b $\frac{2}{x\ \ln 2}$

c $\frac{5}{(5x-1)\ \ln 4}$

6 a $\frac{8x}{4x^2-1}$

b $\frac{15x^2-2}{5x^3-2x}$

c $\frac{2x-1}{(x+3)(x-4)}$

7 0.2

Exercise 14.3

1 a $\cos x$

b $2\cos x-3\sin x$

c $-2\sin x-\sec^2 x$

d $6\cos 2x$

e $20\sec^2 5x$

f $-6\sin 3x-2\cos 2x$

g $3\sec^2(3x+2)$

h $2\cos\left(2x+\frac{\pi}{3}\right)$

i $-6\sin\left(3x-\frac{\pi}{6}\right)$

2 a $3\sin^2 x\cos x$

b $-30\cos 3x\sin 3x$

c $2\sin x\cos x+2\sin x$

d $4(3-\cos x)^3\sin x$

e $12\sin^2\left(2x+\frac{\pi}{6}\right)\cos\left(2x+\frac{\pi}{6}\right)$

f $-12\sin x\cos^3 x$
$+8\tan\left(2x-\frac{\pi}{4}\right)\sec^2\left(2x-\frac{\pi}{4}\right)$

3 a $x\cos x+\sin x$

b $-6\sin 2x\sin 3x$
$+4\cos 2x\cos 3x$

c $x^2\sec^2 x+2x\tan x$

d $\frac{3}{2}x\tan^2\left(\frac{x}{2}\right)\sec^2\left(\frac{x}{2}\right)$
$+\tan^3\left(\frac{x}{2}\right)$

e $15\tan 3x\sec 3x$

f $\sec x+x\tan x\sec x$

g $\frac{x\sec^2 x-\tan x}{x^2}$

h $\frac{1+2\cos x}{(2+\cos x)^2}$

i $\frac{(3x-1)\cos x-3\sin x}{(3x-1)^2}$

j $-6\cot 2x\ \mathrm{cosec}^3\ 2x$

k $3\ \mathrm{cosec}\ 2x-6x\cot 2x$
$\mathrm{cosec}\ 2x$

l $\frac{-2}{(\sin x-\cos x)^2}$

4 a $-\sin x\,e^{\cos x}$

b $-5\sin 5x\,e^{\cos 5x}$

c $\sec^2 x\,e^{\tan x}$

d $(\cos x-\sin x)e^{(\sin x+\cos x)}$

e $e^x(\sin x+\cos x)$

f $\frac{1}{2}e^x\left(2\cos\frac{1}{2}x-\sin\frac{1}{2}x\right)$

g $2e^x\cos x$

h $xe^{\cos x}(2-x\sin x)$

i $\cot x$

j $x[2\ln(\cos x)-x\tan x]$

k $\frac{3\cos 3x-2\sin 3x}{e^{2x-1}}$

l $\frac{x\cos x+\sin x-x\sin x}{e^x}$

5 a -2

b $\frac{3\sqrt{2}-8}{6}$

6 a $\tan x\sec x$

b $-\cot x\ \mathrm{cosec}\ x$

c $-\mathrm{cosec}^2\ x$

7 a $3\cot 3x$

b $-2\tan 2x$

8 $A=3,\ B=-5$

9 $A=4,\ B=-3$

Exercise 14.4

1 $4x-24y=\pi$

2 a $2x+2y=\pi$

b $Q\left(\frac{\pi}{2},0\right),\ R\left(0,\frac{\pi}{2}\right)$

c $\frac{\pi^2}{8}$ units^2

3 $Q(1,0)$

4 a $A\left(\frac{1}{2}\ln 5,0\right),\ B(0,4)$

b $C(-8,0)$

5 $\frac{1}{2}e(2e^2+1)$

6 $\sqrt{2}\,p$ **7** $\frac{2}{3}p$

8 $\frac{1}{4}p$ **9** $\frac{9}{2}p$

10 $2\sqrt{3}\,p$

11 a $(-2, -2e^{-1})$ minimum

b $(-1, e^{-2})$ maximum, $(0, 0)$ minimum

c $(\ln 7, 9 - 7\ln 7)$ minimum

d $(0, 4)$ minimum

e $(-2, -4e^{2})$ minimum, $(4, 8e^{-4})$ maximum

f $\left(e^{-\frac{1}{2}}, -\frac{1}{2}e^{-1}\right)$ minimum

g $\left(\sqrt{e}, \frac{1}{2}e^{-1}\right)$ maximum

h $(-\sqrt{e-1}, e^{-1})$ maximum, $(0, 0)$ minimum, $(\sqrt{e-1}, e^{-1})$ maximum

12 a $(0.927, 5)$ maximum

b $(1.85, 10)$ maximum

c $(0, 5)$ maximum, $\left(\frac{\pi}{2}, -5\right)$ minimum

d $\left(\frac{\pi}{4}, 3.10\right)$ minimum

e $\left(\frac{5\pi}{6}, -\frac{3\sqrt{3}}{2}\right)$ minimum

13 a $A = 2, B = 8$

b $\left(\frac{1}{4}\ln 4, 8\right)$ minimum

14 $A(1, 0), B(e^{-1}, -e^{-1})$

15 a $P(0, 0), Q(-2, 4e^{-2})$

b $B(0, -2e), C\left(0, e + \frac{1}{3e}\right)$

c $\frac{1}{2}\left(3e + \frac{1}{3e}\right)$

16 b 2.7 cm^2 per second

17 $\frac{\pi}{6}$ maximum

Exercise 14.5

1 a $y = 2x - 1$

2 a $\frac{1}{3}\cos 2x \cos\left(\frac{x}{3}\right) - 2\sin 2x \sin\left(\frac{x}{3}\right)$

b $\dfrac{(\sec^2 x)(1 + \ln x) - \frac{1}{x}(\tan x)}{(1 + \ln x)^2}$

3 -0.8

4 a $\dfrac{2x\cos 4x + 4x^2 \sin 4x}{\cos^2 4x}$

b $-\frac{\pi}{2}p$

5 a $2e^{2x} - 2e^{-2x}$

b 2.5

c -7.25

6 a $A(1 + 2\ln 2, 0)$, $B\left(0, \frac{1}{2} + \ln 2\right)$, $C\left(1 - \frac{1}{2}\ln 2, 0\right)$, $D(0, -2 + \ln 2)$

b $k = (\ln 2)^2$

7 a $a = \frac{4\pi}{3}$

b $2y = \frac{19\pi}{6} - x$

8 i $\frac{dy}{dx} = \frac{2x\sec^2 2x - \tan 2x}{x^2}$

ii $y - \frac{8}{\pi} = -\frac{\pi^2}{32(\pi - 2)}\left(x - \frac{\pi}{8}\right)$

9 i $y + \ln 3 = \frac{1}{\ln 3}x$ **ii** $\frac{1}{2}(\ln 3)^2$

10 i $-\frac{8}{9} + \ln 9$ **ii** 0.0393

11 i $(-1, -0.5), (1, 0.5)$

ii $p = 2, q = -6, (-1, -0.5)$ minimum, $(1, 0.5)$ maximum

12 i $2r\sin\theta$ **iii** -17.8

iv -0.842

Chapter 15

Exercise 15.1

1 a $y = \frac{12}{5}x^5 + c$

b $y = \frac{5}{9}x^9 + c$

c $y = \frac{7}{4}x^4 + c$

d $y = -\frac{2}{x^2} + c$

e $y = -\frac{1}{2x} + c$

f $y = 6\sqrt{x} + c$

2 a $y = x^7 + \frac{2x^5}{5} + 3x + c$

b $y = \frac{x^6}{3} - \frac{3x^4}{4} + \frac{5x^2}{2} + c$

c $y = -\frac{1}{x^3} + \frac{15}{x} + \frac{x^2}{2} + c$

d $y = -\frac{2}{x^9} - \frac{1}{x^6} - 2x + c$

3 a $y = x^3 - 3x^2 + c$

b $y = \frac{4}{5}x^5 - x^3 + c$

c $y = \frac{8}{5}x^{\frac{5}{2}} + \frac{x^3}{3} + 2x^2 + c$

d $y = \frac{x^4}{4} + \frac{x^3}{3} - 6x^2 + c$

e $y = \frac{x^3}{6} + \frac{3}{2x} + c$

f $y = -\frac{2}{x} + \frac{5}{2x^2} - \frac{1}{x^3} + c$

g $y = \frac{x^4}{8} - 2x - \frac{1}{2x} + c$

h $y = \frac{6}{5}x^{\frac{5}{2}} - \frac{2x^{\frac{3}{2}}}{3} - 20\sqrt{x} + c$

4 $y = x^3 - 2x^2 + x + 5$

5 $y = 2x^3 - 3x^2 - 4$

6 $y = x^2 - \frac{6}{x} + 3$

7 $y = 8\sqrt{x} - 4x + \frac{2}{3}x^{\frac{3}{2}} + 8$

8 $y = 2x^3 - x^2 + 5$

9 a $y = 2x^3 - 6x^2 + 8x + 1$

10 $y = 2x^2 - 5x + 1$

Exercise 15.2

1 a $\frac{x^2}{8} + c$ b $2x^6 + c$

c $-\frac{1}{x^2} + c$ d $-\frac{4}{x} + c$

e $6\sqrt{x} + c$ f $-\frac{4}{x\sqrt{x}} + c$

2 a $\frac{x^3}{3} + \frac{7x^2}{2} + 10x + c$

b $\frac{2x^3}{3} + \frac{x^2}{2} - 3x + c$

c $\frac{x^3}{3} - 5x^2 + 25x + c$

d $4x^{\frac{3}{2}} + \frac{x^2}{2} + 9x + c$

e $\frac{x^4}{4} - \frac{2x^3}{3} + \frac{x^2}{2} + c$

f $\frac{3x^{\frac{7}{3}}}{7} - 3x^{\frac{4}{3}} + c$

3 a $x + \frac{5}{x} + c$

b $\frac{x^2}{4} + \frac{2}{x^2} + c$

c $-\frac{1}{3x} - \frac{1}{3x^2} - \frac{1}{9x^3} + c$

d $2x^2 - 6\sqrt{x} + c$

e $\frac{2x^{\frac{5}{2}}}{5} - \frac{2}{x^{\frac{5}{2}}} + c$

f $\frac{x^2}{2} - \frac{6}{x} - \frac{9}{4x^4} + c$

Exercise 15.3

1 a $\frac{1}{10}(x+2)^{10} + c$

b $\frac{1}{14}(2x-5)^7 + c$

c $\frac{1}{15}(3x+2)^{10} + c$

d $-\frac{1}{5}(2-3x)^5 + c$

e $\frac{3}{28}(7x+2)^{\frac{4}{3}} + c$

f $\frac{2}{15}(3x-1)^{\frac{5}{2}} + c$

g $12\sqrt{x+1} + c$

h $-\frac{4}{5(5x+3)^2} + c$

i $\frac{1}{4(3-2x)^3} + c$

2 $y = \frac{(4x+1)^5}{20} - 2$

3 $y = \frac{\sqrt{(2x+1)^3}}{3} + 2$

4 $y = 5 - 2\sqrt{10-x}$

5 $y = (2x-3)^4 + 1$

6 $y = \frac{(3x-1)^6 + 8}{9}$

Exercise 15.4

1 a $\frac{e^{5x}}{5} + c$ b $\frac{e^{9x}}{9} + c$

c $2e^{\frac{1}{2}x} + c$ d $-\frac{e^{-2x}}{2} + c$

e $4e^x + c$ f $\frac{e^{4x}}{2} + c$

g $\frac{e^{7x+4}}{7} + c$ h $-\frac{e^{5-2x}}{2} + c$

i $\frac{e^{6x-1}}{18} + c$

2 a $5e^x - \frac{e^{3x}}{3} + c$

b $\frac{e^{4x}}{4} + e^{2x} + x + c$

c $\frac{9e^{2x}}{2} - \frac{e^{-2x}}{2} + 6x + c$

d $e^x - 4e^{-x} + c$

e $\frac{5e^{2x}}{4} - \frac{e^x}{2} + c$

f $\frac{e^{5x}}{5} - 2e^{2x} - 4e^{-x} + c$

3 a $2e^x + 2\sqrt{x} + c$

b $\frac{1}{3}x^3 - \frac{3e^{2x+1}}{2} + c$

c $\frac{e^x}{4} + \frac{1}{3x} + c$

4 $y = e^{2x} - e^{-x} + 4$

5 a $k = -7$

b $y = 7e^{2-x} + 2x^2 - 5$

6 $y = 2e^{-2x} + 6x - 6$

7 a $6 - e$

b $\left(\frac{4e^2 - e - 2}{2e - 2}, \frac{24e - 4e^2 - 21}{4e - 4}\right)$

Exercise 15.5

1 a $-\frac{1}{4}\cos 4x + c$

b $\frac{1}{2}\sin 2x + c$

c $-3\cos\frac{x}{3} + c$

d $\sin 2x + c$

e $-2\cos 3x + c$

f $\frac{3}{2}\sin(2x+1) + c$

g $\frac{5}{3}\cos(2-3x) + c$

h $\sin(2x-7) + c$

i $\frac{4}{5}\cos(1-5x) + c$

2 a $x + \cos x + c$

b $\frac{2}{3}\left(x^{\frac{3}{2}} - \sin 3x\right) + c$

c $\frac{3}{2}\sin 2x + \frac{2}{5}\pi\cos\frac{5x}{2} + c$

d $-\frac{1}{x} - \frac{2}{3}\sin\frac{3x}{2} + c$

e $\frac{1}{2}\left(e^{2x} + 5\cos 2x\right) + c$

f $4\sqrt{x} - 2\cos\frac{x}{2} + c$

3 $y = \sin x + \cos x + 2$

4 $y = x - 2\sin 2x + 3 - \frac{\pi}{4}$

5 $y = 2x^2 + 3\cos 2x - 5$

6 $y = 5\cos 3x - 2\sin x + 4$

7 a $k = 6$

b $y = 2\sin 3x - 4x + 2 + 4\pi$

8 a $y = 5 - 2\cos\left(2x - \frac{\pi}{2}\right)$

b $y = -\frac{1}{2}x + \frac{\pi}{6} + 5 - \sqrt{3}$

9 a $k = 2$

b $\left(\frac{3\pi - 2}{6}, 3\right)$

Exercise 15.6

1 a $8\ln x + c$

b $5\ln x + c$

c $\frac{1}{2}\ln x + c$

d $\frac{5}{3}\ln x + c$

e $\frac{1}{3}\ln(3x + 2) + c$

f $-\frac{1}{8}\ln(1 - 8x) + c$

g $\frac{7}{2}\ln(2x - 1) + c$

h $-\frac{4}{3}\ln(2 - 3x) + c$

i $\frac{1}{2}\ln(5x - 1) + c$

2 a $\frac{7x^2}{2} + x + 2\ln x + c$

b $x - \frac{4}{x} + 4\ln x + c$

c $25x - \frac{9}{x} - 30\ln x + c$

d $x + \ln x + c$

e $-\frac{1}{2x^3} - \frac{5\ln x}{2} + c$

f $3x^3 - \frac{4}{3x^3} - 12\ln x + c$

g $5\ln x - \frac{4}{\sqrt{x}} + c$

h $\frac{2x^{\frac{5}{2}}}{5} - \ln x + c$

i $\frac{e^{3x}}{6} - \frac{\ln x}{5} + c$

3 $y = \frac{5}{2}\ln(2x - 1) + 3$

4 $y = x^2 + 5\ln x - 5$

5 $y = 1 + \ln(x + e)$

6 a $1 - 2\ln 2$

b $(2\ln 2, 2\ln 2 - 3)$

Exercise 15.7

1 b $\frac{x + 5}{\sqrt{2x - 1}} + c$

2 a $30x\left(3x^2 - 1\right)^4$

b $\frac{1}{30}\left(3x^2 - 1\right)^5 + c$

3 a $\ln x + 1$

b $x\ln x - x + c$

4 b $-\frac{1}{x} - \frac{\ln x}{x} + c$

5 a $\frac{2\left(x^2 - 2\right)}{\sqrt{x^2 - 4}}$

b $\frac{1}{2}x\sqrt{x^2 - 4} + c$

6 b $\frac{2}{3}(x + 1)\sqrt{x - 5} + c$

7 a $2xe^{2x}$

b $\frac{1}{2}xe^{2x} - \frac{1}{4}e^{2x} + c$

8 a $k = 1$

b $\frac{5\sin x}{1 - \cos x} + c$

9 a $k = \frac{3}{2}$

b $\frac{2}{3}(x + 8)\sqrt{x - 4} + c$

10 a $k = -2$

b $-\frac{2}{x^2 - 7} + c$

11 a $2x^2 + 6x^2\ln x$

b $\frac{1}{3}x^3\ln x - \frac{1}{9}x^3 + c$

12 a $\cos x - x\sin x$

b $\sin x - x\cos x + c$

13 b $\frac{1}{4}e^{2x}(\sin 2x + \cos 2x) + c$

14 a $\frac{5x^2 - 14x}{\sqrt{2x - 7}}$

b $\left(x^2 + 3\right)\sqrt{2x - 7}$

Exercise 15.8

1 a 127 b 1.5 c 24

d 15 e 10.5 f 7.5

g $12\frac{5}{12}$ h $\frac{52}{81}$ i 75.5

j 26.4 k $3\frac{13}{24}$ l $5\frac{1}{3}$

2 a 68 b $18\frac{2}{3}$ c 12.4

d 0.5 e 0.25 f 8

3 a $\frac{1}{2}\left(e^2 - 1\right)$ b $\frac{1}{4}(e - 1)$

c $\frac{5\left(e^4 - 1\right)}{2e^4}$ d $\frac{1}{3}(e - 1)$

e $\frac{5\left(e^2 - 1\right)}{2e}$

f $\frac{1}{2}\left(e^2 + 4e - 3\right)$

g $\frac{1}{12}\left(3e^4 + 8e^3 + 6e^2 - 17\right)$

h $\frac{9}{2}e^2 - \frac{2}{e^2} - \frac{29}{2}$

i $4e^2 - \frac{3}{2e^2} - \frac{5}{2}$

4 a 2 b $\frac{3\pi}{2}$

c $\frac{\sqrt{3}}{4}$ d $\sqrt{3}-\frac{3}{2}$

e $\frac{\pi^2-8}{16}$ f $\frac{1}{6}\left(3-\sqrt{2}\right)$

5 a $\frac{4}{3}\ln 2$ b $\frac{1}{2}\ln 11$

c $\frac{3}{2}\ln 5$ d $-\frac{5}{2}\ln 3$

e $-\frac{2}{3}\ln\frac{11}{2}$ f $2\ln\frac{9}{7}$

6 a $2+\frac{2}{3}\ln\frac{11}{5}$ b $\ln 9-10$

c $2+\frac{1}{2}\ln\frac{5}{3}$

7 $k=5$

8 $A=-6$

9 a quotient $=2x+1$, remainder $=-1$

10 $2-\frac{5}{4}\ln 3$

Exercise 15.9

1 a $\frac{3x}{\sqrt{2x-1}}$ b $5\frac{1}{3}$

2 a $\frac{6x^2+4}{\sqrt{3x^2+4}}$ b 4

3 a $-\frac{2x}{\left(x^2+5\right)^2}$ b $\frac{1}{9}$

4 a $\frac{3x+2}{2\sqrt{(3x+4)^3}}$ b 2

5 b $\frac{\pi\sqrt{2}}{20}$

6 a $\sin x+x\cos x+c$

b $\frac{1}{2}(\pi-2)$

7 a $x+2x\ln x+c$

b $1+e^2$

8 a $\sin 3x+3x\cos 3x$

b $\frac{1}{18}(\pi-2)$

Exercise 15.10

1 a $6\frac{3}{4}$ b $13\frac{1}{2}$

c 6 d $1+e-\frac{2}{e}$

e 5 f $\frac{2+\pi}{4}$

2 a $1\frac{1}{3}$

b $5\sqrt{2}-5-\frac{5\pi^2}{72}$

c $4\ln\frac{5}{2}$

d $\ln 5$

3 $3\frac{1}{12}$

4 a $\frac{1}{6}$ b $20\frac{5}{6}$

c 8 d $49\frac{1}{3}$

e $32\frac{3}{4}$ f $21\frac{1}{3}$

5 12

6 a 9 b 1.6

7 b $1+e^2$

8 $k=\frac{1}{2}(e^4+1)$

9 b $5\ln 5-4$

10 b $\pi-1$

Exercise 15.11

1 2

2 $3\frac{1}{3}$

3 16

4 $5-\frac{3\pi}{4}$

5 a $10\frac{2}{3}$ b $20\frac{5}{6}$ c $1\frac{1}{3}$

d 36 e $20\frac{5}{6}$

6 a $\frac{1}{3}$ b $\frac{3}{4}$

7 34

8 a $(-2, 0)$ b $42\frac{2}{3}$

9 $4\frac{4}{15}$

10 π

11 $\frac{35}{2}-6\ln 6$

Exercise 15.12

1 a $2xe^{x^2}$ b $\frac{1}{2}e^{x^2}$ c 26.8

2 a $y=2x^2-\frac{1}{x+1}+1$

b $8x+34y=93$

3 a $x+\frac{6}{x}+c$ b $k=2$

4 b 628 units^2

5 a (0, 1.85) b 0.292 units^2

6 $\ln(25e^5)$

7 a $A=4$

8 a $\frac{8x^3}{2x+1}+12x^2\ln(2x+1)$

b ii $\frac{10}{\sqrt{x+2}}+c$ iii $\frac{40}{3}$

9 i $-4xe^{4x}$

ii $4\ln 2-\frac{15}{16}$

10 i $\frac{3}{2}x^2-\frac{2}{5}x^{\frac{5}{2}}+c$

ii (9, 0) iv 16.2

Chapter 16

Exercise 16.1

1 a $12.5\,\text{m s}^{-1}$ b 6

c $-2.4\,\text{m s}^{-2}$

2 a $6\,\text{m s}^{-1}$ b $10\,\text{m s}^{-2}$

3 a $4.95\,\text{m s}^{-1}$ b 5

c $1\,\text{m s}^{-2}$

d

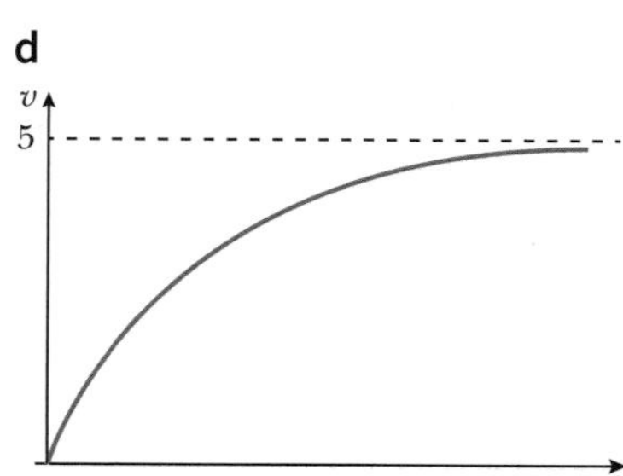

4 a $\frac{1}{3}\left(e^4-2\right)$ b $5.4\,\text{m s}^{-1}$

5 **a** 2 **b** $\ln\left(\frac{7}{5}\right)$ m

c $-0.25\,\text{m s}^{-2}$

6 **a** $\frac{4\pi}{3}$ **b** $-1.90\,\text{m s}^{-2}$

7 **a** $t = \frac{\pi}{4}$ **b** $-3\,\text{m s}^{-2}$

8 **a** $v = 4\sin 2t$, $a = 8\cos 2t$

b $t = \frac{\pi}{2}$, $s = 4$

9 **a** $t = \frac{1}{2}\ln 2$ **b** 0.899 m

c 24.1 m

10 **a** 2 m away from O

b $v = 2 - 4\sin 2t$, $a = -8\cos 2t$

c $t = \frac{\pi}{12}$, $s = \frac{\pi}{6} + \sqrt{3}$

d $t = \frac{\pi}{4}$, $s = \frac{\pi}{2}$

11 **a** $t = \frac{\pi}{8}$

b $a = -4k\sin 4t$

c $k = 5$

12 **a** $2\,\text{m s}^{-1}$

b **i** $2\,\text{m s}^{-1}$

ii $\frac{2}{3}\,\text{m s}^{-1}$

c **i** $0\,\text{m s}^{-2}$

ii $-\frac{2}{9}\,\text{m s}^{-2}$

d

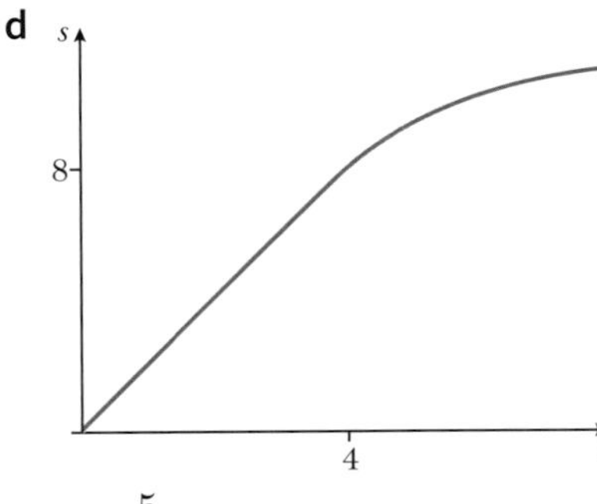

e $2\ln\frac{5}{4}$ m

13 **a** 2 m

b $t = \frac{5}{3}$

c $0 \leqslant t < \frac{5}{3}$ and $t > 4$

d $\frac{5}{3} < t < 4$

Exercise 16.2

1 **a** $16\,\text{m s}^{-1}$ **b** 15 secc[illegible]ds

c $12\frac{2}{3}$ m **d** $166\frac{2}{3}$ [illegible]

e $189\frac{1}{3}$ m

2 **a** $-1\,\text{m s}^{-2}$ **b** $s = \frac{1[illegible]}{t-2}$

c 1.6 m

3 **a** $2(4e^2 + 1)$ m

b $s = 2e^{2t} + t^2 - 2$

c 111 m

4 $\left(\frac{9\pi^2}{8} + 6\right)$ m, $\frac{1}{3}\,\text{m s}^{-2}$

5 **b** $29.75\,\text{m s}^{-2}$ **c** 1[illegible] m

6 $p = 6$, $q = -6$

7 **a** $t = 5$

b

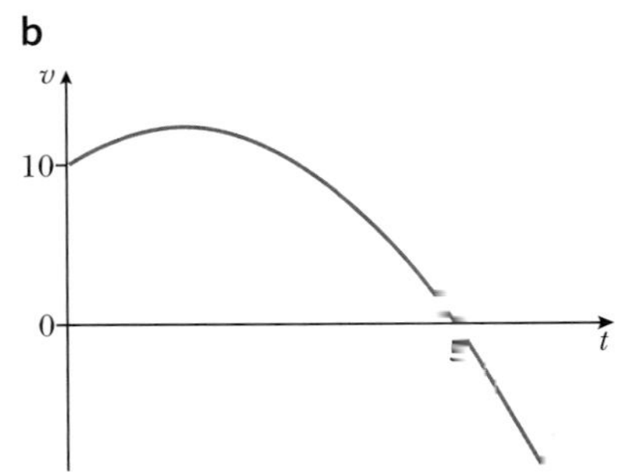

c 62.5 m

8 **a** $t = 2$, $t = 6$ **b** 5.5[illegible]

c 112 m

9 **a** $-12 \leqslant a \leqslant 12$ **b** [illegible]74 m

10 **a** $0.64\,\text{m s}^{-2}$ **b** 12.[illegible] m

11 **a** $t = \frac{2\pi}{3}$

b $\left(4\sqrt{3} + \frac{2\pi}{3}\right)$ m

12 **a** $p = \frac{1}{2}$, $q = -2$

b $s = \frac{1}{12}t^3 - t^2 + 3t$

c $t = 6$ **d** $\frac{11}{12}$ m

13 **a** $v = \frac{2\pi t}{3}\cos\frac{\pi t}{3} + 2\sin\frac{\pi t}{3}$,

$a = -\frac{2\pi^2 t}{9}\sin\frac{\pi t}{3} + \frac{4\pi}{3}\cos\frac{\pi t}{3}$

Exercise 16.3

1 **a** 3.2 **b** 15 **c** 312

2 $\frac{11}{6}$

3 **a** 2 **b** $\frac{\pi}{4}$ **c** 1

d 4

4 **a** 5 **b** $\frac{7\pi}{24}$ **c** 1.14

5 **i** $t = 1$

ii $\frac{2}{3}t^3 - 7t^2 + 12t$

iii -2

6 **a** **i**

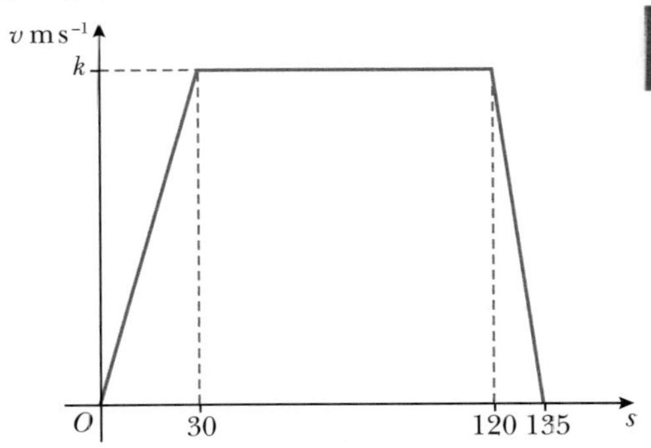

ii $k = 30$, $a = 1$

b $50\,\text{m s}^{-1}$

7 **i** $\frac{1}{2}e^{2t} + 3e^{-2t} - t - 3.5$

ii $\frac{1}{2}\ln 3$

iii 10

8 **ii** 0

iii $3t^3 - \frac{63}{2}t^2 + 90t$

iv **a** 78

b 88.5

Index